'Fraser is at her best here, lucid, authoritative and compassionate' Miranda Seymour, *Sunday Times*

'This sparkling new biography ... Antonia Fraser writes beautifully, with impressively shrewd judgement ... This is a fine book and a very good read'

Desmond Seward, *Daily Mail*

'A hugely well-researched work ... *Marie Antoinette* is a heroic, and tragic, exercise in identification'

Andy Martin, *Daily Telegraph*

'In *Marie Antoinette*, Fraser's superb gifts of narrative, characterisation and eye for salient detail are deployed to greater effect than ever before' Mark Bostridge, *Independent on Sunday*

'Fraser sets out to rescue Marie Antoinette from the shadow of the guillotine, and she does this with resounding success'

Ruth Scurr, *The Times*

'She has written a fine biography ... A fine and rewarding book' Douglas Johnson, *Spectator*

'It would be a stern republican indeed who could finish this life unmoved – and an inert reader who could remain unstirred by the vivid portrait Fraser paints of an age of turmoil'

Michael Kerrigan, *Scotsman*

'A superbly researched book which will clearly become the definitive work on the ill-fated queen'

Margot Lawrence, *Catholic Herald*

'Engrossing ... With this excellent book, Fraser has done something to counteract 200 years of vilification – she has made the doomed Queen human'

Anna Carey, *Sunday Tribune*

Since 1969, Antonia Fraser has written many acclaimed historical works which have been international bestsellers. These include the biographies *Mary Queen of Scots* (James Tait Black Memorial Prize), *Cromwell: Our Chief of Men* and *King Charles II*, and *The Gunpowder Plot: Terror and Faith in 1605* (St Louis Literary Award; CWA Non-Fiction Gold Dagger). Four highly praised books focus on women in history: *The Weaker Vessel: Woman's Lot in Seventeenth-Century England* (Wolfson Award for History, 1984), *The Warrior Queens: Boadicea's Chariot* (1988), *The Six Wives of Henry VIII* (1992) and *Marie Antoinette: The Journey* (Enid McLeod Literary Prize, 2001). Antonia Fraser is the editor of the series *Kings and Queens of England* (Weidenfeld & Nicolson), and wrote the volume *King James VI of Scotland, I of England*. Her latest book, *Love and Louis XIV: The Women in the Life of the Sun King* (2006), is published by Weidenfeld & Nicolson. She is married to Harold Pinter and lives in London. Antonia Fraser was made CBE in 1999, and awarded the Norton Medlicott Medal by the Historical Association in 2000.

By Antonia Fraser

Mary Queen of Scots

Cromwell: Our Chief of Men

James VI of Scotland, I of England

(*Kings and Queens* series)

King Charles II

The Weaker Vessel: Women's Lot
in Seventeenth-Century England

The Warrior Queens: Boadicea's Chariot

The Six Wives of Henry VIII

The Gunpowder Plot: Terror and Faith in 1605

Marie Antoinette: The Journey

Love and Louis XIV: The Women in the Life of the Sun King

Marie Antoinette
The Journey

ANTONIA FRASER

PHOENIX

A PHOENIX PAPERBACK

First published in Great Britain in 2001
by Weidenfeld & Nicolson
This paperback edition published in 2006
by Phoenix,
an imprint of Orion Books Ltd,
Orion House, 5 Upper St Martin's Lane,
London WC2H 9EA

1 3 5 7 9 10 8 6 4 2

A CIP catalogue record for this book
is available from the British Library.

ISBN-13 978-0-7538-2140-4
ISBN-10 0-7538-2140-0

Typeset by Input Data Services Ltd, Frome

Printed and bound in Great Britain by
Clays Ltd, St Ives plc

The Orion Publishing Group's policy is to use papers that
are natural, renewable and recyclable products and
made from wood grown in sustainable forests. The logging
and manufacturing processes are expected to conform to
the environmental regulations of the country of origin.

www.orionbooks.co.uk

FOR HAROLD
the first reader

Contents

Contents

Illustrations

Laxenburg: the 'holiday home' of the imperial family which Marie Antoinette loved, engraving by Johann Ziegler, 1796 (*AKG London*)

Francis Stephen of Lorraine (the Emperor Francis I): Marie Antoinette's father, Martin Mytens (*Kunsthistorisches Museum, Vienna/Bridgeman Art Library*)

Maria Teresa (the Empress of Austria): Marie Antoinette's mother, (*Christie's Images, London/Bridgeman Art Library*)

The imperial family on St Nicolas Day, 1762, by Archduchess Marie Christine (*Kunsthistorisches Museum, Vienna/Weidenfeld and Nicolson Archive*)

Ferdinand and Marie Antoinette dance in the ballet *Il Trionfo d'Amore*, 1765 (*Kunsthistorisches Museum, Vienna/Weidenfeld and Nicolson Archive*)

Maria Teresa in mourning with her four sons (*Schloss Schönbrunn, Vienna/Bridgeman Art Library*)

Marie Antoinette, aged twelve or thirteen, by Martin Mytens (*Schloss Schönbrunn, Vienna/Bridgeman Art Library*)

The Archduchess Marie Christine, Marie Antoinette's much older sister, 1776, by Johan Zoffany (*Kunsthistorisches Museum, Vienna/Bridgeman Art Library*)

Marie Antoinette's favourite sister, Maria Carolina, later Queen of Naples, by Martin Mytens (*Schloss Schönbrunn, Vienna/Bridgeman Art Library*)

Marie Antoinette at the spinet by Franz Xaver Wagenschon (*Kunsthistorisches Museum, Vienna/Bridgeman Art Library*)

Illustrations

Louis XV, King of France and grandfather of Louis XVI, pastel by Maurice-Quentin de la Tour (*Weidenfeld and Nicolson Archive*)

Louis XVI, aged twenty, by Joseph-Siffred Duplessis, c.1775 (*AKG Berlin/Jerome da Cunha*)

Marriage contract of Marie Antoinette and the Dauphin

An early letter home from Marie Antoinette to her mother (12 July 1770)

Letter from Marie Antoinette to Mme Durieu on the eve of her departure to France (*Private collection*)

Marie Antoinette in hunting costume painted the year after her marriage by Krautzinger, 1771 (*Kunsthistorisches Museum, Vienna/Weidenfeld and Nicolson Archive*)

Medallions of Louis XVI and Marie Antoinette as King and Queen of France (*British Library, London/Bridgeman Art Library*)

Marie Antoinette's gambling-purse and jetons (*Private collection*)

Blue enamel and diamond clasp of a bracelet given to Marie Antoinette at her wedding (*Victoria and Albert Museum, London*)

Count Mercy d'Argenteau, Austrian Ambassador to Versailles

The Swedish aristocrat Count Fersen by Noel Halle (*Private collection/Giraudon/Bridgeman Art Library*)

The Princesse de Lamballe

The Duchess de Polignac by Louis Elisabeth Vigée Le Brun (*Private collection/Giraudon/Bridgeman Art Library*)

A group of pictures showing Marie Antoinette's beloved retreat the Petit Trianon, the Temple of Love and the *Hameau* (*Petit Trianon, Versailles/Biblioteca Estense, Modena/Bridgeman Art Library*)

Marie Antoinette's cipher (*Private collection*)

Marie Antoinette's copy of *Manon Lescaut* by the Abbé Prevost (*Private collection*)

Marie Antoinette's passepartout key to the palace of Saint Cloud (*Private collection*)

Archduke Maximilian with Marie Antoinette and Louis XVI, by Josef Hauzinger (*Kunsthistorisches Museum, Vienna/Bridgeman Art Library*)

Christoph Willibald Gluck; Marie Antoinette's former teacher, by Joseph-Siffred Duplessis, 1775 (*Kunsthistorisches Museum, Vienna/Bridgeman Art Library*)

Marie Antoinette with her harp at Versailles by Jacques Fabien Gautier-Dagoty, 1777 (*Château de Versailles/Giraudon/Bridgeman Art Library*)

Marie Antoinette by Jean-François Janinet, aquatint, 1777 (*Private collection*)

Illustrations

The Queen out hunting, with the King in the background, by Louis-Auguste Brun, 1783 (*Private collection*)

Marie Antoinette, aged twenty-eight, 1783, by Louise Elisabeth Vigée Le Brun (*Château de Versailles/Bridgeman Art Library*)

Madame Elisabeth, younger sister of Louise XVI (*Weidenfeld and Nicolson Archive*)

Bust of Marie Antoinette by Felix Lecomte, 1784 (*Private collection*)

The Comte de Provence, brother of Louis XVI, by Joseph Siffrede Duplessis, 1778 (*Musée Condé, Chantilly/Lauros-Giraudon/Bridgeman Art Library*)

The Comte d'Artois, younger brother of Louis XVI, by Danloux (*Château de Versailles/Lauros-Giraudon/Bridgeman Art Library*)

Marie Antoinette in a white muslin dress and a straw hat, by Louise Elisabeth Vigée Le Brun, 1783 (*Darmstadt/AKG London*)

Marie Antoinette's two oldest children, Marie Thérèse, Madame Royale, and the Dauphin Louis Joseph, 1784, by Louise Elisabeth Vigée Le Brun (*Château de Versailles/Lauros-Giraudon/Bridgeman Art Library*)

The Queen with her children in the park of the Trianon, 1784, by Adolf Ulrik von Wertmüller (*Nationalmuseum, Stockholm/Bridgeman Art Library*)

The Diamond Necklace, originally intended to tempt the Comtesse Du Barry (*reconstruction*) (*Weidenfeld and Nicolson Archive*)

Silk cloth woven for Marie Antoinette (*Collections du Mobilier national/Photograph: Sébert*)

The Queen with three of her children, by Louise Elisabeth Vigée Le Brun, 1787 (*Château de Versailles/Giraudon/Bridgeman Art Library*)

Marie Antoinette's second son, Louis Charles, Dauphin, later Louis XVII, c. 1792, by Alexandre Kucharski (*AKG London/Visioars*)

Louis XVI, by Callet (*Château de Versailles/Giraudon/Bridgeman Art Library*)

Extract from Louis XVI's *Journal* (*Weidenfeld and Nicolson Archive*)

The *Nécessaire* Marie Antoinette took with her to Varennes (*Private collection*)

Furniture made for Marie Antoinette by J-H Riesener (*The Metropolitan Museum of Art, Rogers Fund, 1933*)

Madame Campan, 1786, by Boze (*Château de Versailles/Lauros-Giraudon/Bridgeman Art Library*)

Porcelain coffee cup and saucer made to commemorate the birth of the first Dauphin, 1781 (*Weidenfeld and Nicolson Archive*)

Simplified Family Tree

Showing HABSBURG – BOURBON – ORLÉANS connections

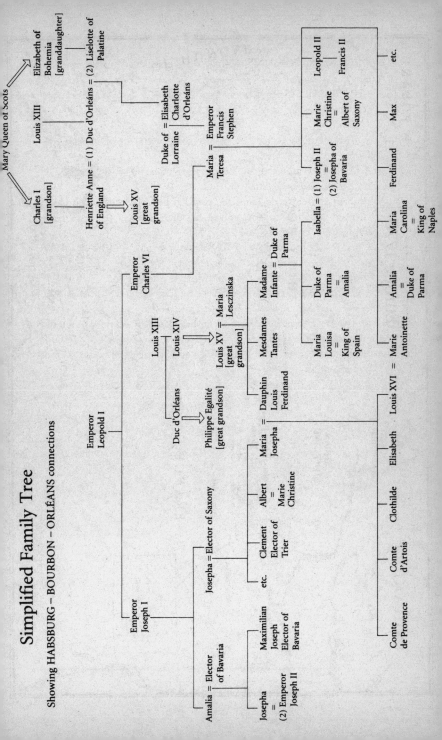

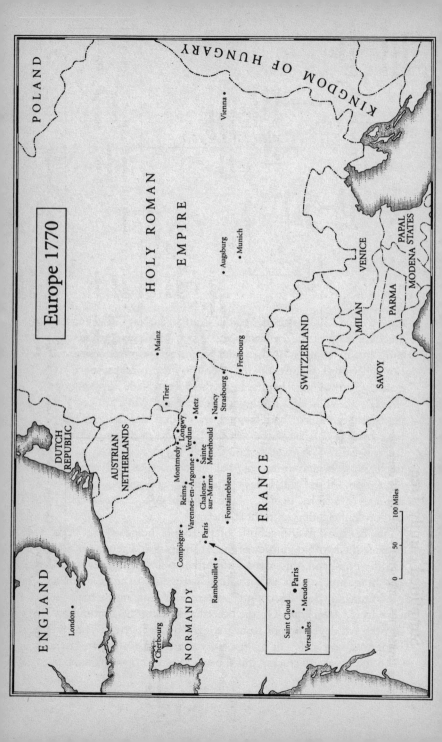

Europe 1770

POLAND

KINGDOM OF HUNGARY

HOLY ROMAN

EMPIRE

Vienna

Augsburg
Munich

ENGLAND

London

Mainz

Trier

DUTCH
REPUBLIC

AUSTRIAN
NETHERLANDS

Compiègne
Reims
Montmédy
Longwy
Verdun
Metz
Varennes-en-Argonne
Nancy
Sainte
Menehould
Strasbourg
Chalons-
sur-Marne
Paris
Fontainebleau

FRANCE

Freibourg

SWITZERLAND

SAVOY

MILAN
PARMA

VENICE

PAPAL
STATES
MODENA
STATES

NORMANDY

Cherbourg

Rambouillet

Saint Cloud
Paris
Meudon
Versailles

0   50   100 Miles

Author's Note

Et in Arcadia Ego: even in Arcadia death is lurking. Madame de Staël, thinking of the 'brilliance and gaiety' of Marie Antoinette's early life in contrast to her later sufferings, was reminded of Poussin's great picture on the theme of the omnipresence of death: the revelling shepherds in the forest glade brought up short by the sight of a tomb with this menacing inscription. Yet hindsight can make bad history. In writing this biography, I have tried not to allow the sombre tomb to make its presence felt too early. The elegiac should have its place as well as the tragic, flowers and music as well as revolution and counter-revolution. Above all, I have attempted, at least so far as is humanly possible, to tell Marie Antoinette's dramatic story without anticipating its terrible ending.

My concern, as the subtitle of the book indicates, has been to trace the twofold journey of the Austrian-born French Queen. On the one hand, this was an important political journey, from her homeland to act as an ambassadress – or agent – in a predominantly hostile country where she was nicknamed in advance *L'Autrichienne.* On the other hand, there was her journey of personal development from the inadequate fourteen-year-old bride to a very different mature woman, twenty odd years later.

In the course of tracing this journey, I have hoped to unravel the cruel myths and salacious distortions surrounding her name. Principal among them must be the notorious incident which has Marie Antoinette urging the poor, being without bread, to eat cake. This story was first told about the Spanish Princess who married Louis XIV a hundred years before the arrival of Marie Antoinette in France; it continued to be repeated about a series of other Princesses throughout the eighteenth century. As a handy journalistic cliché, it may never die. Yet, not only was the story wrongly ascribed to Marie Antoinette in the first place, but such ignorant behaviour would have been quite out of character. The unfashionably philanthropic Marie Antoinette would have been far more likely to bestow her own cake (or *brioche*) impulsively upon the starving people before her. On the subject of the Queen's sex life – insatiable lover? voracious lesbian? heroine of a single romantic passion? – I have similarly tried to exert common sense in an area which must remain forever speculative (as indeed it was in her own day).

Biographers have their small private moments of perception, the importance of which was recognized by the Goncourt brothers, admiring biographers of the Queen in 1858: 'A time of which one does not have a dress sample and a dinner menu is a time dead to us, an irrecoverable time.' Lafont d'Aussonne, author of an early post-Restoration study (1824), found an ear of wheat made out of silver thread on the floor of the Queen's former bedroom at Saint Cloud during a sale and pocketed it. Two hundred years after the death of Marie Antoinette, I found the experience of being asked to don white gloves to inspect the tiny swatches in her Wardrobe Book at the Archives Nationales both appropriate and affecting, the pinpricks made by the Queen to indicate her choice of the day's costume being still visible. I had, however, no desire to emulate Lafont d'Aussonne's act of pious theft – if only because two gendarmes stood close behind my chair.

The Baronne d'Oberkirch, writing her memoirs just before the deluge, gave an unforgettable vignette of the aristocrats returning from an all-night ball at Versailles in their carriages, with the peasants already doing their rounds in the bright morning sunshine: 'What a contrast between their calm and satisfied visages and our exhausted appearance! The rouge had fallen from our cheeks, the powder from our hair ... not a pretty sight.' Such a vision seems to sum up the contrasts of the *ancien régime* in France – including the Baronne's innocent assumption that the peasants were calm and satisfied. Certainly the wealth of female testimonies to the period and to the life of Marie Antoinette gave special immediacy to my researches. The women who survived felt an urgent need to relive the trauma and record the truth, a compulsion often modestly disguised as a little gift to their descendants: 'c'est pour vous, mes enfants ...' wrote Pauline de Tourzel, an eye-witness to some of the horrific incidents of the early Revolution, at the start of her reminiscences. Probably no queen in history has been so well served by her female chroniclers.

In a book written in English about a French (and Austrian) subject, there is an obvious problem to do with translation. Nor does it have an easy solution. What is tiresomely obscure for one reader may be gratingly obvious to another. On the whole I have preferred to translate rather than not in the interests of clarity. With names and titles I have also placed the need for clarity above consistency; even if some decisions may seem arbitrary in consequence, intelligibility has been the aim. Where eighteenth-century money is concerned, it is notoriously difficult to provide any idea of the modern equivalent so on the whole I have avoided doing so. However, one recent estimate equated a pound sterling in 1790 to £45 in 1996; there were roughly 24 livres to the pound in the reign of Louis XVI.' As ever, it has been my pleasure and privilege to do my own research, except where individuals are specifically and most gratefully acknowledged. The references are, with equal gratitude, listed in the Notes and Sources.

I wish to thank H.M. the Queen for permission to use and quote from the Royal Archives, and also Lady de Bellaigue, Keeper of the Royal Archives, Windsor. I thank the Duke of Devonshire for permission to quote from the Devonshire Collections and Mr Peter Day, Keeper of the Collection, Chatsworth; also Dr Amanda Foreman and Ms Caroline Chapman who supplied me with references to the 5th Duke's Collection. Ms Jane Dormer gave permission for me to quote from Lady Elizabeth Foster's (unpublished) Journal; Dr Robin Eagles let me read his D.Phil. thesis 'Francophilia and Francophobia in English Society 1748–1783', Oxford, 1996 (since published). Jessica Beer was invaluable in helping me to set up research in the Hofburg, Vienna, and accompanied me on expeditions into the scenes of Marie Antoinette's childhood; Christina Burton did useful Fersen research in Sweden; Fr Francis Edwards S.J. directed me towards canonical references; Professor Dan Jacobson supplied material about the early Judaic history of the Scapegoat; Cynthia Liebow was at all times a highly able enabler in Paris; Katie Mitchell pointed me towards Genet's feelings for Marie Antoinette; Mrs Bernadette Peters, former Archivist, Coutts Bank, researched their archives there for me; Mlle Cécile Coutin, Vice Présidente de l'Association Marie-Antoinette, supplied information about Marie Antoinette's compositions and the 1993 commemoration; Mr J. E. A. Wickham, M.S., M.D., B Sc., F.R.C.S., F.R.C.P., F.R.C.R., gave advice on phimosis. I am much indebted for conversations, advice and critical comments to Dr Philip Mansel, M. Bernard Minoret, Dr Robert Oresko and Dr John Rogister. Professor T. C. W. Blanning read the manuscript for errors, the remaining ones being, of course, my own.

The Vicomte de Rohan, President, Société des Amis de Versailles, was a distinguished guide to the secrets of Versailles. I wish to thank Doktor Lauger, Press Attaché to the President of the Austrian Republic, for access to the room in which Marie Antoinette was born, and Mag. Christina Schütz, IIASA, Laxenburg for my visit there. The Austrian Tourist Board was helpful with current information about Mariazell; as were Gendarme Klein of the Varennes-en-Argonne Gendarmerie, Madame Vagnère of the Sainte Ménehould Tourist Office and the Gendarmerie at Sainte Ménehould with information relevant to the flight to Varennes.

A host of people assisted me in a variety of ways: Mr Arthur Addington; Mr Rodney Allen; Dr L. R. I. Baker; Professor Colin Bonwick; Mrs Anka Begley; Ms Sue Bradbury, Folio Society; Professor John Beckett; Dr Joseph Baillio; Dr David Charlton;

Dr Eveline Cruickshanks; Professor John Ehrman; Mrs Gila Falkus and my god-daughter Helen Falkus to whom the possibility of this project was first confided; Mr Julian Fellowes; Mme Laure de Grammont; Mr Ivor Guest; Mrs Sue Hopson; Dr Rana Kabbani; Mrs Linda Kelly; Dr Ron Knowles; M. Karl Lagerfeld; Ms Jenny Mackilligan; Mr Ben Macintyre; Mr Bryan Maggs of Maggs Bros.; Mr Alastair Macaulay; Mr Paul Minet, *Royalty Digest*; Mr Geoffrey Munn of Wartski; Mr David Pryce-Jones; Mrs Julia Parker D.F. Astrol.S.; Professor Pamela Pilbeam; Mrs Juliet Pennington; Mrs Renata Propper; Professor Aileen Ribeiro; Lord Rothschild; Sir Roy Strong; Mme Chantal Thomas; Lord Thomas of Swynnerton; Mr Alex M. Thomson; M Roland Bossard, Château de Versailles, Chargé d'études documentaires; Mr Francis Wyndham; Ms Charlotte Zeepvat.

The staff of the following libraries deserve thanks: the British Library; in Paris the Archives Nationales and Mme Michèle Bimbenet-Privat, and the Bibliothèque Nationale; the Public Record Office and Dr A. S. Bevan, Reader Information Service Dept; the Victoria and Albert Museum Library; in Vienna, the Hofburg Haus-Archiv. My publishers on both sides of the Atlantic – Nan Talese, Anthony Cheetham, Ion Trewin and my excellent editor Rebecca Wilson – were extremely helpful; as were my agent Mike Shaw and my assistant Linda Peskin at her magic machine. The incomparable Douglas Matthews did the index.

Members of my family were as usual highly supportive, in particular my 'French family', Natasha Fraser-Cavassoni and Jean Pierre Cavassoni, while my brother Thomas Pakenham supplied an interesting botanical reference. I am also much indebted to my daughter Flora Fraser; with her knowledge of the eighteenth century and its sources, she guided me in particular at Windsor. Lastly, like everyone who has studied Marie Antoinette in the present time, I owe an enormous debt to Liliane de Rothschild. Her unrivalled mixture of erudition and enthusiasm has been a constant inspiration during the five years I worked on this book; in her own words: *Vive la Reine!*

ANTONIA FRASER
Feast of All Saints 2000

PART ONE

Madame Antoine

CHAPTER ONE

A Small Archduchess

~

'Her Majesty has been very happily delivered of a small,
but completely healthy Archduchess.'

Count Khevenhüller, Court Chamberlain, 1755

On 2 November 1755 the Queen-Empress was in labour
all day with her fifteenth child. Since the experience of
childbirth was no novelty, and since Maria Teresa,
Queen of Hungary by inheritance, Empress of the Holy Roman
Empire by marriage, hated to waste time, she also laboured in
another way at her papers. For the responsibilities of government
were not to be lightly cast aside; in her own words: 'My subjects
are my first children.' Finally, at about half past eight in the
evening in her apartments at the Hofburg Palace in Vienna,
Maria Teresa gave birth. It was a girl. Or, as the Court
Chamberlain, Count Khevenhüller, described the event in his
diary: 'Her Majesty has been happily delivered of a small, but
completely healthy Archduchess.' As soon as was practical, Maria
Teresa returned to work, signing papers from her bed.[1]

The announcement was made by the Emperor Francis
Stephen. He left his wife's bedroom, after the usual Te Deum
and Benediction had been said. In the Mirror Room next door
the ladies and gentlemen of the court who had the Rights of
Entry were waiting. Maria Teresa had firmly ended the practice,
so distasteful to the mother in labour (but still in place at the
court of Versailles), by which these courtiers were actually
present in the delivery room. As it was they had to content

3

themselves with congratulating the happy father. It was not until four days later that those ladies of the court who by etiquette would formerly have been in the bedchamber were allowed to kiss the Empress. Other courtiers, including Khevenhüller, were permitted the privilege on 8 November, and a further set the next day. Perhaps it was the small size of the baby, perhaps it was the therapeutic effect of working at her papers throughout the day, but Maria Teresa had never looked so well after a delivery.[2]

The Empress's suite of apartments was on the first floor of the so-called Leopoldine wing of the extensive and rambling Hofburg complex.* The Habsburgs had lived in the Hofburg since the late thirteenth century, but this wing had originally been constructed by the Emperor Leopold I in 1660. It was rebuilt following a fire, then greatly renovated by Maria Teresa herself. It lay south-west of the internal courtyard known as In Der Burg. Swiss Guards, that doughty international force that protects royalty, gave their name to the adjacent courtyard and gate, the Schweizerhof and the Schweizertor.

The next stage in the new baby's life was routine. She was handed over to an official wet-nurse. Great ladies did not nurse their own children. For one thing, breastfeeding was considered to ruin the shape of the bosom, made so visible by eighteenth-century fashions. The philandering Louis XV openly disliked the practice for this reason. The traditional prohibition against husbands sleeping with their wives during this period probably counted for more with Maria Teresa, an enthusiast for the marital double-bed and the conception – if not the nursing – of ever increasing numbers of babies. As the Empress said of herself, she was insatiable on the subject of children.[3]

Marie Antoinette was put into the care of Constance Weber, wife of a magistrate. Constance, according to her son Joseph

---

* Now part of the offices of the Austrian President. The bedroom in which Marie Antoinette was born is today the President's salon, with red- and gold-embroidered hangings; the room is dominated by an enormous portrait of Maria Teresa by Mytens. An adjacent room still contains a collection of *pietra dura* (pictures in semi-precious stones of birds and animals) which Maria Teresa loved, a taste she handed on to Marie Antoinette.

Weber, who later wrote his memoirs, was famed for her beautiful figure and an even greater beauty of soul. She had been nursing little Joseph for three months when she took over the baby Archduchess, and it was understood in the family that Constance's appointment would improve all their fortunes. As the foster-brother of an archduchess, Joseph Weber benefited all his life; there were pensions for Constance as well as his other brothers and sisters. During Marie Antoinette's childhood, Maria Teresa took her to visit the Weber household; there she showered gifts upon the children and, according to Joseph, admonished Constance: 'Good Weber, have a care for your son.'[4]

Maria Teresa was thirty-eight years old and since her marriage nearly twenty years earlier, she had produced four Archdukes as well as ten Archduchesses (of whom seven were living in 1755). The extraordinarily high survival rate of the imperial family – by the standards of infant mortality of the time – meant that there was no urgent pressure upon the Queen-Empress to produce a fifth son. In any case it seems that Maria Teresa had expected a daughter. One of her courtiers, Count Dietrichstein, wagered against her that the new baby would be a boy. When the appearance of a girl, said to be as like her mother as two drops of water, meant that he lost the bet, the Count had a small porcelain figure made of himself, on his knees, proffering verses by Metastasio to Maria Teresa. He may have lost his wager but if the new-born *augusta figlia* resembled her mother, then all the world would have gained.[5]

If the birth of an eighth surviving daughter was not in itself a disappointment, was there not perhaps something inauspicious about the date itself, 2 November? This, the Feast of All Souls, was the great Catholic Day of the Dead, when the departed were solemnly commemorated in a series of requiem Masses, in churches and chapels heavily draped in black. What this actually meant during the childhood of Marie Antoinette was that her birthday was generally celebrated on its eve, the Feast of All Saints, a day of white and gold. Besides which, 13 June, the feast of her patron saint St Antony, tended to be regarded as Marie Antoinette's personal day of celebration, just as the feast of St Teresa of Avila on 15 October was the name-day of her mother.[6]

If one looks to influences, the baby born on the sombre Day of the Dead must have been conceived on or around a far more cheerful feast of the church: 2 February, the traditionally candle-lit celebration of the Purification of the Virgin Mary. An episode during the Empress's pregnancy could also be seen as significant. In April, Christoph Willibald Gluck was engaged by Maria Teresa to compose 'theatrical and chamber music' in exchange for an official salary; this followed his successes in Italy and England as well as in Vienna. A court ball at the palace of Laxenburg, fifteen miles from Vienna, on 5 May 1755, marked his inauguration in this role.[7] Two tastes that would impress themselves upon Marie Antoinette – a love of the 'holiday' palace of Laxenburg and a love of the music of Gluck – could literally be said to have been inculcated in her mother's womb.

In contrast, the fact that a colossal earthquake took place in Lisbon on 2 November, with 30,000 killed, was not at the time seen as relevant. This was an age of poor European communications and news of the disaster did not reach Vienna until some time afterwards. It was true that the King of Portugal and his wife had been engaged to stand as the coming baby's godparents; the unfortunate royal couple had to flee from their capital at about the time Marie Antoinette was born. But, once again, this was not known at the time. In any case, royalties were not expected to be present at the event; according to custom, proxies were appointed in their absence: the baby's eldest brother, Joseph, and her eldest sister, Marianne, aged fourteen and seventeen respectively.

The baptism took place at noon on 3 November (baptisms were always held speedily and in the absence of the mother, who was allowed to recover from her ordeal). The Emperor went with a cortège to the Church of the Augustine Friars, the traditional church used by the court, and heard Mass, including the sermon. After that, at twelve o'clock, as Count Khevenhüller noted in his meticulous diary, which is an important source for our knowledge of events in Maria Teresa's family, the baptism was held in 'the new and beautiful Anticamera' and performed by 'our Archbishop', since the new Papal Nuncio had not yet made a formal appearance at court.[8] The imperial family sat in a row on a long bench. Two galas were ordered: a great gala for the day of the baptism, and a lesser gala for the day after. On 5 and 6 November there were two more spectacles that were shown to the public for free, and on those days there was no charge to the public for entry at the city gates. It was all a very well established ritual.

The baby in whose honour these celebrations were held was given the names Maria Antonia Josepha Joanna. The prefix of Maria had been established for all Habsburg princesses in the days of the baby's great-grandfather, the Emperor Leopold I and his third wife Eleanora of Neuburg; it was intended to signify the special veneration of the Habsburg family for the Virgin Mary.[9] Obviously in a bevy of eight sisters (and a mother) all enjoying the same hallowed prefix, it was not going to be used for everyone all the time. In fact the new baby would be called Antoine in the family.

The French diminutive of the baptismal name, Antoine, was significant. Viennese society was multilingual, people being able to make themselves easily understood in Italian and Spanish as well as in German and French. But it was French, acknowledged as the language of civilization, that was the universal language of courts throughout Europe; Frederick II of Prussia, Maria Teresa's great rival, for example, preferred his beloved French to German. It was French that was used in diplomatic despatches to the Habsburgs. Maria Teresa spoke French, although with a strong German accent (she also spoke the Viennese dialect), but the Emperor Francis Stephen spoke French all his life, not caring to learn German. In this way, both in the family circle and outside it, Maria Antonia was quickly transmogrified into Antoine, the name she also used to sign her letters. To courtiers, the latest archduchess was to be known as Madame Antoine.

Charming, sophisticated, lazy and pleasure-loving, an inveterate womanizer who adored his wife and family, Francis Stephen of Lorraine handed on to Marie Antoinette a strong dose of

French blood. His mother Elisabeth Charlotte d'Orléans had been a French royal princess and a granddaughter of Louis XIII. Her brother, the Duc d'Orléans, had acted as Regent during the childhood of Louis XV. As for Francis Stephen himself, although he had Habsburg blood on his father's side and was adopted into the Viennese court in 1723 at the age of fourteen, it was important to him that he was by birth a Lorrainer. From 1729, when his father died, he was hereditary Duke of Lorraine, a title that stretched back to the time of Charlemagne. This notional Lorrainer inheritance would also feature in the consciousness of Marie Antoinette, even though Francis Stephen was obliged to surrender the actual duchy in 1735. It was part of a complicated European deal whereby Louis XV's father-in-law, who had been dispossessed as King of Poland, received the Duchy of Lorraine for the duration of his lifetime; it then became part of the kingdom of France. In return Francis Stephen was awarded the Duchy of Tuscany.

The renunciation of his family heritage in order to soothe France was presented to Francis Stephen as part of a package that would enable him to marry Maria Teresa. On her side, it was a passionate love match. The British ambassador to Vienna reported that the young Archduchess 'sighs and pines all night for her Duke of Lorraine. If she sleeps, it is only to dream of him. If she wakes, it is but to talk of him to the lady-in-waiting.'[10] Wilfully, in a way that would be in striking contradiction to the precepts she preached as a mother, Maria Teresa set her heart against a far grander suitor, the heir to the Spanish throne. The medal struck for the wedding bore the inscription (in Latin): 'Having at length the fruit of our desires.'

The desires in question, however, did not include the bride-groom's continued enjoyment of his hereditary possessions. As his future father-in-law Charles VI crudely put it: 'No renun-ciation, no Archduchess.'[11] Maria Teresa of course believed in total wifely submission, at least in theory, another doctrine that she would expound assiduously to her daughters. Her solution was to tolerate and even encourage her husband's Lorrainer relations at court, as well as a multitude of Lorrainer hangers-on.

The marriage of Maria Teresa's sister Marianna to Francis Stephen's younger brother Charles of Lorraine strengthened these ties; Marianna's early death left Maria Teresa with a sentimental devotion to her widower. Then there was Francis Stephen's attachment to his unmarried sister Princess Charlotte, Abbess of Remiremont, who was a frequent visitor. She shared her brother's taste for shooting parties, in which she personally participated. In the year of Marie Antoinette's birth, a party of twenty-three, three of them ladies, killed nearly 50,000 head of game and wild deer. Princess Charlotte fired over 9000 shots, nearly as many as the Emperor. This strong-minded woman was so devoted to her native Lorraine that she once said she was prepared to travel there barefoot.[12]

Thus Marie Antoinette was brought up to think of herself as 'de Lorraine' as well as 'd'Autriche et de Hongrie'. In the meantime Lorraine had become a foreign principality attached to France, so that princes of Lorraine who made their lives in France had the status of 'foreign princes' only and were not accorded the respect due to foreign royalties nor that due to French dukes. This ambiguous status was one from which the foreign princes ever sought to escape, while those of superior birth in French courtly terms sought to hold them down. A seemingly small point of French etiquette – small at least to outsiders – was to be of considerable significance in the future of Francis Stephen's daughter.

This was an age of multiple intermarriage where royal houses were concerned. Insofar as one can simplify it purely in terms of her four grandparents, Marie Antoinette had the blood of the Bourbons – the Orléans branch – and of Lorraine on her father's side. More remotely, her Orléans great-grandmother, a Palatine princess known as Liselotte, brought her the blood of Mary Queen of Scots via Elizabeth of Bohemia – but this was to go back 200 years. On the maternal side, Marie Antoinette inherited German blood from her grandmother Elizabeth Christina of Brunswick-Wolfbüttel, once described as 'the most beautiful queen on earth'. Her appearance at the age of fourteen enchanted her husband Charles VI: 'Now that I have seen her, everything that has been said about her is but a shadow devoured

9

by the light of the sun.'¹³ However, if exceptional beauty was to be found in the pool of genes that Marie Antoinette might inherit, it was also true that the lovely Empress became immensely large and dropsical in later years.

Lastly, Marie Antoinette inherited the Habsburg blood, both Austrian and Spanish, of her grandfather the Emperor Charles VI. These two branches of the Habsburg family, which had in theory divided in the sixteenth century, were in fact the result of constant intermarriage, like great rivers whose tributaries flowed into each other so frequently that their waters were inextricably mingled. The failure of the direct Spanish Habsburg line in 1700 led to the accession of a French Bourbon prince, the grandson of Louis XIV, to the Spanish throne (via his Spanish Habsburg grandmother) despite the efforts of the then Archduke Charles who was the rival pretender.

In 1711, however, the death of the Emperor Joseph I, leaving only two daughters, meant that Charles as his younger brother inherited the Austrian dominions. He was elected as Holy Roman Emperor shortly afterwards. Although unable to claim the imperial throne, Joseph's daughters married respectively the Electors of Bavaria and Saxony to provide a plethora of descendants, who would spin webs of alliance and intrigue throughout Europe in the eighteenth century. In the meantime, by one of those historical ironies, Charles VI himself was unable to produce a male heir. He too was left with two daughters, of whom the elder, Maria Teresa, was now to be transformed into his heiress.

Charles VI's attempts to secure the inheritance of Maria Teresa by, in effect, bribing other European powers to respect the arrangement was known as the Pragmatic Sanction. For all these efforts, his death in 1740 merely unleashed a new dynastic struggle, the eight-year War of the Austrian Succession. Silesia was immediately conquered by the Prussian King: this was the most prosperous region under the Habsburg dominion and the twenty-three-year-old Maria Teresa felt the loss keenly. It seemed that she was doomed to preside over the dismemberment of the once great Habsburg Empire. In her own words: 'It would not be easy to find in history an example of a crowned head acceding to government in more unfavourable circumstances than I did myself.'14

It was a measure of the greatness of Maria Teresa that fifteen years later, at the time of Marie Antoinette's birth, she was in fact wreathed in triumph, admired throughout Europe as 'the glory of her sex and the model of kings'. For all her losses in the war – at the Peace of Aix-la-Chapelle in 1748 Maria Teresa still could not recover Silesia – she was nevertheless confirmed in her hereditary possessions. Apart from Upper and Lower Austria, these included Bohemia and Moravia (now the Czech Republic), Hungary, much of what is now Rumania, a portion of former Yugoslavia, as well as the Austrian Netherlands (approximately Belgium*) and the Duchies of Milan and Tuscany in Italy. Meanwhile Francis Stephen had been elected Emperor.

In 1755 the country was at peace, with memories of the War of Succession receding; the army was contented and a series of domestic reforms had taken place, thanks to Maria Teresa's chancellor, Haugwitz. As a result the Empress was not only admired abroad but enjoyed popularity at home. For the twentieth anniversary of her wedding to Francis Stephen in February 1756, Maria Teresa gave a surprise children's party in which all her children, even 'the little Madame Antoine', appeared in masks and costumes.'15 That summed up the Empress's domestic bliss. Of all the children of Maria Teresa, Marie Antoinette was the one who was born at the zenith of her mother's glory.

Six months after the birth of Marie Antoinette, a radical change in the national alliances of Europe put an end to this surface tranquillity. By the Treaty of Versailles, signed on 1 May 1756, Austria joined with her traditional enemy France in a defensive pact against Prussia. If either country was attacked, the other would come to its aid with an army specified to be 24,000 strong. No single event in Marie Antoinette's childhood was to

* The so-called Austrian (southern) Netherlands, in which modern Luxembourg was then included and centred on Brussels, would form the largest constituent part of Belgium when it was founded after 1830; the two areas were, however, not identical and the modern term Belgium is used purely for convenience.

have a more profound influence on the course of her life than this alliance, forged while she was still in her cradle.

It is not difficult to explain Austria's hostility to Prussia: Maria Teresa had neither forgotten nor forgiven the Rape of Silesia which occurred at her accession, and she regularly referred to Frederick II as 'the evil animal' and 'the monster'. (He responded in kind by having a sermon preached pointedly on the text of St Paul: 'Let the woman learn in silence.')[16] France's friendship with Prussia, on the other hand, had long been seen as the cornerstone of the latter's foreign policy; but it had been eroded in a complex series of manoeuvres in which Prussia turned towards England. Not only had hostilities between France and England – rival colonial powers – already broken out in the Americas in 1754, but France also viewed England as an enemy in Europe. Since Austria, once England's friend, felt similarly betrayed by the latter's involvement with Prussia, the way was open for a diplomatic *volte-face*.

Once the will, or rather the need, was there, personalities played their part. The French King Louis XV favoured the alliance, although his only son and heir, the Dauphin Louis Ferdinand, his daughter-in-law Maria Josepha (a Saxon princess), and his formidable array of grown-up daughters still at court, were all resolutely anti-Austrian. But the appointment of a pro-Austrian Foreign Minister, the Duc de Choiseul, meant that, for the time being at least, these family prejudices were unimportant. Meanwhile Maria Teresa's own trusted servant Prince Kaunitz, convincing her that French support would enable her to reconquer Silesia, was sent as ambassador to Versailles in 1750. Maria Teresa, that pillar of conjugal virtue, was even accused (falsely) of despatching messages to the Marquise de Pompadour, Louis XV's all-powerful mistress; there was an ugly rumour that the Empress had actually addressed the mistress as 'cousin'. Afterwards Maria Teresa would indignantly deny this to the Electress Maria Antonia of Bavaria, one of Joseph I's dispossessed daughters: 'That channel would not have suited me.'[17] Nevertheless the fact was that there was opportunism on both sides, and Maria Teresa was certainly not without her share of it.

The imperial Austrian will was firm, as was the royal French will.* As Voltaire wittily expressed it: some people said that the union of France and Austria was an unnatural monstrosity, but since it was necessary, it turned out to be quite natural.[18] Nevertheless the heart and mind of neither country were won over. As we shall see, Austria and Maria Teresa continued to admire France as the fountain of style, just as they continued to employ the French language. At the same time the French were regularly dismissed as frivolous, lightweight, incapable of constancy and so forth, compared with the 'solidity and frankness' of the Germans (the word the Empress and her relations always used to describe themselves). It was an unfavourable stereotype, which could not fail to impress itself upon any child – say, a small archduchess – brought up at the Austrian court.

The French for their part, conscious of their civilizing role, were not backward in their derision for customs other than their own. An alliance could not so easily sweep away the prejudices against Austria that had so long held sway, especially the suspicion that Austria might intend to manipulate and control France in its own best interests. This was a point of view that would impress itself upon another young person, for example, a young French prince, Louis Auguste, son of the Dauphin, brought up at the French court.

The question of an alliance between an archduchess and a prince was not an academic one. Europe was now dividing into two powerful groups, whose rivalries in both the Old World and the New World would shortly lead to a seven-year-long war. Prussia, England and Portugal faced an alliance of Austria, France, Sweden and Saxony, to which Russia would soon be added; Spain, France's fellow Bourbon monarchy, would also become involved on the French side. These various allies would shortly seek to express their future cooperation in the customary manner of the time: royal intermarriage.

---

* A huge set of Sèvres porcelain, white ornamented with a pattern of forest-green ribbons, which was given by Louis XV to Maria Teresa to celebrate the alliance, can still be seen in the Hofburg Museum.

As it happened, the 1740s and 1750s had witnessed the birth of a multitude of young royals, both male and female, within the reigning families of these countries. Austria no longer lacked male heirs as it had under two successive emperors, Joseph I and Charles VI. The days when the direct line of the French monarchy was represented by the frail person of a single child, the great-grandson of Louis XIV (the future Louis XV), were over. Europe was positively crowded with small royal pawns, ready, as it seemed, to be employed in the great game of diplomatic alliance.

In the separate but related Spanish branch of the Bourbon family, there was a number of princes and princesses available; for example Isabella, Maria Louisa and Don Ferdinand of Parma, the grandchildren of Louis XV by his favourite daughter known as 'Madame Infante'. There were the children of the King of Spain: his heir the Prince of Asturias, another Maria Louisa and his younger son, Ferdinand, who assumed the throne of Naples. Then there were the princes and princesses of Savoy. This was a royal house with many historic links to France – Louis XV's mother had been a Savoyard princess – more especially because Savoy's geographical position in what is now northern Italy made it an excellent buffer against Austria. Lastly, of the major players, there were the princes and princesses at Versailles – the Children of France as they were proud to be termed. These were the French grandchildren of Louis XV, the family of his only son.

All in all, fate or nature had provided abundant material for the older generation to weave their dynastic plots, be they Louis XV, Maria Teresa, Charles III of Spain or the reigning King of Sardinia, Charles Emmanuel III, grandfather of the Savoyard family. The so-called Family Pact of 1761, by which Maria Teresa's heir, the Archduke Joseph, married Isabella of Parma, and Isabella's younger sister married her first cousin, heir to the throne of Spain, was an outward manifestation of this. French Bourbons, Spanish Bourbons and Habsburgs were all joining together in opposition to Prussia and England.

What then of the many Habsburg archduchesses who had been born in the space of roughly ten years and who were now joined by another sister? What of Marie Christine? Elizabeth? Amalia? Josepha? Joanna? Charlotte? (The eldest, Marianne, being disabled, was not considered a candidate for marriage.) Without any specific names being mentioned – one princess being much like another when it came to dynastic alliances – it was understood that three of the archduchesses might be destined for, in no particular order, Don Ferdinand of Parma, the young King Ferdinand of Naples – and maybe a French prince.

The new baby, contentedly nursed by Constance Weber, was a sweet little thing. But that was hardly the point when it came to the matter of forging an alliance. From the first Madame Antoine had her value, not as an individual, but as a piece on her mother's chessboard.

CHAPTER TWO

Born to Obey

'They are born to obey and must learn to do so in good time.'

Empress Maria Teresa on her daughters, 1756

L ike many people exiled from the scenes of their childhood, Marie Antoinette would look back on her early years as idyllic. It is easy to see how this might be so. The family portraits of which Maria Teresa was so fond do indeed portray a domestic paradise for which anyone might yearn in later life.[1]

Here was the Empress, supremely confident in herself and her position, still handsome in her forties.* It is true that, like her husband, she had begun to put on weight and no longer reminded older courtiers of the quicksilver young woman of the 1740s who danced and played cards all night, yet could ride and go sledging with equal energy in the day. In her case, given that her mother the Empress Elizabeth Christina suffered from dropsy, her weight gain may have been partly due to an unavoidable heredity, partly due to multiple child-bearing. However, the celebrated physician and educationalist Gerhard Van Swieten, Maria Teresa's guru, regularly lectured the imperial couple on the need to take care and eat less, so there may have been an element of personal responsibility.[2] Yet the Empress's ample appearance only served to emphasize the awesome dignity

---

* Maria Teresa celebrated her fortieth birthday on 13 May 1757 when Marie Antoinette was eighteen months old.

combined with maternal tenderness that was the image she radiated. Who would not be proud to be the child of such a mother?

As for Francis Stephen, in portraits he cut an equally imposing figure. In private life, however – which he infinitely preferred – he was cheerful, teasing, indulgent. In short, he was an ideal father from the point of view of a small child who would not pick up the strains imposed by his frequent infidelities. To these, Maria Teresa, with a characteristic mixture of fieriness and puritanism, was never reconciled. Wifely tolerance of husbandly frailty was yet another eighteenth-century female virtue, like submissiveness and accepting a worldly marriage, which Maria Teresa preached to others but did not apply to herself.

A preference for informality was Francis Stephen's legacy to the Austrian Habsburgs; it was undoubtedly one that he handed on to his youngest daughter along with the Lorrainer blood to which it was generally ascribed. Louis Dutens, a traveller who knew most of the European courts, praised the 'good-natured' Emperor for his innovations. 'The family of Lorraine,' he wrote, 'has contributed not a little to banish from the Court of Vienna the severe etiquette which prevailed there.'

The message was not, however, of the need to abolish all formality. Although the strict customs, including the old-fashioned black court dress inherited from Spain, were gradually dropped, the Austrian court remained a place of much stately splendour when the occasion demanded it. There were still, for example, 1500 court chamberlains in the time of Maria Teresa whose existence was justified by various ritual duties whose origins lay far in the past. What was important was the distinction, encouraged by Francis Stephen and supported by Maria Teresa, between state ceremonial and private life. The one was to be carried out as a matter of duty, and as magnificently as possible. The other was to be enjoyed.

Joseph Weber, Madame Antoine's foster-brother, revealed that the Archdukes and Archduchesses were encouraged to make friends with 'ordinary' children in their everyday lives. In the same way, people of merit were admitted freely to the court, without necessity of birth or title. Except, that is, on the great days of formal celebration; then, as in the old days, ceremonial pomp continued to be observed, including the restrictions of the Rights of Entry.[4] The young Madame Antoine, born when this relaxation had already taken place, grew up taking this distinction at court or in Vienna for granted.

A family group on St Nicholas's Day 1762, painted by the Archduchess Marie Christine, perfectly depicts the bourgeois cosiness of the imperial couple's home life, something that was unthinkable at the parallel court of Versailles. This was the feast at which young children traditionally received presents. The Emperor, at his breakfast, wears a robe and slippers, with a turban-style cap on his head instead of a wig. The Empress's dress is extremely plain and Marie Christine, who put herself in the picture, looks more like a maid than an archduchess. The Archduke Ferdinand is apparently upset with his gift, while little Max, on the floor with his toys, is delighted. A smiling Madame Antoine holds a doll aloft to indicate that she has just been given it; at the age of seven she looks much like a doll herself.

This seemingly perfect childhood had for its background three principal castles, as well as numerous other lesser ones, and the superb houses of the Austrian grandees. The stately and sprawling Hofburg, where Antoine was born, was used in the winter months; it was central to the capital where these same grandees also had their splendid town houses. In spite of its size, the opportunities for freedom for the children could hardly be extensive there. Nevertheless, Marie Antoinette would later remember it with pleasure. She became sentimental at the thought of proposed changes, although she was happy to think of Maria Teresa moving into her old rooms.[5] Only about five miles away, however, lay the magical palace of Schönbrunn.

This enormous imperial abode could compete in size and splendour with most of the palaces in Europe. At the same time it enjoyed a pastoral setting. Its short distance from central Vienna – and a well-maintained road – meant it could be used for state occasions in the spring and summer; the family generally took up residence there from Easter onwards. In contrast, the French court at Versailles had no real base in Paris itself by the middle of the eighteenth century. The Austrian court was thus more like that of England as it developed under George III, able to oscillate between his London residence (now Buckingham Palace), Windsor Castle, and Hampton Court.

Everyone loved Schönbrunn with its beautiful gardens, leading to parkland and woods beyond as far as the eye could see. By the time of Madame Antoine's birth Maria Teresa had made substantial improvements to the residence of her forefathers, not only necessary repairs – it had been destroyed by the Turks in 1683 – but various enhancements. She was seized by the contemporary passion for chinoiserie and Eastern decor, including lacquer, mirrors, vellum miniatures and tapestries, declaring 'all the diamonds in the world' were as nothing compared to 'what comes from the Indies'.[6]

Significant from the point of view of Habsburg family life was the Empress's decision to construct two new wings to meet the demands of her growing family. The Archdukes inhabited the right wing, the Archduchesses the left. Although each child or young person had his or her own suite of five rooms – including an audience room as well as a salon and a bedroom, sisters close in age and in the same wing were in fact thrown further together by this arrangement, which separated them from both their brothers and their parents.*

Francis Stephen loved plants and gardens; the Dutch Botanical Garden at Schönbrunn was created in 1753 and an orangery was built two years later, housing a rich collection of tropical plants. The gardens themselves were planned and replanned with zest, an enthusiasm that Madame Antoine herself would take for granted as one of the natural interests of a civilized royal person. A menagerie, situated so that Francis Stephen could enjoy contemplating it over his breakfast, had been established in 1751; it included a camel sent by a sultan, a rhinoceros that had arrived by boat up the Danube, a puma, the red squirrels favoured by Marie Christine and the parrots

---

* These private apartments can still be seen today, with pictures by Marie Christine. The so-called Marie Antoinette Room, one of the state apartments, is named for a Gobelin tapestry woven after a painting by Madame Vigée Le Brun and donated by the Emperor Napoleon III in the nineteenth century.

that were the favourites of Elizabeth. There was a theatre for those constant musical and dramatic celebrations.[7]

Another theatre was built at Laxenburg in 1753. Like everything to do with Laxenburg, it was on a much smaller scale. That was in fact the point of the Empress's predilection for this charming rococo palace.* It lay about ten miles south of Vienna in the direction of Hungary, at the edge of a small pretty town, and was bordered by thick woods good for hunting. Here there was simply no room for the vast crowds of courtiers thought essential to the imperial dignity at Schönbrunn and the Hofburg; even great officials had to make do with houses in the town.[8] Understandably, the imperial family greatly preferred performances in the Laxenburg theatre, because the scale made it much easier for them to hear.

This was a period when many royalties were embellishing their country retreats by requiring special uniforms (the modern equivalent of this dress code would be that oxymoron casual chic). For example, the colours demanded by the Pompadour at Bellevue were purple, gold and white. Laxenburg's dress code was a red cloth frockcoat (*le frac*), which was considered informal at this period, with a green waistcoat, and red dresses for the ladies. Both had to be ornamented with gold, which made their casual chic expensive for the courtiers to produce.[9] Nevertheless the message was clear: Laxenburg is different; even the clothes are different.

The Empress herself, with all her cares of state, was known to be generally cheerful while at Laxenburg; her father Charles VI had also loved it for the beauty of its surroundings. These were in effect family holidays. It was no wonder that of all the scenes of Antoine's childhood, Laxenburg was the one that exercised the greatest nostalgic pull. Not only was there that cheerful mother but the Archdukes and Archduchesses could also enjoy a measure of personal freedom.

Early in the next century, the Empress Marie Louise, Marie Antoinette's great-niece, would be struck by the similarity

---

* Laxenburg is now the seat of IIASA (International Institute for Applied Systems Analysis); there is a thriving conference centre there.

between Laxenburg and the Petit Trianon at Versailles; no doubt the resemblance was one effect of Marie Antoinette's affection for this first exquisite palace of retreat.[10] In fact Laxenburg was an adapted hunting lodge, rebuilt by Leopold I, like so much else, after the end of the Turkish depredations. It was during Antoine's own childhood that the court architect Nicholas Pacassi designed the so-called Blue Court (a corruption of the original owner's name) as a further enlargement; the need, as at Schönbrunn, was to accommodate the royal family.

A belvedere now crowned the roof of the north wing and there was a sequence of playrooms, like elevated garden rooms, with wide views across the park.* They were painted with a series of *trompe l'oeils*, birds on the ceiling, and romantic pastoral scenes on the walls, glimpsed through pale green latticework up which climbed painted sweet peas. The feeling of freshness, of greenery and light, was intended to be vivid for the children, even when the weather was bad. In eighteenth-century royal terms – the only ones Marie Antoinette was in a position to understand – Laxenburg presented an image of rustic bliss, a paradise that could perhaps one day be recreated.

At Laxenburg and elsewhere, festivities, both outdoors and indoors, punctuated the lives of the imperial family. The heavy Austrian winters offered unrivalled opportunities for sledging and sledging parties. (Memories of such jollities meant that Marie Antoinette would get excited all her life at the sight of any serious snowfall.) One traveller evoked a glamorous vision of the Archduchesses in fur-trimmed velvet and diamonds, gliding by in gilded sledges in the shape of swans; the Archdukes Ferdinand and Max acted as drivers and the whole scene – at Schönbrunn – took place by torchlight.[11] There were cavalry tournaments known as carousels to be watched, and elaborate equestrian displays. Riding and hunting were considered normal occupations for young women.

* This delightful background to the childhood of Marie Antoinette can still be seen today. The park that she would have known was, however, remodelled in 'the English fashion' in 1783.

The court fêtes in theatres, big and small, were dominated by the strong taste for music in the imperial family and its supporting aristocracy, something that was taken for granted and viewed with pleasure, much like the heavy snows. Nor was this appreciation and talent confined to the aristocracy: Dr Charles Burney, the English musicologist who journeyed throughout Europe for his general history of music of the mid-1770s, was struck by the level of musical education not only at court but also among the villagers. 'It has been said by travellers that the nobility keep musicians in their houses,' he noted, 'but in keeping servants, it is impossible to do otherwise.'[12] This was not a new thing. Joseph Haydn, for whose music Marie Antoinette would later display enthusiasm, was born in eastern Austria in 1732, the son of a wheelwright. For nearly thirty years, off and on, he was employed at the court of the great Esterhazy family. Gluck, nearly twenty years his senior, who was at one point singing-master to the young Archduchess and would enjoy a long-lasting and valued connection to her, was the son of the chief forester of Count Kinsky.

In the case of Madame Antoine, the enjoyment of music was from childhood central to her life. It is true that she can hardly have taken an important part in the earliest fête that centred round her. This was the celebration held on 1 November 1756, the eve of her first birthday. However, from an early age she took part in the celebration on her name-day, 13 June, the Feast of St Antony. In the morning her parents would drive to a solemn High Mass at the Church of the Minorities, followed by a gala in honour of the youngest Archduchess.[13]

In 1759, shortly before her fourth birthday, Antoine sang 'a French Vaudeville song' at the celebrations for the name-day of her father, the feast of St Francis, whilst her elder brothers and sisters sang Italian arias. The Empress's own name-day came shortly afterwards, when the Emperor organized an impromptu musical party for his wife, once again with the children singing and performing; the Archduke Ferdinand played an overture on the kettledrum.[14]

The imperial children acted as audience too. On 13 October 1762 'the little child from Salzburg' – Wolfgang Amadeus

Mozart – came with his father and sister Nannerl to Schönbrunn. He played the harpsichord in the presence of the Empress, the Emperor, the court composer Georg Christoph Wagenseil and various of Maria Teresa's offspring, including Antoine who was three months older than the prodigy. The child played 'marvellously', was the verdict, and he was rewarded with an honorarium of 100 ducats and presents from other nobles. He was also presented with a fine outfit that had belonged to the Archduke Max, a coat of lilac colour and a moiré waistcoat, all trimmed with gold braid. The concert was repeated, again at Schönbrunn, a week later.[15]

Perhaps it is not true that the young Mozart flung himself at the young Marie Antoinette and declared that he would marry her when he grew up (an apocryphal story which, if it had in some amazing way come true, would certainly have altered the course of history). But his impetuosity was certainly in evidence; Antoine was present when he rushed up to the Empress and jumped on her lap, receiving a kiss in return. Mozart also responded to the Emperor's teasing by accurately playing with one finger on a covered keyboard, and showed his own play-fulness by demanding that Wagenseil should turn over his music for him, as he played the court composer's own work. Shortly afterwards Mozart travelled on to France, where the French King's daughter Madame Victoire became his patron, receiving a dedication of some piano sonatas in return. The Marquise de Pompadour was, however, less welcoming. 'Who is this that will not kiss me?' enquired the 'little Orpheus' of the haughty mistress: 'The Empress kissed me.'[16]

Much of the girls' education was centred on their need to appear and perform gracefully at court events as they grew older. Their teachers included not only Gluck, but Wagenseil, Joseph Stephan and Johann Adolph Hasse, who later dedicated a book to Marie Antoinette. There were also two English women, Marianne and Cecilia Davies, who played the harpsichord and also specialized in the armonica or 'musical glass'. They lived in the same house as Hasse while they instructed the Empress's daughters. With such influences it was not difficult for anyone with a modicum of natural talent, plus natural inclination, to shine as required. Marie Antoinette would later be described as sight-reading to a professional standard, and able to take part in enjoyable little concerts with her friends. The harp was her favourite instrument and under the guidance of the talented performer, Joseph Hinner, she would make considerable progress.[17]

Of the various arts, however, dancing was the one at which Marie Antoinette was generally held to excel. The particular grace of her deportment, including the distinguished carriage of her head, would become a feature of her appearance upon which every observer, whether friendly or hostile, commented. Its origin lay in the formal dancing lessons that she was given at a time when ballet itself was beginning to develop in a new direction. It was the celebrated French ballet master and choreographer Jean-Georges Noverre, author of a seminal book of 1760, *Lettres sur la danse et sur les ballets*, who taught Madame Antoine.[18] Maria Teresa was the patroness of Noverre, a role that her daughter would also adopt.

Apart from this perceived need to perform, the other emphasis in the Archduchesses' education was on docility and obedience. The crucial text used in their upbringing was *Les Aventures de Télémaque* by Fénelon, written at the end of the seventeenth century for the heir to Louis XIV and imported to Austria by Francis Stephen. This underlined the importance for the female sex of industriousness and dexterity (embroidery, which Madame Antoine loved, was fortunately a suitable feminine skill) but also of modesty and submission. The little dancers, especially Antoine, the youngest, were to be like puppets and manipulated as puppets are. The necessity for total obedience from her daughters was something about which Maria Teresa was quite unequivocal. 'They are born to obey and must learn to do so in good time,' she declared the year after Antoine was born.[19]

But the imperial daughters were not puppets, none of them, not even the littlest one who would in the future be termed by her mother, lovingly but patronizingly, as 'our sweet Antoinette'. Like any other large family, this one contained a collection of diverse individuals and, like any other large family, was inevitably divided by its range of age and experience, which means that it cannot helpfully be regarded as a monolithic entity. As one analyses the internal dynamics of the Habsburgs, the idyllic picture that was promoted by Maria Teresa, which Marie Antoinette obediently remembered, takes on a very different aspect. Even the female submission that the Empress preached contrasted rather oddly with much of her own perceivable behaviour.

It was true that the Empress paraded her wifely deference to the Emperor; on the other hand it was she who worked day and night at her state papers and the Emperor who went happily off hunting. It was Maria Teresa who was the wonder of Europe for her strength and decisiveness, not Francis Stephen. To say the least of it, Maria Teresa presented a complicated role model to her daughters.

Beneath the idyllic surface, there were also currents and rapids and shoals, jealousies and rivalries, which, however common to all large families, took on an added significance in a family of state. In effect the children of Maria Teresa and Francis Stephen, born between 1738 (Marianne) and 1756 (Max), fell into two groups. The first family – and the phrase was apt in more ways than one – consisted, besides the invalid Marianne, of the heir, Joseph, born on 13 March in 1741; Marie Christine born on 13 May, Maria Teresa's own birthday, the following year; then came 'the lovely Elizabeth' as she was known, born in August 1743. The Archduke Charles, born in 1745, died when young; the first family was completed by Amalia born in 1746, and Leopold in 1747.

After that there was an artificial gap of five years caused by the birth and death of a daughter in 1748, compounded when the next-born daughter, Joanna, also died young. The third in line of the row of ill-fated daughters, Josepha, another beauty born in 1751, would not, as we shall see, survive either, with crucial effects on the fortunes of her two younger sisters. Thus the second family began with that Archduchess always called Charlotte by her siblings, just as Marie Antoinette was called Antoine, although she is known to history as Maria Carolina; she was born on 13 August 1752. There followed in quick succession Ferdinand, an extremely pretty little boy, Antoine, and Maximilian, a chubby baby later nicknamed plainly 'Fat Max'; the three of them were born in the space of two and a half years.

It will be seen that Madame Antoine's position in the family was marked on the one hand by distance; the Archduke Joseph was nearly fifteen years older, old enough to be her father by the royal standards of the time. On the other hand this position was marked by closeness; sandwiched as she was between two brothers eighteen months older and thirteen months younger, Antoine's share of maternal attention as a baby can hardly have been great. In any case Maria Teresa, in her late thirties and forties, was no longer the happy young mother who had greeted the birth of Joseph, the male heir, with ecstasy. In fact her energies were now dominated by affairs of state and the halcyon period during which Antoine had been conceived and born was over. From late 1756 until the Peace of Paris in February 1763 – Antoine's infant years – Austria was at war with Prussia and England, and Maria Teresa was at the helm. The Seven Years' War was not a time of serenity for the Empress. Nor was the lost region of Silesia gloriously restored, as predicted by Kaunitz, at the subsequent peace, which marked no more than a stalemate between Austria and Prussia.

Nevertheless it was Maria Teresa, however preoccupied, who was the central figure of her children's lives and whose love – hopefully coupled with respect – they sought, even if, as in the case of the younger ones, a strong dose of awe, even fear, was mingled with these feelings. Much later Marie Antoinette told a lady-in-waiting that she had never loved her mother, only feared her; but this was hindsight, when a great many unhappy adult experiences had distorted the simplicities of childhood. Her comment during her mother's lifetime was probably nearer the truth: 'I love the Empress but I'm frightened of her, even at a distance; when I'm writing to her, I never feel completely at ease.' The evidence of earlier times is of an adoring daughter who on occasion was quite pathetic in her desire to please. She dearly wanted to incarnate 'our sweet Antoinette', the personality at once engaging and docile designated for her by Maria Teresa.[20]

Given the inexorable authority of the Empress, the clear

favouritism that she exhibited for the Archduchess Marie Christine almost from her birth (was it the shared birthday?) was a source of great resentment to all the brothers and sisters. At one point Marianne was said to have been made ill by it.[21] Joseph felt it; and when his wife, Isabella of Parma, that bride, half-French and half-Spanish Bourbon, bestowed on him by the Family Pact in 1761, also professed herself fascinated by Marie Christine, matters were only exacerbated. The phenomenon was so marked that one wonders, as with all parents who indulge in marked favouritism, why the Empress did not sometimes question it herself. On the contrary, Maria Teresa saw 'Mimi', or 'la Marie' as her second surviving daughter was known, as the consolation that was owed to her by life.

Outwardly Antoine resented the bossiness of this sister who was thirteen and a half years older than she; as she saw it, Marie Christine used her paramount position to make trouble with her mother. It was a view shared by her brother Leopold, who was much closer in age to Marie Christine, who denounced her scolding ways, her sharp tongue and, above all, her habit of 'telling everything to the Empress'.[22] Certainly Marie Christine had a strong streak of the 'masculine' or masterful in her nature. This was inherited from Maria Teresa by more than one archduchess – Amalia and Maria Carolina, for example – but not by Marie Antoinette. At the same time Marie Christine was highly intelligent as well as artistically gifted; she was certainly the outstanding sister in that respect.

It was easy as a result for Antoine to conceive a timid disinclination for the company of intellectual, brilliantly self-possessed older women, exactly the sort of sophisticated creatures who by tradition dominated French society. Amalia, although nearly ten years older, was a much less threatening figure; she was not so clever, not so interesting, not so pretty, not so graceful – and for all these reasons she was not so much loved by Maria Teresa. Although Antoine could cope with Amalia, the echoes of her childish jealousy for Mimi, as the years passed, would resonate ever more strongly.

Antoine's relationship with her closest sister in age, Charlotte, on the other hand, set quite a different pattern. The future Maria

Carolina, three years her senior, was raised with Antoine almost as though they were twins. As Frederick the Great said of his relationship with his own sister: 'These first bonds are indissoluble.' From Charlotte, Antoine learnt that loving relationships with delightful female contemporaries could be like bastions in an unkind or puzzling world. The very fact that for some years the two youngest Archduchesses escaped a great deal of official attention meant that they could bond happily with each other. They tended to share experiences; if one got ill, the other would catch the infection, and both would be segregated, then sent off to convalesce together.[23]

These were two lively little girls; at the same time Charlotte was the dominant one, the protectress, Antoine the dependent one. Maria Teresa, besotted as she was with her Mimi, insistent as she was on obedience, nevertheless admired Charlotte's spirit; she was, said the Empress, the one who most closely resembled herself. Perhaps it helped their symbiotic relationship that Charlotte and Antoine 'resembled each other greatly', as the painter Madame Vigée Le Brun later pointed out (portraits of the two can easily be mistaken).[24] As children they shared the same big blue eyes, pink and white complexions, fair hair and longish noses; but for indefinable reasons, it all added up to feminine prettiness in Antoine. Charlotte, if 'not as pretty', was on the other hand attractive with a forceful personality.

The marriage of Joseph to Isabella of Parma, which was intended to solidify the connection of Austria with the France of her grandfather Louis XV, did not in fact last long. In 1762 Isabella gave birth to a daughter, the Archduchess Teresa, and died a year later giving birth to a second daughter, who also died. The latter had been named Christine after the sister-in-law for whom Isabella had felt such a passion, comparing the two of them to Orpheus and Eurydice, following Gluck's opera on the same subject. Broken-hearted, Joseph placed the matter of a second marriage, essential to produce an imperial heir, in the hands of his parents. After some arguments on the subject of rival German princesses in which Marie Christine favoured Cunegonde of

Saxony, the choice was made of a Habsburg second cousin, Josepha of Bavaria.[25]

The wedding, at the end of January 1765, was celebrated with suitable magnificence. Gluck composed an operetta for the occasion, *Il Parnasso Confuso*, with a libretto by Metastasio. The Archduchess Elizabeth played Apollo, with Amalia, Josepha and Charlotte as Muses; the Archduke Leopold both conducted the orchestra and played the harpsichord. The ballet *Il Trionfo d'Amore*, which was considered the essential accompaniment to an opera, was danced by the younger children.[26] A picture by Mytens shows Ferdinand and Antoine, shepherd and shepherdess, while Max, wings and all, enacts Cupid. Antoine is exquisitely poised, her famous deportment already in evidence, the graceful arms well displayed. Her face is also instantly recognizable, not so much for the characteristically long neck on which it is set, as for the significantly high forehead. The Mytens picture was one that Antoine herself loved and she would subsequently receive it with delight to adorn her personal haven.

Six months later the courtly family bliss that this picture epitomized vanished utterly. The Emperor and Empress were setting out for Innsbruck in order to celebrate the marriage of their second surviving son, the Archduke Leopold to the Spanish King's daughter. It was intended to be as splendid an occasion as could be conceived, in order to emphasize not only the majesty of both monarchies, but also the brilliant nature of the alliance. At the last moment the Emperor paused, and on some strange impulse rushed back to give the nine-year-old Antoine one more embrace. He took her on his knee and hugged her over and over again. Antoine noticed with surprise that he had tears in his eyes; leaving her was causing Francis Stephen great suffering. Twenty-five years later she still recalled the incident with pain; she believed that Francis Stephen had had some presentiment of the great unhappiness that would be her lot. For Madame Antoine never saw her father again.

On 18 August 1765 at Innsbruck the Emperor died of a massive stroke. He had lived for fifty-six years and ten days, as Maria Teresa noted in a pathetic list of numbers, which went on to calculate the months, weeks, days and even the hours of his life. She added, 'My happy married life lasted twenty-nine years and six months and six days,' and she listed the details of that period too, down to the hours: 258,774.[27]

The devastation of the Empress was total. It was symbolic of her grief that she cut off the hair of which she had once been so proud, draped her apartments in sombre velvets, and herself wore nothing but widow's black for the rest of her life. The strong young mother, who had once said cheerfully that she would have ridden into battle herself if she had not been perpetually pregnant, was transformed into a figure of tragic severity. Everything about her was and remained 'dark and mournful'.[28] Already awesome to her younger children, Maria Teresa now projected a universal dissatisfaction with their behaviour. It was rooted in her own personal unhappiness but nonetheless constituted a perpetual reproach to those who could still enjoy life and its pleasures.

CHAPTER THREE

Greatness

~~~

'If one is to consider only the greatness of your position, you are the happiest of your sisters and all princesses.'

Maria Teresa to Marie Antoinette, 1770

T he bereft Empress now shared her power – since part of it could only be enjoyed by a male – with her twenty-four-year-old son, who was elected Emperor (as Joseph II) to replace his father. But she allowed nothing, neither mourning nor Joseph's promotion, to interrupt her sedulous policy of planning her children's marriages. There were to be victims of this single-hearted application, giving new meaning to the celebrated family motto in Latin, which can be roughly translated as: 'Others have to wage war [to succeed] but you, fortunate Habsburg, marry!' But there was one beneficiary of the Emperor's untimely death, and that was the Archduchess Marie Christine.

The favourite daughter had set her heart on a cousin on her mother's side, Prince Albert of Saxony. This intelligent and sensitive young man, four years Marie Christine's senior, had arrived in Vienna in 1759 with his younger brother Clement. Both fought in Maria Teresa's army during the Seven Years' War; Clement of Saxony went into the Church and subsequently became Archbishop-Elector of Trier. Albert, however, fell in love with the lively young Archduchess as they shared a sledge on the way to Schönbrunn. Unfortunately for all his qualities, his intelligence and his artistic interests, Albert presented no sort of match for an Emperor's daughter. A brother of the Dauphine Maria Josepha, he was the fourth son in the huge family of August III of Saxony, King of Poland, and could offer no kind of position. In any case Francis Stephen had wanted Marie Christine to marry his sister's son the Duke of Chablais, thus underlining the Lorrainer connection.

The death of her father and the increased dependency of her mother on her Mimi gave Marie Christine her chance. She married Albert in April 1766. It was a brilliant stroke in more ways than one. First of all, Mimi had achieved that ultimate rarity among the marriages of princesses, a love match. That was in itself enough to arouse the jealousy of her sisters for whom less romantic fates were reserved. But there was more to envy. Since Albert was not a rich man, Maria Teresa proceeded to even things up. Marie Christine was given a huge dowry while Albert received the Duchy of Teschen which Maria Teresa acquired for him. The couple were promised jointly the reversion of the governorship of the Austrian Netherlands on the death of Maria Teresa's brother-in-law Prince Charles of Lorraine. In the meantime Albert was made Governor of Pressburg in Hungary, with its vast castle on the Danube.

After the wedding Maria Teresa was 'childish enough', in her own words, to hear her remaining daughters pass through her room and fancy that 'my Mimi' was among them, instead of in her own home at Pressburg. In truth the position of Pressburg made it easy for the Empress to visit this young couple, whom she found it a pleasure to see together. Marie Christine also received the coveted award of a house of her own at Laxenburg. A year after the wedding Marie Christine nearly died in childbirth, and her baby daughter did die; there would be no more children. The consequence was that Marie Christine enjoyed the greatest prize of all, the constant gift of her mother's company. As Marie Antoinette would write wistfully to Maria Teresa: 'How I envy Marie [Christine] the happiness of seeing you so often!'[1]

At the beginning of 1767 the Empress was left with five daughters on her hands. 'The lovely Elizabeth' was twenty-three, Amalia nearly twenty-one, and Josepha, another beauty, was sixteen; then there was Charlotte, who would be fifteen in August, and Antoine, who was in her twelfth year. Due to her youth, the last named was not at this point a vital player in the imperial game, although she was mentioned vaguely in connection with her coevals, the French princes. This game might be termed that of 'alliances and establishments'; the phrase was that of the memorialist Louis Dutens as he congratulated Maria Teresa on that mixture of 'good fortune and address' that had brought her such success in setting up her children.[2]

The two Ferdinands – of Parma and Naples, both born in 1751 – were prizes that Maria Teresa was determined to secure, not so much for her daughters – whose individuality was of no moment – as for the sake of the alliances they would symbolize. Louis XV, advising his grandson Don Ferdinand of Parma, took a worldly-wise attitude to the whole matter: what did it matter who she was, so long as he got a suitable wife? It was true that it was easier to make love to a pretty woman than a plain one, but that was about the measure of the difference.[3] Charles III of Spain on the other hand, as his father, objected to the choice of Amalia for Ferdinand of Naples since she was six years older than her prospective bridegroom. This made the sixteen-year-old Archduchess Josepha the obvious candidate for this Ferdinand. She was also delightfully pretty, pliant by nature and, for all these reasons, her brother the Emperor's favourite.

Then a series of disasters struck, making 1767 Maria Teresa's *annus horribilis*. Already Marie Christine had lost her baby, and she herself had been seriously ill. Then the poor unloved Empress, Joseph's second wife, died of smallpox at the end of May and was placed, as was the custom, in a tomb in the imperial crypt of the Hofburg.* After that Maria Teresa herself caught smallpox, and came close enough to death to receive the Last Sacrament; Europe trembled at the news, while her own family was in shock.

---

* Today the imperial crypt is still a site of respectful mourning (visitors are requested to take off their hats); here 143 Habsburgs and one commoner – Maria Teresa's governess – are buried. Amid the dark shapes of the tombs and the sculpted figures of death, the skulls grinning under their diadems, can be seen bouquets of tribute, including fresh flowers, tied in ribbons of the imperial colours.

The next disaster was in fact indirectly caused by Maria Teresa herself. Once recovered, she insisted that her daughter, the Archduchess Josepha, who was on the verge of making her long bridal journey to Naples, go with her down into the imperial crypt to pray; it was intended as an act of filial piety. But the tomb of Joseph's wife was not sufficiently sealed. As the anticipatory nuptial celebrations were in full swing in Vienna, the Archduchess caught smallpox. On 15 October – ironically enough Maria Teresa's name-day – Josepha died. Leopold Mozart, among others, had attended the celebrations with young Wolfgang, hoping for profitable engagements. As he gloomily put it, in view of the cancellation of all public events: 'The Princess Bride has become the bride of a heavenly bridegroom.' It was a terrible death, which left a permanent impression on her little sister. Antoine remembered Josepha taking her in her arms; with a grim premonition, Josepha told the girl that she was leaving her for ever – not for the kingdom of Naples but for the family vault.[4]

That was not all. Smallpox stalked the royal houses of Europe like a spectre with a scythe. It was fortunate for Antoine personally that she had caught it at the age of two, in a mild version; having recovered completely except for a few practically invisible marks, she was immune to infection.[5] At times, however, the scythe wounded but did not kill. The Archduchess Elizabeth also caught the disease; she lived but her beauty was utterly destroyed. It was a personal tragedy for the Archduchess, who had been extremely vain of her proverbial good looks; according to her mother, 'It mattered not if the look of admiration came from a prince or a Swiss Guard, Elizabeth was satisfied.'[6] But in public terms, it meant that she was immediately and ruthlessly eliminated from the European marriage market.*

The immediate problem was to arrange a bride for King Ferdinand of Naples, he who was expecting the speedy arrival of a young wife. Maria Teresa swung into action once more. In a letter to Charles III of Spain a month after Josepha's death

* Like her elder sister, Marianne, who was an invalid, Elizabeth would live and die unmarried.

she outlined her bloodstock: 'I grant you with real pleasure one of my remaining daughters to make good the loss … I do currently have two who could fit, one is the Archduchess Amalia who is said to have a pretty face and whose health should promise a numerous progeny, and the other is the Archduchess Charlotte who is also very healthy and a year and seven months younger than the King of Naples.' Maria Teresa left it up to the Spanish King as the boy's father to choose as long as 'the association of my house with Your Majesty's' was preserved.[7]

It was true that where Charlotte was concerned, Maria Teresa said she felt a rival obligation to Louis XV and his house. Charlotte happened to be Louis XV's god-daughter, and his granddaughter Maria Louisa of Parma also thought Charlotte would be an excellent choice to marry the heir to the French throne.[8] Charlotte was only two years older than Louis Auguste, the former Duc de Berry, whose father's death in 1765 made him the new Dauphin of France; that was not an impossible gap. Not only was she 'healthy', she was also known to be vivacious and intelligent. But the King of Naples was not to be fobbed off; he was declared by his father to prefer the much younger Charlotte to Amalia. Whatever the claims of the French, the deal was done with the Spanish. That meant that Amalia could in turn be allotted Louis XV's grandson, Don Ferdinand of Parma.

From Amalia's point of view it was a devastating decision, since she was violently in love with Charles of Zweibrücken. But this German princeling was not considered of sufficient stature by Maria Teresa. Not only was Don Ferdinand six years Amalia's junior, but he was only a duke, so that she would be a mere duchess while her younger sister Charlotte would be a queen. Yet the match suited the Empress's strategy and was not to be avoided. It was a ruling in direct contrast to Maria Teresa's treatment of Marie Christine, and left Amalia permanently embittered. As for Charlotte, her name – her new name, Maria Carolina – was simply substituted for that of the dead Josepha in the marriage treaty that had already been drawn up. It was a sensible solution, as all concerned except the unfortunate Amalia were agreed.

By 2 November 1767 – Antoine's twelfth birthday – death and disease had robbed Maria Teresa of all the other available Archduchesses. Certainly Charlotte's disappearance in the direction of Naples meant that there was no longer any question of her making that mooted French royal marriage. The possible consequences of the union of the forceful, highly-sexed Maria Carolina to the future Louis XVI, in place of the gentler Marie Antoinette, must remain for ever in the domain of historical speculation. It was thus the rapid fall of a series of dominoes that made Antoine the focus of her mother's attention. For the first time the Empress properly contemplated the material she had to hand in the shape of her fifteenth child. It had to be said that in many respects, she found it distinctly unpromising.

To the Empress's critical eye, the girl's appearance was satisfactory enough, and where it was not, it could easily be fixed. Her teeth, for example, were noticed to be in a bad state, and crooked; but wires were beginning to be used to straighten unsightly teeth, in a system known as the 'pelican', invented by a Frenchman who was later the royal dentist. Three months of this treatment gave Antoine the required, regular teeth.[9] Her large, well-spaced eyes, a subtle blue-grey, were slightly short-sighted. But the consequent misty look was not unattractive, and for the rest, lorgnettes could be brought into play; fans often elegantly included them.[10]

Of her advantages, her hair was fair: a light ash colour that would probably deepen with the years, but that now set off her pink and white complexion to good effect. It was also as thick as Maria Teresa's had once been. On the other hand Antoine had an uneven hairline. Together with a high forehead, which was considered to be a Lorraine trait and was unfashionable by the standards of the time, this made for difficulties.[11] The long neck was a definite asset but the nose was slightly aquiline; fortunately this was not a period when short noses were admired to the exclusion of all others. Antoine's nose could be described as a distinguished one, suited to an archduchess – or a queen.

There was, however, nothing to be done about the notorious Habsburg lip, a projecting lower lip visible in Habsburg portraits down the centuries. The effect given was that of a slight pout in a girl, a rather more disdainful attitude in a woman. It was something that Marie Antoinette came to sigh over; that haughty *hochnäsig* (literally high-nosed) look, which she felt, as it were, did not correspond to the character of the inner woman. At this time, it was simply a matter of getting artists to avoid portraying her in profile. Sculptors obviously had more of a problem, which is why it is much easier to comprehend the reality of Marie Antoinette's appearance – if not her allure – from the busts.

Where Antoine's figure was concerned, one shoulder was higher than the other but that could be corrected by the proper use of corsetry or concealed by padding.[12] The Archduchess was skinny and flat-chested in an age when a proper feminine bosom was considered an essential attraction; she was also not very tall. But since she had not yet reached puberty, it was hoped that both bosom and height would follow.

For all these minor faults, the general effect was very beguiling. Madame Antoine had a 'smile sufficient to win the heart' and that smile indicated her general wish to please. The eighteenth-century French *philosophes*, in their encyclopedias, in the entry under 'Woman', listed 'this art of pleasing, this desire to be pleasing to everyone' as one of the prime feminine traits; it was certainly one possessed by Antoine – in competition for attention, perhaps, with her more gifted elder sisters – from an early age.

Similarly she fitted in the *Encyclopédistes'* category of prettiness rather than beauty, as in the distinction drawn between *beau* and *joli*: 'The beautiful is grand, noble and regular – we admire it; that which is pretty is fine and delicate; it pleases.' It was a distinction that Antoine's French tutor, the Abbé de Vermond, would also make. 'One can find faces that are more regularly beautiful,' he wrote of his pupil. 'I do not think it would be possible to find one that is more delightful.' As for Maria Teresa, not given to flattery where matters of state were concerned – as Antoine's character and appearance had now become – she commented that her daughter had the gift to win people to her, due above all to her 'affability'. Madame Antoine could not –

could she? – fail to inspire love within marriage.[13]

The trouble was that this affable little creature had managed, it seemed, to avoid more or less the unpleasant experience of education, other than in the arts where her skill in dancing and her taste for music added to her general aura of grace. The sheer irritating inconvenience of this discovery, considering the august fate that the Empress now designed for Antoine, would be almost amusing – until one ponders on the lifelong consequences for Marie Antoinette of her youthful illiteracy.[14]

In August 1767, in another painful development for Antoine during this melancholy year, Maria Teresa had separated the two youngest Archduchesses Charlotte and Antoine, who up until this moment had been raised together. This separation was not connected to Charlotte's future prospects – Josepha was at that point still the designated bride for Naples. It was partly the consequence of their bad – or at least mischievous – behaviour, teasing and tricking the governess. It was also partly due to the perceived failure of this governess herself. 'I shall now treat *you* as a grown-up person,' Maria Teresa told Charlotte.[15] The implication was clear. Antoine was left behind to be the child.

Countess Brandeis was a kindly, not very bright woman who lavished affection on little Antoine, the affection that was perhaps lacking from her imperial mother. She petted and spoilt Antoine who adored Brandeis in return. It seems fitting that her earliest surviving letter – a New Year greeting when she was eleven or twelve – was written to her 'dearest Brandeis' and signed 'your faithful pupil who loves you dearly, Antoine'.[16]

The trouble was that Antoine's 'dearest Brandeis' carried through her spoiling to the extent of neglecting any kind of serious instruction. When periodically the Empress demanded to see her daughter's work, how much easier to get Antoine to trace something written out by the governess than actually teach the girl how to do it herself! It was also a convenient way of placating that stern taskmaster Maria Teresa. Even the drawings allegedly by the Archduchess's hand probably owed a great deal to the helpful Brandeis.[17]

In 1768 'dearest Brandeis' was removed in favour of Countess Lerchenfeld, cleverer and also tougher, who had acted as Mistress of the Robes to the elder Archduchesses. Inevitably Antoine disliked her and continued to mourn for Brandeis. This combination of a late beginning and a personal aversion to her teacher did not do much to remedy her educational situation.

The standard of instruction for princesses in the eighteenth century was not particularly high. But although Antoine's ability to write must be seen in that context, it was well below what was the acceptable norm. 'She has acquired the habit of writing inconceivably slowly,' was Vermond's comment, the blame being distributed between her own idleness and the faults of her writing-masters.[18] Yet the question of her writing, her snail-like pace, the blotches, the misspellings, could be resolved, as indeed to a large extent with time it was. Reading, and Antoine's lack of ability in that respect, was a far more serious deficiency. As a result of her inadequate teaching, Antoine developed a real fear of the subject because of her failure at it – and with fear came its frequent concomitant, guilt.

It is notoriously impossible for those whose chief pleasure is reading to understand the mentality of those to whom it seems at best an arduous task. Maria Teresa was not herself an omnivorous reader – but either by nature or via adversity, she had developed a character that could achieve what it needed to do. Other members of the imperial family were distinctly bookish, including the new Emperor Joseph who would tell his sister that he thought two hours a day should be set aside for her reading. Quite apart from the Habsburgs, there was the French royal family ... At roughly the same age as Antoine was encountering Mozart, Louis Auguste was making an address to the celebrated British historian David Hume, an experience that marked him for life with an enthusiasm for Hume's works.[19] In particular he admired the character of Charles I about whom Hume had written so vividly and so magisterially.* It was a significant difference.

The real betrayal in Marie Antoinette's education was that

---

* Louis Auguste, unlike Marie Antoinette (who descended from Charles I's sister Elizabeth of Bohemia), was descended from Charles I himself; the latter's daughter Henriette Anne, Duchesse d'Orléans (Madame), was Louis XV's great-grandmother.

she was never encouraged to concentrate. This ability, comparatively easy to inculcate in childhood, was generally held to be lacking in Marie Antoinette the adult, even by her admirers; her conversation tended to be disjointed 'like a grasshopper', wrote a member of her intimate circle. Madame Campan, the First Lady of the Bedchamber, who knew her so well, was eager to point out that the problem was not actually lack of intelligence. What Marie Antoinette knew, she knew – or rather what she had been properly taught. She was good at Italian, for example, because she had a good teacher in Metastasio.[20] But this area of knowledge was certainly not very wide.

Her enemies ascribed her lack of concentration to capriciousness, which, by the time they encountered her, it had probably become. But it originated in an upbringing that Marie Antoinette told her foster-brother Joseph Weber had been inadequately supervised. One of the favourite maxims that Weber remembered her repeating on the importance of education had a sad ring of truth: 'To be a king, you have to learn to be a king'.[21] The same might be well said of a queen, whatever her graces, whatever her charms.

The young Dauphin of France, prospective bridegroom of this pleasing but uneducated child, was in quite a different way not particularly promising material. Somehow his life had got off to an unlucky start. His mother was bowed with grief during her third pregnancy, thanks to the death of her second child, the infant Duc d'Aquitaine. It was, however, the death of the eldest boy, the Duc de Bourgogne, in 1761 that left the seven-year-old Louis Auguste with a permanent inferiority complex. Bourgogne's death was long-drawn-out and agonizing. Yet according to the inexorable etiquette of Versailles, Louis Auguste was moved into the apartments of his dead brother on the very day of his death.

His parents made no secret of their lamentations at the death of the favourite (whom Maria Josepha had called that special pet name, her *chou d'amour*). The man in charge of Louis Auguste, the Duc de Vauguyon, Governor of the Children of France from 1758, also took the opportunity to lecture him on his inadequacy for the role once played by his incomparable brother. Perhaps Vauguyon thought this was for his pupil's spiritual good; but the result was a terrible lack of self-confidence in the unwilling supplanter. It was all very well being taught the maxim, 'Firmness is of all the virtues the one most necessary to a king,' but his upbringing was hardly qualified to help him put this firmness into practice.[22] The death of his father, the Dauphin Louis Ferdinand, in 1765 meant that Louis Auguste, now Dauphin, was only a heartbeat away from the throne of France.

What he lacked in confidence, the Dauphin certainly did not make up for in physical attraction. He was heavily built, his weight increasing further as time passed. There was some kind of gene of fatness in this branch of the Bourbon family, which may have been glandular in origin. His father had been enormously fat. Maria Josepha's father Augustus III had also been obese, while the prodigious physique of *her* grandfather Augustus II had been saluted with the cognomen 'the Strong'; at least one of her brothers, Clement, was extremely fat. Wherever the inheritance came from – possibly from the meeting of two similar genes – there was no doubt that Louis Auguste, his nearest brother the Comte de Provence and his younger sister Clothilde all had what would now be called a weight problem. Clothilde was actually nicknamed 'Gros-Madame'. They also all had enormous appetites.

Notoriously clumsy, the Dauphin cut an unfortunate figure at court dances; he had a tin ear so that his singing caused general shudders. His clear 'Saxon' blue eyes – unlike the sparkling black 'Slavic' eyes of his grandfather Louis XV and his youngest brother the Comte d'Artois – were myopic, causing him to peer at courtiers and fail to recognize them; more often he kept his head down so as to avoid the confrontation altogether. Ill equipped for formal life at Versailles, the Dauphin took refuge in a profound passion for hunting, a traditional royal occupation. From the age of nine onwards he recorded his exploits in a hunting journal which constituted a sportsman's log (such as the young Louis XV had kept for seven years), rather than a conventional record of day-to-day events.[23]

The Dauphin was, however, intelligent, naturally studious and well instructed by the rote-learning methods of the time. He liked literature and the 'sublime melodies' of Racine. Above all, he had that love of history that was inculcated at David Hume's visit.[24] He was pious too, in an unquestioning way that seemed appropriate enough to a future King of France; in a country where Church and crown had uneasy relations, a simple approach to religion was probably the most helpful one. Given all these factors, given that the Dauphin would be routinely capable of the marital act like any other husband – surely he would be? – there seemed to be no reason why marriage negotiations between French Prince and Austrian Archduchess should not proceed.

Yet these negotiations were not plain sailing. On the French side it had never been a question of Maria Carolina versus Marie Antoinette; Louis XV held one archduchess to be much like another. At Versailles it was more a question of an Austrian marriage – any Austrian marriage. The dedicated hostility of many members of the French court to such an alliance took the form of suggesting a rival candidate, in the shape of Maria Josepha's niece, Princess Amelia of Saxony. The Dauphine's brother, Prince Xavier of Saxony, took an active role in promoting the match. Amelia's elder brother Frederick Augustus could be united at the same time to Gros-Madame Clothilde. It was a double marriage, which would have much empowered the House of Saxony, while not of course equalling in prestige an alliance with Austria. Indeed, Louis XV's pro-Austrian minister Choiseul referred to Amelia and Frederick Augustus derogatively as 'those Saxon things'.[25]

It was to be some time, however, before Choiseul was able to feel that he had seen off the pretensions of the Saxon things altogether. Louis XV was extremely fond of his 'Pepa', as he called the widowed Dauphine Maria Josepha, and had the habit of spending time cosily in his daughter-in-law's apartments (formerly those of the Pompadour and thus close to his). He was in no hurry to put an end to Pepa's hopes for her children, while having, finally, no intention of gratifying them. The Dauphine died in March 1767 'universally regretted by the whole world' in the words of the official announcement.[26] Yet still Louis XV held back from any public acknowledgement of the

Austrian match, although it was always his private intention to go for a marital alliance that accorded with his own (and Choiseul's) pro-Austrian foreign policy.

The new French ambassador, the Marquis de Durfort, who arrived in Vienna in February 1767, was told to deliver an ambiguous message. As Maria Josepha, with her own agenda, had pointed out, the best way to ensure the goodwill of Austria was to keep the court in a state of expectation, rather than settle the matter. Durfort, however, found that it was not so easy to deliver an ambiguous message to the Empress, when what she wanted to hear was rather different. Received every Sunday at court, he found himself drawn into the Empress's inner circle and subjected to a barrage of charm; as Durfort wrote, no one knew better than the Empress 'how to make herself mistress of hearts'. He also admired her for her active and hard-working way of life. Durfort believed that whatever her talk of retiring as a widow, Maria Teresa had a natural taste for domination, which would always prevent her doing so.[27]

Durfort was certainly powerless to evade the Empress when she told him in a meaningful way that *she* had all the French royal portraits from her half-French daughter-in-law the late Isabella of Parma ... What could Durfort say in reply? Gallantly, he volunteered that his master the French King for his part would definitely love to possess all the Austrian royal portraits. Maria Teresa was quick to put an artist at Durfort's disposal. Unfortunately by this time Durfort had received a reproof from France: things were moving too fast. The French ambassador was left explaining uncomfortably to his master that he had not been the initiator of all this.[28]

It would be over two years from Durfort's first arrival in Austria before he was finally bidden to make a formal offer for the hand of the youngest Archduchess. It was thus a cumulative process, on the French side, gaining pace in 1768 when, as has been seen, Maria Teresa decided to concentrate on Antoine in the absence of any other viable candidate. The Empress started to drop further broad hints. Durfort was showered with hothouse fruit throughout the winter – even grapes in January – whilst his presence was requested for every fête and reception. Some of these ambassadorial duties could be onerous. In January 1768, Maria Teresa insisted on Durfort being at her side on a balcony. The Frenchman was dying of cold but he had to watch a procession of twenty-two sledges pass by, the passengers and drivers including most of the imperial family. When the sledge containing Madame Antoine passed beneath their eyes, the Empress nudged him: 'The little wife,' she whispered.[29]

The physical appearance of the Archduchess now underwent a vital transformation; a real Parisian hairdresser in the shape of Sieur Larsenneur was imported to deal with that forehead and that hairline. So important was this aspect of her appearance considered to be – and of everybody's appearance at that time – that the hairdresser in question was recommended at the highest level, by the sister of the Duc de Choiseul. Everyone was impressed by Larsenneur's 'simple decent manner' of dressing Madame Antoine's hair; young ladies in Vienna were said to be abandoning their curls in favour of a style *à la Dauphine*.[30]

Now Maria Teresa was able to get her own way about the portraits. Along with the hairdresser came Joseph Ducreux, who was commissioned to paint the future Dauphine; the portrait was to be sent to Versailles. (He was bewildered on arrival by the size of Maria Teresa's family and had to ask which of the many archduchesses at court he was supposed to paint.) The painter was not as successful as the hairdresser. Five long sittings did not result in anything very satisfactory and the picture had to be done again, but finally in May 1769 it was despatched.[31]

The education of the Archduchess was another matter. Equal in importance to her hairstyle was the question of her French. Versailles was not impressed when it heard that two French actors, Aufresne and Sainville, who happened to be in Vienna on tour, were teaching Madame Antoine (the two men were specialists in the work of Marivaux, the popular early-eighteenth-century dramatist). Some more respectable instructor was required, and it was this perceived need that led to the arrival of the Abbé de Vermond in the autumn of 1768. His role was officially that of Reader, but he would in fact act as Antoine's tutor while they were both in Austria, and as her confidential advisor later on.

Jacques-Mathieu de Vermond was in his mid-thirties when he arrived in Vienna. He did not come from a particularly distinguished background, but had been put forward indirectly to Choiseul by a grander ecclesiastic, Loménie de Brienne, Archbishop of Toulouse, as the man for the job; he was said to be discreet and tactful as well as devout. Like Durfort, Vermond was quickly adopted as a member of the imperial family circle. It would later be said (by those who were not Vermond's friends and who resented his privileged role) that 'an unlucky star' had brought Vermond into Marie Antoinette's intimate set. It was suggested that where Vermond might have exercised a good influence, he concentrated on making himself beloved by Marie Antoinette, in order to maintain his position.[32] Yet it has to be said that, given Antoine's mixture of timidity and laziness where education was concerned, Vermond would not have achieved very much had he not won her confidence and liking.

When Vermond arrived, Antoine at just thirteen could neither read nor write properly in either French or German. Her spoken French – the language *en famille* – was slapdash and full of German phrases and constructions. As Vermond pointed out, her French would improve immeasurably once she was surrounded by French people speaking 'pure' French and heard no more German. Her attendants spoke French badly on the whole, while in Vienna 'everyone speaks three languages' – Italian being the third – which did not help. A year after Vermond had arrived, Antoine was speaking French with ease and fairly well; even if she was not idiomatically perfect, the ugly phrases were being eliminated. By the time she left Austria, she was speaking fluently, according to an independent witness, although with a slight German accent.[33]

French history was more of a problem; it emerged that Madame Antoine did not even know the history of her own country. Vermond painted a pretty picture of his young pupil's earnest attempts to improve her knowledge; how she was particularly interested in those Queens of France who had been members of the House of Austria. Maria Teresa listened in on some of these lessons. When the mother asked the daughter over which European country she would prefer to rule, the answer, amazing to relate, was France! 'Because it was the country of Henri IV and Louis XIV, the one so good, the other so great.'[34] In this instance, one cannot help suspecting that some prior coaching may have gone on *à la* Brandeis.

Madame Antoine positively liked learning about French genealogy and the French regiments, their names and colours, reported Vermond. No doubt his lectures on the great court families she would find at Versailles, their positions and influence, were listened to with attention – as they should have been. Nevertheless the French would still find that Marie Antoinette's education had been 'much neglected', which led to private accusations of stupidity, so perhaps Vermond struggled finally in vain with a mind without an intellectual or speculative cast.*

Nevertheless the Abbé's reports on her character were generally favourable; he praised the sweetness and kindness of her nature – while deploring her tendency to let herself be distracted. Her appearance had only one fault: that she was rather small. 'If as is to be expected, she grows a little more, the French will need no other token by which to recognize their sovereign.' A secret report to France was more succinct: Madame Antoine was delightful and would give no trouble.[36]

The Marquis de Durfort made the formal application on 6 June 1769 for the betrothal of the Dauphin aged nearly fifteen and the Archduchess aged thirteen and a half. Six days later a fête of more than usual magnificence was held at Laxenburg on the eve of the name-day of the future Dauphine. The gravity and dignity of Madame Antoine ravished every eye. Everyone knew that a glorious future beckoned for the youngest daughter of the Empress, for as in a fairy story, hers was to be the most splendid establishment of all. Or as Maria Teresa told Marie Antoinette: 'If one is to consider only the greatness of your position, you are the happiest of your sisters and all princesses.' To Louis XV, however, the Empress wrote from Laxenburg

---

* The essay on the Queens of France, said to be by Marie Antoinette, now in the Habsburg Archives, is in a completely different handwriting, far more advanced than hers at that period or, indeed, for long after it. It was probably written for her, rather than by her.[35]

along rather different lines: 'Her age craves indulgence.' In this suggestive vein, Maria Teresa asked the French King to act 'as a father' to the future Dauphine.[37]

CHAPTER FOUR

Sending an Angel

~~~~~

'Farewell, my dearest child. A great distance will separate us ... Do so much good to the French people
that they can say that I have sent them an angel.'

Maria Teresa's parting words to her daughter, 1770

As Count Khevenhüller set about the highly elaborate
preparations for a daughter of Austria to marry a son of
France, the Empress decided to spend the modern notion
of quality time with Antoine. It took the form of a votive
pilgrimage made together in August 1769 to Mariazell in northern
Styria. Here, at the shrine in the Basilica, behind a silver grille
donated by the Empress who made her First Communion here,
a twelfth-century wooden image of the Blessed Virgin Mary –
Magna Mater Austriae – was venerated.*

The journey was intended not only to bind Maria Teresa and
Marie Antoinette together but also to symbolize that special
devotion of the House of Habsburg to the Virgin which had
given them both the same prefix in her honour. And now
Antoine too could take Communion at her mother's side. The
Empress subsequently offered a family-tree picture by Antoine-
Assieu Moll to commemorate the occasion: 'because of the
refuge the Virgin Mary has been in all her calamities ... for the
sake of her saved kingdoms and for all her descendants'.[1]

---

* Mariazell, sometimes termed 'the Lourdes of Austria' (although its origins are
far older), is still a place of national pilgrimage; it is popular for First Communions,
as well as a skiing resort.

At this point the future Dauphine was conventionally pious – there was not much chance of being anything else where Maria Teresa as mother was concerned – but unlike Louis Auguste, there is no evidence of anything more ardent. Royal ladies were allotted father confessors; in France Marie Antoinette complained to Vermond about one of them, Bishop Guirtler: 'He wanted to make me a *dévote* [ultra religious]!' Vermond permitted himself to wonder aloud how the Bishop had proposed to carry this out, since he had had so little success himself in correcting her behaviour. Marie Antoinette laughed.[2]

There was a story of Maria Teresa worrying over the future state of Antoine's soul once she was at the morally perilous French court. The Empress was supposed to have consulted a nun who pronounced as follows: the Archduchess would have great reverses, and then she would become pious again. Henry Swinburne heard the story; he was an English Catholic who travelled widely and was especially popular in Vienna where Joseph II acted as godfather to his son. Another tale was repeated to Madame Campan by the governess to the children of Prince Kaunitz. This time the Empress was supposed to have asked the celebrated healer and pretender to miraculous powers, John Joseph Gassner: 'Will my daughter be happy?' His reply was suitably gnomic: 'There are crosses for all shoulders.'[3]

These stories were repeated years later; but insofar as they were true, their importance is surely more as an indication of the Empress's growing anxiety about Antoine's future than anything more sybilline. It was in line with this apprehension that Maria Teresa had already written the first of her worried-mother letters to Louis XV, craving indulgence for Antoine's youth. Further letters would follow. Nevertheless Khevenhüller – and his opposite number in France – ploughed relentlessly on throughout the autumn, preparing the ground for Madame Antoine's sumptuous bridal journey next spring. At the same time Prince Starhemberg, a former ambassador to France and chief assistant to Prince Kaunitz, was appointed as Ambassador Extraordinary. He was in overall charge of her progress including the crucial moment of the handover, known in Austria as the *consegna* and in France as the *remise*.

It was the Court Chamberlain's intention to mobilize a procession whose magnificence would attest to the imperial state of Austria, despite being centred around a teenage girl. Horses were a particular concern, horses to draw the endless carriages that were consonant with the rank of the future Dauphine, horses that had to be changed with sufficient frequency to avoid delays. It was to be a procession of 132 dignitaries, swollen to twice that number by doctors, hairdressers and servants including cooks, bakers, blacksmiths and even a dressmaker for running repairs. For this there was need for 57 coaches and 376 horses; that entailed a total of 20,000 horses altogether posted along the route. The Prince of Paar, grand postmaster, was to be in control of actual movements; this meant that his wife, the Princess, could travel with Madame Antoine.[4]

Arranging food and drink for this travelling court – for such it was – was a problem in itself. Furthermore dignity had to be maintained at all points, even in the most intimate moments of everyday existence. The French accounts show due concern for the furnishing of the rooms in which the future Dauphine was to lodge en route. Curtains were to be of crimson taffeta. Otherwise red velvet and gold embroidery was to be lavished everywhere, not only on furnishings such as the great armchairs for the travelling salon, but also in the royal commode and the royal bidet. In the meantime Khevenhüller had to grapple with the rather different point of view of the Emperor Joseph, who was anxious that expense should, where possible, be spared. The Court Chamberlain had to explain to his imperial master that his pared-down proposal for the Austrian military escort would definitely not create a good impression on the French...[5]

Madame Antoine herself became, inevitably, the focus of courtly sightseeings. At a masked ball in December 1769 nearly 4000 people attended in order to gape at the future Dauphine and were charmed at what they saw, even if the Empress, increasingly lame and leaning heavily on her daughter's arm, gave cause for concern. For those unable to inspect the original, there were beginning to be commercial reproductions of Marie Antoinette's picture, in both Austria and France. Official medals were also struck, with allegorical designs and flowery inscriptions,

most of which alluded to her descent, since there was frankly
little of interest to be said about the bride (or the bridegroom).
One sounded a note of optimism:

> From the most august blood she has seen the light of day
> Yet her high birth is the least of her merits.

The Austro-French alliance was another popular theme. One
medal minted in France as early as March 1769 showed the
young pair holding hands over an altar where a sacred fire was
burning; behind them, the symbolical figures of France and
Austria were seen to embrace.[6]

There was, however, an extraordinary amount of detail to be
settled between the two courts before this allegorical embrace
could be turned into reality. Fortunately the dowry of an
Archduchess of Austria who married a Prince of France was
laid down by custom: 200,000 florins, and jewels worth an equal
amount. In the opinion of Louis XV, as he told his grandson
Don Ferdinand, the dowries of the House of Austria were rather
small. Laid down with equal precision was the income she would
receive as a widow: 20,000 gold écus and jewels valued at 100,000
écus.[7]

The big expense from the point of view of Austria was the
Archduchess's trousseau; her native country paid for it but –
naturally – it had to come from Paris if she was to cut any kind
of sartorial dash at Versailles. In total, 400,000 livres were
allowed for this.* The money was to be provided by Madame
de Nettine, director of the most important bank in Brussels in
the Austrian Netherlands and the trousseau itself chosen by
Count Mercy d'Argenteau, the Austrian ambassador to Versailles.

It was hardly likely that such prolonged negotiations could
pass by without difficulties of etiquette. The question of the

---

* Although 200,000 crowns was – *pace* Louis XV – a handsome dowry to most
people, it was certainly not exceptional among great ones. In 1769, for example,
the heiress Mademoiselle de Penthièvre brought a dowry of 6 million livres with
her when she married the son of the Duc d'Orléans. In terms of British money
of the period, Marie Antoinette's trousseau cost over £17,000: a notional three-
quarters of a million pounds at the beginning of the twenty-first century.

marriage contract was especially tricky. Who was to sign first? The King as father of the bridegroom? Or the Empress and the Emperor? The problem looked momentarily insoluble until it was decided to compromise with two separate contracts. The King of France signed first on one, the Austrians on the other.[8] Poor Durfort, who had upheld the French interests gallantly in Vienna, was told that he would not after all be accompanying the bridal cortège into France; this was a snub to his position, although he was allowed to act as Ambassador Extraordinary (that is, the French King's personal representative) during the actual marriage celebrations.

Durfort also received strict instructions from the Duc de Choiseul in France that he was not to receive Madame Antoine under his own roof once the proxy marriage had taken place; as a French subject he could entertain an archduchess but he could not entertain a Dauphine. Durfort had his own complications with the Austrian court; as the French King's representative, he refused to be outranked by Marie Christine's husband, Albert of Saxe-Teschen (as he was now known) – a mere prince, no matter whom he had married. In the end the two had to be kept apart, going to alternate functions. Albert, who was greedy, settled for the official dinner whilst Durfort got the church service. To maintain his dignity once more, Durfort managed to stop the Archduchess's oath of renunciation being administered to her by the Cardinal-Archbishop of Vienna, in favour of a lesser functionary who did not outrank Durfort himself.

During her own bridal journey to Naples a year earlier, Maria Carolina had written back to the governess Countess Lerchenfeld: 'Write to me everything you know about my sister Antoine, down to the tiniest detail, what she says and does and even what she thinks ... Beg her to love me, because I am so passionately concerned for her.'[9] This natural concern – by remote control – of the elder sister for the younger never ceased although both of them were aware that they might never meet again. Fortunately other friendships were at hand. There were Madame Antoine's ladies-in-waiting to whom she was extremely attached; this was a foretaste of the excellent relations she would have with those who served her (Marie Antoinette was always a heroine to her valets). Then there were two princesses of lesser rank, who were more likely to be able to travel to France than a Queen of Naples.

Charlotte Wilhelmine of Hesse-Darmstadt was the virtual twin of Marie Antoinette (she was born three days later) and like her younger sister Louise, born in 1761, had been brought up at the Viennese court. The two young women were the nieces of the reigning Landgrave of Hesse-Darmstadt. If Antoine's reciprocated affection for Maria Carolina had set the pattern for close and, above all, cosy female relationships early in her life, then her connection to Charlotte and Louise continued the trend. These were to be lasting friendships. Time and duty separated the three of them geographically, but Marie Antoinette, that agonizingly slow correspondent, found it a joy to write to them, the friends of her youth; over forty of these letters survive.[10] She retained the portraits of her 'dear Princesses' among her most intimate possessions for the rest of her life.

Then there was Antoine's feeling for little children; she was one of those girls who had a natural love of them and their unchallenging company long before there was any question of her bearing children herself. When Count Mercy d'Argenteau grumbled about this predilection of the Dauphine on her arrival in France, that she preferred playing with the young ones to reading books, Maria Teresa admitted that her daughter was 'always very fond of amusing herself with children'.[11]

There was a child at the Viennese court: the little Archduchess Teresa, daughter of the Emperor and the late Isabella of Parma, Louis XV's granddaughter. At seven, Teresa was in fact closer in age to the fourteen-year-old Antoine than the latter's nearest remaining sister Elizabeth, who was in her late twenties. Durfort reported a charming scene on New Year's Day 1770. Just as he was arriving at Madame Antoine's apartments in order to present his greetings, she emerged with her brother the Emperor. Together, they went to see Teresa, who had prepared a little puppet theatre for her father and aunt in which the principal events of the reign of Maria Teresa were enacted.[12]

Three weeks later – on 23 January – Teresa was dead of pleurisy, leaving the Emperor Joseph distraught: 'I have ceased to be a father. Oh my God, restore to me my daughter ...' He asked her governess, who by custom received the dead child's belongings, to allow him his daughter's writings and 'her white dimity dressing-gown embroidered with flowers'.[13]

At Versailles the news of the death of a Great-Granddaughter of France was treated with appropriate ceremony and lamentation. The city of Paris went into mourning and money was distributed to the poor in her memory. There was, however, no truth in a subsequent story that Louis XV had really wanted the Dauphin to marry Teresa, only turning to Antoine after his great-granddaughter's death. As has been seen, preparations for the marriage of Antoine were well advanced by the end of January; on the 21st a ring had arrived for her from the Dauphin.[14]

Another death, on 6 February 1770, was a good deal less tragic from Madame Antoine's point of view; the unpopular Countess Lerchenfeld died and was replaced as head of her household by Countess Trautmannsdorf. Antoine was in need of a sympathetic ally. The really tumultuous event of February for her occurred on the 7th when, as the Empress was quick to inform the French ambassador, the future Dauphine 'became a woman'.[15] She had had her first period that very morning but no particular problem had been presented, since the Archduchess had been able to dance in the evening; Maria Teresa was confident that Louis XV would be very happy at the news. Madame Antoine was now on course to become a mother, as and when her marriage was consummated. Furthermore she would be the mother of a child with imperial Austrian blood in its veins. And it was this dynastic aspect of the matter that inspired in Maria Teresa an obsessional curiosity about her daughters' monthly cycles.

It was a preoccupation with which considerations of distance, let alone privacy, were never allowed to interfere. Once her daughters were married, the Empress greeted with indignation the news of the arrival each month of the 'Générale Krottendorf', for such was the nickname given by her to her daughters' periods.* These daughters, the wives of important princes in other countries, were expected to give full and frequent reports on the subject. Envoys such as Count Mercy d'Argenteau were pressed into service, and the French royal doctor, Lassonne, was supposed to report 'every month' directly to her mother with news of Marie Antoinette's cycle so that Maria Teresa was not left to the doubtful 'meticulousness' of the young woman herself. Less appropriately, perhaps, Gluck was at one point asked to bear the vital message. Louis XV himself gave the Empress a news-flash on the subject a few months after her daughter had arrived in France; the *règles* (the French term) of the Dauphine had arrived for the first time 'since we have had the pleasure of possessing her'.[17]

That was the point. The fate of a princess who married into a foreign country was to be a hostage – possessed. But she was also expected to be an ambassador. Marie Antoinette was certainly an egregious example of such a complicated twofold destiny but throughout history there were many, many other princesses who shared it. Isabella of Parma had outlined the unhappy possibilities: 'What should the daughter of a great prince expect? ... Born the slave of other people's prejudices, she finds herself subjected to the weight of honours, these innumerable etiquettes attached to greatness ... a sacrifice to the supposed public good.' Napoleon, marrying Marie Antoinette's great-niece forty years later, expressed the bargain rather more crudely: 'I am marrying a womb.'[18]

Under the circumstances it was scarcely surprising that royal women retained strong feelings for the land of their birth, from which duty had wrenched them and which, in the course of events, it was more than likely they would not see again. The Dauphine Maria Josepha, who was immensely proud of her position in the French royal family, told her brother Prince

---

* In real life the Générale (or *generalin* in German), as her name came to be shortened, seems to have been a lady of the court, presumably married to a General Krottendorf. Maria Teresa mentions her death in late 1779. But the precise origin of the nickname for the monthly period remains obscure; it is, however, to be compared to similar nicknames of the same time. For example, the daughters of the 2nd Duke of Richmond referred to 'the French lady's visit'.[16]

Xavier after fifteen years of marriage that her heart could detach itself neither from France nor Saxony. But this was pre-eminently true when the bride had reason to suppose her own country superior to all others. (Some French princesses, as Marie Antoinette would discover to her cost, enamoured of both their status and their country, would solve the problem by staying there unmarried.) Catherine of Braganza, the Portuguese-born wife of Charles II, tried to cheer up her niece Princess Mary, who was on her way to Holland to marry her cousin William of Orange, with memories of her own apprehensions, which had happily been unnecessary. 'But Madam, you came into England! I am going out of it,' replied the Princess with the cruelty of youth.[19]

Nine years before the wedding of Marie Antoinette, Charlotte of Mecklenburg-Strelitz made a long journey across Europe to marry George III, sight unseen as it were. Arriving in London at three o'clock in the afternoon, she was dressed in English clothes and was married to him a few hours later, with a long reception and the wedding night to follow immediately. The whispered encouragement of the Duke of York – '*Courage, Princesse, courage*' – as he took his future sister-in-law up the aisle was appropriate to Charlotte's situation, as it was to that of many other princesses. It was not as though the bride could necessarily expect sympathetic endorsement in her new family circle. Marie Antoinette was sneeringly baptized *l'Autrichienne** by Madame Adélaïde, eldest surviving daughter of Louis XV, years before it became a popular term of derision. Similarly the French Queen Maria Lesczinska, wife of Louis XV and daughter of the dispossessed King Stanislaus, was known as *la Polonaise*. The shy Infanta Maria Teresa, wife of Louis XIV, had been mocked for her Spanish accent.[20]

The advice of Maria Teresa to her daughters, stepping lightly in their pretty satin shoes across these morasses, was extremely detailed. And yet it did little to reconcile the two covert roles

---

* Meaning literally 'the Austrian woman'; but the coincidental combination of the two French words for ostrich (*autruche*) and bitch (*chienne*) meant that the name would present horribly rich opportunities for cartoonists.

of hostage and ambassador. The two previous Archduchesses had received long instructions, many of which were religious in nature: adjurations to pray long, pray often, read holy books and so forth and so on. To Maria Carolina, Maria Teresa hammered home the precept that marriage was the greatest happiness. Above all, she must try to understand her ill-educated but well-meaning husband, King Ferdinand, who had received the following encouraging rating as a bridegroom: 'Although an ugly prince, he is not absolutely repulsive ... at least he does not stink.' Where her homeland was concerned: 'Do not always be talking about our country, or drawing comparisons between our customs and theirs.'[21]

Amalia was similarly admonished in advance: 'You are a stranger and a subject; you must learn to conform; even more because you are older than your husband, you must not seem to dominate ... you know we are subjects of our husbands and owe them obedience.' Yet for whatever reason, by the time of Antoine's wedding, both the Queen of Naples and the Duchess of Parma were being perceived in Europe as interfering consorts. Maria Teresa bewailed her daughters' reputation for domination: 'This will reflect badly on my Dauphine.'[22] It does not seem to have occurred to her that she herself had not actually led such a visibly meek life.

In contrast to the theme of obedience, there was the crucial question of remaining a good German. Maria Teresa had told Maria Carolina that 'in her heart and in the uprightness of her mind', she should be a German; only in things that were unimportant (although nothing that was wrong) must she appear to be Neapolitan. The Empress's instructions to 'the little one', as she sometimes called Antoine to Maria Carolina, also contained this important admonition. On the one hand Antoine was never to introduce any new custom, or behave in any way other than was strictly ordained in advance at the court of France; she must never ever cite the usages of the court of Vienna. On the other hand she must also see it as her duty to 'be a good German'.[23] How was this apparently contradictory admonition supposed to be effected? As Dauphine, Marie Antoinette would need to find out.

The rest of Maria Teresa's instructions, conveyed in the form of a long letter which Antoine was told to read once a month, were simple enough, if hardly envisaging much independence of action on the part of one who would shortly be the subject of another monarch. It was carefully laid down, for example, to whom the Dauphine would be able to write; her Lorrainer uncle Prince Charles and her Lorrainer aunt Charlotte were on the list, as was Prince Albert of Saxe-Teschen. It must have come as a relief to Antoine that the Queen of Naples was on the list on the grounds that the one sister who had faced a difficult situation in her marriage – 'much more difficult than your own' – would inspire the other.[24]   Antoine was not to read any book without permission of her confessor, since French books, under the veil of erudition, often showed a shocking lack of respect for religion. Antoine must never forget the anniversary of her father's death on 18 August. In time she would of course commemorate annually the death of her mother – not exactly a consoling thought for one shortly to leave her side – but in the meantime Antoine should say special prayers for her mother on her birthday.

It was only in a few sentences that Maria Teresa revealed apprehensions for her daughter based on the terrible (and unacknowledged) inadequacy of Antoine's preparation. The future Dauphine was not to display undue curiosity – a particular fault of hers. She must not cultivate familiarity with 'underlings'.[25] Above all, she must remember that 'all eyes' would be fixed on her; she must give no scandal.

The month of April 1770 – her wedding month – began with a three-day spiritual retreat for Madame Antoine. This programme of prayer and reflection was directed by the Abbé de Vermond. Since he tactfully promised not to make his various little instructive talks too long, it was probably less onerous than the Archduchess's new sleeping arrangements, which were to be in her mother's black velvet-draped apartments. The Empress was making up for lost time in this close last association with her daughter, however gloomy the surroundings must have seemed, however awesome the privilege.

Outside the imperial bedchamber, the onward march of ritual festivities left little space for tranquillity. These included the presentation of a Latin address by the university, to which the Archduchess was said to have responded in kind; since she had not been taught Latin, presumably Vermond took a hand. Then there was the kissing of her hand by mixed German and Hungarian guards. On 15 April – Easter Sunday – the Marquis de Durfort returned in splendour as Ambassador Extraordinary of the French King, having quitted Vienna as a mere ambassador shortly before. In theory Durfort had returned to France to perform this transformation act; but all he had actually done was acquire an enormous cortège of forty-eight carriages, drawn by six horses each, in order to emphasize the new magnificence of his status to a court that had come to know him well over the last three years.[26]

Since Durfort had to find the money out of his own pocket, he would shortly resell all but two of the equipages. But it is to be hoped that in the meantime Madame Antoine, who watched this formal entry from the house of Countess Trautmannsdorf, was suitably impressed. The two remaining carriages were in fact provided by the French; these were to have the honour of conveying the Dauphine personally on her journey, and were the most gorgeous of all. One was upholstered in crimson velvet and embroidered with motifs of the four seasons in gold; the other was upholstered in blue, with motifs of the four elements, and bouquets of flowers made from thin gold wire trembling on the roof.[27]

The next day Durfort was received in audience by the Empress and the Emperor. It was all very courteous. Durfort doffed his hat and was politely told to put his hat back on. Having done so, he took it off again as a sign of respect. When all this was finished, the Ambassador Extraordinary was able to present a letter and two portraits of the Dauphin to Madame Antoine. Primed by Countess Trautmannsdorf, Madame Antoine took one of them, set in diamonds, and pinned it to her corsage. The letter was one of exquisite courtesy and formality, in the contents of which it is unlikely that the Dauphin had much say.

As for the portrait, there had already been trouble behind the scenes on that score when the French despatched a picture of Louis Auguste out ploughing. This was a classical image but not the image of an archduchess's fiancé that was expected in Vienna. The new portraits were more conventional likenesses. However, if Marie Antoinette had any reaction to them, either public or private, it was not recorded; as these ceremonies gradually progressed throughout April, it was as though her small figure was gradually disappearing under 'the weight of honours, these innumerable etiquettes attached to greatness' described by Isabella of Parma as the inevitable fate of a princess bride.

The next day, 17 April, Madame Antoine swore on a Bible to renounce her right through her mother to the Austrian hereditary lands and through her father to Lorraine.[28] This formal renunciation was frequently asked of departing princesses in order to prevent a foreign dynasty from trying to acquire the family throne if the male succession failed.

That evening the Emperor Joseph gave a supper party for 1500 people at the Belvedere Palace in Vienna. There had been some doubt whether he would participate in the ceremonies, given that he was still in mourning for his recently dead child; but to the general relief the Emperor rallied to the imperial cause, in spite of his sorrow, although Khevenhüller's copious records suggest that most of the decisions were taken by Maria Teresa. In addition to the huge numbers invited for supper in the palace, which had been designed in the early eighteenth century for Prince Eugene of Savoy, a further 600 would dance at a ball in a pavilion specially erected in the palace gardens for the purpose; masks and white dominoes or hooded cloaks were to be worn. (But there was a special order that no 'disagreeable' masks would be tolerated.)[29]

The usual rules for any vast entertainment were in place. Court officials were to make sure that there was no admission without invitation; no doubt this was a necessary proviso, given that the general public were to be admitted to the lower gardens of the Belvedere and provided with their own, albeit rather smaller, illuminations. The presence of 800 firemen standing by was another piece of wise planning, given the multitudinous candles – nearly 4000 – needed for such an occasion. Rather less usual was the hiring of dentists, in case of any sudden pangs on the part of guests; the official gazette attributed this to the 'motherly care' of the Empress. Supper at the ball was to be served in stages, 100 people at a time, starting at eleven o'clock, but drink – coffee, tea, chocolate and lemonade as well as liqueurs – was to be supplied without intermission throughout the night. Perhaps this generosity was responsible for the fact that the ball actually lasted until seven in the morning, although the imperial party withdrew at about three.[30]

The following night it was Durfort's turn to show what a French ambassador could do. His last effort, since he was forbidden to receive Madame Antoine once she was married, it was held at the Liechtenstein Palace a little outside Vienna. Eight hundred servants were provided to wait on 850 guests. There were fireworks accompanied by the currently fashionable Turkish music. Gold dolphins, an emblematic reference to the Dauphin, lit by flaming torches were in abundance. Every tree and shrub was heavy with allegory and verse on the general theme of Hymen, the God of Marriage, ordering Louis Auguste to wed Marie Antoinette, the Goddess of Beauty.

As with the medals, the specific alliance of France and Austria was not forgotten. One ornate verse in French ran:

> The Rose of the Danube and the Lily of the Seine
> Mingling their colours, embellish both parts:
> From a garland of these flowers, love forms a chain
> Uniting happily two nations' hearts.

A Latin salutation referred to 'Maria Antonia' as 'Daughter, sister, wife, daughter-in-law' (*Filia, soror, uxor, nurus*) and coyly suggested that she would soon add to all these the 'sweet name' of mother. In spite of all this, however, Count Khevenhüller loyally noted in his diary that the French entertainment had not been nearly as good as that of Austria the night before.[31]

The wedding, which took place at six o'clock in the evening on 19 April, was of course a proxy wedding. This was a familiar concept where the marriage of princesses to foreigners was concerned since, given ecclesiastical approval of its validity, it meant that the young lady could travel with her new rank. Antoine's proxy bridegroom was to be her elder brother, the Archduke Ferdinand; he was as yet unmarried (he would marry Beatrice d'Este, heiress to the Duchy of Modena, the following year) and had already acted as proxy for the Duke of Parma at the marriage of Amalia. In this case Ferdinand simply had to take the Latin vow, 'I am willing and thus make my promise', kneel beside his sister and enjoy the nuptial supper at her side. In bygone times, proxy marriages had been considerably more realistic with the 'bridal pair' being bedded together, in front of witnesses, the proxy inserting a symbolic leg.

Like her mother before her, thirty-four years ago, Antoine got married in the Church of the Augustine Friars, the beautiful austere fourteenth-century edifice in which she had been baptized.* The Emperor Joseph and the Empress, who had first led her daughter up the aisle, sat high on a special dais to the right of the altar; Antoine and Ferdinand were on a lower level, and to the right of Ferdinand, but lower still, was the Marquis de Durfort. Antoine wore glistening cloth-of-silver, her train carried by Countess Trautmannsdorf. The Papal Nuncio, Monsignor Visconti, officiated. The vows were taken. Rings were duly blessed. An act of celebration was drawn up which Prince Kaunitz certified and Durfort legalized. Once the ceremony was concluded, salvoes were fired outside, and the sound of kettledrums and trumpets was heard.[32]

At nine o'clock there was the official marriage supper lasting several hours; this was a testing occasion physically for Count Khevenhüller who had to stand throughout, behind the chair of the Emperor. Nor were the galas over. Yet another took place on the following night, at which ambassadors and others were permitted to kiss the hand of she who could now be officially addressed as 'Madame la Dauphine'. It was time for Durfort to take his leave; he had been displaced by the Baron

---

* The main feature of the church today is the vast Canova monument of 1805 to the Archduchess Marie Christine, Marie Antoinette's disliked elder sister, with references to her as 'the best wife'.

de Breteuil – a character whom we shall meet again in the story of Marie Antoinette. Since Durfort already possessed a pair of imperial portraits for his good offices in the marriage of Amalia to Don Ferdinand of Parma, he was allowed to receive a diamond ring and a diamond-decorated snuffbox instead.

But the main activity of the day for the Empress and her newly married daughter was letter-writing. First of all the Dauphine had to address Louis XV personally, according to the royal convention, as 'Monsieur mon frère et très cher grandpère', for royals were all technically brothers and sisters to each other; thus Maria Teresa addressed Louis XV quite simply as 'Monsieur mon frère'. The Dauphine told the French King how long it was since she had first wished to communicate to him the affection she felt for him; she was now taking the first opportunity to do so. The Dauphine was delighted that, thanks to the ceremony yesterday, she now 'belongs to Your Majesty' (once again the language of possession). The French King may be sure that she will spend her whole life trying to please him and deserve his confidence. 'All the same,' writes the Dauphine, in language, like the letter itself, traceable to Maria Teresa, 'I feel my age and inexperience may often need his indulgence.' She craves it in advance, and that of 'Monsieur le Dauphin' too, as of the whole family into which she now has the happiness to pass. The signature of the new Dauphine is still the familiar one of her childhood: 'Antoine.'[33]

It is no surprise to find that the Empress's postscript, addressed to 'my brother', sounds exactly the same note. She writes of her own unhappiness in losing such a beloved child, and how her entire consolation lies in the fact that she was confiding her to 'the best and tenderest of fathers'. She hopes that the French King will want to direct her daughter's future course of behaviour. 'Her intentions are excellent, but given her age, I pray you to exercise indulgence for any careless mistake ... I recommend her once again as the most tender pledge which exists so happily between our States and our Houses.'[34]

The departure of the Dauphine was scheduled for nine o'clock the following morning, 21 April. The early hour was deliberate. Whatever the bride's glittering future, these partings were not, and could hardly expect to be, happy occasions. Count Khev-enhüller reported in his diary that it was hoped to avoid the distress that had attended the farewells of the Archduchesses Maria Carolina and Amalia. In April 1768, Maria Carolina had sprung out of the coach at the last moment to give her adored Antoine a series of passionate, tearful embraces. On this cold spring morning it was the Empress who clasped her daughter to her again and again. 'Farewell, my dearest child, a great distance will separate us ... Do so much good to the French people that they can say that I have sent them an angel.' Then she broke down and wept. Joseph Weber, with his mother the wet-nurse, was allowed to watch the cortège depart. He always remembered how Madame Antoine, unable to control her own sobs, craned her neck out of the windows again and again, to catch a last sight of her home.[35]

As the procession of fifty-seven carriages passed by Schön-brunn at the beginning of the long road to France, the postilions blew their horns. They were saluting the past of the Archduchess and the future of the Dauphine.

PART TWO

The Dauphine

CHAPTER FIVE

France's Happiness

~~~

Marie Antoinette: 'I shall never forget that you are
responsible for my happiness!'
Choiseul: 'And that of France.'

Exchange in the forest near Compiègne, 13 May 1770

I t was to be two and a half weeks of travelling before the
Dauphine was officially handed over to France.[1] Marie
Antoinette would in effect cross the whole of central Europe
in her passage from Vienna to Versailles. She spent a great deal
of this time cooped up in her velvet-and-gold carriage; sometimes
the day's journey would last over nine hours. Essentially she
was a royal package, sealed with the double-headed eagle of the
Habsburgs and the fleur-de-lys of the Bourbons.

The first overnight stop was at the great baroque monastery
of Melk. Here the Dauphine was received by her brother Joseph,
and some convent pupils performed an opera. Marie Antoinette
was reported as looking bored; but given the gruelling schedule
to which she had recently been exposed, it is more likely that
she was totally exhausted. These partings – having left her
mother, she would part from her brother the next morning –
were in their very nature distressing, despite Khevenhüller's
precautions. In this, she was not unusual. Maria Carolina had
become extremely upset at the last Austrian outpost on her
journey south. Louis XV, giving away his beloved daughter
Madame Infante in 1748, went a short way with her, then
hugged her as she wept. Finally the King had the courage to

say to her coachman, 'To Madrid', and, leaping into his own carriage, cried, 'to Versailles.' Marie Antoinette, in her turn, was said to have burst into tears as she crossed the border of her mother's dominions, exclaiming that she was frightened she would never see the Empress again.[2]

The nature of her reception at the various towns along the route was, however, enthusiastic, if repetitious. Her august birth was naturally emphasized – this was the daughter of that nonpareil Maria Teresa – but otherwise every kind of goddess of youth and beauty was invoked: Hebe, Flora, Venus, and so forth and so on. Thus the Dauphine in her stately caravan, lauded for her virtues and those of her family, finally reached Munich on 26 April. Here she was entertained by the Elector of Bavaria, Maximilian Joseph, brother of the late Empress Josepha and a cousin on her mother's side. In the agreeable surroundings of the Nymphenburg Palace, whose gardens were second only to those of Versailles, and with the Amalienburg Pavilion as her personal lodging, the Dauphine was allowed a day of rest. Then it was on to Augsburg, where master craftsmen of the town had specially decorated her apartments, and where she was made an honorary member of the Academy of Sciences and Fine Arts, before heading for Günzburg and another two-day stopover, this time with her father's sister, Princess Charlotte of Lorraine.[3]

From Marie Antoinette's point of view, despite all the acclamations en route of which Prince Starhemberg was keeping Versailles fully informed, it was pleasant to be greeted by one of the familiar figures of her childhood. This emphasis on Lorrainer family ties as Marie Antoinette headed towards Versailles was deliberate. As the two Princesses prayed together at the Lorrainer chapel at Königinbild, the point was being made that Lorrainer claims and connections were not going to be overlooked. The new Dauphine was 'de Lorraine' as well as 'd'Autriche'.

After that it was on towards Ulm and then Freiberg, which was reached on 4 May. Here, over two days, the celebrations of the Dauphine's arrival were notably elaborate, having been plotted well in advance, with all the ins and outs of city politics.

It was in the evening of 6 May when, having passed through the Black Forest, the Dauphine reached the abbey at Schüttern where she was to spend her last night on German soil before the handover.

This was also the night on which Marie Antoinette encountered, formally, the first of the French court officials who were intended to guide her inexperienced footsteps at Versailles. He came in the person of the Comte de Noailles, Ambassador Extraordinary of Louis XV. A man in his fifties, the Comte was a member of that eponymous family that was 'the most profitably provided with places and favours at court'. In the words of a knowledgeable observer, the Marquis de Bombelles, the family had reached 'the crest of grandeur' by intriguing skilfully.*[4] There was certainly an extensive network of them, in successive generations, available to do so. The Comte's elder brother, the Duc de Noailles, had two adult sons, the Duc d'Ayen and the Marquis de Noailles. The Comte's own sons, of whom the elder was part of the welcoming delegation, added to the total. Most importantly of all, the Comtesse de Noailles, whom Marie Antoinette would meet the following day, was to be in overall charge as her Mistress of the Household (*Dame d'Honneur*).

As a couple, the Comte and Comtesse de Noailles were upright and proud of their unusual marital fidelity. It was a virtue for which they were commended by Louis XV; for, like many roués, he respected what he could not practise. Unfortunately they were also rigid and severe in less admirable ways, obsessed with etiquette and rules for rules' sake. As a member of Marie Antoinette's household pointed out, the desiccated Comtesse de Noailles had little of that natural warmth that would induce young people to pay attention to her good advice.†[5] As for the Comte de Noailles, he insisted on his right

---

* Bombelles' *Journals* are an important source of information. He was a diplomat with experience of many European countries, and his connections to the court included his mother-in-law, Madame de Mackau, deputy Governess to the Children of France, and his wife Angélique, who was a favourite of Louis Auguste's sister, Madame Elisabeth.

† The Goncourt brothers, writing the life of Marie Antoinette in the nineteenth century, referred to the Comtesse de Noailles as 'the bad fairy' in her entourage.[6]

not only to fetch the Dauphine but also to distribute the presents of money and jewels – over 400,000 livres' worth – that were by tradition given to her accompanying Austrian suite before their return to their own country.

Immediately there was a hitch, one of etiquette. The Comte de Noailles demanded a last-minute change in the language of the document of the handover. The phrase 'Their Imperial Majesties having *wanted* [the marriage]' could be conceived as offensive to Louis XV, suggesting that he had been in some way manipulated by Austria. It had to be altered to 'Their Imperial Majesties having been willing to accede to the King's wish': more diplomatically virile. Prince Starhemberg held out in turn for a dais in the handover salon. In the end there were to be two documents, as with the marriage contract. First, France signed before Austria and the order of signatures was then reversed.[7]

It was in keeping with this impartiality, so earnestly maintained, that the handover was to take place on an island in the middle of the Rhine, near Kehl. Handovers were never easy to arrange. Islands were the correct spot for actual brides; Maria Josepha of Saxony, the previous Dauphine, had been handed over on this same island twenty-three years earlier. So when Marie Adélaïde of Savoy, aged ten, was brought to the French court as the mere fiancée of Louis XIV's heir, it was decided after much cogitation to use a hump-backed bridge on a steep slope. A coach was manoeuvred so that its back wheels were in Savoy, its horses and front wheels in France; the doors opened on to neutral territory exactly in the centre of the bridge.[8]

The problem with the island near Kehl was that its building had fallen down since the days of Maria Josepha; something wooden had to be hastily put together for this two-way ceremony. Wealthy citizens of Strasbourg were pressed into service to lend furniture and tapestries while the Lutheran University provided a suitable dais. Some of these hastily assembled tapestries struck an odd note; no official seems to have noticed that one series depicted the story of Jason and Medea, the rejected mother who slew her own children. But a young man named Goethe, then studying law at Strasbourg, was deeply shocked: 'What! At the moment when the young princess is about to step on the soil of her future husband's country, there is placed before her eyes a picture of the most horrible marriage that can be imagined!'[9] To most of the spectators, however, the ritual details of the occasion were far more important.

Immediately after the handover, Marie Antoinette would say goodbye to her Austrian attendants, none of whom, except Prince Starhemberg, were to travel on to Versailles. Her farewells were punctuated with tears, protestations of affection and messages to her family and friends at home. Even her beloved pug Mops was not allowed to accompany her into France. This might seem hard, except that once the ritual ceremony of de-Austrification was over, Count Mercy d'Argenteau, the Austrian ambassador, found himself negotiating for the arrival of the pug from Vienna.[10] With others, all equally ill trained and 'dirty', Mops was soon distracting the Dauphine from life's serious purposes – at least in Mercy's opinion.

Similarly, the ritual by which the Dauphine was stripped of her magnificent Austrian wedding clothes, even down to her stockings and underwear, in order to don French-made garments, was not quite as harsh and humiliating as it sounds. It was of course a symbolic act of possession; in the words of Madame Campan in her memoirs: 'that [the bride] might retain nothing belonging to a foreign court (an etiquette always observed on such an occasion)'. But an eighteenth-century princess, even one raised in a comparatively informal court, had little of the modern concept of personal privacy where dressing, undressing and the performing of intimate functions were concerned. Life at Versailles would be even more public. You did not have to be the Francophile who found the Dauphine 'a thousand times more charming' in her new attire, to realize that parting from her faithful suite was a good deal more painful for Marie Antoinette than the formal divestment.[11] She had, after all, been treated as a doll, to be dressed up in this and that at the adults' whim since childhood; this was just one more example of that process.*

---

* Madame Campan's claim that the Dauphine was totally undressed has sometimes

The fate of the rich Austrian bridal clothes, incidentally, was equally symbolic, representing in this case the way things worked at Versailles. Marie Antoinette's senior attendants, the Dames du Palais, seized them as perquisites of office. A few years later, Charles Emmanuel III of Savoy, negotiating the marriage of his granddaughter Josephine to the Dauphin's brother, was suitably alarmed to hear about this plundering of Marie Antoinette's trousseau.

A rumble of thunder from the nearby Black Forest could be heard during the actual ceremony. Otherwise it went more or less according to the much-debated plan. There were two entrances to the hastily erected building, and two exactly matching rooms, one for the Austrians, one for the French. Marie Antoinette was led from the Austrian room into the salon of the handover by Prince Starhemberg. Here a table covered in red velvet represented the boundary between the two countries. On the other side of it she found the Comte de Noailles, with two aides, awaiting her. A human touch was provided by his son, the eighteen-year-old Prince de Poix, who could not resist peeking through the keyhole from the French side to try to get an advance view of his future Queen. Speeches were made and the deed was done.

It was time for the Dauphine to meet her French attendants. Here there was a slight hiccup which involved, once again, etiquette and the Noailles family. The Comte de Noailles was anxious that his wife should be *handed* into the main salon by a gentleman-in-waiting, which he maintained was her right, as opposed to merely *walking* into it. In order to achieve this, it was arranged that the salon door on the French side should be left slightly ajar, so that it could be nudged open by her heavy flowing skirts at the appropriate moment. Unfortunately this resulted in the door opening too soon ... Once dignity was

been treated sceptically on the grounds that the writer was not personally present; but Madame Campan's father-in-law, to whom she was very close, was part of the handover party. Other sources describe the Dauphine as changing her clothes or being dressed, which presupposed being undressed. That the ritual had not yet been abandoned is clear from the fact that it was applied to Josephine of Savoy, marrying the Comte de Provence three years later.[12]

recovered, an elaborate quadrille of presentations took place. First of all, the Comte presented the Comtesse to her new mistress. In an impulsive gesture that would turn out to be characteristic of her approach to her new French 'family', Marie Antoinette flung herself into the Comtesse's arms.[13]

This, however, was not the way of Versailles. The Comtesse was quick to establish the right of her husband to a ceremonial embrace. This was based on his additional rank as a Grandee of Spain, rather than as a French count. (As Grandees of Spain, people managed to climb up higher on the ladder of etiquette than otherwise entitled, which was the aim of more or less every courtier at Versailles.) So having just been presented by her husband, the Comtesse now re-presented him back again, for his due embrace.[14]

After that the gentlemen of the Dauphine's household were presented. Then the Comtesse presented the ladies, who had originally attended Queen Maria Lesczinska, who had died two years previously in her late sixties. There was the Duchesse de Villars as her Mistress of the Robes (Dame d'Atour) and among the Dames du Palais the Marquise de Duras, who was yet another Noailles, the Duchesse de Picquigny and the Comtesse de Mailly.

Not all the ladies-in-waiting, however, were as formidable as the Comtesse de Noailles, who said herself that she saw her role as that of a governess to a young woman as much as an attendant to a Dauphine, thus reincarnating that feared figure in Marie Antoinette's life, the critical older woman. Although the Duchesse de Duras, as she became, tended to alarm the Dauphine with her superior intelligence, the Comtesse de Mailly was sweet-natured as well as wise, and would inspire great affection in her young mistress. As for the Duchesse de Picquigny, bold and amusing, her appointment was certainly due to her rank rather than her virtues, since she had a disreputable private life; the appointment raised some eyebrows including those of the Austrian ambassador.

Nevertheless, for better or for worse, the Dauphine was now officially French. These ladies, all chosen by the King without consultation for a variety of reasons to do with public policy and private intrigue, together with her various Ladies of the Bedchamber and her lesser waiting-women, were to be the companions of her waking hours, until and unless Marie Antoinette took steps to make alternative arrangements.

Strasbourg, conscious of its importance as the first French city to hail the Dauphine, put on a brave show. It was all witnessed by the sixteen-year-old Henriette de Waldner, from an old Austrian family, who as Baronne d'Oberkirch would write a percipient memoir of her varied life. She watched the picturesque arrival of the Dauphine, surrounded by children dressed up as shepherds and shepherdesses, offering her baskets of flowers. Meanwhile the daughters of the bourgeoisie, in their best clothes, strewed further flowers in her path. Marie Antoinette gathered them up 'as the goddess Flora might herself have done'. In the evening the entire city was illuminated, the cathedral from top to bottom looking like 'one single light'.[15]

'Oh, if I lived a hundred years, I would not forget this day, these celebrations, the cries of joy issuing from a people drunk with happiness,' wrote the Baronne d'Oberkirch at a time when those innocent days of Marie Antoinette's French welcome were a mere memory. Henriette was present when the public orator began to address the Dauphine in German and she stopped him. 'Don't speak to me in German,' she said firmly. 'From now on I want to hear no other language but French.' The fact that Marie Antoinette spoke these engaging words with a slight accent made them especially touching.

Yet even here, as oxen were roasted and fireworks set off 'as though it was the end of the world', there were troubles. Those who had the status of 'foreign princes', for example, chose to arrive 'incognito'. This was an elaborate sham (we shall meet it again at Versailles), since everyone knew perfectly well the identity of the people concerned; but it did mean that the foreign princes were not subject to the rules of French etiquette, which were so unsympathetic where they were concerned.[16] And there was one encounter that would cast a long shadow, or as the Baronne d'Oberkirch wrote: 'What strange connections there are in life!'

Laxenburg: the 'holiday home' of the imperial family which Marie Antoinette loved.

The Empress Maria Teresa,
mother of Marie Antoinette.

Francis Stephen of Lorraine
(the Emperor Francis I),
Marie Antoinette's father.

The imperial family, painted by the Archduchess Marie Christine on St Nicolas Day, 1762, showing the informal style of life they enjoyed in private. *Left to right:* Ferdinand, Marie Christine, Marie Antoinette, Max, Maria Teresa and Francis Stephen.

Opposite: Ballet *Il Trionfo d'Amore*, danced at the wedding Archduke Joseph and Josepha of Bavaria, in 1765, by Ferdina and Marie Antoinette as shepherd and shepherdess, with Max Cupid; this picture, which reminded her of her childhood, lat belonged to Marie Antoinette herself in Franc

Maria Teresa in the heavy mourning she wore for the rest of her life
after the death of her husband in 1765 surrounded by her four sons.
Left to right: Joseph, Ferdinand, Leopold and Max.

Marie Antoinette aged twelve or thirteen.

The Archduchess Marie Christine, thirteen years older than Marie Antoinette, resented her for being their mother's favourite.

Marie Antoinette's favourite sister, Maria Carolina, later Queen of Naples; the two archduchesses, three years apart in age, were often thought to look alike, although Marie Antoinette was generally rated the prettier.

For it was here at Strasbourg that Marie Antoinette had her first meeting with Prince Louis de Rohan, a handsome rather dissolute man in his mid-thirties who was Coadjutor of the see where his uncle Cardinal Louis Constantin was Bishop (the third member of the family to hold the position). In due course the womanizing of Prince Louis would get an angry reaction from the strait-laced Maria Teresa, when he was sent to Vienna as ambassador: 'A dreadful type ... without morals'.[17] Nor did it make things better that Prince Louis, quite apart from his own activities in that direction, also enjoyed gossiping about the sexual failings of other people. But at Strasbourg in 1770, Prince Louis de Rohan simply represented another member of a great French noble family, with whose claims – or pretensions – Marie Antoinette as Dauphine would have to learn to cope.*

Like the Noailles family, that of Rohan consisted of an extensive network, knitted still closer by frequent intermarriage in the clan. For example, Prince Louis' father was a Rohan-Guéméné and his mother a Rohan-Soubise. Despite being Breton princes with origins of great antiquity, the Rohans were 'perpetually occupied with their own elevation', as the critical Baron de Besenval wrote. Their obsession about being treated as sovereign princes had annoyed their contemporaries, including Saint-Simon at the court of Louis XIV, through several generations.[18]

After a night spent in the episcopal palace of the venerable Cardinal Louis Constantin de Rohan, the Dauphine continued on her way across north-eastern France. She and her cumbersome but splendid cortège still had 250 miles to go before they reached Versailles; the cost to the French of this stage of the journey would be 300,000 livres. The route took Marie Antoinette to Nancy, part of her father's former Duchy of Lorraine, where once again the Dauphine was able to emphasize the connection by praying at the tombs of her ancestors. At

---

* It was later suggested by scandalmongers that Marie Antoinette had known Prince (later Cardinal) de Rohan as a girl in Vienna and had been debauched by him. Leaving aside the improbability of such a story, given the nature of her childhood, it was also impossible since Prince Louis arrived in Vienna in 1772, two years after she left.

each stop there were addresses, reviews, theatrical entertainments, which at Châlons-sur-Marne were performed by
actors provided by the royal household. At Soissons, the Dauphine was allowed a day of rest while the French court travelled
on to the château of Compiègne. The first actual encounter of
two young people whose union had already been celebrated in
verse and address almost to exhaustion, was about to take place.

This fabled meeting took place at three o'clock in the
afternoon on 14 May in the forest near Compiègne, where the
road crossed the river at the Bridge of Berne. The French King
arrived in a carriage that contained only his grandson and three
of his four surviving spinster daughters. The curiosity of Louis
XV concerning his granddaughter-in-law was at last to be
gratified. He had already cross-questioned his ambassador to
Austria about her bosom, and on being told with a blush that
the ambassador had not looked at the Archduchess's bosom,
the King replied jovially: 'Oh didn't you? That's the first thing
I look at.'[19]

As the Dauphine stepped out of her carriage on to the
ceremonial carpet that had been laid down, it was the Duc de
Choiseul who was given the privilege of the first salute. Presented
with the Duc by Prince Starhemberg, Marie Antoinette exclaimed: 'I shall never forget that you are responsible for my
happiness!'

'And that of France,' replied Choiseul smoothly.[20]

Then the King and his family left their carriage. The Duc de
Croÿ, First Gentleman of the Bedchamber, duly presented
'Madame la Dauphine' whereupon Marie Antoinette flung herself
on her knees in front of 'Monsieur mon frère et très cher grandpère', now to be 'Papa' or 'Papa-Roi'.

When she was raised up – the King was moved by the
touching gesture of submission – Marie Antoinette saw before
her a distinguished figure with 'large, full, prominent black
piercing eyes and a Roman nose', a monarch who even at the
age of sixty was generally regarded as 'the handsomest man at
his court'.[21] Unfortunately it was a description that the Dauphin
at his side was never likely to merit. Here was a youth with
heavy-lidded eyes and thick dark eyebrows, looking generally

awkward – or was it sulky? – and, although not sixteen until August, already quite portly. In short, Louis Auguste was not quite the idealized figure of the portraits and the miniature that Marie Antoinette had received, which had tactfully and understandably trimmed his jawline and minimized his bulk.

As for the royal aunts, aged thirty-eight, thirty-seven and thirty-six respectively, the malicious English anecdotalist Horace Walpole had described them as 'clumsy, plump old wenches'. In fact the eldest and cleverest, Madame Adélaïde, had had a certain charm in youth, even if it had now long vanished; Madame Victoire was not bad-looking but had become so fat that her father nicknamed her 'Sow'; whilst Madame Sophie, known as 'Grub', tilted her head sideways like a frightened hare.[22] These nursery nicknames bestowed by the King (Adélaïde was 'Rag') cast a deceptively warm and cosy light on these three disappointed women left behind at Versailles, but, as Marie Antoinette would discover, cosiness was not really their main attribute, at least so far as *l'Autrichienne* was concerned. She would also discover that her husband the Dauphin, robbed of his own mother three years ago, was devoted to his aunts.

Louis XV for his part saw a charming little girl who was roughly of an age with the teenage nymphets he had been wont to visit in various establishments (in effect royal brothels) in the district called the Parc aux Cerfs. She was nevertheless very different from those rosy curvaceous creatures, the types of freshness and sensuality, half knowing, half innocent, portrayed by Fragonard. It was easier for the King to relate Marie Antoinette to what he had been told about his own mother, who had died when he was two and for whose memory he had a sentimental veneration. For Marie Adélaïde of Savoy was another little girl who had arrived at Versailles.

Marie Antoinette's complexion was her best feature, the dazzling white skin and wonderful natural colour offsetting the less fortunate 'Austrian lip'. But her undeveloped figure – alas for the King's hopes – was somewhat of a disappointment, even if it had to be admitted that it was satisfactory enough for her age. In general, the King's verdict on the Dauphine was 'spontaneous and a little childish'. What did Louis Auguste see?

His hunting journal, begun four years previously, in which only major events got a look-in, reported briefly: 'Meeting with Madame la Dauphine,' with no comment on his reaction to Marie Antoinette's physical appearance.[23] He now gave his 'wife' a formal embrace.

That night at the château of Compiègne, the Dauphine was introduced to the Princes and Princesses of the Blood, as the relatives of the King were known, this title being the most prized distinction at the French court. Here were the Bourbon-Contis and the Bourbon-Condés; the two branches had separated in the seventeenth century but had frequently intermarried. Foremost among the Princes of the Blood, however, was the Duc d'Orléans (whose late wife had been a Bourbon-Conti). He was present with his son Philippe, currently known as the Duc de Chartres.

Philippe, better known to history as the Duc d'Orléans, the title that he would inherit in 1785, was an energetic if somewhat frivolous character. He was always wonderfully dressed and was rated the best dancer at court. By marrying the great heiress Mademoiselle de Penthièvre a year previously, he had ensured that his fortune was potentially the greatest in France, given that the Orléans wealth was already prodigious. At the time of the marriage Louis XV had commented that the bridegroom was a libertine. The verdict of his English mistress, Grace Elliott, was kinder: Philippe was 'a man of pleasure'. Whatever his character faults, Philippe, as the eventual Orléans heir, was next in line to the throne if the French male Bourbon line failed.*[24]

A charming young widow, the Princesse de Lamballe, was among the ladies whom Marie Antoinette encountered for the first time. Born Marie Thérèse de Savoie-Carignan, she was half Italian and half German, her mother having been a German princess. Her appearance was sweetly soulful, like an angel painted by Greuze; her nature was almost morbidly sensitive. She had a strain of melancholy generally held to come from her German side. It was the early death of her dissolute young

---

* Although Philippe, future Duc d'Orléans, was only a fourth cousin once removed of the future Louis XVI.

husband, only son of the famously charitable Duc de Penthièvre, that had in fact created the vast fortune of Philippe's wife. As a widow, the Princesse de Lamballe concentrated on acting the devoted daughter-in-law to the bereaved Duc, grandson of Louis XIV; his father the Comte de Toulouse, one of the royal bastards, had been legitimated by the King. She was much admired for her dedication and nicknamed 'the Good Angel'; the generous Duc de Penthièvre was known as 'the King of the Poor'.[25] As to the question of remarriage – she was only twenty – it was an important point, by the rules of the game that the Dauphine had to learn, that the Princesse de Lamballe's rank at court derived from her marriage into a legitimated princely house, not her birth. Remarriage to one of lower rank might involve sacrificing her own.

There was another rule of the game that had to be learnt the following next night at the château of La Muette. The Dauphine remarked on another charming young woman present, whose large blue eyes were described by one man with some excitement as having 'a frank caressing regard' and by the English ambassador as having 'the most wanton look in them that I ever saw'. This was the Comtesse Du Barry, born more plainly Jeanne Bécu, and the King's mistress. Her presence at the supper party had already caused enormous discontent behind the scenes; the pious aunts who hated her were furious while the Austrian ambassador, allowed to pay his respects at Compiègne, resented the imposition. The King shrugged it all off. 'She's pretty and she pleases me,' was the royal line.[26] As for the Du Barry's appearance at the supper, although a social outrage, it was technically allowable since the King had recently, with some official manoeuvring, secured her presentation at court by a tame noblewoman.

Marie Antoinette fell into the trap of asking the Comtesse de Noailles the identity of this lady; the Du Barry had obviously not featured in the lessons given by the Abbé de Vermond on the personnel of the French court. When the Comtesse tactfully replied that the lady was there to give pleasure to the King, the Dauphine cheerfully said: 'Oh, then I shall be her rival, because I too wish to give pleasure to the King.'[27]

More in keeping with Count Mercy's sense of propriety was the call paid to Madame Louise on the way to Versailles. Youngest of the Dauphin's aunts, she had recently taken the veil as Sister Thérèse Augustine. One of the nuns in the Carmelite convent always remembered the apparition presented by the young Dauphine: 'The most perfect princess as to her face, her figure and her appearance ...' She had an air 'at once of grandeur, modesty and sweetness'.[28]

Although there had been much lightning at La Muette, the next day, Wednesday, 16 May 1770, dawned brightly, fortunately for the crowds, including many great ones, who had to get up early and make the three-hour carriage journey to Versailles. Admission was by ticket only – with many stern official orders to the effect that this must be respected – but there were probably about 6000 people present of all ranks. For the great ones, full court dress (*grand habit du cour*) was *de rigueur*: swords and silk coats for men, tightly boned bodices, hooped skirts and a long train for women, as well as elaborately dressed and powdered hair. The Duchess of Northumberland for one had to get up at 6 a.m. to have hers done.[29]

Marie Antoinette, not yet officially attired in her wedding robes, arrived with her entourage at Versailles at about half past nine in the morning. Every window of the great façade was thronged with curious spectators. Marie Antoinette also benefited from the brilliant May morning for her first sight of the fabled palace where, as she assumed, she would spend the rest of her life. She was then conducted to the ground-floor apartments that had once belonged to the previous Dauphine Maria Josepha (and where incidentally Louis Auguste had been born) to prepare herself for the wedding ceremony. This was arranged to take place in the colonnaded Royal Chapel, built at the turn of the century.

These were not to be her permanent apartments, as they lacked privacy due to their ground-floor location. They therefore had the slightly depressing air of temporary accommodation. The officials of the King's Works (*Bâtiments du Roi*) had spent two years refurbishing the rooms intended for the

Archduchess's use, starting them, in fact, as soon as the marriage looked likely.* But not for the first time or the last in the history of such things, the projected works were not finished on time.[30]

There was, however, at least one unalloyedly pleasant encounter before her: this was with the two Princesses, Clothilde and Elisabeth, her sisters-in-law, who were too young to be present at the supper the previous night. It was then that Marie Antoinette had met her two brothers-in-law. One was Louis Xavier, Comte de Provence; at fourteen and a half (almost exactly her own age) he was even more corpulent than the Dauphin, although unlike Louis Auguste, he was sharp and intelligent in conversation. Charles Comte d'Artois was two years younger, and of the three brothers was the only one who had inherited something of the celebrated good looks of his grandfather.

Poor plump Clothilde, the Gros-Madame of unkind court nomenclature, was nine, as 'round as a bell' with her circumference thought to exceed her height. She was nevertheless famously good-natured, loved by her little circle and forgiving of those who teased her. Madame Elisabeth was just six years old, and 'scarcely out of her leading-strings', having been under three when her mother died.[31] Shy to outsiders but pretty enough – the family embonpoint had not yet struck – Elisabeth quickly became Marie Antoinette's pet. Because the Princesses were still so young, etiquette could be circumvented and Marie Antoinette could receive them before she put on her court dress: a nice distinction.

An awe-inspiring moment was provided when Marie Antoinette was presented with the magnificent jewels, diamonds and pearls, that were her due as Dauphine. They had previously belonged to Maria Josepha whose wealth of gems at her death had been valued at nearly 2 million livres. Since there was no Queen of

---

* These apartments today have their view masked by large plants in boxes, which gives a good idea of the lack of privacy that they would have without them. Somewhat surprisingly, a large and showy replica of the so-called Diamond Necklace can also be seen there in a case.

France extant, the Dauphine also received a fabulous collar of pearls, the smallest 'as large as a filbert nut', which had been bequeathed by Anne of Austria to successive consorts. This seventeenth-century Habsburg princess who married Louis XIII was incidentally Marie Antoinette's own ancestress as well as that of the Dauphin.* The bride added all this to the various jewels, among them some fine white diamonds, that she had brought with her from Vienna.[32]

There were a multitude of other luxurious gifts provided by the French King, such as a fan encrusted in diamonds, and bracelets with her cipher MA on the blue enamel clasps, which were also ornamented with diamonds. The royal bounty arrived in a crimson velvet coffer, six feet long and over three feet high. Its various drawers were lined with sky-blue silk and had matching cushions; the central feature was a parure of diamonds for the Dauphine herself, but there were also presents labelled for her attendants. (She herself would present Prince Starhemberg with a magnificent set of Sèvres porcelain as a reward for his services.)[33] The wedding ring itself had been fitted from among a dozen provided at Compiègne and was therefore expected to give no problem.

The full panoply of Versailles was now loosed upon a central figure who, in the words of one observer, was so small and slender in her white brocade dress inflated with its vast hoops on either side that she looked 'not above twelve'. Yet the dignity of Marie Antoinette who had 'the bearing of an archduchess' – the result of that rigorous grooming of her childhood, which had been the most efficient part of her education – was universally commended. And this was a place where style and grace of self-presentation were of paramount importance. The

---

* By the standards of European royalty, Marie Antoinette and Louis Auguste were not particularly closely related. On the Habsburg side (Maria Josepha's mother was a Habsburg) they were second cousins once removed. They shared Bourbon descent from Louis XIII and additional Orléans blood, since Louis XV's grandmother Anne Marie had been an Orléans princess; at its closest this amounted to second cousins twice removed. Interestingly, Marie Antoinette had more actual French blood in her than her husband – two grandparents out of four – to his one in the shape of the King.

Dauphin, on the other hand, was generally reported as being cold, sulky or listless throughout the long Mass, in contrast to his bride. And he trembled with apprehension as he placed the chosen ring on her finger.[34]

In the signing of the marriage contract, however, their relative skills were reversed. The entire royal family signed in the appropriate order, first of all 'Louis' for the King, then 'Louis Auguste' neatly and precisely written by the Dauphin. But the third signature, 'Marie Antoinette Josephe Jeanne', had a large blot on the first 'J': the first of those blots – were they careless or nervous? – that would later blight Marie Antoinette's correspondence with her mother. Furthermore her signature began to slope markedly downwards on 'ette' after the half-word 'Antoine' as though the Dauphine had not quite accustomed herself to her new signature. Nor is it clear whether the first 'e' of 'Jeanne' is actually there.[35]

For all these small omens, for all the rain that fell later, disturbing the radiance of the morning, the festivities were widely felt to constitute the finest royal wedding anyone had ever seen; indeed, the King thought so himself. The outstanding nature of the celebrations was generally ascribed to the high rank of the bride: 'The Dauphin does not marry the daughter of the Emperor every day.' Louis XV had married a relatively obscure princess but his grandson was marrying 'the daughter of the Caesars'. The Duc de Croÿ, intoxicated by the idea of seeing the glorious scene *en fête*, climbed up on to the roof: 'It's from here that one should see Versailles.' The lanterns and the lights everywhere, even the canal covered in illuminated boats, left an unforgettable impression.[36]

Yet the key ceremony – on which the Franco-Austrian alliance symbolically focused – was still to come. This was the ritual bedding of the young pair, which would be followed, it was hopefully assumed, by the physical consummation of the marriage. Sex was not a subject from which Louis XV had shied away in the past. He had taken an interest in the wedding night of his grandson Don Ferdinand of Parma and the Archduchess Amalia that was as much prurient as dynastic: 'Send me all the details down to the smallest ones,' he wrote, and as time went on, he asked keenly after the health of his grandson's 'generative organ'.[37]

Nor was it to be expected that Maria Teresa, so rigorously inquisitive about the monthly cycles of her daughters, would neglect to follow through her enquiries to the procreative act itself. In the case of Maria Carolina, the Empress was delighted to hear that King Ferdinand, boorish as he might be with certain disgusting physical habits, had nevertheless performed his marital duties with enthusiasm on his wedding night. The arrival of Maria Carolina's period a few days later, putting a temporary halt to this new sport, had caused much disappointment.[38] The same obsession meant that the Archduchesses were frankly instructed about what was going to happen to them in the marriage bed.

Naturally not every wedding night between two people who had met only days, if not hours, before, went wonderfully well. The Dauphin's father Louis Ferdinand had burst into floods of tears instead of making love to Maria Josepha in 1747 because the occasion brought back poignant memories of his dead first wife. But Maria Josepha exhibited discreet sympathy and matters righted themselves so that they managed to produce a large family. For every George III, who was perfectly happy with his bride from the first although they were total strangers to each other, there was a Frederick II, spending a reluctant hour with his wife Elizabeth Christina of Brunswick-Bevern and then walking about outside for the rest of the night.[39]

On this occasion, nothing ceremonial was left undone. The Archbishop of Rheims blessed the nuptial bed. Louis XV himself, present in the bedchamber, gave his grandson the nightgown, according to preordained etiquette; the young Duchesse de Chartres gave the Dauphine hers. The King then handed his grandson formally into bed. The Duchesse de Chartres performed the same function for the Dauphine. Everyone who had the Rights of Entry to the chamber on this occasion – a remarkably large number of people, based on birth and position at court – now bowed or curtsied and withdrew.

At Versailles there was none of the ribaldry – at least, not recorded – that had led Charles II of England, a hundred years earlier, to whisper to the young William of Orange as he drew the nuptial curtains: 'Hey, nephew, to your work! St George for England.'[40] There were, however, exactly similar expectations on behalf of the patron saints of France and Austria.

Versailles being a palace of rumour as well as a centre of power, it was not long on the following morning before it was being hinted that these expectations had not been fulfilled.

CHAPTER SIX

In Front of the Whole World

'I put on my rouge and wash my hands in front of the whole world.'

Marie Antoinette on her daily routine, 12 July 1770

Louis XV's sensual romps in his private apartments with the Du Barry might be devoid of spectators, but very little else in the life of Versailles went without witnesses. Furthermore these witnesses were not secret pryers and peepers (although they might perform that function as well); they were royal servants of many different ranks who had a legitimate right to be present. Many of their paid positions – known as *charges* – were either bought or were presented by the monarch as a source of income.[1] Ceremonies framed the royal day; these included the ritual morning dressing (*lever*) at which the formal *toilette* was performed with much assistance, and the ritual evening undressing (*coucher*). The Rights of Entry to these ceremonies, which despite their apparently intimate nature had nothing private about them, were prized as an indication of personal prestige. The great ones had Major Rights while quite another category of servitors, including physicians, valets-de-chambres, and the Royal Reader, had Minor Rights.

Then there was the public dinner (*grand couvert*). More or less anyone who was decently dressed could come and gape at the royals at their food, provided, in the case of a man, that he was equipped with a sword; but then swords for the unprepared could be obtained at the gates of Versailles.[2] Since separate households meant on certain occasions separate dinners, the stairs at Versailles might be busy with people scurrying from one prandial spectacle to another. You might catch Marie Antoinette at her soup, the younger Princes at another course and Mesdames Tantes at their dessert. It was characteristic of both Dauphin and Dauphine that Louis Auguste ate with gusto while Marie Antoinette scarcely touched her food in public. Nevertheless it was always presented to her by her Mistress of the Household (the aged Comtesse de Noailles) kneeling on a stool with a napkin on her arm, with four other Dames du Palais in full court dress to assist her. When the whole royal family was gathered at the public dinner (Princes of the Blood were only admitted on the day of their marriage), conversation tended to languish, with the exception of the Comte d'Artois whose irrepressible spirits allowed him to keep chatting away.

The public pomp of Versailles was one thing. It was after all a planned display. A hundred years ago Louis XIV had deliberately constructed a system that centred round himself, the Sun King about whom the galaxies of the nobility were obliged to revolve by their constant attendance at his court. In a sense the spirit of the mighty King lived on in the routines he had established: as late as 1787 Chateaubriand observed that Louis XIV's presence remained 'always there' at Versailles. Presentation at court was the most important ceremony in a young woman's life. Managing the long, heavy train was an art in itself. Candidates needed to rehearse the three vital curtsies beginning by the door with at least two lessons with a special dancing-master in Paris. These 'reverences' had to be at one and the same time 'modest, gracious and noble', wrote Madame de Genlis in her *Dictionnaire ... des Etiquettes de la Cour,* for if style was the man, 'the curtsy had to express the whole woman'. The man in question, Monsieur Huart, was large and imposing. His hair white with powder, he positioned himself at the end of the room in a kind of courtly drag (a billowing underskirt) standing in for the figure of the Queen.[3]

'It was all very funny,' wrote the Marquise de La Tour du Pin much later, describing the whole rigmarole of the presentation. But it was also all very serious, in view of the fact that the new girl's appearance would generally be torn to pieces by the spectators at Versailles. For example, was her skin really white enough to endure the contrast with the fine lawn chemise that was deliberately allowed to peep through the lacings at the back of her dress?[4]

For all this incredible formality, service was often by contrast extremely slapdash owing to the nature of an organization where menials actually performed the tasks for which the great ones had the official *charge*. Thus the favourite fish of Marie Antoinette, destined for a royal dinner given in her honour by the Comte d'Artois, was stolen and ended up being served to the Scottish gardener at Versailles for his breakfast; on another dreadful occasion a piece of glass was swept into the gruel (*panade*) of a Child of France by an incompetent kitchen servant because the Royal Governess was too haughty to prepare the dish herself. What struck foreign observers was the ease of access to Versailles of those who by no stretch of the imagination could be described as great ones (nor were even decently dressed). The common people thronged the antechambers: 'It appears that no questions are asked.'[5] This was in direct contrast to the laborious formality of the court and came from a very different tradition by which every French subject had the right of access to the sovereign.

The market-women – originally confined to fishwives (*poissardes*) – were a case in point. Their right to address the Queen of France on certain prescribed celebratory occasions had become transformed into a general right of access for these mouthy battleaxes. Brawny and unafraid, they were generally allowed to go unchallenged in their self-endowed mission to comment on the failings of queens and princesses. The English agriculturalist Arthur Young on a tour of France was amazed to find a group of 'poorly dressed blackguards' thronging into the King's apartments only minutes after he had gone hunting. It was true that when Young tried to push his luck and see the Queen's apartments too, he was told: 'Good heavens, Sir, that's another matter.' Nevertheless there was an extraordinary lack of security about life at Versailles. It was a fact acknowledged by the searches made by the royal bodyguards, who were equipped with spaniels as sniffer-dogs; their task was to try to rout out vagrants and others who had simply established themselves in its numerous nooks and crannies.[6] Apart from this kind of sporadic effort, it was the sanctity of the royal majesty, so endlessly paraded in public, that was supposed to provide its own security.

As Marie Antoinette quickly learnt, the minutiae of this system of parade were astonishingly significant. For what had once been a method of control exerted by Louis XIV had developed into a power struggle among the nobility, played out on the field of etiquette. When the Duc de Coigny handed the candle to the King at his *coucher*, he did more than perform an apparently menial function: he established himself literally close to the centre of influence. The right to sit on a sofa or a stool (*tabouret*) in the royal presence meant far more than the mere physical comfort of the noble concerned.

Modes of address were also jealously guarded privileges. Thus to address the King or Dauphin simply as 'Monsieur', as opposed to 'Monseigneur' or 'Majesté', was in fact a sign of great privilege or intimacy; Marie Antoinette would formally address her husband as 'Monsieur'. (When Count Mercy d'Argenteau heard the Comtesse Du Barry call Louis XV 'Monsieur' in public he was deeply shocked.) Madame Adélaïde, a king's daughter, hearing herself described as 'Royal Highness', was furious, the simple address of 'Madame' being so much grander.[7]

At the same time the rules were intensely complicated. On one occasion in Louis Auguste's childhood he complained about Philippe Duc de Chartres addressing him as 'Monsieur'. Since he was a member of the royal family, and Chartres was one rank down as a Prince of the Blood, the correct term was 'Monseigneur'. At this point his younger brother, the Comte de Provence, intervened: Chartres should actually address Louis Auguste as 'Cousin'. Marie Antoinette, at her formal morning *toilette*, had to learn the correct degree of acknowledgement for every person who came in. It might be appropriate to nod her head or to incline her body or – most graciously of all, in the case of a Prince or Princess of the Blood – to make as if to rise up without actually doing so. The fact that anyone with the

Rights of Entry might choose to attend without prior notification also made the actual routine of the *toilette* infinitely complicated. Marie Antoinette could reach for nothing herself; the handing over of a garment to the Dauphine (or the Queen) for her to put on was a jealously guarded privilege.[8]

On one notorious occasion, Marie Antoinette had actually undressed and was about to receive her underwear, put out by the First Lady of the Bedchamber, from the hand of the Mistress of the Household. All this was according to plan and the Mistress of the Household had already stripped off her glove in preparation to take the chemise. At this point a Princess of the Blood, the Duchesse d'Orléans arrived, her entry indicated by that peculiar scratching sound that was the Versailles equivalent of a knock. The Mistress of the Household, according to etiquette, relinquished the chemise to the Duchesse, who proceeded to take off her own glove. Marie Antoinette, of course, was still naked. And she remained so when yet another princess appeared, the Comtesse de Provence, who as a member of the royal family took precedence in the ceremony and was in turn handed the chemise. When the Comtesse tried to speed things up by omitting to remove her glove, she managed to knock off the royal mob cap. All this time Marie Antoinette stood with her arms crossed over her body, shivering. She tried to cover her impatience by laughing, but not before muttering audibly: 'This is maddening! This is ridiculous!'[9]

Marie Antoinette's own account of her daily routine, written to her mother in July 1770, makes it clear that this constant element of the private-performed-in-public was present from the very beginning. Waking between nine and ten, she would dress informally, say her morning prayers, eat breakfast, and after that visit the royal aunts. 'At eleven o'clock I have my hair done. At noon, all the world can enter – I put on my rouge and wash my hands in front of the whole world. Then the gentlemen leave and the ladies remain and I am dressed in front of them.' This was followed by Mass, with the King if he happened to be at Versailles, otherwise with the Dauphin. After Mass the two of them dined together 'in front of the whole world'.[10]

In many ways the young Marie Antoinette, with her grace

and amiability, was well equipped to play the part of a hieratic figure at Versailles. The Dauphine certainly had nothing to fear from being exposed to the whole world, morally or physically. At this point she accepted all the conventions of the role, to be played on the stage of what was, in essence, an ageing court. The earlier deaths of the Dauphine Maria Josepha and of the Queen meant that the fourteen-year-old Marie Antoinette was the First Lady of Versailles from the start. In effect, a generation had been skipped. There were courtiers present whose experience stretched back half a century, and even in one or two cases still longer to the last days of Louis XIV. The old man who as a boy had accidentally set light to the wig of the great monarch as he tried to guide his passage with a candle still trembled at the memory. The Duc de Richelieu, widely thought to be the original of Valmont in *Les Liaisons Dangereuses*, had been born in the previous century, and in the words of the Comte d'Hezecques, who had been his page, the roses of love and the laurels of glory had been showered on him throughout three reigns (as well as a few other less admiring accolades).

Then there were various old ladies, described by the Prince de Ligne as impressive like the ruins of Rome and gracious like classical Athens. The ageing Maréchale de Mirepoix, for example, was so charming 'that you would imagine that she had thought of nothing but you for the whole of her life'.[11] It would be a great mistake to underestimate the power of the old at Versailles, especially the older women. For all the sentimental attachment to the fresh appearance of youth – possessed so markedly by the Dauphine – prestige did not vanish with the first wrinkles. A woman was generally held to grow old at thirty, or at least lose the seduction of her beauty (although the *bal des vieux* at court was actually for women over twenty-seven). Louis Petit de Bachaumont, author of numerous volumes of anecdotal reminiscence, put the masculine point of view crudely enough when he repeated a contemporary saying: a girl of fifteen was a coffer whose lock had to be forced, while a woman of thirty was 'venison well ripe and good to put on the spit'. After that a forty-year-old woman was 'a great bastion where the cannon had made more than a breach' and at fifty 'an old lantern in which one only places a wick with regret'.[12]

However, the bastions and the lanterns had, from the feminine point of view, lost neither their strength of character nor their influence with the passing of time. The mocking, mischievous spirit that Madame Antoine had developed in Austria to cope with her own fears of older, cleverer women, was going to be inappropriate at Versailles. Nicknaming the Comtesse de Noailles 'Madame Étiquette' and sending to know the correct procedure for a Dauphine of France who had fallen off her donkey was amusing enough for Marie Antoinette. Such levity was understandable in a girl. 'At the age of fifteen she laughed much,' wrote the Prince de Ligne.[13] But it was perilous laughter.

Where court conventions were concerned, however, Marie Antoinette was for the time being completely docile. With her natural dexterity, she could manage with ease the cumbersome court dress with its wide hoops and long train, and the famous 'Versailles glide', by which ladies seemingly moved without their feet touching the ground, their satin slippers mysteriously avoiding the dirt, was something of which she would become the supreme exponent. For lesser mortals, the glide was practical too; by this means ladies avoided stepping on the train of the lady in front of them. There were two other practices that symbolized the courtly way of life. First was the essential powdering of the hair. So all-embracing was this practice – in 1770 you could not come to court without it – that the smell of powder (and the pomatum that was applied first to fix it) became one of the pervading perfumes of eighteenth-century Versailles, remembered long afterwards by those who had been there. Huge capes had to be draped round those in court dress, men and women, while the powder was blown on to their coiffures; Louis XVI would need a vast peignoir. But these monstrous edifices of wool, tow, pads and wire, looking as if they had been 'dipped in a meal-tub' (in the words of Eliza Hancock, Jane Austen's cousin), that were so often identified with Marie Antoinette actually predated her and were already part of the normal usage of Versailles.[14]

The second symbolic practice was the lavish application of

rouge to the cheeks: not delicate shading but huge precise circles of a colour not far from scarlet. Casanova believed that rouge emphasized ladies' eyes and indicated 'amorous fury', while widows like Maria Teresa and the Dauphine Maria Josepha gave up wearing it as a measure of austerity. In the case of Marie Antoinette, with her superb complexion, it still had to be formally applied every morning in front of 'the whole world'. Rouge, however, was not worn at Versailles in order to allure. It was a badge, or rather two badges, of rank and distinction. It was for this reason that the market-women, who ignored the prohibition on those outside court using rouge, made themselves look like 'raddled old dolls', according to Madame Vigée Le Brun, in an attempt to ape the great ladies; by 1780 French women were said to use 2 million pots of rouge a year.[15]

Visitors from other courts were often appalled by what they saw; in the 1760s Leopold Mozart thought the aristocratic French women looked like wooden Nuremberg dolls on account of this 'detestable make-up ... unbearable to the eyes of an honest German'. The Emperor Joseph II was equally scathing; he would mock his little sister for her grotesque appearance. In wearing her rouge, however (and spending a great deal of money on it; rouge was so expensive that poorer people used red wine to stain their cheeks), Marie Antoinette was for the time being loyally obeying the convention for Versailles, even if it made her unbearable to German eyes.[16]

'Everything that characterizes the public spirit of a court ... is always interesting to note,' wrote the Baron Grimm in one of his witty reports on Versailles life, which were sent back to his master the Duke of Saxe-Gotha.[17] For this reason, a row about etiquette that broke out immediately after the Dauphine's arrival, although apparently trivial, took on a significant aspect. It was all a question of a single dance – a minuet – and two masterful women. The first was the Empress Maria Teresa who liked the idea of family connections abroad being favoured. The second was the Comtesse de Brionne. Born a Rohan (of the Rochefort line) she was the widow of Charles Louis de Lorraine, from the cadet branch of the House of Lorraine established in France.

Once beautiful, and reputedly the mistress of Choiseul, the Comtesse de Brionne in middle age was one of those powerful women mentioned earlier; in her case she had settled into the solid pursuit of her children's advantage. In particular, the Comtesse had social ambitions for her daughter Anne Charlotte, known as Mademoiselle de Lorraine. At Versailles, the Comtesse was determined to use the new Dauphine's family connection with Lorraine to advance Anne Charlotte (who was exactly the same age as Marie Antoinette) above the duchesses. This Lorrainer Cinderella was to be among those who opened the court ball.

The duchesses were predictably – and according to court rules quite justifiably – furious over this breach of etiquette. Collectively, they indicated that they would not attend the ball, and although many of them did in the end, they managed to spoil the occasion by drifting around Versailles for some hours, parading the fact that they had not yet changed into court dress; as a result the ball got off to a late start.

So grave indeed was the threat perceived to be to the established order from Mademoiselle de Lorraine's elevation that the Archbishop of Rheims and the Bishop of Noyon, the first and second ecclesiastical peers, actually addressed a memorandum to the King on the subject. It was not long before a little rhyme was being circulated:

> Sir, the great ones at your dance
> Will see with much pain
> A Princess of Lorraine
> Be the first at the ball to advance.

Louis XV, who hated this kind of trouble, refused to make any kind of ruling beyond saying that the presence of Mademoiselle de Lorraine did not create any kind of precedent. Since an invitation to the opening minuet was in his personal gift, he had merely intended to honour the Dauphine. As for Mademoiselle de Lorraine (or her mother), her dreams of grandeur were blighted by a complicated ruse. The Comte d'Artois danced for a second time *after* Mademoiselle de Lorraine. Since he was a member of the royal family and unarguably her superior in rank, it was obvious that the strict rules of etiquette were not being observed on this occasion. No precedent had been set for the future about the position of Mademoiselle Lorraine. Thus the Brionne triumph was negated.[18]

This was the affair of 'the famous minuet of Mademoiselle de Lorraine', as the Duc de Croÿ called it. It left an early, damaging impression of a foreign Dauphine determined to favour her own relations in defiance of the rules of Versailles. Yet the responsibility for all this unnecessary brouhaha lay, surely, with Mercy d'Argenteau, the Austrian ambassador who had been in France for the past four years (where he had also served a previous tour of duty) rather than with the newly arrived, rather dazed and extremely youthful Marie Antoinette. He should have headed off demands of the Empress that her relation be honoured and with equal tact disposed of the pretensions of the Comtesse de Brionne. Florimond, Count Mercy d'Argenteau, now takes the stage as the most important person in the Dauphine's life in practical terms, and her major advisor. Nearly thirty years older than the Dauphine, he was intended to be, and did become, a kind of father figure to Marie Antoinette.[19]

Tall, spare and elegantly dressed, rich – and keen on riches – Mercy d'Argenteau had been born in the prince-bishopric of Liège, part of modern Belgium. He adored life in Paris, having also experienced Turin, St Petersburg and Warsaw, and accompanied his single status with a splendid lifestyle, which included the fascinating singer Rosalie Levasseur as his mistress. (She had made her debut in 1766, the year of Mercy's arrival in France, and would create the role of Amour in Gluck's *Orphée* when it came to Paris.) This relationship flourished despite the prayers of the nuns at Liège for his reform, and the efforts of his uncle to arrange a good marriage. Mercy shrugged his shoulders and declared that Providence would decide. But since that was not how eighteenth-century marriages were brought about, he remained theoretically a bachelor; although it is notable that Mademoiselle de Lorraine and her elder sister were at one point considered candidates for the honour, thus emphasizing Mercy's links to the Comtesse de Brionne.[20]

Fundamentally Mercy was a cold man and remarkably centred on his own material interests. Bad health of a peculiarly enervating kind (haemorrhoids) may have contributed to a sort of irritable detachment where Marie Antoinette was concerned. Yet he did show real and selfless devotion throughout his long life to one individual: the Empress Maria Teresa, and through her, to the interests of Austria. That was, unfortunately, not necessarily to the advantage of her daughter. Of course in one sense it was hardly surprising that the Austrian ambassador would put the interests of his own country first. But, as has been stressed, this management of double loyalties was a matter of enormous delicacy where foreign princesses were concerned.

Mercy, who was supposedly helping Marie Antoinette find her feet at the French court, actually perpetuated a Rule-by-Maria-Teresa with consequences that were increasingly dubious. He was not at all abashed about this, telling the Empress at one point, with some satisfaction, that he saw no reason why her influence with her daughter would ever fade. In October 1770 the Abbé de Vermond who had been allowed to rejoin her household in France as Reader, summed up Marie Antoinette as having above all 'a desire to please her august mother'; it was questionable whether this was an appropriate motivation for the Dauphine of France.[21]

Marie Antoinette was supposed to write to her mother every month. On exceptional occasions, such as a royal illness, an extra courier might be despatched. But in general the imperial couriers left Vienna at the beginning of each month, travelling to Brussels for despatches, before going on to Paris and picking up further letters there. They were expected back in Vienna around the 28th of the month. Since the whole process took eight or nine days either way, Marie Antoinette had to cope with a quick turnaround; in any case she tended to write her letters at the last minute, for fear of being spied on by her new family. Mercy commented on how the Dauphine was forever locking things up against unlawful inspection; he defended the blots on the letters on the grounds of this necessary speed. The

Empress herself dictated her letters to her secretary, adding personal comments in the margin which the latter did not see. Similarly, Mercy sent his own letters attached to the Dauphine's correspondence after she had already handed it over to him.[22]

The first surviving letter of Marie Antoinette to Maria Teresa from France, dated 9 July 1770, is certainly an ill-written missive, full of crossings-out. The signature was evidently intended to be 'Antoine' since 'tte' is cramped by the margin as in the wedding certificate, but the Dauphine now had to sign herself 'Antoinette' to her mother, 'Marie Antoinette' being reserved for formal documents. It was not, however, until the following year that the signature was really flowing and easy.*[23]

In addition to these rather desperate dutiful letters from one who was never a natural correspondent, the Empress was receiving regular, detailed and intimate reports on her daughter's behaviour from Count Mercy. These were kept utterly secret from their subject. Confronted by her mother's omniscience, which never seemed to work to her advantage, only to her discredit, Marie Antoinette does not appear to have suspected the true culprit. How could the Empress be so well informed about much that was quite trivial gossip? 'My sister Marie', the Archduchess Marie Christine, known in the family as a tale-bearer, was a prime suspect; her aunt, Princess Charlotte of Lorraine, was also blamed. It all added up to a feeling of inferiority, of personal failure. Praise from the Empress was extremely rare; criticism – such well-informed, guilt-inducing

* This first letter, and many others that are also authentic, can still be seen in the Habsburg Archives. During the nineteenth century, however, the letters of Marie Antoinette were frequently forged; inauthentic examples flooded Paris, Vienna and London. One editor printed a number of letters for which the 'originals' had vanished; other forgeries of an allegedly early date were blatantly copied from the handwriting of her later years. The situation was unravelled and a definitive edition, with all forgeries eliminated, was printed in 1895 in Paris by Maxime de la Rocheterie and the Marquis de Beaucourt. Nevertheless, at this point the correspondence between mother and daughter was censored according to nineteenth-century standards; the most intimate aspects of Maria Teresa's advice, although partly printed in 1933 by Georges Girard in *Correspondance entre Marie-Thérèse et Marie-Antoinette*, were not published in full until 1958, by Paul Christoph in *Maria Theresia und Marie Antoinette: ihr geheimer Briefwechsel.*[24]

and therefore often unanswerable criticism – inexorable.

At the heart of Marie Antoinette's personal failure – as the Empress saw it – was her inability to inspire sexual passion in her husband. In her marriage to the heir to the throne, she represented the future, including future preferments for courtiers, as well as the present. Or did she? Nothing was quite certain about her position until the final physical act was performed that was intended to crown the Franco-Austrian alliance.

The Dauphin's continued refusal to perform this act, or even to contemplate doing so, could at first be ascribed to his youth and shyness. That was Marie Antoinette's hopeful scenario. Outwardly all seemed well. The two of them had the air of a gracious royal pair whose innocence in the public eye contrasted favourably with the debauched reputation of the King, his nymphets and now his wanton mistress. One popular rhyme on the subject contrasted two ruling women: Joan of Arc, who had saved the country, with 'the Harlot' – the Du Barry – who was now ruining it.[25] Even a frightful tragedy, which marred the magnificent fireworks set off in Paris on 30 May, did not redound to the discredit of the Dauphin and Dauphine.

Elaborate preparations had been made for the celebration of the royal marriage by France's capital city. Merchants agreed to put up their shutters both on the day of the wedding itself and for the setting off of the fireworks. Detailed police orders were also issued. But for some reason workmen had dug a series of trenches which blocked the exits from the Place Louis XV (now the Place de la Concorde). As the colossal crowds sought to move with the progress of the illuminations, men, women, children and, even more disastrously, horses and carriages plunged in. Altogether, 130 people were crushed to death. Lord Edward Beauclerk could not open his carriage door for the pile of corpses and when his groom finally got out, he found his own father dead in the heap. Fifty-five years later, the Comte de Ségur wrote of the dead in his memoirs: 'Methinks I still hear their cries ...'[26] They were buried in a certain common grave by the Church of the Madeleine off the rue d'Anjou (which would later be used for those executed by the State).

The next day the appalled young royal couple dedicated a month's income each for the relief of the dependents.

A little while later, Marie Antoinette further established her public reputation for sweetness and mercy by stopping her carriage for over an hour to aid an injured postilion. She would not continue until she had established the presence of a surgeon. She then insisted on a stretcher for the wounded man, instead of an uncomfortable post-chaise, and followed its progress. This behaviour was much acclaimed, Mercy reported to Vienna. Another celebrated incident confirmed the image. When a peasant wine-grower was gored by a stag in the course of the royal hunt, the Dauphine conveyed the unfortunate man in her own coach, while making arrangements for the family he left behind and for his ruined crops. Wide publicity was given to the scene, commemorated in engravings, tapestries and even fans, under the general title, 'An Example of Compassion'. This much-disseminated image of the lovely, caring Dauphine was felt to be completely appropriate for a future Queen of France.[27]

For once publicity did not lie. The impulse of compassion was genuine enough and was deeply rooted in Marie Antoinette's character. 'She was so happy at doing good and hated to miss any opportunity of doing so,' wrote Madame Campan of a much later occasion when some country people addressed to her a petition on the subject of a predatory game-bird, reserved for the King's sport, which was destroying their crops. Marie Antoinette ordered the bird to be destroyed. Six weeks later, when the arrival of a second petition made her aware that her orders had not been carried out, she was upset and angry.[28]

It is true that Marie Antoinette's insistence on personal involvement in humanitarian enterprises – a tradition in which she had been brought up in Vienna – was privately thought to be rather unnecessary at Versailles. Louis XV pointed this out when the Dauphine requested permission to go to Paris to comfort one of her Dames du Palais, the Comtesse de Mailly, who had lost her only child: 'We are not accustomed to paying visits at a distance, my dear daughter.' All the same, he agreed that she might act according to the dictates of her 'kind heart'.[29]

This lauded public style contrasted dismally with what was actually going on behind the royal bedroom door. In short, *rien*, the word actually used by Louis Auguste in his hunting journal to denote a day without sport but curiously appropriate to his marital situation. Marie Antoinette herself attached much importance to his sixteenth birthday – 23 August 1770 – and the Dauphin seems to have made some promise to her that matters would be remedied when the royal family went to Compiègne around this date. Then 'he would make her his wife'. Unfortunately the visit passed without any change in a situation that was at once puzzling and deeply humiliating. In September a further promise was made, but Marie Antoinette made the mistake of boasting about the impending glorious event to Mesdames Tantes who quickly spread the news. The Dauphin used this as an excuse to renege yet again.[30]

No doubt out of embarrassment, having to run the gauntlet of speculative courtiers as he made his way there and, worse still, back again, Louis Auguste stopped visiting his wife's bed on a regular basis. The proper apartments of the Dauphine, to which she had attached some hopes, were readied at last. In the process there was a considerable clash of wills between the royal architect Gabriel and the Dauphine, supported in this case by the Dauphin. The young couple wanted something plainer, simpler than the magnificent gilded style that had prevailed before. Above all, they wanted something that could be finished quickly. Marie Antoinette's constant pleas were for the project to be most quickly realizable: 'a white dais, any dais'. But Gabriel thought a square white platform would produce 'a monstrous dissonance', and in any case 50,000 livres had been allowed for the gilding thought suitable for a Dauphine. In the end roses and fleurs-de-lys alternated, together with sphinxes holding the arms of France. Over the bed itself loomed the great double-headed eagle of Austria.[31]

In avoiding the predatory gaze of the eagle – and the expectant little eagle lying below it – Louis Auguste was helped by the custom of the French court by which married couples did not necessarily share beds. This became an enduring bone of contention between the Empress and her daughter. Maria Teresa, who, believing in the marital double bed herself, attached enormous importance to this spending-the-night-together, presumably hoping that passion might strike the Dauphin in some unguarded moment in the middle of the night or the early morning. Austrian ways in this respect were in her opinion definitely preferable. Maria Teresa refused to listen to Marie Antoinette's citation of the usages of France – those usages that in another context she had specifically told her daughter to respect.

The irritation of the Empress with a situation that even she could not control – although she tried hard – grew with the months. Her personal solution (quite apart from a double bed), which she advocated relentlessly over the coming months, was caresses and 'redoubled caresses'. Had she not given her own recipe for a happy marriage – a subject on which she was an acknowledged expert – in May? 'Everything depends on the wife, if she is willing, sweet and *amusante*.'[32]

The attitude of the French King, whose flagrant enjoyment of extramarital bliss provided such an embarrassing contrast to the laggardliness of his grandson, was rather more laid back. A royal doctor made a physical inspection and for the time being had nothing adverse to report. An enquiry to Louis Auguste himself brought about the temporizing reply that although he found the Dauphine delightful, he could not as yet conquer his shyness. So there was no progress. When the Duchess of Northumberland, making diplomatic small talk, suggested that the Dauphin, who had been hunting all day, must have been impatient to get back to his wife, the King answered drily: 'I can't say he mentioned anything on the subject.' Privately he told his favourite grandson, Don Ferdinand of Parma: 'It will happen when we least expect it.'[33]

Yet there was a more serious aspect to the situation than the implied refusal of a gawky adolescent boy ('The Dauphin is not a man like others!' wrote Maria Teresa crossly) to act the husband. This was the manifest public coldness that he showed to his young wife. In the summer of 1770, Mercy optimistically predicted of Marie Antoinette's relationship with Louis Auguste: 'There can be no doubt that with a little caution, she will be able to dominate him completely.'³⁴ But of that there was little sign.

It was true that the influence of the Duc de Vauguyon, the Dauphin's anti-Austrian Governor, began to wane. Marie Antoinette reported proudly that she had managed to elude the appointment of a confessor in the Vauguyon camp by appealing directly to the King to appoint one. (Although the rules of the Catholic Church concerning the secrecy of the confessional were strict enough for the Dauphine's spiritual faults to be safe from inspection, a confessor could still exercise considerable influence merely by the advice he gave.) Marie Antoinette also told a comic tale of catching Vauguyon listening at the keyhole when she was in conversation with the Dauphin; in her version the two young people laughed together at Vauguyon's discomfiture.

Nevertheless the lessons of his tutor had been well learnt by Louis Auguste in his youth. He had been warned in advance against the domination of an Austrian archduchess – in the interests of Austria – and dark stories had been told about the Habsburgs. Here was the Archduchess in person. From the point of view of Maria Teresa, it was an error to suppose that sexual incompatibility was the only problem facing her daughter, and that if that was solved, everything was solved. Louis Auguste's uncommunicative *Journal* does, however, give details of his health. Throughout the summer he suffered a series of digestive upsets, which although attributed to his habit of guzzling sweet pastries (about which Marie Antoinette ticked him off) were surely linked to the pressure he felt.³⁵

In this way Marie Antoinette's efforts to share the Dauphin's predominant interest by attending the hunt even if she did not actually hunt herself, in short, to make herself part of his daytime life if not his night-time occupation, were well advised. Maria Teresa, however, waxed furious about the fact that she rode. It was true that a riding mishap would have been most unfortunate if the Dauphine had actually had any chance of being pregnant; but since she had none, that issue could hardly be said to arise. Nevertheless the Empress, ignoring her own sporting past, preached against the practice. In vain the Dauphine pointed out that the King of France himself – to whose wishes she was supposed to be subject – had given her money for horses and had welcomed her presence. Maria Teresa merely told an anecdote of a princess of Portugal who had had a miscarriage through riding.[36] The implication that her daughter had really only one function, one that she was not fulfilling successfully, was inescapable.

Illogically – but then the Empress, like many people who believe themselves to be always in the right, was not necessarily logical – Maria Teresa praised a portrait of her daughter in riding-costume carried out by Joseph Krantzinger in 1771, and rated it her favourite. This charming equestrian study showed the Dauphine wearing a raking tricorne-hat (which concealed her high forehead), her eyes wide and doe-like, her pretty hands well displayed. It was found to be 'very like' by the mother and also incidentally by the ambassador. Maria Teresa kept it in her study and another in the private little room where she worked at night: 'Thus, I have you always with me, under my eyes.'[37] These were words, of course, that were capable of a metaphorical interpretation.

Mercy, who in principle deplored the Dauphine's spontaneity, while paradoxically praising her for her 'good instincts', was similarly critical when she handed out cold meats at a hunting party to young people of the court. This was conduct unbecoming in the Dauphine of France. And yet the attempt to secure Louis Auguste's friendship by undemanding friendliness – and hunting was, so far as could be seen, his only unequivocal passion – was surely as good, if not better, a method of proceeding as Maria Teresa's 'redoubled caresses', which had no appearance of being welcome. In December 1770, the Dauphine began to give little dances in her apartments which the Dauphin attended; they might at least enjoy a normal social life if a normal sexual one still eluded them. The sight of his wife dancing even elicited a wistful comment from the Dauphin who was so clumsy himself. When a court lady praised Marie Antoinette, Louis Auguste replied: 'She has so much grace that she does everything perfectly.'[38]

Coming to terms as she was with her husband's lack of sexual interest, Marie Antoinette also had to cope with the implications of his grandfather's continuing sexual energy. The presence of the Du Barry at court constituted a problem – but only if it was allowed to become one. Morals at Versailles were lightly worn. The nobility married young, their marriages being more or less arranged, and then lapsed gracefully into extramarital relationships, which were generally tolerated provided they were conducted in sufficiently elegant style. The polite expostulation of the Duc de Richelieu on finding his wife in bed with her lover, expressed the mood: 'Just think, Madame, of the embarrassment if anyone but myself had discovered you.' The Duc de Guiche apologized to his wife for returning unexpectedly and finding her in a similar situation; he was the one at fault for not giving due warning.[39]

There were many long liaisons established at court, such as that of the Prince de Guéméné with the beautiful half-Irish Madame Dillon. The conduct of their affair demonstrated the cool manners of the day. The Comtesse d'Ossun said that when she first arrived at court she understood they were lovers, but six months later she no longer believed it. Affairs with actresses, singers and dancers were accepted with similar sophistication. When the Prince d'Hénin began an affair with the famous singer Sophie Arnould, the Princesse professed herself delighted that her husband had found an occupation on the grounds that 'an unemployed man is so dull'.[40]

In such a climate, the presence of a royal *maîtresse-en-titre* as such was hardly likely to raise many eyebrows among the majority of the French courtiers who had been accustomed to a changing cast of such ladies for most of the long reign, even if the Du Barry's disreputable origins were more difficult to accept. Nevertheless by now 'the new lady', as she was known, was simply a force with whose influence they had to reckon. Unfortunately there were three reasons why Marie Antoinette found herself unable to take such a pragmatic view of simply accepting the fact that 'the Harlot' pleased the King (the attitude she had innocently expressed at La Muette when she declared herself the rival to the unknown charmer). In that first surviving letter of 9 July 1770, Marie Antoinette described the Du Barry as 'the most stupid and impertinent creature that you can imagine' and she expressed pity for the King's 'weakness' for her.[41] She now began to pride herself on giving the favourite no formal acknowledgement.

The first of these reasons was the prudish nature of her own upbringing in which Maria Teresa, ignoring the mistresses of Francis Stephen, had preached a straightforward morality based on the teachings of the Catholic Church. At fourteen, a protected and virginal girl, Marie Antoinette had not lived long enough at the Viennese court to understand the currents of extramarital desire that swirl beneath the surface of any community; she was naturally chaste as she was brought up to be. Now she was launched into a society where the undercurrents were more like rapids. This, however, might have been overcome with time and suitably discreet worldly instruction. Unfortunately there was a second reason. Marie Antoinette's instinctive revulsion (which cannot have been unaffected by the sense that the Du Barry was succeeding where she was failing) was enhanced by the counsels of the spinster royal aunts and used for their own ends.

The third reason why Marie Antoinette declined to give the Du Barry the brief acknowledgement, required not so much for the favourite's *amour propre* as for the King's, lay in her developing character. Desperately insecure for obvious reasons, she took refuge in that kind of obstinacy that is often the refuge of the weak.

Marie Antoinette did have one little victory over the Du Barry when she pleaded prettily for one of her Dames du Palais. The Duchesse de Gramont, Choiseul's sister, had been exiled to the country for refusing to make room for the favourite in a coach. Although the Duchesse now needed to reach Paris for urgent medical reasons, the Du Barry refused to allow a waiver of the terms of exile. 'But Papa,' said the Dauphine in the most winning way, according to Mercy, 'quite apart from compassion and justice, think of the hurt to me if a member of my household was to die while still being in disgrace with you.'[42]

In general, however, dignity not sweetness was her stance where the favourite was concerned. It was a dignity that concealed an ability to hold a grudge, on this occasion aided and abetted by Mesdames Tantes. Of course Marie Antoinette was not the only person at Versailles who harboured grudges; but for her there was a danger that her judgements, both private and political, might be warped, where wiser heads knew when to abandon resentments that no longer served their purpose.

The aunts, of course, rested their case on their father's danger of hell-fire due to his immorality. But a good deal of jealousy also went into the mixture, and sheer trouble-making. It was especially delightful that *l'Autrichienne* could be led into offending Louis XV by simply upholding decency, at the same time as ditching her own prospects. Count Mercy deplored the influence of the royal aunts in this respect, understanding how crucial it was that the Dauphine should please the grandfather if she could not please the grandson. Yet to Marie Antoinette, lonely and rather homesick, the daily company of the aunts at Versailles was highly comforting; they were surrogate mothers, who unlike her own mother had nothing to do but fulfil the royal routine. If she was easily led by them, getting involved in mischiefs not her own, as Mercy told the King, it was hardly surprising. That letter quoted earlier, describing her daily life, makes it clear how much Marie Antoinette saw of the aunts: four extremely long visits daily, in the morning, the afternoon, in the early evening and again later. She spent more time in their apartments than her own.

The year 1770 had begun so promisingly for Madame Antoine, Archduchess of Austria, heralded by the arrival of the Dauphin's ring, jewelled harbinger of a glorious and contented future. It ended sadly for the Dauphine of France with the exile of the Duc de Choiseul from court. It was he who had brought about 'her happiness ... and that of France' and she felt a fierce loyalty to him as to all those she believed to be her early supporters. As it was, Choiseul was the victim of various elements in the political scene, including intrigues centred round the Du Barry who had conceived one of her rare personal dislikes for him.

Rancour was not generally part of her nature; the Du Barry saw herself as sent into the world to seduce not to snub. Although the Dauphine refused to address her, the Du Barry had asked to install a portrait of the Dauphine in her apartments.[43] But Choiseul had had the audacity to launch an 'open war' against the favourite and – even more mortifying perhaps – had indulged in amusing sallies at her expense along with his intimates and relations. Perhaps the great minister, who had been in power since 1758, might have ridden out the enmity of the Du Barry and her political allies, but his own influence with the King had been gradually eroding. For all Choiseul's energetic reforms of the army and navy, so necessary following the Seven Years' War, he had not been able to solve the problem of the country's finances, which had been severely strained by that conflict. Furthermore Louis XV, looking for a way to curtail the activities of the Parlement de Paris, found his Foreign Minister siding with it over such measures as the suppression of the Jesuits; this was a ban that enraged the King's devout daughters, the Mesdames.

The Duchesse de Choiseul reacted to the unexpected appearance of her husband at dinner – she had believed him to be at court – with some style. 'My dear friend,' she said, 'you have the air of a man who has been exiled, but pray sit down, our food will not taste any the worse for that.'[44] Such sang-froid could not conceal the fact that with the disappearance of its architect, the Franco-Austrian alliance and its upholders had been dealt a major blow. Maria Teresa was aghast at the loss of Choiseul, as she told Mercy. Nothing seemed to be going right in France, according to her carefully laid plans, neither politics nor sex.

Only the Dauphin reacted to the fall of the Foreign Minister with apathy, greeting it with neither pleasure nor pain. But then, in contrast to his wife's emotional nature, apathy was his usual reaction to everything.

CHAPTER SEVEN

Strange Behaviour

 ~◦~

'If a young girl as charming as the Dauphine cannot
fire up the Dauphin ... it would be better to do nothing
and wait for time to remedy such strange behaviour.'
Maria Teresa's doctor, Van Swieten, quoted 6 June 1771

D uring the Carnival celebrations of 1771, which traditionally preceded the dour Catholic Lent, the Comtesse
de Noailles gave a weekly series of dances in her
apartments. As Mistress of the Household, that was not only
her right but her duty; an argument for the steep emoluments
attached to the position was the necessity for such expensive
entertainments. One of these dances was the setting for the
beginning of a sentimental relationship between the fifteen-year-
old Marie Antoinette and the twenty-one-year-old Princesse de
Lamballe.[1]

Although it was in one sense ironic that Madame Etiquette –
the Dauphine's mischievous nickname for the Comtesse de
Noailles – should have been the catalyst for a relationship that
diminished her own influence, in another sense this was an
inevitable development. Every Dauphine – every princess at
Versailles, every young woman in this society – needed her
friends not only for intimacy but for support. In particular Marie
Antoinette sought to reproduce the close ties she had enjoyed
with her sister Maria Carolina (in whose welfare in faraway
Naples she continued to take the keenest interest).

This kind of friendship, common among young women of
the time, was heavily influenced in its expression by the style of

Rousseau's epistolary novel *La Nouvelle Héloïse*.* It was a thing of hearts and flowers, not bodily embraces, and in 1771 about as far as could be imagined from the outright lesbian practices of which both Marie Antoinette and the Princesse de Lamballe were later accused. When Marie Antoinette addressed the Princesse de Lamballe (and many others, including her sister-in-law Madame Elisabeth) as 'my dear heart' and addressed her as 'angel' or signed herself with 'a heart entirely yours', she was in the tradition of Rousseau's heroine Julie d'Étange writing to her confidante and cousin Claire: palpitatingly sensitive rather than passionately sensual.

As it happened, the Princesse de Lamballe was for many reasons a suitable candidate for such a friendship at this juncture. Her status as the widow of the Duc de Penthièvre's heir, a (legitimated) descendant of Louis XIV, meant, for example, that Louis Auguste, before his marriage, paid his single recorded visit to a private house to console the Princesse on the death of her husband.[3] According to the usage of Versailles, the Princesse was entitled to be addressed by both Dauphin and Dauphine as 'Cousine'.

But there was trouble when the egregious Comtesse de Brionne, with her Lorrainer connections, mooted a marriage between her son the Prince de Lambesc and the Princesse de Lamballe. Count Mercy was quick to point out the damage that would be done if the Dauphine threw her influence behind this plan. Not only would Marie Antoinette have to compensate the Princesse de Lamballe for her loss of rank in some appropriate material manner, but she would also be landed yet again with the uncomfortable burden of the Comtesse's pretensions. The ambassador suggested handing over the whole matter of the Prince de Lambesc's marriage to the King – as a result of which the Comtesse abandoned the project and the Princesse remained unmarried.

---

* It is impossible to exaggerate the influence of *La Nouvelle Héloïse*, a story of (heterosexual) love and renunciation. First published in French in 1761, it went through seventy-two editions before 1800, as well as ten in England and others in America.[2]

In general, however, Mercy approved of the Princesse de Lamballe, as an excellent corrective to the undue pressures of Mesdames Tantes. He believed that they had recently created trouble for the Dauphine by influencing her against the Prince de Condé, although Condé himself had always supported Marie Antoinette. Mercy told the Dauphine that she must simply avoid expressing political opinions, despite her protests that it was impossible to be the only one who did not speak in the family circle. As she put it, she was never 'the first'.[4]

These tensions stemmed from a royal edict confirming the dissolution of one Parlement and the formation of another, promulgated at a *lit de justice*, so called because historically the King had dispensed this justice from the royal bedchamber and still sat on cushions for the occasion. The finality of such an edict, the imposition of the King's will against the general wishes, was, however, beginning to be questioned. On this occasion the Princes of the Blood protested against a curtailment of some of their privileges and wrote what Marie Antoinette described to her mother as 'a very impertinent letter' to the King on the subject.[5] The result was that the Princes, and those Ducs who had supported them, were exiled from the court. Even if the influence of the aunts was generally harmful, on this particular issue they simply encouraged the Dauphine to follow the King's own line, which was, after all, what everyone wanted her to do in theory.

Fortunately Marie Antoinette's new friend the Princesse de Lamballe was not an intriguer. This was what Marie Antoinette indicated to the Empress when she wrote proudly that her new friend 'didn't have the Italian character'.[6] She was, on the contrary, thanks to her mother's blood, that desirable commodity, a good German. Furthermore she was famously pure and unsullied (in revulsion perhaps from her early experiences of being married to a debauchee). Everyone, rich and poor, admired her father-in-law, the Duc de Penthièvre, for his decency and charity; he in turn admired the dignified young widow of his son.

This respectability of the Princesse de Lamballe, even at Versailles, was maintained. Several years later when other royal friendships had developed, the Abbé de Vermond reproached the Dauphine with the quality of her women friends. Marie Antoinette ignored the generalization and concentrated on defending the Princesse alone as being 'pure'. Vermond responded by wondering grouchily how long that purity would survive, before pointing to the Princesse de Lamballe's stupidity.[7] Here he was on safer ground. The Princesse de Lamballe was not clever. She was, rather, the sort of young woman whose sensitivity was so excessive that she was said to have fainted in public at the sight of a bunch of violets; she was not particularly amusing either. Neither the Princesse's lack of intelligence nor her lack of sparkle was at this stage a disadvantage where Marie Antoinette was concerned. On the one hand the Dauphine disliked clever women; on the other hand she had not yet discovered the entertaining possibilities of life at Versailles. It was more important that the Princesse's big sad eyes, her gentle melancholy regard, spoke of devotion not criticism. There was also something that the two women had in common: although their experiences of the male sex were the exact opposite, neither of them had found much happiness there.

In the spring of 1771, Marie Antoinette certainly had need of a sympathetic friend. Nearly a year after their marriage, the Dauphin was apparently no closer to 'making her his wife'. In the meantime arrangements for a second marriage – that of the Comte de Provence to Josephine of Savoy – were far advanced. This was seen by the apprehensive Maria Teresa as a threat on two fronts. First of all, she feared that a pliant new grand-daughter-in-law would win the French King's affections and advance the influence of Savoy – a traditional rival due to its geographical position in northern Italy – over that of Austria. Second, and still more menacing to Marie Antoinette's fortunes, was the prospect – at last – of an heir to the throne in the next generation. But this heir would be begotten by 'Monsieur' and borne by 'Madame' – that is, by Provence and his Savoyard wife. (These plain appellations, vastly more honorific than more grandiose titles, were generally given to the second son and his wife.)

The stream of nagging letters from Vienna continued. Some

of the criticism was on a petty domestic level. For example, the Empress heard that her daughter was not wearing her corsets, which would certainly ruin her figure. When Marie Antoinette contended that such corsets were not worn in France, her mother offered to send her Viennese corsets. Increasingly, however, the Empress picked on her daughter's inadequate character, her preference for pleasure over duty, her lack of application and so forth and so on, to the extent that even Count Mercy respectfully suggested that the leaven of a little sweetness might get better results.[8]

When Maria Teresa denounced her daughter for laughing with her younger ladies and making fun of others at the court, she was certainly drawing attention to unwise behaviour. Sins that would be venial in any other girl were far more consequential in the future Queen of France. It was a question of how the passage of the Dauphine from adolescence into maturity was to be handled. With the Comtesse de Noailles over-strict and stuffy, with the critical Empress apparently all-knowing of the slightest trifle at the French court, there seemed to be no one to bolster Marie Antoinette's confidence on the one hand, and supervise her intelligently on the other.

Certainly the letter that the Empress wrote to the Dauphine on 8 May 1771 was more like a collection of skilfully directed blows with a dagger than a helpful maternal missive. Maria Teresa began by bemoaning the fact that her daughter's looks were deteriorating; a recent miniature no longer showed that look of youth Marie Antoinette had had when she left Austria. She added the surely unnecessary reminder that a change in the Dauphine's condition (that is, pregnancy) was not the cause.* On that subject, there followed the usual admonition – 'I can't repeat it to you often enough' – about employing patience and charm, never ill humour, to remedy the unfortunate situation, for it was the Empress's strongly held view that everything in

* It was an additional torment for Marie Antoinette that she had from the beginning an irregular menstrual cycle. In those reports on the arrival of the Générale (period) demanded by her mother of all her daughters, Marie Antoinette was obliged to mention a gap of four months before adding that there was no reason for it.[9]

this respect depended on the wife. After that Marie Antoinette was criticized on 'an essential point'. She should for reasons of public prestige be inducing Louis XV to pay her daily social visits in her apartments, just as he had paid to the late Dauphine, Maria Josepha.[10]

It was, however, on the subject of Count Mercy and the reception of the 'Germans' generally that Maria Teresa waxed most eloquent. Why did Marie Antoinette receive her own ambassador so rarely, a man of such qualities, so much esteemed at court? Why did she not show more favour towards what the Empress called 'your nation'? 'Believe me,' wrote the Empress, 'the French will respect you much more and hold you in much greater account if they find in you the seriousness and straightforwardness of the Germans. Don't be ashamed of being German even to the point of awkwardness.' Thus Marie Antoinette was to make a point of singling out distinguished Germans with her attentions, and to extend her patronage towards the lesser ones who did not have the right to appear at court. This was her royal destiny: to make herself loved. And how well she had done so far! After this apparent tribute, the Empress proceeded to wield the dagger again. Marie Antoinette must be quite clear about what had helped her to do this. Otherwise disaster would follow.

'It's not your beauty, which frankly is not very great,' wrote the mother to the daughter. 'Nor your talents nor your brilliance (you know perfectly well that you have neither).' It was solely her good nature and her pretty ways, so well deployed, that had enabled Marie Antoinette to please. Without these, she was nothing. For a fifteen-year-old girl accused of losing her youthful freshness, who was conspicuously failing to please the most important man in her life, and was yet expected to cement the 'German' fortunes at court, it was not an encouraging report.

In one potentially disastrous area of the Dauphine's life, at least, there was a reprieve. It quickly became clear that no offspring was to be expected from the Provence marriage – not now, and probably not ever. Josephine, who at eighteen was over three years older than her husband, was small, plain, with a sallow skin and with what Louis XV unkindly described in a letter to his grandson in Parma as 'a villainous nose'. She was certainly no match for the Dauphine, being timid, gauche and ill educated in all those graces considered so important at Versailles. Nor was she a quick learner. A subsequent ambassador to France from Savoy had to ask Josephine's father, Victor Amadeus III, to drop a hint about the necessity for a careful *toilette*, in particular with regard to her teeth and hair: 'It is embarrassing for me to discuss such things,' admitted the ambassador, 'but these mere details to us are vital matters in this country.'[11]

Nevertheless the new Comtesse de Provence was anxious to do the right thing. When her Mistress of the Household, the Duchesse de Valentinois, advanced on her with the mandatory pot of rouge, Josephine flinched. Coming from the very different court of Savoy, she found rouge repugnant. But on learning that this was the custom of France and she must adhere to it in order to please her husband, Josephine gamely requested a great deal of rouge 'so as to please him the more'.[12]

It would take more than a couple of bright red circles on the cheeks to excite the Comte de Provence. Josephine duly received 300,000 livres' worth of jewels from Louis XV (scaled down to three-quarters of the Dauphine's casket) and from Provence his portrait as 'a pledge of the sentiments that are engraved in my heart for you'.[13] But he showed no sign of bestowing upon his wife anything more than that. At fifteen he was already so fat as to be almost obese. Due to a deformity of the hips he waddled rather than walked, could not ride and took no other exercise. He also ate a great deal. It was probably Provence's corpulence that made him impotent although there may have been other physical causes as well.

But Provence was quick-witted. If he had a problem all his life with the fact that 'he was not born master', as Marie Antoinette once noted, he was certainly far more adept than Louis Auguste at handling the question of marital consummation. Instead of obstinacy and silence, he met the situation with lewd boasts of four-times-nightly sex. The cognoscenti – a great many people in the inquisitive society that was Versailles – knew perfectly well that nothing had taken place. Marie Antoinette, making it her business through her household to be well informed on this subject, soon assured her mother that Provence's boasts were baseless: 'It would need a miracle.' An interested gossip like Bachaumont quickly dismissed such tales. A couple of years later the incoming Savoyard ambassador reported that there had never been any question of a physical union. Josephine herself confirmed this in February 1772; she was quite sure she was not pregnant 'and it's not my fault'.[14]

None of this stopped the wily Provence from dropping hints about his wife's condition whenever he could most conveniently bait his brother and his Austrian wife with their own failure. It remained a fact that the birth of a son to the Comte and Comtesse de Provence would considerably undermine the position of the senior couple, the Dauphin and Dauphine – especially that of the Dauphine. It was undeniable that a marriage that was not consummated could be safely annulled by the laws of the Catholic Church – and the failure-bride sent packing. The Dauphin's boyhood Governor, the Duc de Vauguyon, was said to be angling for this and Count Mercy was well aware of the possibility. Something of Marie Antoinette's suffering on the subject can be gauged from a sad little aside in a letter to her mother. When the Duchesse de Chartres gave birth to a dead child, Marie Antoinette wrote that for her part, she would be happy to give birth to any child – even a dead one.[15]

Despite the innate family rivalry of the two Princesses, one Austrian, the other Savoyard, Marie Antoinette seemed to be handling her relationship with Josephine well. 'My sister', as the Dauphine called her, was on the surface made into a friend. It was the ambassadors of their respective countries who maintained an open rivalry. The presence of four young married people at Versailles, whose ages ranged between eighteen and fifteen, led to the formation of an informal society that was perfectly in accord with the rules of etiquette. The unvarying precedence of 'Monsieur' and 'Madame', in other words the Comte and Comtesse de Provence, was immediately after that of Dauphin and Dauphine. Musical parties (Marie Antoinette had resumed her music and singing lessons), games of billiards (a sport to which the French royal family was devoted), games of cards (equally popular), hunting parties: all these pleasures led to an existence that was certainly not unpleasant, if hollow in one respect.

On that subject, however, Maria Teresa's doctor, the great Van Swieten, advised patience in the following practical terms: 'If a young girl as charming as the Dauphine cannot fire up the Dauphin ... it would be better to do nothing and wait for time to remedy such strange behaviour.'[16] In the meantime it certainly added to Marie Antoinette's contentment that by the autumn the French King showed no sign of preferring the Comtesse de Provence's company to her own, as had been feared.

Unfortunately he was not paying those daily visits to the Dauphine either. The problem of the Du Barry and her acknowledgement would not go away, more especially because Choiseul's replacement, the Duc d'Aiguillon, was part of the Du Barry's set. Politics as well as prudence thus dictated a realistic approach to the situation at the French court on the part of 'the Archduchess', as Mercy significantly described Marie Antoinette in his letters to Maria Teresa.

It was the aunts, whose influence over their niece by marriage was now well established, who bedevilled the situation. Mercy in France and Maria Teresa in Austria urged on Marie Antoinette the absolute necessity of seeking the King's favour. This merely involved a simple greeting to the Du Barry, who by the rules of Versailles was entitled to be in the presence of the Dauphine. As Maria Teresa pointed out, anything else begged the question of exactly *why* the Dauphine would not receive a lady who was part of the royal circle, making her by implication most inappropriately and publicly critical of the King's behaviour.[17] But the aunts managed to scupper the first occasion when this brief greeting had been set up to take place, by sending for their beloved niece to join them at the last minute. This gave Marie Antoinette the excuse she needed to duck out of the encounter.

On 31 October 1771 – to mark Marie Antoinette's sixteenth birthday two days later – the Empress sent another of her lethal missives. This one related, with a joy verging on the sadistic, how well Marie Antoinette's brothers and sisters were doing in their marriages – and their marriage beds. Maria Carolina was at last pregnant after three years of marriage, and her first child would be born the following June. The Archduke Ferdinand, who had married the heiress of Modena, Beatrice d'Este, was 'enchanted' with her and had 'made her his wife' at once. 'All this news,' wrote the Empress, 'which should fill me with contentment, is diminished by reflections on your dangerous situation, all the worse because you either don't understand the danger, or don't wish to. You simply will not employ the necessary means to get yourself out of it.' The French King – 'such a good father, such a good prince' – was the clue to it all. Seeking out the King's company had to be her daily occupation, not just when she wanted something.[18] Whatever the moral implication, the worldly implication was clear: she must placate the monarch if she was to survive at Versailles.

It was under these circumstances that on New Year's Day 1772 at Versailles, the Dauphine surrendered at last. There was a big crowd of courtiers paying their respects. In their midst Marie Antoinette made a remark of superb royal banality in the general direction of the Du Barry: 'There are a lot of people here today at Versailles.' After that she allowed herself to explode to Louis Auguste, vowing that she would never address another word to the dreadful creature. Writing to her mother Marie Antoinette took a less explosive line but she made it clear that she had sacrificed 'all her prejudices and repugnances' on being assured that there was nothing dishonourable about doing so. After all, it would be the greatest unhappiness of her life if she were to be the cause of trouble between the two families, Habsburgs and Bourbons. However, 'my heart will always be with my own,' she added to the Empress. Marie Antoinette meant of course the Habsburg family. 'My duties here are sometimes hard to fulfil.'[19]

For all these complaints, Marie Antoinette's behaviour towards the Du Barry became more circumspect. In the summer at Compiègne, where the atmosphere was not so ostentatiously formal, Count Mercy, who as a diplomat saw it as his business to pay visits to the favourite, brokered another public acknow-ledgement. First of all the Dauphine made conversation with the Duchesse d'Aiguillon and then, since the favourite had just arrived with the King, *turned her body* in the Du Barry's direction. She proceeded to chat on easily about the weather and the hunts without making it clear to whom her remarks were being specifically addressed. Louis XV, ignoring the ambiguity, was delighted, and that night at the royal supper, showered his granddaughter-in-law with attentions.[20] It marked the beginning of Marie Antoinette's realization that Mesdames Tantes had been wrong in the rigorous stance they had preached to her.

The Dauphine's Habsburg 'heart' – if that was what it was – became relevant in the summer of 1772, when she was sixteen and a half. Poland and its partial dismemberment was the issue. The reforms in that country by King Stanislaus Poniatowski (who followed the Saxon ruler, part of the late Dauphine's family, on the throne) had led, in effect, to civil war. This in turn was a cynical opportunity for the great powers – Russia, Austria and Prussia – to help themselves to large chunks of Poland, provided they could agree with each other to do so without going to war. The problem was France, traditionally a friend and ally of Poland. How would she react to the forcible removal of over one third of Polish territory? Would the Franco-Austrian alliance stand the strain? Prolonged negotiations between the three aggressors were finally concluded in the summer of 1772 by the Conventions of St Petersburg. As Frederick II observed, unpleasantly but accurately, of his old enemy Maria Teresa, now his collaborator in robbery: 'She wept and she wept but she took and she took.'[21]

The Empress's anxiety about Louis XV, expressed privately to Mercy in June, was a great deal more sincere: 'I know very well that the line we have just taken with regard to Poland will have created a sensation in France.' Nevertheless the French alliance was still the cornerstone of Austrian policy; nothing that had happened to Poland changed that, although Maria Teresa admitted that France might feel a certain grievance, if only because there had been no warning. Who would smooth over this family crisis? 'There is only my daughter, the Dauphine, to do so, assisted by your counsels and local knowledge,' she told Mercy in a long memorandum of 2 July. This way the Dauphine

could do a real service to 'her family and her homeland' (*patrie*).*
The Empress demanded nothing that could be held demeaning,
only due consideration and attention to her 'grandfather and
master'. Her last words were the most menacing: 'Perhaps the
alliance depends on it.'[22]

   As it happened, the alliance proved to be impregnable simply
because Louis XV had no intention of breaking it. He had little
means to rescue Poland in the face of a united and powerful
force on the other side. Choiseul's replacement, the Duc d'Aiguillon, was much disliked by Marie Antoinette for his loose life
and his connection to the Du Barry; he also had a malicious
tongue, which she suspected mocked her amusingly behind her
back. But whatever his dislike of the Austrian connection,
Aiguillon too was helpless. Mercy was able to reassure Maria
Teresa that since Aiguillon perceived the Austrian alliance was
'in the heart of his master', he would make no attempt to
dissolve it. The following year Louis XV stated categorically: 'I
have made that alliance and it will continue as long as the
Empress lives and the Emperor as well ... I do not want a
war.'[23]

   The interesting aspect of the Polish affair from the point of
view of Marie Antoinette is the real fear with which she greeted
her diplomatic instructions from her mother. (She was somewhat
in the position of a modern spy, left in a foreign country for
several years as a 'sleeper' and now ordered to spring into
action.) She ended a letter to the Empress of 17 July 1772, after
she had received these instructions from Mercy, simply enough:
'I shall certainly not forget what Mercy has said to me; this is
very important and I'm very anxious about it; but I shall be
only too happy to contribute to the union [of the two families]
and to prove to my dear mother the deference and loving
respect which I shall accord to her all her life ...' But the next
day, in one of his long private communications to the Empress,
Mercy revealed a more agonized reaction. 'Where will I be if
there is a rupture between our two families?' the Dauphine had

---

* *Patrie* was the word always used by Marie Antoinette to denote Austria in her
correspondence with her family.

asked desperately. 'I hope that God will preserve me from this misfortune, and guide me as to what to do. I have prayed fervently to Him.'[24]

The truth was that for better or worse Marie Antoinette showed none of the instincts of a political intriguer, that sheer zest for the art of manipulation shown by her sister Amalia, who was no longer on speaking terms with her mother due to her machinations and general bad behaviour. At least the Dauphine was developing physically; the childishness of appearance that Louis XV had marked on her arrival at Versailles was vanishing. In the autumn of 1772 Marie Antoinette boasted to Maria Teresa that she had grown a lot and put on some weight, through drinking milk, although unfortunately that started ill-founded rumours of pregnancy. When it came to her character at seventeen, that was developing too. Her reading habits were improving and in June she reported proudly that she had been reading some history with Vermond. This was obviously a ploy intended to appeal to Louis Auguste, noted since early youth as a lover of historical works. The following January, Marie Antoinette dutifully recorded her own impression of her husband's favourite book, Hume's *History of England*: 'It seems very interesting to me, although one must remember it was written by a Protestant.'[25]

With her experience of family life, Marie Antoinette began to act as peace-maker between the sparring royal brothers, Louis Auguste and Provence. On one occasion when the clumsy Louis Auguste broke a piece of porcelain belonging to Provence and the younger brother flew at him, Marie Antoinette actually interrupted the fight; the two of them were roughly the same age as her own brothers. But the natural instinct of Marie Antoinette was for giving affection, not for taking control, although she was guiltily aware that she was supposed to be in some way 'controlling' the Dauphin, as references in her letters show. In the absence of any real corroborative evidence for the Dauphine's growing ascendancy over her husband, we must assume that these little boasts were what her mother wanted to hear (and Mercy wanted to convey) rather than anything more serious.

Her love of other people's children, on whom she lavished 'her tenderest caresses' according to Madame Campan, maddened Mercy because he thought it distracted her from more serious things. If she spotted a child in the crowd, she might send to ask its name. One little English 'Miss' in the company of Dr Johnson turned out by a happy coincidence to be called 'Queeny'. Touchingly, under the circumstances, the Dauphine even tried to choose her ladies for the sake of their children – Madame Thierry, for example, who had a four-year-old son. The offspring of her household were always welcome in her apartments where they might break the furniture and tear the clothes with impunity.[26] Her dogs were just as undisciplined, which irritated Mercy equally, although in this case Marie Antoinette was merely following the custom of Versailles.

For the great palace was a pets' paradise, if not a very clean paradise; foreigners commented on the dirt. Cats were everywhere. Louis XV adored them, having one particular spoilt Persian white which he refused to allow his courtiers to tease; perhaps significantly the Dauphin disliked cats. A celebrated race of grey angora cats were to be found on the lotto tables, patting the pieces with their furry paws. For the Du Barry it was a parakeet and white monkeys as well as a dog that received a propitiatory diamond necklace from the visiting Prince of Sweden. The Princesse de Chimay also favoured monkeys, despite the celebrated occasion when her monkey ran wild in her boudoir, plastering himself with rouge and powder in imitation of his mistress before bounding into the supper room and terrifying all those present.[27]

The Dauphin's sister Elisabeth favoured greyhounds. Mesdames Tantes loved spaniels. Comte d'Hezecques, from his days as a page at Versailles, remembered a chaotic scene when the royal family emerged into the great gallery, each with their attendant familiar. Suddenly something frightened the animals and they all began to panic, barking and fleeing through the vast, dimly lit salons 'like shadows'. The Princesses added their cries to the tumult as they shouted, then yelled after the departing dogs, and finally went in pursuit.[28]

Such pleasures could certainly palliate the central unhappiness of Marie Antoinette's existence. When the Comtesse de Noailles reported in the summer of 1772 that the Dauphine had 'moments of sadness' over the 'incomprehensible behaviour' of her husband towards her, she added that they did not last long. Yet caresses for dogs and other people's children, or even the round of formal and informal entertainments that constituted court life, could not forever mask the inexorable question: what on earth was going on with the Dauphin and Dauphine? Or rather, since nothing was going on, why was that? And what was the cure? In the autumn of 1772 it was suggested that the problem might lie in a physical impediment, a condition known as phimosis.* The radical cure for phimosis was circumcision. The trouble with such an intimate operation, performed on an adult in an age before anaesthetics or effective painkillers, was that it might put off a nervous patient from the sexual act altogether, as one royal doctor sensibly pointed out later: 'It was just as bad to have it done as not.'[29] Proper instruction might be the answer.

In the spring of 1773, when the young couple had been married nearly three years, the King ordered Doctor Jean-Marie Lassonne to examine the Dauphin and, after that, to talk very frankly to both husband and wife. Lassonne had been physician to the late Queen and was now in Marie Antoinette's household. Lassonne found the Dauphin 'well made' and, as Marie Antoinette told her mother on 15 March, gave the opinion that 'clumsiness and ignorance' were what were preventing this vital event from taking place. Marie Antoinette also reported to Maria Teresa that the Dauphin handled the occasion well, speaking without embarrassment and with a lot of common sense. Dr Lassonne expressed himself as 'very satisfied and full of hope'.[30]

And hope suddenly became the order of the day. Marie Antoinette declared herself happily confident that she would soon be at last the Dauphin's real wife. The 'strange' and 'incomprehensible' behaviour would soon be at an end. She could view the imminent announcement of the marriage of

* Tightness of the foreskin, due to insufficient elasticity, which does not, however, make erection, or even ejaculation, impossible, although it might inhibit both.

Artois to another Savoyard Princess, Josephine's younger sister Thérèse, with far more equanimity than she had greeted that of Provence two years earlier.

No one was happier at the prospect of the consummation than Count Mercy. He too was giving instructions – political in his case. Mercy told the Empress that Marie Antoinette was beginning to ask intelligent questions on subjects such as Poland and Sweden and would benefit from more instruction in the future. It was true that her apprehensions about the alliance and her own responsibility in maintaining it remained strong. Letting everyone down in this respect would be 'the greatest unhappiness' for her. She also boasted once again of her ascendancy over her husband. She could guarantee that if the Dauphin had 'more authority', relations between the two courts would be extremely warm.[31] (Time would show whether this was a fantasy, intended to impress her mother, or the truth.) Yet as Mercy admitted, all his plans for Marie Antoinette to influence the King as well as the Dauphin really needed a pregnancy to clinch them.

CHAPTER EIGHT

Love of a People

~⁀⁀

'How fortunate we are, given our rank, to have gained
the love of a whole people with such ease.'

Marie Antoinette on visiting Paris, 14 June 1773

O n 14 June 1773 Marie Antoinette was at last able to
report a triumph to her mother. This was the official
visit of the Dauphin and Dauphine to Paris – their
first – which had taken place six days previously. This expedition
had been strongly advocated by the Empress over a long period.
She envisaged the public display of her daughter's charms as
doing wonders for her prestige or what would now be called
her image. Making a graceful appearance before crowds was
exactly what the Dauphine was capable of doing.

Royal women in general, such as the late Queen, the late
Dauphine and Mesdames Tantes, usually led a life confined to
Versailles and the other palaces. This was Maria Teresa's point.
There must be no timidity. She wanted the Dauphine to shine
in comparison to the rest of the French royal family, with what
the Empress identified as their lack of geniality and their
unpolished manners.[1]

In the summer of 1772 there had been a suggestion that,
curious to see the fabled city, the Dauphine would ride through
the boulevards, with only one lady in attendance so as not to
arouse suspicions about her identity. It foundered, however, like
many other plans, on the question of etiquette. Madame Adélaïde

announced her intention of coming too, which meant that her lady-in-waiting would attend both, and this slighted the Dauphine's lady-in-waiting who had the right to attend her mistress when on horseback. But since this particular lady happened to be the daughter of the Comtesse de Noailles, of course she could not be slighted ... In short the Comtesse de Noailles made so many difficulties that the project had to be abandoned. Mercy was left to lecture Marie Antoinette in the abstract on the essential duty of a great princess: to draw the hearts of the people to her.

A year later, the lesson had been well learnt. Marie Antoinette had also discovered for herself the sheer delight of the people's acclaim. Her letter was ecstatic. When the Dauphin and Dauphine tried to promenade in the gardens of the Tuileries Palace, they were stuck for three-quarters of an hour, unable to move forwards or backwards due to the enthusiasm of the crowds. Furthermore, the royal couple had jointly given orders to their bodyguards that no force was to be used to ease their passage – which had the gratifying effect, unusual for such occasions, that no one was injured.

'I can't tell you, my dear mother,' she wrote, 'the transports of joy, of affection, that were shown to us despite all the burdens of these poor people,' by which she meant taxes. Before finally retiring, the royal couple, again unusually, acknowledged the crowd by waving to them, 'which gave great pleasure'. Marie Antoinette reflected: 'How fortunate we are, given our rank, to have gained the love of a whole people with such ease.' At seventeen, it was easy for Marie Antoinette to believe that it would be a lifelong love affair.

A week later Marie Antoinette and Louis Auguste made a state visit to the opera, which for the Dauphine at least, with her passion for music and singing, was sheer pleasure. There was such a full house that the balcony boxes on either side of the stage had to be restored for the court officials and the royal attendants. The programme of separate pieces (of the sort that perennially make up galas) included performances by the ballerina Anne Heinel, fresh from a London triumph, with the equally famous Gaëtan Vestris. Marie Antoinette showed her natural enthusiasm when it came to the applause. Theoretically, this was forbidden at court performances, so that the few claps in the pit were usually quickly stopped by the guards. But when Marie Antoinette asked the lady beside her to applaud, there was a general ovation.[2] The Dauphine could do nothing wrong.

Another welcome development of the Paris visit, reported by Marie Antoinette, was the increased social grace of the Dauphin who received the addresses of the crowd with aplomb. The stress that Marie Antoinette placed on her husband's new ease of manner contrasted, however, with the rather different emphasis in Mercy's secret report. The ambassador was concerned to praise the Dauphine's triumph and the enthusiastic exclamations of the crowd – 50,000 of them 'without exaggeration' – who cried out over and over again: 'How beautiful she is! How charming she is!' But he also indicated that the Dauphin had been generally regarded as a mere 'accessory' to the occasion, compared to the radiantly smiling young woman who was the centre of everybody's attention.

That was not all. Many of the acclamations that Mercy heard had by a strange coincidence linked Marie Antoinette to her mother. People had apparently cried out that in the Dauphine's charms and her air of benevolence they recognized 'the daughter of the august Maria Teresa'.* In the same way, Marie Antoinette was careful to lace her letters of rejoicing with the usual protestations of gratitude to the mother who had made her great position possible. 'I was the last of all [the daughters] and I have been treated as the eldest.'[3] The shadow of the dominant mother still crept across the new sunshine that warmed her happy daughter.

The Dauphin's departure from the awkward behaviour to which the French court was wearily accustomed also signalled a new kind of ease in his relationship with his wife. During the summer of 1773, the wise counsels of Dr Lassonne took their effect. Louis Auguste managed to achieve some kind of physical

---

* These particular acclamations, if they took place, would have been a tribute to the European reputation of the Empress since she had, of course, never visited France, let alone Paris.

union with Marie Antoinette. Naturally the momentous news was conveyed as soon as possible to Maria Teresa: 'I think I can confide to you, my dear Mama, and only to you,' wrote Marie Antoinette on 17 July, 'that my affairs have taken a very good turn since we arrived here [Versailles] and that I consider my marriage to be consummated; even if not to the degree that I am pregnant. This is the only reason why the Dauphin does not want it to be known. What happiness it would be if I gave birth to a child in the month of May!'[4] She went on to give details of her 'indisposition' (her period) and to assure the Empress that she did not go riding during that time.

Two days after this letter was written, the Dauphin agreed that the two of them should break the exciting news to the King. Louis XV kissed Marie Antoinette with great tenderness and called her 'his daughter'. It was then thought that the time was ripe to spread 'our secret'. As Marie Antoinette told her mother: 'Everybody is very pleased with it.' Although the annoying period or 'Générale' had arrived, 'as usual a few days in advance', she still did not give up hope for a Maytime birth. The Empress was naturally exultant. This did not stop her remonstrating with the Dauphine yet again on the subject of her riding now that she was 'a woman'; it was a pastime that notoriously caused miscarriages, and which she would not permit if she was the French King. Nevertheless: 'The joy is incredibly great everywhere,' wrote the Empress. 'What delight!'[5]

Time would, however, reveal the precise nature of the act that had taken place and its possible limitations. Marie Antoinette's faith in her future pregnancy was not, for example, shared by the Spanish ambassador, Count d'Aranda. The Count made it his business to be extremely well informed on this tricky subject, probably through contacts among the royal doctors, supplemented by gossip from the royal valets. It was not a prurient interest but a worldly one; the Spanish Bourbons, despite having resigned their rights to the French throne some half a century earlier, were not necessarily content to see the lesser Orléans branch succeed to the French throne if the main line failed to produce male heirs. In 1773, this was a possible development. Supposing Artois' marriage, projected for

November, ran the same unfortunate course as those of his elder brothers, then Louis Philippe, grandson of the Duc d'Orléans, born on 6 October of this year, was the closest heir in the next generation.

Aranda's reports were detailed. In August he noted that both Louis Auguste and Provence had a certain impediment, which prevented them being husbands. On 23 November he reported with regard to the Dauphin there was certain physical evidence ('stains') that emissions were taking place outside the proper place because of the pain of introducing the member. In other quarters, expectations of pregnancy began to fade. 'Three grandchildren this year and a fourth expected,' but nothing from the Dauphine, moaned the Empress in November. Count Mercy had to admit to her that 'this happy event' was not quite as imminent as might be wished. By January of the following year, Maria Teresa was back on her familiar line of complaint; the coldness of the Dauphin, a young husband of twenty (he was actually nineteen and a half), towards a pretty woman was inconceivable to her. And she began to meditate some more serious action from Marie Antoinette's family; in short, to get her son the Emperor Joseph 'to stir up this indolent spouse'.[6]

Nevertheless, from the point of view of Marie-Antoinette herself, something had been achieved in the shape of an increased intimacy with her husband, which boded well for the future. Even as he admitted that the situation was not going to be remedied overnight, Mercy reported a significant dialogue confided to him by the Dauphine. Marie Antoinette told Louis Auguste that she would be humiliated both before the court and the public if the new Comtesse d'Artois became pregnant before she did. At this, Louis Auguste enquired rather touchingly: 'But do you love me?' Marie Antoinette replied that he could hardly doubt it. She loved him sincerely and respected him still more. Tender caresses followed, with the Dauphin promising, on return to Versailles, to 'resume his regime', at which point he hoped everything would go well.[7]

That was for the future. As for the present, in November 1773 the young royal circle at court was increased by the addition of Thérèse Comtesse d'Artois. However, this new princess provided – with one exception – no threat to the position of the Dauphine. Mercy, who never erred on the side of generosity where Savoyards were concerned, described her as being silent and interested in absolutely nothing. Furthermore her posture was hopeless, her bearing without grace and she was a clumsy dancer. Certainly Thérèse, seventeen at the time of her marriage to the sixteen-year-old Artois, was no beauty. She was extremely small and burdened, like her sister Josephine, with an exceptionally long nose; a cruel English observer would later describe her as looking like 'a starved witch'. At least the French King was pleased to note that Thérèse had a good complexion, and, his favourite area of contemplation, a good bosom.[8]

The exception – which did constitute a threat to the Dauphine – was Thérèse's ability to 'please her husband', in the words of Louis XV. Here was a royal bridegroom who did not fall at the fence but performed his duties manfully from the wedding night onwards. Quite apart from marital satisfaction, there was no doubt that in terms of looks and beguiling manners, the Comtesse d'Artois had got the best of the bargain where the three princely husbands were concerned. Tall and slim in youth, with the bright black eyes of his grandfather, Artois had the precious gift, so lacking in his two elder brothers, of high spirits; he was affable with a 'free and open air' that endeared him to the people. Court ladies would think back with misty eyes to his charms: 'The graces, goodness and spirit of Henri IV' was one – perhaps hyperbolic – description. He was also extravagant and fond of display, although in business matters he would show some acumen. Of course it was hardly to be expected that a vigorous royal prince would confine his attentions to his wife. Nor were these extramarital attentions themselves unwelcome: 'Few beauties were cruel to him, if one believes the legend,' wrote the Comte d'Hezecques.[9] Yet for all Artois' mistresses, it was Artois' wife who had the possibility of a pregnancy just as Marie Antoinette had feared in her exchange on the subject with the Dauphin shortly before the wedding.

For the time being, however, it did not happen. Marie Antoinette began to alleviate the desperate homesickness of her early years in France, and the continued frustration of her marriage, with a lifestyle that was to say the least of it agreeable. She had been accustomed to dream of Vienna and her friends there in her first year abroad, reading about Vienna in the newspapers to catch up on their news. Her beloved former governess Countess Brandeis also kept her in touch with chatty weekly letters on the doings of her mother, brothers and sisters. When Marie Antoinette wanted to send presents home to her old friends, she was reproved for the unnecessary gesture. Nevertheless she insisted for once on having her own way; these gifts were acts of charity. It is obvious from later references in her letters to two women in her Austrian household and to their personal troubles, in which she advocated resignation as being the greatest grace God could grant, that she had kept in touch with them.[10]

Thoughts of Schönbrunn or Laxenburg permeated Marie Antoinette's letters to Maria Teresa. How fine the waterfall at Schönbrunn must be! 'If only I could transport myself there ...' She particularly liked her mother telling her details of summer fêtes at Laxenburg so that she could imagine herself being present. The arrival of two miniatures of her 'little' brothers, Ferdinand and Max, set in a ring, aroused sentimental recollections; the Dauphine would be able to keep them with her 'always'. In a similar vein, Marie Antoinette showed the great Austrian general, Count Lacy, who was visiting France for his health, porcelain vases decorated with views of the Austrian palaces. And when Countess Brandeis' stream of letters unaccountably dried up in April 1773, Marie Antoinette was distraught. She burst into tears on learning from Mercy that the Countess had been stopped by order of the Empress and pleaded with the ambassador to get the edict reversed, on the grounds that she depended on Brandeis more than anyone else to give her news of her mother. Mercy agreed to assist, on condition that Brandeis wrote less often and more circumspectly. Helping Brandeis and her relations – such as a young cousin destined for the Church – was something that Marie Antoinette continued to do, whatever the imperial disapproval.[11]

Nevertheless the pleasures of France – above all, the pleasures of Paris where she seemed to receive the love of a whole people – began to weigh in the balance against memories of her home. As the Abbé de Vermond pointed out contentedly, the Dauphine's spoken French, once bedevilled by German phrases and constructions, had improved immeasurably with her actual sojourn in the country. She now used the language 'with ease and vivacity'. In June 1770 Marie Antoinette had greeted the sight of her mother's letter with the involuntary exclamation of a polyglot childhood: 'Thank God!' (*Gott sei dank*). A few years later, Maria Teresa found it necessary to throw into her letters 'a little German so you do not forget it'. Despite this motherly precaution, less than five years after her arrival in France, Marie Antoinette had achieved that ambition to which she had referred at Strasbourg on her wedding journey. Even Mercy had to admit to the Empress that 'the Archduchess', although she had not forgotten the German language, was unable to speak it properly, still less read it or write it.[12] In short, outwardly, in her speech at least, Marie Antoinette was well on her way to becoming an ideal and idealized French princess.

The opera and the theatre began to necessitate frequent visits. After all, at the age of eighteen, she was young and she was pretty. She had endured three and a half years of an unsatisfactory marriage, one that she could fairly claim she had tried hard to implement – for even her mother now blamed the Dauphin as not being a man like others. But she could no longer make the mourning of her condition her main preoccupation. Those 'moments of sadness' mentioned by the Comtesse de Noailles in the summer of 1772 had unfortunately not been banished by the renewed marital offensive – as one might term it – of 1773, despite the high hopes of all concerned, including, perhaps, those of the Dauphin. In between these sad moments, however, there were a great many distractions to be enjoyed.

It was not yet a question of gallantry or even courtly flirtation. With the awkward business of the marriage bed still unresolved, Marie Antoinette had every incentive to dislike the morals of Versailles, as incarnated by the ever-triumphant Du Barry. The combination of these two factors made her, as her brother the Emperor Joseph would point out a few years later, rather more 'prudish' in sexual matters than otherwise.[13] Admiration, the love of a people, rather than that of a particular man, given that the man was not her husband, was the intoxicant at this point.

On New Year's Day 1774 a young Swedish nobleman, Count Axel Fersen, made his first appearance at Versailles. Born on 4 September 1755, he was two months older than Marie Antoinette; he had been making the Grand Tour of Europe for several years, in the course of which he had met her brother, the Archduke Leopold, in Florence. Fersen spoke fluent French, in which language he wrote, as well as Italian, German and English. He was the son of an aristocratic mother and the Marshal of the Armies, 'the richest man in Sweden', supposedly with £5000 a year, to the £3000 of the next-richest man. Apart from this material advantage, Fersen was dazzlingly good-looking. He was tall and slim, with a narrow face, intense dark eyes beneath strongly marked eyebrows and a slightly melancholy air. These were romantic looks, which caused the Duc de Lévis to write that he looked like the hero of a novel – but not a French novel since Fersen was too serious. Another part of his attraction was what Georgiana Duchess of Devonshire called 'the most gentleman-like air'; the Count was always extremely concerned to present an elegant appearance.[14]

This particular New Year's Day was extremely cold and snowy; the Dauphine was looking forward to going sledging the next day. In such weather, according to his *Journal intime*, Fersen was preoccupied with the delivery of a new fur cloak ordered for the occasion from his tailor. When it failed to arrive, Fersen had to delay his planned early departure for Versailles until nearly nine o'clock in the morning. After that his diary recorded the delights of being a young and personable man abroad. A few days later he was received by the Comtesse de Brionne who was at her *toilette* being coiffed. Fersen watched with amusement as she scraped off spare powder with a special little silver knife, and then selected various types of rouge, so dark it looked almost black, from six separate pots. As for her daughter, he found Mademoiselle de Lorraine, she of the minuet, not as pretty as had been claimed, but vivacious and good company.[15]

On 30 January, Fersen went to the opera ball in Paris, arriving at one o'clock in the morning. There was a huge crowd, and those present included the Dauphin and the Comte de Provence as well as the Dauphine. According to custom, the royal party and others were masked in order to preserve their incognito. It was in this way that the eighteen-year-old Fersen fell into conversation with a young and unknown masked woman. As he recorded in his *Journal intime*: 'The Dauphine talked to me for a long time without me knowing who she was; at last when she was recognized, everybody pressed round her and she retired into a box at three o'clock: I left the ball.'[16] Thus the myth of the instant love affair, a *coup de foudre* (perhaps literally so) in the opera box, so beloved of novelists and film-makers, remains just that. What did happen was the conventional establishment of Fersen's social credentials. He was subsequently asked to a few *bals à la Dauphine* before departing for England.

It is significant that Fersen's *Journal intime*, which frequently passes comment on the attractiveness or otherwise of the various women he met, does not at this date mention the charms of the Dauphine. Fersen's real agenda in 1774 was marriage to the English heiress Catherine Lyell, hence his departure from France. Leaving aside her 'moments of sadness', Marie Antoinette herself was more interested in her patronage of her former teacher Gluck who had recently arrived from Vienna.

'The Chevalier Gluck', in his seventieth year, had chosen to make this second journey – he had already been to Paris in 1762 – at a moment when his Austrian career, successful for so long, was beginning to decline. The presence of his imperial pupil near to the throne of France, and in a position to help him, was a strong element in his decision. Nor was he disappointed. Soon after Gluck arrived, he was admitted to Marie Antoinette's formal *toilette*. The Dauphine's excitement was so great that she never stopped talking to the composer so long as he remained; in every way, including musically, the Chevalier was a link with home. Marie Antoinette was soon receiving Gluck 'at all times' and he could certainly be confident of her attendance if and when he presented his new opera *Iphigénie en Aulide* in Paris.[17]

Gluck certainly had need of the Dauphine's support since the new, simple, emotionally restrained yet fervent style of the opera that Gluck hoped to introduce met with little favour in advance from the French artistic world. He had anticipated this. 'There will be considerable opposition,' Gluck wrote on the eve of his departure for Paris, 'because it will run counter to national prejudices against which reason is no defence.' The composer's methods of rehearsal did not help to smooth things over. 'Blunt and quick-tempered', he did not care for the star-system. He told Sophie Arnould, who wanted great arias instead of perpetual recitative in her role of Iphigénie: 'To sing great arias, you have to know how to sing.' For where national prejudices were concerned, Gluck himself was no mean exponent; he was once overheard saying at a banquet that the French could not sing, and that the only point of being in France was to make money. He quarrelled with the dancer Gaëtan Vestris who wanted to end the opera with a ballet, as was customary. 'A Chaconne! A Chaconne!' cried Gluck. 'We must recreate the Greeks; and had the Greeks Chaconnes?' Vestris, learning to his surprise that they did not, retorted with some spirit: 'So much the worse for them.'[18]

As predicted by Gluck, patriotism was partly responsible for this hostile reaction. 'Their French vanity was sorely wounded to be taught all these things by a Teutonic master,' wrote Mannlich, who as court painter to the German Duke of Zweibrücken had his own axe to grind. The French had a natural partiality for their own earlier composers such as Lully, opera director to Louis XIV, and Rameau, ennobled by Louis XV; they also had a liking for the contemporary Italian composer Niccolò Piccinni since it was easier to bend to 'the yoke of an Italian'. The matter was also mixed up with court faction.[19]

Relations between the Du Barry and Marie Antoinette existed at this point in a state of barbed neutrality. From the Dauphine's point of view she had to put up with the situation, since 'the lady' could not be dislodged. This did not mean, for example, that she had to accept the Du Barry's gracious offer of some diamonds. The Dauphine replied that she had diamonds enough. Now the Du Barry was persuaded that espousing the cause of Piccinni would enable her to inflict a further defeat on the Dauphine and so she duly took it up. It was said that she carried her investigations in pursuit of the vendetta to the degree of attending a rehearsal of *Iphigénie* concealed behind a grille.

For a while, it appeared as if musical matters were going the way of the Du Barry. There were philistines who continued to detest the alien sounds of Gluck, although not everyone went as far as the English Lord Herbert, visiting Paris, who would describe his music as 'worse than ten thousand Cats and Dogs howling'. But as it happened, the conversion of Rousseau, who also attended a rehearsal a week after the Du Barry's secret visit, was a more significant portent. He congratulated the composer for achieving what he had hitherto thought impossible. In the words of Baron Grimm, Rousseau became convinced that the French language could be as apt as any other for 'strong, passionate and expressive music;[20] later he would leave *Orphée* with tears running down his face, quoting the celebrated lament of its hero: '*J'ai perdu mon Eurydice.*' Yet at the opening night, on 19 April 1774, victory was still in doubt.

The Dauphine attended, together with her husband, the Comte and Comtesse de Provence and various Princesses of the Blood including the Duchesse de Chartres, the Duchesse de Bourbon and the Princesse de Lamballe. The performance took place, as was customary, at 5.30 p.m. and lasted for five and a half hours. It did not take that long to establish the success of the piece. Spontaneous applause – or was it to please the Dauphine? – broke out after the overture. Agamemnon makes an opening plea to the implacable moon goddess Diana, who is demanding the propitiatory death of his daughter:

> Shining author of light
> Could you witness without turning pale
> The most dreadful of all sacrifices?

That was when Marie Antoinette led the applause herself. The clapping lasted for several minutes.[21] Hereafter, although the row between Gluckistes and Piccinnistes rumbled on, Gluck's own position as Marie Antoinette's protégé was assured.*

---

* It should, however, be noted that Marie Antoinette also had the works of Piccinni in her library, as well as French music.

A real-life drama was about to unfold, which would have the consequence – minor except to Gluck – of putting to an end the run of *Iphigénie en Aulide* in a Paris where, as a result of its success, 'they are thinking and dreaming of nothing but music'.[22] Its major consequence was a change in Marie Antoinette's life for ever and, no less radically, in the life of the Comtesse Du Barry too. *Iphigénie* was the story of a girl who was to be sacrificed by her father in the flower of her youth, whereas this real-life drama concerned an older man, with a younger mistress who was desperate to avoid being sacrificed.

The physical collapse of Louis XV at the end of April 1774 took the court by surprise and for a while frantic efforts were made to pretend that he was capable of recovery. The Baron de Besenval analysed the phenomenon: 'When illness comes to princes, flattery follows them to the grave and no one dares admit to them being ill.' Yet at sixty-four the French King had long outlived his father and grandfather. He had also outlived the extraordinary popularity that he enjoyed as a young man. As the Comte de Ségur wrote in his memoirs, he was 'in his youth, the object of an enthusiasm which was too little deserved; and in his old age, of severe reproaches which were equally exaggerated'. When a large statue of Louis XV was erected in the square to the west of the Tuileries gardens bearing his name, it showed the King magnificently aloft on his steed with the various Virtues grouped below. The subject was too good for the satirists to ignore:

> Grotesque monument! Infamous pedestal!
> Virtues on foot, vice on horseback.[23]

On 27 April 1774, the King, who was staying at the Grand Trianon, went out hunting, but felt sufficiently weak to stay in his carriage. Fever and nausea the next day caused his doctor La Martinière to recommend a return to Versailles. It was at this point that the drama began. When kings were dying – or conceivably dying – a delicate balance had to be maintained by those around them between their physical needs in this world and their spiritual needs in the next. That is to say, even a king could not expect absolution for his sins unless he sent away his current mistress and made a full act of repentance. If the fateful act of exclusion was not performed in time, he risked dying in a state of mortal sin, with the prospect of eternal damnation. Unfortunately from the King's point of view the decision could not be reversed; to repent totally of a particular relationship and then cheerfully renew it with the return of health was against the rules of spiritual etiquette, which, however lax and casuistical, still existed.

No one was more aware of this dilemma than Louis XV himself as his health deteriorated, since he had already experienced it once. Thirty years earlier the King had fallen seriously ill, and after a period of agitated conjecture, his then mistress the Duchesse de Châteauroux was sent away. The King duly received absolution. But he did not die. Regrettably, this meant that the Duchesse could not return; her reign was over, if that of the King was not. Other mistresses followed, principal among them the Pompadour, last among them the Du Barry.

It was not until 3 May that the King, looking at the pustules on his body, said aloud the dreaded words that no one else had dared to pronounce to him: 'It is smallpox.' Hitherto he had been buoyed up by believing that he had already suffered smallpox as a young man and was therefore immune. The diagnosis meant that his confession became a matter of urgency. It also meant that his spiritual advisors, including the Cardinal de la Roche-Aymon and the Archbishop of Paris, had a duty to see that it was made; otherwise criticism within the Church of their pusillanimous conduct would have been severe. As for his devout daughters, they were understandably determined that his spiritual welfare should now take precedence and that the favourite should be banished. The Duc d'Aiguillon, on the other hand, as the favourite's protégé, had a more complicated hand to play. In all of this, the one person nobody thought of consulting was the Dauphin. It seemed to occur to nobody that in a few days' time 'he might be master'.[24]

On the evening of 4 May the King finally ordered the Du Barry to leave for Ruel (Aiguillon's own château, not far away from Versailles). His words were dignified: 'Madame, I am sick, and I know what I have to do ... Rest assured that I shall always have the most tender feelings of friendship for you.' But perhaps he did not even then give up all hope because a few hours later he sent for his mistress again, only to be told that she had already departed. Two large tears rolled down the King's cheeks. It was then that he finally confronted the truth of his own mortality. Yet in spite of increasing sickness, which gradually swelled up his whole face and turned it dark 'like a Moor's head', the King did not die.

Was the drama of thirty years ago to be re-enacted? Fifteen carriages containing various courtiers were noted by Mesdames Tantes as going to call at Ruel just in case ... This insurance policy would be held against the courtiers concerned for many years to come. Meanwhile the King's daughters, defying the possibilities of infection, nursed him devotedly.

It was not until three o'clock on the afternoon of 10 May 1774 that the candle that stood in the window of Louis XV's room during his ordeal was extinguished. Suddenly the young couple, Louis Auguste and Marie Antoinette, waiting anxiously together in the Dauphine's apartments and still ignorant of what happened, heard 'a terrible noise, exactly like thunder'.[25] It was the sound of rushing feet. The crowd of courtiers hanging around the antechambers of the royal deathbed had instantly deserted them when the news of the King's decease was broken. All ran towards the rising sun, every man and woman intent on being the first to pay compliments to the new monarch and his wife.

The King and Queen of France, as they had thus become, fell on their knees and, in a scene that touched everyone who witnessed it, prayed together: 'Dear God, guide us and protect us. We are too young to reign.' After that Marie Antoinette leant on her husband's arm and touched her eyes with her handkerchief as she received the compliments of the courtiers. The first person to present herself, as of right, was the Mistress of the Household, the Comtesse de Noailles, just as she had proudly greeted the Dauphine on her arrival on French soil, four years earlier.

No one, however, lingered at Versailles. The danger of contagion was extreme for everyone but especially for Louis

Auguste who had never had smallpox, nor even been inoculated. By four o'clock the royal party was organized to depart for the palace of Choisy, five miles from Paris on the banks of the Seine, famous for its freshness and its flower gardens. One carriage took the aunts, following their heroic stints of nursing, and the younger Princesses, Clothilde and Elisabeth, with their Governess, the Comtesse de Marsan. The other carriage conveyed the new King and Queen, and his two brothers with their wives. A little while later some English visitors were able to ramble freely through Versailles due to that indifference to security already remarked. Having enjoyed the loud sound of birdsong in the gardens, they inspected the state apartments and found them dirty and neglected. The rooms of Mesdames Tantes, with their books, were more appealing. Here a majestic cat was wandering. The name on the silver collar was that of Madame Victoire, once daughter to the King, now aunt to Louis XVI – for the new King quickly indicated he was ridding himself of the name Auguste.[26]

As for the corpse of Louis XV, that was hastily sealed up in its coffin and driven at breakneck speed to the cathedral of Saint-Denis, so that the infection would not be spread. The spanking pace caused much merriment among the waiting crowds of his erstwhile subjects. Lady Mary Coke described how 'so far from showing the least concern, they whooped and hallooed as if they had been at a horse-race instead of a funeral procession.' The once familiar cry of Louis XV out hunting was heard again in mockery: 'Tally ho! Tally ho!'

Nor was the atmosphere in the new King's carriage on its way to Choisy any more sombre. For a while the solemnity of what had just happened meant that the six young people – the Comtesse de Provence at twenty-one was the oldest, Artois at seventeen the youngest – were plunged in sadness. But then that peculiar mixture of mirth and mourning that often attends deaths took a hold. A word inadvertently pronounced wrongly by the Comtesse d'Artois sent everyone in the carriage into fits of hysterical laughter.[27] The tears were dried. A new life was beginning.

PART THREE

Queen Consort

CHAPTER NINE

In Truth a Goddess

Vera incessu patuit dea: the goddess walks in constant truth.
Virgil, quoted by Horace Walpole about Marie Antoinette

Shortly after the death of Louis XV, a fashionable jeweller made a fortune by selling mourning snuffboxes which showed a portrait of the young Queen surrounded by black and bearing the inscription 'Consolation in Grief'. There was no doubt that the new reign was immensely popular at its outset. Not only the general indifference felt for the memory of the late King, but also the vivid expectations entertained for his successor contributed to this. The accession to the throne of 'a young virtuous prince' was expected to lead to 'a regeneration'.[1]

Few could remember the coming to the throne of Louis XV as a child of five, in 1715. This new accession, only the second in the eighteenth century, brought an adult to the role. In contrast to his grandfather, Louis XVI might provide that domestic propriety that was gradually beginning to be expected of royal families – as witness the English royal family across the Channel. For Louis XVI, in the popular perception, was a king with a gracious consort. The glamour of Marie Antoinette – to use a twentieth-century word which nevertheless seems appropriate – appeared to fit her admirably for the position of Queen of France. During the next few years Marie Antoinette's beauty, or the illusion of beauty that she gave, reached its prime, fulfilling that promise hinted at when she had been a child in Vienna. Her figure, especially her bosom, filled out. Her large wide-apart blue-grey eyes were notably expressive, their short-sightedness only giving a softness to her gaze; her hair, insofar as the natural colour could be discerned beneath the 'meal tub' of powder, had darkened from the childish ash to a light brown and was very thick. Her defects of course remained. Her nose was aquiline and, as such noses generally do, became more pronounced with age. Although increasingly elaborate hair-dressing concealed the notorious forehead, there was nothing to be done about the Habsburg lower lip, other than ignore it, as the artists tried to do, concentrating on the Queen's short and pretty upper lip.

In 1774 Jean-Baptiste Gautier-Dagoty painted Marie Antoinette in her bedroom in Versailles at her favourite pursuit of the harp, one beautiful hand well displayed. It was a charming composition. She wore a light grey gauzy dress under a wrapper with a hint of peach-coloured ribbon at her breast; a Reader (female) held a book, a singer (male) held out music, a waiting-woman extended a basket of plumes to put in her hair and in the corner the artist surveyed his palette. The next year Gautier-Dagoty painted a portrait that was widely copied in different versions, showing the Queen with a diamond *aigrette* pinned to her coiffure, pearl and blue ribbons threaded through her locks, lace on her pale blue dress and a cloak of blue velvet, richly ornamented with fleurs-de-lys and ermine, surrounding her. It was a cunning study of femininity and majesty combined. Both pictures showed Marie Antoinette full face. Jean-Baptiste Lemoyne's marble bust, which was sent to Vienna a few years earlier, is, given the rigidity of the medium, inevitably a good deal less flattering.

The radiance of the Queen's smile was celebrated; it contained 'an enchantment', which the future Madame Tussaud, an obser-ver at Versailles, would say was enough to win over 'the most brutal of her enemies'. But the Comte de Tilly, who first saw Marie Antoinette in 1775 when he was fourteen, and judged her with the critical eye of youth, thought it ridiculous to pretend that the heavy 'and at times drooping underlip' lent nobility and distinction to the Queen's appearance. Whatever the sweetness of her smile, it was a mouth that only came into its own when the Queen was angry.[2]

Yet even Tilly had to admit that her skin, her neck, her lovely shoulders, her arms and hands, were the most beautiful he had ever seen. The brilliance of her complexion caused the Prince de Ligne, who adored the Queen, to remark that her skin and her soul were equally white, and in a letter home Eliza Hancock picked out the Queen's 'very fine white complexion' for mention.[3] It was this that led Mrs Thrale, touring France with Dr Johnson in 1775, to rate Marie Antoinette 'the prettiest Woman at her own Court', even better by day than she was by night (when of course she was still obliged to deface herself with the obligatory rouge). The artist Madame Vigée Le Brun was honest enough to say that since the Queen's skin was 'so transparent that it allowed no shadow', paint could never quite capture it.[4]

It was, however, the graceful whole rather than the perfect individual elements that made such an impression on those who knew Marie Antoinette. Above all it was her bearing; in Baron de Besenval's words, 'Something delightful about the carriage of her head, a wonderful elegance in everything, made her able to dispute the advantage with others better endowed by nature and even beat them.'[5] Of course the physical charms of royalty are seldom cried down, the lustre of a crown enhancing even the most mediocre appearance in the eyes of the public. Yet in the case of Marie Antoinette there is such unanimity of report from so many sources, including foreign visitors as well as her intimates, that it is difficult to doubt the truth of the picture.

The result was a plethora of comparisons to goddesses and nymphs – much as had been made on her wedding journey, the difference being that Marie Antoinette was now a visible woman, rather than an unknown girl. Madame Campan compared her to the classical statues in the royal gardens, for example, the Atalanta at Marly. There was the story of the twelve-year-old boy, educated in the classics, who flung himself at the Queen's feet at court, seeing in her the embodiment of 'all my father's goddesses'. At least two writers chose to cite the famous passage in the *Aeneid* when Venus appeared incognito to her son Aeneas. But as Venus turned away 'by her gait she revealed that she was in truth a goddess' (*vera incessu patuit dea*). The novelist and essayist Sénac de Meilhan was reminded of Virgil by the Queen's manner of walking, so light of foot and yet so majestic. Horace Walpole would never forget seeing her following Louis XV into the Royal Chapel, how she 'shot through the room like an aerial Being, all brightness and grace and without seeming to touch earth'. Madame Vigée Le Brun, watching her outdoors with her ladies at Fontainebleau, thought that the dazzling Queen, her diamonds sparkling in the sunlight, might have been a goddess surrounded by nymphs.[6]*

It was on this occasion that Marie Antoinette turned to the painter and asked, half humorously, half regretfully: 'If I were not the Queen, they would say I looked insolent, is that not so?' Yet it was not a totally unconscious posture. An English child at Versailles, petted by Marie Antoinette, was 'astonished and terrified' to witness the deliberate change in her countenance when she had to receive some ambassadors; 'the striking air of dignity' she assumed where minutes earlier there had been a friendly, playful woman.[8] It might not always be so advantageous for Marie Antoinette to indicate by her very bearing that she was born an Austrian archduchess. However, there was no such shadow on the popular mood at the time of the accession of Louis XVI.

The new King and Queen did not stay long at Choisy because it was feared that the royal aunts had become infected with smallpox. The court then moved on to the château of La Muette, on the outskirts of Paris, and then progressed to Marly and Fontainebleau. Altogether the court stayed away from Versailles for six months, until that palace was deemed safe for habitation again. During this period there were two dismissals. Both were predictable and both were attributed to Marie Antoinette.

* In 1775, with more originality, Lady Clermont told Marie Antoinette that she was put in mind of the English beauty, eighteen months younger, Georgiana Duchess of Devonshire; the French Queen professed herself 'much flattered'.[7]

The Comtesse Du Barry could not expect her reign to outlast that of the former King. For the time being she was instructed to reside in a convent; later she was able to live at her château of Louveciennes where she received the curious, and on occasion the amorous. For the Comtesse still remained beautiful, still wanton, into her forties; the 'full-breasted' figure that had pleased the late King was still appealing, if ampler. All this meant that the late King's favourite had been treated without vindictive severity by the standards of the time. Gossips were furthermore wrong in ascribing her exile to the Queen. It was Louis XVI, under the influence of his pious aunts, who had every intention of banishing their old enemy. Marie Antoinette might have demanded the banishment of the Du Barry, but it was not necessary.

Sorting out a scandalous situation left behind from the previous reign was one thing. A far more serious question of rearrangement was needed where the question of the new King's advisors was concerned. In theory the monarch possessed absolute power but in practice he could hardly operate alone. The prevailing method of government was to use a series of committees and even more informal consultations, some of them tête-à-tête with a minister, known as the King's *travail* (labour). Louis XVI was an honourable and conscientious young man, but even those who wished him well referred to his indecisiveness, the need for a stronger nature to dominate him, a relic no doubt of the lack of confidence inculcated during his unloved childhood. Furthermore there is no evidence that he had been prepared by his grandfather to be 'the master'. Under the circumstances, the character and inclinations of his chief advisor and other ministers were likely to be of the greatest significance.

It was unthinkable, however, that the Duc d'Aiguillon should continue to fulfil the role he had played under Louis XV. His connection to the Du Barry, together with suspicions of his disloyalty in conduct and conversation, made him personally odious to both King and Queen. Here too his speedy dismissal was attributed to Marie Antoinette alone whereas the truth was very different. Anxious as the Queen was to see Aiguillon dismissed, she was equally anxious to see him replaced by the man, still exiled from the court, to whom she remained loyally attached, the Duc de Choiseul. In the event the Comte de Maurepas was appointed to be the King's chief minister. This was the first example of Marie Antoinette's inability, whatever the hostile propaganda to the contrary, to sway her husband where their interests diverged.

Many other examples would follow. Ten years later the Queen wrote ruefully to her brother the Emperor that 'the natural suspiciousness of the King had been strengthened long before his marriage by his boyhood Governor'. The Queen added that the Comte de Maurepas, although less forceful and less wicked than Vauguyon, thought it useful for the maintenance of his own credit 'to maintain the King in the same ideas'.[9] More philosophically, Count Mercy reflected that a chief minister would inevitably try to curb the influence of the Queen.

Maurepas, a man in his seventies, had been in exile for twenty-five years for allegedly circulating scurrilous verses about the Pompadour. He seems to have been a candidate of the King's aunts who, during the period when quarantine from smallpox meant that Louis XVI was cut off from many other potential ministers, exerted a particular sway. In short, the King preferred the advice of his French aunts to that of his Austrian wife. Cynical by nature – people mistook the stylish indifference with which he had greeted his disgrace for wisdom – Maurepas was an excellent manager of the court system. According to the Comte de Ségur: 'All his policy consisted in taking men and times as he found them and maintaining peace at home.' The Duc de Lévis, more critically, described him as having no feeling at all for the public good.[10]

This man would now be the closest advisor of the young French King for the next seven years. An even longer span of influence was enjoyed by the Comte de Vergennes, fifty-five at the time of his appointment as Foreign Minister in 1774. A career diplomat, Vergennes had been hampered in his rise by what was regarded as an unsuitable marriage to his mistress, of Turkish origin, whom Louis XV called 'that dreadful woman'. But he was clever and hard-working, his main character fault being a strong mercenary streak – 'the man of his age who most loved money'.[11] Vergennes would serve the King in various capacities for nearly thirteen years.

Looked at from the angle of Marie Antoinette, the important point was that both men, although not in favour of abandoning the Austrian alliance altogether, were anxious to keep it on a purely defensive level. In particular, they feared the expansionist nature of Joseph II, once his mother succumbed altogether to her failing health. A letter from Vergennes of December 1774, at a moment when Maria Teresa was believed wrongly to be dying, expressed this worry about the 'restless and ambitious spirit' of the Emperor. In their suspicion of Austria, Maurepas and Vergennes found a convenient identity of view with their sovereign. And all three men looked warily on the Habsburg Queen.[12]

Maurepas' intimate status was conveyed by the fact that he occupied the Du Barry's old apartments at Versailles. In time he would even be allowed to use the secret staircase that joined the royal apartments to that of the favourite, if for a very different purpose. Symbolically, the Queen's apartments were now considerably further away from those of the King. It was not until the summer of 1775, at the urgent insistence of Mercy, that a long subterranean staircase linking the two was constructed.* Up until that time Louis had been condemned to make his sporadic marital visits by going through the so-called Oeil de Boeuf antechamber (named from its ox-eye window) in which courtiers lounged speculatively.

What theoretical powers did Marie Antoinette have, in order to combat the insidious propaganda of the King's advisors? The fact was that there was no agreed official role for a French queen. The status of the French royal female was generally low: a reflection of the fourteenth-century Salic Law by which no woman could ascend to the throne. In contrast women had succeeded to the thrones of Spain, England and Hungary,

---

* This staircase would play a dramatic part in the subsequent story of Marie Antoinette.

whatever the powers of the queens concerned, whatever their subordination to their husbands. This obviously lifted up the position of princesses because they were capable of inheritance. Certainly there was a tradition in the Habsburg family, from which Marie Antoinette sprang, of strong female rulers, either as Regents appointed by their close male relatives (as Margaret of Austria had ruled the Netherlands) or Queens Regnant such as Isabella of Castile and, of course, Maria Teresa.

What were the other possibilities for royal women? Motherhood could lead to an improvement in status. Maria Carolina, in her marriage contract, was promised a place in the Council of State when she produced a male heir. Her first son, following two daughters, who was greeted with unselfish joy by Marie Antoinette, was born in 1775 and a second in June 1777. Altogether the Queen of Naples, emulating her mother in fertility, would undergo eighteen pregnancies, but it was the birth of the heir that was crucial. Given that an official position for the Queen in the French King's Council of State was unthinkable, there was obviously no such clause in Marie Antoinette's wedding contract. It was true that a widowed Queen of France could be Regent for her young son, as had happened in the case of three foreign-born princesses, Catherine de'Medici in the sixteenth century, Marie de'Medici and Anne of Austria in the seventeenth. In France the powers of the mother (as opposed to the wife) were acknowledged. So far, however, Marie Antoinette had not even managed to take the first step up this particular ladder of power.

In the absence of a more formal structure, unofficial influence was the proper sphere of the female and the French court was well used to it. But it was the influence of the mistress not the wife. Throughout the long reign of Louis XV, the mistress had been a force to be reckoned with, whether it was the intelligent, tasteful Pompadour or the Du Barry, who was so much less gifted that the Prince de Ligne said of her that she would have to use important documents as curling papers 'in order to get them into her head' (the Du Barry had particularly long thick hair of which she was inordinately proud). The last consort, Maria Lesczinska, trained by her father to be intensely grateful for her position, had made one little venture at a political action nearly fifty years earlier, and had thereafter subsided into a formal, pious, secluded life.[13] She was, however, seen – by the French – as a model of a queen.

The role designed for Marie Antoinette by Count Mercy was intended to be more like that of the mistress, taking advantage of the unique advantage she did have – personal access to the monarch in a period when this was a crucial element in all court intrigues. The fact that she was not fulfilling the most significant function of a mistress was an irritating weakness in such calculations. However, it did at least mean that the 'indolent' King showed no penchant for other women, a palliative seized upon by Maria Teresa. In the meantime Marie Antoinette was supposed to infiltrate herself into the confidence of the King, while being careful always to wait for *him* to consult *her*, as Mercy emphasized (not an easy mission to fulfil). There was some difference of aim between Mercy and the Emperor Joseph. Whilst Mercy saw Marie Antoinette as playing her part in these court intrigues, Joseph was more interested in his sister exerting a notional 'German' influence. But the method of operation was to be the same: her access to the King was to be used.[14]

The Queen did have other weapons at her disposal. She had considerable patronage. Here she was on safe ground, with the custom of the country behind her. Even if particular appointments of hers were criticized, there was nothing unusual in her making them. When her mother protested at members of the Queen's household being rewarded, Marie Antoinette pointed out that it was expected of her, and her supporters would otherwise miss out. Furthermore, showering people she liked with benefits was exactly suited to the temperament of Marie Antoinette, where political infighting was not. This lack of any real interest in politics – the game for its own sake – was an aspect of her character that struck all those who knew her well. The Comte de La Marck said that she had 'a repugnance for the whole subject common to women', ignoring the fact that the Queen's close female relations felt no such repugnance. It was certainly a cause of despair among her Austrian advisors that she remained fundamentally uninterested, 'both by principle and inclination', in Vermond's words, except where questions of personal distaste or gratitude were concerned, as with Aiguillon on the one hand (where she succeeded because the King agreed with her) and Choiseul on the other (where she failed because he did not).[15]

If not political by temperament, Marie Antoinette was generous and loyal – good qualities in a royal person but expensive ones. The household of a Queen of France traditionally consisted of about 500 people all paid for by the Minister of the Royal Household (*Ministre de la Maison du Roi*) at a cost of 4 million livres. These ranged from its official Mistress, the Comtesse de Noailles, down to the footmen who turned the royal mattress because it was too heavy for the women to manage. They included the numerous functionaries, who generally worked in a quarterly rota in squads of four, for the stable and the kitchen as well as the bedchamber.[16] Looked at with a twenty-first-century eye, this is a vast establishment; it needs to be considered, however, from an eighteenth-century perspective. The King's household was even larger – that was only to be expected. But the respective households of his younger brothers and their wives were almost as large as the Queen's, the Mistress of the Household and the Mistress of the Robes for the Comtesse de Provence receiving the same financial reward, for example, as those for Marie Antoinette.

In general, the royal system, which had been established long before the arrival of Marie Antoinette, was incredibly lavish. And there were many, many people, mainly but not entirely noble, with a vested interest in continuing it. In addition, it was not as if the rest of the world adhered to a different standard of life. The Spanish ambassador had at least seventy servants, the English ambassador over fifty; at the château of Chantilly, an amazed English visitor watched a supper party given by the Prince de Condé at which eight people were waited on at table by twenty-five attendants. As Thomas Jefferson wrote of the French and their lifestyle: 'The roughnesses of the human mind are so thoroughly rubbed off with them that it seems as if one might glide through a whole life among them without a justle [sic].'[17]

It was theoretically to smooth out roughnesses, then, that Marie Antoinette had, for example, a Grand Almoner, a First Almoner, an Almoner in Ordinary, four almoners who rotated quarterly, four quarterly chaplains, four quarterly chapel boys, down to two chapel summoners. Of course the effect of such gross overmanning was the reverse of smooth and it was also very expensive. All these people, like all the other courtiers, watched each other perpetually to see that no extra advantage was being taken, no privilege neglected. The Queen's trainbearer, to take only one example, had to be of noble birth; otherwise the First Gentleman Usher, who had to provide a place for him in his coach, could not tolerate the association. The trainbearer also had to surrender the train to a page when the Queen entered the chapel of the *private* apartments of the King, although he was entitled to carry it in the State Apartments and the Gallery of Mirrors. He was also in charge of her cloak, although he had to hand it to an usher or equerry if she actually wanted to put it on ... Woe betide the trainbearer who overstepped the limits of his role, committing crimes like carrying the train into the chapel, or handing the Queen her cloak himself.

This honeycomb of privilege and payment was well described in her memoirs by the Queen's First Lady of the Bedchamber, Henriette Campan, née Genet.* One of the few intelligent women that Marie Antoinette liked and trusted, Madame Campan was three years senior to her mistress, having begun her career as Reader to the Mesdames Tantes when she was fifteen. In a period rich for the first time in female testimonies, that of Madame Campan stands out not only for her intelligence and education but also because she had access to the Queen and the court over a long period at a particular intermediate

* Madame Campan became something of a hate figure to the ultra-royalists after the Bourbon Restoration, because she had taught the step-daughter of Napoleon, and her testimony, first published in 1823, was criticized for that reason alone. Although she does make mistakes (like many other memorialists) and is not averse to self-glorification in order to atone for her 'Napoleonic' affiliations, Madame Campan is nevertheless a vital witness. A recent French writer, Jean Chalon, has compared her status to that of Figaro in the song: 'Figaro here, Figaro there.' But of course Figaro, like all domestics, saw a great deal of the game.[18]

level where much information could be gathered.

Shortly before the death of Louis XV, Henriette had been married off to a widower, François Campan, the son of Pierre Campan, Marie Antoinette's librarian. The junior Campan proved to have been reluctant to remarry; his rapid disappearance abroad meant that Henriette had plenty of time to concentrate on court affairs, her single child, Henri, being born ten years later when she was in her early thirties.[19] Apart from being daughter-in-law to the Librarian, Henriette Campan had a sister in the Queen's household, Adélaïde Auguié, known to Marie Antoinette as 'my lioness' because of her exceptional height, and another sister, Julie Rousseau, also in royal service.

Madame Campan, while defending Marie Antoinette for following the existing structure of a Queen's household, was critical of her where an innovation of 1775 was concerned. The Princesse de Lamballe was made overall Superintendent of the Household, that is to say, superior to the Comtesse de Noailles and the Duchesse de Cossé, Mistress of the Robes. In theory this was a revival of an ancient post. But since the post itself had been abolished as being too powerful, its reappearance marked an unfortunate decision by a Queen determined to give the Lamballe 'greater personal consideration'.[20]

Nor was the Princesse de Lamballe's handling of her post diplomatic. She interfered with the running of the household, but did not issue the requisite invitations for lavish suppers, for which her stipend was intended, on the grounds that it was beneath her status as a Princess of the Blood to solicit others. The other Princesses of the Blood took offence at this. Lamballe was only the widow of a prince of legitimated royal descent, so it could be argued that if the post was to be recreated, it should have gone to someone with a superior claim: Mademoiselle de Clermont, for example, the daughter of the impeccably royal Prince de Condé, whose aunt had been the last incumbent.[21]

It was ironic that the Queen, while generously determined to please her friend, was also beginning to tire of her. Was the Princesse de Lamballe, with all her devotion and her famous sensitivity, becoming, to put it delicately, somewhat of a bore? She certainly did not provide the kind of amusing society to which Marie Antoinette was beginning to turn in compensation for the other deficiencies in her life. The new favourite, Yolande de Polignac, was a far more fascinating and seductive character. Yet by the rules of Versailles, the post of Superintendent, once given, could not be withdrawn. The Princesse de Lamballe continued disconsolately to haunt Versailles and to insist on such prerogatives as putting the Queen's breakfast on her bed, while the Queen's feelings of sentimental friendship for her demonstrably waned.

Comtesse Jules de Polignac, as she was known, had been born Yolande de Polastron, of an ancient but poverty-stricken family, and when very young had married Jules de Polignac, who was similarly noble, similarly poor. She was now twenty-six, but her particular freshness of appearance, giving an impression of 'utter naturalness', was undiminished; Yolande with her cloud of dark hair, her big eyes, her neat nose and pretty pearly teeth was generally likened to a Madonna by Raphael – even if the Duc de Lévis thought her rather an insipid Madonna. People enjoyed themselves in her company; her manner was gently pleasing and she had a delightful laugh.[22]

Not everyone could see her attraction. Count Mercy for one thought that neither the Comtesse's wit nor her judgement made her suitable for the Queen's favour. He could not understand that it was her apparent passivity, her languid sweetness which convinced bystanders of her lack of 'avidity or egotism', that attracted Marie Antoinette.[23] Afterwards the satirists were happily convinced that the Queen's emotional dependence on Yolande de Polignac was accompanied by a full-blown sexual relationship which lost nothing in the telling, as though affection between two women must invariably take this form. But what Marie Antoinette wanted at this point was an intimacy based on sentiment rather than sex; nothing in her life so far had made her look on sex as anything but duty and a rather disagreeable duty at that. The pattern of intense friendships in France had been set by the Princesse de Lamballe. This was another, deeper version.

It was the Comtesse who was now, for better or for worse, to form the emotional centre of the world of Marie Antoinette.

She came to mean to her what Maria Carolina had meant for so long in the Queen's early life, and the Princesse de Lamballe more briefly. Furthermore, because Yolande saw to it that all her relations were part of the new royal circle, her family life came to be in effect that of the Queen, who predictably adored the two small Polignac children Armand and Agläié. As for Yolande's character, it was appealing that she was notably calm by nature; she had neither the ultra-sensitivity of the Princesse de Lamballe, nor the capricious moods that increasingly swept over Marie Antoinette.

None of this corresponded to an active lesbian relationship, if the test of that is physical consummation. But it is plausible to believe that Marie Antoinette was in some romantic sense in love with Yolande de Polignac (or, in girlish language, had a crush on her), at least in the early years of their relationship. The French saying that in love there is always one who bestows kisses and the other who extends the cheek was not irrelevant; Marie Antoinette, metaphorically speaking, bestowed the kisses on the apparently gently indifferent cheek of Yolande de Polignac.

What were the favourite's own feelings? Gentle indifference in a love object, however fascinating to an affectionate nature, may mask self-centredness on a large scale. Yolande had an accepted lover, the clever, artistic but dominating Comte de Vaudreuil. For one seemingly lacking in avidity, she would amass an amazing amount of positions and rewards for herself, her large family, her connections and, of course, Vaudreuil.

In terms of the court, 1775, which was destined to be the year of the coronation of Louis XVI, also heralded a series of humiliations for his consort. In December, Marie Antoinette had had to break to her mother the news that she had been personally dreading for two years, and she did not expect Maria Teresa herself to receive it with 'much joy'. The Comtesse d'Artois was pregnant.[24]

The patronage of Gluck continued. *Orphée*, attended by the Queen, had been a success in the previous August, and at the beginning of January there was a new production of *Iphigénie en*

Aulide, which led to a spontaneous outburst of enthusiasm for the Queen. In a moving moment in the second act, Iphigénie's bridegroom Achilles began to praise her, predicting eternal happiness for the kingdom as a result of their marriage. As the chorus duly responded, 'Let us sing, let us celebrate our Queen …' loud applause brought them to a halt. The tribute was acknowledged with graceful embarrassment and tears by Marie Antoinette, while others present also wept at the touching spectacle. Once the chorus was allowed to complete the verses, there were shouts of *bis* and the whole thing was repeated. Then cries of 'Long live the Queen' filled the air for fifteen minutes. The Baron Grimm was moved to reflect: 'What prologues, what panegyrics can compare to these outbursts of tenderness and public admiration!'[25] The popular ecstasy, the worship of the true goddess, was in sad contrast to Marie Antoinette's private despair over the good fortune of her sister-in-law, which she hid behind a veil of solicitation.

In February, a visit that should have brought consolation to the Queen turned sour; once again, as in the case of Mademoiselle de Lorraine's minuet, it was mishandled by Count Mercy. The Archduke Max, the Queen's youngest brother, chose to pay an incognito visit to Versailles using the name of the Comte de Burgau. A picture painted by Joseph Hauzinger to mark the occasion shows a gloomy-looking Marie Antoinette, hair piled high, cheeks well rouged, and a melancholy Louis XVI, with a complacent Archduke, whose corpulence at the age of eighteen was already earning him the nickname 'Fat Max'. The French royal couple had reason to look depressed. The Archduke showed himself tactless in his behaviour on every level.

To Marie Antoinette's polite French, he insisted on answering in German. Then he wore uniform, something that was expressly forbidden to the French at court in order to promote the wearing of the French silk civilian dress, as Mercy should surely have warned him. Max was gauche to a degree that appalled the civilized French; when presented with one of Buffon's works at the Jardin du Roi by the great naturalist himself, he waved it aside, saying casually that he would hate to deprive the author of his own book. All this was, naturally enough, fodder for the

Austrophobes at court. But it was the Archduke's tactless behaviour to the Princes of the Blood, which Mercy also allowed to pass, that created a really unfortunate impression, redounding inevitably to the discredit of the Queen.

When it came to rank, an Archduke, the son and brother of an Emperor, was obviously superior to a French Prince of the Blood, who was already one rank below that of the French royal family. If, therefore, Max had arrived in full archducal fig, the Princes would have been bound by the rules of etiquette to call on him first. The 'Comte de Burgau' was another matter. Since he was a foreigner of no particularly distinguished rank, it could be argued that the Comte should call on the Princes first. The situation was aggravated by the fact that Mercy bear-led Max to call on various ministers without waiting for them to make the first move. So the Princes of the Blood sulked and did not call. The Queen, misled by the ambassador, was both indignant and upset on behalf of her family. As for Max, he left behind him the sobriquet, 'the Arch Fool'.[26]

It was not altogether surprising that as the coronation, planned for mid-June, approached, Mercy's efforts to get the Queen crowned at Rheims alongside her husband were rebuffed. The burgeoning pregnancy of the Comtesse d'Artois – her baby was due in August – emphasized the tenuous nature of Marie Antoinette's claim. Maurepas advised the King to resist the pressure of the ambassador, using the expense of a double ceremony as an excuse, but Louis XVI himself certainly went along with the decision.[27]

Marie Antoinette expressed herself indifferent to the whole matter. She would accompany her husband, and she would order a magnificent dress from the fashionable new couturier Rose Bertin. The weight of this robe, due to the richness of the jewelled embroidery, was so great that Bertin, a woman of fearless spirit where her creations were concerned, proposed that the Duchesse de Cossé, as Mistress of the Robes, should convey it to Rheims on an expensive stretcher. When the Duchesse declined to do so, suggesting a more humdrum trunk, the Queen was reduced to carrying it in her own luggage. The expense of the Queen's dress was, however, a comparatively minor item in the extravagance of the whole occasion. The King's own clothing was enormously costly. Since the crown of Louis XV was found to be too small, there was a special new gold crown made for the King by the royal goldsmith, Auguste, at a cost of 6000 livres, which included rubies, emeralds, sapphires and 'the finest known diamond', the Regent. A further 150 livres went on a morocco case for it, lined with velvet.[28]

The costs of such an elaborate coronation had already been queried by Anne Robert Turgot, the King's new Controller General of Finance, who had been appointed in August 1774. Through a series of edicts, he was attempting to remedy the finances of government, never properly stable since the Seven Years' War. There was now a deficit of 22 million livres with a projected further 78 million still to come. Turgot intended to reform the tax system, with measures that involved reducing the fiscal privileges of the nobility. He also tried to establish a free market in grain. Unfortunately a disastrous harvest in 1774 compounded the hardship caused by a system that was ill received in the first place. Prices rocketed and there were rumours that they were deliberately held high for profit. Violent protest in the shape of grain riots followed, the 'Flour War', as it was known, reaching Versailles on 2 May.

Turgot had argued for a simplified coronation in Paris. This would have given the impression of a King crowned by popular acclamation, with the double effect of bringing extra commerce to the capital. Perhaps it was the May riots that persuaded the King and his advisors to go for the security of Rheims, so much further from the capital. At all events, this excursion of the King and Queen, exposing themselves to the public gaze a long way from Versailles and in the direction of the north-eastern border, at a time when the physical appearance of royalties was generally speaking an unknown factor, was to have unforeseen consequences in years to come.

The day of the coronation, 11 June, was intensely hot and the long ceremony was exhausting. Nevertheless Marie Antoinette was deeply moved by the occasion. First of all her husband's dignified concentration caused her to weep as the Te Deum was being sung. The King too had tears in his eyes, but the Queen's emotion was so overwhelming that she was forced to withdraw for a short while. On her return, the eyes of the royal couple met tenderly. All of this was noted and received much approbation: 'The people loved her for her tears.' Second, as Marie Antoinette told her mother afterwards, she was affected by 'the most touching acclamations' on the part of the people and the evident devotion shown to them both; this despite the shortage of bread, which continued. In the evening both the King and Queen promenaded outdoors informally through the city, stoically enduring the stifling heat, Marie Antoinette on the arm of her husband.[29]

Now, if at all, during the period of the Flour War, was the occasion when Marie Antoinette might have uttered the notorious phrase: 'Let them eat cake' (*Qu'ils mangent de la brioche*). Instead, she indulged to her mother in a piece of reflection on the duties of royalty. Its tenor was the exact opposite of that phrase, at once callous and ignorant, so often ascribed to her. 'It is quite certain,' she wrote, 'that in seeing the people who treat us so well despite their own misfortune, we are more obliged than ever to work hard for their happiness. The King seems to understand this truth; as for myself, I know that in my whole life (even if I live for a hundred years) I shall never forget the day of the coronation.' This was the tender-hearted Marie Antoinette who, alone among the French royal family, refused to ruin the peasants' cornfields by riding over them, because she was well aware of the minutiae of the lives of the poor.[30]

In fact that lethal phrase had been known for at least a century previously, when it was ascribed to the Spanish princess, Marie Thérèse, bride of Louis XIV, in a slightly different form: if there was no bread, let the people eat the crust (*croûte*) of the pâté. It was known to Rousseau in 1737. It was credited to one of the royal aunts, Madame Sophie, in 1751, when reacting to the news that her brother the Dauphin Louis Ferdinand had been pestered with cries of 'Bread, bread' on a visit to Paris. The Comtesse de Boigne, who as a child played at the Versailles of Marie Antoinette, attributed the saying to another aunt, Madame Victoire. But the most convincing proof of Marie

Antoinette's innocence came from the memoirs of the Comte de Provence, published in 1823. No gallant guardian of his sister-in-law's reputation, he remarked that eating *pâté en croûte* always reminded him of the saying of his own ancestress, Queen Maria Thérèse. It was, in short, a royal chestnut.*[31]

While Marie Antoinette was still at Rheims, she attempted to alleviate the condition of the Duc de Choiseul, exiled from court for the last four and a half years. It was not a notably successful manoeuvre. The best the Queen could do was persuade the King to let her receive her former patron personally. While Choiseul's enemies shivered at the thought of his return to power, and the Queen herself tried to present the whole episode as a political triumph for herself in an unwise letter to an Austrian diplomat Count Rosenberg, the truth was that, thanks to Maurepas and Vergennes, she simply did not have sufficient influence with the King to restore Choiseul.

In vain Marie Antoinette boasted to Rosenberg that 'the poor man' – a reference to Louis XVI – had been induced to arrange the visit himself without having any idea how his wife had manipulated him. When Maria Teresa heard of the 'style, the fashion of thinking' of this letter, she delivered a stunning reprimand to her daughter. The Empress was shocked! How could she refer to her royal husband in such a manner?[33] The hypocrisy of the rebuke – delivered to one constantly adjured to govern her husband by stealth – was breathtaking.

Nor did the Queen fare any better in the case of Choiseul's ambitious protégé, the Comte de Guines. A cultured man, an accomplished flautist who commissioned a concerto from Mozart, Guines was a member of the Polignac set, quite apart from his Choiseuliste origins. He was also vain; the Duc de Lévis, whose sharp tongue got him the nickname 'Mosquito' from Marie Antoinette, reported that as Guines got fatter, he had his clothes made tighter and tighter to minimize his bulk

---

* But a peculiarly symbolic one, given that the staple food of the French peasantry and the working class was bread, absorbing 50 per cent of their income, as opposed to 5 per cent spent on fuel; the whole topic of bread was therefore the result of obsessional national interest.[32]

so that in the end he had to have two identical sets of breeches cut according to whether he had to stand up or sit down. Guines had been for several years French ambassador in London. Now a 'louche and cruel' scandal blew up, known as the Guines Affair, in which the ambassador was framed by his own secretary who used his master's name to sell information to speculators. The resolution of the affair turned into a contest of political wills. Vergennes as Foreign Minister was determined to take the opportunity to get rid of Guines from this embassy, and if possible from other future embassies as well. As for the Queen, it has been suggested that she viewed the vindication of Guines as a stepping-stone towards the return of Choiseul himself.[34]

Vergennes, enjoying the confidence of the King where the Queen did not, won. Guines was dismissed without a future. A curt note from Louis XVI to his Foreign Minister early in the following year was explicit: 'I have made it quite clear to the Queen that he cannot serve either in England or in any other Embassy.'[35] The dukedom that Guines received subsequently in order to propitiate Marie Antoinette could not mask her actual defeat.

The dreaded *accouchement* of the Comtesse d'Artois took place on 6 August 1775. The result was a large healthy baby and it was a boy. Immediately Louis XVI granted him the royal title of the Duc d'Angoulême. The birth of this first Bourbon prince in the new generation was a blow to the Orléans family, immediately relegating their claims to the throne. It was more than a blow to Marie Antoinette; it was a ritual humiliation. For by the rules of etiquette she, along with all the other courtiers with the suitable Rights of Entry, was compelled to attend the birth and witness its most intimate moments. The Queen was present when the Comtesse d'Artois, hearing that she had gone further than merely produce a baby and had given birth to a male, cried out to her husband: 'My God, how happy I am!'

When it was all over, and Marie Antoinette had embraced her sister-in-law most tenderly, she was free at last to retire to her own apartments. At this point, however, this woman, so maternal that she had even envied the Duchesse de Chartres when she gave birth to a baby that died, had to run the gauntlet of the raucous market-women. Exercising their traditional right to hang around Versailles on occasions of state importance, they pursued the departing Queen with their cat-calls: 'When will *you* give us an heir to the throne?' Marie Antoinette's demeanour was as ever calm and dignified and she showed nothing outwardly of her mortification. But once she arrived at the safety of her own suite of rooms, the Queen shut herself up in her inner sanctum, alone with Madame Campan, and wept bitterly. As the First Lady of the Bedchamber wrote: 'She was extremely affecting when in misfortune.'[36]

This was the kind of experience that made one of Marie Antoinette's more desperate acts of charity comprehensible. The Queen was in her carriage near Louveciennes when a little village boy of four or five with fair hair and big blue eyes fell under her horses' hoofs. He was unhurt. By the time the boy's grandmother had emerged from her cottage, the Queen was already clutching him to her with the words: 'I must take him. He is mine.' It helped that the boy's mother had died, leaving five other orphans. The grandmother certainly raised no objection when Jacques was whirled away to Versailles, especially since Marie Antoinette promised to maintain the whole family financially. It was poor little Jacques who howled with home-sickness as he was thoroughly scrubbed, before being dressed up in white-edged lace to be presented anew to the Queen. Undaunted, the Queen proceeded to share her food with Jacques whenever possible, as well as supervising his education and of course keeping her word about the financial arrangements.[37] The sweet but desperately unreal impulse was characteristic of Marie Antoinette at this time.

The marriage celebrations for the King's sister, Gros-Madame Clothilde, which followed in the second half of August, were also no great comfort to an Austrian Archduchess. The bride-groom was the Prince of Piedmont, heir to the kingdom of Sardinia, which made the third Savoyard marriage in a row within the royal family, to say nothing of a half-Savoyard heir to the throne, the infant Duc d'Angoulême. Poor Clothilde's notorious weight caused the wits to say that two Savoyard Princesses had been received in exchange for one very heavy French one. That weight had indeed caused some concern to the grandfather of the bridegroom, King Charles Emmanuel III, on the grounds that if the fourteen-year-old Clothilde was fat already, she would certainly get fatter still in Savoy, as French women always enlarged on Italian food; his anxiety focused on the question of heirs. Clothilde herself worried that her bridegroom might recoil from her appearance although in the event the Prince behaved with style. She was, he said, much less fat than had been reported and in any case, 'I find you adorable.'[38] About the only consolation for Marie Antoinette in all this was the increased companionship of her younger sister-in-law Madame Elisabeth, now aged eleven, who was able to graduate from the care of the Royal Governess, the Comtesse de Marsan.

There was an epidemic of satiric and grossly obscene pamphlets or *libelles* in the autumn of 1775, a phenomenon that Marie Antoinette felt obliged to report to her mother. 'No one was spared,' she wrote, 'not even the King.' One pamphlet in particular was dangerously wounding, producing a flood of angry tears from Marie Antoinette, because it was, unlike the majority of them, horribly true.[39] This was against the background of the continuing fecundity of the Comtesse d'Artois who was almost certainly pregnant once more.*

The pamphlet was entitled *Les Nouvelles de la Cour*, centring on the despair of the 'sad Queen' with the refrain: 'Can the King do it? Can't the King do it?' The verses themselves were extremely graphic, to the extent that even Bachaumont was shocked, although he printed it happily in his *Correspondance Secrète*. The Lamballe was said to be working at alleviating the Queen's frustration with her 'little fingers', Maria Teresa to be advocating a lover:

> My daughter, to have a successor
> It little matters whether the maker
> Is in front of the throne or behind it.

* She did in fact give birth to a daughter on 5 August 1776, one year after the birth of the Duc d'Angoulême.

The problem of the King's foreskin (*prépuce*) was contrasted with the Queen's enthusiasm for puce, the new fashionable colour. Speculation on the royal emissions suggested 'clear water' to be the most likely substance.[40]

Count Mercy's pronouncement on the whole matter of the unfulfilled marriage, made at the end of the year, was much less ribald than the crude verses of the *libelliste* that provoked the disloyal courtiers to snigger behind the backs of their royal master and mistress. But it conveyed the same message. It was not enough to be a true goddess to the people, and listen to the cries of 'Let us celebrate our Queen!' at the opera. 'However brilliant the Queen's position at the moment,' wrote Mercy to Maria Teresa on 17 December, she would never consolidate it until she produced an heir to the state. She needed 'the quality of a mother to be regarded as French' by this 'petulant and frivolous nation', which would otherwise resent her influence.[41]

CHAPTER TEN

An Unhappy Woman?

'You are getting older and you no longer have the excuse of youth. What will become of you? An unhappy woman and still more unhappy princess.'

*The Emperor Joseph II to the Queen of France
(aged twenty-one) in 1777*

The New Year of 1776 was unusually severe with six weeks of snow. As time passed, ancient sledges were rooted out, last used by the King's father in his youth. The noise of the bells on the gold-decked harnesses filled the air; horses were caparisoned with white plumes; masked ladies of the court took to visiting the Champs-Elysées. Two years previously Marie Antoinette had been in ecstasy at such an opportunity to recreate the pleasures of her youth. But there was a chill in the air quite independent of the weather; in this case, criticisms of the pastime as being too 'Viennese' caused her to abandon it after a while. Her relationship with the King, which had failed to develop into warmth in the past year, now became visibly cool.

Their lack of similar interests was obvious. In a revealing letter, written to Count Rosenberg in April 1775 (he was one of the Austrian correspondents approved by her mother because he passed on the contents), Marie Antoinette did not try to disguise the fact. Her tone, however, as invariably when writing to Vienna, was defensive. She suggested that the experienced diplomat should pay no attention to the tales about her conduct that were reaching Austria: 'You know Paris and Versailles, you have been there, you can judge.' The Queen would be frank with him. 'For example, my tastes are not the same as the King's, who is only interested in hunting and his metal-working. You will agree that I would cut an odd figure at a forge; I am not one to play Vulcan [the god of Fire] there and if I played the role of Venus that would displease him a great deal more than my actual tastes of which he does not disapprove.'[1]

Eighteen months later, however, this gracious state of compromise outlined by Marie Antoinette, the basis for so many satisfactory royal marriages past and future, was no longer visible to interested observers. Baron Goltz, the well-informed Prussian envoy, heard that there were new scenes, which indicated a complete estrangement between the royal couple. In the view of the Austrians, this would only be solved by a visit from the Emperor Joseph; Goltz reflected that given the absolute diversity of their natures, his task was not going to be easy.[2]

At least the Queen always maintained a 'most submissive' attitude to her husband in public. But she was beginning to incarnate what Maria Teresa angrily called 'the spirit of dissipation' both by night and day; for the Empress had lost none of the vitriol of her pen with the passing years.[3] In what did this 'dissipation' consist? Some of it was harmless enough. The Queen began to enjoy going racing in the Bois de Boulogne escorted by her husband's cousin (and her own), Philippe Duc de Chartres. The heir to the first Prince of the Blood himself extended his violent Anglomania – from her political institutions to her tailoring – to the English style of racing and English bloodstock.

More dangerous was the Queen's growing passion for gambling at the various card games with which the court passed its time. Here neither Marie Antoinette nor the court of France was unique. Gambling was an endemic danger at such leisured and privileged places, extending back to the notorious occasion in the previous century when the Marquise de Montespan, mistress of Louis XIV, had won 700,000 écus gambling on Christmas Day. The current furious craze had actually started in the reign of Louis XV. In the previous generation both Marie Antoinette's parents had adored cards. Unfortunately the late-night card parties of Marie Antoinette, concentrating on the games of lansquenet and pharaoh, had two particular effects. They kept her away from the sleeping King, which she probably intended, and contributed to her financial problems, which she certainly did not. (They also contributed to the financial problems of her courtiers when she won.) It was not even that profit was the point of it all; the Queen gambled to be in the fashion and to amuse herself, not to win. By January 1778 Count Mercy contended that the Queen was so straitened that she no longer gave fully to the charities that she loved.

There is a vignette of the Queen's life – and that of the King – in an account of a gambling session on the eve of the Queen's twenty-first birthday in 1776. Marie Antoinette cajoled Louis XVI into importing players from Paris who would act as bankers. Play started on the night of 30 October and continued to the morning of the 31st, and then went on again until 3 a.m. on the morning of the Feast of All Saints. When the King taxed his wife with this, she replied naughtily: 'You said we could play, but you never specified for how long.' The King merely laughed and said quite cheerfully: 'You're all worthless, the lot of you.'[4]

The so-called frenzy did not, however, consist of a full-blooded amorous intrigue of the sort practised by most of the inhabitants of Versailles. On the contrary, Marie Antoinette had, wrote the Prince de Ligne, 'a charming quality of obtuseness which kept any lovers at a distance'. Courtly admiration and innocent but gallant flirtation with men who initially were a lot older was what pleased her. Saint-Priest, in his *Mémoires*, noted that there was 'coquetry at the bottom of her nature'.[5] These admirers were expected to be able to sing and of course dance to a certain elegant level – arts in which the King was singularly lacking. She herself listed a few of such men for herself in that letter to Count Rosenberg which rejected 'Vulcan's forge'. Her singing parties consisted of chosen ladies with good voices and 'certain agreeable men who were, however, no longer young'. Apart from Comte Jules de Polignac, who was thirty, these included the Duc de Duras, father-in-law of one of her Dames du Palais, who was sixty, the Duc de Noailles who was seventy-two and the Baron de Besenval who was in his fifties.

The Baron de Besenval, a lieutenant colonel of the Swiss Guards, was typical of the kind of older man who appealed to the young Queen as an amusing companion. As the Comte de Ségur wrote, 'His agreeable levity, entirely French, made one forget that he was born a Swiss.' He was rated the best raconteur in the Polignac set, a virtue that weighed heavily in those circles against his minor vices of drinking and womanizing. Besenval was later accused by contemporaries of encouraging the Queen's spirit of mockery (to her friends this was merely her sense of fun) although he stepped out of line with an inappropriate declaration of passion. It seems that there was a misunderstanding on both sides. Marie Antoinette imagined that Besenval's 'grey hairs' were security against serious attentions, whereas as a result of the Queen's friendship Besenval deluded himself into thinking that they would be welcome. When Besenval fell on his knees, it was the Queen of France who rebuked him in icy tones: 'Rise, sir, the King shall not be informed of an offence that would disgrace you for ever.' Besenval stammered an apology and withdrew.[6]

Almost exactly the same thing happened when an even more celebrated roué, the Duc de Lauzun, was encouraged by the spectacle – as he saw it – of a beautiful young Queen for the taking and similarly declared himself. In his case the false impression arose over a misunderstanding connected with a magnificent plume of white heron's feathers sported by Lauzun at the salon of the Princesse de Guéméné and which the Queen admired. Her admiration forgotten, the Queen was startled to receive the plume subsequently as a present via the Princesse. Wrote Madame Campan: 'As Lauzun had been wearing it, the Queen had not imagined that he could think of giving it to her.' Etiquette being all-important, Marie Antoinette now calculated that a single airing of the plume in her own coiffure in Lauzun's presence would be sufficient to avoid giving offence. Unfortunately Lauzun's vanity led him to magnify the favour. He too pressed his suit, and was also rejected, with the chilling regal words: 'Go, sir.'[7] Whereas Besenval remained part of the

Polignac set, finally being too amusing to be banished, Lauzun moved to the Orléanist opposition circle.*

There is a sense of hysteria about these rejections. But it was an understandable hysteria; the Queen was only too well aware that her chastity, like the state of her marriage, must always be a subject of gossip and conjecture. For example, a whole romance was built round an incident in which a good-looking if slightly foolish young man in the household of Artois, called '*le beau* Dillon', fainted in public. The alarmed Queen placed her hand over his heart to check for signs of life – a spontaneous gesture, which was either 'imprudent' or concerned, depending on the point of view.[9] She repaid those who badmouthed her on the subject with an intense dislike. One notable example was the malicious Prince Louis de Rohan, French ambassador in Vienna, about whom she began to share her mother's feelings of acute disapproval.

More seriously, her undeniable enjoyment of the company of the Comte d'Artois himself, the most attractive royal brother, would become a long-running favourite of the *libellistes*. They drew obscene conclusions about the Queen's pleasures by contrasting Artois' evident virility with Louis XVI's impotence. In fact the attitude of Marie Antoinette to Artois had something of the big sister about it (she was two years older than he) even if she did have more tastes in common with him than with her husband. In any case, had Marie Antoinette indeed chosen to embark on a real love affair at this stage, her brother-in-law was the last man she would have chosen. The danger of revelation was far too great in view of the fact that Artois' own children had much to gain from the Queen's ruin; their chances in the succession would have been improved still further.

With the whole question of physical intimacy in her marriage

* Lauzun's own memoirs were written many years later, probably by others using his own manuscript; they were generally regarded as untruthful by contemporaries. He has Marie Antoinette (among many other eager women) throwing herself at him in a novelettish scene in which he breathes, 'You are my Queen ...' and 'her eyes seemed to be asking me to give her yet another title; I was tempted to enjoy the good fortune which appeared to be offered to me.' However, even Lauzun admits that he then drew back.[8]

Marie Antoinette's youthful education under teachers who
included Gluck led to a lifelong love of music in all its forms.

Louis XV, King of France and
grandfather of Louis XVI; at the
age of sixty he was still regarded
as 'the handsomest man' at his
own court.

Louis XVI at the age of twenty.

Marriage contract of Marie Antoinette and the Dauphin, whose signature 'Louis Auguste' is below that of his grandfather Louis XV as 'Louis'; her signature is marked by a blot and it seems that the full name 'Antoinette', as opposed to 'Antoine', is unfamiliar; the 'e' of Jeanne may also be missing.

evitte deux jours de
suitte a la toilette n'ayant
pas d'autre temps a moi
et si je ne lui repond
pas exactement qu'elle
croyez que s'est par trop
d'actitude a brulé sa
lettre. il faut que je
finisse pour m'habiller
et aller a la messe
du Roi j'ai l'honneur
d'etre

choisy ce 12 juillet
1770   la plus soumise
je lui envoye fille Antoinette
la liste des present
que j'ai recu croyant
que cela pouvoit l'amuse

je vais un veste pour
le Roi qui n'avance gere
mais j'espere qu'avec
la grace de Dieu et
de sera fini dans quelque
année.   a 3 heures
je vais encore chez ma
Tante ou le Roi vient
a cette heure la   a 4 heure
vient   chez moi a
5 heure tous les jours
le Maitre de Clavecin
ou   chanter jusqu'a 8
heures. a 6 heure et demi
je vais presque toujour
chez mes Tantes quand je
ne vais point me promener
il faut
j'avoir que mon chary
vais presque toujours

An early letter home
from Marie Antoinette to
her mother (12 July 1770);
spelling and writing are
shaky and she is still
uneasy with the full
name 'Antoinette'.

Auspice Deo

Soyer persuadé chere Durieu
que je penserai toujours
a vous et que je n'oublire
jamais les peines que vous
avez eu avec moi c'est
dont vous assure

ce 19 avril   Votre Tres fidelle
1770   Antoine Archiduchesse

Letter from Marie Antoinette,
on the eve of her departure
to France, to Mme Durieu
showing her childhood
signature of 'Antoine'.

Marie Antoinette in hunting costume painted the year after her marriage; her mother loved this picture, which she thought 'very like', and hung it in her study: 'thus I have you always with me under my eyes'.

Medallions of Louis XVI and Marie Antoinette as King and Queen of France.

Marie Antoinette, like most of the French court, had a passion for gambling: her velvet gambling-purse embroidered with the royal arms, and jetons.

Blue enamel and diamond clasp of a bracelet given to Marie Antoinette at her wedding, showing her cipher MA.

Count Mercy d'Argenteau, Austrian Ambassador to Versailles; nearly thirty years older than Marie Antoinette, he was viewed by her as a father-figure.

The Swedish aristocrat Count Fersen; his romantic looks were much praised and he was thought to look like the hero of a novel.

The Princesse de Lamballe, Marie Antoinette's first favourite, who was admired for her soulful appearance; a widow, she also enjoyed a reputation for purity.

unresolved, it would be natural for Marie Antoinette to feel awkwardness if not outright disgust at the whole sexual process. Certainly Madame Campan called her personal modesty 'extreme'.[10] Marie Antoinette understandably appreciated admirers who courted her without pressing their suit, either out of respect or because they were in fact romantically engaged elsewhere. With the handsome young Swedish aristocrat Count Fersen far away from France (insofar as their brief encounter had been remembered by either party), it was the gallantry of older men that bolstered the Queen's self-confidence and allowed her to give vent to her taste for harmless flirtation. The Duc de Coigny, for example, one of her clear favourites, was almost twenty years her senior. He had been a good soldier in the Seven Years' War, and was now the pattern of a faithful servant. His elegant manners and devotion were much commended, but to those in the know, it was clearly not an ardent relationship.

Where younger men were concerned, the foreign-born were particularly welcome because their material expectations at Versailles would not match those of the French and they might also avoid some of the many interfamilial intrigues that plagued the court. Marie Antoinette was fascinated by several of the other personable young Swedes at court, with their dashing appearance and excellent French. Then there were various British aristocrats from across the Channel who made an appearance at Versailles as part of the constant Anglo-French connection at the court level, which somehow floated lightly above more mundane political differences. Indeed, the Emperor Joseph (who had an extremely low opinion of Austria's former ally) accused his sister of flirtatiousness where 'useless' young English people were concerned. A few years later, whether flirtatiously or not, Marie Antoinette certainly relished the spectacle of the young Lord Strathavon, who possessed a famously well-turned pair of legs, dancing the Highland Fling at Versailles. She also danced with 'this charming Scot' herself, presumably something more conventional.*[11]

---

* Subsequently Marquis of Huntly, this spirited Scottish nobleman was still able

More serious and long-lasting relationships were enjoyed by Marie Antoinette with the Prince de Ligne and Count Valentin Esterhazy, respectively twenty years and fifteen years her senior. The Prince's roots were in Belgium but he had come to Vienna at the age of sixteen; his mother was a princess of Salm and his wife – to whom he had been married about the time Marie Antoinette was born – a princess of Liechtenstein. Thoroughly cosmopolitan, he could claim cousinage of sorts not only with the Habsburgs but also with the Kings of France, Prussia and Poland. Such a man, who described himself as feeling 'an Austrian in France [where he had a house in Paris in the rue Jacob] and a Frenchman in Austria', could not fail to appeal to the expatriate Marie Antoinette. Furthermore, for 'elegance of mind and manners', the Prince de Ligne never had an equal, according to Madame Vigée Le Brun.[12]

Count Valentin Esterhazy was of Hungarian origin but he had been brought up in France and had fought well in the Seven Years' War. Madame de la Tour du Pin wrote that the Queen addressed Esterhazy as 'brother' and treated him as friend. The Empress expressed surprise that such a 'whippersnapper' of no particular distinction should be a member of her daughter's circle; her view was coloured by the part that Esterhazy's Hungarian family had played in an uprising against her. But Esterhazy showed himself unselfish as well as a dashing courtier; the Queen rewarded his fidelity by helping to arrange his marriage to a wealthy young heiress, to whom Esterhazy became notably attached. He was also approved by Louis XVI, who wrote him a delightful little note on the arrival of his son: 'A little Hussar has been born,' signed 'A Person at Versailles'.[13]

The Queen's innate chastity, the fact that her virtue was 'intact, even strict' in the words of Emperor Joseph, who kept himself well informed on the subject of his sister's failings, did not

to dance the quadrille when he was seventy and he died in 1853 at the age of ninety-one. As a result of his prowess, he could boast of dancing with Marie Antoinette, Princess Charlotte, the daughter of George IV, and Queen Victoria.

mean that she was without faults. It meant merely that she was without that particular one – sexual promiscuity – that would be generally ascribed to her in the future by those who did not know her. There was beginning to be something desperate about her enjoyment of pleasures, that rapidity with which she turned from one to the other. The levity, the lightness of spirit, the volatility, that quality called by the French *légèreté* for which there is no exact English equivalent, with which Marie Antoinette is so much associated in the popular mind (and in many historians' minds), can be traced back to this period, when disappointment in her marriage began to be masked by enjoyment of her position.[14]

The girlish laughter of her early years in France had not gone away. But as the Prince de Ligne observed, 'the great queens of history' did not laugh. This irreverent spirit – defensive in origin – was not denied by those who admired Marie Antoinette. 'The gaiety of her character led to mockery,' wrote the Comte de La Marck and that was a fault in someone in her position, especially as the people around her pandered to her desire to be amused in this manner. The older women of the court in particular were affronted. Marie Antoinette the *moqueuse* should perhaps have borne in mind the saying of the cynical Marquis de Merteuil in *Les Liaisons Dangereuses*: 'Old women must not be angered for they make young women's reputations.'[15]

Of course the stories became exaggerated, especially in circles where 'the Austrian woman' had not been welcome in the first place. There was a persistent tale of the Queen making fun of the dowagers in their old-fashioned black, come to pay their respects on the accession of the King. According to Madame Campan, the truth was very different. It was the Queen who tried desperately not to laugh, hiding her face behind her fan, at the mischievous behaviour of the old Marquise de Clermont-Tonnerre. Although she should have been standing up, the Marquise actually sat down unseen behind the wide-hooped skirts of the court ladies, twitching them as she indulged in 'indiscreet drollery'. A malicious little verse commemorated the supposed incident:

> You've given offence a-plenty
> Little Queen of only twenty
> You'll go home to Austria
> Fal lal lal, fal lal...[16]

When all was said and done, the Queen was now officially answerable to no one – except the King. For example, Louis agreed readily to the idea of a Rousseau-esque adventure on behalf of the Queen and courtiers to watch the dawn, so long as he personally, devoted to his sleep, did not have to participate. The presence among others of the Comtesse de Noailles, still at this point Mistress of the Household, who stayed close to the Queen's side at all times, was sufficient guarantee of the respectability of this outing. There were also, of course, body-guards present. The Queen, who had got the idea from Mar-montel's *Histoire des Incas*, was ecstatic, exclaiming over and over again: 'How beautiful it is! How truly beautiful!' She said that she now understood why Incas worshipped the sun. This innocent scene, so characteristic of the sensitivities of Marie Antoinette, was transformed into an outright orgy in the first scurrilous pamphlet that was addressed to the Queen personally, *Le Lever d'Aurore*. She was said to have overcome the problem of her ladies' attendance by stealing away into the shrubberies for amorous encounters.[17]

The King was furious; he always reacted chivalrously to insults to his wife. The state censorship common to the eighteenth century meant that a licence was necessary for printing, which was why a great many of the obscene *libelles*, including those of the previous reign against the Du Barry, were printed in Holland and England for clandestine importation. The author, identified as the Abbé Mercier, was imprisoned in the Bastille. But the *libelles* did not cease. The Queen was accused of dalliance in yet another thicket immediately after the coronation, in the so-called *Aventure de la Porte-Neuve*. The continuing need to emphasize the outdoor setting of the Queen's illicit couplings was due to the demonstrably large entourage that generally surrounded her in public. Here the physique and performance of an unknown lover was said to have been greeted with enthusiasm by Marie

Antoinette: 'Prince, lord or simple gentleman, you're Hercules in the form of Adonis.'[18]

The satirical attacks at this point were, however, no more than an unpleasant douche of cold water. Marie Antoinette herself was left with the alternatives of weeping or shrugging them off with laughter that was intended to show disdain. In fact, she did both by turns. Tears were provoked by the sheer unfairness of it all – 'these miserable gazettes', as she termed them to Maria Teresa. She took to singing the refrain of *Les Nouvelles de la Cour*, the obscene attack on the King's potency referred to earlier, in an effort to demonstrate a sophisticated indifference.[19]

For the time being the disdainful mode of reaction prevailed, as though the Queen found it impossible to take these anonymous ambuscades seriously. When Maria Teresa was shocked by the 'inveterate hatred' manifested in such publications against 'the Austrians, my person and my poor innocent Queen', her daughter urged her not to condemn a whole nation for the sins of a few scandalmongers. An important factor in Marie Antoinette's attitude, ironically enough, was her belief that the French people were fundamentally volatile and inclined to express things with 'their pens and their tongues' that were not actually in their hearts. She herself in contrast prided herself on her own German sobriety: 'I shall always glory in being one,' she told her mother and she only wished that the people of 'this country' (*ce pays-ci**) had some of the good German qualities.[20] As the Queen's lack of seriousness became a target of the anonymous *libelles*, she herself thought it was the satirists who were not to be taken seriously. There was the possibility of a dangerous misunderstanding here.

In fact the *libelles* and the gazettes, while inventing freely on the subject of Marie Antoinette's lewd conduct, had more of a case when it came to her extremes of fashion. Maria Teresa waxed indignant when she read about these coiffures. Three feet high, and so many feathers and ribbons! 'A young and pretty

---

* 'This country' was how Marie Antoinette always referred to France in her correspondence with her family.

Queen, full of charms, has no need of these follies,' fulminated the Empress.[21]

But then it could be plausibly argued that one of the duties of the Queen of France – the centre of the world of fashion, which had a strong commercial motive to remain so – was to see that the modes flourished by leading them. The feathers that annoyed the Austrian Empress were made so popular by Marie Antoinette that a lucrative trade sprang up. If Louis XVI gave his wife a jewelled feather (*aigrette*) that was ornamented with diamonds which he already owned, as a hint to put it in her hair instead of real feathers, this was not an option open to every husband. As for the elaborate headdresses, nicknamed *poufs*, these might allude to the wearer's state – a miniature baby and nurse to indicate the recent childbirth of the Duchesse de Chartres, a tiny funeral urn for a widow – or to a current craze such as ballooning, or to political events such as the American Revolution.[22]

It was easy for Maria Teresa to condemn these as ridiculous, from the viewpoint of another country and another generation. To put it at its most practical, Paris was a city dependent on the financial support of the noble and rich to maintain its industries, which were in the main to do with luxury and semi-luxury goods. For foreigners, fashion was part of the point of being in Paris; Thomas Jefferson subscribed to the magazine *Cabinet des Modes* and sent fashion plates back to ladies of his acquaintance in America. As the Baronne d'Oberkirch remarked on her first visit to the French capital, the city would be sunk without its luxurious commerce.[23] In a country where details of appearance, costume and presentation were 'vital matters', as the Savoyard ambassador had observed on the subject of the Comtesse de Provence, Marie Antoinette was an appropriate consort.

It was the personal extravagance of Marie Antoinette that could be criticized rather than her modishness. The Queen's relationship with the imaginative, talented and extremely domineering couturier Rose Bertin was either a magic union or a *folie à deux*, depending on the point of view. It was Mademoiselle Bertin who gave orders to the tailor, receiving back a plain, unadorned shape on which she proceeded to let her fruitful imagination play. Against the spectacle of an exquisitely dressed Queen, her appearance a work of art in itself – French art – must be put in the balance the dress bills that mounted, and the dress allowance that was never ever enough. (Although even here one might point out the vast bills run up with Bertin by the Du Barry in the previous reign – 100,000 livres a year on silks and laces alone.)[24]

The arrogance of Rose Bertin in her shop in the rue de Saint-Honoré became a byword as news of the Queen's custom spread. There was a story of the provincial lady who came to ask for something new for her presentation at Versailles. Bertin surveyed her from top to toe and then with a regal air turned to one of her helpers: 'Show Madame my latest work for Her Majesty.' About eight years older than Marie Antoinette, Bertin was introduced to court circles by the Duchesse de Chartres, and was swiftly nicknamed 'the Minister of Fashion'. Her clients included the Princesse de Lamballe, who spent extremely freely, as well as numerous foreign royalties, with Russian aristocrats particularly plentiful among them.[25]

It has been estimated that the couturier visited the Queen roughly twice a week from the accession onwards, being received in her inner cabinet. In contrast the celebrated hairdresser Léonard only came to Versailles once a week, on Sundays, leaving the daily work to others including his assistant, known as '*le beau* Julian'; but that was because Léonard's salon in Paris in the week was so violently busy, rather than a measure of economy. A lively, good-humoured Gascon, with a sharp wit – and a star's temperament – his triumphal arrival as a coiffeur was described by Madame de Genlis: 'Léonard came, he came and he was king.' As for Bertin, it was not helpful that the dressmaker did not bother to present detailed accounts, as one of Marie Antoinette's Mistresses of the Robes, the Comtesse d'Ossun, complained. However, succeeding Mistresses of the Robes themselves were not always competent accountants, although handling of the royal accounts was supposed to be one of the duties of the position.[26]

By the end of 1776, the Queen, who had a dress allowance

of 150,000 livres, had managed to incur liabilities of nearly 500,000 livres. Six months earlier she had bought a pair of chandelier diamond earrings, partly on credit and partly by exchanging some of her own gems, from the celebrated Swiss jeweller Boehmer. The King paid up 'at her very first word' according to Mercy. Again when she bought a pair of diamond bracelets for 400,000 livres, she had to borrow from the King, who did not complain.*[27]

Of course to complete the picture, it should be pointed out that the entire royal family was prodigiously extravagant, seeing little connection between what they spent and what they had to spend. This included the pious royal aunts, capable of using up 3 million livres in a six-week expedition to Vichy to drink the waters. Then there was the Comte d'Artois, a noted spendthrift who regularly had his debts paid by his elder brother; they soon reached a total of 21 million livres. The Comtesse de Provence, quickly forgetting her modest Savoyard upbringing, also began to spend lavishly. As for the Comte de Provence, he would have debts of 10 million livres paid by Louis XVI in the early 1780s.[28]

Similarly, the Queen's household had managed by immemorial custom to build in fantastic elements of extravagance to their own benefit. Bills were sent in for four new pairs of shoes a week, three yards of ribbon daily to tie the royal peignoir (that is, brand-new ribbon) and two brand-new yards of green taffeta daily to cover the basket in which the royal fan and gloves were carried. And these were only minor items. The 'right to the candles' (candles were replaced even if unused) brought four of her women 50,000 livres a year each. The extraordinary amount of new outfits ordered annually – twelve court dresses, twelve riding habits and so forth and so on – was in part explained by the privileges of her household to help themselves to these garments once discarded but hardly worn. It was typical of the way things were run that a fresh chicken was provided every

* Earrings were chosen to draw attention to the much-praised long neck, and bracelets for the beautiful hands; according to her portraits and accounts, the Queen did not care particularly for necklaces.

night –and subsequently sold by the Queen's servants – because she had on a single occasion happened to ask for some chicken for her dog.[29] Yet for all these extenuating circumstances, the impression given by Marie Antoinette on the eve of the arrival of her brother the Emperor is of someone for whom shopping, like gambling, has become a central compensation.

The passion of the Queen for her new *Jardin Anglais* – the eighteenth-century English style of planting being much less formal than the grand planning of seventeenth-century France – was more imaginative. This garden was to ornament the small palace attached to Versailles, known as the Petit Trianon. She had long wanted a country retreat, something to which she had been accustomed in her youth. The idea that the King should bestow the Trianon upon her was actually the suggestion of the Comte de Noailles, Governor of Versailles and husband of the Mistress of the Household. It was approved by Count Mercy who told the Queen to make the request. Louis XVI readily agreed with the gracious words: 'This pleasure house is yours.' According to another story, he replied even more gallantly that he agreed on the grounds that 'These beautiful places have always been the retreats of the King's favourites.' The order came through on 27 August 1775.[30]

The Queen's taste encompassed the kind of romantic garden that could be created by the designs of the painter Hubert Robert and the royal architect Mique. Tree-planting became a passion.* With gardening in her blood – her father's love of horticulture was a childhood memory – Marie Antoinette plunged herself into creating a sylvan paradise that would perhaps recall the lost Eden of Laxenburg. Her impatience to see its realization, even if it was deplored by her administrators, was an understandable mark of her enthusiasm: 'You know our mistress ... she likes to enjoy her pleasures without delay'.[31]

Contemporaries referred to the Petit Trianon snidely as 'Little Schönbrunn', alternatively as 'Little Vienna'. In later centuries

---

* Many of the trees whose planting was inspired by the Queen were felled in the terrible gale of December 1999 when Versailles lost 2000 trees. They are being replaced in an ambitious restorative scheme.

Marie Antoinette's involvement with her 'pleasure house' would be the subject of misinterpretation on a scale with her alleged reference to cake. It would be suggested, for example, that she had had the palace built herself before plastering it in 'gold and diamonds'. Trianon had in reality been designed and built by Gabriel in the previous reign, and the whole point of its interior was its exquisite simplicity. This desire for simplicity and retreat was in fact the key to the whole enterprise – that and the desire to have something personal to her. Significantly, Marie Antoinette hung family portraits in her boudoir there, including one of her father in a Franciscan habit, and one of her aunt Charlotte of Lorraine in similar religious attire.[32]

Of course it was easy afterwards to contrast these expensive activities (not only those of the Queen, although hers were inevitably more visible) with a worsening financial situation. The Controller General Turgot was dismissed in May 1776, as the King and the other ministers increasingly resented the reforms which seemed to represent a usurpation of the royal authority. Although Marie Antoinette was in favour of his dismissal because of Turgot's attack on her protégé Guines, the will was that of Vergennes and the King.

Turgot was also disinclined to support French participation in the American struggle for independence. This intervention in America was the brainchild of Vergennes, who viewed it in terms of traditional French hostility to England: what hurt England (that is, an American revolt) helped France. Louis XVI's agreement was not secured without some heart-searching on the subject of rebellion and monarchy; was it really right to go to the assistance of those who were rejecting their sovereign, King George III? In the end he submitted to Vergennes' desire, although years later he would complain that the minister had taken advantage of his youth.[33]

The fact was that the hideous expense of despatching thousands of French troops and ships to fight in the New World plunged the government still further into the giddy spiral of deficit, just as Turgot had predicted. The incoming financial minister, Jacques Necker, hoped to pay for the war by ambitious borrowing schemes. Even if Mercy clucked over Marie Antoinette's acquisition of further diamonds 'in these circumstances', the fact was that the personal extravagance of the Queen of France was of very little monetary consequence compared to this vast American venture, masterminded by Vergennes.

The Emperor Joseph finally arrived in France on his mission to save the royal marriage on 18 April 1777. He came at a time when the Queen's personal credit had recently been weakened still further. Louis XVI sided with the Governess to the Children of France during his youth, the Comtesse de Marsan, against his wife over a court appointment. It was a question of the Prince de Rohan, who had finally been edged out of his ambassadorial role in Vienna to the delight of Maria Teresa. Of his return to France, Marie Antoinette observed with a certain prescience to her mother: 'If he behaves himself as he has done in the past, the result will be plenty of intrigues here.' It was the intention of Rohan to claim that position – Grand Almoner – to which family custom entitled him, when the present incumbent died. It was, however, an intimate post, involving constant attendance on the King (and Queen) at family ecclesiastical functions. Marie Antoinette, furious about the tales that Rohan had told in Vienna, including his relaying of the contents of the pamphlet *Le Lever d'Aurore*, saw no reason why he should be rewarded. On the other hand, the Comtesse de Marsan, as the Prince's aunt, claimed that the appointment had long been promised on the word of the King. Louis protested feebly to his former Governess that he had also given his word to the Queen that it would not take place. 'Your Majesty cannot have two words,' riposted the Comtesse and hinted that if thwarted, she would publicize the King's unfair favouring of the Queen.[34]

In the end, as so often, it was the Queen who was defeated. Nevertheless she assured her mother that the 'bad principles' and 'dangerous intrigues' of Rohan would ensure that she personally ostracized him.[35] The cut-off was to be as far as possible complete. Rohan would only see the King at his *lever*, to which he had the Rights of Entry, and at Mass, where Rohan had a professional role. The Queen's stance over Rohan was one of those seemingly minor decisions, born of hurt pride, perhaps a little provocative towards the Rohan interest but understandable enough, that were to have momentous consequences.

Marie Antoinette was apprehensive about her brother's arrival. On the one hand she longed for this contact with home, particularly from the 'august' elder brother she 'tenderly loved', in Mercy's words. There had been no further family visit since the disastrous visit of 'the Arch fool' two years previously, and Maria Teresa's occasional promise – or threat – to arrive in Flanders, close enough for a visit from France, had not materialized. On the other hand, the Emperor, now thirty-six, had a scornful, even brutal style when he chose and had already weighed in with his own critical letters. Mercy told Maria Teresa apropos of the imperial visit that the Queen of France was afraid of being scolded.[36]

The Emperor, or rather 'Count Falkenstein', the incognito name under which he travelled, arrived wearing plain grey and was sporting none of his many Orders. It was pouring with rain. In an open carriage, without an escort, Joseph was soaked to the skin. He did not complain. The next day he set off in similarly unadorned style for Versailles. Count Mercy, his ambassador, could not, however, accompany him as protocol demanded; the unfortunate Mercy was laid low with an attack of haemorrhoids, whose severity became a general talking-point. As a result his house in Paris was besieged by people come to suggest the most diverse remedies; these included a messenger from the Abbess of Panthémont, a sufferer for the last ten years, recommending pills and pomade on the one hand, the avoidance of agonizing coach journeys on the other. She would confide still more if a person of discretion came to visit her in person.[37]

The absence of Count Mercy had the effect of underlining the intimacy that King, Queen and 'Count Falkenstein' now enjoyed for the next six weeks. It was true that Joseph insisted on being lodged in a hostelry in the town of Versailles, where he slept on a wolf skin. Rising early on the first morning, he visited the menagerie before 8 a.m. and admired a female elephant. Later in the day the Emperor commented jovially to the Duc de Cröy that since there was a male elephant in the Austrian menagerie, 'we could make a marriage'. Cröy resisted the temptation to point out that there could be another more important match. The Emperor had remained unmarried since the death of his second wife Josepha; there were rumours (as it happened, unfounded) of the Emperor's interest in the thirteen-year-old Madame Elisabeth as a third wife.[38]

Joseph II's determination not to be involved in the time-wasting and costly rituals of Versailles meant that he was able to enjoy the best of the informal life of the Queen – and the King. His relationship with the Queen began with a long, wordless embrace. Thereafter, on 22 April, she took him for a walk alone in the gardens of the Petit Trianon, having dined with merely two ladies in attendance. Marie Antoinette then received her first lecture, the topics of which included the unsuitability of her friends and her mad passion for gambling, as well as her neglect of the King.

In many respects the Emperor did not abrogate the natural harshness of his tone. His savage mockery of the Queen's use of rouge was intended to show his total contempt for the Versailles way of life: 'A little more!' he exclaimed sarcastically. 'Go on, put it under the eyes and the nose, you can look like one of the Furies if you try.' His reaction to one of the Queen's towering headdresses showed more wit. The Emperor told his sister drily that he thought the fabulous plumed creation 'too light to bear the burden of a crown'.[39]

What made all this endurable from the point of view of Marie Antoinette was the genuine warmth that Joseph demonstrated towards her, a warmth lacking perhaps from the maternal relationship. As Mercy told the Empress, Joseph had struck the right note to get the Queen to promise amendment. Given the fifteen-year gap in their ages, it was an attitude that was quasi-paternal, quasi-amorous. To the Emperor, who no longer had a daughter – or any child – living, she was 'my dear and charming Queen' and 'my little sister'. But the long-widowed Emperor also said jokingly that if Marie Antoinette had not been his sister, he would have liked to have married her in order to have the 'pleasure of her company'. In a confidence, Joseph revealed that he had forgotten how sweet existence could be until he entered his sister's life again.[40]

The fact was that Joseph, unlike Maria Teresa, was thoroughly captivated by Marie Antoinette. A few years later she had become 'this sister, who is the woman I love best in the world'. It was a fact acknowledged by another sister, Maria Carolina, after he had visited her in 1784: 'He spoke about you with such tenderness that we have great reason to be jealous of you, because without flattery I believe that you are his darling.' Of course this only proved his good taste, added the Queen of Naples hastily.[41]

The Emperor's reports at the time to his brother, the Archduke Leopold in Tuscany, were more outspoken. He began by describing their sister as a delightful young woman who had not yet found her proper role. Many of her pleasures were in fact perfectly appropriate, but dangerous insofar as they distracted her from the sober reflections in which she badly needed to indulge. After studying Marie Antoinette he came to the conclusion that she was good-natured and honest, a little thoughtless due to her age, but fundamentally a decent, virtuous person. She was also intelligent with good instincts, so long as she trusted them, and did not listen to the advisors who were her weakness because they preyed on her love of amusement.[42] The Emperor meant the Polignac set.

The 'Reflections' that the Emperor left behind with his sister, written the day before he departed on 31 May, were on the contrary extremely tough, like his mockery of her fashionable appearance. 'What are you doing here in France,' wrote the Emperor, 'by what right should one respect you, honour you, except as the companion of their King?' He went on to list all her faults extensively and unsparingly, beginning with her lack of 'tenderness and pliancy' towards her husband when in his presence. Did she not show herself 'cold, bored, even disgusted'? There was her attendance at opera balls in Paris or race meetings in the Bois in place of a solid programme of serious reading. On and on went the Emperor, culminating with the following: 'It is time – more than time – to reflect and construct a better way of life. You are getting older and you no longer have the excuse of youth. [She was twenty-one.] What will become of you? An unhappy woman and still more unhappy princess.'[43]

The reason the Queen accepted all of this gratefully, reading and rereading the 'Reflections', was because she now believed – and would continue to believe – that she enjoyed the protection and understanding of her brother. Quite as important as the criticisms made by the Emperor of his sister, and in many ways more so, were the intimate lectures given to Louis XVI. On arrival Joseph had judged Louis as 'rather weak but no imbecile', but unfortunately there was 'something apathetic about both his body and his mind'.[44] He set out to remedy this in the most candid manner. On 24 May the King's *Journal* recorded: 'Walked alone on foot with Emperor.' Five days later there was another walk, just the two of them.[45] Whatever the Emperor said to his brother-in-law on these two crucial occasions can only be deduced, but it is clear that he broke to him not so much the 'Facts of Life' as the 'Facts of a King's Life'.

In the end it was not in fact a case of phimosis, the overtight foreskin mocked by *Les Nouvelles de la Cour*. Even if that had been a factor contributing to the King's psychological disinclination to complete the sexual act, it need not continue to do so. In the latter half of 1775 there had in fact been considerable discussion of the possibility of an operation, as Marie Antoinette reported to her mother, the birth of the Duc d'Angoulême in August no doubt contributing to the urgency. But by 15 December she confided to Maria Teresa: 'I doubt very much that the King will decide to undergo it [the operation].' The new Savoyard ambassador, the Comte de Viry, heard similarly of the King's reluctance. Marie-Antoinette reported that the doctors disagreed, hers being in favour, and the King's own doctor – 'an old blatherer' – opposing it on the grounds that it would do as much harm as good. In the meantime she would hold her peace on the subject.[46]

In January 1776, Moreau, a surgeon of the Hôtel-Dieu hospital, was pronouncing the operation unnecessary and a few months later Marie Antoinette was increasingly sure that the surgeon was right. One year later, on the eve of the arrival of the Emperor, the Prussian envoy, Baron Goltz, heard that the King had definitely declined to undergo the operation, either because of the possible harmful consequences or because he had become indifferent to the whole matter.[47] Once again the birth of the Duc d'Angoulême made the problem of the succession less urgent from the purely Bourbon point of view, while remaining just as crucial to the Habsburg interest.

So there never was an operation.* Joseph II described the true situation in graphic terms to his brother Archduke Leopold: 'Imagine, in his marriage bed – this is the secret – he has strong, perfectly satisfactory erections; he introduces the member, stays there without moving for about two minutes, withdraws without ejaculating but still erect, and bids goodnight. It's incredible because he sometimes has night-time emissions; it is only when he is actually inside and going at it, that it never happens. Nevertheless the King is satisfied with what he does.' As Louis XVI confessed to the Emperor, all this was done in the name of duty, never for pleasure.

'Oh if only I could have been there!' wrote the Emperor furiously to the Archduke. 'I could have seen to it. The King of France would have been whipped so that he would have ejaculated out of sheer rage like a donkey.' Joseph concluded with a reflection on his sister's lack of 'temperament' in this respect, meaning lack of sexual appetite leading to lack of sexual initiative. It underpinned her virtue in which from personal observation he strongly believed; it was a virtue that arose 'less from forethought than an inborn indisposition' towards it. The King and Queen of France were 'two complete blunderers'. In short, there was nothing wrong with Louis XVI, other than laziness, apathy, and the inevitable consequences of this situation being 'ill handled'.[48]

It was in this way, thanks to the outspoken orders of the Emperor, that Louis XVI did at last stop being 'two thirds of

---

* A fact confirmed in a negative sense by the detailed record of the King's unremitting hunting activities in his *Journal*. A painful operation of this sort (anaesthetics not being available) would have involved several weeks' convalescence out of the saddle at the very least; but there is no such cessation.

a husband' to Marie Antoinette, seven years and three months after their marriage. The crucial nature of the Emperor's intervention in this sensitive but hitherto insoluble matter was made clear by the fact that both King and Queen subsequently wrote to the Emperor thanking him and 'attributing it', the consummation, to his advice. The King also wrote again in December 1777. As the Emperor told Leopold, this advice had been quite basic.[49]

What the Emperor called 'the great work' was accomplished shortly before the King's twenty-third birthday. On 30 August, no longer an unhappy woman, an ecstatic Queen was able to write to her mother about her feelings of joy – 'the most essential happiness of my entire life' – beginning eight days ago. This 'proof' of the King's love had now been repeated and 'even more completely than the first time'. There is something touching about Marie Antoinette's first instinct, which had been to send a special courier to her mother; she had held back first for reasons of security and then to make absolutely sure.[50]

Nothing was now so threatening, not even the third pregnancy of the Comtesse d'Artois in two and a half years. The Queen had in mind a Temple of Love to be built in the grounds of the Petit Trianon. Under the circumstances, the Temple seemed a happy augury of the future, rather than the unhappy reminder it might once have been.

CHAPTER ELEVEN

You Shall Be Mine...

'You shall be mine; you shall have my undivided care;
you will share all my happinesses and you will alleviate
my sufferings...'

Marie Antoinette, quoted by Madame Campan,
19 December 1778

The death of the fifty-year-old Elector Maximilian Joseph
of Bavaria on 30 December 1777 produced a crisis in
Europe. At the same season, encouraged by the American
victory over the English at Saratoga, Louis XVI assured the
deputies from the new 'United States' of America of his 'affection
and interest' in their case. France concluded an offensive and
defensive alliance with the United States in the following February.[1] This ensured another crisis – between France and
England. Cries of joy from the French courtiers greeted the
news of the American alliance when it was broken to them by
the Comte de Provence, fresh from the King's Council, at a
pre-Lenten *bal à la Reine*. The merry days of Anglo-French
junketing at the court level were for the time being in abeyance,
in favour of the hereditary rivalry last expressed during the
Seven Years' War.

It was, however, the Bavarian crisis that confronted Marie
Antoinette with her first real political test. At the time of the
Polish Partition in 1772, she had merely been the Dauphine,
and the potential conflict had in any case been settled by the
compliance of Louis XV with Austria. Now the Habsburg
'sleeper' was to be animated more vigorously in the interests of

that alliance made so long ago, of which she was the visible pledge. All this occurred at the same time as the Queen's newly fulfilled married life proceeded, with hopes of pregnancy, even if these were dashed on a regular monthly basis. For example, on 15 January 1778 Marie Antoinette felt it necessary to explain to her mother how 'ashamed and upset' she felt at the recurrence of her 'indisposition'.[2] Yet the royal couple were undoubtedly drawing closer together. Even the birth of a second son to the Comtesse d'Artois on 24 January, created Duc de Berry, was no longer the humiliation it might once have been.

The trouble was that, politically at least, the question of the Bavarian succession, far from uniting King and Queen further, pushed them apart. Since the Bavarian Elector was childless, this crisis had in a sense been brewing for some time, although his apparently vigorous health meant that the actual event took everyone by surprise. His heir was a comparatively remote cousin, the Elector Charles Theodore of the Palatine, and Joseph II had already begun to negotiate with this Elector in order to secure Bavarian territory, possibly in exchange for Austrian territory in Belgium. The Emperor also brought into play the claim to certain lands of his late wife the Empress Josepha, who had been a Bavarian princess; he argued that this claim had passed to him.[3]

This acquisitive tendency of Joseph II had been deplored by Vergennes for several years past. Both by temperament and through instruction, his master Louis XVI fully agreed with him. The alliance that linked France so closely to Austria did not oblige her 'to share the ambitious and unjust element' in the Austrian Emperor's plans. What, for example, would be the reaction of Frederick II of Prussia and the Elector of Saxony to any bad-neighbourly aggression on their own frontiers? For it was obviously the Emperor's intention to build up his own power bloc at the expense of these two countries. The reputation of France in Germany, as opposed to Austria, could not be simply ignored.[4]

The matter was certainly delicate, not only at Versailles but in Vienna. On the one hand Vergennes was concerned about the prospect of Austria turning to England if totally rebuffed by her ally; France could then be threatened by both land and sea. On the other hand the Empress Maria Teresa herself was extremely worried about her son's militaristic intentions. The Bavarian claim, she felt with justice, was weak, and she protested that 'a universal conflagration' was a heavy price to pay for 'a particular convenience'. The Empress also had her own agenda, thanks to the 'great ascendant' that her daughter, the forceful Archduchess Marie Christine, had over her. As the wife of a Saxon prince who was loyal in the service of Austria, Marie Christine thoroughly disliked the idea of her husband having to fight against his own native country of origin – and his own blood relations. The Empress's beloved 'Mimi' did not let up on her entreaties to her mother, using tears in public while she worked actively behind the scenes. As a result, relations between Marie Christine and her brother Joseph, never good, deteriorated further.[5]

On 15 January 1778 the Emperor took action. He ordered 15,000 Austrian troops into Lower Bavaria. At roughly the same moment, the Queen of France was writing to her brother, boasting of her reformed way of life, which she thought was sure to delight him. For example, she was dancing so much less at Versailles that there was a rumour that she had lost her enthusiasm for the pastime altogether. Under the circumstances, she felt able to point out that it would be 'a great piece of good fortune', above all for her, if the 'Bavarian affair' was settled peacefully.[6]

Unfortunately this was not to be the case. Predictably Frederick II threatened his own invasion – of Bohemia – if Joseph II did not immediately quit Bavaria. The conflagration dreaded by the Empress was building and would shortly break out. But was it necessarily to be a universal one? Would France actually send troops in support of Austria? Coached by Count Mercy, Marie Antoinette pleaded with her husband to carry out his obligations under the treaty.

The mission was not a success. The Queen was reported to have spoken 'heatedly' to the King. Equally, she let her tears flow, but to no avail. Louis XVI's line was to refer to 'the ambition of your relations', which he said was upsetting the whole of Europe; first Poland, now Bavaria. This 'dis-membership' of Bavaria was certainly being done against the will of the French King. As to the alliance, France took the line that there was no obligation in the terms of the treaty to come to the aid of territories only recently annexed to Austria.[7]

When the French ambassador delivered this message to Prince Kaunitz in Vienna, the Austrian statesman exploded with rage. On 3 March Marie Antoinette was similarly reported to have been extremely bad-tempered on the whole subject, asking – in vain – for the removal of Vergennes.[8] Her ill-humour was comprehensible. First, the real limits of her influence had been exposed. To be seen as manipulative in politics was not a good thing, but to be seen as unsuccessfully manipulative was even worse. Second, she had allowed herself to be branded publicly as pro-Austrian and anti-French.

It was at this moment that Providence, so long neglectful of her interests, came at last to the rescue of Marie Antoinette. Part of the Queen's bad temper on 3 March may have been privately attributable to the arrival of her period, yet another 'indisposition' that had to be explained away in apologetic terms to her mother.* It was three days early, while that of February had been six days in advance. The beginning of April, however, came and went without the appearance of the dreaded Générale. By 11 April the Queen suspected – unimaginable joy – that she might actually be pregnant. Eight days later she dared to write to the Empress with the caveat that nothing was yet certain, and would not be so until the beginning of the next month. Nevertheless she hastened to assure her mother of her excellent health: she was eating well, sleeping well, all better than before – and of course absolutely no journeys by carriage; her expeditions were now limited to little promenades on foot.[10]

The rest of the letter consisted of an account of her interview with the errant ministers, Maurepas and Vergennes, whom she had summoned to her presence, apparently at the insistence of Mercy. 'I spoke to them rather strongly,' the Queen wrote

* This was the occasion when the services of Gluck, returning to Vienna, were used to break the annoying news.[9]

proudly, 'and I think I made an impression on them, especially Vergennes.' She was proposing to hold forth again on this subject in the presence of Louis XVI. For all these boasts, the ministers had not actually given way on the subject of French troops in support of Austria and neither did the King. He remained as lukewarm as possible without actually breaking the alliance. Nevertheless the possibility of an heir at long last shored up the Queen's position. Naturally a boy was expected, at least if Maria Teresa was anyone to go by, who promised that on the Feast of St Antony (her daughter's name-day) the saint would be 'tormented' with her prayers on the subject.[11]

The method chosen to break the news to the public was characteristic of Marie Antoinette. In mid-May, the Queen asked the King for 12,000 francs to send to the relief of those in the debtors' jail of Paris – but these were not to be random debtors; they were to be those languishing in jail for failing to pay their children's wet-nurses, as well as the poor of Versailles. 'Thus I gave to charity and at the same time notified the people of my condition,' wrote Marie Antoinette.[12] Unfortunately this neat display of compassion did her no good with the satirical pamphleteers. Having made merry at the expense of the King's impotence, they were not likely to give up their scatological trade now that the condition was seemingly cured. Various fathers were suggested for the coming baby, most prominently the Duc de Coigny and, most unpleasantly, the Comte d'Artois. It is very likely that the Comte de Provence and other courtiers had at least some clandestine connection to these effusions, or at any rate read them and disseminated them. In contrast to that, the pregnancy itself went forward healthily, and the Queen was able, in the flush of her happiness, to maintain her studied indifference to these manifestations.

On 16 May 1778 Dr Lassonne made an examination of the Queen and pronounced himself satisfied.* At the same time the

---

* It would seem that the baby had been conceived on roughly the date when Benjamin Franklin was officially received at Versailles, as one of the accredited envoys of the United States. In contrast to the French custom, Franklin wore

Queen interviewed the future *accoucheur*, the brother of the Abbé de Vermond. She rejected, perhaps understandably, Sieur Levret who had been *accoucheur* to the Comtesse d'Artois; nevertheless the choice of Vermond was criticized at the time since he was felt to be more interested in his fees than his patient. For all these practical preparations, including the choice of wet-nurse, swaddling clothes and an apartment for the new baby on the ground floor of Versailles to benefit from the air, Marie Antoinette herself admitted touchingly that there were 'moments when I think it all a dream'. She had, after all, 'lived for so long without hoping to be so happy as to bear a child'. However, she wrote,' 'the dream continues...'[13]

By the end of May Marie Antoinette declared that she was getting 'amazingly fat' and the following month boasted that she had put on over four inches, mainly on her hips. By mid-August she was pronounced much bigger than was usual at five months. That summer was intensely hot and Madame Campan described how the Queen found relief walking in the cool of the night air, for she kept up her daily promenades as she had promised Maria Teresa she would. Rose Bertin and other couturiers responded to the new situation with gauzy flowing silk garments known as *Lévites* in the light cool colours the Queen loved: pale blue, turquoise and soft yellow. (The name was taken from the costumes worn by the actresses playing Jewish priests in Racine's *Athalie*.) It was a sign of the growing intimacy between Marie Antoinette and Rose Bertin that the latter was paid to make a special expedition to her native Abbeville; there she prayed at the local shrine of the Virgin on her mistress's behalf.[14]

The hairdresser Léonard had to cope with the changing situation too. The wonderful thick hair that Marie Antoinette had once enjoyed was turning into problem hair. In the autumn of 1776 – a time of depression over her relationship with the King – her hair had reportedly fallen out, or at least thinned dramatically, according to an English lady at the French court.[15] Daily coiffeuring, pomading, and powdering, and now pregnancy,

neither sword nor powdered wig. Perhaps the King found this first contact with the virile New World inspirational.

did not help. Yet in general the Queen's health remained good throughout the long autumn.

She was bled once or twice, according to custom, although her delicate veins meant that it was not a great success. The Queen was also given iron. The waiting period was naturally punctuated by communications from Maria Teresa, who had already been appointed godmother well in advance, with King Charles III of Spain as the godfather. This meant that the Empress would have the privilege of naming the child, also well in advance, since royal baptisms were held immediately after the birth. A Bourbon baby prince would obviously have some variation on the theme of Louis. An unwelcome girl would certainly be called the French version of her famous grand-mother's name, since the Empress required all her first-born granddaughters to be named in her honour.*[16]

Social life and entertaining according to the prescribed pattern did not cease although there were some restrictions. One sufferer from this was the musical prodigy whom Marie Antoinette had last encountered as a child in Vienna. Now aged twenty-two, Wolfgang Amadeus Mozart had arrived in Paris in late March 1778 accompanied by his mother, who, given the Habsburg connection, hoped for 'a letter of introduction from someone in Vienna to the Queen'. But the coincidence of Marie Antoinette's first pregnancy meant that Mozart was unable to secure her patronage as he might otherwise have done. A separate offer of employment as organist at Versailles was rejected as unworthy despite Leopold Mozart's emphatic advice that an appointment of this kind would be the surest way to win 'the protection of the Queen'.[18]

Mozart departed from France in late September having got no nearer Marie Antoinette herself than the household of her favourite, the Duc de Guines, where he gave lessons to the untalented daughter. As the French argued over the respective merits of the rival composers Gluck and Piccinni in a frenetic cultural battle, Mozart denounced their musicality in patriotic

* This meant that there would in the end be a grand total of six princesses in various countries named Maria Teresa.[17]

terms, which echoed the sentiments of Gluck five years earlier. Where music was concerned, the French 'are and always will be asses', he wrote on 9 July, 'and as they can do nothing for themselves, they are obliged to have recourse to foreigners'.[19]

The senior foreigner, Gluck, the Queen's former teacher, old friend and protégé all in one, fared better. His operas continued to be supported unfalteringly by Marie Antoinette. Even her enthusiasm could not make *Alceste* and *Armide* of 1776 and 1777 respectively such rapid popular successes as their predecessors *Iphigénie en Aulide* and *Orphée*. But she took a detailed interest in Gluck's creations and whenever he was in France, it was remarked how the Queen instantly admitted him to her company, chattering away 'in the most lively fashion'. Since Gluck (back in Vienna) projected a new opera, *Iphigénie en Tauride*, it was thought that his return to Paris would solace the Queen in her last months of pregnancy. Here the awkward diplomatic situation between France and Austria ruled out a direct request from the French Queen in the interests of her own amusement.

Fortunately the Empress now thought of her daughter's amusement as a legitimate concern 'especially if a Dauphin came into the world'. Gluck received permission to return on 1 November 1778. He was once more in the orbit of France 'of which Your Majesty [Marie Antoinette] is both ornament and joy ... a sensitive and enlightened Princess, who loves and protects all the arts ... applauds them all and carefully distinguishes them'. These were the words of his formal dedication of *Iphigénie en Tauride* to the French Queen the following year.[20]

Two episodes that occurred at court as the Queen became increasingly weighed down by her pregnancy presaged the extremes of loyalty and disloyalty to which Marie Antoinette would one day be subject. On 25 August, the Queen saw a handsome face that she recognized among the crowd being presented to her. Count Fersen, last seen four and a half years ago at the end of the reign of the old King, had recently returned to France from Sweden. He had failed to persuade his English heiress to marry him; she did not care to leave her family for a foreign country. Fortunately love had not been involved, merely the suitability of the match in worldly terms. Fersen was now determined to pursue a military career instead. As he told his father, 'I am young and I still have a great deal to learn.' Fersen did not bother to record this royal meeting in his *Journal intime*, but he did mention it in a letter home. The day he was at Versailles to be presented, 'The Queen, who is charming, exclaimed when she saw me: "*Ah, it's an old acquaintance!*" The rest of the royal family did not speak a word to me.' In his letter, Fersen underlined the Queen's spontaneous and gratifying reaction.[21]

On 8 September he returned to the subject of the Queen in a further letter to his father. Marie Antoinette was declared to be 'the prettiest and most delightful princess that I know' and she was taking a real interest in him. She enquired, for example, why he did not turn up at her regular Sunday salons for cards and entertainment. On hearing that Fersen had done so, but had found no salon that particular Sunday, the Queen expressed her apologies. The evidence of Marie Antoinette's immediate predilection for Fersen in 1778 is clear – another gallant and good-looking foreigner to add to her circle. Fersen's admiration for her, openly related to his father, is similarly unabashed. But his concluding sentence on the subject points eloquently to the Queen's real preoccupation at this time: 'Her pregnancy advances and her condition is extremely visible.'*[22]

The return of Philippe d'Orléans, Duc de Chartres, from the naval campaign against the English off the coast of France was a less happy affair. The Battle of Ouessant, in which he had had an official position, was hailed as a French victory. The Duc de Chartres rode to Versailles, arriving at 2 a.m. on 2 August, and had to wait for the King's *lever* the next morning to break the news. He then travelled on to Paris where the Palais-Royal, the family's official Parisian residence, was filled with rejoicing multitudes, before appearing at the opera to a hero's welcome.

After that, things got worse. It turned out that the Duc de Chartres was not exactly the hero of the occasion that he

* It has been suggested (yet again as in 1774) that there was a *coup de foudre* between the pair on this occasion, ignoring the fact that the Queen was going on for six months' pregnant.

purported to be. There were accusations of cowardice, alternatively incompetence. His culpability is open to question. Was
he in fact a coward? Over-promoted, thanks to his royal rank,
did he mistake the naval signals during the battle through
ignorance? Philippe's frivolous insistence on leaving the scene
of the battle for the rapturous Parisian welcome of his dreams
was less easy to defend. The satirists went quickly to work:

> What! You have seen the smoke!
> What a prodigious achievement...
> It is absolutely right
> That you should be an august sight
> At the opera.[23]

A few months later the Duc de Chartres was ogling various
beauties at a ball, when he designated the looks of one particular
noble lady as 'faded'. The lady in question overheard him. 'Like
your reputation, Monseigneur,' was her curt retort. As if this
was not enough, the heir to the Orléans dukedom allowed
himself with characteristic lack of judgement to be involved in
a squalid intrigue to do with ministers and corruption. Humiliated, the old Duc d'Orléans pleaded for his son. But Louis
XVI, who – unlike his wife – had never enjoyed the company
of this light-hearted, dashing cousin, banished Philippe from
court for a month. The Queen, feeling that her personal position
was too vulnerable in view of the Austrian démarche, detached
herself from his cause.[24] The estrangement of the main Bourbon
line and that of Orléans began to take root.

The Queen's *douleurs*, the expressive French phrase for labour
pains, began very early in the morning of 19 December 1778.
Marie Antoinette had gone to bed at eleven o'clock without any
sign that the baby was starting. Shortly after midnight she felt
the first pains and rang her bell at 1.30 a.m. As Superintendent
of the Household, the Princesse de Lamballe had the right to
be told immediately, as did those who enjoyed the 'honours', in
other words the privilege of being present. At three o'clock the
Prince de Chimay came to fetch the King.

Never was the etiquette of Versailles held to be so vital. It was the duty of the Princesse de Lamballe personally to tell members of the royal family and the Princes and Princesses of the Blood who were at Versailles. She then sent pages to inform the Duc d'Orléans who was at his nearby palace of Saint Cloud with the Duchesse de Bourbon and the Princesse de Conti. The Duc de Chartres (still sulking), the Duc de Bourbon and the Prince de Conti were all in Paris.

At the same time as these measured steps were being taken, there was another totally disorganized rush in the direction of the Queen's apartments from the moment the cry of the royal *accoucheur* was heard: 'The Queen has gone into labour.' These avid sightseers – for that is what they were – were mainly confined to outer rooms such as the gallery, but in the general pandemonium, several got through to the inner rooms, including a couple of Savoyards, who were discovered perched aloft in order to get a really good view.[25]

The Queen was still able to walk about until about eight o'clock in the morning when she finally took to the small white delivery bed in her room. Around her, besides the King, were the royal family, the Princes and Princesses of the Blood, and those with the 'honours' including Yolande de Polignac. In the Grand Cabinet were members of her household, the King's household and those who had the Rights of Entry. Throughout the labour, Louis XVI remained helpfully practical. It was he, for example, who insisted on the immense tapestry screens that surrounded the bed being fastened with ropes; otherwise they might well have fallen down on the hapless Queen.

The baby was born just before 11.30 a.m. It was a tiny Maria Teresa, in other words a daughter.

The position of the Comte d'Artois, proud father of two sons, the Ducs d'Angoulême and de Berry, was still unchallenged in a country where females could not succeed. From the point of view of the Comte de Provence, still the heir presumptive to his brother's throne, things had also turned out well. His continuing status was acknowledged by the fact that the grand title of 'Madame', borne by his wife, was not removed from her in favour of the newborn princess, even though the latter was the daughter of the reigning monarch.[26] The baby, given the names Marie Thérèse Charlotte (for both her godparents), was to be Madame Fille du Roi, or by the time she was five years old, Madame Royale.

Was the King disappointed? Much later the girl-child born that day happened to ask her father the age of the new King of Sweden. Louis XVI replied that he knew exactly the date of his birth because it was when they had all been awaiting her mother's *accouchement*. Louis XVI had proceeded to warn Marie Antoinette to prepare herself for a girl, 'because two Kings would not have two sons in the same month'. Marie Thérèse could not resist asking with great respect whether her father regretted her birth. Naturally the King assured her he did not, and embraced her while the watching courtiers wept with emotion and Marie Thérèse herself also burst into tears. Thirteen years later, this was surely true, the trauma having long faded as with most parents whose first child is not the desired sex. At the time his *Journal* recorded no disappointment – only his attendance at the ceremony of the swaddling up of his infant daughter in the Grand Cabinet next door – but then his personal feelings were almost entirely absent from his diary.[27] After that Madame Fille du Roi was handed to the Princesse de Guéméné, who had the right to the post of Governess to the Children of France.

As for the Queen, she had had a convulsive fit and fainted. The press of people, the heat and the lack of fresh air in the rooms, whose windows had been sealed up for months against the winter cold, was too much for her after her twelve-hour labour. She may also have been physically damaged by the birth and have haemorrhaged as a result, her *accoucheur* having been chosen more for his connections than his skill. The Marquis de Bombelles, via his courtier mother-in-law and wife, heard that the Queen had been 'wounded' in the course of her labour, and Maria Teresa, learning of some 'terrible accident', even believed in her paranoid way that it had been done on purpose to stop her daughter having more children.[28]

For a while nobody seems to have noticed her swoon, in a scene so crowded and noisy that in the words of Madame Campan, 'anyone might have fancied himself in a place of public entertainment'. When the Queen's inanimate condition was eventually registered, some strong men tore down the nailed-up shutters and winter air streamed into the room, saving her.*

Thanks to this mishap, the Queen was not informed of the sex of her child for at least an hour and a quarter after Marie Thérèse's birth. When she heard, she wept – or so the relatives of the Duc de Cröy told him. These tears were, however, likely to have been a reaction to her labour and the general intensity of emotion at having produced a living child, especially when silence had originally caused her to think the baby was born dead. Her first reported words on the subject were touching in their unconscious reflection on the fate of a princess in a patriarchal society: 'Poor little girl, you are not what was desired, but you are no less dear to me on that account. A son would have been the property of the state. You shall be mine; you shall have my undivided care; you will share all my happinesses and you will alleviate my sufferings...'[30]

As to the real implications of the child's gender – the need to try again as soon as possible – they were summed up for the Queen and many others in a popular little rhyme:

> A Dauphin we asked of our Queen,
> A Princess announces him near;
> Since one of the Graces is seen
> Young Cupid will quickly appear.

Certainly for Marie Antoinette, with her lifelong passion for children in practice as well as in theory, the birth of a daughter who was exceptionally robust and healthy was not the straight-forward 'domestic misfortune' it was rated in Vienna. It was the Prince de Lambesc, son of the Comtesse de Brionne, who was despatched to Austria to make the official announcement on behalf of the King of France. By etiquette, Count Mercy's

---

* It was not actually Louis XVI who performed this Herculean act, as is sometimes suggested, although he certainly possessed the physical strength. His own *Journal* does not relate the incident, making it clear, as Mercy confirmed to the Empress, that he had already left the chamber of the birth, accompanying his infant daughter.[29]

own messenger was supposed to follow forty-eight hours later (although Mercy managed to cut that delay in half). Marie Antoinette had wanted to scribble a few lines in pencil to her mother but was stopped on the grounds that the Empress would be worried by the thought of her daughter's unnecessary effort at such a critical moment.[31]

The Queen was not present at her child's instant baptism. Thus Marie Antoinette was spared the incident when the malicious Comte de Provence protested to the officiating Archbishop that 'the name and quality' of the parents had not been formally given, according to the usual rite of a christening. Under the mask of concern about correct procedure, the Comte was making an impertinent allusion to the allegations about the baby's paternity made in the *libelles*. The allusion was certainly not lost on the courtiers present. In Paris, the Duc de Chartres mounted a different sort of protest by decorating the Palais-Royal with an extremely modest set of illuminations; this meanness was attributed by the crowds to his continued state of dudgeon with the King and Queen. Marie Antoinette, more easily able to overlook such insults because she did not hear or see them herself, concentrated on celebrating her daughter's birth with donations to appropriate charities. She asked the King for 5000 livres to be used as dowries for one hundred 'poor and virtuous' girls who were marrying 'honest' workmen.[32]

The Queen stayed in bed for eighteen days, her ladies watching over her night and day in large armchairs with backs that let down as beds. Léonard visited her to cut her hair short and give it a chance to repair the ravages of the past few months. During this period, Marie Antoinette bravely attempted to breastfeed her baby, in accordance with the theories of Rousseau about natural healthy motherhood. This was the advantage of having produced a daughter – 'you are mine' – since a Dauphin would have been borne away immediately to the best wet-nurse in the land. But the belief that maternal nursing acted as a contraceptive meant that Maria Teresa greeted the news with open disapproval. It was up to the King of France and the doctor to decide, wrote the Empress, although she would not have permitted it herself; the idea that the Queen of France, still in the happy dream of having given birth, might have some kind of will of her own on the subject was ruled out. Although a wet-nurse for the baby Princess was obviously employed as well, Marie Antoinette seems to have managed to nurse her daughter for a certain period; four months later she told her mother she still had traces of milk.[33]

In April 1779, as the Empress called forcefully for 'a companion' for Marie Thérèse, she received the unwelcome news that Marie Antoinette had been struck down with an 'exceptionally severe' case of measles. Since the King had never had the illness, the Queen decided to keep her three-week quarantine at the Petit Trianon. This was the first occasion on which she actually spent the night in her beloved little paradise, instead of returning to Versailles to sleep. The size of the Petit Trianon meant that the Queen's household had to be lodged at the nearby Grand Trianon. The days were spent in such therapeutic activities as drinking asses' milk and boating on the Grand Canal. Certain aristocratic ladies came down from Paris to provide company. So far, so good; there was nothing here that Count Mercy could not explain away to the Empress.[34]

More difficult to gloss over was the ostentatiously chivalrous behaviour of four male members of the Queen's circle who went to watch over their liege lady like so many mediaeval squires. In other words, the Duc de Coigny, the Duc de Guines, Count Esterhazy and the Baron de Besenval (rated as too entertaining to be omitted) were there to amuse the Queen during her convalescence. With the Princesse de Lamballe and the Comtesse de Provence as fellow members of the merry crew, the whole escapade was an innocent frolic rather than anything more sinister. There had been a similar incident in March when the Queen and her ladies were stranded in a broken-down coach on their way to Paris for late-night revelry and had to hire a hackney carriage. 'The very next day' this innocent adventure was 'blared all over the town'. Such episodes were open to misinterpretation.[35]

A question went the rounds: if the King got measles, would he be tended by four ladies? In fact the King did not get the measles and he did miss the Queen; their relationship became noticeably deeper following the birth of their child. Finding three weeks too long to be apart, Louis XVI made his own romantic gesture. He stood for a quarter of an hour in a private courtyard of the Petit Trianon while the Queen leant out of a window. No one else was allowed to be present at this touching encounter but it was learnt afterwards that tender words had been exchanged on both sides.

In a further step forward, that bone of contention between the King and Queen, the matter of the Bavarian succession, was removed when the military action came to an end. The Peace of Teschen, of 13 May 1779, gave none of the warring powers exactly what they wanted, although everyone received something. Charles Theodore, the Elector Palatine, was acknowledged as the legitimate heir to certain lands, while Austria's Joseph II got a small piece of Bavarian territory – he called it 'a morsel' – known as the Innviertel.[36] Frederick II of Prussia had, however, blocked the Emperor's major plan of aggrandizement. The 'co-guarantors' of the Peace were to be the Russia of Catherine II – who had brilliantly succeeded in imposing herself on European councils as a result of the war – and, of course, France.

Subsequently Vergennes was exultant on the subject in a memorandum to his sovereign: 'Your Majesty has prevented the house of Austria getting dominions, and has established the influence of France in Germany; also harmony between herself and Prussia.' Marie Antoinette's attitude was somewhat different. For her it was naturally a 'much desired peace' and her happiness was overflowing at its arrival, as she told her mother. Nevertheless, she ascribed the pacification largely to Maria Teresa's efforts, praising the Empress's goodness, sweetness, and, if she dared say so, her patience towards 'this country' (France).[37]

The American war with England, on which Vergennes was concentrating France's efforts, was certainly a more remote prospect for her personally. When the Comte d'Estaing returned from capturing Grenada in July, he was crowned with flowers by Marie Antoinette and her ladies who wore white satin 'Grenada' hats. Léonard created a special coiffure *aux insurgents* in honour of the rebels. A new ballet, devised by Gardel and performed in the autumn of 1779, had an American island as a setting and the American hero [John] Paul Jones as a leading character. There were dances by 'American officers and their ladies', and a display of military drill in the third act, which in the early stages of the ballet was prudently performed by professional infantrymen.[38] So far, the distant military struggle had no more substance than the passing fashion; no more reality than the ballet.

Naval warfare was different. The autumn visit to Fontainebleau had to be cancelled because of its expense. An outbreak of dysentery among the fleets in Brittany and Normandy was inconvenient, particularly as it had spread to the Spanish fleet. The Spaniards, who had finally allied themselves with France the previous April, remained reluctant partners, given that their colonies made them more vulnerable in the New World than France. They demanded that there should be a joint operation against England in Europe – possibly using Ireland as a back door – in exchange for supporting France in America. Marie Antoinette hoped that this unfortunate outbreak of disease in the fleet would not encourage the English to be obdurate in refusing to make peace.[39]

Yet as the year drew to a close with the first birthday of Marie Thérèse, Madame Fille du Roi, the main preoccupations of Marie Antoinette were not political. Her chief joy was in the precocious development of her daughter. Marie Thérèse had the big blue eyes and healthy complexion that in babies make for admiration. She was also tall and strong, walking in her basketwork stroller by the time she was eight months old and shouting out, 'Papa, Papa.' These preferential cries did not offend her mother; on the contrary she was delighted that father and daughter were in this way linked more strongly. As for Marie Antoinette, she could hardly love her more than she did – the child who was 'mine'. Marie Thérèse had four teeth by the time she was eleven months old, and at fifteen months, by which time she was walking easily, could have been taken for a child of two. In her letters to her mother, Marie Antoinette apologized disingenuously for babbling on about her daughter...[40]

Her chief worry was her own health, if a 'young Cupid' (that is, a Dauphin) was to follow quickly. Marie Antoinette believed herself to have had a miscarriage in the summer of 1779, as a result of reaching up to close a carriage window.* The relentless questioning of the Empress on this intimate subject continued. A typical comment was evoked by the death of the Austrian court lady, Générale Krottendorf, who had – presumably because of the unfortunate association of the French word *crotter* (to dirty) – been the origin of the nickname given by the Empress and her family to their periods. In her New Year letter of 1780, Maria Teresa hoped that her death was an omen that meant the annoying monthly Générale would not visit her daughter again.[42]

This was a period when marital relations with Louis XVI had fallen into an amicable pattern. They did not share beds – that was not the French way, as Marie Antoinette tried in vain to persuade her mother – but they did live together as man and wife, and the 'two thirds husband' was a thing of the past. However, Marie Antoinette endured persistent gastric troubles. This was an icy winter, which laid low everyone except Louis XVI and the Comte de Provence, so that the Queen's illnesses may have been due to the general epidemic. On the other hand, they may have been a portent of something more serious as a result of that badly handled labour.

At least the Queen was able to send a novel New Year present to her mother: a souvenir containing a lock of the King's hair, her own hair – and that of 'my daughter'. Now the seemingly interminable letters of official congratulation that the Queen of France had to write to the King of England on the frequent deliveries of his wife could at last strike a genuine note. The birth of Princess Sophia in December 1777 was greeted with 'sincere interest' but that of Prince Octavius, shortly after that of Marie Thérèse, met with 'real satisfaction'.[43] Where royalties were concerned, Marie Antoinette was no longer the odd – infertile – one out.

---

* But her periods were so troublesome at the end of her short (three-weekly) cycle that this may not actually have been the case.[41]

CHAPTER TWELVE

Fulfilling their Wishes

⟋⟋⟍⟍

'Madame, you have fulfilled our wishes and those of France...'

Louis XVI to Marie Antoinette, 1781

In the spring of 1780 a prolonged visit from those friends of Marie Antoinette's youth, the Hesse Princesses, enabled the Queen to demonstrate in eloquent fashion the style that she was beginning to develop in her own private life. For like the rest of Europe, royalties not excepted, Marie Antoinette had a growing belief in the right to some kind of personal privacy. The contrast between the magnificent state rooms and the network of poky little cabinets or private rooms behind them (which is so striking to the modern visitor to Versailles) represented a chasm between two worlds.

Of course the older generation in France resented such changes as older generations tend to do. Even such obviously appropriate modernizations as allowing men and women to eat together, and the Queen being present at the King's 'little suppers', which was instituted by Marie Antoinette in 1774 at the suggestion of Count Mercy, had met with furious disapproval. Previously the Queen and the Princesses were forbidden to sit down with the non-royal males. Mercy made the excellent point that the loose morals of the court of Louis XV had been enhanced by this artificial segregation, which led directly to 'licentious' social occasions presided over by the Comtesse Du Barry.¹

The senior women at the French court, according to the memoirs of the Vicomtesse de Fausselandry, had always found it difficult to pardon the Queen for her beauty and her 'sweet familiarity'. Her friendship with the kind of young people who shared her own predilection for an escape from court traditions provided further ammunition; in revenge they called her proud, when the reverse was the truth. Yet it is important to note that Marie Antoinette's instinct towards a simpler and more private way of life was actually welcome to the monarch himself. As Louis XVI would confide to one of his servants much later, 'These manners, new at Court, were too suitable to my own taste to be opposed by me.'[2]

The pleasures of this privacy included the enjoyment of her burgeoning gardens, the introduction of private theatricals and wherever possible the adoption of much plainer clothes in place of the rigid court dress, with its stiff structures of panniers and train. For it was at about this time that Marie Antoinette, abandoning heavy traditional make-up, began to wear her classic white muslin gowns. These consisted of a plain piece of material put over the head, with a drawstring neck. A few ruffles and ribbons were added, and it was tied at the waist by a silk sash, pale blue or striped. With a straw hat to complete it, this was the costume of Marie Antoinette immortalized in 1783 by the brush of Madame Vigée Le Brun. The following year, when Mrs Cradock, wife of a wealthy Englishman, was shown the Queen's Robes of State, it was as though she was inspecting museum pieces. In a sense, that was true, even if those concoctions of rose satin and blue velvet, heavily embroidered with pearls and other jewels, garnished with lace and gold and silver tissue, were still let out of the museum from time to time.[3]

The Wardrobe Book of the Queen was presented to her daily by her Mistress of the Robes together with a pincushion; Marie Antoinette would prick the book with a pin to indicate her choices. The porters attached to the Queen's Wardrobe (this was three large rooms filled with closets, drawers and tables) then carried in the huge baskets covered in cloths of green taffeta. The Wardrobe Book of 1782, in the care of the Comtesse d'Ossun, survives. Each outfit is categorized and accompanied by a tiny swatch of material. There are samples for the court dresses in various shades of pink, in shadowy grey-striped tissue and in the self-striped turquoise velvet intended for Easter.

But what is notable is the preponderance of swatches for the more casual clothes, the loose *Lévites* shown together on one page in an array of colours, from pale grey and pale blue through to the much darker shades of maroon and navy, sometimes with small sprigs embroidered between the stripes. There are redingotes (from the English word riding-coat) in the same palette of blues, as well as a particular mauve marked Bertin-Normand, coupling together the names of the couturier and the silk-merchant. Swatches for the so-called 'Turkish' robes are shown in self-striped pink and very dark mauve, for the *robes anglaises* in turquoise and self-striped mauve as well as dark maroon striped in pale blue. One swatch of material, supplied by the other celebrated silk-merchant, Barbier, uses the Queen's favourite cornflower to good effect, set in a design of wavy, cream-coloured stripes.*[4]

The muslin dresses added simplicity of material to that of shape. Originally imported to France by the Creole ladies of the West Indies, her muslin dresses suited Marie Antoinette's romantic idea of a simplified life to the extent that she came to present them to her English friends, such as the Duchess of Devonshire, as a token of esteem.[5] Although the Queen of France was denounced by the French silk industry by failing in her duty to them, it has to be said that, once again, Marie Antoinette was not so much innovating fashion as flowing instinctively with it. All over Europe costumes were becoming simplified (as were hairstyles) as if in response to some shared *Zeitgeist*. In Vienna the Emperor Joseph even tried to ban the cumbersome panniers and expensive paraphernalia of official court dress. Although he did not succeed, the liberating intention was much like that of his sister in France. Similarly Marie Antoinette's permission for gentlemen to wear frockcoats (*le*

---

* In the Wardrobe Book, in the Archives Nationales, Paris, the actual pin-pricks that the Queen made can still be seen; in recent years some of the long pins she used were recovered from the floor of her room at Versailles.

frac) in her private company might be denounced by con-
servatives. Twenty years ago, fulminated the Marquis de Bombelles, gentlemen wearing such a costume would not even have
dared present themselves to the wife of a notary! Nevertheless
it was the way the world was going.[6]

It was the same instinct that led Marie Antoinette, with a
bevy of courtiers (but not the King), to visit the tomb of
Rousseau. All present admired the simple good taste of the
tomb, the soft romantic melancholy of the site, without, in the
opinion of the sardonic Baron Grimm, having any thought to
the memory of the man. And yet all of them, including Marie
Antoinette, were being influenced by the man's ideas ... Sensibility, even excessive sensibility, was much admired; appreciation
of Gluck was another mark of it. When *Iphigénie en Tauride* was
first performed, many people, anxious not to be thought coarse-
grained, took the precaution of weeping the whole way through
the opera.[7]

For their taste of the Queen's new style, the Hesse Princesses
came in a large family party, their visit being connected to a
law-suit in Paris. There was the unmarried Princess Charlotte,
Marie Antoinette's special friend: 'All your family can be quite
sure of my affection, but as for you, my dear Princess, I can't
convey to you the depth of my feeling for you.' Then there was
the nineteen-year-old Princess Louise, with her husband (also
her cousin) Prince Louis, who was heir to the Landgrave of
Hesse-Darmstadt, and his younger brother Prince Frederick.
Unlike Marie Antoinette, Louise was pregnant – she would give
birth at the end of August – and a great deal of concern on the
subject of her health was displayed by the Queen throughout
her visit; this vicarious solicitude made up for the continued
blighting of her own hopes in this direction, despite courses of
iron pills.[8]

The father of the Princesses, Prince George William, although
badly afflicted with gout and failing eyesight, was also in Paris,
for the sake of the family lawsuit, together with his wife, another
unmarried daughter Princess Augusta and his son Prince George
Charles. The latter, as a foreign prince in his mid-twenties, was
someone whose interests Marie Antoinette could try to promote,

in the patroness's role that she enjoyed. The Landgrave of Hesse-Homburg and his wife the Landgravine Caroline, herself the sister of Princes Louis and Frederick, completed this interwoven family group, which brought with it memories of another time and a shared past.

Immediately the Queen sought to involve her friends in her favourite pursuits. On the evening of her arrival, Marie Antoinette's 'dear Princess' Charlotte was bidden to the Queen's own box at Versailles for a theatrical performance. To reestablish their friendship, Charlotte and her family were to be sure to arrive an hour or so in advance. Such an invitation was a sign of great favour since the Queen's box was extremely small. Huge panniered skirts would obviously be a disaster, so Marie Antoinette added the important words to her handwritten note: 'I beg you all not to be too dressed up.' On 2 March an invitation to a ball given by the Comtesse Diane de Polignac, sister of Comte Jules and Mistress of the Household to Madame Elisabeth, was accompanied by a similar instruction regarding informality. Since this was to be a ball 'without ceremony', beginning at 11.30 p.m., the Princesses should wear 'little' dresses or polonaises, robes where the light silk overskirts were conveniently looped up instead of grandly sweeping the floor.[9]

An invitation came to Princess Louise, her husband and brother-in-law from Marie Antoinette to see the garden at the Petit Trianon: 'It's looking so beautiful that I should be charmed to show it to you.' There was the provision: 'I shall be quite alone so don't dress up; country clothes and the men in frockcoats.' Midday was the best time to see the garden and lunch would be offered. A note to Princess Charlotte with arrangements for picking her up in order to go for a walk in the forest (at Marly or Saint-Germain) warned once again: 'Don't be dressed up and don't wear big hats, because the carriage is only a barouche.'[10]

The Queen took a keen personal interest in the transformation of her gardens at the Petit Trianon. A series of little models made by the sculptor Deschamps were produced for her inspection. Trees and grass were represented by wood or moss or scrapings of horn dyed green; columns of the sort that were to feature in this romantic landscape, devised in part by the painter Hubert Robert, were modelled in wax. Fourteen models had to be produced before the Queen was satisfied. At Choisy, Marie Antoinette indulged her 'real passion' for flowers; she particularly enjoyed painting the *rose-modèles* who posed for her, as it were, along a great white trellis nine feet long, where all her favourite species were grown. Appropriately enough, the young Pierre Joseph Redouté, who shared her love of roses, would be appointed her official draughtsman in 1787. Hyacinths – with blue the favourite colour – tulips and irises were among those flowers she favoured, not only in her gardens but as a theme of decoration for her various boudoirs. One of her ladies had special responsibility for seeing that everywhere in her apartments huge Chinese pots and small vases of crystal, Sèvres or Venetian glass were filled with flowers. Then there was her love of wild flowers such as violets and the flowery essences that were replacing the heavier musky perfumes, now thought to be old-fashioned.[11]

The theatre, including opera and the ballet, had long been an obsession; Madame Campan reported how Marie Antoinette was always eager to hear news of the latest plays and performances while at her *toilette*. In Paris, of course, she had her boxes at the Opéra, the Comédie Française and the Comédie Italienne (later the Opéra Comique), whose retiring rooms included dressing tables. Ballerinas such as the exquisite Madeleine Guimard, perennially youthful and so thin that she was known as 'the skeleton of the Graces', fell under her patronage.[12]

But amateur theatricals were also part of eighteenth-century court tradition, the Pompadour, for example, having a great taste for them, whilst in Paris well over a hundred private theatres flourished. In the summer of 1780 Marie Antoinette graduated from minor performances in her own apartments, where she had been coached by her erudite Librarian, Monsieur Campan, to something more ambitious. On 1 June a new theatre was inaugurated at Versailles adjacent to the Petit Trianon. Designed by Richard Mique, its decor was blue and gold, with blue velvet and blue moiré, and papier-mâché to simulate marble.* Active participation in the theatricals was a great favour, and even an invitation to watch was a sign of approval. Aristocrats who were kept out were indignant when it was a nobody, the Librarian Campan, who acted as director and prompter, rather than some more suitable Duc. The celebrated theatrical companies came down from Paris to perform, but on 1 August some 'little trifles', to use Count Mercy's careful phrase to Maria Teresa, were given by the courtiers themselves and their mistress.[13]

Mercy's tact in breaking the news to the Empress was part of his general policy where any new pastimes of Marie Antoinette were concerned. In fact, in this case her reaction was hardly relevant since the King himself thoroughly enjoyed his wife's performance on the stage. With the Princes and Princesses of the Blood, Louis XVI watched enchanted, unaccompanied by any great train of courtiers, and with only the body of ordinary domestic servants present who were performing their usual duties. Furthermore, as Mercy himself commented, the passion for theatricals now took over from the passion for gambling at late-night card parties, and it diverted the Queen from giddy expeditions to Paris. Expert tutors were imported: the actor Joseph Dazincourt from the Comédie Française for theatrical technique and Louis Michu from the Comédie Italienne as singing master.[14]

The amateur actors included the talented Comte d'Artois; Yolande de Polignac's lover, the Comte de Vaudreuil (who was generally agreed to be the most skilful); another member of the Polignac set, the Comte d'Adhémar; and Yolande's ravishing young daughter Agläié who, from her recent marriage to the Duc de Guiche, was nicknamed 'Guichette'. Significantly, Marie Antoinette's chosen parts had absolutely nothing to do with the gorgeously attired stately role she played day by day at Versailles. She played shepherdesses, village maidens and chambermaids, just as Artois played gamekeepers and valets. Rousseau's *Le Devin du Village* (*The Village Soothsayer*) ended with the village

* The theatre where Marie Antoinette blithely trod the boards can still be seen, an exquisite souvenir.

devin adjuring everyone to return to the countryside, away from the court; a happy dance round the maypole followed. Marie Antoinette played the faithful – but simple – Colette with Artois as her admirer Colin and Vaudreuil as the eponymous soothsayer.

In the summer of 1780 Marie Antoinette needed distraction, and not only from gambling sessions and late-night trips to Paris; she had also lost a member of her circle for whom she had an acknowledged *penchant*. This was Count Axel Fersen. He succeeded at last in leaving for the American war as ADC to the French General Rochambeau on 23 March, having been kicking his heels since the previous autumn when a Franco-Spanish invasion plan in which he hoped to take part was aborted. Where this particular phase of the relationship between Marie Antoinette and Fersen is concerned – the first real phase – it is as ever important to beware of hindsight. The Swedish ambassador, in a report to his king of April 1779, wrote of the Queen's 'leaning' towards Fersen: 'I confess that I cannot help believing it ... I have seen signs too unmistakable to doubt it.' She had regarded him so 'favourably' that this had given offence to several people.[15]

A weakness for a young and good-looking man is, however, a very different matter from an adulterous liaison, especially since the fondness concerned was expressed in the kind of patronage that would inevitably absent Fersen from her side, by going to America. At the age of twenty-five Fersen also had an agenda that was clear enough. Putting the needs of a military career first, he wanted to be part of the French support of independence in the New World.

Already, young French aristocrats, inspired by a mixture of idealism and ambition, were beginning to cross the Atlantic under their own impetus, despite the theoretical need for government permission. The rebels were beginning to capture the imagination: 'Their cause was our cause. We were proud of their victories, wept for their defeats,' wrote one noblewoman. The young red-haired radical, the Marquis de La Fayette, backed by his colossal private wealth – a rumoured income of 100,000 livres a year – defiantly chartered a boat and departed for the war. Another voyager was La Fayette's brother-in-law, the Vicomte de Noailles, son of Marie Antoinette's first Mistress of the Household (the two men were married to sisters, Noailles cousins). While some might have privately agreed with Yolande de Polignac's verdict in a letter to an English friend – 'This dreadful America, since it has been discovered, has produced nothing but evil!' – others including Fersen saw there the opportunity for glory and self-advancement.[16]

Fersen certainly placed the perceived need for action above his other need to marry an heiress, although even here he was prepared to contemplate the widowed daughter of the Baron de Breteuil as a possible bride. Apart from that, he was thoroughly beguiled by the Queen – particularly as she was so helpful. Fersen's candid letters on the subject to his father in Sweden are the best possible proof of the lack of any deeper level to their relationship at this point. 'She is a charming princess,' Fersen wrote in the same terms he had used two years previously, adding, 'she has always treated me very kindly.' He also pointed to the influence of Breteuil, the French ambassador in Vienna who was currently visiting France: 'Since the Baron spoke to her, she singles me out even more. She almost always walks with me at opera balls ...' But it was his next comment that was the real clue to Marie Antoinette's favour: 'Her kindness has aroused the jealousy of the younger courtiers who cannot understand a foreigner being better treated than they are.'[17] This, of course, was the whole point; Fersen, apart from his attractions, brought no baggage from the court of France, something that was fully understood by the Polignac set. The Polignacs were quite content that the Queen should have an admirer who wanted a commission for America rather than richer pickings in France itself.

In his concern to leave, did Fersen also feel that he was being sucked too far into the Queen's circle – and the Queen's affections? It is possible. Certainly Fersen wrote of his appointment to Rochambeau's expedition, which he attributed finally to Vergennes' feeling for the senior Count Fersen: 'I am in a state of joy that cannot be expressed.'[18] The Queen, on the other hand, was said to have wept when Fersen took his departure, having invited him to a series of her supper parties in the weeks before.

When Fersen originally planned to depart, one of the Queen's Dames du Palais, the Duchesse de Saint-James, had teased Fersen about his 'conquest' of the Queen, a light remark that probably would not have been made if it had had serious substance. Then she asked him: 'Are you abandoning your conquest?' Fersen was quick to reply with that modesty and discretion he would show throughout his life: 'If I had made one, I would not abandon it.' He went on: 'Unhappily I depart ... without leaving any regrets behind me.' It was not strictly speaking true. When Marie Antoinette wrote to her mother in April of her fervent prayers for the embarkation of the French expedition – 'May God grant that they arrive successfully!' – it is plausible to think that she had the Swedish Count as well as the French soldiers in mind. Fersen, on the other hand, as ever turning to attractive female company, was soon finding the women of Newport, Rhode Island, to his great satisfaction, 'pretty, friendly and *coquettes*', while the people in general were 'cheerful and straighforward'.[19]

It was the Polignac set that remained Marie Antoinette's 'family'. It formed the basis of the group known as the Queen's Private Society (*Société Particulière de la Reine*), which included at least six Polignac relations. As such exclusive clubs always are, the Private Society – a form of salon, something that had a long tradition among ladies in France, both grand and intellectual – was resented and criticized by those outside it. None of the members was a very 'elevated character', wrote the Comte de La Marck, and there were many to point out how greedy all of them were.[20] Certainly the Queen gave lavishly or rather saw to it that the King gave. Comte Jules was created a Duc and 'Guichette's' magnificent dowry at her wedding in the summer of 1780 was the talk of the court.

Yet it is important to note that Louis XVI felt about the Polignac set rather as he felt about the theatre: here were people and activities who diverted his wife. In the case of the Duchesse de Polignac, as she had become, she understood how to handle Marie Antoinette's mercurial moods, one of her methods being to stand silently and offer a concoction of soothing orange-flower water into which sugar had been stirred. On a personal level, the charming Yolande was one of the few women the King actually liked and trusted. On 5 May 1780 she gave birth to a son whose paternity was generally ascribed to her lover, the Comte de Vaudreuil. Wags asked whether the father was perhaps the Queen, since it could not be the Duc de Polignac (there had been a gap of nine years since the births of Agläié and Armand).[21] Louis XVI, undeterred by such gossip, paid the new mother a visit of courtesy; hers was the only private house in Paris he had entered since his accession.

Since this was the court of France, and for the first time there was no royal mistress in sight, sporadic efforts were made to put other women in the King's way. In January 1778 even Marie Antoinette had braced herself for the King taking a mistress now that their marriage was fully consummated. She promised her brother Joseph in a letter that if there were liaisons, she would do everything to win the King back. It was not for nothing that Henri IV, of celebrated virility, was the most popular king in French history; the image of both Louis XIV and Louis XV included sexual prowess. Thus the King's supposed interest in an actress at the Comédie Française or even his casual inspection of a young woman at a card party through his lorgnette – he asked who she was – caused prurient excitement. To all of this the King's reaction is best summed up by an incident in which the Duc de Fronsac, heir to the dissipated Duc de Richelieu, dangled his own mistress, an opera singer known as 'la petite Zacharie', as bait in front of the King. 'Be gone, Fronsac,' said the King in disgust. 'It's obvious whose son you are ...'[22]

In February 1782 the King himself made his position quite clear: 'Everyone would like me to take a mistress but I have no intention of doing so. I do not wish to recreate the scenes of the preceding reigns ...'[23] Louis XVI's way of dealing with such rumours consisted of sitting safely beside the gentle and unthreatening Yolande de Polignac at a ball. The obstinacy that had enabled him to hold out against the consummation of his marriage for so many years was not likely to desert the King now in favour of behaviour that he found both distasteful and immoral. Nevertheless the position of royal mistress remaining unfilled meant that there was in a sense a vacancy at court. Courtiers could not seek out favours from the *maîtresse-en-titre* as they had been accustomed to do; nor could they play off the royal mistress against the royal consort. The future would show whether the Queen of France was, against precedent, to fill the position and enjoy the influence of both wife and mistress.

The politics of the autumn of 1780 presented the Polignacs with an opportunity for advancing their own. On 13 October Necker managed to secure the dismissal of Antoine de Sartine, the Minister for the Navy, whose management of the finances of the fleet had earned his disfavour. The Polignac candidate to replace Sartine was the military aristocrat the Marquis de Castries, a brilliant soldier in the Seven Years' War who had been a protégé of the Duc de Choiseul. It was, however, the approval of Necker that clinched the job for Castries rather than purely and simply the influence of the Queen. Mercy and Vermond were in any case anxiously counselling her to step back from the Polignac intrigues, in order to concentrate her talents on supporting Austria.[24]

The Minister of War was also to be replaced. This time the Polignacs strongly forwarded a member of the Queen's Private Society, the Comte d'Adhémar. But once again Mercy struck home. Adhémar was passed over and a second military aristocrat, also a hero of the Seven Years' War, the Marquis de Ségur, was appointed; a man of great authority, Ségur was descended illegitimately from that Duc d'Orléans who had been Regent. Marie Antoinette now had two service ministers, Castries and Ségur, who owed their advancement at least partly to her patronage, to parallel the increasing interest she was taking in military and naval appointments.[25]

None of this amounted to a genuine power base. The Queen's influence was limited and the Polignac influence more limited still. Maurepas, although nearly eighty and increasingly debilitated by ill health, continued to exercise political domination over the King, in alliance with Vergennes. Where the Queen scored small victories, it was because these ministers had decided to avoid unnecessary confrontation. Significantly, Mercy still complained of the Queen's lack of a really intelligent commitment to politics. Her general, rather vague, benevolent attitude to patronage led her rather to please those she liked than think the matter through.[26]

The death in the summer of 1780 of Marie Antoinette's uncle on her father's side, the veteran Prince Charles of Lorraine, presaged a far greater family loss in the late autumn. Marie Antoinette, ever conscious of the need to promote Lorrainers in France in order to please her mother, wrote a nostalgic letter to Maria Teresa about her sadness at the end of the (royal) House of Lorraine. For the Prince, the childless widower of Maria Teresa's younger sister, had never remarried; instead, as Governor of the Austrian Netherlands he had pursued the arts and women with equal zest, showing a true Lorrainer's instinct for enjoyment of life.

Maria Teresa herself was failing. Her last letter to her daughter was dated 3 November, the day after Marie Antoinette's twenty-fifth birthday. It struck a wistful note about the child she had not seen for over ten years: 'Yesterday I was all day more in France than in Austria.' The Empress was only sixty-three but dropsy had been aggravating her sufferings with her legs for some years. Now her lungs began to 'harden'; she complained of a burning sensation inside, and repeatedly demanded the opening of her windows. There were five days of intense illness, which would later be movingly described by her eldest daughter, the Archduchess Marianne, the invalid who had never left home.[27]

To the very end the Empress still exercised her formidable will. She sent away her daughters (the Archduchesses Marie Christine and Elizabeth as well as Marianne) because she did not want them to see her die; they were also forbidden to attend the funeral. The three daughters who were the repositories of her dynastic ambitions were of course far away: the Queens of France and Naples, and the Duchess of Parma. And the Empress firmly refused to go to sleep: 'At any moment I may be called before my Judge. I don't want to be surprised,' she said. 'I want to see death come.' Finally death did come – on the morning of 29 November.

It was a full week before the information reached the French court, where Louis XVI decreed grand mourning for his fellow sovereign and mother-in-law. He requested that the Abbé de Vermond should break the news to the Queen on his regular morning visit to her apartments. Louis XVI even went so far as to express his personal thanks to Vermond for doing him 'this service'; the King had never chosen to speak to Vermond before, although the latter had been his wife's confidential advisor for all the years of her sojourn in France. Louis' tenderness, coming from this notoriously awkward man, left Marie Antoinette touched and grateful.

It was to Joseph II that Marie Antoinette, on 10 December, expressed her full despair: 'Devastated by this most frightful misfortune, I cannot stop crying as I start to write to you. Oh my brother, oh my friend! You alone are left to me in a country [Austria] which is, and always will be, so dear to me ... Remember, we are your friends, your allies. I embrace you.'[28]

It remained to be seen, once mourning was over – the merry pastimes of the Private Society were all temporarily abandoned – whether the Emperor really did remember that he was supposed to be the friend and ally of France, or whether, as Vergennes feared, his current offers of mediation in the American war meant that Joseph was actually veering in the direction of England.

Without Marie Antoinette immediately realizing it, her own situation apropos her homeland had subtly changed. It was not so much that the opportunity to live up to her august mother's expectations had gone for ever although that was true enough. It was more that Count Mercy's secret channel of communication with Maria Teresa was not replaced by anything at all similar with Joseph II. As a result, Marie Antoinette's own relationship with her brother assumed greater importance. How fortunate then that at the beginning of 1781 the Emperor was careful to soothe the French on the subject of the alliance: 'Our links with France are natural, advantageous and infinitely preferable to those with England.'[29]

It was in this favourable atmosphere that the Queen of France began to hope that the great event for which Maria Teresa had so fervently hoped – but had not lived to see – might actually be happening. As February wore on, she knew it was possible that she might be pregnant once more. Such a secret, of course, could hardly be kept in Versailles. As early as 2 March the Marquis de Bombelles, in Ratisbon on a diplomatic mission, heard the news from his mother-in-law. The Queen herself had told Madame de Mackau in graceful terms: 'I am going to cause you further bother because I am *enceinte*. I assure you that in spite of my joy, I regret the increase in your trouble.' On 17 March – what she took to be the two months' mark – Marie Antoinette broke the great news to Princess Louise of Hesse; she continued to keep her informed of progress. On 7 May, for example, she reported that her health was 'perfect' and that she was putting on 'a lot of weight'. The Queen added that Louise's witchcraft (*sorcellerie*) was very charming to predict a son for her.[30]

The attitude of the Emperor Joseph was typically blunt. He told Count Mercy that the news had given him personally great pleasure. As for his sister, the pregnancy would essentially contribute to her happiness, 'if she knows how to make use of it'. In the course of the summer, as the Queen's condition progressed – her health in general was excellent, better than in 1778 – the Emperor decided to come and once more in person give his advice to his sister on 'matters of state'.[31]

French internal politics were certainly intricate enough. While the expensive American war wound on into its fourth year, Necker took a calculated risk. Necker's official accounting, which was made public (his so-called *compte rendu au roi*), proposed against all the odds that there was actually a surplus rather than a deficit in the royal finances. This conjuring trick caused more than one raised eyebrow among observers of the political scene. Nevertheless it was not for his accounting but for his demands over status that Necker found himself in crisis in May. Necker's Protestant religion had always been a complication in a country where certain titular offices could not be occupied by a non-Catholic. When Necker attempted to better his public position, given his existing responsibilities, he failed, whereupon he allowed himself to be provoked into resignation by Maurepas.[32]

'Count Falkenstein' – once again the Emperor came incognito – arrived in France on 29 July. And once again he demanded a hotel in Versailles rather than more lavish apartments within the palace itself. His suite consisted of two servants only, with an official from his chancellery. This low-key style suited the Queen. Joseph's visit was only to last a week, but Marie Antoinette was determined to see as much of him as possible; it was helpful that her activities were by now considerably curtailed given that she was in the seventh month of her pregnancy. Ridiculous rumours were being reported by the Chief of Police, Lenoir, that the Queen was using her brother's visit to pass him immense amounts of money from 'the royal treasure'. They seemed at the time to be no more than rumours – and were very far from the truth. Economy was to be the watchword of the French court. When a performance of *Iphigénie en Tauride* was given in the new theatre at the Trianon, the Queen was careful to point out that the limited seating meant the event would not be all that expensive. The sum of 500 livres spent on the burning of 'good wood' to illuminate the Temple of Love was less frugal.[33]

It was the Emperor Joseph who was invited to act as godparent to the expected baby on this occasion, as his mother had been three years before. This gave him the right to choose the baby's name, and also to appoint proxies at the instant baptism. On 14 October, Joseph wrote to Count Mercy that the two younger brothers, the Comtes de Provence and d'Artois, should take his place at the christening.* He told the ambassador that he wanted to know every single detail of the Queen's impending *accouchement*, for he yielded nothing to his mother in that respect. For his part, Mercy assured the Emperor that Marie Antoinette was showing real zeal and affection 'in everything that concerns your Majesty'.[34]

---

* Nobody was particularly concerned over the sudden claims of the Comtesse de Provence that she too was pregnant; there was a general suspicion that these would fade away when the Queen gave birth, as indeed happened.

*

The Queen went into labour on the morning of 22 October. She had spent a good night, according to the meticulous account of her progress in the King's *Journal*, had a few pains on waking, but was still able to have her morning bath. It was only at midday that the King gave orders to cancel the shoot that was about to be held at Saclé. In the next half an hour the *douleurs* increased. There were present, according to the King, 'only' the Princesse de Lamballe, the Comte d'Artois, Mesdames Tantes, the Princesse de Chimay, the Comtesse de Mailly, the Comtesse d'Ossun, and the Comtesse de Tavannes.[35] The most important personage allowed into the royal bedchamber was, however, the Princesse de Guéméné. At present the Royal Governess only had Marie Thérèse, not quite three, in her care, but it was in her hands that the new baby would immediately be placed. Members of the two households were, as in 1778, close by. This time the King had taken precautions that the flow of fresh air should not be impeded, for fear of a recurrence of the Queen's fainting fit.

Finally Marie Antoinette lay down on the little white delivery bed. Then: '*At exactly a quarter past one by my watch she was successfully delivered of a boy.*' The italics are those of the King. For those outside, there were fifteen minutes of suspense, before one of the Queen's women, her dress dishevelled and in a state of tremendous excitement, rushed in and cried out: 'A Dauphin! But you must not mention it yet.' Inside, the Queen herself was still unaware of the sex of her baby, and imagined from the profound silence around her that it must be another girl. It was the King himself who broke the news. These were his words, as he wrote them down: 'Madame, you have fulfilled our wishes and those of France, you are the mother of a Dauphin.'[36]

Afterwards a tender story was told about the Queen's anxiety. 'You can see I'm behaving very well,' she said. 'I'm not asking you anything.' At this point the King thought it time to put her out of her agony. Holding the baby, with tears in his eyes, he told his wife: 'Monsieur le Dauphin asks to come in.'[37] Yet the King's actual words – for his own account of what he said must be preferred – if less playful, are in a sense even more touching.

For they indicate formally that Marie Antoinette had at last achieved what as a foreign princess she had been sent to do. It had taken eleven and a half years. She had borne an heir, half Habsburg, half Bourbon.

Outside the bedchamber, the world went mad. Good intentions of secrecy went for very little. Count Curt Stedingk, a Swedish soldier who was a great favourite with the Queen (like Fersen, he had served bravely on the French side in America), was among those present. He gave an unforgettable picture of his encounter with the Comtesse de Provence, rushing towards the apartment of her sister-in-law 'at a great gallop'. Forgetting in his enthusiasm exactly whom he was addressing – a woman whose husband had just been demoted from his position as heir presumptive – he cried out: 'Madame, a Dauphin! What joy!' Elsewhere the Marquis de Bombelles ran through his own house like a madman, shouting to his wife: 'A Dauphin? A Dauphin! Is it possible? Yes, it's really true. What are they saying, what are they doing at Versailles?'[38]

The scenes at Versailles were indeed almost religious. For they centred on the adoration of a tiny child, arriving as a saviour. As Royal Governess, the Princess de Guéméné took the baby in her arms. Carried in a chair, she paraded him through Versailles on the way to her own apartments. The noise of the acclamation and the sound of clapping penetrated even the Queen's room. Everyone wanted to touch the baby, or failing that, the Princesse's chair. 'We adored him,' wrote Stedingk. 'We followed him in a great crowd.'

PART FOUR

Queen and Mother

CHAPTER THIRTEEN

The Flowers of the Crown

~

'She as yet knew nothing of the crown but its flowers ...'
Marquis de Ségur on Marie Antoinette, 1783

'The happiest and most important event for me': so Marie Antoinette described the birth of her son in a letter to her friend, Princess Charlotte of Hesse-Darmstadt. Such a jubilant reaction was not confined to the baby's mother. The baptism, according to custom, was performed in the afternoon following the birth. The child was named Louis Joseph for his Bourbon forefathers and his Habsburg godfather (and uncle) with the additional names of Xavier and François. The King wept throughout the ceremony. Soon, as Madame Campan noted, he was framing his conversation so that the words 'my son the Dauphin' could be introduced as frequently as possible.'

'Oh Papa!' exclaimed the little Duc d'Angoulême when shown the Dauphin. 'How tiny my cousin is!'

'The day will come,' replied Artois with meaning, 'when you will find him great enough.'²

It was true that Angoulême had just been dispossessed of the illustrious position of heir in the next generation, which had been his since his birth in August 1775. More importantly, the Comte de Provence, displaced in his own generation, was now one step further away from the throne.

At this baptism, however, there were no impertinent allusions as there had been in 1778. Provence held his peace. Nevertheless there was a discordant note. As with the baptism of Marie Thérèse, the ceremony had by right to be performed by the Grand Almoner. This was none other than that Prince Louis de Rohan, now Cardinal, whose appointment the Queen had tried so hard to block. Even the Cardinal's hat, granted in 1778, had been the subject of dispute. Louis XVI, egged on by his wife, had refused to exercise his prerogative – the so-called 'nomination of crowns' – to put forward Rohan's name. But the Queen was foiled once again by the Rohan family's skill at intrigues; as a result Prince Louis was nominated by the King of Poland.³

The presence of this bad man – as the Queen firmly believed he was, bad as in immoral, bad as in trouble-making – in such a prominent role at the baby's christening could not dampen the happiness of the royal parents. The coral and multi-diamonded rattle donated by the Tsarina of Russia, valued at 24,000 livres, represented an alternative and splendid omen of the baby's future happiness.⁴

The response of the French nation as a whole was summed up in a letter from Count Mercy to Prince Kaunitz in Vienna: 'Tumultuous joy reigns here.' Some celebrations were more elegant than others. On 27 October the new Opera House – built to replace one that had burnt down – opened with a free performance of *Adèle et Ponthieu* by Gluck's rival Piccinni. Eighteen hundred people were expected; in the event 6000 forced their way in, jamming the boxes. Cries of 'Long live the King', 'Long live the Queen' and 'Long live Monsieur le Dauphin' came from the happy audience. In the world of fashion, however, a new colour was termed *caca-dauphin*, as though even the royal baby's natural functions needed somehow to be fêted. Perhaps the new and widely copied short feathery hairstyle created for the Queen by Léonard, to help with her hair-loss, named *coiffure à l'enfant*, struck a better note.⁵

In Austria, pride in the achievement of 'their' princess was uncontained. Gluck reported how all Vienna rejoiced, not so much for the sake of the French, of course, as for the sake of the Queen. As for the Emperor, Joseph confessed that he had thought himself incapable of a young man's enthusiasm (he was forty), yet now found that he was staggered by his own emotion. After all, 'this sister, who is the woman I love best in the world' was at this very moment 'the most happy' being on earth.[6]

About this time the eleven-year-old Henrietta Lucy, daughter of Madame Dillon, who as the Marquise de La Tour du Pin would write perceptive memoirs of the period, saw the Queen for the first time. Marie Antoinette was wearing a blue dress strewn with sapphires and diamonds, and she was opening the ball given by the royal bodyguards at Versailles with one of the guardsmen: 'She was young, beautiful and adored by all; she had just given France a Dauphin ...' This was the outwardly brilliant period of which the Comte de Ségur would later write that the French 'of every class' regarded the Queen as one among the sweetest ornaments of the fêtes that embellished the court. Encouraging literature, protecting the arts, dispensing many benefits and disobliging no one, 'She as yet knew nothing of the crown but its flowers.' The Queen did not foresee that she was soon to feel 'the crown's dreadful weight'.[7]

Of course it was not literally true that the Queen had not felt this weight. The *libellistes* did not ignore the birth of the Dauphin, any more than they had ignored that of Madame Fille du Roi. The official medal might bear the legend in Latin 'Public Happiness'. But a malicious engraving showed Marie Antoinette cradling her baby, accompanied by Louis XVI wearing a cuckold's horns and an angel with a trumpet who was supposed to 'announce to all parts' the birth of the Dauphin: 'But be careful not to open your eyes to the secret of his birth.' The Spanish chargé d'affaires passed on another scurrilous rhyme whose refrain on the subject of the Dauphin was: 'Who the Devil produced him?' Suggestions included the Duc de Coigny as before, and the Comte d'Artois. One of the most notorious embroideries on this latter theme had appeared during the Queen's pregnancy. This was *Les Amours de Charlot* [Artois] *et Antoinette*, a lewd and ludicrous romp in which a page kept appearing to interrupt the moment of climax because the Queen inadvertently pressed the bell beside her as she thrashed about in ecstasy.[8]

Similarly Jean Lenoir, the Chief of Police, whose business it was to see to these things, reported with horror that a pamphlet printed in English, *Naissance du Dauphin*, ascribed the paternity of the baby to 'another royal prince'. Another scabrous pamphlet, which would go through many stages (and numerous editions), began life in December 1781 as *La Vie d'Antoinette*. Yet for the time being the Queen was able to continue her policy of studied indifference, enjoying the flowers of the crown while the police in France and the French ambassador in London attempted the impossible task of buying up all the editions and pulping them.[9]

The welfare of the baby himself was her prime concern at this time. There was no talk on this occasion of the Queen nursing him. Louis Joseph was entrusted to a woman nicknamed 'Madame Poitrine' for the vast bosom that would nurture the little Prince. This strong-minded lady, the wife of a gardener, absolutely refused to have her hair powdered, according to court custom, saying that a lace cap was just as good. She also introduced a little rhyme, which she crooned over the baby's head, beginning: '*Malbrouck s'en va-t-en guerre ...*' This folk-song, referring to the English general engaged in the wars of Louis XIV, had remained popular in her village down the years. It now became the fashion at a court that was enchanted by every manifestation of Madame Poitrine's rusticity.[10]

Where a more recent war was concerned, it seemed a wonderful augury for France that there had been a great victory overseas on 19 October 1781, three days before the birth of its long-awaited Dauphin. At Yorktown, Virginia, George Washington's forces, supported by the French fleet under Admiral de Grasse, defeated the English army led by General Cornwallis. As the news reached Europe, even more important than the military reverse was the sapping of the English will to continue the struggle. The way was open for peace negotiations, not only with the former colony but with her allies France and Spain. Although these negotiations themselves would be protracted, the French 'heroes' of the American struggle now began to return to their own country, regaling their compatriots with stories brought back from the New World. These stories concerned a country where American rebels – with French assistance, of course – had taken charge of their own destiny and cast off the oppressive rule of a king, creating thereby a very different political system.

The Marquis de La Fayette, for example, arrived back in Paris to his wife's family home of the Hôtel de Noailles on 21 January 1782. This happened to be the day set apart for the official celebrations of the birth of the Dauphin, now three months old. There was the ceremony of 'churching' for the royal mother at the cathedral of Notre-Dame (a rite of purification after childbirth), followed by a banquet at the Hôtel de Ville, and in the end a huge display of fireworks. The Queen, taking the Marquise de La Fayette, a member of her household, into her own coach, proceeded to the Hôtel de Noailles, where she graciously received La Fayette himself at the door. It was the kind of considerate gesture at which Marie Antoinette excelled. It did not, however, stop La Fayette observing of a subsequent lavish court ball that the cost would have equipped a whole regiment in America ... He was literally and metaphorically coming from a different place.[11]

There was another rite of passage a month after the Dauphin's birth. On 21 November 1781 Louis XVI recorded in his laconic *Journal*: 'Nothing,' meaning no hunting, then: 'Death of Monsieur de Maurepas at eleven-thirty in the evening.' Joseph II was quick to point out that the disappearance of the King's mentor, his chief servant for over seven years, presented an obvious political opportunity for the Queen in the first flush of her triumph as the mother of the Dauphin. Marie Antoinette's advisor, the Abbé de Vermond, put forward the name of the ambitious Archbishop of Toulouse, Loménie de Brienne, as a substitute, who would act as the Queen's man. But the King, with a new sense of his own independence, declined angrily.[12]

The real gainer from Maurepas' death was not Marie Antoinette but Vergennes, who was able to slip unostentatiously into the position of confidence that his patron Maurepas had formerly occupied. By February 1782 Mercy was back with his usual litany of complaints about the Queen's unreliable behaviour where politics were concerned; how she let the King believe she was bored with affairs of state and did not even want to know about them. Her 'great credit' with her husband was used only to dispense favours.[13]

It might have been better for Marie Antoinette's reputation in France if she had maintained the apolitical stance that obviously accorded with her own deepest wishes, despite family pressure from Austria. Unfortunately – for her – she continued to be an important chess piece in the predatory foreign schemes of Joseph II, as she had once been a pawn in her mother's game of matrimonial alliances. Over the next few years, the Emperor made relentless demands on his sister. She must assure him of French support by exerting her influence with the King. Yet in most areas, the foreign policy of Austria, as interpreted by the Emperor, brought him into conflict with French interests. Nevertheless Joseph urged on Marie Antoinette what he called 'the finest and greatest role that any woman ever played'.[14] (He had forgotten the late Empress Maria Teresa, it seems, in his attempt to galvanize his sister.)

The previous year, the Emperor and the Tsarina Catherine of Russia had concluded a secret alliance against Turkish attack. Now Joseph gave Marie Antoinette instructions for the warm reception to be accorded to the Tsarina's heir, the Grand Duke Paul, and his Grand Duchess, a German princess. Arriving in May as the 'Comte and Comtesse du Nord', the imperial couple were subjected to the full panoply of Versailles, including a performance of *Iphigénie en Aulide*. There was also a masked ball in which Marie Antoinette appeared as Gabrielle d'Estrées, mistress of Henri IV, in shining silver gauze and a black hat whose massive white plumes were fastened by diamonds including one vast jewel. The customary lavish display of fireworks was only marred by the discovery of the Cardinal de Rohan who had bribed a porter to smuggle him in, despite his marked lack of invitation. The Cardinal was unmasked because he wore his trademark red stockings beneath his coat. The unforgiving Marie Antoinette was predictably furious and had the porter in question sacked, until Madame Campan – by her own account – successfully pleaded for him to be reinstated.[15]

A visit to the porcelain factory at Sèvres was part of the entertainment. Louis XVI loved the traditional royal patronage of the factory, including the annual 'Sèvres week' instituted in 1758. The new season's porcelain would be laid out in the King's private dining room, and the courtiers were heavily encouraged to buy, the King and Queen themselves setting an example with their purchases. In 1782, for example, there was 'jewelled' Sèvres for sale whose garniture made it extremely expensive.* Such things were, as Bombelles wrote, objects of luxury 'but a luxury essential to support'. At the factory the Grand Duchess was enchanted to discover that a ravishing service of lapis lazuli and gold, including a mirror with two Cupids at its base pointing to the words 'She is yet more beautiful', was intended for her.[16]

In fact the stout Grand Duchess was not a beauty, whatever the Cupids might pretend, and Marie Antoinette found her rather formidable with her stiff 'German demeanour' despite her tactful interest in French sculpture and opera.[17] Nevertheless, the Queen was eager to display goodwill towards the Russians, given her brother's new foreign initiative. Yet this initiative could hardly be pleasing to France. On the one hand Turkey, which was menaced by Catherine of Russia, was her natural ally; on the other hand France feared the increased influence of the meddlesome Emperor in the Balkans. In any case, the expense of the American war ruled out any military reaction. The French had to confine themselves to diplomatic manoeuvres.

Over the Emperor's next two projects, however, he needed French cooperation rather than French passivity. Joseph II planned to reopen the mouth of the Scheldt River; this was for the sake of the city of Antwerp upstream, which had been blocked from access to the sea by the Treaties of Westphalia of 1648 that had ended the Thirty Years' War. On this occasion it was the energetic Dutch Republic with its great commercial port of Amsterdam which could be expected to resist. Undeterred, the Emperor took the line that France was bound to approve his conduct not only by the terms of their alliance but also

---

* But there is no truth in the legend that Sèvres cups were modelled on Marie Antoinette's breasts, which would have been a quite uncharacteristic activity for this 'modest' and 'prudish' woman, conscious of her dignity as Queen of France.

because he had upheld their campaign against England.

At the end of 1782 Marie Antoinette promised Mercy that she would raise the issue with Louis XVI, and throughout February she mounted a campaign on the subject. Yet by June her efforts were still not bearing the fruit that the ambassador expected, and he begged her yet again to 'prove her devotion to the august house and family'. (He did not mean the Bourbons.) The following year Mercy despaired once more over Marie Antoinette's reluctance to use her personal ascendancy over her husband in a constructive political way. She remained maddeningly content merely to implement her 'persistent desire' to help people who petitioned her, springing, in the words of the Comte de La Marck, from 'a rare goodness of heart'. The Emperor was less interested in his sister's goodness of heart than in what he hopefully termed her 'feminine wiles'.[18] Alternately wooing and bullying Marie Antoinette, he instructed her to make use of these weapons of a pretty woman when dealing with her husband's ministers. Nevertheless, the Scheldt Affair languished, thanks to the absolute hostility of the King and his ministers. This was guided by Vergennes, for whom no feminine wiles could make up for such an extension of the Emperor's influence.

The second of Joseph's projects concerned an exchange of territories: the Elector Charles Theodore of Bavaria and the Palatine would receive the Austrian Netherlands in return for his own lands. But the French were equally hostile to this scheme, which would immeasurably strengthen the Emperor in Germany. None of this was liable to lead to good relations between France and Austria. Vergennes wrote frankly to the French ambassador in Vienna: 'We have stopped the progress of the Emperor three times and that's not easily forgiven' – the first occasion having been the War of the Bavarian Succession in 1778.[19]

On 1 September 1784 Joseph irritably accused his 'dear sister' of being '*the dupe*' (his italics) of the French Council of State, headed by Vergennes. In reply Marie Antoinette wrote a revealing letter to her 'dear brother' about her relationship with her husband and its limitations.[20] Whilst she did not contradict

Joseph on the subject of French policy, having spoken to the King on the subject 'more than once', the Queen described quite forcefully 'the lack of means and resources' that she had available to establish contact with him, given his character and his prejudices. Louis XVI was 'by nature very taciturn' and often did not speak to her about affairs of state, without exactly planning to hide them from her. 'He responds when I speak to him, but he hardly can be said to keep me informed, and when I learn about some small portion of a business, I have to be cunning in getting the ministers to tell me the rest of it, letting them believe that the King has told me everything.' When she reproached the King with not informing her about certain matters, he was not angry, but merely looked rather embarrassed; sometimes the King confessed that he had simply not thought to do so.

It was at this point that Marie Antionette made an important reference to the King's Austrophobe upbringing. The King's innately suspicious nature had been fortified by his tutor, the Duc de Vauguyon. Long before Louis' marriage, Vauguyon had frightened him with tales of the dominance – *empire* – that his Austrian wife would wish to exert over him. Vauguyon's 'dark spirit' was pleased to frighten his pupil 'by all the phantoms invented against the House of Austria'. As a result, the Queen had never been able to persuade the King of Vergennes' various deceits and trickeries. 'Would it be wise of me,' she asked pointedly, 'to have scenes with his minister over matters on which it is practically certain the King would not support me?'

Of course, Marie Antoinette let the public believe that she had more influence than she actually had, 'otherwise I would have still less'. This confession to her brother was not good for her self-esteem but she wanted to make it so that Joseph could understand her predicament. Was there a glimmer of realization that the proper duty of the Queen of France, the mother of the Dauphin, was not necessarily to pursue all the interests of the House of Austria? Not so far. The habit of family loyalty, encouraged by Joseph II at a distance and Mercy closer to home, was still too strong.

*

Domesticity – the care of her own precious family – was where Marie Antoinette's heart lay at this point, not surprisingly when one considers her strong maternal instinct on the one hand and the difficulties she had encountered in producing this family on the other. The Queen was, for example, personally concerned with the education of her daughter, 'keeping her with her all day long' and certainly not wishing to hand her over entirely to the grand court servants who believed it was their right – not the mother's – to rear the Children of France. Such a pre-occupation ran through her letters to her friends the Hesse Princesses, while Count Mercy groaned over the childish talk and games that distracted the Queen from her true political duties.[21] An unexpected and horrifying bankruptcy of a noble family in the early autumn of 1782 was therefore of particular concern to the Queen because it involved the Royal Governess of her children. This was the Princesse de Guéméné who only a year previously had so happily paraded the newborn Dauphin round the ranks of applauding courtiers.

Afterwards the Prince de Rohan-Guéméné – to give him his full title – issued the following sympathetic explanation of his bankruptcy. He invoked the name of the notary Sieur Marchand who had produced all the trouble by his creative way with annuities: 'I was deceived and I have deceived the whole world. To do Monsieur Marchand justice he was led on by the desire to give us a splendid lifestyle.' To provide the Prince and Princesse with income, Marchand had in fact encouraged all types of people to invest their savings in these annuities by offering enticing and therefore exorbitant rates of interest. Then he – or rather the Prince de Guéméné – could not pay. It was the latter who went bankrupt to the tune of 33 million livres although it was Marchand who went to prison, a fate preferable to facing the creditors in the outside world.[22]

The Rohan-Guéménés, as a couple, had been dazzling, and for a while it was difficult to believe in the collapse of their brilliant future. The Prince, aged thirty-two in 1782, was a nephew of the former Royal Governess, the Comtesse de Marsan, and the Cardinal de Rohan. His wife came from another branch of the family, Rohan-Soubise, headed by her father, a Marshal of France who had been an intimate of Louis XV. It was an eighteenth-century marriage. The handsome and courteous Prince had been the accepted lover of the beautiful Madame Dillon until her recent death, in her early thirties, from consumption. The Princesse for her part was amusing, intelligent and rather eccentric, with a love of dogs that led her to believe that through them she was in touch with the spirits.[23]

Much royal favour was enjoyed. At the time of the King's coronation, seven years earlier, it was Marie Antoinette who had negotiated for the Prince to take the post of Grand Chamberlain. This had previously been occupied by the Prince's uncle on his mother's side, the Duc de Bouillon. The latter would have much preferred to have kept the position himself for his lifetime, allowing his nephew the 'reversion' – to receive it on his death. But Guéméné had his way. The lofty standing of the Prince and Princesse was confirmed by the fact that the whole royal family signed the marriage contracts of their son the Duc de Montbazon and daughter Josephine who in the Rohan fashion had married a cousin, Prince Charles de Rohan-Rochefort.[24]

As for the role of the Princesse, for a while it seemed that she might weather the storm if only because a Royal Governess, in common with other similar office-holders at Versailles, could not be dismissed. Yet it was unthinkable by the standards of the time – of any time – that someone tainted with such a disgrace should occupy such a position of trust and power, even if rumours of the Princesse's maladministration were probably not true. It was resignation or nothing, and this resignation was the subject of delicate negotiations. The Princesse finally gave up her post exactly a year after the birth of the Dauphin, the day of her greatest triumph. The King and Queen behaved as well and generously as it was in their power to do, despite the advice of Mercy and Vermond that the Queen should avoid any entanglement in this distressing affair.[25] Marie Antoinette secured an enormous pension for the Princesse on the surrender of her post, while the King bought the Guéméné property at Montreuil and presented it to Madame Elisabeth. Guéméné himself was similarly rewarded on his surrender of the post of Grand

Chamberlain, which was restored to his uncle the Duc de Bouillon.

Nevertheless there were elements in the whole affair that had uncomfortable repercussions for the future, despite the desperate efforts of the Rohan family, closing ranks, to pay off the debt. The Cardinal de Rohan lost a valuable contact in the departed Royal Governess, who was doubly related to him both by blood and by marriage. His sense of exclusion could only be enhanced. Naturally, the fall of the arrogant Rohans, with their high-flown pretensions to independent princedom, was greeted with sardonic glee by the rest of the court. One exchange had a member of the stricken family declaring: 'Only a King or a Rohan could go bankrupt on such a scale,' and receiving the rejoinder: 'I hope this is the last act of sovereignty of the House of Rohan.' On the surface the stain of the disgrace remained. When the old Duc de Bouillon finally died six years later, Louis XVI still felt strongly enough on the subject to refuse to give the post of Grand Chamberlain to Guéméné's son.[26]

The filling of the vacuum created by the resignation of the Princesse also had a long-lasting effect on the reputation of Marie Antoinette. With her strong views on the education of her children, her unfashionable desire to be closely involved with it, it was certainly comprehensible that she wanted to award the post of Royal Governess to a beloved friend. On any normal level, the Duchesse de Polignac, sympathetic and sweet-natured, was a suitable choice. She shared the concerns of motherhood; her fourth child, Camille, was born three months after the Dauphin.

But Versailles was not a normal world. The danger did not lie in the vices portrayed in the pamphlets about the Polignac with titles like *La Princesse de Priape* or *La Messaline Française*. Nor did Louis XVI object to the appointment. He took the trouble to assure the Duchesse in advance that he would readily entrust his children to her. His grateful reliance on Yolande's ability to manage the Queen and her mercurial moods did not falter. A significant report had the King entering the Queen's apartments and asking the Duchesse: 'Well, is she still in a bad temper today?'

Yolande drew the King aside, and although the subsequent conversation could not be overheard, it was clear from her manner that the Duchesse was advocating patience in the face of a storm that would soon pass.[27]

The new appointment was added to the list of benefits enjoyed by the Polignacs, from the thirteen-roomed apartment in Versailles to the reversion of the profitable position of Director General of the Posts, given to the Duc de Polignac. It is true that by 1782 Marie Antoinette was no longer totally dominated by the Polignac set. It was her affection for Yolande herself that was constant, although even here the Queen's mercurial nature meant that the friendship was likened by the Comte de Tilly to a beautiful day, not without clouds and changes, but always ending fair.[28]

As the King and Vergennes thwarted the Queen's will over certain appointments, passing over the Queen's candidate of Loménie de Brienne for the Archbishopric of Paris in favour of Vergennes' cousin, so the Queen herself stood out against the Polignacs over the question of the Comte d'Adhémar. He was proposed for the important role of Minister of the Royal Household, a post that had some of the connotations of a modern Minister of the Interior or Home Secretary. Marie Antoinette thought it an unsuitable appointment, preferring the Baron de Breteuil.

These signs of a decline of royal favour towards the Polignacs were optimistically charted by Mercy. But they paled beside the evident favouritism by which the Duchesse was made Governess to the Children of France. The rank at birth of the Duchesse de Polignac, if not modest by ordinary standards, was modest enough to be used as an excuse by Mercy to criticize the Queen's choice. What this meant was that some lady of higher birth was deprived of her perceived due. Thus the Queen created 'implacable enemies' for herself, in the words of her friend Count Esterhazy.[29] Where her children were concerned, Marie Antoinette preferred to let her affections dictate her choice. It is possible to admire on a human level the Queen's instinct for real warmth in her family circle – birth apart, the Princesse de Guéméné had never been a very suitable candidate as Royal

Governess – and at the same time to perceive the difficulties that such an instinct created in court terms.

The question of the Queen's affections sprang into renewed prominence in late June 1783 when that 'old acquaintance' Count Fersen returned at long last from America – he had been away for over three years. Marie Antoinette was once again pregnant, if not in such an advanced state as she had been at the time of their second meeting in August 1778. The baby seems to have been conceived in May if one is to go by the Marquis de Bombelles, with his intimate connections to the court, who thought the Queen was six months' pregnant in early October.[30] She was certainly pregnant throughout Fersen's three-month sojourn in France.

Furthermore this pregnancy was also a matter of satisfaction to both her and the King since it was becoming painfully clear that the miraculous Dauphin lacked the robust health of his sister. Although Louis Joseph's delicacy was at first denied by the Queen in letters to her brother, the evidence of his fragility grew cumulatively stronger as the years passed until it was tragically obvious. At any rate, the need for a second son as a safeguard was recognized early on in the life of the Dauphin Louis Joseph – apart from being an agreed principle in all royal families.

The point has some importance in reference to the marital relationship of Louis XVI and Marie Antoinette since it indicates the necessity for continuing efforts at procreation on the part of the King. Whatever his initial reluctance, this dutiful monarch did not now question this need. While hardly a sexual athlete, a Duc de Lauzun, Louis XVI had already impregnated the Queen successfully twice, possibly three times (the miscarriage in between) and had now done so again.

This particular pregnancy of 1783 was to end in a bad miscarriage throughout the night of 2 November, the Queen's twenty-eighth birthday; she had lost the child by the morning. It was ten days before Marie Antoinette even began to recover and her health caused general concern. Her foster-brother Joseph Weber, who had followed his fortune to France in 1782, testified to this. 'Look, Weber, I'm not dying!' said the Queen sharply to him as he expressed his worries. Yet on 1 December her uncharacteristically solemn demeanour on a public occasion still struck an English observer. After that, although Marie Antoinette confirmed to her brother Joseph at the end of the year that she was anxious to have a second son, she believed that she should have to wait for a few months until her health was fully recovered.[31] It is clear from Louis XVI's attitude to these not infrequent pregnancies that he continued to have sexual relations with his wife in the hopes of enlarging his family.

It is against this background that the developing relationship of Marie Antoinette and Fersen must be considered. In theory, nothing precluded Marie Antoinette from sleeping with Fersen as well as with the King, and conceiving a child by her lover rather than her husband. But it is worth pointing out that birth control had been known to the aristocracy for a hundred years by this time, and although described in the confessional as 'the baleful secrets' of society, it undoubtedly helped to cover up some of the extramarital goings-on at Versailles. Louis XV for example, another man with a long career as a lover, had used 'preventive machines' or condoms.[32]

But did the Queen in fact sleep with the handsome Count? On balance of probabilities, the answer must be yes. The idea of a great pure love that is never consummated, although propagated by some sympathetic historians, does not seem to fit the facts of human nature. There was no question of his supreme attraction. Tilly said that he 'was one of the best-looking men I ever saw', even 'his icy countenance' working to his advantage, since all women hoped to 'give it animation'. The hairdresser Léonard, who knew the court so well, described him more romantically as being like Apollo: someone with whom all women fell in love and of whom all men felt jealous.[33] Furthermore, Fersen adored women in general and in the particular, and his progress both in America and Europe was punctuated by dramatic love affairs. At the same time he prided himself on his chivalrous nature and knew how to be discreet. He understood how to appeal to a Queen who, all things considered, had

had a fairly lugubrious experience of sex during the last thirteen years.

Nobody expected Fersen to offer sexual fidelity to the Queen; that was not the mode. She was, after all, not offering it to him; that was not the mode either. His affairs did not cease, with possible candidates in at least two Englishwomen, Emily Cowper and Lady Elizabeth Foster, who was mistress of the Duke of Devonshire. What he did offer was exactly what she wanted: romantic devotion, accompanied from time to time, one must believe, with physical proof of it.

Very little was known of this at the time. Contemporaries were markedly reticent, while the *libellistes*, with their guns fixed on incest with the Comte d'Artois and lesbianism with the Duchesse de Polignac, were facing the wrong way.* There were a few nineteenth-century stories depending on hearsay, which hardly constituted proof. Nevertheless the verdict of the Comtesse de Boigne – 'Intimates scarcely doubted that she yielded to his passion' – is significant. For the Comtesse, although born at Versailles in 1781 and thus too young to remember these events, was old enough when she wrote her memoirs to have heard all the gossip within the bosom of the court; her uncle, who survived until 1839, was that *beau* Dillon, a member of the Polignac set once accused of being the Queen's lover himself. The earlier testimony of Lady Elizabeth Foster in her private journal is even more conclusive, given her own connection to Fersen and the fact that she moved in the aristocratic Anglo-French circle among which Marie Antoinette numbered many friends. On 29 June 1791 Lady Elizabeth wrote in her journal that Fersen had been 'considered as the lover and was certainly the intimate friend of the Queen for these last eight years'. She then went on to praise him for being 'so unassuming in his great favour ... so brave and loyal in his conduct that he was the only one to escape the general odium heaped upon her friends'.[34]

Nevertheless, documentary proof was slow to arrive. In 1877

---

* Madame Campan is discreetly silent on the subject in her memoirs, presumably anxious to recover favour with the Bourbons after her Napoleonic connection.

Fersen's great-nephew, the Baron R. M. de Klinckowström, who published Fersen's *Journal intime* and his letters, censored them heavily; the Queen's responses had long ago vanished, presumed destroyed. In 1930, however, a Swedish writer, Alma Söderhjelm, had the intelligent idea of investigating Fersen's Letter Book (which was still extant), a kind of filing system in which from 1783 onwards he noted details of his own correspondence. A correlation was discovered between a mysterious 'Josephine' and the Queen, Josèphe or Josepha being one of her baptismal names. As the years passed, Josephine did not always represent Marie Antoinette; confusingly there was a maid with the same name who features in his correspondence. But the evidence of unusual intimacy was there.[35]

After Fersen left Paris on 20 September 1783 he wrote eight letters to 'Josephine' before his return in June the following year. It is therefore perfectly possible that a reference to 15 July 1783 written in his *Journal intime* exactly fifteen years later ('I remember this day ... I went *chez Elle* for the first time')[36] was a code for the beginning of their liaison proper. On the other hand, Fersen was also extremely anxious to secure a military appointment and the Queen was equally anxious to help him – patronage that once again would have the paradoxical effect of taking him away from her side. Since at the time the Count and the Queen had not met for well over three years, it is also quite possible that Fersen was reporting with joy on his renewed access to her Private Society.

Similarly, one can interpret in various ways his letter to his beloved sister Sophie Piper on the subject of a future wife. Fersen had continued to toy with marriage plans that were always based on money, never on love. One prospective spouse was Germaine Necker, the Swiss Protestant heiress, daughter of the former Finance Minister: 'Her father has a big fortune ... I don't remember what she looks like,' he commented. But she preferred Fersen's fellow Swede, the Baron de Staël. Another prospective wealthy bride, already mentioned, was the only daughter of the Baron de Breteuil, the Comtesse de Matignon, who had been widowed in 1773; one of Fersen's Swedish friends, Baron Evert Taube, thought he was 'very much in love with her' – or was it her money? In any case the 'dissipated and elegant' Comtesse preferred to remain unmarried.[37] 'Unless marriage vastly increases my own wealth, it's hardly worth the trouble, with all its burdens, embarrassments and deprivations,' wrote the gallant bachelor to his father, declaring himself happy in his state. Therefore when Fersen also told his sister on 31 July that he thought the married state was not for him, he may have been inspired by his own cynical philosophy – 'the conjugal life is against nature' – or he may have been referring anonymously to his new relationship with the Queen: 'I can't be with the only person I want, the only person who really loves me, so I don't want to be with anyone.'[38]

One cannot know for certain, then, exactly when Fersen became the Queen's lover, although it is suggested here that he did, either in the high summer of 1783 or, if his long absence (and the Queen's early pregnancy) was an inhibition, the following year. It is noteworthy that Lady Elizabeth Foster's assertion that they had been lovers for 'eight years' prior to June 1791 would bring the date for its inception almost exactly to that of Fersen's return to Versailles from America. Unquestionably the Queen toiled away to help Fersen buy the colonelcy of the Royal Swedish Regiment, a French force originally founded to give Swedish prisoners the option of service or the galleys. The purchase of the colonelcy involved Fersen's father in the enormous expenditure of 100,000 livres, something that needed delicate negotiation. This had not been fully ironed out by the time Fersen left France on 20 September 1783 although he had already become 'proprietary colonel'. For a while Fersen had to endure accusations of profligacy and time-wasting from his father in Sweden, somewhat reminiscent of the reproaches of Maria Teresa to Marie Antoinette. Angrily Fersen pointed out how he had left the delights of Paris to follow General Rochambeau, spending three whole winters in America...[39]

Fersen's claim to the regiment was backed by his own sovereign, Gustavus III, who described him to Louis XVI as 'having served with general approval in your armies in America'. Marie Antoinette for her part wrote warmly to Gustavus himself along the same lines: how Fersen's father was not forgotten while the son had 'greatly distinguished himself in the American War'.⁴⁰ All was set for Fersen to return to Sweden to sort out the financial details of the vast purchase price with his father when a sudden summons came from Gustavus, who was about to tour Europe. Instead of returning to Sweden, Fersen was expected to join the royal party as Captain of the Bodyguard.

His brief presence in France – July until September – could well have contributed to the glamour of the relationship from the point of view of Marie Antoinette. And then there was Fersen's aura as a soldier in an age when soldiering was the proper, manly thing to do. (One of her early gestures of friendship was to ask to see him in his Swedish uniform.) Kings as well as counts were respected for being militaristic, as witness the general admiration enjoyed by Frederick II. Louis XVI, on the other hand, was that rare thing, a pacific monarch who did not relish going to war. The French King's indifferent attitude to military matters was a subject of contemptuous astonishment to his brother-in-law the Emperor, who suffered from no such inhibitions. On one of his visits to France, Joseph could not get over the fact that Louis XVI had never even visited the École Militaire, the military training ground. In the same vein, the King closed down the military camp at Compiègne and neither held drills nor reviews of his troops.⁴¹

The King, who as a child had dutifully learnt the lesson that one should not take up arms except for a legitimate cause, knew little by temperament of that kind of soldier's glory that it could be said the dashing Fersen incarnated. In the eyes of Marie Antoinette, Fersen – with his ardour, his celebrated discretion, his foreign birth, which distanced him from court feuds, his charm that made Louis XVI also enjoy his company – was the ideal cavalier. In fact Fersen might be termed one of the flowers of Marie Antoinette's crown.

The pleasures of Versailles continued although with time the development of a model village (*hameau*) at the Petit Trianon occupied more of Marie Antoinette's energies, and the amateur theatricals less. Despite the myth, she never actually dressed up as a shepherdess or a dairymaid, neither guarding sheep nor milking cows personally. These were, however, the roles that she regularly played on stage – in the spring of 1783 she portrayed Babet and Pierrette, both country girls – hence perhaps the evolution of the legend. Unlike Mademoiselle de Condé who at Chantilly dressed up as a farmer's wife, or Madame Elisabeth who had herself painted for the cover of a *bonbonnière* in a dairymaid's bonnet, Marie Antoinette considered her new simplified costume of white muslin topped by a straw hat quite sufficiently pastoral. Her dairy has been aptly described as a kind of 'summer drawing room' where the guests could help themselves to fruit, milk and other healthy products.[42]

The model village was the conception of the romantic painter Hubert Robert, and the design of Richard Mique, but, like Marie Antoinette's notion of a rustic retreat, it was scarcely original. It was in fact copied from that of the Prince de Condé, while the Duc d'Orléans at Raincy and the Comtesse de Provence, a great country-lover and gardener, at Montreuil enjoyed similar projects. The Comtesse ended up with a pavilion of music, and a model village with twelve houses, dovecotes and windmills, a dairy made of marble with silver vessels, as well as allegorical temples consecrated to love and friendship, a hermitage and a belvedere. The Duc de Chartres at Mousseaux had a remarkable garden including windmills in its design. Mesdames Tantes, never to be outdone where expensive living was concerned, enjoyed a country retreat at Bellevue and then at L'Hermitage. So the Baronne d'Oberkirch, who accompanied the Comte and Comtesse du Nord on their visit, stoutly defended the French Queen against the accusations of extravagance: 'All that fuss about a Swiss village!' Others spent far more on their gardens.[43]

Whilst that was true, what the Queen of France spent was inevitably more visible. A better defence lay in the fact that Marie Antoinette had created or commissioned things of great delight. Over 1000 white porcelain pots, with the Queen's monogram on them in blue, were designed to be filled with flowers so as to ornament the exterior of the model village's twelve cottages, with their lattice windows and stucco made to imitate worn, cracked brickwork and half-timbering.* Jasmine, roses and myrtle were rampant; the perfume of lilacs filled the air; there were butterflies in the sunlight and later the sound of nightingales. The Marlborough Water Tower, whose name came from Madame Poitrine's song, had pots of gillyflowers and geraniums on its steps. There was a mill and a dovecote. Its animals included a bull, cows with names like Blanchette and Brunette, calves, sheep and a Swiss goat; there was an aviary and a henhouse. However, a working farm nearby provided most of the produce needed for the Queen's visits. These expeditions, carefully noted by the King in his *Journal*, totalled 216 days over ten years, with 1784 accounting for thirty-nine of them, by far the largest annual amount.[44]

The Petit Trianon was a place where Marie Antoinette rejoiced in organizing country dances at which children were especially welcome, asking her English friend Countess Spencer for details of folk tunes like 'Over the hills and far away.' Life there clearly represented some attempt at finding a lost paradise. Yet not all the inclinations of the French court were similarly nostalgic. On 19 September 1783 – the eve of Fersen's departure – Versailles saw the amazing launching of the hot-air balloon of Dr Montgolfier in the presence of the royal family. Even the two-year-old Dauphin was brought along and the sovereigns duly inspected the balloon's interior before it set off. Azure blue, with the King's cipher on it in yellow, the balloon, according to one observer, looked like 'an exotic new plant'; the King, with his intellectual curiosity, was full of enthusiasm for this scientific advance.[45] Fashionable women sported fans with images of courtiers and balloons commemorating the event.

Among the spectators were two young Englishmen in their early twenties, William Pitt and William Wilberforce, who were visiting France with the aim of learning the language. Both were already members of the House of Commons. The official peace between France and England of the spring of 1783 had brought the English travellers, diplomats and aristocrats flooding back. They were busily prosecuting anew their complicated love affair

---

* Nine of them are still standing.

with the French in which their yearning for the French way of life had to be accompanied by a paradoxical contempt for these frivolous people. In Rheims, Pitt and Wilberforce had somehow struck it unlucky socially; the man who was supposed to introduce them to society turned out to be a grocer who neither could nor did fulfil his promise. The story caused some royal mirth at Fontainebleau, when Pitt and Wilberforce, hoping to see 'all the magnificence of France', encountered the Queen at a stag-hunt.

Marie Antoinette, apart from jokes about the grocer – she 'often rallied them on the subject' – was exceptionally gracious to the young Englishmen; she looked perhaps to enlarging her circle of foreign protégés. In return Wilberforce rated her 'a monarch of the most engaging manners and appearance', as the Englishmen continued to meet the Queen in the salons of the Polignacs and the Princesse de Lamballe, at billiards, over cards and at backgammon. Louis XVI in contrast got a less favourable verdict. The King was physically 'so strange a being (of the hog kind)' that it was worth going a hundred miles for a sight of him, especially out boar hunting. It was a young outsider's frank description of a king who at the age of twenty-nine conspicuously lacked the dignity commonly expected in a man of his position. The same comparison between husband and wife had been made a few years earlier in a slightly kinder version by Thomas Blaikie, the bluff Scottish gardener at Versailles; whilst the Queen was 'a very handsome, beautiful woman', the King was 'a good rough stout man, dressed like a country farmer'.[46]

Of the loftier Britons arriving in France, the ambassador and ambassadress, the Duke and Duchess of Manchester, belonged to a certain diplomatic tradition of hauteur. The Duchess complained of her accommodation at Versailles: 'As Duchess of Manchester I can accept this lodging, but as ambassadress of England, I cannot.' But the second ambassador, who replaced Manchester in December 1783, was on the contrary made for acceptance in the Queen's circle. This was the Duke of Dorset, a bachelor in his thirties and a man of extraordinarily handsome appearance and superb manners who would occupy the post for the next five years. He loved the opera, he loved the ballet (the ravishing dancer Giovanna La Baccelli was his mistress and he once took her to a ball with his insignia of the Garter on her forehead). The Duke entertained lavishly and he was prepared to send to London for novelties that the Queen might desire, such as an ivory-handled billiard cue. Although inevitably Marie Antoinette was accused of taking him as a lover, she actually found him cosy, terming him 'une bonne femme'.[47]

On one occasion Marie Antoinette was amused to see the young Comtesse de Gouvernet (later Marquise de La Tour du Pin) shaking hands with the Duke according to the English custom. As jokes like that about Pitt's grocer do not die easily in royal circles, the Queen made a habit of asking the Duke whenever both were present: 'Have you shaken hands with Madame de Gouvernet?' Marie Antoinette also expressed her disapproval in jocular fashion of the Duke's yellow buckskin breeches, known as Inexpressibles: 'I do not like dem Irrestistibles.'[48]

Apart from such companions, there were other amusements to hand to assuage the tiresomeness of political endeavours that satisfied neither her brother nor her husband. It would be an exaggeration to list reading among the Queen's pleasures; she never really recovered from that unfortunate late start. Like most European women of her time and class, Marie Antoinette enjoyed reading light novels, the so-called 'livres du boudoir.* References in her letters to more serious stuff tended to be directed at her mother or brother, with the obvious intention of impressing them. (One notes that she was still no more than 'quite advanced' in her reading of the Protestant Hume four years after she boasted of beginning it.) Nevertheless Marie Antoinette seems to have enjoyed historical novels, of the sort that could relate to her own experiences, judging from the amount of them in her collection. *L'Histoire de Madame Henriette d'Angleterre* by Madame de La Fayette referred to another foreign

---

* Clumsy attempts by her detractors much later to pretend that her library was full of pornography, illustrating her general depravity, ignored the fact that such books, which were romances rather than pornography, were read by the most respectable women of her time.

princess who had married into France, Charles II's favourite sister, who wed a seventeenth-century Duc d'Orléans. Of foreign novels, both *Amelia* by Fielding and *Evelina* by Fanny Burney were in her library in translation. The Queen's books were generally bound in red morocco, with an occasional deviation towards green suede, and the cover was stamped in gold with her arms, those of France and Austria. The books at the Petit Trianon, however, continued the tradition of simplicity there; they were bound, or half-bound, in speckled calfskin, and marked CT, for Château de Trianon, on the spine.[49]

Many of the books in Marie Antoinette's collection contained the words 'Dedicated to the Queen' inscribed on the title page. These included plays such as *Mustapha et Zéangir* by Sébastien Roch Nicolas de Chamfort, a tragedy in five acts, in verse, performed at Fontainebleau 'in front of Their Majesties' in 1776 and 1777, and later at the Comédie Française. Marie Antoinette proved a useful patron to Chamfort, helping him to become a member of the Académie Française and securing a pension for him of 1200 francs as a result of this particular play; it exalted brotherly love, something that the Queen chose to believe was also a feature of her husband's family.[50]

Even if the formation of her various libraries in her various palaces – by the end there were nearly 5000 volumes – owed more to the energies of her Librarian Pierre Campan than to her own, it is safe to assume that the music books in Marie Antoinette's collection were in frequent use. They were certainly very extensive, ranging from sonatas for her favourite harpsichord, via Italian songs, to the operas she enjoyed. Each new opera by Gluck was duly dedicated to her, and bound in its morocco, while the Queen owned almost the whole of the works of André Grétry.[51] When her brother asked her to look after Gluck's protégé – and successor in terms of Viennese opera – Antonio Salieri, Marie Antoinette was happy to extend to him her protection.

Such protection extended to personal contact, as it had with Gluck. In February 1784 the Queen wrote to Mercy. He was to tell Salieri to copy out various pieces from *Les Danaïdes*, his first piece on the Paris stage and dedicated to her, including a duet.

He should bring them on Saturday at noon: 'She will be happy to perform (*faire la musique*) with him.' As this letter indicates, Marie Antoinette was an enthusiastic amateur performer. There is also a lively tradition that she composed the music for songs herself, such as Jean Pierre Florian's Provençal ballad '*C'est mon ami*', even if her various directors may have assisted or guided her. Haydn, so favoured in Austria, never came to Paris. However, of his 'Paris Symphonies' performed in the Salle de Spectacle of the Société Olympique, that in B Flat (No. 85), probably composed in 1785, found particular favour with Marie Antoinette. When Imbault engraved the first edition in parts, No. 85 bore the title of *La Reine de France*.[32]

However, none of these diversions, not music, not 'romantic' reading, could allay Marie Antoinette's chief private worry. This was the 'languor and ill health' of the Dauphin Louis Joseph. On 7 June 1784 the King was out hunting near Rambouillet when he received an urgent message from the Queen. It was significant that many people at court assumed that the emergency was connected to Louis Joseph and that it denoted some kind of collapse. In fact, far more pleasantly, it was connected to the unexpected arrival of King Gustavus III of Sweden.[33] Among others, he brought in his train Count Fersen, who had been absent from France for the last eight and a half months.

CHAPTER FOURTEEN

Acquisitions

*'An interesting acquisition for my children and for me
... The Duc d'Orléans is selling me Saint Cloud.'*
Marie Antoinette to the Emperor Joseph II,
5 November 1784

The unexpected arrival of the King of Sweden – incognito as 'the Count de Haga' – on 7 June 1784 meant the hasty organization of a suitable royal welcome. Like Joseph II, the Swedish King preferred not to lodge in a richly furnished apartment at Versailles, bearing in mind the 50,000 livres' worth of presents that he would have to dispense afterwards. Count Fersen was put in charge of finding alternative accommodation; the Marquis de Bombelles directed him to the Hôtel des Ambassadeurs next door to his own house. Although Bombelles considered that Gustav's instinct for simplicity lacked 'noblesse royale', one could also see it as part of his general enlightenment.[1] Nearly ten years older than Louis XVI, Gustav III was a lover of French literature, an admirer of Voltaire and the *philosophes*; in fact, a passionate admirer of all things French. In Sweden he had instituted widespread reforms including the abolition of torture, while encouraging agriculture and science.

The next day 'the Count de Haga', dressed informally in a frockcoat, walked in the park at Versailles. Later he was found by the Queen bending affectionately over the cradle of the little Louis Joseph, as she entered holding Marie Thérèse by the hand. A certain coincidence may have been in both their minds – it was the birth of Gustav III's own son, another Gustav, in 1778

that had convinced Louis XVI that his own imminent child
would be a daughter. This meant that Marie Thérèse and the
young Gustav were already a possibility in the game of royal
marriage-alliances.

It was not the only one mooted for the five-year-old Madame
Royale, as Marie Thérèse was now generally known. Royal
daughters had been known by tradition in France as 'the King's
choice', on the grounds that their marriages provided a useful
opportunity for making alliances or cementing relationships. The
possibilities for Marie Thérèse included her first cousin on the
Habsburg side, the son of Maria Carolina, as well as her Bourbon
first cousin, the Duc d'Angoulême. This latter was the match
that Marie Antoinette preferred because it would keep her
daughter with her in France: 'Her situation would be far
preferable to that of the Queen of any other country.' Then
there was the more complicated question of Louis Philippe, five
years older than Marie Thérèse, who was the heir to the
Orléans dukedom.* The King's daughter represented a highly
advantageous match for the Orléans family by which they might
hope to leapfrog their way up the pecking order of the court.
There seems to have been some question of the marriage being
promised (or at any rate his father believed that it was promised,
which was not quite the same thing).²

The girl in question was not an easy character. A portrait
painted of her this year shows the wide eyes of the mother, but
also a small mouth with the corners turned down; the impression
given is of a certain despondency, confirmed by her nickname
of 'Mousseline la Sérieuse'. She was also haughty, very much a
Bourbon. Although the Comte d'Hezecques as a Frenchman
said that it was 'the Austrian pride' of her mother in her that
had to be corrected, in fact the reverse was true. It was
Marie Antoinette, aware of the disastrous results of the endless
deference paid to the Children of France by self-promoting
courtiers, who took various measures to curb her daughter's

---

* His father Philippe Duc de Chartres (much later known as Philippe Egalité)
succeeded his own father as Duc d'Orléans in November 1785. Louis Philippe
then moved up to become Duc de Chartres.

arrogance. Poor children were imported as playmates; Madame Vigée Le Brun, who painted Marie Thérèse several times, described how a peasant child was sat down with her at dinner, Madame Royale being instructed to do the honours; on another occasion her toys were given away to the needy by the Queen.[3] The result, not surprisingly, was that Marie Thérèse much preferred the father who bestowed on her uncritical adoration.

In one notorious episode, the Abbé de Vermond was deeply shocked at Marie Thérèse's reaction to her mother's fall from her horse. Hearing the news, the child merely enquired whether her mother had been in danger of death, adding: 'I wouldn't have minded.'

'Madame Royale doesn't understand,' replied Vermond; 'that means the Queen might have died.'

When Marie Thérèse repeated her indifference, Vermond asked incredulously: 'Surely Madame Royale doesn't understand what death is?'

'Oh no, I know perfectly well,' came the answer. 'You don't see people any more. I would never see the Queen again.' On being taxed further, Marie Thérèse refused to budge, saying that she would be absolutely happy not to see her mother again because then she would be able to do whatever she wanted.[4]

In her anxiety not to let her daughter be spoilt, was Marie Antoinette too severe? She may have had in mind her own childhood with its unhappy mixture of indulgence and neglect – and tried to do the opposite in both cases. The deputy Governess Madame de Mackau displayed a more graceful technique when she handled Marie Thérèse's rudeness towards the Baronne d'Oberkirch. The Baronne exclaimed with innocent admiration at how pretty the little girl was. 'I am delighted, Madame la Baronne, that you find me so,' replied Marie Thérèse with hauteur, 'but I am astonished to hear you say it aloud in my presence.' The poor Baronne was covered in confusion until Madame de Mackau remarked pointedly: 'Please don't excuse yourself. Madame Royale is a Daughter of France, and as such she would never let the demands of etiquette deprive her of the pleasure of being appreciated.' At which point Marie Thérèse hastily extended her little hand to be kissed and then swept a low curtsy.[5]

Louis Joseph, unlike his sister, was a beautiful child. He was, however, fragile-looking because of the frequent fevers that racked him, causing desperate anxiety to his parents and to the dedicated Royal Governess, the Duchesse de Polignac. His appearance bore a certain Habsburg stamp, resembling the Emperor Joseph when young if one allows for his delicate looks; he was sweet-natured as invalid children often are. Fortunately he had sufficiently recovered from the attack that coincided with the arrival of the Swedish King for the Duchesse de Polignac to give a supper in honour of King Gustav in her apartments. The Queen arrived very late, having been in Paris attending a performance of the latest artistic sensation at the Comédie Française, Beaumarchais' play *Le Mariage de Figaro*. She had been late at the theatre too, due to the conflicting demands of the Swedish visit, and the first act was already over. Nevertheless the enthusiastic public seized the opportunity to insist that it should be given all over again.

Figaro, first performed publicly in April 1784, was a triumph despite an inauspicious start when the King banned it. By September Mrs Thrale commented on the French mania for the piece, which struck her – ironically enough – as quaintly old-fashioned: 'The Parisians are not thinking about Pictures or Poetry; they are all wild about a wretched Comedy called *Figaro*, full of such Wit as we were fond of in Charles the Second's Reign; all Indecent Merriment and gross Immorality mixed however with Satire.' French women now carried fans with Beaumarchais' verses on them as they had done with Gay's *Beggar's Opera* in London. Others wore bonnets *à la Suzanne*, with garlands of white flowers as worn by the actress in the role of Figaro's betrothed. Baron Grimm described how the pressure for tickets was so great that duchesses were compelled to jostle with women of the town in the balcony.[6]

Louis XVI's initial hostile reaction was not based on ignorance but on a secret reading of the play by Madame Campan, instigated by the Queen. One might interpret his hostility as prescient where this radical work (*pace* Mrs Thrale) was concerned.

In this he showed more awareness than his own court. As the Baronne d'Oberkirch observed of the nobility applauding the witty diatribes against their own order, the triumph of the valet and maid over the noble master, these were people 'slapping their own cheeks'. The First Lady of the Bedchamber was told to arrive at 3 p.m. for a long session, having taken care to eat dinner first. In the event the reading was punctuated by involuntary cries of disgust from Louis XVI: 'But that's monstrous! How dreadful!' And again: 'What bad taste! What terrible taste!'[7] If Marie Antoinette's intention had been to manipulate the King to allow a performance, it certainly backfired since he ended by swearing that it would never be allowed.

Fortunately for Beaumarchais and the history of the theatre, if not Louis XVI, it was the 'bad taste' which prevailed. Private performances of 'the celebrated Nuptials' became all the rage, the Comte de Vaudreuil giving one for the Polignac set at his country house at which Monsieur Campan was present. Clandestine readings became so common that soon everybody was boasting of being on the way either to or from one of them. Bazile's cry in Beaumarchais' *Barbier de Seville* came to mind: 'I don't know who's being deceived since everyone is in the secret.'[8] So the King gave way.

Marie Antoinette never flouted her husband's wishes publicly, maintaining that womanly attitude of submission so strongly advocated for wives by the late Empress. Now she was able to attend Beaumarchais' great hit in person. *Figaro* in its speckled calfskin, stamped C.T. and under its original title *La Folle Journée*, was placed in the Trianon library. In her enjoyment of *Figaro*, Marie Antoinette could not imagine the consequences to her personally of the piece's wild popularity. This was not a question of its radicalism – the 'slapping' of their own cheeks by the nobility even as they applauded. It was the plot itself that contained unsuspected seeds of danger; a story of amorous and not-so-amorous conspiracies, of cases of mistaken identity with disguised ladies making rendezvouses in dark shrubberies, had become the staple of the Parisian stage – and Parisian gossip.

King Gustav – and Count Fersen – stayed in France until 20

July. After that Fersen returned at last to Sweden, where he occupied himself among other matters with securing a dog for 'Josephine', probably of a breed similar to his own beloved Swedish dog Odin; at any rate 'not a small dog' and as he ultimately admitted in order to smooth away difficulties, it was intended for the Queen of France.* After some discussion about the name, the new Swedish dog seems to have received the same Nordic name of Odin. Such canine presents were a proof of friendship or favouritism rather than passionate love, dogs as such being an important element in aristocratic society. Marie Antoinette, for example, gave Count Valentin Esterhazy a large, fierce-looking dog, who was named Marcassin and like Fersen's Odin became a somewhat spoilt feature of his life.[9]

Yet it is clear from Fersen's frequent communications after he left France that Marie Antoinette's intimacy with him continued during his six weeks' visit, punctuated as it was by prodigious entertainments. These included that given by the Queen herself on 27 June 1784 at the Trianon, with a performance of a piece by Marmontel in the theatre, music by Grétry, ballets, supper in the various pavilions of the garden, all against a background of the illuminated Jardin Anglais. Everyone had to wear white to be admitted, the result being that it was said to look like a party being held in the Elysian Fields (a reference to the celebrated Dance of the Spirits in Gluck's *Orphée*). At some point during this hectic period, Marie Antoinette became pregnant again, for the fourth or fifth time, as she had been wishing to do ever since her health had recovered from the miscarriage of the previous November. It was an event tacitly linked to the declining health of little Louis Joseph and the anguish of both King and Queen on the subject; for every optimistic report of his recovery, another one would follow describing a high fever.

It was therefore with peculiar happiness that Marie Antoinette was able to report to her friend Princess Charlotte on 17 August the healthy progress of a new pregnancy. (She believed herself to be two months' pregnant, the time-span Marie Antoinette

---

* This is a clear identification of the Josephine in question with Marie Antoinette, although as has been noted, it was not universally the case.

generally let elapse before making the announcement to intimates.) Poor Charlotte, with many misgivings, was about to marry Prince Charles, future Duke of Mecklenburg-Strelitz, the widower of her eldest sister Frederica, who had died in childbirth. Marie Antoinette tried to rally her with a radiant picture of Charlotte's future existence surrounded by the five stepchildren, who were also her nieces and nephews. But the Queen, ever conscious of the fate of foreign princesses, confided to Louise that she was apprehensive for Charlotte having to go abroad and change her life when she was nearly thirty...[10]

Could the child have been Fersen's? Since the Count had been in France at the right date, it was at least theoretically possible, which had not been the case with the Queen's previous pregnancies. It would obviously be from one angle a romantic solution. Nevertheless the fact that a solution is romantic does not necessarily make it the correct one. The baby's parentage was certainly never questioned by the King, which is proof in itself that he continued from time to time to make love to his wife. The Abbé de Véri confirmed this fact in his *Journal*. Even the most evil-minded gossips (those who knew the scene at the court, not the scurrilous outsiders) had to admit that the dates of the Queen's conceptions 'fitted only too well with the King's conjugal visits'.[11]

One more point should be made on a subject that can never be more than speculative. Fertility and sexual prowess are two very different things. It was Louis XVI, despite his deficiencies in the arts of love, who unquestionably begot at least two children. It was Fersen, the great lover, who did not. A likely explanation is provided by Fersen's celebrated expertise in all matters to do with gallantry; part of this expertise would have been knowing very well how to avoid procreation. Many years into his long amatory career, when his current mistress, Princess 'Ketty' Menchikov, announced she was pregnant, Fersen wrote: 'The news came as a complete surprise and made me very unhappy.'[12]

The future enlargement of her family was the motivation behind Marie Antoinette's desire to acquire a new property in the autumn of 1784. Saint Cloud, hitherto the property of the

Orléans family, was the palace in question. With three children, La Muette would be too small in the summer. Saint Cloud would be 'an interesting acquisition for my children and for me'; she also had to think of the younger children's future, compared to the dazzling prospects – in the material sense – awaiting the little Dauphin. Marie Antoinette believed she could leave Saint Cloud to 'whichever of my children I wish' because it was going to be her personal property. All of this appeared reasonable enough, at least from the Queen's point of view. The price – 6 million livres – was high, but could be covered by other sales such as the château of La Trompette at Bordeaux. Naturally the Emperor saluted with enthusiasm 'this new mark of tenderness' on the part of the King because it would bolster his sister's position.[13]

Unfortunately there were other interests at work beyond maternal preoccupation. The idea of acquiring Saint Cloud as a piece of personal property was probably the inspiration of the new Minister of the Royal Household appointed in November 1783, the Baron de Breteuil, who saw it as 'a ring on the Queen's finger'. He may have planned to be Governor of the palace but he also had a larger aim: to make the Queen rule or, put more elegantly in French, *'faire regner la Reine'*. The circumstances were hardly propitious for the furtherance of such an ambitious project. The Scheldt Affair had ended in frustration for the Emperor; he had not secured access to the mouth of the river for Antwerp, the French backing the Dutch Republic in its resistance, and had finally been obliged to agree to French mediation.[14] As for the matter of the Bavarian exchange, that had not yet been settled satisfactorily. Joseph had, as he thought, secured the agreement of the Elector's heir, the Duke Charles of Zweibrücken, who had been brought up in Brussels and was consequently not opposed to returning there. But the French, including Louis XVI, remained resolutely opposed to such a redrawing of territorial alignments.

In the end the scheme came to nothing because Duke Charles rejected it, but not before Marie Antoinette, six months' pregnant, had denounced Vergennes furiously in the King's presence for his deceitfulness. Vergennes offered his resignation, and the whole matter had to be smoothed over by the King himself. Vainly he tried to persuade his wife that the minister had no intention of causing trouble between Austria and France. Under the circumstances, Mercy's simultaneous complaint that the Queen was really only interested in the education of her daughter makes rather sad reading; it is certainly an eloquent testimony to the continuing gap between her inclinations and the duties expected of 'my dear and charming Queen' by Joseph II.[15]

If the Austrian ambassador deplored the Queen's 'frivolous' interest in her child's education, her efforts to secure her younger children's future by the purchase of Saint Cloud were no more popular in France. Breteuil's own character played its part in this. Now aged fifty-one, Breteuil was a wealthy widower with a magnificent lifestyle including a permanent mistress in the Duchesse de Brancas. As a diplomat he had served in Stockholm where he had formed a friendship with the Fersen family (hence that mooted alliance between his heiress-daughter and the young Count). It was, however, his eight years of service in Vienna, where Breteuil, unlike Rohan, had earned the approval of Maria Teresa, that constituted the bond with Marie Antoinette. Breteuil was an intelligent man of liberal ideas in politics; unfortunately there were those, his opponents, to whom Breteuil appeared 'tyrannical, haughty and silent'.[16]

For example, Breteuil greatly disliked Rohan and was disliked in return; his appointment as Minister of the Royal Household had exacerbated the latter's feelings of his niece's social exclusion, already stirred up by the forced resignation in 1782 of the Princesse de Guéméné, from the position of Governess to the Children of France. More important at the time, however, was the breach that Breteuil's handling of the Saint Cloud sale occasioned with the Controller General of Finance, Charles Alexandre Calonne. Marie Antoinette had never liked Calonne, despite his studied deference towards the Polignac set. This resulted not only in their further enrichment by 100,000 livres a year but also in further lucrative positions, such as the English embassy for Comte d'Adhémar, who had been passed over by the Queen as Minister of the Royal Household in favour of Breteuil.[17]

Fifty years old, Calonne was a passionate art collector, famously witty and with a sophisticated appreciation of women. Coming from the so-called Noblesse de Robe, the administrative aristocracy, his manners were so elegant as to call down the condescending comment from the Duc de Lévis that they were quite uncharacteristic of his class. One might have supposed such a man to have appealed to Marie Antoinette, even before Calonne, a close friend of Vaudreuil and Artois, embarked on his deliberate policy of placating the Polignacs. In fact the roots of her dislike seem to stretch back into the past, as is so often the case with Marie Antoinette; Calonne had been early associated with the Duc d'Aiguillon, the unforgiven minister of Louis XV. Now Calonne struggled to right the finances of the kingdom, including the appalling yearly sum needed to service the national debt which had originally been incurred by the Seven Years' War and which had recently been much increased by the struggle in America. His negative reaction to the acquisition of Saint Cloud was on the surface a predictable revulsion against the expense; but Calonne also resented Breteuil's personal handling of a transaction that he considered to be his own due. Lastly, he did not care for the Queen sitting in on his meetings with the King to do with the sale.[18]

Given Marie Antoinette's lament, expressed to her brother at this time, that she never really knew what was going on from the King, and had to fake knowledge in order to acquire it, one can understand her interest in being present at the negotiations. The real nub of the Saint Cloud problem – as it became, forming part of the groundswell of her unpopularity – was the unwise decision to make it her personal property. There was no tradition of such gifts to a French Queen Consort, and Saint Cloud was not a secluded 'pleasure house' like the Trianon. It was, in fact, near enough to Paris for everyone to take note of the unfamiliar command 'by the orders of the Queen' (*de par la Reine*) as well as the Queen's special livery.* It was enough to start the ridiculous rumour that if the Queen died, the property would

---

* A large pass-key to Saint Cloud, which still exists, firmly marked 'La Reine' in large letters, makes the point.

go by default to the Emperor. More seriously, there were protests when the letters patent of the King's gift were registered with the Parlement de Paris. One member of the junior chamber cried out that it was 'impolitic and immoral' to see the palace belonging to the Queen.[19]

Whatever the hostility incurred by its possession, Saint Cloud provided Marie Antoinette with a new opportunity to indulge her ardent love of interior decoration. There were the colours she loved, a spectrum not unlike the colours she chose for her clothes, pale blue and pale green for painted panelling, a kind of lavender-grey for the Great Bathroom at Versailles with its Neptune-like motifs of tridents, waterfalls, shells, fossils and corals; apple-green for the draperies at the Trianon. (But she hated orange according to Madame de La Tour du Pin and would not let the colour into her presence, even in the form of ribbons.) White material sprigged with blue flowers was used for summer in her private apartments; white muslin might be draped over the apple-green. Marie Antoinette, animatrix of the Petit Trianon, had a special fancy for the cotton *toiles de Jouy*, introduced into France in the 1770s, for chinoiserie or pastoral scenes in the style of Boucher. On the other hand the decor of the so-called Salon Doré in her private apartments, created about 1783, looked to a neo-classical future – white and gold with sphinxes prominent among the gilded decorations in the Pompeian style.[20]

A major part of the Queen's enthusiasm for decoration concerned furniture. Here too there were many interesting acquisitions. Marie Antoinette was an ardent connoisseur and showed discernment in what she chose and commissioned. Indeed, the elegant spirit of Marie Antoinette is perhaps better represented by those exquisite pieces of her known furniture that survive than almost anything else.* Favourite pieces were made of inlaid wood or lacquer and ornamented with gilded

---

* Apart from the French palaces, these can also be appreciated nowadays in many collections abroad, including the Wallace Collection, London; Waddesdon, Bucks; the Frick Collection and the Metropolitan Museum in New York.

bronze, often with flower motifs or children playing. Designers were celebrated *ébénistes* (cabinet-makers) such as Jean Henri Riesener who made more than 700 pieces for the Royal Collection overall.

Marie Antoinette had a weakness for furniture incorporating mechanical devices; David Roentgen of Neuwied, *ébéniste mécanicien* to the King and Queen, made her a writing-table surmounted by the realistic figure of a lady playing arias on a little clavichord. Riesener also collaborated with the German Merklein to produce pieces of furniture with mechanical devices to smooth away any possible difficulties in the Queen's luxurious routine. For example, a special mechanical table was constructed for her to eat in bed following her *accouchement*; it was so cunningly constructed that 'even the weakest hand' could lower it without making any noise. A dressing-table revealed little compartments for pomades, pins and furbelows, as well as producing a mirror at the touch of a button; another button transformed it into a desk or a music stand, which could be adapted for use either sitting or standing.[21]

This pretty but practical object, its wood edged with gilded bronze, was so popular with the Queen that she often took it with her on her travels. In general Marie Antoinette tended to move her furniture about, having a range of residences in which to arrange it within a comparatively small geographic compass,* including the Tuileries Palace in which she had a small pied-à-terre. Certain types of chairs – *bergères* or *fauteuils* often made by Georges Jacob – or the large chests of drawers known as commodes, were in effect reordered in exactly the same models. She also had a passion for little tables, and especially for the lightly built writing-desks called *secrétaires*. The name indicated their origin as places where writings could be kept secret. Also, from the psychological angle, one might point out that the hiding of her correspondence had been one of the Queen's

* Apart from her formal bridal journey through north-eastern France fourteen years ago, and the expedition to Rheims for the King's coronation, Marie Antoinette knew nothing of France; she had never, for example, seen the sea – neither on the French coast nor for that matter during her childhood in land-locked Austria.

prime concerns ever since her arrival in France. Sometimes furniture was specially adapted in order to be upholstered with the embroideries for which the Queen, surrounded by her ladies, had such enthusiasm, making her the ideal customer of Madame Éloffe, the fashionable purveyor of wools and silks as well as lingerie.[22]

None of this came particularly cheap and it was not helpful that the prices of objets d'art in general rose sharply after 1750. It would, however, be quite wrong to give the impression of an economical King married to a free-spending Queen, to say nothing once again of the extravagant habits of the rest of the royal family, including the aunts. All of them paid top prices for their own interesting acquisitions – up to 5000 francs each for commodes and *secrétaires*. Louis XVI, ordering from Adam Weisweiler, Jacob and others as well as Riesener, suffered from his familiar indecision as he tried out an ornate commode at Saint Cloud or ordered two beds in 1785 and then changed his mind. More sympathetically, he asked for furniture without sharp corners to avoid those painful encounters that threaten short-sighted people. Marie Antoinette, on the other hand, liked carvings of all sorts: rams' heads, fruit, flowers, of course – and the heads of her dogs.[23]

At the great sale of the belongings of the Duc d'Aumale in 1782, the King as well as the Queen bid lavishly, the latter acquiring two wonderful jasper tables as well as yet more commodes, which were then altered at yet further expense.[24] Nor did their expenditure on their apartments lighten with the years, despite the kingdom's worsening finances. One can point to the custom of the society in which they lived; that is what royalties did, in the process patronizing great artist-designers and furniture-makers. A more effective defence, as with the Petit Trianon, is to do with the creation of beauty. One might cite Marie Antoinette's boudoir at Fontainebleau as the supreme example of this. Of all the surviving rooms associated with her, this is the one that still ravishes the eye. Created on the theme of the pearl by Barthélémy, the Rousseau brothers and Roland in 1786, delicate flowers, cherubs and ribbons decorate the pale iridescent silk of its walls and furnishings; Riesener's glimmering mother-of-pearl *secrétaire* with its diamond-shaped paillettes evokes the graceful ghost of its royal owner.*

Oddly enough in one who had such a vivid interest in her personal setting, the Queen was not particularly interested in painting. She was unimpressed by the great classical and biblical compositions hanging in the Louvre on which her husband, for example, expended a lot of money. Marie Antoinette preferred the romantic seascapes, sunsets and storms of Claude Joseph Vernet, a follower of Claude Lorraine. Sending for Vernet after she had admired his works in the Salon of the Académie Royale de Peinture et Sculpture, Marie Antoinette made royal small talk: 'Ah, Monsieur Vernet, I see that it is you who are responsible for our rain and fine weather.' She also liked animal pictures – the painter Anne Vallayer Coster was given lodging in the Louvre and helped to become a member of the Royal Academy and there were of course cosy little pictures of her favourite dogs, to complement the little black lacquer dogs, of Japanese work decorated in gold, sent to her by Maria Teresa. Still lifes were also popular; like Louis XV she admired Chardin, whose clear vision of the beauty of everyday things was so sympathetic to her own spirit. A picture of a pineapple in a pot by Jean-Baptiste Oudry, the famous painter of nature who designed for the Beauvais tapestry factory, was hung in an inner cabinet.[26]

Although Marie Antoinette enjoyed having family likenesses around her, and took the trouble to visit Habsburg family portraits executed in tapestry at the Louvre, she regarded pictures of herself with indifference, much as modern royalties must view official photographs. According to Madame Campan, she was only interested in resemblance.[27] The tremendous public fuss made about the group portrait painted by Adolf Ulrik von Wertmüller for King Gustav, showing Marie Antoinette with her two first children in the grounds of the Petit Trianon, seems to have left her personally unaffected. It was denounced on the

---

* The visitor to Fontainebleau, passing from the ornate nineteenth-century taste of King Louis Philippe to that of Queen Marie Antoinette, is likely to feel refreshed. The mother-of-pearl furniture was thought to have vanished for ever in the time of the Revolution, but was miraculously rediscovered in 1961 and replaced in its original position.[25]

one hand as too casual for a queen, on the other hand as unflattering.* Certainly King Gustav thought the picture did not do her justice, whilst to the modern eye the children are wooden and Marie Antoinette's face, beneath a dominating Rose Bertin *pouf* of feathers and ribbons, verges on the caricature. Yet Wertmüller was allowed to paint the Queen again in 1788 when the results were even plainer.

The main result of the unfortunate Wertmüller portrait was to advance the career of the charming young Frenchwoman Louise Vigée Le Brun, who was commissioned by the Minister of the King's Works to do something both more stately and more beguiling. One of her earlier portraits, a study of the Queen in one of her ruffled and sashed dresses, wearing a straw hat, had also courted trouble for an informality thought unsuitable in a Queen of France. Yet, as the new commission demonstrated, Madame Vigée Le Brun, a true Frenchwoman in contrast to the interloping Swede, was a natural image-maker for the Queen.

The same age as Marie Antoinette, Elisabeth Louise Vigée was the daughter of a minor artist and had married a fellow painter, Jean Baptiste Le Brun. She was the protégée of Vernet, whose portrait she painted. But it was in fact the direct intervention of Marie Antoinette that secured membership of the Académie Royale for her in May 1783. Extremely pretty, Louise's delightful appearance led to rumours that she was the mistress of various of her subjects including Calonne (possibly correctly) and Vaudreuil. She also shared the Queen's taste for simplicity, dressing in the kind of muslins and lawns that Marie Antoinette loved. She wore little powder in her hair at a time when the Queen herself was increasingly sparing with it, just as the latter's rouge was by now barely perceptible.[28]

In 1788 Louise would give a celebrated 'Greek' dinner in honour of Vaudreuil, with the guests wearing unadorned classical white. When the guest of honour arrived, he discovered the whole party singing Gluck. It was hardly surprising that a creature of such gratifying tastes, conveyed in the simple but

---

* Now in the Nationalmuseum, Stockholm.

The Duchesse de Polignac,
Marie Antoinette's long-term favourite;
contemporaries praised the freshness of
her complexion and 'her utter naturalness'.

Opposite and above: A group of pictures showing
Marie Antoinette's beloved retreat the Petit Trianon,
the Temple of Love and the *hameau* (model village).

Marie Antoinette's cipher.

Manon Lescaut by the Abbé Prevost, part of Marie Antoinette's library and showing her arms on the cover.

Passepartout key to the palace of Saint Cloud, Marie Antoinette's personal property, marked 'La Reine'.

This painting commemorates the visit of Marie Antoinette's brother,
the Archduke Max, to Versailles in spring 1775; Max's tactless behaviour
stirred up trouble for the Queen.

Christoph Willibald Gluck, Marie Antoinette's former teacher, whom she helped to success in Paris in 1774 with *Iphigénie en Aulide*.

Marie Antoinette with her harp at Versailles; she is surrounded by her ladies and members of her household including a singer, an artist and a reader.

Marie Antoinette, aquatint
by Jean-François Janinet, 1777.

sensuous beauty of her work, should have received the Queen's patronage. In her *Souvenirs*, Louise summed up the essence of her most famous subject: 'I do not believe that Queen Marie Antoinette ever allowed an occasion to pass by without saying an agreeable thing to those who had the honour of approaching her.'[29] That innate charm, based on a wish to please, which had characterized Marie Antoinette since childhood, was something the portraitist's talent made her ideally qualified to convey.

The birth of the Queen's third child took place at seven-thirty in the morning on Easter Sunday, 27 March 1785. The Queen had been so large that Calonne, as the appropriate minister, was said to have prepared two blue ribbons of the Order of the Saint Esprit for twin princes.[30] But it was in fact a single healthy boy, who was named Louis Charles at his instant baptism half an hour later and was equally immediately created Duc de Normandie. Since the godmother was to be Queen Maria Carolina, the name Charles, the French version of Carolus, was a tribute to Marie Antoinette's favourite sister, and to the shared childhood of Charlotte and Antoine.

This was the first child borne by the Queen since the Duchesse de Polignac had taken over the position of Royal Governess, and it was therefore into her waiting arms that the desired second male baby was placed; the emotion felt by this sensitive creature was so great that Madame de Mackau, as deputy Governess, had to stand and assist. Already, however, the Duchesse had done Marie Antoinette a favour by making sure that she endured the inevitable ordeal in circumstances less traumatic and less frankly humiliating than had attended the births of her previous children, not forgetting the Queen's life-threatening convulsions in 1778, when she was stifled by lack of air amid the press of spectators.

Royal women in Europe were beginning to revolt against this archaic ritual. It will be remembered that in Austria, Maria Teresa had done away with the custom of courtiers actually being present in the delivery room, banishing them to the next room; similarly in England, the German-born Queen Charlotte, who gave birth to fifteen children from 1762 onwards, permitted members of the Cabinet and the Archbishop of Canterbury only in the room next door – although the door was left open.[31] Now the Queen of France managed to give birth without the usual debilitating crowds.

In this case, it was helpful in the interests of the Queen's privacy that her *douleurs* were short-lived, and even more helpful that the Duchesse de Polignac, as Governess, was in a position to suppress the news that labour had actually started. The fact that this time labour took place on the morning of so great a feast of the Church as Easter Sunday was no disadvantage either, in terms of distracting attention. Marie Antoinette was well enough to sup with the Princesse de Lamballe that evening.

Like his sister Marie Thérèse, the baby Louis Charles impressed everybody with his strong constitution, as the Queen happily reported to Joseph II. In May, Marie Antoinette referred to his health again; he was definitely stronger than usual for a baby of that age. In time his sweetness, his lively winning ways and, above all, robust physique which gave such promise for the future, would make Louis Charles the chief source of pleasure in Marie Antoinette's life. His very presence would later remind her of the days when Yolande had been his Governess and they had all been happy together. She used the same tender endearment, *chou d'amour*, that the pious Dauphine Maria Josepha had applied to her beloved Duc de Bourgogne, Louis XVI's eldest brother.*[32]

The Queen had need of comfort at home. The Scheldt Affair had still not been settled, despite French mediation, and despite the fervent wish of the Queen for an end to 'this Dutch nuisance'. Her discomfort was also due to the fact that the war of attrition that had been fought by the satirists over a number of years was beginning to succeed. The birth of the Duc de Normandie was accompanied, naturally, by the usual accusations,

---

* Meaning literally 'cabbage of love' although *chou* has moved to have a secondary meaning of 'darling' or 'sweetheart'. It is unconvincing to cite Marie Antoinette's use of this endearment as a proof that Louis Charles was Fersen's son as has been suggested; leaving aside the unlikelihood of Marie Antoinette making an allusion to her child's bastardy in this manner, Maria Josepha's reference makes it clear that this was simply a pet name given to a beloved child.

although the name of Fersen, incidentally, did not figure in them. One sacrilegious parody of the Christmas Story had Marie Antoinette, like her patroness, the Virgin Mary, bearing a baby who was not conceived by her husband. Louis XVI was seen as a complaisant St Joseph figure, whose chief interest was stuffing himself with food and drink while the Queen gave birth to an heir to the throne 'engendered by love'.[33]

A picture was being painted, for the benefit of those who had never met Marie Antoinette, of an extravagant, foolish woman, without a thought in her head (except lecherous ones towards sundry unsuitable love objects, female and male), presiding over a dissipated court where Dionysian feasts were a regular occurrence in order to pursue these lusts. Her waning popularity with the French as a whole was noted by Count Fersen, who returned to France on 10 May 1785 and stayed until June before joining his regiment in Flanders. He noted how coldly Marie Antoinette was received when she entered Paris, as was customary for a queen following an *accouchement*: 'not a single acclamation' broke 'the perfect silence', although that night at the opera she was applauded for a quarter of an hour.[34]

At the same time, completely contradictorily – but when did that bother a satirist? – this frivolous creature was credited with machiavellian wiles where the manipulation of her gross and apathetic husband was concerned, mainly in the interests of Austria. But that was not the whole of it. Marie Antoinette was also being made the useful female (and, of course, foreign) scapegoat for the general political troubles of the King, troubles that had at their root the impossible financial situation of the crown. In this way rumours of grandiose feasting, against the background of a Petit Trianon pasted with diamonds and glittering with gold, became symbolic of resentment with the governing power as a whole – but focused on the Queen.

It was in this climate of public suspicion that, on 12 July 1785, Marie Antoinette received a strange letter at the hand of the leading jeweller, Charles Auguste Boehmer. She had received Boehmer briefly after Mass on behalf of the King, as Louis XVI had commissioned the usual bejewelled presents for the official baptism of his ten-year-old nephew, the Duc d'Angoulême. Like most of the celebrated international jewellers of the time, Boehmer was Jewish; he was regarded in the courts of Europe, where he was much at home, as 'a most amiable man'. With his partner Paul Bassenge, who acted as designer to his salesman, Boehmer ran a shop in Paris; but when their customers were the Queen of France or other great ladies, including the Comtesse Du Barry in the previous reign, Boehmer naturally brought his wares to them. In the past he had had many dealings with Marie Antoinette.³³ But this was before a passion for her children had taken over, coupled with an enthusiasm for decoration that went better with domesticity than diamonds.

In particular Marie Antoinette had rejected on several occasions an elaborate, many-looped diamond necklace, which Boehmer and Bassenge had probably produced with the Du Barry in mind. It consisted of a total of 647 diamonds, gemstones of the highest quality; its weight was 2800 carats. Taste surely played a part in her decision – it was certainly not the sort of thing that appealed to her personally – but also her change in lifestyle. The answer that the Queen gave was polite but firm: 'She found her jewel cases rich enough.' The jewellers, becoming slightly desperate over their investment, at one point asked her Librarian, Campan, to intercede, but he refused, as did several others. France not being the only option, a paste copy of the necklace toured other European courts – but without takers.

Boehmer and Bassenge also substantially reduced the price and suggested various easy methods of payment, which made the necklace, if an object worth nearly two million francs can ever be so described, something of a bargain. Since Boehmer had purchased the position of Crown Jeweller, he could not, for all his unwelcome pestering on the subject, be banned from the court. Nevertheless Marie Antoinette was resolute; she believed that the money would be better spent on the navy: 'We have more need of ships than diamonds.' If the necklace was such a bargain, the King might buy it in trust for his young family and in fact he did toy with the idea before deciding that the money would be locked up for too long. In short, the Queen of France did not want the necklace and never had. In her own opinion she had made this amply clear to the ambitious jewellers.

The letter that Boehmer handed to the Queen ran as follows:

Madame,

We are at the summit of happiness to dare to think that the latest arrangements which have been proposed to us and to which we have submitted with zeal and respect, are a new proof of our submission and devotion to the orders of Your Majesty. We have real satisfaction in the thought that the most beautiful set of diamonds in the world will be at the service of the greatest and best of Queens.[36]

Marie Antoinette's first instinct was to interpret this letter as a new solicitation for her custom. Nevertheless, even in that context the letter remained slightly baffling. The Queen read it aloud to her First Lady of the Bedchamber with the casual aside that, since Madame Campan was so good at solving the riddles printed in the newspaper the *Mercure de France*, perhaps she could cast light on this one.

But Madame Campan could not. So the Queen twisted this odd little missive into a spill and lit it at the candle kept burning on her desk to melt the sealing wax for her correspondence. The Queen remarked, most inappropriately as it turned out: 'This letter is hardly worth keeping.' As for Boehmer, she was determined never to use him again. She instructed Madame Campan to make it clear that she no longer liked diamonds: 'If I have money to spend I prefer to add to my properties at Saint Cloud.' After thinking it over, she was sure that Boehmer must have created some new piece of jewellery to sell to her.

What Marie Antoinette did not know, and had indeed absolutely no way of knowing, was that she was wrong on both counts. Boehmer had not created a new piece of jewellery and he was not trying to sell her anything. It was the magnificent if flashy diamond necklace of previous history to which he referred. And Boehmer was under the impression that he had already sold it to the Queen of France.

CHAPTER FIFTEEN

Arrest the Cardinal!

'By orders of the King, arrest the Cardinal!'
Baron de Breteuil, Minister of the Royal Household,
15 August 1785

The inexplicable letter presented to the Queen on 12 July 1785 had in fact been dictated to the jeweller Boehmer by Cardinal de Rohan. This step on his part marked the culmination of a series of terrible anxieties, starting with the fact that it was he who had actually paid for the diamond necklace. Like Marie Antoinette, the Cardinal believed two things about the situation, both of which were untrue. First, he understood that the Queen had wanted to acquire the necklace but lacked the immediate funds to do so. Second, he was under the impression that by advancing – in stages agreed with the jewellers – the large sum of money required, he would secure his heart's desire of gaining the Queen's favour. She had not spoken to him publicly – let alone privately – since that distant day in Strasbourg when she was the bride of the Dauphin, and he, as Prince Louis, had been Coadjutor to his uncle the Bishop.[1]

Just as Marie Antoinette could not begin to guess at the meaning of Boehmer's letter, so the Cardinal was equally at sea with what was happening. He could not understand, for example, why the Queen had not yet worn the necklace, although its public display was, as he thought, to be an indication of her gratitude. Most importantly, he could not understand why there had been no marks of royal favour, not even the slightest acknowledgement of his new status when that, after all, had been the whole object of the exercise.

Here then were two baffled people, Queen and Cardinal, neither of whom could in all fairness be expected to have guessed at the other's assumptions; as a result both were to be rapidly seized with a violent sense of injustice. This indignation based on genuine ignorance, these raised passions, felt by both sides, were present in the Diamond Necklace Affair from the beginning and were to have a devastating effect on its course. The enormous gap between their two perceptions of reality, Queen and Cardinal, might indeed have made the whole matter material for a farce – except that in both cases, it turned out to be a tragedy.*

A visit by Boehmer to Madame Campan at her country house on 3 August did little to clear matters up so far as the Queen's role was concerned. Boehmer himself was by now extremely worried at not having received an answer to his letter. He asked the First Lady of the Bedchamber if she had anything to pass on to him, and when Madame Campan told him that the Queen had simply burnt his note, he lost his famous blandness and burst out: 'That's impossible! The Queen knows she has money to pay me!' So the full story emerged, or at least the full story as Boehmer knew it. It was a shocking and also an astonishing tale for anyone who, like the First Lady, had had long experience of the character of the Queen.

Here was Boehmer declaring that the Queen had acquired the Diamond Necklace for one and a half million francs. He also explained why he had put it about that he had sold the necklace in Constantinople: 'The Queen desired me to give that answer to all who spoke to me on the subject.' Even more amazing was Boehmer's statement that it was the Cardinal who had actually purchased the necklace on behalf of the Queen.

---

* The respective points of view of Queen and Cardinal were put later by their acolytes, Madame Campan, and the Cardinal's Vicar General, the Abbé Georgel; both writers, although not necessarily present at the crucial scenes in the affair, received the confidences of their employers at first hand immediately afterwards.²

When Madame Campan retorted that the Queen had not spoken to Rohan since his return from Vienna, Boehmer suggested that she must have been seeing him in private, for she had already given the Cardinal 30,000 francs.

'And the Cardinal told you all this?' gasped the First Lady.

'Yes, Madame, the Cardinal himself.'

Madame Campan's advice was that Boehmer should go immediately to Versailles and seek an interview with Breteuil, the Minister of the Royal Household, since as Crown Jeweller, Boehmer was officially in his department. At the same time she expressed her amazement that such a 'sworn officer' should conduct an important transaction like this, without direct orders from King, Queen or even Breteuil. At this point Boehmer made the most troubling statement of all: far from acting without direct orders, he had notes signed by the Queen in his possession, which he had shown to several bankers in order to stave off making his own payments. So Boehmer departed, leaving behind a bewildered Madame Campan to consult her father-in-law. The Librarian advised her not to go to the Queen at the Trianon but to leave it to Breteuil to sort out this unhappy business. Boehmer, however, did not go to Breteuil; he went straight to the Cardinal de Rohan in Paris. As a result of their confabulation, Rohan made a memorandum about the results of Boehmer's visit to Madame Campan: 'She told him that the Queen had never had his necklace and that he had been cheated.' The Cardinal and Boehmer now knew that some kind of disaster was in the making although neither of them quite knew the whole of it as yet. Only the Queen remained in ignorance.

Two or three days later, Marie Antoinette, who was at the Petit Trianon, refused to see Boehmer again. It was not until the Queen casually asked Madame Campan if she had any idea what the persistent jeweller wanted that the latter felt she must speak out, in spite of her father-in-law's advice. Significantly, it was the question of the notes that she was supposed to have signed that was seized upon by Marie Antoinette: 'She complained bitterly of the vexation.' Yet the Queen still could not conceive of the Cardinal being involved in such a business. The whole affair was 'a labyrinth to her and her mind was lost in it' – a fair comment, perhaps, then and now.

Unfortunately the introduction of Breteuil, aided by Vermond, to discuss 'what was proper to be done', ended the Queen's original non-committal and certainly not ungenerous attitude to Rohan. Breteuil was quite clever enough to see his chance to destroy his enemy, or at least to attempt to do so. Neither Breteuil, nor at a lower level of influence Vermond, nor indeed Count Mercy d'Argenteau, seems to have given any real thought as to the best way to handle this unpleasant imbroglio – as yet imperfectly understood – in a manner sensitive to the nuances of French court politics. Mercy's agonizing physical condition had flared up again, making even travel to Versailles an endurance test.[3] All three of them – the Queen's protégé-minister, the Queen's Reader, the Queen's chief advisor over fifteen years – thought of the narrow advantage of destroying Rohan, rather than the protection of the Queen's reputation. Already so much damaged by the *libelles*, her good name should have been their prime concern.

So the stage was set for the confrontation between Queen and Cardinal, in the presence of the King and various ministers including Breteuil, on 15 August, the Feast of the Assumption of the Virgin Mary (Marie Antoinette's patronal feast). Even the method by which this confrontation was engineered was deliberately provocative, rather than firm but discreet. The Cardinal was already dressed in his sweeping scarlet 'pontifical' robes, ready to celebrate Mass, when he was summoned to the King's inner cabinet at noon. Here Louis XVI taxed Rohan with purchasing the diamonds from Boehmer and then asked him what he had done with them. 'I was under the impression that they had been delivered to the Queen,' replied Rohan. 'Who commissioned you to do this?' asked the King. Then for the first time, the name was mentioned in public that was to haunt all the participants of the Diamond Necklace Affair. 'A lady called the Comtesse de Lamotte Valois,' was the Cardinal's answer. He added that when he received a letter from the Queen at the hands of the Comtesse, he believed he was pleasing Her Majesty by taking the commission upon himself.

With indignation that had evidently been rising during this

colloquy, Marie Antoinette interrupted Rohan. How could he believe that she would select him of all people for her emissary, a man to whom she had not spoken for eight years since his return from Vienna, 'and especially through the mediation of such a woman'? With dignity, the Cardinal replied that he now saw plainly that he had been a dupe: 'My desire to be of service to Your Majesty blinded me.' He then produced a note from the Queen to Jeanne de Lamotte, which commissioned him to purchase the necklace. It was signed 'Marie Antoinette de France'.

It was the King who took the note and read it. His own outrage now took over. The letter was neither written nor signed by the Queen. How could a prince of the House of Rohan, the Grand Almoner himself, ever think that the Queen would sign 'Marie Antoinette de France'? All the world knew that queens signed only their baptismal names. The Cardinal did not answer. Pale and bewildered, he felt unable to speak further in the royal presence. On being pressed by Louis XVI on matters to do with his own notes to Boehmer, Rohan agreed to write down a full account of 'this enigma', in the King's words, in an inner cabinet. Rohan returned fifteen minutes later with an account that was as confused as his verbal answers had been.

This forged signature 'Marie Antoinette de France' turned out to be a key element in the Diamond Necklace Affair because it prejudiced Louis XVI against the Cardinal. Breathing royal etiquette since birth, the King simply could not understand how a courtier, and above all a Rohan, a member of a family so keen on the details of status, could make such a mistake.* There was indeed general amazement on the subject at court. It was not as if the question of queens (and other royalties) using simple baptismal names was blurred. On the contrary, it was a privilege proudly maintained; a friend of the Prince de Ligne once advised him, as a rule of self-advancement at court, to keep close to

---

* The contemporary equivalent would be a signature by Queen Elizabeth II of 'Elizabeth of Great Britain'. People remote from royal circles might not realize that her usual signature is 'Elizabeth R' (for Regina); but someone in public life, let alone a courtier, would react at once.

those whose forenames were sufficient for their signature.[4] Marie Antoinette, who had used 'Antoine' as a child, still used 'Antoinette' alone very occasionally in family letters where she signed them (mainly she did not). On all her formal correspondence, the Queen of France was loftily 'Marie Antoinette', with no need of qualification.[5]

Echoing the question of Louis XVI, how could the Cardinal have been taken in by such a signature? This is to assume that the Cardinal did not actually forge it himself. Although for some time this would be the King's angry conviction, he was wrong on this issue. Rohan's own trial brief for his defence would later make the reasonable point that if the Cardinal had really been either the forger or his accomplice, the matter would have been handled more intelligently. 'While it was certainly surprising that he accepted such a signature as genuine, it would have been quite amazing if he had been the author of it.'[6]

The simplest explanation of the Cardinal's credulity is probably the true one. It lies in humanity's infinite capacity for self-deception where some perceived (and in this case long-desired) advantage is at stake. In short, the Cardinal was part of a system that made the royal favour so essential that people resorted to desperate measures to acquire it. Added to this must be the undoubted genius of that seductive 'Circe', Jeanne de Lamotte Valois, as a con woman. The Cardinal was not the only prey of tricksters to find his own gullibility impossible to credit afterwards when the spell was broken. Besides which there was something naive about his character. This streak no doubt was the product of his vanity, the vanity of a man brought up since childhood to believe himself superior just because he was a Rohan, and thus unused to being checked; it was this that made the Queen's hostility – inexplicable to him – so hard to bear.

The Cardinal de Rohan was, for example, equally impressed by the brilliant charlatan known as Count Cagliostro, who, despite origins in the Sicilian peasantry, 'seduced him into the treacherous bypaths of the occult and supernatural', in the words of his own Grand Vicar, the Abbé Georgel. It is true that Cagliostro's claims to know the mysteries of the ages, having been born an Egyptian thousands of years ago, fascinated all

Europe at the time, along with his hypnotic appearance; the expression in his eyes was 'all fire and yet all ice', wrote the Baronne d'Oberkirch. (But she did at least spot that his accent was Italian, despite his supposed Arab birth.) This was, after all, a society in which the claims of Franz Mesmer to effect cures by the use of 'animal magnetism' were also taken seriously. The Baronne d'Oberkirch visited him too, and he fascinated among others the Marquis de La Fayette as well as Marie Antoinette herself, although it was the scientific-minded Louis XVI who initiated the investigation that caused Mesmer's fall from Parisian favour.[7] But the fact was that Prince Louis was no match for adventurers in whatever guise they came. Where worldly wisdom was concerned, he may have been a Rohan, but he was also a fool.

Psychologically the King could not accept that, so he took the easier step of believing Rohan to be a villain. By now Marie Antoinette, who had begun as a sceptic, found it only too easy to agree; her low opinion of Rohan was only reinforced by the production of the forged signature. Armand de Miromesnil, who was present as Keeper of the Seals, had the sense to query the propriety of arresting the Cardinal in such a sensational manner while he was wearing his pontifical robes. But that is in fact exactly what now happened, when the Cardinal returned from writing down his personal account of the affair. Breteuil, Rohan's enemy, was put in charge, ordered to seal all the Cardinal's papers in his Paris house and have him taken to the prison of the Bastille.

Perhaps the King still smarted inwardly over Rohan's appointment as Grand Almoner in 1777; on that occasion the former Governess to the Children of France had defeated the wishes of Marie Antoinette, leaving Louis XVI himself to cope with his wife's resentment. When Rohan was told of his fate, he protested by invoking the names of his powerful relatives, the Comtesse de Marsan and the Prince de Soubise, and 'the reputation of my family name'. This certainly exasperated the King. He replied sharply that he would try to console the Cardinal's relations as best he could. In the meantime, he did what he must 'as a king and a husband'. It was a reiteration of his words to Miromesnil over the need for immediate action: 'The name of the Queen is precious to me and it has been compromised.'

Louis XVI's instinctive and honourable support of his wife was the next key element in the affair. The King's chivalry was evoked, and as has been noted over the various libellous publications, he was always quick to rush to the defence of her reputation. Commenting on the news to Vergennes about how the Cardinal had made use of the Queen's name to secure a valuable necklace, Louis XVI declared that 'it was the saddest and most horrifying business that he had ever come across'.[8] From the Queen's point of view, this firmness from a man normally so vacillating was a heart-warming development. Ironically enough, the royal couple, still not quite grasping what could happen to them in terms of public opinion, were entering a newly harmonious stage in their relationship. Marie Antoinette repeatedly and happily praised the King's behaviour to her brother, relating how she had been much touched by the prudence and resolution he had displayed. When details of the affair were discussed with his ministers, the King took care to do so in the presence of the Queen; this was quite a new development, which sprang directly from his feeling that his wife had been hatefully traduced.

The trouble was that the chivalry of the husband prevented him from appreciating the wisest course for the sovereign. Whatever the Cardinal had done – and it was quite reasonable at this point for both King and Queen to see him as a conspirator, if not a forger – he still held a prominent ecclesiastical position at court and was a member of a family powerfully vociferous in the interests of its own. Vergennes, supported by the Marquis de Castries, who was not normally in agreement with him, believed that some special discreet tribunal should be used. If only Vergennes, an experienced and sagacious negotiator who was on good terms with Rohan, had been allowed to manage the affair! But Vergennes and Breteuil were enemies, while Mercy, who might have offered wiser counsels, also disliked Vergennes personally and was jealous on the Queen's behalf of his influence over the King. Instead Rohan was offered a choice of pleading openly for clemency to the King or being tried by the Parlement de Paris. Rohan's choice of the Parlement, whatever the verdict, both prolonged matters and took them into the political arena. Matters such as the rights of princes and the independence of the Parlement became inextricably entwined with the quite separate issue of the Cardinal's guilt and the Queen's reputation.[9]

Breteuil had a face 'beaming with satisfaction' as on 15 August he issued the orders of the King: 'Arrest the Cardinal de Rohan!' He did not know that there was in fact very little cause for rejoicing. A performance of Beaumarchais' *Le Barbier de Séville* at the Trianon Theatre found Marie Antoinette playing the girl Rosina, the young Duc de Guiche as her crabbed guardian Doctor Bartolo, Vaudreuil as Figaro and Artois as the amorous Count Almaviva. The Queen was equally unaware that it was to be her last appearance on the stage there.[10]

Even now the Cardinal showed that, gullible as he might be in many ways, he remained quick-witted. Taking advantage of an inexperienced guard, he managed to get a rapidly pencilled note to Georgel back at his house, instructing him to burn all his papers to do with the Comtesse de Lamotte. By the time Breteuil came to impose his seals, much of the evidence about the Diamond Necklace Affair, the 'labyrinth' in the words of Marie Antoinette, this 'enigma' in the words of Louis XVI, had vanished for ever. Added to this must be the fact that Jeanne de Lamotte Valois herself proved to be an imaginative liar on a grand scale, so that very little she said can be trusted.

The result is that the affair can never be unravelled with complete conviction as to all its details, although some things can be stated with absolute certainty about it. One of these is the innocence of the Queen; she had no prior involvement with or advance knowledge of the affair. Wild suggestions that Marie Antoinette manipulated the whole case in order to ruin the Cardinal not only ignore the fact that she had for years been successfully using her own best weapon of the freezing royal silence against him, but they also seriously misread her character. Never politically machiavellian, as Mercy constantly complained, the Queen was incapable of conceiving, let alone carrying out, such an elaborate conspiracy. It involved among other things deliberately signing 'Marie Antoinette de France', first to hoax Rohan, then to expose him, a ploy that could, of course, easily have gone wrong if Rohan had exercised normal common sense about the signature of the Queen.*

The Queen's complete surprise and shock is well attested, as is the way she persistently underrated the seriousness of what was happening in the months to come. On 22 August she told Joseph II about the 'catastrophe' of the Cardinal de Rohan in a letter that reiterated the fact that she had never in her life signed 'Marie Antoinette de France', the point on which she felt so keenly. She now thought the actual signature was that of Jeanne de Lamotte, a woman of low rank who had never had any access to her personally. Marie Antoinette was confident that all the details would soon be made clear to the whole world, which would put an end to the matter. A month later, it was the Cardinal whom Marie Antoinette castigated as a 'vile and clumsy forger', motivated by the need for money to pay his own debts to the jewellers. 'For my part I am delighted we shall hear no more of this horrible business,' wrote the Queen blithely to her brother.[12] Her main concern was the inoculation of the Dauphin, who was not quite four, against smallpox, which took place at Saint Cloud under her supervision. It went well enough although the poor delicate little boy had suffered terribly with two different sets of pustules erupting.

What then did actually happen and how did the Cardinal de Rohan end up with a forged note of repayment from the Queen of France at the hands of an adventuress? For that matter, why were contemporaries so fascinated by the whole tangled affair? The second question is easier to answer than the first. As an intrigue the affair had every element over which the prurient could gloat: the wicked Queen; the corrupt Prince of the Church;

---

* It was well put by a modern historian, Sarah Maza, in 'The Diamond Necklace Affair Revisited' (1991), that although the total innocence of Marie Antoinette was obvious, standard accounts of the affair viewed her as guilty 'because large numbers of people wanted to believe in her guilt'.[11]

the beautiful impoverished heroine, Jeanne, with her royal blood (as in a fairy story – princess-as-beggar-maid) caught up with these lascivious monsters … Even the theme of the diamonds was a help to pornographers since the word for jewels (*bijoux*) was a code for the female genitalia. (*Les Bijoux Indiscrets*, a tale by Diderot, had the eponymous 'jewels' relating their adventures.) One caricature showed the Queen with open legs being regarded by the Duc de Coigny as the Princesse de Lamballe held the necklace aloft. In another way the drama was much to contemporary taste because it echoed the kind of plot to be seen currently on the French stage.[13] All this meant that the web of fantasy spun around the innocent Queen and the foolishly naive Cardinal was much easier to accept than the actual truth: that the whole thing was a criminal conspiracy.

So far as it can be pieced together, this is the outline of what had happened behind the scenes before the 'catastrophe' of the Cardinal in August 1785.* About the only thing that was true in the contemporary perception of the affair was Jeanne's background. Although she was brought up in virtual beggary by her peasant mother, she did have royal Valois blood, her wastrel of a father being descended illegitimately from King Henri II. Whether or not he told her on his deathbed never to forget she was a Valois – he also incidentally told her, 'Never dishonour the name' – Jeanne certainly emerged from a fairly louche girlhood with ambitions.

Married in 1780 at the age of twenty-four to Nicolas de Lamotte, who simply assumed the rank of Comte and added Valois to his name, Jeanne had several other protectors. Her aim, however, was to secure some kind of pension by right of her Valois blood, for which reason she was among the crowds haunting Versailles, seeking advancement by personal petition. Her special wish was to get access to the Queen, who was renowned for her impulsive philanthropy, but it is unlikely that this happened in any formal manner – that is, if she ever came

---

* The fullest and most impartial study remains *The Queen's Necklace* by Frances Mossiker, first published in 1961, where the various contemporary accounts are compared side by side.

anywhere near to Marie Antoinette during the frequent daily ceremonies of Versailles that the public attended, for she was certainly not presented to her. Once Jeanne's portrait was engraved and widely disseminated for the general delectation, a copy was procured discreetly by Madame Campan at the Queen's orders to see if it would jog her memory.[14] It did not. In the meantime Jeanne's Valois story did secure some patronage from the Comtesse de Provence, and finally a modest pension.

Jeanne met the Cardinal de Rohan as early as 1783; they had some kind of liaison, although Jeanne was by now living virtually *à trois* with her husband and her lover Rétaux de Villette. It was no doubt the presence of Rétaux de Villette in her household that encouraged Jeanne to show the Cardinal friendly letters addressed to 'my cousin the Comtesse de Valois' by the Queen of France, since Villette, among his other talents, was an accomplished forger. By spending time in the Cardinal's company, Jeanne became well aware of his obsession about Marie Antoinette's favour. And so the elements for the sting were in place.

At some point Jeanne and her husband, with the active participation of Rétaux de Villette, conceived of a plot to rob the Cardinal (and the jewellers) of a large sum of money – as well as of the gemstones themselves. The Queen's commission to the Cardinal to acquire the necklace that she apparently coveted, and the arrangements she made for gradual repayment, were of course forged. The happy jewellers were delighted to negotiate the exceptionally low figure of 1,600,000 francs for the necklace, a reduction of 200,000 francs on the original asking price. At all points the false Queen in her notes urged the Cardinal to be discreet. It was the impersonation of Marie Antoinette at night in the gardens of Versailles – in the well-named Grove of Venus – that was, however, the master stroke. The Comte de Lamotte went to the promenade of the Palais-Royal, frequented by the ladies of the town, and picked out a young professional called Nicole d'Oliva whose salient characteristic was her astonishing resemblance to Marie Antoinette. Although Nicole d'Oliva was in her early twenties, with the fresh air of a girl painted by Greuze, she did have the well-known profile, including, one assumes, the Habsburg lip. In any case she was to appear to the Cardinal with her face obscured by some kind of headdress, and wearing one of the white muslin dresses the Queen often wore, all in semi-darkness.

The impersonation succeeded. A rose was offered to the Cardinal – a flower adopted by the Queen as her symbol, as everyone had seen in Vigée Le Brun's recent portrait – and the magic words were uttered that the Cardinal wanted to hear above all others: 'You may now hope that the past will be forgotten.' The resemblance between this scene and that at the end of *Figaro*, where the Countess Almaviva appears, veiled, in a dark shrubbery, to her own husband in the guise of her maid Suzanne, is too great to be coincidental. The pity of it was that the Cardinal did not reflect on the coincidence himself. As to the Queen's notes that followed, the Cardinal might also have reflected on a notorious case in which the Dame Cahouet de Villers used notes forged in the Queen's handwriting in order to secure goods from Rose Bertin for herself. At one point the Queen had even been seen to signify her approval of this transaction as though at a prearranged signal, (the forger had in fact taken advantage of one of Marie Antoinette's unconscious traits which was to nod her head regularly at a certain point on her journey to Mass.[15]) The Dame had ended up in the Bastille. With the false courage of audacity, Jeanne and her associates were confident of succeeding where she had failed.

Once the diamond necklace was secured from Boehmer, its fate was to be taken to London by the Comte de Lamotte. There it was shown to the English jewellers Grey and Jefferies in the form of loose gems, some of which had been so roughly prised out of their settings that they were damaged. Lamotte's story was that he had inherited the diamonds from his mother, but he was prepared to accept such an astonishingly low price, given their real value, that the English jeweller prudently checked first with the London police as to whether there had been a recent burglary. Satisfied, he accepted the gems. And so the controversial diamond necklace proceeded on its mysterious way.*

---

* It cannot be known for certain what happened to the stones. Some of them

The conspiracy, unlike the diamond necklace itself, began to emerge into the open when Jeanne de Lamotte was unable to maintain the modest repayments by which 'the Queen' kept the Cardinal and Boehmer quiescent; she could not, of course, secure that display of the necklace at the white throat of the Queen of France that her victims continued to expect. So Cardinal and jewellers both found themselves owed money; questions began to be asked, which led to Boehmer's note to the Queen, dictated by the Cardinal, of 12 July. Shortly after the arrest of the Cardinal, and following his statement, Jeanne was arrested; her lover, the forger Rétaux de Villette, was brought back from Geneva where he had fled; the hapless Nicole d'Oliva, who had imagined she was being hired for sexual services, not to impersonate the sovereign, was also arrested. Cagliostro too was detained as being part of the plot but he at least mounted a magnificent defence; he was guilty, he said, of no crime beyond the murder of Pompey at the orders of the Pharaoh in ancient Egypt. (He was subsequently acquitted either for his sheer audacity or more likely because he was actually not guilty.) The Comte de Lamotte remained at liberty in London.

The Queen's thirtieth birthday fell on 2 November 1785. It was a date that she took seriously. Marie Antoinette told Rose Bertin that her outfits must have more gravity; she renounced wearing her beloved flowers in her headdresses in favour of more matronly (and, to the modern eye, far less becoming) velvet *poufs*. Six months later the Duke of Dorset told Georgiana

may have been acquired by the Duke of Dorset and remained in his family, according to tradition, in the form of a tasselled diadem. It used to be claimed that twenty-two of the most fabulous brilliants were made into a simple chain, worn by the Duchess of Sutherland; this chain was exhibited in the Versailles Exhibition of 1955. But it was pointed out by Bernard Morel in a study of the French Crown Jewels that the diamonds of the so-called Sutherland Necklace were for the most part 'irregular in shape', which did not accord with a contemporary drawing of the 'Cardinal's Necklace', including annotations about the weights. Boehmer and Bassenge eventually went bankrupt. The case that their legal heirs brought against Princesse Charlotte de Rohan-Rochefort, heir to the Cardinal de Rohan, dragged on until 1867. The Rohan family finally paid off this 'debt of honour' towards the end of the nineteenth century.[16]

Duchess of Devonshire that their mutual friend 'Mrs Brown' (meaning Bourbon), as they nicknamed Marie Antoinette in correspondence, now looked on herself as 'an old woman', though he added loyally that she 'never was handsomer' than when she had appeared yesterday at the hunt at Marly. The fact was that the Queen was beginning to put on weight, and was in the majesty of her appearance; spring had given way to summer and a ripening summer at that. The Comte d'Hezecques made the point that her carriage became especially proud and regal as she faced the anonymous slanders over the diamond necklace. She might now be 'rather stout' but to illustrate her dignity, he quoted a passage from Fénélon; as the Queen proceeded to Mass in stately fashion, the plumes of her headdress shook, and she dominated all the other ladies of the court as a great oak rises above all the other trees of the forest.[17]

Some of this perceived stoutness can probably be attributed to a new pregnancy that began about the time of her birthday, when the Queen had not completely recovered her figure from the birth of the Duc de Normandie earlier in the same year. It was certainly an important point that throughout the months that followed, in which her unpopularity would reach unprecedented heights, the Queen herself was not only pregnant but feeling ill with it. This pregnancy, unlike the previous three which resulted in live births, never seems to have gone well from the start. For some time there was real doubt about whether the Queen was actually *enceinte*, and it was not until February that she confirmed the fact to Princess Louise of Hesse-Darmstadt. Count Mercy, having believed at the end of January that the suspension of the Queen's *règles mensuelles* was due to her distress over the Diamond Necklace Affair, wrote only on 10 March 1786 that she was expecting a child at the end of July. Court rumours sped around that the Queen was annoyed to find herself pregnant once more, on the grounds that she had already produced two male heirs; she herself told Joseph that she thought she had enough children and that this birth might have severe implications for her health. The Duke of Dorset told Georgiana Duchess of Devonshire that he would keep 'a sharp eye on the bambino: *without spectacles* I can guess who it will most resemble'. But this was enjoyable if scurrilous gossip among friends. Once again Louis XVI never questioned the baby's paternity so one may assume that his conjugal visits had not ceased – and Fersen's measures to avoid conception also continued.[18]

Marie Antoinette's reluctance may have simply been due to feeling ill; alternatively she may have felt that the gap between the two pregnancies was too short. It is more likely that she was expressing a kind of generalized melancholy at the way things were turning out for the worst in every department of her life. The Treaty of Fontainebleau of 9 November 1785 brought to an end 'the Dutch mischief' at last as the Emperor abandoned his claims to the Scheldt. But France's subsequent defensive alliance with the Dutch manifestly did not advance the interests of Austria. Marie Antoinette was left protesting – as usual – to her brother that the Franco-Austrian alliance was more precious to her than to anyone, without having any opportunity to exercise her influence in its favour.

If there was no comfort to be derived from France's foreign policy, neither did matters nearer home provide solace. By the beginning of December, all Paris was agog at the publication of Jeanne de Lamotte's trial brief, which contained a torrent of abuse directed at the Queen, filling in the details of the latter's supposed sexual intrigue with the Cardinal. Humiliating as the charge was for Marie Antoinette, given her total dislike for Rohan, it was gleefully accepted by the public. As Fersen reported to the Swedish King as early as September 1785, everybody believed that the Queen had fooled the King. These trial briefs, in theory addressed to the courts, were printed in advance and read avidly; Nicole d'Oliva's trial brief, for example, appearing in March 1786, sold 20,000 copies. They provided an excellent opportunity to disseminate sensational and scandalous stories without the possibility of contradiction.[19]

Private sadness completed the cycle. On 12 December 1785 Princess Charlotte, who had married her sister's widower with the 'terrible presentiment' that she too would die in childbirth, fulfilled the gloomy prophecy. She died at the age of thirty, having been married for not much more than a year, leaving a son, Auguste. Marie Antoinette was devastated. She told Princess

Louise: 'I shall conserve all my life my memory of her and my regret at her death,' and she asked for her own portrait, originally given to Charlotte, to be handed on to Auguste.[20]

The trial of the Cardinal by the Parlement de Paris in May 1786, and of the other accused conspirators, took place in a charged atmosphere in which the truth of the Diamond Necklace Affair was likely to be the first casualty. Almost everyone involved had another agenda. The King refused to allow the Queen to appear on the grounds that he himself was the fount of justice in the country and it would therefore be inappropriate. So her testimony was written down and submitted. She herself was anxious that the details of the spurious meeting in the Grove of Venus should not enter the public record because she knew perfectly well the use that the *libellistes* would make of such colourful material. (In the event it was not struck out and she was quite right in her prediction.) The Parlement de Paris in turn was anxious to assert its independence, while the Princes were determined not to allow this attack on their rank – as they saw it – to succeed. Vergennes, preferring to injure Breteuil rather than protect his master, chose to involve himself behind the scenes with Rohan's interests.[21]

For the King and Queen all of this took place against the bizarre background of a family visit from Marie Antoinette's brother and sister-in-law, the Archduke Ferdinand and his wife Beatrice d'Este, who, incognito as 'the Count and Countess Nellembourg', arrived on 11 May and left on 17 June. Marie Antoinette had not seen Ferdinand, the brother who had acted as her proxy bridegroom, for sixteen years.

The Archduchess Beatrice had gone down well at the English court in the autumn of 1785, her appearance being gallantly described by Queen Charlotte as 'not handsome but pleasing which lasts longer'.[22] Her remarkable intellectual achievements – she read Greek and Latin – were also pardoned on the grounds that she was extremely modest about them. At Versailles, however, the Archduchess's birth, which was not strictly speaking royal, was liable to cause predictable problems. It was particularly complicated since the Princesse de Conti, a Princess of the Blood, but not of course a member of the inner royal family, was her aunt ... As the great ladies decided who should call and when, and a series of lavish entertainments was given at the Trianon and elsewhere, a far greater drama was being played out in Paris.

On 4 June 1786 the Queen, still concerned with the details of her brother's seemingly endless visit, wrote a short note of instruction to Count Mercy. She added a short meaningful postscript: 'What do you think of the verdict?' She might well ask. The Parlement had delivered it on 31 May. The underlings were treated comparatively lightly, Nicole d'Oliva being acquitted with only a reprimand for impersonating the sovereign, and the forger Rétaux de Villette banished with his goods forfeit. But the Lamottes – he *in absentia* – were handed out ferocious sentences, including flogging, branding and life imprisonment. However explicable by the penal standards of the time, considering the nature of their criminal acts, these punishments still have a chilling sound.

But the Cardinal de Rohan was acquitted by the Parlement de Paris. He had to apologize publicly for his 'criminal temerity' in believing he had had a night-time rendezvous with the Queen of France and he must seek the monarchs' pardon; he had to divest himself of all his offices, make a donation to the poor and be banished from the court for ever. But he was free. The Parlement had believed in his good faith. As to that fatal assumption on the part of the Cardinal that the veiled figure in the Grove of Venus was the Queen murmuring invitingly in his direction, it was by implication a legitimate assumption.[23] It was the most damning denunciation of the Queen's way of life, as it was intended to be.

Dressed in purple robes, the colour of mourning for a Cardinal, Rohan received his sentence. Around him were eighteen members of the family of Rohan, all dressed in the less striking mourning colour of black. His fate, however, was enviable compared to that of Jeanne de Lamotte. She was stripped naked and beaten by the public executioner, then publicly branded as a thief, with the letter V for *voleuse*, in front of a huge crowd of prurient spectators. Jeanne struggled and screamed so much that the burning brand missed her shoulder and marked her breast. She was then taken to the women's prison of the Salpêtrière to serve a life sentence.

The marks upon the Queen's reputation were equally searing. Although not physically painful, they too would prove a source of torment. They were also ineradicable. When the news of the verdict was first conveyed to her, Marie Antoinette shut herself up in her inner cabinet and wept. To Madame Campan, she burst out in indignation that there was no justice in France. If she, the Queen, had not found impartial judges in a matter that sullied her good name, how would an ordinary woman like Madame Campan hope for justice in a matter that touched her honour? The King's comment to the First Lady was brief but eloquent. It also showed that he did not accept the Cardinal's innocence: 'You will find the Queen greatly afflicted and she has good reason to be so. But what can one say? They [the Parlement de Paris] were determined only to see a Prince of the Church, a Prince de Rohan, while he was in fact just a greedy man who needed money.'[24]

Finally the Archduke and Archduchess left, their last days clouded by the verdict; a great fête on 7 June had to be cancelled as inappropriate. Count Fersen left too for England, where he was goggled at by the smart English, who were friends of Marie Antoinette, and nicknamed 'the Picture' for his handsome looks. Even the King left the Queen's side. He went to Cherbourg and other seaports on an eight-day visit. His *Journal* recorded inspection of harbours and coastal works, and dinners aboard ships such as the *Patriote*. He arrived back at Versailles on 29 June 1786.[25]

As the father of the family returned, the Queen greeted him on the balcony of the palace with her three children, Madame Royale aged seven and a half, the Dauphin approaching five, and the Duc de Normandie at fifteen months. Touching cries of 'Papa! Papa!' were heard from the balcony. The King flung himself hastily out of his carriage to embrace them all. He was flushed with the success of his journey, during which he had demonstrated real technical and naval knowledge with his questions; in consequence he had conducted himself with an ease and bonhomie unknown at Versailles. After his departure from Harcourt, the people, much impressed by his goodness, were said to have kissed the sheets left behind on the royal bed. The day after his return, Louis XVI returned to his normal routine of hunting, which he had briefly interrupted for the coastal tour.[26]

Ten days later the Queen began to feel unwell. At first she denied that these could be labour pains. She continued with her own routine, which included Mass in the Royal Chapel. It was not until four-thirty in the afternoon that the ministers whose presence was obligatory, including Breteuil, were summoned. Three hours later, at seven-thirty in the evening on 9 July, the baby was born. It was a girl, instantly named Sophie Hélène Béatrice, and to be known as Sophie for the late Madame Sophie, the King's aunt, who had died of dropsy four years earlier. Mesdames Tantes were consulted about the choice of name; would it revive painful memories of their beloved sister? The royal aunts replied that they had absolutely no objection; on the contrary they would love their new (great-) niece more than ever.[27]

The Emperor Joseph was his usual frank self when he observed that it was a pity the baby was not a third son. The King on the other hand was extremely cheerful when he told the Spanish ambassador: 'It's a girl.' The ambassador was equally so when he replied with a gallant reference to the marriage prospects of the new Princesse: 'As Your Majesty keeps his Princes at his side, he now has a means [his daughters] of bestowing presents on the rest of Europe.'[28] From the first, however, such an august destiny for the new Madame Sophie seemed unlikely. There must be a strong presumption that she was premature, not only taking into account Mercy's original prediction of the end of July, and the Queen's unwillingness to believe she was in labour, but also the fact that the King had gone on his coastal tour so close to the baby's birth.

The baby did not flourish. The Dauphin's fevers continued to torment him, and to agonize his parents. As for Marie Antoinette's mood, it was one of rising 'outrage' over the treatment of her 'honour'. As Count Mercy told the Austrian Foreign Minister, Prince Kaunitz, she felt she had not been in any way avenged for all the disgust and pain she had felt.[29]

CHAPTER SIXTEEN

Madame Deficit

~~~

'Behold the Deficit!'
Note pinned to an empty frame, intended for the Queen's portrait,
at the Royal Academy, 1787

As Marie Antoinette continued to feel anguish at the acquittal of the Cardinal, and Louis XVI grappled with financial problems so acute that they threatened national bankruptcy, there was a second Habsburg family visit. On 26 July 1786, the Archduchess Marie Christine and the Archduke Albert arrived from the Netherlands where they had been made joint Governors in succession to Prince Charles of Lorraine. They stayed for a month, incognito, as 'the Comte and Comtesse de Belz'.

The timing was not good. The baby Sophie was only three weeks old. The Queen was slow to recover her health; she suffered throughout the autumn – and beyond – from problems that were probably gynaecological in origin: that 'terrible accident' in her first *accouchement*, which Maria Teresa had thought might be malicious. She was also frequently breathless and began to have problems with her leg. Joseph II thought it quite extraordinary that the two sisters had not met, given their proximity, but the omission had a perfectly good explanation. In the past Marie Antoinette had disliked Marie Christine for trouble-making with their mother. In the Empress's lifetime, the Queen had combated her plan to arrange such a visit with convenient invocations of the problems of etiquette, given Albert's comparatively minor status as a mere Prince of Saxony; it was the same point made by the French ambassador at the time of her wedding. With sisterly sweetness, Marie Antoinette had protested that she would not wish 'la Marie' to experience any difficulties at the French court.[1] Currently, the Queen resented the fact that Marie Christine sent scurrilous publications about her to Joseph.

Now 'the old ideas of the Queen', according to Mercy, made her fearful that Marie Christine would seek to dominate her once more as she had done in their childhood. All the same, Mercy trusted that the visit would result in warmth between them. Afterwards he had to admit that this was not the case. Put diplomatically, 'The renewal of acquaintance between the two august sisters had not been without its clouds.' Marie Christine wished to spend a great deal of time at Versailles, while Marie Antoinette was determined to curtail their meetings. Nor was the Archduchess invited to the Trianon. Consequently she did not receive the special souvenir album of this private retreat, which Marie Antoinette usually had made for bestowal upon her favourites, including Joseph II, the Comtesse du Nord, King Gustav of Sweden and the Archduke Ferdinand.[2] Perhaps the sisters might have been more genuinely sympathetic to each other, had they had some prevision of the storms that lay ahead not only for Marie Antoinette but also for the superior and critical Marie Christine.

A week before the Governors returned to the Netherlands, on 20 August, the Controller General of Finance, Calonne, presented an important memorandum to the King. It was entitled *Précis d'un plan pour l'amélioration des finances* and he had been working on it throughout the summer with a young assistant named Talleyrand. Calonne's bold attempt to combat the rising chaos in France, which was not only financial but administrative, suggested ways in which taxation would be far more uniformly and fairly spread. For example, a land tax was to be payable by all landowners without exception – even the Church – only the poor being protected against yet further burdens. Calonne also believed in the use of provincial assemblies in order to remedy a country-wide administration that was becoming unmanageable.[3]

Obviously the legal enactment of these reforms – quite apart from their implementation – was something that needed careful handling. Trouble could be expected from the Parlement de Paris, which was already in an obstreperous mood as the acquittal of Rohan had shown, as well as from the various provincial Parlements. The expedient chosen, an Assembly of Notables, was one that had not been used for 160 years, when Cardinal Richelieu employed it in an effort to outwit the Parlements in the reign of Louis XIII. This Assembly was now supposed to express its formal approval for the reforms, which would only then be passed on to the Parlements for their endorsement. They would then be officially registered by edicts of the King in that special process, the *lit de justice* (which could also be used to enforce edicts that the Parlement resisted). The point about the Assembly was that its members were nominated by the King from various categories; in this it was in sharp contrast to another body, the Estates General, which had been in abeyance for even longer – since 1614. In that body, the Three Estates of nobility, clergy and commons chose their own representatives.

The opening of the Assembly of Notables was on 22 February 1787; there were 144 members, few of them commoners. The Queen did not attend the opening, at which the King appeared with as much majesty as it was possible for him to muster, in purple velvet, flanked by his two brothers. According to Besenval, Marie Antoinette's absence was a deliberate indication of her disapproval for Calonne and his policies; she sided with those Notables – and there were many of them – who constituted an informed opposition and who would not be managed by Calonne. Afterwards Marie Antoinette herself denied this angrily: 'Me!' she cried. 'Not at all. I was absolutely neutral.' Besenval, a member of the Polignac set and a supporter of Calonne, replied smoothly: 'Madame, that was already too much.' He told her that it was a great mistake to be neutral in such circumstances, since it gave exactly the opposite impression of partiality; thus she was open to the charge of overriding the will of the King.[4]

In fact the Assembly of Notables was destined to fail for a

more fundamental reason than the 'neutrality' of the Queen: it simply did not provide the obedient endorsement that was its *raison d'être*. What it did provide was a plethora of debates, arguments and discussions, with demands that fiscal and administrative reforms should receive proper acceptance from the Parlements – or even for the summoning of that dread spectre, an Estates General. La Fayette asked his friend Thomas Jefferson whether the Notables should really be called the 'Not Ables'. At all events Calonne could not secure any form of closure. By Easter Week, the King was refusing to receive Calonne, and on Easter Sunday, 8 April, it was indicated that he was dismissed. At the same time Miromesnil lost his position as Keeper of the Seals, for exactly the opposite crime of having connections to the Notables who were in opposition.[5]

In other ways this period marked a time of change. Vergennes' health had begun to give way; he died on 13 February 1787, having served the King since his accession thirteen years earlier. On the one hand Vergennes' management had created an enormous dependency in Louis XVI, who was an irresolute character as even his admirers agreed; on the other hand Vergennes had held out successfully against the influence of the Queen in foreign affairs. It remained to be seen what his main legacy would be: an emotional void that needed to be filled, or an ineradicable distrust of Marie Antoinette on the part of her husband.

Naturally Count Mercy did not allow the death of Vergennes to pass without badgering the Queen over the appointment of a new Foreign Minister. Bracingly he told her that she must perform 'a service to the two courts' of Austria and France. The preferred Austrian candidate was the Comte de Saint-Priest who had had a varied diplomatic career over twenty-five years. An enemy of Vergennes, he was known to have favoured Austrian interests; he was also incidentally a close friend of Count Fersen, despite the fact that his wife was one of the Swedish Count's numerous mistresses. Privately, however, Mercy confided to the Austrian Foreign Minister Prince Kaunitz that although the Queen continued to have a leaning towards her homeland, an attachment to her own blood and feelings of friendship for her brother, she was 'incapable of acting positively in any of these interests'.[6] Marie Antoinette passively accepted that it was the Comte de Montmorin, a boyhood friend of the King, a former ambassador to Spain and a man personally unfavourable to Austria, who would actually replace Vergennes as Foreign Minister. Insofar as she promoted Saint-Priest, she did so with a conspicuous lack of energy.

There was, however, one small but significant alteration in the sentiments of the Queen. She now had a 'scruple'. Mercy himself seems not to have realized the importance of this change, dismissing it as part of Marie Antoinette's lack of interest in 'serious things'. Her scruple – her principles as she termed them to Mercy – struck him as merely annoying. Yet what the Queen was saying was in fact nothing if not serious. She felt that it was not right 'that the Court of Vienna should nominate the ministers of the Court of France'.[7] For the first time, over matters of Austrian interest, here was a Queen of France speaking.

Whatever Marie Antoinette's tentative new direction, Prince Kaunitz's attitude to her, expressed to Mercy on 18 March 1787, was shockingly cynical, given the years the Queen had spent struggling to represent the Austrian alliance, however unsuccessfully. 'If she were Queen anywhere but in France,' wrote the Austrian Foreign Minister, 'in another place with another government, frankly she would not be allowed any meddling in affairs neither interior nor exterior, and she would be a nonentity as a result in every sense of the term. Let us suppose for a moment that it is the same in France, and in that case, let us count on her for nothing, and let us just be content, as with a bad payer [of debts] with anything we can get out of her.' Even Mercy demurred at this crudeness, arguing that he preferred to continue to nurse the Queen along towards 'doing great things' as he had done for so long.[8]

The fact was that Mercy's own influence was beginning imperceptibly to decline. It was noticeable that the Queen evaded Joseph's invitation to visit him in Brussels where he projected a visit, on the grounds of her own health, her children's health (meaning that of the Dauphin) and then finally because such an expedition would be extremely expensive, and the Queen must set an example of economy. All of these excuses were undoubtedly true. But the impression is left nevertheless that the Queen was at last feeling her political way; there was plenty to occupy her in France, without visiting Belgium for an admonitory lecture on their shared interests from her eldest brother.

In early 1787 the Emperor's restless energies were darting in new directions. A radical reform programme drove the Habsburg-dominated Netherlands into revolt. When the Governors – Marie Christine and Albert – were obliged to negotiate certain concessions, Joseph was furiously angry. In the meantime his alliance with Russia meant that Austria was almost certainly on the verge of a new Turkish war, which the Tsarina was eagerly contemplating. As in 1783, there was a conflict of interests here between Austria's treaty with France and her understanding with the predatory Russia, which was made still more acute when the latter seized the Crimea.[9] Although Marie Antoinette continued to pay lip-service to the needs of the Austro-French alliance, it is clear that events in France were driving home – at last – the message that she might have to decide which came first, the needs of the Habsburgs or the Bourbons.

What caused this shift, in a woman uninterested at heart in politics, as many close to her attested, to someone with a very different agenda? Seventeen years is a long time at a court with such a powerful atmosphere as that of Versailles; in this case, it represented over half the lifetime of Marie Antoinette. It would be surprising if the character of the thirty-year-old Queen had not altered in some way from that of the childish if charming Dauphine who arrived in 1770. But Marie Antoinette's shift was comparatively recent. It is therefore plausible to argue that it had causes other than this natural development, which culminated in the famously 'serious' thirtieth birthday of 2 November 1785.

One obvious cause was the enlargement and growing-up of her family – not her Habsburg family but the Children of France, that little clutch of Bourbon Princes and Princesses to whom she had given birth, one of whom would inherit the throne. A deeper reason lay in the frightful adversity that Marie Antoinette had endured over the Diamond Necklace Affair, and the vicious, unfair libels surrounding it. This evidently brought new steel to a fundamentally pliant character. Increasingly, Marie Antoinette would find herself rising to challenges and, in doing so, transcending any previous expectations of a gentle, rather lightweight nature.

Of course she was hardly unique in being strengthened by adversity; but this neither is, nor was, the case with everyone. Louis XVI, for example, was by no means transformed by the purgations he was currently enduring. His apathy, his indecision, his tendency, surely psychological, to fall asleep in Council meetings – he even snored on occasion – all those characteristics so long bewailed by the courtiers, were only intensifying. There was a direct connection between the positive approach of the Queen – for better or worse – and the negative state of the King. Since she had been trained since youth to respect the male figure of her husband and her sovereign, it was as though she could only spring properly into political life when the natural order was reversed; then residual memories of the true power wielded by the dominant female in her life, the Empress Maria Teresa, might come into play. Nevertheless, this womanly sense of reverence for the King's immutably superior position was deeply ingrained and would linger to compete with her new activism. The following year Marie Antoinette would write: 'I am never more than the second person' in the state 'and despite the confidence that the first person [Louis XVI] has in me, he often makes me feel it'.[10]

In May 1787, however, the King was coming to the Queen's apartments daily and weeping. By August, Louis XVI was exhibiting all the signs of a major depression, in his own terms, brought on by the failure of his recent policies. Count Mercy described only too vividly the low state of the King's morale, which had led to actual physical degeneration. He hunted 'to excess' – as though to escape, where previously he had hunted to enjoy – and then indulged in 'immoderate meals'. Worst of all there were 'occasional lapses of reason and a kind of brusque thoughtlessness which is very painful to those who have to endure it'.[11]

The outside world interpreted this behaviour as ordinary drunkenness; Jefferson heard that the King hunted half the day and was drunk the other half. It is difficult to disentangle the question of the King's drinking from that of his physical awkwardness (including his short sight) since both could lead to stumbling. His enormous corpulence did not help either. The King's defenders promoted the idea that he was often taken to be collapsing with drink when it was actually with sheer physical exhaustion after the hunt.[12] It is only fair to point out that the Queen – who drank no alcohol out of choice, only mineral water from Ville d'Avray – was also accused of drunkenness and drunken orgies. Nevertheless there seems to have been a connection between the King's depression and his desperate seeking of escape in alcohol.

There was something gallant about the Queen's attempts to make good this situation. Her health continued to give trouble, not only in breathlessness but in headaches, which may have been at least partly psychological. Unfortunately her new seriousness did not transform her at a glance into a successful politician. Her lack of concentration, which can be traced back to an inadequate education, continued to undermine her own efforts. She loved to tell the story of one of her Lorrainer ancestors who, when he wanted to levy a tax, went to church and stood up after the sermon. He waved his hat and mentioned the sum he needed. If she yearned for this kind of feudal paradise, she was not alone in eighteenth-century France. It was nevertheless an illusion of paradise rather than a policy. As the Prussian envoy, Baron Goltz, reported in November 1787, the Queen has 'quitted her frivolous [Private] Society and occupies herself with affairs, but as she doesn't have a systematic brain, she goes from caprice to caprice ...'[13] However, the Queen, unlike the King, was also decisive and she had great courage. There were circumstances in which these qualities might be more important than the more sustained deviousness necessary in a natural politician.

The fall of Calonne, applauded by the Queen but also desired by the King, represented melancholy news for the Polignac set on whom he had deliberately lavished ingratiatory benefits. Ministers were never allowed much grace in the manner of their departure in eighteenth-century France, but Calonne was particularly bitter at the manner in which he was stripped not only of office but also of his Order of the Saint Esprit. Subsequently he went to Holland and then to England.

In the meantime the increasing coldness of Marie Antoinette towards the Duchesse de Polignac was the subject of general comment. It also produced a desire in Yolande to absent herself from court. Following his fifth birthday, the Dauphin had been handed over by the Governess to a Governor, the ageing Duc d'Harcourt, a decent if slightly dull man. Despite the continuing presence of the two smallest children in the royal nursery, the Duchesse de Polignac now set off for England in early May. There she was welcomed by her smart friends, to whom she was known as 'Little Po', and where she expected to form 'a female treaty of opposition' with Georgiana Duchess of Devonshire.[14]

It is possible to see this declining favour of Yolande de Polignac as part of the same alteration in the nature of the Queen's priorities. For all Yolande's charms and the hold that her delightful personality had had over the Queen for so long, she had never shown any real allegiance to the Queen's interests. Marie Antoinette took to sending a page to find out who was at the Polignac salon – for which she was, after all, paying. When she made some critical comment about the company, the Duchesse replied, with that exquisite effrontery so characteristic of her time and type, that just as she would not dream of commenting on the Queen's company, she could not tailor her own to the Queen's desires. The implication was quite clear. Yolande de Polignac was willing to provide entertainment and, above all, intimacy for a Queen who had been searching for all these things, but at a price. She needed to receive in return not only tremendous material and social advancement for herself and her family but also recognition of her power. The affection that Louis XVI felt for the Duchesse was a bonus. In spite of all his financial difficulties in July he would pay the debts of her unmarried sister-in-law, Comtesse Diane de Polignac, to the tune of 400,000 francs, on the grounds that this spirited and diverting woman had incurred them entertaining the Queen.[15]

On 1 May 1787, the man who was to be the Queen's political partner for the following vital months was put in control of finance, following the dismissal of Calonne. This was Étienne de Loménie de Brienne, who was sixty years old and had been Archbishop of Toulouse for the last thirty-four years. His appointment was proof enough of the King's depression since Louis XVI disliked Brienne personally for his unorthodox religious views. Clashing with the Queen, who had wanted to promote Brienne in 1783, the King was said to have exclaimed angrily: 'An Archbishop of Paris must at least believe in God!'[16]

The Queen's preference for Brienne was well established and she was said by Castries, the Navy Minister, to be 'madly happy' on the night of his appointment. Like so many of her likes and dislikes, this preference was rooted in the past, for her confidential advisor, the Abbé de Vermond, had been in Brienne's service before he joined her own twenty years earlier. Although Germaine de Staël would dismiss Brienne as 'neither enlightened enough to be a *philosophe* nor firm enough to be a despot', that was by virtue of hindsight and besides, hers was the point of view of Necker's daughter. Brienne's health was not generally good: among other things, he suffered from a disfiguring eczema, which repelled the King. He was seen by some as arrogant and taciturn, by others as 'a sly, artful fellow'.[17] But then reflection and cunning might be necessary to achieve results.

The worst thing that could be said about him, given the extreme unpopularity of the Queen a year after Rohan's acquittal, was that he was clearly her man. Marie Antoinette was now being hissed at the Opéra by the people of Paris. Once Gluck's line, 'Let us sing, let us celebrate our Queen' had been interrupted by popular enthusiasm; it was now the terrible invocation in Racine's *Athalie* – 'Confound this cruel Queen . . .' – that received the wild applause. Nevertheless it was still possible that Brienne, as a former member of the opposition party in the Assembly, could deliver where Calonne had failed.

That was not the case. Cutbacks at court had already been instituted under Calonne. When the Assembly proved no more malleable than before under Brienne's management, the latter fell back on this policy of retrenchment. The Assembly of Notables was sent away on 25 May 1787 and 173 posts were eliminated in the Queen's household alone. In terms of public opinion, this curtailment of court extravagance was a useful exercise, although it is noticeable that much of the heavy private royal expenditure on furniture and so forth continued as before. In these years, the King (who greeted reduction in the numbers of horses sulkily) bought the château of Rambouillet to improve his hunting prospects still further, and there were redecorations both at Rambouillet and at Fontainebleau.

The blame was generally attached to a single individual, the Queen, who in the summer of 1787 was derisively called Madame Deficit. But it was in fact the sheer number of French royals with the current or future right to their own households that was the real problem: the King's two brothers and their wives, who did not share households; the King's two nephews; the King's sister; the King's surviving aunts; and, of course, his own growing family.

The trouble was that this retrenchment was fiercely resented by the nobles who had come to see such positions as their inalienable right. Even Louis XVI's apathy was shaken when the Duc de Coigny seemed to be about to strike his sovereign at the news of his disbandment. The Duc de Polignac was generally admired for having taken the abolition of his *charge* as Postmaster General so 'tamely' yet he could surely expect to make some sacrifice for the monarch who had so singularly advanced him. Besenval for his part thought it quite disgusting how someone could lose one of their 'possessions' from one day to the next: 'That sort of thing,' he wrote, 'used only to happen in Turkey.' At the same time these economies did nothing to tackle the real problem at the heart of it all. By 1788, court expenditure accounted for between 6 and 7 per cent of the total national spend, while over 41 per cent went on servicing the national debt.[18] With the disappearance of La Fayatte's 'Not Ables', the need for proper taxation, falling on the aristocracy (hitherto exempt), and a proper administrative system to carry it out, was as acute as ever.

The Queen, with Brienne at the helm, was beginning to attend ordinary committees of the King and his ministers, not just those that concerned her directly. She was also mounting her own propaganda exercise in a wider sphere, promoting her image as the fecund Mother of the Children of France. Not only was this an historic role but it also went happily with the *Zeitgeist* influenced by Rousseau who praised women in proportion to their enthusiastic adoption of family values. It was no coincidence that allegations of bastardy were made against Marie Antoinette's children from Marie Thérèse onwards; these were pre-emptive strikes against the Queen's area of greatest strength, her royal motherhood.

The group portrait commissioned from Madame Vigée Le Brun, to replace that of the Swedish Wertmüller with a proper French work, was intended to disseminate just this image. Gone were the white muslins, the sashes, the roses and the straw hats. Dressed probably by Rose Bertin, the Queen looked conspicuously and consummately regal in red velvet edged in black fur, with white plumes in her matching red velvet *pouf*, red, white and black being the ancient royal colours. Enormous care was taken to get the details right; accessories were borrowed from the Queen's Wardrobe in July 1786 and returned a year later. The Queen wore earrings – but significantly no necklace. A large jewel box was intended as a reference to that Roman paragon of virtue Cornelia, mother of the Gracchi, who had famously designated her own children when asked to display her greatest treasures.[19] The arrangement of the Queen's 'jewels' was carefully orchestrated. Madame Royale leant tenderly towards her mother – unfortunately not a flattering angle; the Dauphin pointed to Madame Sophie's cradle, while the plump little Duc de Normandie, in a white baby dress displaying the Order of the Saint Esprit, which was granted to the King's sons at birth, perched on his mother's lap.

The royal mother at the centre of it all was by now a substantial figure. Her comportment had not altered, that 'way of walking all her own' so that you could not see her steps as she glided with 'incomparable grace'. This was attested to by three Lorrainers, who spied on her unobserved in the grounds of the Trianon, noting that she carried her head even more proudly when she believed herself to be alone. Her hair had once again been cut short before the birth of Sophie. As the Queen ran her fingers through it in a nervous gesture that became characteristic, Count Esterhazy, Marie Antoinette's devoted admirer, even detected the first grey hairs ...[20] None of this mattered when a queenly coiffure could be constructed with the aid of powder and false hair.

The weight increase, begun the previous year, was now so considerable as to inspire rumours of further pregnancies on a regular basis; the Queen told the Emperor crossly, reacting to one of these stories, that if she had been pregnant as often as people pronounced, she would have sixteen children like her sister-in-law, Archduke Leopold's wife. Although her waist was still neat, the ample proportions of her bosom, well over forty inches when she herself was only of medium height, are confirmed by the records of the couturiers. Then there are the measurements of surviving corsages, supple structures made of taffeta embroidered with the royal arms (not stiff, like the modern corset), on which her bodices were built, and the records of couturiers. Even the superbly flattering brush of Louise Vigée Le Brun did not seek to conceal altogether a fullness below the chin, which would be further visible in the 'blue velvet' portrait of 1788. With a lack of gallantry, King Gustav of Sweden said in public that the Queen of France had grown too fat to be any longer counted as a beauty, while Joseph II took patriotism to its limits when he told Marie Christine that their sister had 'the fine face of a good fat German'.[21]

Comparisons to fresh young nymphs were no longer likely to arise, but the Mother of France was not supposed to be a nymph. She was supposed to inspire reverence. It is clear from Louise Vigée Le Brun that much care was taken in order to project an image not far from that of a Holy Family. Louise herself was frequently inspired by Raphael. Her fellow painter Jacques-Louis David suggested that Louise should look at the

Holy Families of the High Renaissance in the Louvre, especially that by Guilio Romano. When Louise – who was being paid the high price of 18,000 francs – asked David whether she would be accused of plagiarism, David replied robustly: 'Do as Molière does. Take what you want, where you want.' He believed that the use of modern clothes, fashions and furniture would protect the artist from criticism.[22]

For all the care taken, and for all the faithfulness of the resemblance, which the Comte d'Hezecques praised as he looked from Queen to portrait when it hung at Versailles, it was not a lucky picture. The youngest member of the group, the baby Sophie, died on 19 June 1787, a few weeks short of her first birthday. Her figure had to be painted out; the Dauphin's finger pointing in the direction of the empty cradle was a sad memorial to his sister's short life. The Queen – 'greatly afflicted' – told Princesse Louise that the baby had never really grown or developed. This was confirmed by the autopsy, which was signed by the deputy Governess Madame de Mackau in the absence of the Duchesse de Polignac in England. It made pathetic reading, down to the details of three little teeth that the baby had been about to cut and which had been responsible for the five or six days of convulsions that ended her life.[23]

When Madame Elisabeth was invited by the Queen to view the corpse of 'my little angel', she was struck by the pink and white appearance of the baby. Elisabeth added in her pious way that baby Sophie was quite happy now, having escaped all life's perils, while her elder sister Marie Thérèse was left desolate 'with an extraordinary sensibility for her age'. Now the tiny form lay in a salon at the Grand Trianon, under a gilded coronet and a velvet pall. The Queen's foster-brother Joseph Weber tried to cheer her by saying that the baby had not even been weaned when she died, implying that the grief for one so young could not be very great. But he struck the wrong note. 'Don't forget that she would have been my friend,' replied the Queen, a reference to her daughters, who were 'mine', unlike their brothers who belonged to France, that sentiment first expressed at the birth of Marie Thérèse.[24] Her tears continued to fall.

The Vigée Le Brun portrait was intended to be shown at the

Salon of the Royal Academy at the end of August. In fact it needed to be withdrawn, as the Queen's unpopularity was so great that demonstrations were feared; Lenoir, the Chief of Police, had to tell her not to appear in Paris. The empty frame was left. Some wag, alluding to the scornful new nickname for the Queen, pinned a note to it: 'Behold the Deficit!'

It was yet another affliction for the Queen in this troubled time that Jeanne de Lamotte had managed to escape from the Salpêtrière prison a few days before the death of Sophie, probably with connivance. She reached England where she proceeded to pour forth ghosted publications which, however, she autographed personally in true celebrity-bestseller fashion.[25] The worst of these concerned her 'Sapphic' relationship with the Queen – 'Ye Gods, what delights I experienced in that charming night!' – because the allegations chimed so happily with the popular notion of the Queen as viciously perverted, not simply immoral. The 'affair' with Artois was one thing, but the sexual bouts with the Lamballe and the Polignac, all gleefully narrated with much circumstantial detail, were unnatural. Another aspect of these denigrations was the comparison of the Queen – 'the monster escaped from Germany' – to the other notoriously evil or lascivious women in history. She was worse than Cleopatra, prouder than Agrippina, more lubricious than Messalina, more cruel than Catherine de' Medici ... This was the vicious misogynistical chant that would continue to Marie Antoinette's death and beyond it.

In the meantime the 'monster' struggled to support Brienne, to cope with the depression of the King and to come to terms with the death of one child, while the health of her elder son was ever present in her mind. Since the endorsement of Parlement could not be secured for the reforms, these were forcibly registered at the King's *lit de justice* on 6 August, at which point Parlement itself was ordered by Brienne to go into exile at Troyes. At the end of August, Brienne was made Chief of the Council. When Castries and Ségur resigned over the decision not to intervene in the Dutch Republic, the Archbishop's brother replaced Ségur as War Minister. Still the angry disputes continued. Parlement, discontented with its situation, did eventually vote a twentieth part of the money wanted. On 19 November another edict was issued by the King at a meeting termed a *séance* (session) *royale* in order to receive loans.

This led to further trouble. As Marie Antoinette confided to Joseph II, the King pronounced the simple words: 'I ordain registration,' which had always sufficed to give the force of law to an edict at a *lit de justice*, when his cousin Philippe, now Duc d'Orléans, dared to issue a strong protest. The registration, he said, was illegal, since the votes had not been counted during the session; if, on the other hand, it was not a proper session but a *lit de justice*, they should all remain silent. The King was furious at this challenge and departed with his brothers, leaving the Duc d'Orléans to read out a protest that he had evidently written in advance.[26]

The result was that the Duc was exiled to his château at Villars Cotterets, and two other colleagues, who had spoken 'insultingly' in front of the King, were sent to prison. Marie Antoinette's reporting of the whole matter to her brother was resigned: 'I am upset that these repressive measures have had to be taken; but unhappily they have become necessary here.' She added perhaps the most significant phrase in her letter: that the King had also indicated that he would call a meeting of the Estates General in five years' time, as a way of calming the whole situation down.

The turbulence in France was by no means ended by the King's emollient words. During the next months, the battles over the registration of the edicts continued to rage, with provincial disturbances adding to the furore. A few months earlier, Arthur Young, the English agriculturalist who had returned for another tour of France in May 1788, got the impression from dinner parties in Paris that France was on the verge of 'some great revolution'. But it was not at all clear what meaning was to be attached to that dangerous term. After all, it was easy – and rather enjoyable – for foreign nationals to predict insurrection in countries that they did not precisely understand. Marie Antoinette had told her English friend Lady Clermont in January 1784 that England was surely on the verge of a revolution and

that '[Charles James] Fox will be King'; she had been inveigled
into this belief by the nature of the English parliamentary system,
with its vociferous opposition.[27] In France at this time, such a
theoretical revolution would envisage no more than a limitation
on the King's powers, especially his unpopular use of the *lit de
justice* to register edicts. Along with the cries for an Estates
General, demands for reform at this point were essentially
coming from the nobility rather than the people.

Throughout the first half of 1788, the wrangles continued.
Various expedients were considered – 'great changes' in the
words of Marie Antoinette on 24 April.[28] These included a new
body, a plenary court, which would register edicts, and the use
of forty-seven provincial organizations, largely replacing the
Parlements, which would allow the King to disseminate his
commands throughout the country more easily. On 8 May
members of the Parlement were summoned to Versailles to hear
fresh edicts registered by the King at a *lit de justice*, and they
were then told that they were suspended until this new order
of administration had been brought into being. These so-called
May Edicts, however, simply aroused further fierce disturbances
while Brienne's new measures were seen as despotic.

There was a melancholy subtext to all this political uproar in
the physical agonies of the Dauphin Louis Joseph. By early 1788
it was accepted by those around him, other than his parents,
that he could not live very long, and in certain realistic circles
the prospect even came as a relief, given that the Duc de
Normandie was so much healthier and livelier, in short, fitter to
be King. Marie Antoinette gave her own description of Louis
Joseph's sufferings in a letter to Joseph II, now fully involved
in a Balkan campaign against Turkey.

'My elder son has given me a great deal of anxiety,' she told
her 'dear brother' on 22 February in a letter whose frequent
crossings-out bore witness to her agitation (her letters had
generally much improved since her youth).[29] 'His body is twisted
with one shoulder higher than the other and a back whose
vertebrae are slightly out of line, and protruding. For some time
he has had constant fevers and as a result is very thin and weak.'
The Queen tried to comfort herself with the notion that the

arrival of his second teeth was responsible; but since remedies were being sought to start the Dauphin growing again, it was obvious that the situation was far more serious than some natural childhood process. The symptoms that the Queen described to her brother were in fact those of tuberculosis of the spine: the constant fevers and weakness by the angular curvature produced by the gradual crumbling of the vertebrae, the deformity worsening as the pressure on the spinal column increased.

Nevertheless, hopes were now pinned to a period of convalescence by Louis Joseph at the château of Meudon, the official residence of the Dauphin of France but hardly used as such since the death of Louis XIV's son, the Grand Dauphin. Not too far from Versailles, or the other royal residences such as Fontainebleau and Compiègne, Meudon was on a high plateau and said to have the most beautiful view in Europe. Its air was considered to be specially therapeutic ever since Louis XVI had convalesced there as a child. Contemplating the robust physical specimen that the King had turned out to be made everyone feel better about the prospects of his infinitely fragile son. Meudon's park had been virtually abandoned, but its neglected state ensured some privacy for the little boy, which he would not have had at Versailles or Saint Cloud. Instant refurbishment was now carried out, including tapestries to make his bedroom more 'comfortable', a large yellow damask bed for his tutor, the Duc d'Harcourt, and a crimson damask one for the Duchesse.[30]

So, on 2 March, the Dauphin, still feverish, made the journey to Meudon. For a while he did feel slightly better and more cheerful too. But by June the Marquis de Bombelles found him a pitiable sight, with his horribly curved spine and his emaciated body; he would have wept in his presence if he had dared. The wretched boy was beginning to be ashamed of being seen, while the various doctors disagreed about his treatment. In June, the Queen – 'Mrs B' – was described as 'amazingly out of spirits' by the Duke of Dorset. In July she gave another bulletin to the Emperor: her son had 'alternating bouts of being better and being worse'.[31] This meant that she could never quite give up hope, nor ever quite count on Louis Joseph's recovery.

It was an analysis that also fitted the political situation in

France. In some ways the outward life of the court went on seemingly unchanged. Old rituals died hard. On the eve of Lent there was a *bal d'enfants*, that charming juvenile counterpoint to the *bal des vieux*. A fine banquet was given for Mesdames Tantes at the Petit Trianon. About the time of the May Edicts, the official baptism took place of the two teenage Princes of the house of Orléans, Louis Philippe Duc de Chartres and Antoine Duc de Montpensier. Relations with their father had never improved since his conduct at Ouessant in 1778 and subsequent political intrigues. The Duc d'Orléans had not hesitated to align himself with the Queen's enemies over the Diamond Necklace Affair. Yet the King and Queen acted as godparents to the boys and despite the need for royal economies, gave them the traditional bejewelled gifts. In the same way the Duc d'Orléans still dreamed of marrying the Duc de Chartres to Madame Royale, and his daughter Mademoiselle d'Orléans to the Duc d'Angoulême, as though nothing had happened to interrupt the family-oriented matrimonial policy of the French royals.[32]

Finally, on 5 July 1788, at the height of the unrest of the nobility, the King made a preliminary declaration concerning the meeting of the Estates General that had been so long sought. This declaration invited suggestions as to the composition of the body, taking into account the changes in French society since 1614. It was made clear that increased representation of the Third Estate was the issue; Brienne's intention, in short, was to weaken the power of the nobility by strengthening that of the commoners – that is, the bourgeoisie – the Third Estate being seen as the royal ally. It was on this optimistic note that discussions concerning the Estates General were initiated. As the Queen told her brother, what with 'your war that threatens Europe' and 'our domestic troubles', it had not been a good year. She concluded her letter: 'God willing, the next year will be better!'[33]

CHAPTER SEVENTEEN

Close to Shipwreck

'The boat is being placed in his [Necker's] hands so
close to shipwreck that even my boundless admiration
is scarcely enough to inspire me with confidence.'

Germaine de Staël, 4 September 1788

On 8 August 1788 it was at long last formally announced
that there would be a meeting of the Estates General.
That left the question of its composition – on which
the King had invited comments in early July – to be hotly
debated in the coming months. Brienne's measures had demonstrably failed to restore financial credit; by mid-August the
Treasury was hovering on the verge of bankruptcy, with one
official calculating that there were only enough funds 'for state
expenditure for one or two days'.[1] It was becoming apparent
to the anxious Queen, still in her political role, still trying to
galvanize her phlegmatic husband, that it might be necessary to
recall the one man thought capable of restoring public confidence. This was Jacques Necker, widely seen as the solid
incarnation of Swiss Protestant financial virtues, who had been
edged out of office seven years previously and whom the Queen
personally disliked. Her protégé, Breteuil resigned as Minister of
the Royal Household at the end of July; it hardly seemed possible
that her other protégé, Brienne, would survive much longer.

Yet the ceremonial life of Versailles did not cease. An exotic –
and expensive – State visit provided a brave public show as the
politicians, including the Queen, manoeuvred behind the scenes.

The three envoys of the Indian potentate Tippoo Sahib came to France to plead for assistance against the English in the East. Madame de La Tour du Pin wrote: 'But we gave them only words, as we had done to the Dutch.'² She referred to France's inertia in 1787 when Frederick William II, the new King of Prussia, attacked Holland in order to reinstate his brother-in-law as Stadtholder. In fact the envoys were entertained lavishly even if France's domestic troubles precluded further support.

In Paris, Gluck's *Armide* was thought a suitable offering and everyone flocked to gaze at the three visitors, richly dressed, of a 'fine light Hindu complexion' with white beards to their waists. Seated in special armchairs, they propped their slippered feet on the edge of the box 'to the delight of the public who ... had no fault to find with this custom'. At Versailles spectators were similarly amazed at the sight of the envoys' special cooks sitting cross-legged in the Grand Trianon, sifting rice and meat in their hands. The strange smells of simmering peppers and pimentos flavoured with cumin drifted in the air. Marie Antoinette gamely tried to eat some of the food, before being driven back by the spices.³

There was once again a large crowd to witness the last formal audience of the envoys; they departed the day after the announcement of the Estates General. Unfortunately the envoys' time-keeping was as exotic as their food; they were invited between five and six and arrived long after eight. Their speech to the King had to be translated by Sieur Ruffin, the King's secretary-interpreter; he used a specially low voice since some of the sentiments expressed by the Indians were notably disobliging towards England and might have caused offence to those English present. The envoys also demanded to be seated in the King's presence, a privilege not even allowed to his own brothers. Nevertheless, for the great gathering of fascinated royals and courtiers, including 'the little people' (children) who gazed at the colourful strangers, this show provided a welcome distraction from more serious affairs.⁴

Even the nine-year-old Madame Royale was there, seated among the distinguished ladies on a special platform draped in brocade, although the previous week she had been so ill with a fever that her mother had watched over her for two whole nights, and her father for one.[5] The collapse of the normally healthy Marie Thérèse was a special strain upon parents who alternated between dealing with affairs of state and visiting the Dauphin, who was invisible to the rest of the world at Meudon. It would not have occurred to Marie Thérèse, nor to the little children of the Duchesse de Polignac and the Marquis de Bombelles who were all allowed to watch from an embrasure, that this might be the last state visit of the reign ... But the thought must have crossed the minds of some of their elders.

Necker was summoned to see the Queen at ten o'clock on the morning of 26 August. He was made Controller of Finance, and was also admitted to the Council of State, a position that had eluded him in 1781 on the grounds of his Protestant religion. The departure of Brienne was personally 'affecting' for Marie Antoinette and she made sure that he was rewarded with various emoluments including a Cardinal's hat on the nomination of the King (that nomination he had refused to bestow on Rohan). Necker's brilliant daughter, Germaine de Staël, who was now married to the Swedish ambassador and was ecstatic at her father's return, noted caustically how much less well she was received by the Queen on the feast of Saint Louis than the niece of the outgoing Brienne. Germaine was able to add with satisfaction that the courtiers' attitude was very different: 'Never have so many people offered to conduct me back to my carriage.'[6]

Nevertheless, two things emerge clearly from Marie Antoinette's correspondence on the subject of Necker. First, for all her aversion, she alone was responsible for his recall. The King continued to behave sullenly, merely commenting that he had been forced to recall Necker without wanting to do so: 'They'll soon regret it.' For the time being, Necker's appointment did indeed lead to a surge of popularity for the government – cries of 'Long live the King' were heard again – as well as an equally welcome rise on the Stock Exchange. It was true, as Germaine de Staël wrote to the King of Sweden on 4 September, that 'the boat is being placed in his [Necker's] hands so close to shipwreck that even my boundless admiration is scarcely enough to inspire me with confidence.' Yet for the time being shipwreck had been undeniably averted by her father's return.[7]

Second, and more important in the long term, it is evident that Marie Antoinette felt some kind of dark presentiment about the outcome of the new arrangement. This was due to the role that she had personally played in it. She wrote to Count Mercy on the subject, two days before her meeting with Necker, a letter that is the key to her growing feelings of dread: 'I am trembling – forgive me this weakness – at the idea that it is I who am bringing about his return. My destiny is to bring misfortune; and if vile scheming makes things go wrong for him once more, alternatively if he diminishes the authority of the King, I shall be detested still further.'[8]

In part, this reaction sprang from that new strain of 'German melancholy', which the hairdresser Léonard, in constant attendance upon the Queen, noticed in her character. She took to saying, 'If I began my life again ...' before breaking off and asking him to cheer her up with one of his stories.[9] This melancholy coexisted with the new determination that she had developed as a result of the Diamond Necklace Affair. It sapped her spirits if not her resolution. The death of one child and the serious illness of another obviously contributed to this depression. More than that, however, Marie Antoinette was beginning to feel ill-fated, even doomed. She could no longer maintain that elegant studied indifference to the insults dealt out to her both in print and when she appeared in public. The Queen was forced to appreciate the horrible malign power of such things. The contrast between the wicked Messalina of the public imagination and the benevolent mother-figure of her own was becoming too painful to be ignored.

Under the circumstances, the friendship of Count Fersen – both romantic and supportive – was more important to the Queen than ever. Fersen played a double role. He was the Queen's admirer but he was also the emissary of the King of Sweden in various connections. For example, it was Fersen who brought a letter to Louis XVI from Gustav III in May 1787. It was Fersen who acted as the Swedish King's proxy at the baptism of the child of Germaine de Staël and her husband, the

Swedish ambassador to France, a few months later. Although the colonel of a French regiment – the Royal Swedish garrisoned at Maubeuge – Fersen continued to be part of King Gustav's entourage. His role as a kind of liaison officer between the French and Swedish courts made Fersen valuable to Louis XVI, quite apart from his notional position as Marie Antoinette's lover.

In the past years, Fersen had travelled constantly between France and Sweden, his absences from the Queen's side always marked by correspondence with 'Josephine' being noted in his Letter Book. In the spring of 1788 he went to Sweden in order to take part in King Gustav's Finnish campaign against Russia, but by 6 November he was back in Paris, twenty-two letters marking this particular six months' absence.[10] His account books reveal the extent of his visits to Versailles in the critical period that followed, since the tips he had to give to servants were also written down.

Did his sexual relationship with Marie Antoinette continue? The same common sense which suggested that the Queen and Fersen had an affair starting in 1783, now suggests that their relationship, if far from over, was nevertheless being gradually transformed into something more romantic than carnal. The Queen's ill health, the Queen's melancholy, the Queen's family worries, the deteriorating political situation, even developing religious scruples: none of these would necessarily prevent her continuing a full-blown affair although any one of them might inhibit it. Yet one cannot help speculating – as with the nature of their original relationship, it can be no more than speculation – that with the passage of time Marie Antoinette and Fersen began to play rather different parts. They lived, after all, in an age of romantic role-playing, the supreme example being the relationship of Julie and Saint Preux in Rousseau's *La Nouvelle Héloïse*, much of whose epistolary language is strangely similar to that of Marie Antoinette and Fersen.[11] The novel ended with Julie's renunciation of carnal love.

Fersen was now her devoted cavalier, and he was also increasingly her vital political ally. According to the Comte de La Marck, Marie Antoinette liked the fact that Fersen did not let himself be drawn into the Polignac set; he was her kindred spirit, not theirs, or as the English put it, he was 'Mrs B's special friend'.[12] Marie Antoinette had originally been attracted to Fersen not only for his handsome face and gallant manners but because he was an outsider, alien to the intrigues of Versailles. This foreign status was to become even more important in the future.

There was also the critical question of how Fersen saw Marie Antoinette. It is clear from a letter to his father, written the following year, that he was one of the few people who saw her exactly as she had always wished to be seen. 'You cannot fail to applaud the Queen,' he wrote, 'if you do justice to her desire to do good and the goodness of her own heart.'[13] Fersen, of course, as a true lover of women, had always had mistresses, in whatever country he found himself. But it is not irrelevant that the most physically passionate relationship of his life – so very different from his romantic devotion to the Queen – began in the spring of 1789.

The fascinating Eléanore Sullivan, five years older than Fersen and the Queen, had arrived in Paris in 1783. She had, to say the least of it, a colourful past. The daughter of a Tuscan tailor, she had first become a dancer and a trapeze artiste. Originally married to an actor, Eléanore had then become the mistress of the Duke of Württemberg to whom she bore a son. In Vienna, Eléanore was rumoured to have been the mistress of Joseph II; in Paris she married an Irishman, Sullivan, who swept her off to Manila; there she met a rich Scot, Quentin Craufurd, who brought her back to Paris again.[14] Fersen was erotically enchained by Eléanore Sullivan and his connection to her was long-lasting. But it was to be a three-cornered relationship, that included Eléanore's wealthy protector Craufurd.

With the Queen as the object of his devotion, Fersen also entered into another three-cornered relationship but of a political complexion. This time the King was the third party. There is no evidence that Louis XVI ever tried to oust Fersen from his wife's life, or that he even contemplated doing so. Fersen for his part paid tribute to 'the goodness, honesty, frankness and loyalty of the King', which at this period he genuinely believed must prevail with the people, returning France to the weight

Marie Antoinette

and influence she had always enjoyed in Europe.[15]

One story that has sometimes been linked to Fersen's name scarcely fits the known facts. A servant reported that the King had received certain letters while out hunting, and had been so upset by their contents that he had begun to weep silently; finally Louis XVI was too devastated to continue with his sport. But the servant in question had not seen the content of the letters and as a result attached the name of no particular individual to them. Bombelles recorded the incident in his journal as 'a fact, a distressing fact, but I have absolutely no idea what caused it'.[16] At this stage, the King's distressing reading matter was far more likely to be some freshly obscene publications emanating from England to do with the Lamotte than Fersen's love letters (which would in any case have been addressed to 'Josephine').*

For some time it seemed that Marie Antoinette's gloomy presentiments were unjustified. The popular mood was vividly described by Fersen in a letter to his father: 'It's a delirium; everyone sees himself as a legislator, and everyone talks of nothing but progress; in the antechambers the footmen are reading pamphlets, ten or twelve new ones appear every day.' Fersen also commented – a typical perspective, perhaps – that young men who wished to woo the ladies were having to tailor their conversation to their new interests: 'To please them, they have to talk about Estates General and governments and constitutions.' Another foreigner, Jefferson, had a slightly different view of the situation. All this talk of politics, he grumbled, was ruining the gaiety and the insouciance of French society – 'The tender breasts of ladies were not formed for

---

* Saint-Priest, whose memoirs were written in old age (he died in 1821 aged eighty-six) and were not published until 1929, told a story of the Queen deliberately manipulating her husband. She offered to send Fersen away, confident that Louis XVI would refuse.[17] There is no confirmation of this. If this scene had really taken place in private between husband and wife, Saint-Priest could only have heard about it third-hand from Fersen, passed on by the Queen; but Fersen, as all his contemporaries including Saint-Priest agreed, was legendarily discreet; such a tasteless confidence would be quite uncharacteristic.

political convulsion' – so that French women were miscalculating their own happiness when they wandered 'from the true field of their own influence into politics'.[18] In this climate, Necker did indeed manage to ride the storm, if more by pliancy than coherent policy.

As part of the holding operation in the continuing financial crisis, the Parlements were recalled. The Assembly of Notables was invited back for consultation on the composition of the Estates General. The *Mémoire des Princes* was also drawn up, denouncing the alteration of 'institutions held sacred and by which monarchies for so long have prospered' in response to public agitation. This conservative princely protest was not, however, signed by the increasingly radical Orléans, nor by Provence (although Artois did sign). Both of these Princes accepted the principle of *doublement* by which the representation of the Third Estate would be increased to twice that of the past. In spite of the indecisiveness of Necker, compounded by that of Louis XVI, *doublement* was finally accepted on 27 December 1788, although the law that allowed nobles and clergy also to stand as deputies for the Third Estate meant that their influence was not completely diminished. The Queen, although silent on the subject in Council, was believed to approve the measure. In the case of both Louis XVI and Marie Antoinette, it was the idea of the Third Estate, as the crown's natural ally against the other two, that prevailed. 'Ah, their illusions will be short lived!' wrote the Marquis de Bombelles, gloomily, after a New Year's Eve visit to Versailles.[19] Yet the popular salutations of 'Long live the King' coupled with 'Long live the Third Estate' could not but give rise to hope.

Concurrent with her belief in the usefulness of the Third Estate was Marie Antoinette's realism concerning the relationship of France and Austria. On 27 January 1789, in a letter to Mercy, she pointed out the impossibility of France coming to the aid of Austria (and Russia) with troops at the present time. She wrote with full knowledge of Joseph II's own declining health but that fact could not alter her verdict. Although the impending Estates General were not supposed to treat of peace and war, they would certainly give vent to 'complaints and cries of protest' at the idea of such expense. She went on: 'You know the prejudices against my brother, you know how some people here are even on the point of believing that I have sent millions to Germany [*sic*]. Inevitably they would attribute this new treaty to me, and so the ministers of the Estates General would excuse themselves, using the excuse of my credit and influence. Judge for yourself the odious role I would be made to play!'[20]

By a coincidence, Nature herself now struck a blow against the finances of France. Eighteen months earlier a bad summer had resulted in poor harvests throughout most of the country. Now the winter of 1789 was the most severe in living memory. Beginning with a heavy snowfall on New Year's Eve, there were to be two months of freezing temperatures, so that couriers en route between Versailles and the capital froze to death, and Jefferson felt he was in Siberia rather than in Paris. The rich skated and sledged happily (as Marie Antoinette had done in her careless youth, before abandoning the practice as appearing too 'Austrian'). But the sufferings of the poor were terrible as the all-important bread prices rose. In such conditions of misery, it was easy for rumours of a famine plot to spread; the great ones, including Artois and the Queen, were supposed to be conspiring to produce a shortage of flour in order to make further profits. Meanwhile Orléans made a number of very public and 'very liberal' donations to alleviate the condition of the poor.[21] Master of the art of propaganda, he richly enjoyed his position as the people's champion and took every opportunity to underline it.

In the months leading up to the meeting of the Estates General, the private hell of the King and Queen continued with the illness of the Dauphin, who had a bad relapse on 1 February. Meanwhile the unhappy parents were as before ritually denounced in the *libelles*, he as an impotent drunkard, she as a vicious adulteress. Public scorn was one thing. But it was a remarkable demonstration of the lack of respect into which even the courtiers had slipped – without any wisdom as to where their best interests lay – that one particular set of satiric rhymes was actually sung in the salon of the Comtesse de Brionne, on 23 January, in the presence of the most elegant Parisian society;

the hostess was the same ambitious woman who had previously sought so much favour from Marie Antoinette.

The verses that had been circulating everywhere for the previous two days had left no member of the royal family untouched: not the Comtesse de Provence with her growing addiction to the bottle; not the Comtesse d'Artois who had given birth to a bastard child; not Provence – 'I am neither princely nor a king' – and, of course, not the King and Queen. Louis XVI was quoted as reproaching the Duc de Normandie for being a bastard. It ended with a chorus of the Three Estates together, after which Louis XVI sang merrily: 'What need is there for me to think? When I can hunt and I can drink!' The priorities of French society in early 1789 were summed up by the fact that one of those present at the Comtesse's salon criticized the men for wearing the informal frockcoat, while pardoning the *libelles* as being the welcome return of a little spark of 'our old French gaiety'.[22]

The solemn High Mass that would precede the inaugural meeting of the Estates General at Versailles was to be held on 4 May. At various levels, Marie Antoinette's gloomy presentiments were now beginning to be fulfilled. On 26 March the King himself was nearly killed taking the air on the leads of the roof at Versailles, when a ladder on which he was leaning gave way; he was only saved from plunging to his death by the prompt action of a workman.* The Queen herself was beginning to spend more and more time alone in her private cabinet, according to the Saxon envoy, Count Salmour, who, because his mother had been a favoured member of the Austrian imperial household, had been immediately accepted as an intimate.[23]

Then, in late April, a serious riot broke out in Paris, named after the wallpaper manufacturer Réveillon whose supposed decision to cut wages brought it about. Obviously such an action

---

* For connoisseurs of the 'What-might-have-been' (or Counterfactual) school of history, it is interesting to speculate on the possible results of Louis XVI's death in March 1789. He would have left a young child as his heir, and at this stage Marie Antoinette's strong claim to act as Regent, according to precedent, might have been allowed. It is at least possible that things would have gone better.

was as fire to tinder in a time of violently rising prices; in fact it was rumour and misunderstanding rather than Réveillon's actions that caused the revolt. Nevertheless 300 people were killed before the riot was dispersed by troops. Apart from the loss of life, the Réveillon riot had the serious consequence of persuading the government that the people of Paris were becoming unmanageable, while the people themselves saw the government as ready to use military action against them.[24]

Six days later, the whole royal family were due to exhibit themselves publicly in a procession through the town of Versailles. The route between Paris and Versailles became like a boulevard on a fine day, it was so crowded with traffic. Marie Antoinette sent for Léonard – this was not an occasion for his deputy, *le beau* Julian – to dress her hair grandly enough for the court dress she had to wear. He attested to her sadness on that occasion: 'Come, dress my hair, Léonard, I must go like an actress, exhibit myself to a public that may hiss me.' He found her physically bowed in private, her bosom sunken and her arms thin. The next day, however, an American observer new to the scene, the American Gouverneur Morris, put a different gloss on her dramatic style: 'She looks with contempt on the scene in which she acts a Part and seems to say: for the present I submit but I shall have my Turn.'[25]

Morris – his forename Gouverneur came from his Huguenot ancestry – had arrived in Paris in February, in pursuit of a contract for imported tobacco. Trained as a lawyer (he had assisted in the final wording of the United States Constitution), he was to prove an important and a lively witness in the events that followed. A foreigner from a republican country, Morris was still able to view the Queen with humanity, in a way that it seemed many of the French had forgotten: 'I see only the Woman and it seems unmanly to break a Woman with unkindness!'[26] Most of the spectators, lacking Morris's chivalry, saw a woman indeed, but a woman for whom their feelings went much further than unkindness; she was a Queen they hated, whom it was safe to scorn where public derision for the King was still a step too far.

The procession from the Church of Notre-Dame to the

Church of Saint Louis was led by the whole royal family and the Princes and Princesses of the Blood – with one significant exception. The royals were to be followed by the deputies of the Estates General who had been chosen the previous month. Protocol had never been more rigid than in the orders given about the costumes that each rank should wear. The clergy were to wear their ecclesiastical dress; the nobility were to wear black silk and white breeches, lace cravats and plumed hats, and would carry swords; but the Third Estate were to wear plain black and, as an indication of their lowly status, were forbidden to carry swords. The Duc d'Orléans, as one of the nobility's deputies, decided on a move of calculated provocation. Against the King's express orders, he mingled with this swordless black-clad throng, leaving his son, the Duc de Chartres, to take his own place.

All the windows of the houses on the route were jammed with spectators for whom the appearance of Orléans was the signal for loud cheers. The Queen on the other hand was received with icy silence. At one point, a loud 'Long live the Duc d'Orléans!' shouted more or less in her face as she passed actually caused her to stumble briefly before recovering her dignity. For Louis XVI, the acclaim for his cousin and the lack of applause for his wife was a double insult; according to Virieu, the Duke of Parma's envoy, his anger was noticeable. Only one small spectator caused the royal mood of both King and Queen to soften. The Dauphin had been brought from Meudon to see the show. He lay on cushions in an embrasure with a window belonging to the Little Stables. When his parents caught sight of the tiny wizened figure, smiling so bravely in their direction, their tears came involuntarily. Virieu noted that Orléans too had tears in his eyes: tears of pleasure at the warmth of the salutations given to him.[27]

Both King and Queen wore glittering costumes and were heavily bejewelled; it is easy to understand how one observer compared the dazzling scene to the opera, lacking only lamps and chandeliers. For once, however, it was Louis XVI who literally outshone Marie Antoinette, even if he 'walked with a waddle' that inevitably contrasted with the celebrated grace of the Queen. The King wore cloth of gold scattered with brilliants, and the great white diamond known as the Regent which he had worn at his coronation. (The name derived from the Regent Duc d'Orléans, under whose auspices the crown of France had acquired it in 1717.) The King also sported the diamond sword made for him five years previously, new diamond buttons, diamond shoe buckles and diamonds on his garters; all this was in addition to the ornamentations he wore, denoting the order of the Golden Fleece and the Order of the Saint Esprit.[28]

The Queen for her part shimmered in cloth of silver, the moon to the King's sun. In her hair she wore another costly diamond, 'perfectly flawless and brilliant', known as the Sancy, and on her person a series of other diamonds including those called the De Guise and the Mirror of Portugal with vast drops of single gems. These were known as the Fifth and Sixth Mazarins because the English Queen Henrietta Maria, born a Princess of France, had sold them to Cardinal Mazarin in the time of her misfortunes.[29] The Queen, however, did not wear a necklace.

Unfortunately once the service began in the Church of Saint Louis, the sermon given by the Bishop of Nancy recalled to the minds of the spectators, whether royalties or deputies, how much of this brave show was mere camouflage for the ugly situation. The Bishop saw his chance and took it, contrasting the luxury of the court with the sufferings of the poor in the countryside. The Queen merely drew in her lips in that disdainful expression that would become increasingly familiar in the time to come. The King, on the other hand, dealt with the issue in his own way by falling asleep. When he awoke, he was to find the Bishop's audience applauding vigorously, something that had never been known to happen before in a church where the Blessed Sacrament was exposed.[30]

The next day the 1100-odd deputies met together in the Salon of the Menus Plaisirs, a short distance from the château. Marie Antoinette on this occasion wore white satin with a violet velvet mantle and train, and a simple diamond aigrette in her hair. She sat on a large chair to the left of that of the King and below it; the Princesses were ranged beyond her, and the Princes to the right of the King's throne. The Queen carried a huge fan.

Madame de La Tour du Pin, who was sitting uncomfortably with the other ladies of the court on backless benches, noticed that she fanned herself in an 'almost compulsive way' as though deeply agitated. Meanwhile Marie Antoinette scanned the faces of the Third Estate, many of whom were of course completely unfamiliar to her, as though trying to fit the faces to the names.[31] One man, however, was unmistakable: Honoré Comte de Mirabeau. At the age of forty, this radical nobleman was sometimes called 'the tiger', but with his great height, and mass of shaggy hair, he more nearly resembled a bear.

Mirabeau's scandalous private life and his debts had already caused a considerable frisson in French society; now he was present, not as a deputy of the noble Second Estate, but as a deputy of the Third, because he had failed to be elected to the Second Estate in his country district. When Mirabeau entered, there was a widespread murmur, low and sibilant. Those in front moved one bench forward and those behind moved one back. Smiling contemptuously, Mirabeau sat down.

The King spoke on the theme of the financial crisis and the State debt, which he attributed – with justice – to the expenses of 'an exorbitant but honourable [American] war'. Afterwards he was thought to have done well and to have shown some strength and dignity, although critics commented on his harsh and rather grating voice. But Louis XVI did, in one felicitous phrase, term himself 'the first friend of his peoples'. Necker, on the other hand, spoke at enormous length, his monotonous voice eventually giving way to hoarseness so that his speech had to be completed by another. Length alone could not mask the fact that he was proposing no effective solutions. Nor did he give any firm guidance on the voting procedure of the Estates General – whether the Estates should vote separately or as one body – although the arguments on the subject needed urgently to be resolved.[32]

Louis XVI personally was greeted by cries of 'Long live the King' at the end of it all, and now there were again a few cries of 'Long live the Queen' in contrast to the silence with which she had been greeted at the start. She responded in the gracious fashion that she had made her own, with the lowest of curtsies.

According to one account, the cries were prompted by the tragic expression on Marie Antoinette's face. Most people, however, thought that the acclamations for the Queen were simply intended to please the King.

The Queen's deep sadness was easy to understand. When young Harry Swinburne arrived at Versailles on 10 May to be a page, a 'much altered' Marie Antoinette told his mother: 'You arrive at a bad moment, dear Mrs Swinburne. You will not find me very cheerful; I have a great deal on my heart.' Her melancholy was due at least as much to the condition of the Dauphin as to her sense of her own unpopularity. The emaciated little boy, who had smiled so bravely at his parents from his cushions as the royal procession passed, was swiftly returned to Meudon. It was evident that he was being taken back to die. As the shipwreck of the State – in Germaine de Staël's phrase – approached, the royal couple spent every possible moment at Louis Joseph's side; the King's visits, chronicled in his *Journal*, being five or six a day.[33] At the same time the deputies of the Third Estate were discovering new rights and, having discovered them, were clamouring for their implementation. The rivalry between the conservative faction of the nobility and the popular party (which included some aristocrats) was beginning.

Under the circumstances, the King's pervading silences and his chronic indecision were more unhelpful than ever, even if his personal circumstances made these signs of depression comprehensible. The public confidence in Necker, once so great, was also vanishing as it became obvious he was not in fact 'the Man', in Gouverneur Morris's phrase, who would save them all.[34] Meanwhile the Queen's grasp of her political role was also beginning to slip.

As Count Mercy reported to Prince Kaunitz on 10 May, everyone blamed her for the King's inactivity, but by now what she proposed was rarely followed. Provence and Artois used her as a conduit to the King, but then the Princes had their own agenda. Artois in particular was increasingly hardline, his attitude being reflected by that of his adoring sister Madame Elisabeth, who wrote in May: 'If the King does not have the severity to cut off at least three heads, everything will be lost.'[35]

This was not the stance of Marie Antoinette. But her brief period – two years – of real political intervention, following that night when she was so 'madly happy' at the appointment of Loménie de Brienne, was almost over. Her new role as a hate figure or, one might say, a scapegoat at the King's side, was beginning to take over; it was increasingly difficult to combine it with that of an active and influential politician.

On his return to Meudon, Louis Joseph had a whim to sleep on top of the new billiard table. A bed was made up, although the ladies around him exchanged glances at the sight; it looked all too much like a lying-in-state of a corpse. Since he could no longer walk, a mechanical wheelchair upholstered in green velvet with white wool cushions was installed. The whinnying of his favourite chestnut horse from the stables was a reminder of the days of his short childhood. Afterwards many stories would be told of his sweetness: how he would not hurt the feelings of a clumsy valet by sending him away and therefore endured his painful ministrations in silence. He told one of Madame Campan's sisters, Julie Rousseau, in his household: 'I love you so much, Rousseau, that I shall still love you after I am dead.' He was anxious to do the honours to his mother at dinner although Marie Antoinette on these occasions 'swallowed more tears than bread'.[36]

The Dauphin's precocity was also recorded. Louis Joseph, like his father, had a taste for reading history. The Princesse de Lamballe paid a visit with her companion, the Comtesse de Laage de Volude. The latter related a conversation on the subject of the fifteenth-century King of France, Charles VII, for whom Joan of Arc had raised the standard. It was, said the Dauphin, 'a very interesting period in our history; there were many heroes then'. The Princesse and her companion found his beautiful eyes, as he spoke, 'the eyes of a dying child', unbearably moving.[37]

Marie Antoinette was actually at Meudon, and at her son's bedside, when the end came very early on 4 June. Louis XVI, who had visited him the previous day, was told at 6 a.m. by the Duc d'Harcourt. He wrote only in his *Journal*: 'Death of my son at one in the morning.'[38] The boy whose birth had been saluted by his father to his mother with these triumphant words,

'Madame, you have fulfilled my wishes and those of France,' was dead, 'a decayed old man', covered in sores, at the age of seven and a half. After that, etiquette robbed the bereaved parents of that consolation that ritual can sometimes bring. The royal parents, by custom, could take no part in the obsequies. Marie Antoinette was left like Gluck's Alceste, to call for 'some ray of pity' to comfort her suffering, and to believe with that unhappy heroine:

> No one understands my ills nor the terror that fills my breast
> Who does not know ...
> The heart of a mother.

Later that morning, the King went to Mass before nine and then shut himself away. In an unhappy repetition of the scene when he himself had succeeded to his elder brother, his own second son aged four and a half was simply told that he was now the Dauphin and was given the Order of Saint Louis. Louis Charles wept and so did Marie Thérèse, the other surviving child. Meanwhile Louis Joseph lay in state at Meudon according to custom, visited as a mark of respect by those with the right to do so. This privilege was even claimed by deputies of the Third Estate. Four days after the death, they exercised their rights to sprinkle holy water on the little corpse. Others came from Paris, Versailles and nearby Ville d'Avray. Since it was early June, the powerful perfume of rampant unchecked roses, jasmine and honeysuckle came from the neglected gardens of Meudon.[39]

According to custom, once again, Louis Joseph's heart, in an urn, was taken to the Benedictine convent of Val-de-Grâce. The Duc d'Orléans, as senior Prince of the Blood, was supposed to escort it, but he declined to do so, giving the ungracious reason that his role as deputy 'did not leave him time to attend functions', so his eldest son deputized for him once again. For the funeral, Louis XVI decided that elaborate arrangements would be inappropriate; the proper rites for a Dauphin of France could cost 350,000 livres. Like baby Sophie two years before, Louis Joseph was to be given a simple funeral, on the excuse that he had not yet made his First Communion. The Princesse de Lamballe, as Superintendent of the Queen's Household, presided, with files of monks praying ceaselessly in the background. The little coffin was covered in a silver cloth, with the crown, sword and Orders of the Dauphin of France on top of it.[40] After that it was taken to the crypt of Saint-Denis, to lie with the remains of Louis Joseph's ancestors in eternal undisturbed rest – or so it seemed in June 1789.

Madame Vigée Le Brun's unlucky portrait, showing the late Dauphin pointing to the newly empty cradle of Madame Sophie, was removed from the Salon de Mars in Versailles at the Queen's orders; she found it too painful a reminder of the recent deaths. At the official visit of condolence of the court on 7 June, she made a touching sight, leaning against the balustrade of her chamber, trying hard to choke back her tears. The King had to endure all this, and also the determined efforts of the Third Estate, led by the celebrated astronomer Jean Sylvain Bailly, to come and see him in order to discuss arrangements for the impending meeting of the Estates General. He refused to receive the Third Estate either on the day of his son's death or on the following two days, saying that it was not possible in 'my present situation'. When they insisted on visiting him on 7 June, the King commented bitterly: 'So there are no fathers among the Third Estate?'[41]

At this same season, Arthur Young, on a visit to the Palais-Royal where political pamphlets were being sold in shops in the Duc d'Orléans' private gardens, was struck by the fact that a new one was being issued every hour: 'Nineteen twentieths of these productions are in favour of liberty and commonly violent against the clergy and nobility.' It was no coincidence that the trade flourished on the Duc d'Orléans' property where the police could not intervene; the radical Duc had sold the sites to cover his lavish expenditure. The coffee houses were crowded; the mood was high, in spite of the terrible want of bread. The contrast between the royal mourning and the national exhilaration was something that Marie Antoinette never got over. Eighteen months later she commented to her brother Archduke Leopold on how the French had been in 'a delirium' while she struggled to control her sobs. In short, 'At the death of my poor little Dauphin, the nation hardly seemed to notice.'[42]

It was all a cruel demonstration of the clashing demands of public and private in the existence of kings and queens. At this great crisis in French national life, of what real significance was the death of a child, even a royal child? Given that he had a younger brother. But to Marie Antoinette, an emotional and deeply affectionate woman who was stricken by her loss, it represented something else: the callousness that the French could show, this people whose fundamental goodness of heart she had so often praised in the past, even if they were volatile and somewhat childish. She had largely lost the esteem of the French; it remained to be seen whether they would keep hers.

In this mood Marie Antoinette went to Marly with the King on 14 June for a week's court mourning.

CHAPTER EIGHTEEN

Hated, Humbled, Mortified

∼

'The Queen [is] hated, humbled, mortified ... to know that she favours a Measure is the certain Means to frustrate its Success.'

Gouverneur Morris, 1 July 1789

Crucial decisions of the Third Estate were taken during the week beginning 14 June 1789 when the King and Queen were at Marly, mourning the 'first Dauphin' (as Louis Joseph became known with time, the little ghost who had to be distinguished from Louis Charles). Louis XVI's geographical separation from Versailles, where the political action was taking place, had the effect of subjecting him further to the conservative pressures of his brothers, especially Artois. On this occasion, Marie Antoinette did not mount an independent initiative. The King continued to vacillate, something that for the last few years had given her the opportunity to display contrasting firmness. Recent events had, however, sapped her strength. Whether it was due to the private grief she felt or the public odium she had to endure, the Queen's confidence had waned. That feeling of being ill-fated, one whose destiny was to bring misfortune, haunted her anew.

This was the woman about whom it was earnestly believed in certain quarters that she intended to poison the King and install Artois – on the grounds that he was her long-term lover – as ruler of France. This was the woman who, according to a play of 1789 called *La Destruction de l'Aristocratisme*, loathed the

French people with such intensity that 'with what delight I would bathe in their blood'. She was also the woman of whom it was believed that she had secretly spirited away millions to her brother Joseph.[1]

And always the pamphlets poured forth their lubricious slime. Artois in *L'Autrichienne en Goguette* took the Queen from behind in public with obscene exclamations about her 'firm and elastic' body. If not an ardent lover of men, Marie Antoinette was an ardent lover of women; the message was always hammered home that the Queen was insatiable – even when alone. In *Le Godmiche* [Dildo] *Royal* of 1789 the Queen was satirized as the goddess Juno, in a text which began with Juno sitting alone 'with her skirts hitched up ...' and went on from there.[2] Perhaps it was her 'Germanic vigour' that was responsible, which had led to her deflowering even before she left Austria. Now it led her to indulge in orgies with bodyguards where drink featured as well as constant sex, although Marie Antoinette was in fact, as has been noted, a teetotaller.

Who could respect such a creature as a woman, let alone a queen? A woman who, quite apart from her sexual appetites, was a dangerous agent of a foreign power. It all *had* to be true. The stories had, after all, been printed over and over again, repetition being a cynical substitute for veracity. In the words of the radical 'Gracchus' Babeuf about this time, Louis XVI was a donkey, weak and obstinate but not cruel, who should have been mated to a young and gentle she-donkey; instead he had been given a tigress.[3]

Gouverneur Morris summed up the situation harshly in a report back to the United States. Little was to be expected in any way from the King. As for Marie Antoinette, she was 'hated, humbled, mortified' and although she was intriguing to save 'some shattered Remnants of the Royal Authority', it was enough to know that she favoured a measure for that to be 'the certain Means to frustrate its Success'. But Morris's words were no harsher than the reality of the Queen's situation in June and early July. An English doctor, John Rigby, an ardent Whig freshly arrived in France, saw her at Versailles about this time and was struck by how the Queen's countenance had assumed 'the character of severity'. As she went on her way to Mass, that familiar journey in which the grace of her passage had once caused general remark, her brow was deeply 'corrugated' and she looked from side to side with narrowed eyes and an expression of suspicion that he found quite spoilt her beauty.[4]

Hardly a natural politician, let alone a brilliant political thinker, the Queen floundered in an unprecedented situation. But then so did the King, Necker and the vast majority of politically minded people in France. Artois might think that strength was the solution but it remained to be seen whether such strength would not arouse an even more perilous counteraction. On 17 June, three days after the court reached Marly, the Third Estate declared itself unilaterally to be a National Assembly, and that it was intent on providing France with a new Constitution. On 20 June, locked out of the usual salon in which they met, the deputies adjourned to one of Versailles' tennis courts and a general oath was administered. This oath ignored the theoretical powers of the monarch and, as such, was a gross – or courageous – act of defiance. Necker, the moderate, the conciliator of the Third Estate, advocated concessions to defuse the situation. Artois and Provence on the other hand urged the King strongly the other way, carrying the Queen along with them.

In a scene probably stage-managed by the Duchesse de Polignac, Marie Antoinette appeared in the King's presence with her two surviving children. Pushing them into his arms, she pleaded with him to remain firm. The maternal card was, after all, the one good card in her hand. Five days later Marie Antoinette would receive the deputies charmingly, holding little Louis Charles, the 'second Dauphin', by the hand. On 27 June she once again appeared on a balcony with both her children this time, at the King's side. According to the Parman envoy, Virieu, the Queen, mourning her lost son, looked pale and her eyes were red.[5] But she was still able to make the point of her position in the state. And she could still put on a show, recreate the impression given to the young Chateaubriand at Versailles. He received a smile from a Queen who seemed 'delighted with life', something that he would remember nearly thirty years later under bizarre circumstances.[6]

As for Louis XVI, who was as temperamentally disinclined towards firmness as he was disinclined towards the strife, he first adopted one attitude, and then reversed it. In the process, he sacrificed any possible advantage that strength and clarity of purpose might have brought. The Tennis Court Oath, he muttered disconsolately, was 'merely a phrase'. On 23 June the King held a *séance royale* – that is, a session in which edicts would be promulgated; the Queen was not present. He refused to permit all three Estates to meet together although he recognized the need for the Estates to approve taxation in the future. Four days later he went back on his decision and accepted the composite meeting of the Three Estates, since the Third Estate showed no sign of going to their allotted (separate) chamber. Meanwhile Mirabeau, whose eloquent speeches given without notes were holding the deputies in thrall, declared of the Third Estate turned National Assembly: 'We are here by the will of the people, we shall only go away by the force of bayonets.'* The desperate atmosphere at court was reported by the Comtesse de Provence to her close friend Madame de Gourbillon in a letter of 2 July: 'You have no idea what life at Versailles is like ...' Stones were being thrown and shots fired at night.[7]

On 4 July, Count Mercy reported to Joseph II that the King, wavering once more, was now inclining towards the interests of the clergy and nobility, while Necker continued to believe in the potential of the Third Estate to throw its weight on the side of the monarchy. As Gouverneur Morris wrote, Louis was 'an honest Man and wishes really to do Good' without having either 'Genius or Education' to discover what that good might be.[8] In the meantime, with the royal brothers holding firm conservative views on the authority of the monarchy, it was not likely that Necker would last long in the seat of power.

On 9 July there was another revolutionary step forward as the previous National Assembly turned itself into a Constituent National Assembly, with the power to make laws. La Fayette, the deputy for Riom where his estates were, put forward a draft

* The words, which inspired innumerable popular engravings, may be apocryphal, but the sentiments were for real.

declaration concerning human rights that was based on the American Declaration of Independence. Meanwhile the plotting against Necker went forward, also at Versailles, while in Paris troops, up to 30,000 of them, were brought in against possible repetitions of those sinister Réveillon riots of April. On 11 July Necker was dismissed (for the second time) by the King, and with him went Montmorin and others associated with his ministry. In Necker's place came the notoriously conservative Breteuil, and other aristocrats such as the aged Marshal Duc de Broglie as Minister of War, and the son of the Duc de Vauguyon, Louis' Governor of years before.

Since Necker had remained popular with the public, his disappearance – the King told him that he counted on his departure being 'prompt and in secret' – was one more element in the savage general discontent.[9] Rioting on 12 July, which led to the closure of the theatres and the opera, was succeeded by much worse violence on the 13th. There was a seemingly minor incident, when the troops of the Royal German Regiment, under the Prince de Lambesc, were pelted with stones. But the situation erupted when they responded. Later, Lambesc and his men were accused of cutting down not only rioters but also innocent civilians with their sabres.

Perhaps Lambesc was not guilty of inordinate brutality; he was subsequently acquitted after an investigation. His own explanation was that he had to stop the mob seizing the Pont Tournant leading to the Tuileries. Marie Antoinette remained loyal to him: 'How wrong that someone should be punished for being faithful to the King and obeying orders!' she told Mercy. Lambesc, son of the Comtesse de Brionne, was a distant cousin, a non-royal Lorrainer, and the Queen retained her sympathy for him after he emigrated, advocating his cause to her brother Joseph.[10] However, she kept these feelings private, declining, for example, to plead Lambesc's cause with the Marquis de La Fayette, the dominant figure of the National Assembly. Her explanation – 'I would give the impression of believing him guilty if I spoke for him' – was probably not the real one; the truth was that the Queen knew that her days as a successful petitioner were drawing to a close.

The Lambesc Affair certainly did great harm to the royal reputation with the idea that the king's troops were deliberately assaulting his people. It was only a portent of the trouble to come. The following day the great prison fortress, the Bastille, was stormed by a determined crowd who wanted the weapons and powder that they believed were stored there, in order to arm themselves against the depredations of the State. Some of their members who rifled the Opéra for the weapons used on stage were frustrated, 'the axes and clubs being only made of cardboard'.[11]

There were nearly a hundred deaths and over seventy wounded in the course of the assault. These were mainly minor tradesmen and artisans, one of whom was a woman, a laundress. Such casualties became instant martyrs in the legends of the city. The Governor of the fortress, the Marquis de Launay, was killed by the furious crowd after his surrender, together with another official; their heads were paraded through the streets on pikes. There were fantastic reports afterwards of the discovery of secret cartloads of grain intended for the King's personal consumption, or of wagons, emblazoned with the Queen's arms and loaded with clothes for her to use as a disguise. In fact a total of seven prisoners of state – two madmen, four forgers and one nobly born criminal – were released.[12]

The security of Paris against mob rule was immediately thrown into question by this day of bloodshed and destruction. The ordinary Gardes Françaises, who had held to their duties at the time of the Réveillon riots in April, could no longer be counted upon to keep order. Where, then, were the Swiss Guards, under their colonel, the Baron de Besenval, that amusing man who had enjoyed membership of the Queen's Private Society for so long? Besenval was widely blamed by both sides for withdrawing the Swiss to Saint Cloud instead of standing fast to prevent the tumult spreading. Royalists believed that Besenval, now in his late sixties, had acted thus in order to distract the mob's attention from his Paris home, which was stocked with art treasures. Revolutionaries were convinced of the exact opposite: that Besenval had deliberately left the mob to do their worst, in order that Paris itself might be destroyed.[13]

This was symptomatic of the growing incomprehension between the various parties. The Parisian bourgeoisie began to see in the National Assembly their bulwark not so much against royal authority as against mob rule. Meanwhile the King wrote 'rien' for 14 July in his *Journal*.[14] It was true that there had been no hunting; but Louis XVI did not even give the Fall of the Bastille that brief mention he had accorded to the death of Vergennes, the departure of Necker and a few other major political events.

So the ancient stones of the Bastille, that symbol of oppression, were beaten down. As Bailly wrote in his memoirs: 'Holy august Liberty, for the first time, was introduced to the reign of horror, that fearful abode of despotism.' Thereafter fragments of the stone were set into brooches and bracelets, as symbols of liberty. In a further outbreak of radical chic, buckles were fashioned in the shape of the towers of the Bastille, and a bonnet *à la Bastille*, also a tower but trimmed with tricolour ribbon, became all the rage.[15] The red, white and blue tricolour itself sprang into prominence in the shape of innumerable cockades. Green, the traditional colour of liberty, was originally suggested by a radical deputy and journalist called Camille Desmoulins; awkwardly enough, this was also the colour of Artois' livery. In the end red and blue, the colours of Paris, separated by the Bourbon white, were adopted; fortunately these were the colours of the popular Duc d'Orléans – the subject of so much enthusiastic acclamation these days.[16]

The Queen, who would come to dislike the tricolour enormously – but in private – passed the day of 14 July, like the rest of the court, in ignorance of what was taking place in Paris. Nor was anyone, it seemed, in a hurry to tell the King. He was in bed when the Duc de Liancourt, an aristocrat of liberal sympathies, broke the news.

'Is it a revolt?' asked Louis XVI.

'No, Sire,' came Liancourt's reply (which there is no reason to suppose he did not make). 'It is a revolution!'[17]

In seething Paris, a National Guard or citizens' militia was formed, under the command of La Fayette, with the tricolour as its badge, to replace the Gardes Françaises; further militias were created all over France. The astronomer Bailly was elected Mayor of Paris. These developments were less immediately important to Versailles than the future of the court. There was an acute sense of panic at the violence, apparently unstoppable, that had recently taken place. King and Queen united in believing that particular targets of popular wrath should probably withdraw for the time being from France.

The day after the storming of the Bastille – 15 July – the King visited the National Assembly in its salon at Versailles. Mirabeau put a stop to the applause that greeted the sovereign with the ominous words: 'The people's silence is a lesson for kings.' Louis was, however, acclaimed as he returned 'on foot', as he noted in his *Journal*. It was not until the next day that he made the real concessions demanded by the Assembly: the abandonment of the new ministers including Breteuil who had held office for a mere 'Hundred Hours', and the recall of Necker on the simple but radical grounds that the people wanted him back. Before that, a vital discussion took place behind closed doors as to who should flee where and when. The timing was the easiest thing to decide. In view of the hatred felt for the Duchesse de Polignac (back from England), notorious as the extravagant and vicious favourite of the Queen, it was thought right for the Polignac family, husband, wife and children, to leave at once for the Swiss border. Others counselled to go were the Comte and Comtesse d'Artois, the Princes of the Blood, Condé and Conti, and Marie Antoinette's Reader, the Abbé de Vermond, her confidential advisor for twenty years.

Everyone wept at the scene of farewell. At first Yolande de Polignac refused to go, but the Queen was in agonies of fear every moment the favourite remained in France. In floods of tears, Marie Antoinette told her: 'I am terrified of everything; in the name of our friendship go, now is the time for you to escape from the fury of my enemies.' She pointed out that in attacking the Duchesse, they were really attacking the Queen, adding: 'Don't be the victim of your attachment to me, and my friendship for you.' At this point the King entered. Marie Antoinette asked him to help her persuade 'these good people, these faithful friends' that 'they must leave us'. The King then joined his pleas to hers, telling them that he had just commanded the Comte d'Artois' departure, and he would repeat the same order to them: 'Don't lose a single minute.'[18]

By now the King, whose genuine affection for Yolande was not simply a by-product of her usefulness to the Queen, was in tears as well. It was an intimacy that would be attested in the future by his informal correspondence with Yolande when she was in exile; some of these letters would be unwontedly self-revelatory, as when he disclosed how much popular accusations of greed had hurt him. But perhaps his last reported words to her, which were most kindly meant, went to the heart of the Polignac character: 'I will keep on your *charges*.' By this the King meant those paid positions for which the Polignacs could no longer carry out their duties.

At midnight Marie Antoinette sent a last message to Yolande: 'Adieu! the most tender of friends. This word is terrible to pronounce but it must be said. Here is the order for the horses. I have no more strength left except to embrace you.' The Polignacs took three days and three nights to reach Switzerland, during which time the Duchesse was disguised as a maid. In Basle she adopted for the time being the pseudonym of 'Madame Erlanger' for the purpose of correspondence, as not only Louis XVI but also Marie Antoinette poured out their fears to her in their letters; the Queen followed the progress of Yolande's family, whom she considered her adopted children, with as much keenness as if they had been her own.

The significance of the flight of the most right-wing members of the royal entourage, including the Polignacs, was twofold. First of all, Marie Antoinette was back in that position of loneliness which she had taken so much trouble to avoid by forming intense female relationships, by joining, in effect, the Polignac set and by creating her Private Society. Whatever the ups and downs of her feelings for the Duchesse, those clouds and changes that sometimes marred the beauty of the day, in the words of Tilly, it had been an enormously long friendship – it was fourteen years since Count Mercy had first bewailed Yolande's rise to favour. At this sad time, it was natural for the

Queen to dwell more on her memories of emotional dependency, than on the recent cooling-off, particularly as the summer had once more brought the Queen closer to Artois and the Polignacs, in the political sense. In September, Louis wrote to Madame Erlanger (Yolande) about her unnamed 'friend' (Marie Antoinette). She was 'keeping well' but, being 'much tormented by all that passed', was especially sad that she did not have 'the consolation of friendship round her'.[19]

The second, more politically serious effect of the flight, which was followed by a flood of emigrating aristocrats, was to create a centre of would-be royal policy outside France. Provence, next heir to the throne after the four-year-old Louis Charles, was still at Versailles, but Artois and his sons were outside the reach of the revolutionaries, whatever their intentions might be towards the monarchy. The first stop of Artois, with his Savoyard wife, was Turin, the capital of his father-in-law the King of Sardinia; the Duchesse de Polignac also subsequently arrived there. The Princes of the Blood ended up in Coblenz in Germany. Here rumours and conspiracies were equally rife. In particular there was a story that the Duc d'Orléans might be adopted as king, or even as Regent for Louis Charles. The pamphlets pouring forth from the Palais-Royal were extremely favourable to the radical Duc, and 'Long live Orléans!' became a popular placard. All this might be nothing more than provocation but certainly the potential royal rights of Artois and his sons were threatened by any suggestion of an Orléanist succession. The Queen, however, who had remained in France, was no longer part of their counsels, as she had been during the summer interlude. Insofar as her interests and those of her surviving son were bound up with the fate of Louis XVI, she was now in a subtle sense on the opposite side to the émigré Princes.

Why did the Queen stay behind? The question must arise, because she was by far the most unpopular member of the court. The answer lies in Marie Antoinette's concept of duty. Frightened as she was by the grim spectre of her unpopularity and apprehensive that there might be worse to follow, Marie Antoinette was nevertheless determined to preserve her position as the King's wife and the Dauphin's mother. In some quarters there was beginning to be talk of putting aside the wicked Queen – possibly into a convent, that traditional receptacle of inconvenient royal females. It was relevant in this connection that, while there was as yet no legal divorce in France, one of the penalties for adultery on the part of the wife was to be shut up in a convent for two years (after a whipping); if her husband happened to die during this period, the erring woman was obliged to remain cloistered for the rest of her natural life.[20]

The immurement of Marie Antoinette was not a new idea. As long ago as the Diamond Necklace Affair, the benevolent Duc de Penthièvre, father-in-law of the Princesse de Lamballe, had supposedly declared that in view of the threat to public morality, it would be prudent to shut up the Queen in the convent of Val-de-Grâce. The rumour continued to circulate. Now Queen Charlotte in England reported on 28 July 1789 that apartments were being prepared for the French queen at Val-de-Grâce: 'for Safety as some say but others say that the Third Estate insist upon her going there'. It was not true; neither was it true that Marie Antoinette was obliged to go first to Paris, accompanied by the Dauphin, and give formal thanks at Notre-Dame 'for the Revolution that has taken place'. Yet a madman who declared publicly at the Palais-Royal that the Queen should be shut up in a convent, after taking the King and his son to Paris, was loudly applauded.[21]

There was general talk of excluding queens from the role of Regent – despite the traditional right of a Queen of France to act for her young son – citing the same Salic Law that forbade females from succeeding to the French throne. These observations were deliberately pointed at Marie Antoinette: no 'stranger', that is, one foreign born, should have any part in a Regency.[22] Rumours apart, getting rid of the Queen in a non-violent manner remained an interesting option for those, like La Fayette, who did not envisage the abolition of all royal authority, yet saw in the Queen an obvious area of weakness in the King's situation. The Queen, however, viewed this same situation in quite a different light. Latterly it had become her explicit double duty to bolster up the King with her wifely strength, while providing maternal care for the Dauphin. Separation would prevent her carrying out those duties on the one hand, while providing ammunition for her enemies to make an assault on her status.

If the Queen would not go alone, why did the King, Queen and royal children not move to some more secure place after the outrageous demonstration of violence on 14 July? One possibility was Metz, in eastern France on the Moselle. This was one of the strongest fortresses in Europe and it was also not far from the borders of both Germany and the Netherlands. It was the suggestion of Breteuil, endorsed by Artois, and according to Madame Campan, Marie Antoinette approved the idea, ordering her packing to begin.[23] Then the King, as usual, took advice. Unfortunately it was conflicting, and the strongest character present, in terms of influence over Louis XVI, the Comte de Provence, advised staying put. The old Marshal de Broglie also challenged his master's decision to go.

Much later the King told Fersen, in a confidence that was not without self-pity, that he regretted missing the opportunity of 14 July. 'I should have gone then and I wanted to, but what could I do when Monsieur [Provence] himself begged me not to go, and the Marshal de Broglie, as commander, replied: "Yes, we can go to Metz, but what shall we do when we get there?"' The King then repeated sadly: 'I missed my opportunity and it never came again.'[24]

Instead of departing for the frontier, the King went to Paris on 17 July – without the Queen – with the intention of promoting calm. The Queen stayed at Versailles in a state of trepidation, having a presentiment that her husband would not return, a feeling underlined by the fact that Provence was instructed to assume full powers in his absence as Lieutenant General of the kingdom. But this presentiment at least was unjustified; the King was not detained. The Duke of Dorset thought it was 'certainly one of the most humiliating steps that [the King] could possibly take', describing him as being 'like a tame bear' as he was 'led in triumph' by the deputies and the city militia. One of those deputies leading 'the bear' was a lawyer from Arras in his early thirties named Maximilien Robespierre who had, as a student, delivered a Latin address to the King on his coronation, but now embraced rather different political opinions.

Louis XVI approved the appointments of Bailly as Mayor and La Fayette as commander of the National Guard, and in an important speech, mumbled something about his people being always able to count upon his love. Most significantly of all in this time of symbols, Louis XVI allowed himself to be displayed on the balcony of the Hôtel de Ville (the City Hall) with the tricolour cockade, which Bailly called 'the distinctive emblem of the French Nation', in his hat.[25]

'The Revolution in France has been carried out,' wrote the Russian Minister in Paris, Jean Simolin, to his Chancellor in St Petersburg on 19 July, 'and the royal authority annihilated.' He went on to comment on the ferocity that the French had displayed in its course – he was referring to the deaths of Bastille Day, the parading of heads on spikes. One read 'with horror' of this same kind of French ferocity in accounts of the St Bartholomew's Day Massacre (of Huguenots, 200 years earlier). But as Simolin pointed out, there was a difference: this was political rather than religious fervour. Count Mercy, writing to Kaunitz, was equally emphatic that a revolution had taken place, 'however unbelievable it may appear'. Mercy himself had had to retreat to the country and ask for guards at his Paris house, due to the hatred felt by the people for 'the representative of the brother of the Queen'. Although the guards were granted, there was also a thorough (if unsuccessful) inspection of Mercy's house for the great store of armaments that it was generally believed that he, being an Austrian, must have stored there.[26]

So began that eerie summer at Versailles. Against a background of peasant revolts in various regions, inspired by a powerful if irrational emotion known as the 'Great Fear' – in essence a panic about the safety of property – a number of measures were suggested in the National Assembly.[27] It concentrated the mind that stones were thrown at the windows of the Archbishop of Paris, breaking them, on the night of 3 August. Males everywhere were transformed into members of the National Guard, mere valets becoming lieutenants and even the musicians in the Royal

Chapel wearing military uniform, although Louis XVI drew the line at an Italian soprano dressed up as a grenadier. On the same date, the abolition of all feudal privileges was suggested; at the end of August La Fayette's *La Déclaration des Droits de l'Homme* was given official status.

Meanwhile the Queen adopted the lowest possible profile. Although she was popularly supposed to have remained in France with the aim of destroying the National Assembly, while asking for 50,000 troops from her brother, she actually devoted her time to her children. As Joseph II told his brother Leopold on 3 August, the private role of mother was the only one that really suited their sister (something that the Emperor might perhaps have appreciated earlier).[28] It was a foretaste of what life was to be like without the adult friends who were so vital to her.

Yet all ceremony at Versailles could not be abandoned, any more than the King thought of abandoning the routine by which he hunted three or four times a week, including at the moment when the abolition of feudal privileges was raised. In England, Queen Charlotte reflected in her diary: 'I often think that this cannot be the eighteenth century in which we live at present for Ancient History can hardly produce anything more Barbarous and Cruel than Our Neighbours in France.' She cheered herself up by reading a history of the reign of the absolutist Louis XIV, when things had been done so much better.[29] Yet if much of Louis XVI's royal authority had been stripped from him, he was still condemned to carry out the same court routine that his great ancestor had instituted – as was his Queen. Marie Antoinette gave the traditional party to celebrate the Feast of St Louis on 25 August and found herself receiving the market-women, who arrived in some force from Paris. On the one hand they were exercising another traditional right – to pay their respects; on the other hand their presence reminded everyone exactly how short the twelve-mile route from Paris to Versailles really was. The figure of the majestic Queen who still presided over the most formal court in Europe contrasted with that of the despised woman, who by September was unable even to stroll upon the terraces for fear of hostile comment.

In the meanwhile nothing that had happened so far had alleviated the food crisis. There were bread riots in Versailles itself where a baker was half-hanged on 13 September for allegedly favouring his richer customers with better-quality loaves. In Paris, approaching starvation made the women increasingly aggressive on behalf of their families. Mayor Bailly at the Hôtel de Ville had to receive angry deputations on the subject of the bakers from women who shouted publicly that 'men understood nothing'.[30] These demonstrations existed in parallel with the discussions of the National Assembly on the King's surviving powers. Should he have an absolute right of veto on legislation or was the legislative power of the Assembly paramount? And there were, of course, many shades of opinion in between. What both movements had in common was a growing feeling that matters would go better if the King, absent since 17 July, returned to Paris.

There were changes. The vanishing of the Duchesse de Polignac, Royal Governess for nearly seven years, meant that she had to be replaced in this position of such vital concern to the royal mother. The new choice was summed up by the Queen herself. She was confiding her children to 'Virtue', whereas with the Duchesse they had been confided to 'Friendship'. The Marquise de Tourzel was at the age of forty a widow with five children; her husband, like herself a devoted adherent of the royal family, had been killed in 1786 while out hunting with Louis XVI, but they had enjoyed twenty years of perfect conjugal felicity. A strong character as well as a famously upright one, the Marquise de Tourzel would be nicknamed 'Madame Sévère' by the lively little Dauphin although he also loved her, and in particular he adored her eighteen-year-old daughter Pauline who accompanied Madame Sévère into the royal household.

The Marquise's rectitude was, however, accompanied by two absolute beliefs. The first concerned the divinely ordained place of royalty in the world, at the head of a hierarchy where others also had their allotted places. Her motto was 'Faithful to God and the King', the latter being only a little lower than the former. It was this consciousness, as well as the kindnesses she had received from the King and Queen, that made the Marquise accept the post, although she foresaw dangers ahead that might threaten Pauline. The second belief concerned 'the precious trust' that she personally had been given by their 'august' Majesties. As a result, the Marquise intended to dedicate her life to the royal children she called 'divinities'.[31] In 1789 this concept of duty, which meant she must always be at the Dauphin's side, seemed to have no disadvantages.*

The arrival of the new Royal Governess gave Marie Antoinette an opportunity to display her common-sense approach as a mother in a long memorandum on the subject of her son's character.[32] It was not a starry-eyed document and the child delineated was not quite the healthy, merry little peasant boy of her letters to Princess Louise of Hesse-Darmstadt. One may discern in it not only Marie Antoinette's dissatisfaction with the way her husband had been brought up (a dissatisfaction that he himself shared) but also, perhaps, memories of her own less than helpful upbringing, an injudicious mixture of spoiling and neglect. Certainly the admonition to the Royal Governess not to neglect Marie Thérèse entirely for her brother – a temptation generally felt by servants where the male heir is concerned – may also have its roots in Maria Teresa's favouritism of Marie Christine. The very frankness of the document also makes it valuable as a clue to certain aspects of Louis Charles's nature, already present at the age of four and a half.

The Queen described Louis Charles's chief fault as being a strong tendency to indiscretion. He would repeat all too easily what he had overheard and at the same time, without exactly meaning to lie, he would embellish the truth still further with things that he imagined he had witnessed. The Marquise de Tourzel was to take particular care to curb the Dauphin in this weakness. He was also nervous, with a hatred of loud noises; in particular the barking of the many Versailles dogs, if allowed to

---

* The memoirs of the Marquise (later Duchesse) de Tourzel, and her daughter Pauline (later Comtesse de Béarn), are crucial testimonies to the life of the royal family from this time forward, since in their different ways they were so intimately involved.

The Queen out hunting, with the King
in the background, 1783.

Marie Antoinette aged twenty-eight by
Louise Elisabeth Vigée Le Brun.

Madame Elisabeth, younger sister of Louis XVI.

Bust of Marie Antoinette by Felix Lecomte, 1784; her aquiline nose and the disdainful Habsburg look discerned by her enemies are more evident in sculpture than in painting.

The Comte de Provence, brother of Louis XVI, who was for many years the next in line in the succession.

The Comte d'Artois, younger brother of Louis XVI, who was generally held to be the handsomest in the family.

The simplicity of Marie Antoinette's costume in this portrait by
Mme Vigée Le Brun was criticised as unbecoming on the Queen of France.

Marie Antoinette's two oldest children, Marie Thérèse, Madame Royale, and the Dauphin, Louis Joseph, 1784.

This portrait of the Queen with her children by Adolf Ulrik von Wertmüller was considered to be unflattering and insufficiently formal, possibly because the artist was Swedish. (Marie Antoinette herself bore no resentment and commissioned him again in 1788.)

The Diamond Necklace, originally intended
to tempt the Comtesse Du Barry; such an
elaborate and showy piece was not the kind
of thing that appealed to Marie Antoinette
(*reconstruction*).

come too close, frightened him. The little boy was, however, loyal, affectionate and especially fond of his sister; if he was given anything, he immediately asked for the same gift to be bestowed on her. But Louis Charles was also quick-tempered and hated to have to say the word 'sorry' above all things, going to great lengths to avoid it. Yet as his mother admitted, this 'inordinate pride' in himself might one day be to the Dauphin's advantage if he conducted himself well; she was presumably thinking of his father's unfortunate lack of self-esteem.

The scene was set for the events of October 1789, when the inviolate image of the French monarchy – that image cherished, for example, by the dutiful Marquise de Tourzel – was shattered for ever. Tragically, it was the very attempt to prove the security of the royal family in such an ominous situation that turned out to be the spark that led to the conflagration. The Royal Flanders Regiment was brought from Douai to Versailles and on 1 October a banquet was given in the theatre at Versailles, at which the King's bodyguards fraternized with the new arrivals, being seated alternately. The King and Queen, the latter with her new policy of retirement, did not, however, plan to attend. It was only the wild enthusiasm of the soldiers that prompted an unwise courtier to suggest that they appear.[33]

So not only Louis XVI, but Marie Antoinette also decided to be present. The Queen was dressed in white and pale blue, with matching feathers in her hair and a turquoise necklace. She carried Louis Charles, wearing a lilac-coloured sailor suit, in her arms and led Marie Thérèse, in green and white, by the hand. The young Pauline de Tourzel never forgot the enthusiasm that greeted her, the cheers, the tears, the cries of loyalty and devotion ... As Saint-Priest wrote later in his memoirs, the whole scene was inspired by 'wine and zeal'.[34] Appropriately enough, as it seemed at the time, it was a celebrated song by the composer Grétry from his opera of 1784, *Richard Coeur-de-Lion*, that provided the theme of the evening. With the words 'O Richard! O mon roi!' the minstrel Blondel called for his imprisoned master, and it now found an echo in a mass of loyal hearts.

Unfortunately the whole occasion was transformed in the

Parisian press the next day into something that was a deliberate affront to the new national regime. 'In the course of an orgy', according to the revolutionary newspaper *L'Ami du Peuple*, the tricolour cockade had been trampled underfoot. This was a charge strongly denied by those who were there, although Madame Campan, a witness at the behest of the Queen, admitted that certain cockades worn by the few National Guards present were turned inside out to show their white linings; white being the royalist colour.[35] The fervent songs of Grétry and others were construed as incitements to counter-revolution. Thus were the flames lit.

On Monday, 5 October, the routine at Versailles still had a semblance of normality. The Queen was at the Petit Trianon. Count Fersen had arrived at Versailles a week earlier, to spend the winter there in a house he had acquired in the town. It is therefore not improbable that he was present at some point with the Queen on what was to be the very last day she spent in her 'pleasure house'. The King was out shooting in the woods above Meudon and was having some good sport. He had killed some eighty-one head when he received an urgent message from Saint-Priest as Minister of the Royal Household, and, as his *Journal* recorded, this prowess was 'interrupted by events'.[36] The events in question concerned a march of market-women who had set out from Paris at ten o'clock that morning. They were intending to demand grain or flour from their sovereign at Versailles, as well as his assent, hitherto denied, to certain constitutional changes proposed by the Assembly which would have formally diminished his authority (Louis argued for seeing the new Constitution as a whole). The King turned immediately for home at top speed, galloping all the way up the Grand Avenue. He was back by three o'clock. At the same time a message was sent to the Queen, and she too returned. The Dauphin's daily outing in his carriage was cancelled.

A series of agitated discussions took place as to how the royal family should prepare for the expected invasion. They knew the mob to be surging towards them, undaunted by patches of thick fog on the road and heavy downpours of rain. Would it not be more secure to decamp to Rambouillet, twice the distance of

Versailles from Paris and far more secure than the latter ever-open palace? There was a strong body of opinion that the Queen and children at least should be transported away; this would not be difficult to achieve, since, as the Marquise de Tourzel pointed out later, the horses were still hitched to the Dauphin's carriage. François Huë, the Dauphin's premier valet for the last two years, an intelligent and loving man, thought the advice to go to Rambouillet, urged by Saint-Priest, was good: 'If only it had been God's will that it should be followed.' It was Marie Antoinette who initially rejected the idea and for the same reasons that she had elected to remain in France in July: her place was at the King's side. Louis XVI, for his part, could not make up his mind to flee, expressing deep reluctance to become a 'fugitive King'.[37]

No decision had been made by the time the first market-women reached Versailles at about four o'clock, with the main body arriving between five and six. A message from La Fayette – that he was bringing his National Guards to secure the situation – was also received about six, giving the royal family the impression that they still had an opportunity to reconsider their position. When a deputation of market-women made its way to the Oeil-de-Boeuf antechamber of the King's apartments, Louis was conferring with his ministers. In the end he consented to receive a single woman whose appearance and dress, according to one observer, indicated neither 'misery nor an abject condition'. (Nonetheless, one of the strongest memories of the ten-year-old Madame Royale was of the near-nakedness of the women – she had never witnessed such utter poverty before.) This individual was certainly strong-minded enough to harangue the King on the need of the people of Paris for bread. When the King offered to tell the directors of two granaries to release all possible stores, she went away to join her comrades, only to return so as to get the King's order in writing. He gave it to her.[38]

There was now an uneasy stand-off between the seething crowds in the courtyard of Versailles and the royal family and their bodyguards. The original objective of securing food had now been overtaken by the idea of transferring the King bodily to Paris. The idea of the royal family departing for Rambouillet, now revived, was found to be impossible since all the traces of the King's carriages in the courtyard of Versailles had been cut. At the request of the National Assembly, the King – greatly upset – did sign their preliminary decrees to do with the Constitution in an attempt to alleviate the situation.

There were rumours that men in disguise had participated in the market-women's march when its members had first been summoned by the tocsins in Paris. That was certainly not impossible. What was extremely unlikely was that the Duc d'Orléans himself had marched as a woman. Although contemporaries were generally convinced that he had encouraged the march, it was psychologically implausible for the Duc to adopt female dress when he was enjoying his popularity with the crowd.* But there were now numbers of 'armed brigands' present as well as women like one Louise Renée, who was reported in the *Journal de Paris* as having been straightforwardly excited at the idea of going to Versailles to ask for bread. Louise, incidentally, strongly denied having ever said that 'she wanted to come back with the head of the Queen on her sword'; in proof of this, she ingenuously pointed out that she did not have a sword, 'only a broomstick'.[40]

If Louise Renée personally did not utter threats against the Queen, there were plenty who did. The royal bodyguards were quickly alarmed by the oaths they overheard – vows to cut off Marie Antoinette's head and worse. There were, for example, the proud declarations of the market-women that they were wearing their traditional working aprons in order to help themselves to her entrails, out of which they intended to make cockades. The Queen's role as scapegoat for the weaknesses and failures of the monarchy as a whole had never been more evident. In the uneasy calm that spread across the palace of Versailles after midnight, when La Fayette departed, it was the Queen who recognized her peculiar vulnerability. She refused

* Nor is it plausible that Fersen marched among the women in order to find out what was going on and warn the Queen; he never mentioned this – surely vital – detail in his account to his father of the events of Versailles on 5–6 October; the evidence rests solely on the *Souvenirs* of the Comtesse d'Adhémar, published years later.[39]

to share the apartments of the King, where she would surely have been safer, in order not to put him – and her children – in danger, but at two o'clock went to lie sleepless on her own bed. Madame Auguié, sister of Madame Campan, was in attendance with Madame Thibault. The Queen told them to go to sleep but their 'feelings of attachment' to her prevented them. The Marquise de Tourzel, as was her custom, shared the Dauphin's bedroom and was instructed in a crisis to take the little boy to his father.*

The attack came at about four o'clock in the morning. Madame Auguié heard yells and shouts. Afterwards Marie Antoinette believed that it was inspired by the Duc d'Orléans who wanted to have her killed at the very least. It was a view she passed on to her daughter Marie Thérèse who recorded that 'the principal project [of the attack] was to assassinate my mother, on whom the Duc d'Orléans wished to avenge himself because of offences he believed he had received from her.' There was another rumour that Orléans himself, dressed in a woman's redingote and hat, had guided the surge of people, shouting, 'We're going to kill the Queen!' But although Orléans, as his mistress Grace Elliott admitted, was 'very, very violent' against the Queen, there was no need of his active participation.[42] The real work of destruction had been done long before by satire, libel and rumour; Marie Antoinette had become dehumanized. The actual assault by a body of people inspiring each other with their bloodthirsty frenzy was the culmination of the process, not the start of it.

When Madame Auguié went to the door of the antechamber leading to the guardroom, she was appalled to see a guard covered in blood who cried out to her: 'Save the Queen, Madame, they are coming to assassinate her!' Now the ladies dressed their mistress with frantic haste in the exact obverse of the elaborate daily routine to which she was accustomed, in their panic leaving one ribbon of her petticoat untied. The

---

* The Marquise de Tourzel's narrative is thus a first-hand source; Madame Auguié related everything to Madame Campan the next day, which makes the latter's relation of events another good source even if she was not personally present.[41]

decision was taken to flee to the safety of the King's apartments and here the secret staircase played its part – that staircase that had been constructed years before in order that the King might make his nervous 'conjugal visits' in more privacy. Scarcely had the Queen left than the howling mob, having put to death two of the bodyguards, broke in. According to several accounts, they pierced the Queen's great bed with their pikes, either to make sure she was not hiding or as a symbolic act of defiance.[43]

It can never be known for sure what they would have done if the bed had still had its royal occupant. After all, it took only one of the invaders to carry out the demonic threats that they were all making for the situation to ignite. The temperament of any crowd is uncertain and this one had just killed two people. Marie Antoinette's absolute conviction that her assassination had been intended – which marked her for the rest of her life, becoming as formative an experience in its own way as the Diamond Necklace Affair – was therefore hardly unreasonable.* Marie Thérèse paid tribute later to her mother's extraordinary courage and sang-froid throughout her ordeal; Pauline de Tourzel also always remembered her calming gestures and her kind words: 'Don't be frightened, Pauline.'[45] But her outwardly brave demeanour coexisted with an inward terror from which she never totally recovered.

Once the royal family were gathered together in the King's apartments, he too behaving with commendable resolution, there were hasty conferences as to what to do. With the coming of day, a mass of people had assembled in the courtyard outside the balcony that led from the King's apartments, and they demanded a royal appearance. Such had been the confusion of the night past that various members of the crowd may have believed that the Queen had been killed or wounded, or even the King; they wanted to check, as it were, the casualty list. But when the King duly appeared, accompanied by his wife and

---

* The London *Times* had as its headline the next day, 'The Attempt to Murder the Queen', with which Marie Antoinette would have agreed; the more lurid but inaccurate story in the *Morning Post* had the Queen being paraded around with a noose about her neck, to symbolize her humiliation.[44]

children, that was not what was desired. Marie Antoinette was not to be allowed to make the point that she was still the Mother of the Nation ... The image was sharply rejected with cries from down below: 'No children! No children!'[46] Louis Charles and Marie Thérèse, already terrified by the night-time ordeal, in which they found themselves quickly dressed and removed from their familiar apartments, were duly taken away. Marie Antoinette, very pale and uncertain whether she was supposed to appear alone in order to be shot down by an assassin, nevertheless continued to stand there.

Soon the loudest cries drowned out all the rest. 'To Paris! To Paris!' they were demanding. In view of what had happened and what was happening – the gross insults and threats to the Queen proceeding unabated from an anonymous and perhaps murderous crowd, to say nothing of his children's security and his own – it was hard for the King to feel he had any alternative. The mob might want to separate the King from his power base at Versailles but on the other hand the National Guard promised more control in Paris than they had been able to exercise at Versailles.

At twelve-thirty an extraordinary procession set out on the road from Versailles to Paris. It would take nearly seven hours to reach the capital. The raucous crowd cried out in joy the words of a popular song, that they were taking 'the Baker, the Baker's wife, and the Baker's boy' to Paris, with the implication that bread would now be freely available. Yet this procession – 'What a cortège! Great God!' exclaimed the King, as though in sheer disbelief – contained in its midst not only his immediate family still in France, but also the decapitated heads of the bodyguards who had been their familiar companions. The sixteen-year-old Duc de Chartres watched them go, these cousins who had been brought so low, from a balcony at Passy. He raised his eyeglass in order to make out some odd objects carried by the crowd – and found himself staring at the bloody heads.[47]

In the King's carriage, where the occupants were in a state of slumped horror, a significant exchange took place between Louis XVI and Madame Elisabeth. He saw her gazing out of the window as they passed her beloved Montreuil. 'Are you admiring your lime avenue?' he asked in his kindly way. 'No, I am saying goodbye to Montreuil,' replied his sister.[48]

Back at Versailles, the coiffeur Léonard, left behind in a situation that for once did not require his ministrations, found that nothing had changed in the Queen's apartments. There were the slippers Marie Antoinette had not put on, lying there; there was a fichu, and half-turned silk stockings ready for the royal foot. The gilt panels were, however, desecrated and the wind of this blustery day blew through the splintered door. Some members of the diplomatic corps actually travelled to Versailles from Paris on that day because it was a Tuesday, the usual day of their reception; they found complete disorder and they also encountered bands of marauders who offered them some bloody relics. Being diplomats, they indicated cautious approval before departing.[49]

Henceforward Versailles, the château out of whose windows eager spectators had watched the arrival of the young Dauphine nearly twenty years ago, would have the desolate air of a place fallen under a spell.

PART FIVE

The Austrian Woman

CHAPTER NINETEEN

Her Majesty the Prisoner

'Your Majesty is a prisoner ... Yes, it's true. Since Her
Majesty no longer has her Guard of Honour, she is a
prisoner.'

Secretary Augeard to Marie Antoinette,
7 October 1789

'I'm fine; don't worry.' With this note Marie Antoinette
attempted to allay the fears of Count Mercy the day after
her arrival in Paris. (The ambassador himself had only
been preserved from attack by the fact that he was wearing an
overcoat over his ambassadorial silks due to the heavy rains.) If
the Queen was bravely reassuring, the King was phlegmatic. In
his *Journal* he summed up the extraordinary day of 6 October
1789 following the devastating night as follows: 'Departure for
Paris 12.30, visit to the Hôtel de Ville, dine and sleep at the
Tuileries.'[1]

These economical words hardly covered the ordeal suffered
by the King of France, the Queen, their two young children,
his sister Madame Elisabeth, his brother and sister-in-law the
Comte and Comtesse de Provence – and the reputation and
authority of the French monarchy. When the cortège arrived at
the gates of Paris, it was met by the Mayor, Bailly, who managed
an aphoristic reference to history, about the King's ancestor
Henri IV having conquered the city, and now the city had
conquered Louis XVI. Matters went better at the Hôtel de Ville.
Madame Elisabeth, who was present, noted how affably the
King spoke: 'It is always with pleasure and confidence that I

find myself amid the worthy inhabitants of my good city of Paris.'
When Bailly repeated the royal words, he left out 'confidence' but
the King made him put it back. As for Marie Antoinette,
outwardly she was her usual serene self as though nothing
untoward had happened in the last twenty-four hours.[2]

The scene that greeted them at the Tuileries was, however,
hardly likely to inspire the confidence of which the King spoke.
Furthermore their familiar royal bodyguards were now removed
in favour of the National Guards under La Fayette. It was
undoubtedly a prudent move from the point of view of the
former's safety; Marie Antoinette never ceased to mourn those
'brave and faithful' men who had died in her defence. But the
change increased the feeling of alienation for royalties who had
been accustomed to a special kind of security since childhood.

The trouble was that the palace of the Tuileries was both
decayed and populated. Begun by Catherine de' Medici in the
sixteenth century, the sprawling structure, overlooking the Seine
on the south side, had three pavilions and nearly four hundred
rooms; a long gallery built by Henri IV linked it to the Louvre.
But by the 1770s there was duckweed growing in the ornamental
waters of the gardens, once thought to be the most beautiful in
Europe, while prostitutes preferred to ply their trade in the
grounds there because they were quieter than those of the Palais-
Royal. Most of the interior was dark and depressing, with
ancient, faded tapestries and workmen's ladders everywhere. The
King's grandfather had ignored the Tuileries after a brief visit
over forty years ago. Although Marie Antoinette maintained a
small pied-à-terre in the royal apartments for late-lasting visits
to Paris, the real inhabitants were the royal servants and their
relations, about 120 of them, who had seized the opportunity
to move in.[3] There was also the Théâtre de Monsieur (the
Comte de Provence), which had recently been installed in the
Salle des Machines; still more people slept in the actors' dressing
rooms there. All of these human barnacles now had to be
summarily ejected.

So ramshackle were the arrangements, so great the lack of
preparation, that the Dauphin was obliged to spend the night
in a room barricaded with furniture because the doors did not

shut, with his faithful Governess the Marquise de Touzel sitting on his bed, sleepless with anxiety. It was understandable that the little boy should wake up the next morning and ask in dismay: 'Is today going to be like yesterday?' Nevertheless when he told the Queen, 'Everything is very ugly here, Maman,' she replied firmly: 'My son, Louis XIV lodged here comfortably enough; we must not be more particular than him.'[4]

At least the Queen herself was able to occupy the ground-floor apartments of the south wing, which had been recently decorated by the Comtesse de La Marck, a seventy-year-old member of the Noailles family, for her own use. However, the King, at the insistence of the Queen, had to buy out the Comtesse's furnishings of marbles, *boiseries* and mirrors at an estimated cost of 117,000 livres.[5] The royal children slept on the first floor, above the Queen. The King had three rooms on the ground floor, a cabinet for study on the mezzanine and his bedchamber on the first floor. (Once again the Queen thought it right that she, as the target of popular wrath – something amply confirmed by the shouts and insults throughout their journey – should not put the King in danger by her presence.) Madame Elisabeth was also on the ground floor, which she found so repugnant when the market-women pressed their faces to her windows that she asked to be rehoused in the Pavillon de Flore. Mesdames Tantes occupied the so-called Pavillon de Marsan, named for Louis XVI's Governess. The Comte and Comtesse de Provence went to their own handsome palace of the Luxembourg.

Saint-Priest and Fersen greeted the King and Queen on their arrival from the Hôtel de Ville. The latter had travelled as part of the cortège in one of the King's carriages and as he told his father: 'I was a witness to everything.' Although Saint-Priest subsequently expressed himself shocked at Fersen's presence, it merely underlined the fact that Fersen was one of the surviving members of the Queen's Private Society, even if his precise status might defy definition. Fersen now sold the house and horses that he had acquired in Versailles and took up residence in Paris. Here he would soon be able to visit 'Elle' – the Queen – while at the same time acting as the unofficial observer for the

King of Sweden, Gustav being increasingly worried about the effects of French revolutionary violence on the rest of Europe. Other supporters of the Queen also rushed to greet her, including the Princesse de Lamballe, who had been absent for some time due to ill health. Madame Campan was also summoned; she found her mistress very flushed, although still exercising her charm and kindness towards those around her, winning them over by personal contact in a way that would have been incomprehensible to the mob at Versailles.[6]

'Kings who become prisoners are not far from death,' murmured Marie Antoinette to Madame Campan. But were they prisoners? It remained an interesting and for the time being unresolved question, since the events of recent days meant that no one in the royal family was going to test the limits of their freedom. The Queen poured out her thoughts on her future to Mercy; her emphasis was on the waiting game she now needed to play. She might personally need time to recover from the tragic deaths of her guards, but she also realized that the people needed time to rid themselves of their 'horrible mistrust'. The only method of getting the royal family out of its present situation was 'patience, time and inspiring [in the French] a great confidence'.[7]

With this in mind, the Queen would make a memorable comment to one deputation from the Commune of Paris on the subject of the events of 6 October: 'I've seen everything, known everything and forgotten everything.' To Mercy in private her tune was very different. She worried about the effects of the recent risings in Alsace; if something went wrong there, the people would be persuaded it was the fault of 'the Germans' and that would rebound on her. With this in mind, she intended to lead a secluded life and play no part in public appointments.[8]

There was more to the Queen's fears than identification with 'the Germans'. For the first time she was appreciating that the actions of those in the royal family who had emigrated would inevitably be attributed to her, the Austrian woman, however much she disagreed with them, however much they acted against her own husband's interests. 'Prudence, patience are my lot,' the Queen repeated in conclusion. 'Above all, courage. And I can tell you that I need much more of it to support the everyday afflictions than the dangers of the night of the fifth of October.' It remained to be seen whether prudence and patience, let alone courage, would be enough to deal with the double challenge of royalty confined at home and royalties rampant abroad.

Once the desolation of the arrival was over – we must try to forget how we got here, Marie Antoinette told Mercy, in a show of oblivion belied by her memories – life at the Tuileries approached a kind of weird normality. Besides the royal apartments, there were several antechambers and more formal rooms including a salon, and a billiard room in the Galerie de Diane. A large convoy of vehicles brought furniture from Versailles. The Queen had her favourite mechanical dressing-table imported. Further furniture was commissioned from Riesener and others to brighten up those rooms that the Dauphin found so ugly. Léonard arrived and paid his visits, becoming ever more of a confidant. Mademoiselle Rose Bertin continued to be in attendance, although the Queen's bills were down by a third from the peak in 1788 and her accounts showed more evidence of alterations and adaptation of existing garments.[9]

On 8 October, when the psychological wounds of what had happened were still raw, there was a traditional diplomatic reception at the Tuileries of the sort that some diplomats had actually expected at Versailles on the day of the ignominious royal departure. Lord Robert Fitzgerald, the English Minister, deputy to the Ambassador, commented on the extreme melancholy of the occasion; how the Queen looked very pale, and her eyes were full of tears. Nevertheless the reception took place. As time passed, the Princesse de Lamballe even attempted to give some soirées in her apartments, one of her duties as Superintendent of the Household. Marie Antoinette attended for a while until, according to Madame Campan, the sight of an English lord playing with a ring that contained a lock of the regicide Cromwell's hair upset her.[10] Ladies present sported more royalist tokens – white ribbons and white lilies at the breast – although in the streets they put up with the tricolour to avoid embarrassment.

The Comte and Comtesse de Provence continued to arrive from the Luxembourg for the family supper that they had been enjoying together for so many years. In the circumstances the cheerful company of the Comtesse, reading characters from faces in a way that made Pauline de Tourzel giggle, was most welcome, even if the girl felt stupid on being subjected to Provence's carefully polished discourses. As for Madame Elisabeth, she might have said goodbye to Montreuil but she was nevertheless able to have her own milk and cream sent in from her country estate, and to receive happy news of the pregnancies of both her maidservants and of her cows.[11]

The financial allowance given by the National Assembly to the King for his living expenses – 25 million livres – was not ungenerous and there were still the revenues of his estates. The National Guards who attended the King were not monsters but sensible and well-educated members of the bourgeoisie, under the immediate command of a member of the Noailles family. Presentations were still made, and in a gesture of accommodation to the new order Mayor Bailly was granted the Rights of Entry. Public dinners were still given twice weekly; the King had his *lever* and his *coucher*. Routine bulletins about the King's health continued to be given as though no serious threat to that health had ever existed.

There were still over 150 people attached to the court and nearly 700 people at the Tuileries altogether, without counting troops. Even the Duc d'Orléans, making an appearance in a somewhat shamefaced manner, was there, for he was, after all, the first Prince of the Blood. Marie Antoinette, despite her hardening conviction of his implication in her ordeal, had learnt diplomacy since the distant days when she would not speak to the Comtesse Du Barry. Calmly, the Queen addressed a few words to her 'cousin'. Orléans then departed for the more salubrious atmosphere of the English court, although even here Queen Charlotte was careful to note in her diary that he was received 'not in a public capacity'.[12]

Marie Antoinette's own domestic life was singularly unchanged. The royal family continued to go to Mass in public as they had done at Versailles. She worked at her tapestry with her ladies, as she had always liked to do, including large-scale projects for covering furniture. She played billiards with the King, who delighted in teaching 'our dear Pauline' the game.* Above all, the Queen spent time with her children who were, as she told Princesse Louise, growing up: 'They are always with me and give me my sole happiness.'[14] Madame Royale now had all her lessons in her mother's presence, Marie Antoinette being at last able to play that assiduous maternal role that she had originally planned for herself.

As for the Dauphin, he made everyone happy with his innocent gaiety. He was able to profit from the gardens of the Tuileries, for that fresh air and exercise which the Queen had told the Marquise de Tourzel were essential to his health; there (in sharp contrast to his mother) he was generally admired by doting spectators. Many people, whatever their political views, found it possible to see in the lively, handsome little boy a more agreeable symbol of the future of France than that represented by his corpulent, graceless father or his malevolent Austrian mother. Playing in the palace gardens, he became one of the sights of Paris, on one occasion presenting flowers to a large body of visiting Bretons until they ran out and then tearing lilac leaves in two to complete the process. Soon, with the resilience of youth, the Dauphin had quite forgotten his original disgust with the Tuileries. When asked whether he preferred Versailles or Paris, Louis Charles replied: 'Paris, because I see so much more of Papa and Maman.'[15] It was true.

Perhaps it was the balm of her children's constant presence that caused the Queen's health – long a cause for concern – to improve once she was settled in the Tuileries. Although her confidential communications to Count Mercy referred without cease to her 'agitation', the fact was that, according to Madame Campan, her frequent 'hysterical disorders' vanished. Or perhaps it was simply, in Madame Campan's words, that 'all the faculties of her soul were called forth to support her physical strength.'[16]

---

* Writing her memoirs as an old lady for her descendants, Pauline Comtesse de Béarn recalled the King's instruction gratefully: 'It is thanks to him that I can beat you today, my dears.'[13]

In other words, Marie Antoinette, the daughter of Maria Teresa, knew how to put on a good show.

Marie Antoinette – for all the abuse heaped upon her, the people who deliberately splashed her with their carriages when she was out walking, the others who talked loudly and insultingly about her a short, safe distance away – was still expected to exercise that traditional benevolence that was an integral part of the duties of the Queen of France. Demands were quickly made that she should fund the many poor women encumbered with debt who had pawned their vital goods. The King merely authorized the redemption of pledges for goods worth one louis or less, but still the principle of the Queen's innate compassion was maintained. In early January 1790 she presided over a committee meeting of a *charité maternelle* in aid of poverty-stricken mothers, at which a report was submitted to about forty women present. Marie Antoinette impressed the rich ladies in attendance by inviting everyone to sit in her presence. When she was asked to state her preferences, since funds did not permit helping more than two mothers at a time, she tactfully announced that she had consulted the National Assembly on the subject. Miraculously their two candidates were also her own. The Queen then gave a further financial gift, which in the words of one of those present, Madame Necker, would enable them to help further unfortunates in 'the asylum of misery'.[17]

In February various visits were paid to a foundling hospital. The Queen showed the Dauphin, shortly to have his fifth birthday on 27 March 1790, a baby recently discovered on the steps of Saint-Germain l'Auxerrois, the parish church of the Tuileries, and gave him a little lecture: 'Don't forget what you have seen and let your protection extend one day to these unfortunate children.' Easter Week saw the royal family, accompanied by La Fayette, paying a visit to the working-class Faubourg Saint-Antoine where most of the trouble in July had started. There were demonstrations of joy, according to the *Journal de Paris*, and acclamations when alms were presented. Mayor Bailly remarked to the Queen that Her Majesty could see for herself 'the joy of these good people'. The Marquis de Bombelles (who was not present) heard that Marie Antoinette replied: 'Yes, the people are good when their masters visit them, but they are savage when they visit their masters.' At which the Mayor blushed. Whether the Queen gave such a pointed answer or not – it has an apocryphal ring at a time when Marie Antoinette was bending every effort to show 'patience, prudence' – she certainly impressed a member of the National Guard on the same date. Standing very close to her, he admired the display of composure and even enjoyment that she put on at the public dinner.[18]

The next day, Maundy Thursday, both King and Queen washed the feet of the poor in an ancient ceremony to commemorate Easter Week. Another member of the National Guard, who watched, was impressed by the efficiency of the ritual: twelve poor people, dressed in new clothes at the expense of the King, sat on a bench, their right foot bare and resting on the edge of a basin of hot water. The King 'washed' the foot by flinging water over it from a little scoop in his hand. Next the Queen took a napkin from the stack on the silver platter held out to her and passed it over the newly pristine foot before moving on to the next foot – and the next napkin. Alms were then presented as the beneficiaries hastily resumed their right shoes and helped themselves to provisions set out in wooden boxes.[19]

Only the First Communion of Marie Thérèse, planned for 8 April at Saint-Germain l'Auxerrois, showed signs that the old routines were in some way diminished. The King did not attend, although the Queen did so, incognito. It was traditional for a Daughter of France to receive a handsome set of diamonds from the monarch on such a sanctified occasion but Louis XVI judged that such a present would be intolerably extravagant in view of the general financial need. He told Marie Thérèse that she was too sensible to worry about such artificial pleasure, and would undoubtedly prefer to go without her jewels rather than that the public should go without bread. In a tender blessing, as his daughter knelt before him later, the King told Madame Royale that her destiny remained unknown, whether she would stay in France or live in another kingdom ... And he prayed openly for the necessary grace to satisfy those other 'children' of his, the subjects over whom God had given him dominion.[20]

On 12 May the Mayor of Paris presented the King with a commemorative gold medal with the inscription, 'Henceforth I shall make this my official residence.' Bailly in his speech said that those words were engraved in the hearts of all citizens. The Queen and the Dauphin received similar medals, in silver and bronze. Marie Antoinette was assured by Bailly that the people wanted her to be always at the side of the King, while the Dauphin ('Monseigneur') was to be instructed by the Queen's example as well as the King's.[21] It was all very flowery. Ten days later the King and Queen walked on foot, as was customary, in the procession of the Blessed Sacrament, which marked the feast of Corpus Christi, and proceeded to Saint-Germain l'Auxerrois. The National Assembly, invited to participate, did so happily, with its president walking on the right of the King.

This seemingly unchanged royal round masked the fact that vast political changes were not only taking place but were being accepted by the King. Catherine the Great, in a letter handwritten from despotic Russia and which Marie Antoinette showed to Madame Campan, advocated showing magnificent indifference to recent events: 'Kings ought to go their own way without worrying about the cries of the people, as the moon goes on its course without being stopped by the cries of dogs.' This was not an option available to the King of France as a new Constitution was slowly – very slowly – hammered out by the National Assembly. There was a growing and deleterious gap, from the point of view of the King, between the apparent executive and the actual legislative arm of the government, since the National Assembly decreed that the King's ministers could not be chosen from among its deputies. Political compromise seemed of the essence to preserve the King's remaining authority. On 4 February, on the advice of Necker, the King went so far as to describe himself as 'at the head of the Revolution' in a speech to the Assembly, having spent a rather pleasanter portion of the day stag-hunting.[22] This placatory scene infuriated royalists abroad, who from exile found it easy to denounce the diminution of the King's power.

Louis XVI's perceived weakness also had its critics within the bosom of his Parisian family. Madame Elisabeth, for so long the devoted pious gentle sister, was developing into a figure of proud conservatism, under the remote control of her brother Artois. She interpreted the events at Versailles from a paternalistic angle as being examples of the people's dreadful ingratitude, adding, 'If I were the King, I'd do something about making them regret it.' Revealingly, she told a correspondent that the memories of that night – an outrage of the divinely prescribed order – had almost turned her against praying. By May 1790, Madame Elisabeth admitted to Artois, in sentiments that divided her sharply from the brother and sister-in-law with whom she resided, that she regarded civil war as 'necessary' with bloodletting being somehow therapeutic.[23]

Like Louis XVI and unlike Elisabeth, Marie Antoinette believed in compromise. On 4 February 1790, when the King spoke to the National Assembly, she received some deputies on the terrace of the Tuileries where she was playing with Louis Charles. She made a gracious speech beginning, 'Messieurs ... behold my son,' and was told by one deputy to watch over 'this precious kid'. The Queen had, in fact, had a speech prepared for her by the Keeper of the Seals, but in the event she spoke without a text. Her words summed up her public philosophy. In referring to France as 'the nation I had the glory to adopt when I united myself with the King', she went on to say that 'my title of mother assures my links [with it] for ever.'[24]

Yet even as these aspirations were entertained towards a state where the king still had some limited powers – a kind of constitutional monarchy, a parallel world was being developed. In this world the notion of escape was ever present. Immediately after the events of 6 October 1789, Marie Antoinette summoned the Secretary of the Queen's Commandment, Augeard, to the Tuileries and gave him one of the little keys that enabled her confidential servants to slip in and out without observation. Augeard suggested that a loyal person should proceed to Vienna and ask for help. When the Queen asked him, 'And who should that be?' the Secretary replied, 'Your Majesty.' 'What!' exclaimed the Queen. 'I would leave the King alone.' But Augeard was full of practical plans: the Dauphin could be dressed as a girl, in clothes matching those of Madame Royale, while the Queen herself would be totally unadorned. And she would leave a letter for her husband (which could be made public) along these lines: 'It is impossible for me to disguise the fact that I have had the terrible misfortune to displease your subjects.' She would rather condemn herself to 'a secluded retreat outside your dominions' than be seen to interfere with the making of the new Constitution.[25]

According to Augeard, the Queen listened to him seriously before rejecting the plan. On 19 October 1789, she told him: 'All reflection is over; I shall not depart; my duty is to die at the feet of the King.' Nevertheless it is evident that not only Marie Antoinette but well-wishers around her were looking anew at her situation. On 12 November, for example, Mercy inspected the marriage contract hammered out nearly twenty years earlier. He noted that in the case of her widowhood, the Queen was free to stay in France or go to Austria.[26] In late 1789, it is clear that her freedom of action rather than her widowhood was the issue.

What is also clear is that one element already present in discussions of escape at Versailles on 15 July 1789 – the reluctance of the Queen to leave the King's side – remained firmly in place. As plans to legalize divorce in France were debated in 1790, being finally enacted in November, this reluctance gained rather than lost its strength, as Augeard would testify to Marie Antoinette's sister Maria Carolina. Another element present from the beginning was the pathological indecision of the King.[27] This, however sympathetic in a good man who feared to make things worse for his subjects, yet could not see how to make them better, combined fatally with the ultimate respect for his royal authority of those around him. At this stage Marie Antoinette hesitated to make up the King's mind for him as she had once tried to do, so conscious was she of herself as a liability to the monarchy.

All of this was seen to disastrous effect in various abortive schemes during the spring of 1790. The details of the Favras Affair, including the participation of the Comte de Provence, remain mysterious since the conspiracy never came to fruition. The Marquis de Favras, accused of a plot to kidnap the King and take him to Péronne, was tried and executed on 19 February 1790, leaving Louis XVI and Provence to grant his widow a pension. The Queen, who wanted to comfort the widow and her child but did not dare do so publicly, also sent fifty louis. When a similar scheme was mooted by the Comte d'Inisdal, it was resolved to seek the King's agreement. The King first of all took refuge in silence, and then when his wife insisted that he must say something, muttered: 'Tell the Comte d'Inisdal that I cannot consent to being abducted.' Was that tacit approval – so long as Louis himself could not be blamed? If not, what was it? The fact was that the attitude of the King was crucial and he was, as he had always been, 'irresolute'.[28]

It would not have been at all difficult to 'rescue' Louis XVI in the early summer of 1790 or, indeed, for the King himself to take flight. His *Journal* shows that in May he was riding out almost every other day to Bellevue and other places in order to keep up the frantic exercise that he found so necessary to his health, and there were no objections. The uniting of the Queen and the children with the head of the family later might have caused more problems, if not at this stage insuperable ones. However, in June the entire royal family was permitted to go to Saint Cloud as they would normally have done at this season to avoid the summer heat. Not only, as the Queen observed, did they all need fresh air desperately but they could also be more isolated from the menacing atmosphere of Paris where insults were hurled at her person daily. At Saint Cloud the King, riding by permission without guards for as much as five hours daily, was in an even stronger position to take evasive action. According to Madame Campan, the Queen had a plan to meet the King with the children in a wood a short distance from Saint Cloud ... Her plan foundered because it would have meant abandoning the elderly royal aunts.[29]

At this point the destination of the royal family in any proposed secret flight – or dignified departure – became an issue. Were they actually to cross the borders of France? Going abroad, to become the visible puppet of the émigrés led by Artois and the Princes de Condé and Conti, would be a perilous move for the King in terms of propaganda. As for the situation in Austria, the death of the Emperor Joseph II on 20 February 1790 – he had been worn out by hard work and ravaged by tuberculosis – caused Marie Antoinette great grief. It also complicated her relationship with her homeland. In Joseph she mourned the loss of a 'friend and brother' and she might have added a 'quasi-father' too. But she had had in effect no real contact with his successor, Leopold, Grand Duke of Tuscany, he of the prolific family, for twenty-five years.

Of course, the new Emperor hastened to assure his sister that he would be giving her his full support, asking in return for the same friendship and confidence she had given Joseph. Marie Antoinette for her part told Leopold touchingly, if rather optimistically, that he could count on 'a good ally' in Louis XVI. More candidly, Count Mercy admitted that Marie Antoinette and Leopold had never really got on. Yet this was the powerful brother on whom Marie Antoinette now depended to control the émigrés on the one hand and to prop up their own position – possibly with money – on the other. As the Bourbons abroad revealed their selfishness, Artois with his father-in-law the King of Sardinia in Turin, the lesser Princes in Coblenz, Marie Antoinette began to think wistfully of her original family. The thought of the marriage festivities of Leopold's heir Francis to his first cousin, Maria Carolina's daughter, who was said to resemble Marie Antoinette herself, made her misty-eyed. 'You are in the middle of wedding feasts: I wish all the happiness possible to your children.'[30]

Even the Archduchess Marie Christine, who had had her own troubles, was the subject of a new benevolence. Ejected with the Archduke Albert from Belgium by rebels known as the Patriots, Marie Christine had taken refuge at Bonn. Here the youngest Habsburg, Max, now Elector of Cologne, had given them a castle. Marie Antoinette was becoming increasingly wary of her correspondence falling into the wrong hands – people could so easily take the opportunity to forge her handwriting, with damaging interpolations – so that to Marie Christine she emphasized that their letters were simply 'two sisters giving proof of friendship' and who could object to that? Her tone in May was infinitely sad. All the Queen wanted was for order and calm to return to 'this unhappy country' and – a key phrase – to 'prepare for my poor child [the Dauphin] to have a happier future than our own'; for they had seen 'too many horrors and too much blood ever really to be happy again'. 'When you are all three together,' Marie Antoinette concluded, referring to Marie Christine, Albert and Max, 'think of me sometimes.'[31]

In view of 'the extravagance of Turin', as Marie Antoinette described Artois' increasingly martial behaviour, it made sense for the King and his own family to remain within the boundaries of France. The taint that an invasion, theoretically intended to help them, would bring to their cause had to be avoided. In July 1790, probably at the insistence of Count Mercy, Marie Antoinette returned to the political role that she had eschewed in the aftershock of 6 October 1789. But it was to be a strictly behind-the-scenes affair; she did not, for example, attend committees as she had done during the brief period of her real political influence. She did, however, allow herself to be drawn into delicate secret negotiations with the radical aristocrat, the Comte de Mirabeau, in the relative privacy of Saint Cloud. Mirabeau, whose dissolute lifestyle had left him with a mountain of debts, needed money; the King needed an ally who still believed that there was a place for the monarchy in the new Constitution.

The Queen had feelings of revulsion for Mirabeau, referring to 'the horror that his immorality inspires in me'. But she agreed to suppress these feelings in the interest of making Mirabeau's constitutional plans work. (He on the contrary admired her 'manly' strength of purpose.) The person she referred to as 'M' was to be paid 5000 livres a month, all in the strictest secrecy. It was part of Mirabeau's strategy that the King should leave Paris, and quite openly as well. Aiming at some system by which ministers were responsible to the National Assembly, he needed the King to be free to operate, without apparently being under duress. Mirabeau suggested that Louis XVI should adjourn either to Rouen, which lay in a loyalist area of the country, or to the château of Compiègne.[32]

Another strong advocate of flight from an early stage was Count Fersen, now the Queen's closest confidant. Whether or not an active sexual relationship still flourished, on which some doubt has already been cast, he continued to be Marie Antoinette's passionate admirer, as he repeatedly confided to his sister Sophie Piper. To Fersen she was a heroine, misused, misjudged, sensitive and suffering – above all, so full of goodness, at a time when this kind of opinion of Marie Antoinette was rare enough. Although it was incidentally a loyalty shared by his mistress, Eléanore Sullivan, who with her official protector Quentin Craufurd, 'ce bon Craufurd' as Marie Antoinette called him, was an enthusiastic supporter of the Queen. As early as January 1790, Fersen wrote that only a war – be it 'exterior' or 'interior' – could re-establish the royal authority in France; but how could that be achieved 'when the King is a prisoner in Paris?'[33] Fersen borrowed a house at Auteuil from the Queen's friend and a member of her Private Society, Count Esterhazy. He was thus able to take full advantage of the presence of the royal family at Saint Cloud, which continued, with certain intermissions, until the end of October.

Fersen's influence as an active and practical promoter of an escape plan was further increased with the departure of Count Mercy, at the request of the Emperor Leopold. Marie Antoinette described herself as being 'in despair' at this development and it is easy to see why. Although she staunchly tried to see that it was better for him personally to depart, Marie Antoinette had, after all, depended on Mercy's advice, for better or for worse, for twenty years. Now he was leaving her at the most critical moment in her fortunes and she was terrified of 'being mistaken in the course I must take'.[34]

The Queen told the Emperor that Mercy had for her 'the feelings of a father for a child', but the reverse was actually the truth; it was Marie Antoinette who nourished childish sentiments of respect for and dependency on the ambassador, which were not necessarily reciprocated.[35] Unlike Marie Antoinette, Mercy was not sentimental. The fact that he had known the Queen since she was a nervous fourteen-year-old fiancée weighed less with him than the duties imposed by his career, as he saw them. How could the emotional Marie Antoinette foresee that these duties would divide them, once the former ambassador to France became Minister in Brussels? His new task would be the pacification of Belgium following the Patriots' revolt, which was brought to an end by Austrian troops in December 1790. The 'Austrian woman' was left with only Counsellor Blumendorf and a skeleton staff representing her homeland in Paris.

One of the forays made by the royal family from Saint Cloud to the Tuileries concerned the official celebration of the anniversary of the Fall of the Bastille. Marie Antoinette dreaded the occasion in advance, saying that she could not think back to that terrible time without trembling: 'It brings together for us everything that is most cruel and sorrowful.' Nevertheless all the royals were dutifully present. In fact the Fête de la Fédération, as it was described in honour of patriotic 'federal' movements nationwide, had none of the violence associated with the previous years; it simply illustrated the bizarre contradictions as yet unresolved in the future of the government of France. There was, for example, the position of the Church. Two days earlier a Civil Constitution of the Clergy had been adopted, involving the popular elections of bishops and clergy; the pious King sanctioned it, with a heavy heart, perhaps, but he sanctioned it. On 14 July 1790 a commemorative Mass was said at the Champ-de-Mars by the Abbé Talleyrand, once assistant to Calonne in his financial reforms, then a deputy of the First Estate, now allied to Mirabeau. The Duc d'Orléans, returned from England, was present, as was the Duc de Chartres. Nearly seventeen and sharing his father's political tendencies, Louis Philippe had taken to attending the Jacobin Club* – one of the many lively debating clubs or 'pressure groups' springing up in Paris. The young radical was recognized and carried shoulder high by the crowd.[36]

Yet there was comfort to be derived from the event for a

* The term, taken from the disused convent where the Jacobin Club met, was beginning to be used for the revolutionary wing of the National Assembly.

sovereign who still could not make up his mind to be 'a fugitive King'. The event was immensely popular, with advertisements carried in the newspapers for houses to rent with a good view. Even the appallingly wet weather, which effectively doused the Queen's tactful red, white and blue plumes and extinguished the illuminations, did not put the crowd off. Three hundred thousand people watched, some of them wearing the *bonnet rouge*, based on the red Roman cap that slaves sported when they gained their liberty. Eighteen thousand National Guards took part. When royal umbrellas were raised, the crowd shouted 'Down with them!' and 'No umbrellas!'; they wanted to see their King. The oath that La Fayette proposed from the altar included the royal name; La Fayette suggested it should be 'to the Nation, the Law and the King'. That night at the public dinner following the fête, there were cries of 'Long live the King!' outside the windows of the Tuileries.[37]

Even the Queen was momentarily entitled to believe that she had her uses. On the eve of the ceremony, delegates from the various provinces were received. Those from Maine congratulated Marie Antoinette on her courage on 6 October, although she turned the compliment aside in favour of a reference to the superior bravery of her loyal bodyguards. Watching the troops file past the King, the Queen's attention was caught by a particular uniform. She asked its wearer, 'Monsieur, from what province do you come?' The answer was: 'The province over which your ancestors reigned,' and the Queen, happily, was able to point out to her husband: 'These are your faithful Lorrainers.' For these delegates 'the presence of the august daughter of Francis I, the last Duke of Lorraine' made an impression that was 'visible on their countenances'.[38]

The fact was, however, that the situation of the royal family was as unresolved as ever. In August the Marquis de Bouillé, at the head of the Royal German Regiment, succeeded in putting down a mutiny at Nancy in the north-east of France. This news had the effect of encouraging the royal couple to see in the politically constitutionalist Bouillé a loyal and efficient soldier; it was a view that was to have some bearing on their future in the year ahead. Yet when the news reached Paris, there were demonstrations at the Tuileries against the King's ministers and fears that there might be another violent march, this time to Saint Cloud. Unable to control its course, Necker vanished for the third time from the government, this time unmourned. Mirabeau, for his part, wrote a memorandum that horrified the Queen, since he advocated civil war as the way of introducing order, and the kind of constitutional rule he wanted, into France. 'He must be mad to think that we would provoke civil war!' cried the desperate Queen.[39]

The royal family returned from Saint Cloud on 30 October 1790. The Dauphin was no longer able to enjoy that freedom which had benefited him so much, and all of them were more constrained in the goldfish-bowl that the Tuileries had become. The next day saw the publication (in England) of Edmund Burke's famous tract, *Reflections on the Revolution in France*. He turned his previous Whig pro-American convictions on their head, urging the King to resist all further negotiations. It was, said George III approvingly, 'a book every gentleman should read'. In France alone it sold 16,000 copies in three months. In due course, Marie Antoinette may well have read *Reflections*, the book that made her a legendary heroine in her own lifetime. Burke certainly handed the Duke of Dorset one copy, which he hoped would be passed on, and another copy, in a translation by the cosmopolitan Louis Dutens, was presented to the Queen by the Duchesse de St James. Madame Elisabeth also read it, in French, unlike one of her ladies, Bombelles' wife Angélique, who was clever enough to read it in English.[40]

In a famous passage, Burke recalled his sight of Marie Antoinette, then Dauphine, at Versailles: 'And surely never lighted on this orb, which she hardly seemed to touch, a more delightful vision. I saw her just above the horizon, decorating and cheering the elevated sphere she just began to move in – glittering like the morning star, full of life, and splendour, and joy. Oh! what a revolution! and what a heart I must have to contemplate without emotion that elevation and that fall! ... Little did I dream that I should have lived to see disasters fallen upon her in a nation of gallant men, in a nation of men of honour, and of cavaliers. I thought ten thousand swords must have leaped from their scabbards to avenge even a look that threatened her with insult. But the age of chivalry is gone ...'[41]

For the Queen, no longer glittering like the morning star, the question of the swords leaping from their scabbards to avenge her was urgently in need of solving. What swords from which scabbards? And given that the age of chivalry was undoubtedly gone (with the exception perhaps of Count Fersen), what were the terms that these modern chevaliers would demand in return for rescuing the royal family?

CHAPTER TWENTY

Great Hopes

> 'At the end of last year ... I had great hopes.'
> *Marie Antoinette to the Princesse de Tarante,*
> *31 December 1791*

'It is only from here and only we who can judge the moment and the favourable circumstances that might at last put an end to our woes and those of France.' With these anxious words, written to the Emperor Leopold on 19 December 1790, Marie Antoinette addressed the problem at the heart of any plan of escape: its timing. There was indeed much to disquiet her. France abounded with wild rumours about her future, as Prince Charles of Liechtenstein, the envoy of Leopold II, discovered: the Queen was about to be seized and shut up in a fortress; alternatively she was to be put to death for adultery so that the widower Louis XVI could marry Orléans' daughter. Meanwhile the Queen's own perturbation over the possible invasive action of the Princes increased with the months, and not without reason. Artois was reported to be planning to take Lyons and to hive off Alsace from France. The Queen told the Emperor that Louis XVI had written formally to the King of Sardinia and his son-in-law Artois to say that if they persisted in these damaging conspiracies, allegedly on Louis' behalf, the King would have to disown them officially. For all this, Marie Antoinette was beginning to have 'great hopes', as she would confess to the Princesse de Tarante later.[1]

If the counter-revolutionary Princes signified trouble abroad, the French Catholic clergy offered similar complications at home. The Civil Constitution of the Clergy of July 1790 was followed up at the end of November by the idea of an oath to the State. All priests had to swear it, 'non-jurors' being forbidden to exercise their priestly functions. Torn between his duty as a loyal son of the Church, and that of a monarch concerned with his country's welfare, Louis XVI tried desperately to get the Pope to tolerate the oath. The alternative was the introduction of 'a division into France', in other words a damaging schism in the French Catholic Church between jurors and non-jurors.[2]

Pius VI, a man in his seventies who had been Pope since 1775, had no sympathy with the ultramontane tendencies of monarchs in his own time, nor, for that matter, with the libertarian ideals of their subjects. He had already clashed with Joseph II over the latter's projected limitations of papal power in his own dominions, known as 'Josephinism'; as for France, he had condemned *La Déclaration des Droits de l'Homme* of August. Now Pius VI declined to compromise. Nevertheless Louis XVI signed the decree on 26 December. January 1 1791 was the 'fatal day' when the clergy had to decide whether or not to take the oath.

It was also the day on which the Dauphin Louis Charles was given dominoes made of stone and marble torn from the ruins of the Bastille as a New Year's gift by members of the National Guard. The verses that accompanied the gift alluded to the Bastille when its walls had enclosed 'the innocent victims of arbitrary government'; now these toys were intended as the homage of the people and – significant postscript – 'to teach you the extent of their power'. The Marquise de Tourzel had a slightly different version: the boy received the gift from Palloi, an architect, one of the chief destroyers of the Bastille, with outward politeness – and inner fury.[3]

Battle lines were being drawn. On 10 March 1791 the Pope issued a condemnation of the French Revolution in general and the Civil Constitution of the Clergy in particular. Three days later, an answer to the chivalrous rhetoric of Burke's *Reflections* was published in England. The author was Thomas Paine, a Quaker-educated political writer who had spent thirteen years in America and was a passionate advocate of its independence. *The Rights of Man*, written in support of this new revolution and dedicated to George Washington, resulted in Paine being accused of treason in England; he fled to France. The book was, however, an instant bestseller, both in English and in translation.[4]

On quite a different level the scabrous pamphlets attacking the Queen were also bestsellers. Drink, lesbianism, sexual voracity generally ('three quarters of the officers of the Gardes Françaises had penetrated the Queen'), featured as before in works such as *The Memoirs of Antonina*, printed in London in two volumes. Here, due to the demands of such numbers on her time, she was described as preferring lovers in the style of a grenadier 'who abridges preliminaries and hastens to the conclusion'. Marie Antoinette was also credited with a new admirer, La Fayette. The story was ridiculous enough to those who knew Marie Antoinette's personal dislike for the man she derisively nick-named 'Blondinet' for his sandy looks and whose clumsy dancing she had scorned years ago; but it was a useful twist for his enemies in the saga of her debauchery. *Soirées Amoureuses du Général Mottier* [La Fayette] *et la belle Antoinette* was a piece of pornography supposedly written by 'the Austrian woman's little spaniel'. Having enjoyed a rich sexual education at the hands of his mistress, the pet, jealous of being supplanted in the royal bed by La Fayette, had decided to describe the Queen's bawdy nights with the revolutionary.[5]

The anguished King was left with the approaching problem of his Easter duties, the absolute necessity of taking Communion to celebrate Easter Sunday – 24 April in 1791 – that was enjoined on all the faithful. How could he accept the sacrament at the hands of a juror priest? How could he manage to avoid it?* He had, after all, signed a decree officially condemning the non-jurors. There was another unhappy consequence to the split engendered by the Civil Constitution of the Clergy: the King's pious aunts reacted to it with horror.

---

* Easter Communion had been obligatory since the fourth century and is still today a precept that must be fulfilled 'during paschal time' by members of the Catholic Church.[6]

It was unthinkable for the two surviving Mesdames Tantes, Adélaïde and Victoire (the nun Louise had died in 1787), to make *their* Easter Communion at a Mass said by a juror. No conception of their nephew's good, nor that of the royal family as a whole, troubled these royal ladies. There were to be no compromises with the manners of the old order; for example, the aunts made a fearful fuss at the idea of dining at Saint Cloud with Pauline de Tourzel who had not been officially presented – what a precedent! According to etiquette, the girl ought to eat alone. (But the King simply said: 'There will never be similar circumstances. Admit her!')[7] Now the aunts began to make arrangements to depart for the more wholesome spiritual atmosphere of Rome, finally leaving on 19 February.

The flight of Mesdames Tantes turned out to be a public relations disaster. A dragoon charge was needed to clear away hostile crowds as they went; then the aunts were halted for eleven days in the course of their journey by other angry demonstrators. In order to proceed, they were, ironically enough, obliged to appeal for the implementation of the National Assembly's new law by which all citizens could travel as they pleased. The Assembly spent four hours debating the issue, all because, as one deputy furiously exclaimed, 'two old ladies prefer to hear Mass in Rome rather than in Paris'.[8] Finally agreement was reached.

Nevertheless a deputy named Antoine Barnave, a Protestant lawyer from Grenoble, made an important point when he argued for the symbolic importance of this departure: Mesdames should not be allowed to go while the position of the royal family was still being discussed by the Committee of the Constitution. Certainly this contested departure made two points for the future: first, royalties who were dissatisfied with the present situation in France, for all their emollient words, were preparing to flee; second, they could be stopped ... 'You know that my aunts are going,' wrote Marie Antoinette to Leopold in advance. 'We do not believe that we can prevent them.'[9] But a more resolute sovereign than Louis XVI, one who had indeed learnt that early lesson about 'firmness' being the most necessary virtue to a king, might have done so.

The fact was that the situation regarding the departure – or escape – of the main royal family was at the most delicate stage. And it was Marie Antoinette who found herself, perforce, the practical instigator of the action. The King's depression as ever took the form of semi-stupor. When he discussed business with his Minister of the Royal Household, the King might have been talking about the affairs of the Emperor of China, said Montmorin sadly in January 1791. Louis' personal unhappiness, caused by the odious religious situation to which he had reluctantly agreed, was not helped by serious illness in the spring. He suffered from high fever and began to cough up blood: was it the fatal tuberculosis that had carried off so many members of his family including his elder son? He was treated with a series of debilitating emetics and purges. For about a week, the King lay in bed. His strongest emotion seems to have been a deep, hurt bewilderment. As he told his favoured confidante the Duchesse de Polignac in a letter some weeks later: 'How can I have these enemies when I have only ever desired the good of all?' He quoted Molière in *L'École des femmes*: 'The world, my dear Agnes, is a strange thing.'[10]

Marie Antoinette, on the other hand, was developing a more positive attitude, although she still had a residue of melancholy. 'Oh my God!' she wrote to her brother Leopold in October 1790. 'If we have committed faults, we have certainly expiated them.' She too felt misunderstood by the French, who were 'a cruel, childish people', while at the same time she felt equally misunderstood by the émigrés, so blithely ignorant in their exile of the true conditions in France.[11] But Marie Antoinette had also begun to believe fervently in the cause of kingship, for a reason indicated in that letter to her sister Marie Christine of the previous May. She wanted 'her poor child' to have a happier future than their own, and that was a future in which he sat on the throne of France.

It was 'the monsters' in France – both Marie Antoinette and her critics were free in their use of this word – who threatened this future, and in this connection, she warned her brother Leopold against the Freemasons, whose societies had been used by the monsters to link themselves together: 'Oh God, guard my homeland and you from similar perils.' The émigrés, especially Artois, might come into this threatening category too, if they sought to circumvent the role of the King on the grounds that he was a virtual prisoner and thus subject to unlawful pressures. At the same time any wife who becomes obsessed by her son's heritage – in the lifetime of his father – must have a slightly different agenda from that father himself. Marie Antoinette was by now quite convinced of the need to escape in order to save the crown: 'Too much delay risks losing everything.'¹² Louis XVI still wavered.

He could hand a kind of roving commission to the Baron de Breteuil to approach the European powers with a view to restoring his 'legitimate authority', as he did on 26 November 1790. He could despatch the young Comte Louis de Bouillé, son of the soldier Marquis, to the Emperor in an ambassadorial capacity, as he did in early January 1791. On 4 February there was a further tentative step forward when the Comte de La Marck was sent off to the Marquis de Bouillé himself at Metz with a commission from the King.¹³ But as yet, unlike Caesar crossing the Rubicon, Louis could not decide to burn his boats.

Of course the logic of Marie Antoinette's position – that the crown of France must be preserved at all costs – dictated that she should have escaped accompanied only by the Dauphin. (Madame Royale's gender, which prevented her accession, also meant that her security was never seen as an issue; unlike her Austrian mother, the Daughter of France was not subject to personal threats.) Originally put forward by Marie Antoinette's secretary, Augeard, with the idea that Louis Charles should be dressed as a girl, this plan of a mother-and-son flight was always the one with the best hope of success. Comte Louis de Bouillé reiterated it to the Queen in January 1791.¹⁴ A plainly dressed woman in an age when garments automatically spoke a person's rank, an obscure little girl ... There were few to connect such a limited party with the glorious goddess of Versailles (or its wicked Queen for that matter) and the boy prince who was the hope of the nation.

There was a further impetus to removing Louis Charles from

the nation's acquisitive gaze. Both his status and his future education were becoming a matter of debate. A memoir on the subject by the Abbé Audrein, Vice Rector of the Collège des Grassins, was presented to the National Assembly on 11 December 1790, and printed in the newspaper *L'Ami du Roi* shortly after Louis Charles's sixth birthday on 27 March 1791. The Dauphin should be put through an elaborate programme of education in various colleges that would report on his prowess to four carefully chosen governors once a month. He would eat 'frugal but healthy' food and be attended to only by the small number of servants necessary. As an adolescent, he was to do military service under an assumed name, the final summary of his progress to be circulated throughout the nation. Such a regime was not harsh – resembling perhaps the education of a modern heir to a throne – but it was the principle that was sinister from the point of view of the Dauphin's parents: that royal children 'belong to the Nation and must be brought up by it'.[15]

A debate on the Regency took place in the National Assembly on 22 March, in the wake of the King's serious illness. Women, including of course the boy's mother, were specifically excluded, with cries at one point of 'Males only!' Yet it was notable that Marie Antoinette was not eliminated altogether from the care of her son in these circumstances; if the possibility of the Regency was stripped from her in the new Constitution, she was still envisaged as his Guardian, given the strength of the mother's traditional role.[16] The boy's closest male relative was in fact to be chosen – but only so long as he was still in France, and provided he was not the heir to another throne. The former provision excluded Artois (but not, for the time being, Provence) while the latter carefully ruled out Louis Charles's Austrian relatives. The order of regency would therefore be: Provence, then Orléans ... and after that a Regent was to be elected.

These dark clouds gathering over the head of her son did not convince Marie Antoinette to change her mind and escape with Louis Charles alone. As she told Comte Louis de Bouillé, the royal family had sworn to stay together after the events of 6 October and she intended to honour that promise. This was a woman who was fully capable of courage; ruthlessness was another matter.

The commissioning of a large and durable travelling coach, a *berline de voyage*, on 22 December 1790 was a significant moment in the Queen's escape plans. The berlin stood for several things. One was the large size of the party to which Marie Antoinette was inexorably committed, for it could transport six adults inside. Another was the intimate participation of Count Fersen in all the practical details. Ostensibly the berlin was commissioned by one of Fersen's friends, the Franco-Russian 'Baronne de Korff', in order to travel to Russia – one of those endless trans-European journeys common at the time among a cosmopolitan aristocracy with which Fersen himself was so familiar. In fact the man who paid the 5000-odd livres for the berlin was Fersen himself. At all events, this was a carriage 'unknown' to belong to the King and Queen, whose official carriages were highly recognizable.

Afterwards, the nature of the coach, apparently both cumbersome and awesomely opulent, was the subject of much ill-informed comment; it was seen as some kind of doomed symbol. But there was in fact 'nothing extraordinary' about it, in the words of the Marquise de Tourzel, given the purpose for which it was designed: a long, long traverse of roads that would at best be unreliable. Such a berlin, apart from being well sprung, had to be strong, which inevitably made it slow. Sometimes described as bright yellow, the berlin was actually green and black, with a white velvet interior, the only flashes of yellow being on the wheels and undercarriage as was customary at the time.[17]

Hospitality along such a notional route would be quite as unreliable as the roads, so the voyagers would expect to be virtually self-sufficient. In the case of the real journey that was projected, such containment was of course equally vital. So the berlin was to be 'a little house on wheels', with a larder, a cooker for heating meat or soup, a canteen big enough for eight bottles, a table that could be raised for eating, concealed beneath the cushions, as well as leather *pots de chambre*: all 'very convenient' as the Governess noted.* The same practical convenience applied to the Queen's *nécessaire*, a kind of superior picnic basket made of beautiful smooth walnut with a silver basin, tiny candlesticks and a teapot, which doubled as a dressing-case, whose furnishings included little tortoiseshell picks as well as a mirror. She actually had two made, one going as a blind to Marie Christine in Brussels: 'I'll be delighted if she uses it since I have another just the same for my own use.'†[18]

Such elaborate arrangements underlined another important aspect of the projected journey. If the royal party set out as fugitives, they certainly did not intend to arrive as such. It was as the King and Queen of France, with all the appurtenances of majesty, that Louis XVI and Marie Antoinette intended to disembark. The King's crown and royal robes were therefore to be included in the baggage. The loyal crowds who were confidently expected to flock to their ill-used sovereign had, after all, to be able to recognize him when they saw him. Where kings were concerned, appearance and ceremony made the monarch. In short, Louis XVI was to remain within the frontiers of France itself.

In Marie Antoinette's lengthy correspondence throughout the spring, via couriers since she no longer trusted the posts, she was quite as inflexible on this subject as she was over the nature of their joint escape. Precisely what 'the Austrian woman' did not actually want was for the King to be seen to flee to Austria or its dominions; these included Belgium and its capital, which already housed many of their supporters. Even if things went badly inside France, Marie Antoinette preferred to head for Switzerland, via Alsace, rather than Austria.[19]

On the other hand, the Queen did expect assistance from her

---

* A *berline de voyage* was the eighteenth-century version of a modern touring coach.
† Both these royal dressing-cases survive, one in the Louvre and one in a private collection; originally the latter belonged to Madame Auguié, sister of Madame Campan, to whom it was given by the Queen. The sheer weight of such a dressing-case on the knee, let alone when carried, is the remarkable feature to a modern observer, apart from its luxuriousness – but the Queen of France, accustomed to the daily ritual of being dressed at the hands of others, was not expecting to handle it herself.

homeland, as she always called it, and many of her letters to Count Mercy, himself in Brussels, concerned her attempts to secure it. What was wanted was a massing of Austrian troops on the north-west frontier. This would in turn give the Marquis de Bouillé at Metz an excuse to move his own troops in order to combat the imperial menace. In reality these troops were intended to act in support of the King when he arrived.[20]

The real trouble with this plan was that Emperor Leopold was not only the brother of the Queen of France but he was also the head of a great power with an ambiguous attitude towards France, alliance or no alliance. As the Comte de La Marck saw for himself, the Emperor was by no means displeased by France's weakened state, due to its inner turmoils. The requested Austrian troops would cost money to move, and that would need subsidizing: a difficult task for the French King (or in fact the Queen) who were so short of finance. More money had to be borrowed – from bankers in Belgium and from Fersen, Fersen's mistress Eléanore Sullivan and her protector, Quentin Craufurd.

The real key to the Emperor's behaviour was expressed by Count Mercy himself in a long and embarrassed letter of 7 March 1791.[21] He told the Queen – who touchingly but unwisely still imagined that he had her best interests at heart – that she should not count on exterior help. Nor should she have any illusions about the general behaviour of great powers who famously 'do nothing for nothing'. However humiliating this truth might be, the Queen should try to come to terms with it. She should concentrate on how they might be propitiated – or in other words how they might be bribed to help the royal family. The King of Sardinia, for example, wanted Geneva and the King of France would lose little by supporting this claim. Spain was interested in the territorial limits of Navarre. The German feudal princes with lands in Alsace, anxious about their privileges, could be won over. Although Mercy claimed that the Emperor himself was above all this, he did touch on Austria's interests with regard to Prussia, which must be borne in mind.

Writing to the Queen himself a few days later, the Emperor was similarly negative as well as circular in argument. The foreign powers could not think of interfering while the King and Queen were not in a state of safety. Although their only method of achieving that state was obviously to flee, the Emperor went on to say that the King and Queen should not be encouraged to do that, since the foreign powers were in no position to help them. Leopold could not even fix a date for an escape while his Austro-Turkish war – a legacy from Joseph II – went on. So the Emperor advised his sister and brother-in-law to wait until such time as they had developed their own resources – or were in pressing danger.[22]

Against this self-interested caution the Queen cried out with increasing desperation. Surely the other powers would help them? It was, after all, 'the cause of Kings, not simply a matter of politics'. Furthermore 'the cause of Kings' in France received an additional blow with the death of Mirabeau on 2 April. The Jacobins, including their newly elected president Robespierre, were secretly delighted, although the eight-day public mourning, plus a grandiose funeral cortège and a public burial, paid ostentatious tribute to the great man. Mirabeau had at least envisaged the continued need for a sovereign, or, as the Duc de Lévis put it, Mirabeau loved 'liberty through emotion, the monarchy through reason and the nobility through vanity'.

On 14 April, still lacking a positive response from Vienna, Marie Antoinette wrote asking whether they could count on Austrian help, *Yes* or *No*? (Her italics.)[23]

It was Louis XVI's determination to perform his Easter duties at the hands of a non-juror priest that brought about a cathartic resolution to the drama of delay. In spite of the advice of various counsellors to yield to duress, the King could not bring himself to take Communion at the hands of a juror at the parish church of the Tuileries, Saint-Germain l'Auxerrois. He therefore turned to the expedient that had been so successful the previous summer, when it was a question of fresh air rather than spiritual sustenance. He decided to make an expedition to Saint Cloud where, of course, it would be far easier for a non-juror to be slipped in.

Departure was scheduled to take place on the Monday of

Easter Week, 18 April. It was now that the ugly consequences of the flight of Mesdames Tantes were seen. Rumours that the King was to follow suit had already led to demonstrations at the Tuileries. In this case, no sooner were the royal party and servants installed in their coaches in the Grand Carrousel courtyard of the palace than the cry went up that the King was trying to escape. A jeering mob surrounded the King's own carriage, where he sat with his wife, sister and children, and prevented their progress. One courtier, the First Gentleman of the Bedchamber, was beaten, leaving the Dauphin to shout, 'Save him! Save him!' before the Queen was able to take her son back inside the Tuileries. Even worse for the future was the fact that the National Guards refused to force the King's passage. They announced that they too were committed to detaining the King, despite the best efforts of Mayor Bailly and La Fayette, their commander, to dissuade them. So the King sat immobilized for nearly two hours listening to the howls of abuse.[24]

Louis XVI remained outwardly calm, putting his head out of the carriage to remark that it was strange that he who had granted the nation liberty was not allowed it himself. Inwardly, however, the scene, with the mob in control of the guards, left a profound impression on him. Having disembarked, the King celebrated Easter at Saint-Germain and took the Sacrament from 'the new curé' who was, of course, a juror. The Queen wore her court dress, garnished with Alençon lace and especially ordered for Easter from Rose Bertin, but at the Tuileries and not at Saint Cloud. She also purchased a length of ribbon *à la nation* (that is, tricoloured) to put in her hat. The *Journal de Paris* gave an emollient version of events: how numerous 'citizens' had 'pleaded with the King to remain'. The King in his *Journal* put it more succinctly: 'They stopped us.'[25] This incident meant that Louis XVI had at last joined his wife in realizing the necessity of escape.

The Queen told Mercy at the beginning of May: 'Our situation here is frightful, in a way that those who do not have to endure it cannot hope to understand.' The religious split was emphasized by the fact that an effigy of the Pope was burnt in the gardens of the Palais-Royal. The 'pressing danger' that was demanded by the Emperor to justify their flight had arrived. It was only when the King was free to show himself in some 'strong city' that the people would, she believed, flock to him in astonishing numbers.[26]

It was now a question as to where that 'strong city' might be. Metz was unreliable; although only a few of the officers were said to be 'infected', the whole of the infantry was 'detestable' in its revolutionary sympathies, as was the municipality with its local Jacobin Club. Of the various possibilities, Montmédy, thirty-five miles from Metz, near the border of the Habsburg-led Empire (but outside it) and possessed of good communications, was the most popular choice. Montmédy was in Lorraine; hopefully the King's 'faithful Lorrainers' who had been pointed out to him at the Fête de la Fédération by Marie Antoinette would justify their reputation. The troops of the Royal German Regiment at Stenay on the Meuse, ten miles west of Montmédy, between Sedan and Verdun, were also supposed to be reliable.[27]

Other possibilities were Valenciennes, slightly north-west of Paris, which was originally favoured by the King but subsequently rejected for being too close to the Austrian Netherlands; and Besançon in the east, close to the Swiss border. The idea of leaving France via the Ardennes and then crossing back to a 'strong city' was also rejected because even the briefest departure might give an unfortunate impression of flight. If the choice, then, was to be Montmédy, what route should be followed to reach it? It was not exactly a light journey, 180-odd miles from Paris through terrain where anybody's loyalty, whether soldier or citizen, might turn out to be doubtful. The obvious way was to go via Meaux and Rheims, and on to Montmédy itself: a straightforward route and the one favoured by the Marquis de Bouillé and Count Fersen, both experienced campaigners.

Suddenly the King asserted himself. He feared being recognized in and around Rheims, which was one of the few areas of France where he was known, thanks to the coronation ceremony there sixteen years ago. So the route chosen was to the south: Châlons-sur-Marne, then Sainte-Ménehould, before turning north, through a small place called Varennes on the river Aire, on to Dun, crossing the Meuse, to Stenay and so to Montmédy. This involved using a minor road after Sainte-Ménehould and in Bouillé's view was just as dangerous. But the habit of obedience was too strong in the Marquis to allow him to disagree further with his sovereign. This was the way it was to be.[28]

Mid-month, Bouillé assured Fersen that the road from Sainte-Ménehould to Stenay would be guarded by loyal troops. Fersen actually questioned the security of such a display. Might it not be better, more of a subterfuge, if the small party travelled unattended by any kind of military presence? Fersen's logic, however, was not accepted by Bouillé; as with his deference to the King over the route, Bouillé's habit of protecting the King was deeply ingrained.

It now became a matter of personnel – and personalities, as ever in any risky enterprise – both in the military command and in the composition of the berlin party. Those in the know in January 1791, according to Marie Antoinette, had originally been limited to the Baron de Breteuil (now abroad), the Marquis de Bouillé and the Marquis de Bombelles, who had close connections to Breteuil. Then there was the Baron François de Goguelat, ADC to Bouillé and 'Monsieur Gog' to the Queen, who used him as an emissary to Fersen. He was, said Marie Antoinette, 'a man of action, rather zealous but devoted'.[29] Now, however, it was a question of extending the network. A key role was to be played by the young Duc de Choiseul, Colonel of the Royal Dragoons, a relation of Louis XV's minister.

The character of Choiseul was already the subject of criticism in the early stages of planning. At thirty-one Choiseul was young and 'immature' for his command. Although fervent for the royal cause – he had honourably stayed with his regiment instead of emigrating – Choiseul was not a good organizer. 'Inclined to be chaotic,' said Fersen to Bouillé, worried that Choiseul might commit some indiscretion. Nevertheless Choiseul had some useful attributes. He might be rash but he was both grand and rich and he could therefore pay for the necessary relays of horses along the way. So the values of the court were in a sense allowed to permeate strategy.[30]

These values also affected the composition of the coach party. Originally it had been expected that Madame Elisabeth would join in the separate escape of the Comte de Provence and his wife. (In order to travel conveniently, Provence, obese as he might be, had taken up riding again.) But in accordance with her own fixed principle not to leave her brother, Madame Elisabeth was now to be a member of the main party. This meant that five people were already designated for the berlin, with, theoretically, room for one more. At this point protocol and duty dictated, at least to the Marquise de Tourzel, that she should be that one. Had she not given her word never to leave the Dauphin's side? As a result of which she slept in his room every night, or, on that first dreadful night back at the Tuileries, had sat sleepless on his bed as a guardian. In spite of her health – the Marquise suffered badly from renal colic – she would not desert him now in his hour of danger.[31] And that was that.

While it is true that Marie Antoinette had counted on the Marquise in her secret plotting of early February, that was before Madame Elisabeth planned to travel in the berlin. At that point the Queen believed that the remaining space would be allotted to some responsible senior courtier, such as the Duc de Villequier or the Duc de Brissac, both in their mid-fifties, both accustomed to decision-making, both trusted by the King. The two Ducs had, however, recently emigrated, the King fearing reprisals upon them following the debacle of Easter Monday, although 'ce bon' Brissac was lofty enough about facing peril. He had done what he had done, he said, for the sake of the King's ancestors – and his own.[32]

There was no further attempt to insert a man of this calibre into the heart of the party, although it would certainly not have been physically impossible, given that two out of the designated six were children, one of them very small. For example, the Comte de Damas had expected that Vicomte d'Agoult, another loyal servant who had been accredited to him as an ADC by the King the previous autumn, would be fitted in.[33] Instead, two equerries were to ride outside as bodyguards, along with a courier, the Comte de Valory. Two waiting-women, Madame

Brunier for Madame Royale and Madame de Neuville for the Dauphin, were to follow in a light carriage. (Madame Thibault, for the Queen, had a separate passport to Tournai, from where she intended to join her mistress.) Count Fersen, who was to drive the berlin on the very first stage of its journey getting out of Paris, was to separate from the royal party after that was accomplished.

Fersen had originally expected to go the whole way to Montmédy, seeking permission from King Gustav to wear a Swedish uniform for the occasion, since his own French uniform was not with him, and he dared not order another one. But Louis XVI banned it. There has been some speculation as to his reason: did Louis XVI choose this moment for an uncharacteristic outburst of jealousy? It seems an unlikely development at this stage, given that Fersen was allowed to perform the risky task of driving out of Paris, with all the possibilities of discovery that that entailed. Perhaps it was snobbery, those court values again. The Duc de Lévis said afterwards that the role of coachman should have gone to 'a grand French seigneur'.[34] The most probable explanation lies in the fact that Fersen was a foreigner, for all his French military command, and everything was being done to avoid any foreign taint touching the King's escape when he arrived at Montmédy.

Whatever the reason, the end result was a highly vulnerable composition to the berlin party: three adult royals who had spent most of their lives in a magnificent cocoon where ritual took the place of decision, a middle-aged woman in uncertain health and two children. As for Louis XVI, up until this point he had never even been involved at first hand in the question of the escape, having used a series of intermediaries; he was hardly prepared to act as leader in a crisis. The three male equerries were also comparatively junior and unused to command. It was important, under these circumstances, that nothing should go wrong.

The attitude of Mercy in Brussels and the Emperor in Austria did not become more encouraging throughout May and the early part of June, while the difficulties of raising money continued to bedevil the royal family's preparations. Mercy bewailed the dangers of discovery – was it really the time for such a bold venture? – and Leopold continued to counsel prudence: 'Calculate well the risks ...' As late as 5 June, Leopold sent an indirect message that the royal family should stay in Paris and await rescue from outside. This provoked a horrified reaction from Marie Antoinette: 'The glory of the escape must be *ours* ...' But the Emperor did manage to embargo Artois from military action, telling him that he must obey his brother, while Louis XVI told the Duchesse de Polignac that he was being caused 'a lot of disquiet' by Artois' premature plans.[35]

The first date seriously put forward was 12 June, once a hostile chambermaid had finished her tour of duty. But that was the eve of the Feast of Pentecost and the King feared that there would be an inordinate amount of people in the streets. On that day the coiffeur Léonard went to the Tuileries at ten o'clock at night through a side door, and was admitted, armed with a note from the Queen, through the dark and deserted apartments. Then he was entrusted with the baton of a Marshal of France, to be given to the Marquis de Bouillé at Montmédy. He was also entrusted with the Queen's personal casket of jewellery intended for Brussels, the Queen retaining only a set of pearls, some diamond drops and certain *bijoux de fantaisie* (coloured semi-precious stones) as well as the two diamond rings that she always wore. The Crown Jewels of France, being national property and liable to inspection, had already been handed over, to be inventoried by the National Assembly. Whit Sunday itself – 13 June – was Marie Antoinette's patronal feast of St Antony, that day of celebration in her distant childhood. Now there were those in the Royal Chapel who sang, in Latin, 'God protect the Nation!' as well as others who sang, 'God save the King!'[36]

Discreet preparations made the next day included the stopping of the medicine with which the King had been purging himself since his spring illness, for the possible embarrassment it might cause him. Publicly, the King and Queen went to the opera, where payments for the royal box had been kept up through thick and thin. The new piece given, Candeille's *Castor et Pollux*, was a revision of Rameau's opera performed at their wedding twenty-one years earlier. Counsellor Blumendorf, left behind at the Austrian embassy, sent Mercy a coded message from the Queen that departure was imminent; Mercy's reaction was to advise Blumendorf to burn all compromising papers in his possession – and at the first hint of trouble, to lodge Mercy's money and *assignats* (the new revolutionary currency) care of the banker Laborde.[37]

During the week that followed, a number of loyal servants of the monarch were given a tip-off for the sake of their own security. These included the Vicomte d'Agoult, one of the rejected candidates to accompany the berlin, who was now provided with an excuse to emigrate. Joseph Weber, the foster-brother, had a private letter from the Queen: 'Take shelter, get out.' The Princesse de Tarante, Marie Antoinette's beloved friend – 'If anything happened to her I should never forgive myself' – was sent away, but the Princesse de Lamballe, judged to be in too close touch with her brother-in-law the Duc d'Orléans, was not warned in advance. Madame Campan, whose tour of duty stopped on 1 June, was told to go and take the waters, while hiding a portfolio of papers with the painter Anne Vallayer Coster, that member of the French Academy whom Marie Antoinette had patronized.[38]

The new date was 19 June. According to the Duc de Choiseul, who visited the Tuileries in disguise having had a meeting with Fersen, the King now objected to the fact that this was a Sunday and insisted on yet another day's delay. Choiseul headed back to Metz. Finally it was to be Monday night, 20 June. 'All is decided,' wrote the Queen to Mercy, still angry at not having heard from the Emperor about his troops advancing. 'We go, Monday, at midnight, and nothing can alter that plan, we should expose those who are working for us in this enterprise to too much danger.'[39]

Throughout the day itself Marie Antoinette was desperate to preserve an air of normalcy about her routine. The King gave one last interview to Fersen; they would meet next, if everything went according to plan, when the Count was dressed as a coachman on the box of the berlin. But if the rescue failed, Louis ordered Fersen to get out himself, to reach Brussels and try to organize something from there. The Queen also said farewell to Fersen – temporarily, it was to be hoped – but still she shed a few tears. At five o'clock she then took her children on a drive to the beautiful Tivoli gardens belonging to Monsieur Boutin, a financier, and made a display of walking in public with them. It was under cover of this expedition that Marie Thérèse, aged twelve and a half, was instructed by her mother not to be surprised by anything that might shortly happen to her. If she seemed upset, the girl was to tell the accompanying waiting-women that her mother had scolded her. The six-year-old Dauphin was thought to be too young to be let into the secret, and then there was his indiscreet tongue. As she returned to the Tuileries, the Queen instructed the National Guards to be ready to take them on a similar expedition the next day.[40]

The Dauphin went up to his apartments for his supper at eight-thirty, and the Marquise de Tourzel joined him in his room, as usual, at ten o'clock. The Provences arrived from the Luxembourg for a family supper that night as was customary. Everyone was in high spirits, Provence said later, and full of hope because they all expected to be meeting again in happier circumstances in four days' time. Provence himself was riding out – thanks to his new lessons – disguised as an English merchant with one gentleman in attendance; the target in his case was Belgium where the Archduchess Marie Christine and the Archduke Albert had returned a few days previously. It was at this meal that the King confided to his brother for the first time the secret of his Montmédy destination; he ordered Provence to join him, via Belgium, at Longwy. Josephine de Provence, who knew nothing about any plans until this moment, was instructed to flee separately with one lady in attendance. All four, King, Queen, Provence and Josephine, embraced tenderly at the end of the evening.[41]

The adult royals at the Tuileries went up to bed just before eleven. The King was last seen by his two valets, the senior Lemoine and the boy Pierre Hubert, at twenty past the hour, when the heavy curtains of his great bed were formally drawn.

CHAPTER TWENTY-ONE

Departure at Midnight

'Departure at midnight from Paris ... at Varennes-en-
Argonne at eleven o'clock in the evening.'
Journal of Louis XVI, 21 June 1791

It was seven o'clock the following morning, Tuesday, 21
June, when Lemoine and Hubert went into the King's
bedroom as usual and drew back the curtains; Lemoine dealt
with the bed and the boy Hubert with the windows. To
Lemoine's amazement, the royal bed was empty. Passing on to
the Dauphin's room, they found that to be empty too. When
Hubert suggested anxiously that they should inform the Queen,
Lemoine was taken aback and pointed out that it was not yet
the designated hour to draw Her Majesty's curtains ... The
mystery deepened when it was discovered that Madame Royale
had asked to be left to sleep for an extra half-hour, while the
maidservant of Madame Brunier reported that her mistress was
not there either.[1]

At a quarter to eight, the ritual awakening of the Queen
began. Here too there was an empty bed behind the curtains.
Very soon the cry was all over Paris: 'They've gone! They've
gone!' By eleven o'clock a huge and angry crowd was assembled
outside the windows of the Tuileries, shouting insults of the
grossest sort concerning the family who were no longer apparently in residence. The only portrait of the King that could be
found was torn to shreds. It was La Fayette who summed up

the situation when he rushed round to see his friend Thomas Paine: 'The birds are flown!' The republican Paine merely replied, 'Let them go,' but the National Assembly took the opposite line. It was now on full and furious alert. In Brussels, the news was broken to Count Mercy d'Argenteau by the arrival of a chest from the Queen containing a little red morocco box for 'the sister' (Marie Christine), letters of exchange worth 600,000 or 700,000 livres and about 20,000 livres in cash. There was no note or letter.[2] But there was no need; Mercy, who had opposed the escape up to the last minute with Cassandra-like warnings, knew that the die was cast.

As to the King's intentions in this flight, these were made quite clear by the declaration that he left behind him, dated 20 June and signed as customary with the simple name 'Louis'.[3] This extensive document rehearsed the events of recent years including the King's reasons for remaining in France after the violence of October 1789. He could certainly have departed, but preferred not to evoke civil war. Instead he had then taken up residence at the Tuileries as requested, and surrendered his own bodyguards, a painful loss. All these sacrifices had been made in vain; under the new order, the King was deliberately sidelined, stripped of the right to agree or refuse constitutional measures. In these circumstances, 'What remains to the King except the empty sham of royalty?'

A recital of the affronts that Louis had endured followed, prominent among them being the 1789 plan to take the King and his son away to Paris 'and shut the Queen up in a convent'. Then there were the efforts to stop Mesdames Tantes going abroad, and his own experience of being barred from travel to Saint Cloud when the National Guard sided with the mob; he had been condemned in consequence to hear 'the Mass of the new curé' at Saint-Germain at Easter. Was it surprising that the King should now seek to recover his liberty, putting himself and his family in safety? Louis ended by addressing all 'Frenchmen and above all Parisians' and reminding them that the King would always be 'your father, your best friend'. How happy he would be to return to a proper constitution, which he could accept of his own free will, one in which 'our ancient religion' was respected! A postscript forbade the King's ministers to sign any order in his name, until they had received his latest instructions.

While this declaration was being read and while the crowd howled outside the Tuileries, a respectable party of travellers were trundling happily through the roads of north-eastern France. It consisted of Monsieur Durand, a valet; Madame Rochet, a waiting-woman; Rosalie, a children's nurse; Agläié, a girl of about twelve; and her little sister, Amélie, around six years old. Also present was the Baronne de Korff, a middle-aged woman who was the owner of the coach.

To the casual observer, these people were dressed appropriately enough for their degree; for example, the waiting-woman and the nurse wore plain dark clothes, mantles and big shady hats, while the girls were in simple cotton dresses and bonnets.[4] It was only a closer inspection, perhaps by one who was familiar with the scene at Versailles in the old days, that would reveal the characteristic features of Louis XVI, the heavy face, strongly marked eyebrows and beaked nose, seen for example on the new paper currency, the *assignats*, followed by those of Marie Antoinette, Madame Elisabeth, Marie Thérèse, Louis Charles in girl's clothing – and the Marquise de Tourzel. Also disguised as servants were the Comte de Valory, Monsieur de Moustier and Monsieur de Malden. All had been appointed three days earlier when the Queen graciously enquired what their first names were, since she would have to address them as such in their menial capacity. The answers turned out to be François, Melchior and Saint-Jean respectively.[5]

Everything so far had really gone very smoothly, given that the actual escape from the well-guarded Tuileries had always been the danger point. At the last *poste* (posting-station) before Châlons-sur-Marne, the Queen observed to Valory: 'François' – as he had become – 'it seems to me that things are going well and if we were going to be stopped, it would have been before now.'*

---

* These posting-stations, where the exhausted horses were changed for relays of fresh ones, were of vital importance in any journey in eighteenth-century France. The *postes* existed, every fifteen miles or so, along the main routes; if travellers

Believing himself safe, even the taciturn King opened up a little to the Marquise de Tourzel. How happy he was to be free of all the bitter experiences of Paris! He told her jovially: 'Now that I have my backside in the saddle [*cul sur la selle*] I intend to be quite a different person from the one you have known up until now.'[6]

It was true that the exact schedule of departure had not been kept. But some delays were to be anticipated, were they not, in such a delicate operation and would surely be factored into the equation by those at the other end. Actually the escape of the royal children went like clockwork. The Marquise de Tourzel awakened Louis Charles at ten-thirty. Increasingly militaristic in his play and loving to dress up as a knight in specially made miniature armour, the little boy on awakening was convinced that he was going to command a regiment. He began to shout: 'Quick, quick! Give me my sabre and boots and let's be on our way.' Imagining that he was his hero Henri IV, Louis Charles was somewhat put out now to be dressed in the girl's clothing prepared by Pauline de Tourzel but he still believed that he must be taking part in some kind of play. His sister, however, thought that the sleepy Louis Charles, with his long fair hair, made a very pretty little girl.[7]

Marie Thérèse described herself later as having been bewildered, in spite of her mother's warning. Nevertheless a procession of adults on foot (the children were carried) now filed unchecked out of the Tuileries. They used the ground-floor apartments of the departed Duc de Villequier as an exit, since they were not guarded. The party included the two waiting-women, Madame Brunier and Madame de Neuville, who were to go ahead. The Royal Governess and her charges, escorted by Malden, easily reached a plain carriage waiting in a side courtyard on the north side of the Tuileries, known as the Petit Carrousel. This courtyard beyond the Cour des Suisses connected to the outside world by the rue de l'Échelle, leading to the modern rue de Rivoli; a passageway went back to the Grand Carrousel. Here

---

intended to deviate to the byways, arrangements had to be made in advance for fresh horses to be found.

they found Fersen, sitting on the box in coachman's garb, whistling and smoking tobacco for the sake of verisimilitude.[8]

A wait was expected at this point; the Dauphin snuggled down on the floor beneath the Marquise de Tourzel's skirts and went to sleep. In order to avoid suspicion by remaining stationary for so long, Fersen took the carriage for a drive round the nearby streets. Further enlivenment was provided by the sight of La Fayette's carriage, passing into the Tuileries on the way to the King's official *coucher*. After 'a long hour' had passed, according to Marie Thérèse, a woman was seen lurking in the shadows of the Petit Carrousel. It was Madame Elisabeth. Stepping hastily into the carriage, she trod on Louis Charles but he bravely stifled his cries.

The presence of Mayor Bailly as well as La Fayette at his *coucher* meant that the King had to be careful not to hurry matters. But when he did eventually slip out past the guards, escorted by the Comte de Valory, he did so easily enough thanks to a ruse. These guards had become accustomed to seeing the Chevalier de Coigny, who bore a remarkable physical resemblance to the King, leaving at roughly the same hour through the same exit for the last fortnight. Once arrived at the Petit Carrousel, the King boasted of his self-possession, which had even enabled him to bend down and casually fasten the loose buckle on his shoe.

The only person missing at this point was Marie Antoinette. She had decided to leave after the King so that her absence, if discovered, should not prejudice his own escape. She therefore had to await the end of the long-drawn-out *coucher* and La Fayette's departure. Minutes later when she did arrive – at most, fifteen – the King, in a rare gesture of public emotion, took his wife in his arms and embraced her, saying over and over again: 'How happy I am to see you!' It was not so much the duration of the delay as the sheer adrenalin produced by the danger of the situation that caused the King's outburst. Malden, once more acting as escort, may have got muddled among the courtyards, but even so, it is clear from the various accounts that the Queen arrived shortly after the King.*[9] The delay that had crept into the schedule so far

* The story that the Queen and Malden, having taken a wrong turning, wandered

was due to the inexorable ritual of court and *coucher*.

It was after one-thirty in the morning by the time Fersen, as coachman, reached the berlin waiting outside the city barrier at the Porte Saint-Martin. Out of caution,* he did not take the more direct public route but looped round, and this again caused a certain delay in the projected timings. At the first *poste* they reached, at Bondy, Fersen surrendered his role as coachman according to the King's previous decision, and left the royal party.

On rolled the berlin, keeping up a good steady pace which has been estimated at between six and seven miles an hour. After Meaux, La Ferté-sous-Jouarre was reached, then Montmirail, Étoges and Chaintrix, with Châlons-sur-Marne about thirteen miles away. There were few stops, except briefly for fresh air for the children, and once for the King, since the berlin contained all the necessary amenities. At one point the King looked at his watch and observed with some complacency: 'La Fayette is now in real trouble.'¹⁰ It was around two o'clock. The royal party was expected to make contact with the Duc de Choiseul and forty officers at an inconspicuous *poste* at Pont de Somme-Vesle, fourteen miles beyond Châlons, between two-thirty and four-thirty. Clearly the original schedule had been over-optimistic but, unlike La Fayette, the royal family did not expect to be in real trouble as a result.

It was now that the party encountered its first bit of bad luck. One horse after another stumbled and fell, causing a break in the harness, which then had to be mended. This was not an unexpected feature of travel at the time but it did mean that the berlin was now over two hours behind its projected schedule. At this point the Duc de Choiseul, having waited for about two hours at the Somme-Vesle *poste*, lost his head. He had zeal – he would have died for the King – but he lacked the kind of calm resourcefulness that was needed in this situation. Choiseul, on his own initiative, decided that the whole mission had been aborted.¹¹

about the rue du Bac on the Left Bank of the Seine, having crossed the river from the Tuileries by the Pont Royal, is implausible; this would have needed not one but a whole series of wrong turnings, to the right, then out on to a quai and over a bridge, without their realizing what was happening.

* Not out of a foreigner's lack of knowledge of the city; Fersen had been living in Paris on and off for many years.

Without waiting for the arrival of the courier Valory, who was supposed to ride ahead to report progress, he proceeded to take his dragoons back in the direction of Montmédy. Goguelat did not argue against the decision, nor did he remain at the *poste*. Instead he helped to warn those further down the line that everything had gone wrong. Choiseul had Léonard with him, who had accompanied him on his trip back from Paris on the instructions of Marie Antoinette (the coiffeur kept bemoaning the fact that he was in tell-tale silk stockings and breeches). He now told him to take his cabriolet and spread the news that 'the treasure' would after all not be arriving.[12]

At six o'clock Valory arrived at the *poste* at Somme-Vesle and was appalled to find no sign of the dragoons. When the berlin itself arrived at six-thirty, there was similar consternation. What did Choiseul's absence mean? What should they do now without the military escort which had been so carefully planned in the weeks before the escape? No one had any idea, not the three junior bodyguards accustomed to taking orders rather than giving them, and not the King. As to Choiseul's motivation, the Marquise de Tourzel's explanation was hardly too extravagant: 'Heaven, who wanted to test our august and unfortunate sovereigns to the end, let him leave.'[13]

In the end, for want of any more imaginative solution, the berlin simply rolled on again, reaching Orbeval – where there was still no sign of Choiseul – and thence to Sainte-Ménehould. It was now about eight o'clock, and the royal family had been travelling for eighteen hours. Here there were in fact forty dragoons of Choiseul's regiment, under the command of Captain d'Andouins; they had been installed in order to safeguard the passage of this mythical 'treasure'. But these troops had unsaddled and d'Andouins, who in any case believed that everything had gone wrong, kept his distance from the family to avoid suspicion. All the time the royal luck was running out. Someone now recognized the King in a brief moment when he put his head out of the carriage, or at least suspected his identity.

This was one Drouet, in his late twenties, an official of the Sainte-Ménehould *poste*, who was a strong supporter of the Revolution. Afterwards a colourful story was spun concerning Drouet's recognition, how he quickly compared the face when he saw it with the *assignat* in his pocket, which the King himself had given him. The fact was that the 'the infamous Drouet', as he became from the royalist point of view, had served seven years in the army; his attention, like that of the rest of the town, might have been caught in the first place by the sight of the dragoons, added to which Louis XVI had quite a distinctive appearance, *assignat* or no *assignat*. Furthermore the gossip about the berlin's contents was spreading in the district. Fresh horses always had to be accompanied by local postilions in order to take charge of them when their relay was over. It is possible that the King had in fact been recognized as early as Chaintrix and Châlons; but there the inhabitants were more discreet – or more respectful.[14]

Drouet's suspicion was not yet certainty and the berlin was allowed to depart. It was not until an hour and a half later that Drouet and another man, Guillaume, set off in pursuit; they did so at the orders of the municipality.* By this time, the royal party had reached Clermont. Here the Comte de Damas, Colonel of the Dragoons of Monsieur (the Comte de Provence), had been ordered to await the King's passing with 140 men. Unlike Choiseul, Damas had only been let into the secret of the escape fifteen days before its execution and was sufficiently out of touch to believe that the Vicomte d'Agoult would be with the King in the berlin. Wrongly alerted by Léonard that there would be no arrival of the 'treasure', Damas was put under pressure from his officers to stand down. He had thus allowed the horses to be unsaddled and his men to go to sleep at about nine o'clock.[15]

By the time Damas was in a position to send a quartermaster named Rémy and a few troops after the King, Drouet and Guillaume had arrived. They now received some vital information about the berlin's route from another quarter. It might have been expected that the King would roll on east to Verdun. In fact, Verdun, like Metz, had all along been seen as a potential hazard.

---

* Today a plaque at the modern *gendarmerie* at Sainte-Ménehould commemorates the site of the former *poste* from which Drouet and Guillaume 'launched the pursuit of the King Louis XVI'.

After Clermont, it was intended that the berlin should turn sharply north on a more obscure route, through wooded hills. Unfortunately Rémy missed this turning, and continued for some time towards Verdun, delaying his meeting with the berlin. It was Drouet and Guillaume who learnt of the fateful words spoken to the postilions of the fresh horses at Clermont: 'Take the road to Varennes.'[16]

The royal party reached Varennes-en-Argonne, a 'miserable little town' of perhaps one hundred inhabitants, at about eleven o'clock at night. Miserable as it might be, Varennes' peculiar layout turned out to be crucial to the royal fortunes. The main street descended a steep hill to a bridge over the Aire River, with a further section of the town, including its castle and the Hôtel Le Grand-Monarque, on the far side; this meant that Varennes was effectively divided into two. There was now an urgent need for fresh horses, especially as the postilions of the current relay had been instructed by their employer, a woman, to get home without fail the next day for the harvest. Yet – almost unbelievably – no one in the party had the faintest idea where the new horses were supposed to be found.

This was essential information, given that Varennes was too small and insignificant to have its own *poste* and arrangements had therefore had to be made in advance. There was a vague supposition that their best bet was 'the Clermont end of the town', yet no horses were to be found there and the town was in darkness. It was one of the unfortunate but lethal effects of Choiseul's withdrawal that the horses' whereabouts – altered by Goguelat to the far (Stenay) end of the town – was never passed on by either man.

As it was, the King's party was left knocking on doors in the darkness in the upper part of Varennes, while in the lower part, across the bridge near the castle, at the Hôtel Le Grand-Monarque, two comparatively junior officers waited with the missing horses, as well as a detachment of the Royal German Regiment. One officer, Charles de Bouillé, younger son of the Marquis, had been chosen because the presence of his father or Comte Louis might have drawn too much attention; the other, Raigecourt, was also a younger son. These officers had posted no lookout and were thus for some time in complete ignorance of the events happening only a short distance away from them – and their men.[17] Once Drouet and Guillaume rode by, giving the alarm at the local inn, Le Bras d'Or, the town began to wake up. But at this crucial point, the bridge over the Aire was blocked by a conveniently overturned furniture wagon.

Not only were Charles de Bouillé's hussars now cut off from the royal party but so, in theory, were the additional one hundred hussars on the road further north at Dun. Their acting commander, Lieutenant Rohrig, was also quite junior, Goguelat having sent back the experienced commander of the squadron, Deslon.[18] There were in fact several fords over the Aire. But no one among the royalists seemed to know where they were. When Charles de Bouillé was at last alerted to the King's arrival, he found that a deep trench in the water, which had been cut for a nearby mill, made the only ford he knew impassable. He then turned north. In short, the lack of preparations at Varennes was a disaster. Unlike the delays, it was an avoidable disaster. This was something about which both Valory and Choiseul agreed afterwards.

The Queen, on the arm of Malden, took temporary refuge at the large house of an invalid, a Monsieur de Préfontaine; since he had worked for the Prince de Condé, here was a friendly contact that could have been established in advance, but had not. Meanwhile about half an hour was wasted while Valory and Moustier tried to coerce the postilions into going further.[19] They resolutely refused. It was said later that their royalist employer bitterly regretted the intransigent orders she had given about the priority of the harvest. The two bodyguards looked in vain for the fresh horses.

By this time the procurator of the local commune, Monsieur Sauce, had become involved, thanks to Drouet. Another barrier was set up at the top of the town, while the postilions were told: 'Your passenger is the King.' The alarm for fire in the town was set off, a traditional method for rousing the sleeping inhabitants. National Guards began to be summoned. Six passing dragoons, who happened to observe the commotion and might have assisted the royal party, had no officer to command them and therefore did nothing. In all of this, time was of the essence if the berlin was to go on its way with the new relay, or alternatively if the royal party was to be rescued by other means.

Procurator Sauce also understood the value of time, or rather delay, since the task of arresting the King of France in the middle of the night, without any authority, was to say the least of it delicate. In such an extraordinary situation, the appearance of coercion had to be avoided. It was thus, on the excuse of the irregularity of their passports, that the royal family was persuaded to accept the 'hospitality' of Sauce's house until morning, when no doubt they would be continuing on their journey.

The Sauce house had two upper rooms. The royal family congregated in the back one, which was about fifteen feet by twenty, and the bodyguards sat outside under the window. The Queen asked for hot water and clean sheets for the children, who sank into instant sleep, and wine for the rest of the party (with the exception of herself). The King sat slumped in an armchair. Here at last at midnight, Choiseul and Goguelat reached the King, the former with his dragoons, having been lost in the wooded terrain. Damas also got through with a small party of loyal troops. Although crowds were beginning to gather outside the windows, these were mainly peasants. There was as yet no authority for the arrest. Therefore it was still perfectly possible at this point for the various bodies of troops in the neighbourhood to have simply forced through the liberty of the royal family, either by the threat of superior weapons, or by the use of them, as Choiseul and Goguelat suggested. No order was given to do so.

Whose failure was this? Louis XVI must take part of the blame. Fearing as ever the effects of violence on those around him, including his own family, he declined the sword that the Duc de Choiseul offered, telling him to put it away. Louis XVI clung to his paternalistic role, the only one he understood. At one point the King attempted to pacify the gathering crowds by appearing before them and announcing that he had no intention of leaving France and furthermore would return to Varennes, after he had been established at Montmédy. But there is a story that someone shouted from the crowd: 'And what if your foot slipped [over the frontier]?' Even if apocryphal, it is one of those stories that capture the mood of the moment; it was not credible to simple people (nor, of course, to many more sophisticated ones) that the royal journey would really stop at Montmédy, so close to the frontier of the Empire.

Once again, however, Choiseul must bear a responsibility. The Duc had actually received an order in advance from the Marquis de Bouillé to go into the attack if the King was arrested at Châlons; that would have justified his action, if justification were needed. He was a soldier, not a courtier. It was a risk of course, like all unplanned military actions, but there were other soldiers in French royal employ who would have taken it.

After all, the King himself was never likely to take real command. When Goguelat, the ADC, managed to make his way to the King, the latter asked him when they were to depart. 'Sire, we await your orders,' replied 'Monsieur Gog'. As a soldier he at least was not afraid of violence. Goguelat tried to disperse the National Guards gathering outside and, drawing his sword, found himself the victim of an officer's bullet; it struck his collarbone and his horse then threw him. Later Deslon, the commander of the squadron of hussars who had been at Dun, also got back into Varennes, although without his men. Asking for orders, he was told by Louis XVI that he had no orders to give, since he was a prisoner.[20] Once again the lack of a senior advisor at the King's side was a terrible disadvantage – even that cool plotter and professional soldier Count Fersen, the lack of whose 'courage and sang-froid' the Marquis de Bouillé would later lament.

The arrival of emissaries from the National Assembly at about six o'clock in the morning, bearing orders for the immediate return of the King to Paris, changed the situation entirely. The anxious debate at the Hôtel de Ville about the King's future was at an end. One of them, Romeuf, was familiar to the Queen because he was La Fayette's ADC. At the sight of him, so thickly coated in dust from the journey, she exclaimed: 'Monsieur, I would not have recognized you!' Nor, it seems, did she recognize their legitimacy. For the Queen's exhausted despair gave way to rage – in which some criticism of the King may perhaps be implied. Valory reported how she cried out: 'What audacity! What cruelty! Subjects having the temerity to pretend to give orders to their King!' And 'the Daughter of the Caesars' – meaning her imperial parents –

threw the order down on the bed where the Dauphin was sleeping.[21]

It was true that there was one last chance: the Marquis de Bouillé
and that large force he had assembled on the excuse of defending
the frontier, which was intended to support the King at
Montmédy. Deslon knew German and Marie Antoinette remembered enough of the language of her childhood to ask him whether
the Marquis de Bouillé would reach them in time; they expected
him to rescue them. The Comte de Damas, who also knew
German, was able to reply: 'On horse and will charge,' before there
were cries from their guardians: 'Don't speak German.'[22]

Bouillé, however, had only got as far as Stenay by about four
o'clock, having waited on the Varennes–Dun road for some time,
hoping to escort the berlin. He was aroused at four-thirty and his
troops were ready to set out at five o'clock. But it needed several
hours to make the journey to Varennes, given the rough nature of
the road. The King pleaded to delay their departure and one of
the waiting-women, Madame de Therville, even feigned illness in
order to provide an excuse. It was in vain. They could not hold
out beyond seven-thirty in the morning. So the wretched cavalcade
set off.* The Marquis de Bouillé finally arrived in Varennes about
an hour and a half too late.

The journey that followed was a nightmare. The weather, which
had been overcast, became intensely hot. The dust on the roads
was so great that the outriders were lost in a kind of fog. The royal
family was not, however, permitted to close the windows of the
carriage. As a result the dust clung to their clothes – the same
clothes they had been wearing at their departure – which had
become saturated with perspiration. The press of hostile people

---

* Today at Varennes a plaque on the clock tower commemorates the arrest. The
town also has a museum with a room dedicated to Louis XVI, which includes
memorabilia such as a silver soup tureen left behind. The town's position on the
Argonne front during World War I means, however, that mine warfare is also
remembered here and there is a memorial to the many American soldiers who fell
in the campaign in 1918. There is still a Hôtel Le Grand-Monarque. At the time
Varennes was presented with a tricolour flag in recognition of its services to the
nation.[23]

around them meant that the pace was intolerably slow. It had taken twenty-two hours to reach Varennes from Paris; during many of them the family had been buoyed up with hope. It now took nearly four days to return and the mood throughout was one of desolation.

Three deputies from the National Assembly were in charge; two of them, Jérôme Pétion and Antoine Barnave, crammed into the berlin. Barnave sat at the back between the King and Queen, who had Louis Charles on her knee; Pétion sat with Madame Elisabeth and the Marquise de Tourzel in front, the ladies taking it in turn to have Marie Thérèse on their laps. The third, Maubourg, offered to travel behind with the waiting-women to protect them from the abuse being hurled at them.

Pétion, a lawyer from Chartres in his early thirties who had been a member of the Estates General, was one of the many who had attached themselves to Robespierre's rising star. At this point he was loud-mouthed and crude rather than overtly cruel – his pulling of the Dauphin's long fair hair was probably meant as rough teasing rather than anything more sinister. As for his conviction that Madame Elisabeth, that earnest and devout spinster, succumbed to an instant physical attraction for him – he would recall her 'smiles on a summer's night' in his memoirs: that was more ludicrous than anything else.[24] But of course his very presence in the stifling coach was itself offensive.

Barnave was a different matter. He was blessed with undeniable good looks, fine regular features and a wide mouth, and was 'very well made', according to the Duc de Lévis, despite his short hair. At the age of twenty-nine (six years younger than Marie Antoinette) he was a man who had acquired an intellectual interest in the whole notion of liberty and what it meant, through wide reading. It was he who had attacked the departure of Mesdames Tantes as being improper during the debate on the Constitution. Barnave now found himself launched into an argument with Madame Elisabeth, who far from joining in intimate caresses with Pétion was actually determined to bring home to the deputy the sheer outrage of what had been done to the royal family. She herself would never abandon her brother unless all practice of religion was forbidden, when her conscience might tell her to leave France. But how would

Barnave understand that? He was 'not only said to be Protestant' but was probably without any religion at all.'[25]

The Princess also turned to politics. 'You are too intelligent, Monsieur Barnave,' she said, 'not to have appreciated the love of the King for the French people and his genuine desire to make them happy … As for that liberty which you love to excess, you have considered only its advantages. You have not taken into account the disorders that come in liberty's wake.' It was a spirited defence of an essentially conservative position. On the whole Marie Antoinette left the talking to her sister-in-law who was doing so well. It was not realized at the time that it was the Queen-in-distress, not the robust Princess, who made a striking impression on Barnave.

In effect, the return journey retraced the earlier route of the berlin: Clermont, Sainte-Ménehould, Châlons and on to La Ferté-sous-Jouarre, Claye and Meaux, leading finally to the Paris barrier. Not every experience along the way was unpleasant. The first night was spent at the intendancy at Châlons where people who remembered the lovely young Dauphine staying there on her bridal progress twenty-one years earlier wept for pity, even if recruits from the Jacobin clubs of nearby Rheims interrupted the Mass being said for the feast of Corpus Christi at the Sanctus; Marie Antoinette heard 'with horror the indecent abuse that assailed her ears'. Nevertheless young girls tried to present the Queen with flowers and were annoyed to be prevented from reaching her by orders of the deputies. At La Ferté, the hostess of the inn where a meal was taken pretended to be the cook in order to serve the royal family decently. The King was supposed to have been shown a secret staircase by which he alone could have escaped, the Queen another exit. Neither consented to a plan that went against their shared concept of duty – to stay together to the end.[26]

At Dormans, on the other hand, where the second night was spent with the King dozing in an armchair, they were kept awake all night by cries of 'Long live the nation!' and 'Long live the National Assembly!' There were threats to shoot the Queen at Épernay – if she could be got without hitting the King. And although the King and Queen were decently treated by the

Bishop at Meaux – a juror – in whose house they spent the third night, there was real trouble from Claye onwards. It was 25 June, 'one of the hottest days I ever felt,' wrote Grace Elliott, but the people would not allow the berlin to travel faster than at walking pace. The swearing, which was meant to be heard by the royal party, added to their discomfort, and the insolent smoking outside the open windows even more so. It was symbolic of the way the Queen was now demonized that various stories of her offering food out of the window to hungry people along the route all had the same denouement. The recipients of her charity were speedily warned off with the cry: 'Don't touch it! It's sure to be poisoned.'[27]

At the barriers of the city of Paris, there was a vast crowd. But the reception of the royal family was now subject to organization and there was no more danger of mob violence. La Fayette ordered that the normal sign of respect to the King was to be ostentatiously ignored; every head was to be covered as he passed and even the kitchenhands had to put their greasy cloths on their heads. At the same time an order was posted: 'Whoever applauds the King will be flogged; whoever insults him will be hanged.' So the infinitely slow, infinitely melancholy cortège of exhausted would-be fugitives reached the Tuileries through crowds that were for the most part silent.

The Queen's 'proud and noble air' even in these circumstances did not fail to arouse comment, both adverse and sympathetic. The press was as ever busy inflaming public opinion against her, this Medea who had been ready to plunge her arms into the blood of the French people. Now it was 'the rage of Madame Capet at this terrible contretemps' that they claimed was visible on her face. The envoy from Bourbon Parma, Virieu, saw on the contrary a woman who was 'defeated' even though she remained every inch the Queen. But the angelic looks of 'the dear little Dauphin' – still the Child of the Nation whatever his parents' misdemeanours – received general approbation.[28]

When the party finally reached the Tuileries at eight o'clock at night, having travelled since seven that morning, Louis XVI was almost too exhausted to get out of the coach. The three bodyguards and two waiting-women were taken to the Abbaye prison as much for their own protection as for punishment and the Marquise de Tourzel was also held. François Huë, the Dauphin's chief valet, had rushed back to the palace in time to receive his charge, although when the little boy put out his arms to him, Huë was brushed aside by a National Guard. It was not until later that they were reunited. Once in bed, Louis Charles called out to Huë: 'As soon as we arrived at Varennes, we were sent back. Do you know why?' Huë told him quickly not to talk about the journey. That night Louis Charles had a nightmare in which he was surrounded by wolves and tigers and other wild beasts who were going to devour him. 'We all looked at one another,' remembered Huë, 'without saying a word.'*[29]

By this time the Comte and Comtesse de Provence, successfully accomplishing their individual escapes with one attendant each, were reunited at Namur in Belgium. Fersen had also reached Brussels, bearing a letter from the King to Mercy d'Argenteau, conveying to him the money and letters of exchange that had reached him earlier. Count Esterhazy, referring to Fersen under the coded name of 'Le Chose' (literally, The Thing) described Fersen's absolute despair on hearing the news of the recapture although, like the Queen herself, Fersen put on a brave face in public. The reaction of Provence, now the senior royal at liberty, was to be rather different: 'There wasn't a trace of tears in those eyes as dry as his heart,' wrote the Marquis de Bouillé, who even discerned 'a few sparks of perfidious satisfaction'.[31]

The Dauphin's innocent question, although brushed aside by Huë, deserves answering. What did go wrong at Varennes? There is a supplementary question: what would have happened if the King had successfully reached Montmédy?

The first point that should be made is that the risky escape from the Tuileries was in itself successful. The King turned to

* It seems to have been – not inexplicably – a recurring dream of the little boy about this time, since the Marquise de Tourzel recounts a somewhat similar dream en route at Dormans; in this case the wolves were threatening his mother, and he had to be shown the Queen in order to be reassured.[30]

412

Valory at Varennes when there were no horses to be found and exclaimed: 'François, we are betrayed!' In fact, that was not the case. No one betrayed the royal family and up until the devastating absence of Choiseul at the *poste* of Somme-Vesle after which 'everything was abandoned ... to the caprices of fortune', things went remarkably well, with only minor – and commonplace – incidents like the breaking of harness with which to contend.

Afterwards the responsibility for the disaster of the royal family's recapture was the subject of a long war of words in which successive generations also took part, supporting the respective roles of the Duc de Choiseul and the Marquis de Bouillé; belligerent declarations were made such as 'Defence forces me to be on the offensive.' Among other first-hand accounts were those of the Comte de Damas, who was arrested like Choiseul on 22 June and who wrote a *Rapport* while in prison; of the courier Valory; and of the equerry Moustier. Madame Royale gave her child's-eye view four years later. The Marquise de Tourzel was chiefly concerned in her *Mémoires* to rebut the charge – 'I cannot pass over it in silence' – that it was her presence in the berlin that caused all the trouble, on the grounds that she had only carried out her duty at the orders of the Queen.[32]

Choiseul's account of events was written up in prison in August 1791 and he contended that it had subsequently been passed by the King and Queen (although Comte Louis de Bouillé strongly denied that they would have done this). Choiseul explained his defection at Somme-Vesle as due not only to the worrying delay in the schedule but also – even less plausibly – to his need to facilitate the King's route to Châlons. Among the explanations that were variously offered for the disaster, he cited the lack of preparations at Varennes; that, however, was the overall responsibility of the Marquis de Bouillé.[33]

On the other hand, the Marquis himself, who turned back from Varennes on finding the King taken away and who later emigrated to England, did receive a brief note of exoneration from the King: 'You did your duty,' and signed 'Louis'. The best epitaph on Bouillé's failure at Varennes is that of his son

Comte Louis, an avid memorialist. Comte Louis had originally remarked to his father on how happy he must feel at the prospect of liberating the King. While he was retreating from Varennes, in a state of profound dejection that his son never forgot, the Marquis reminded him of the conversation: 'Well, do you still call me happy?'[34]

There is, of course, the question of the route chosen by the King, the fact that Louis XVI 'was unwilling to quit the French dominions, although but in travelling', as was reported later to George III in England. It certainly would have been easier to head for Belgium. But that was to negate his plan to appear as the father of his people whom he would never abandon; afterwards, he described the attempted flight as one of the 'most virtuous acts' of his life.[35] Arguably the party for the escape was from the start too large. But that would not have mattered so much if some bolder, more authoritative personage had either been the sixth passenger in the berlin, rather than the Marquise de Tourzel, or else had been squeezed in as well. Then again, this lack of a proper advisor for the King would not have mattered so much if a crisis had not arisen, first at Somme-Vesle and then at Varennes as a result of the missing relay horses, whose whereabouts Choiseul had not had an opportunity to impart. For the want of a nail, the kingdom was lost, as the folk-rhyme has it. The Duc de Choiseul, to whose appointment both King and Bouillé had agreed, was that nail.

The escape, then, could have succeeded. The outcome of the proposed royal appearance at Montmédy is more difficult to predict. The point has been made that Louis XVI was not the first French King to use retreat from Paris as a method of advance, Henri IV being one notable example and the young Louis XIV under the tutelage of Anne of Austria another. As Madame de Staël wrote afterwards, if the flight had succeeded, it would have put an end to the hypocritical situation whereby the actions of the National Assembly, with which Louis did not agree, were purported to be his.[36]

Yet the combined vision of the King and Queen, in which happy and relieved subjects flocked to their father–sovereign, was surely unrealistic by the summer of 1791. The presence of

Bouillé's force, with the strong possibility of émigré assistance, meant that civil war was a more likely outcome, a solution that had been persistently rejected by the King (and the Queen). Added to which Louis XVI would hardly have made a stirring military leader, a role for which he had neither experience nor inclination. As it was, Louis XVI wrote in his *Journal*: 'Departure at midnight from Paris; arrived and stopped at Varennes-en-Argonne at eleven o'clock in the evening.' And at the end of the year, as was his custom, he recorded the journeys he had made: 'Five nights spent outside Paris in 1791.'[37]

CHAPTER TWENTY-TWO

Up to the Emperor

'It is up to the Emperor to put an end to the troubles of the French Revolution.'

Memorandum by Marie Antoinette,
8 September 1791

As the Duc de Choiseul conducted Louis XVI back to the berlin in Varennes, he felt 'an inexpressible anguish' as if he was seeing King Charles I handed over to his executioners.[1] For the time being, however, that appeared to be an exaggerated prophecy of doom. On 26 June deputies came from the National Assembly and cross-examined the King. By dint of taking to her bath – or sending a message that she had done so – Marie Antoinette managed to avoid being examined until the next day, by which time she was able to coordinate her evidence with that given by her husband. The Queen was very firm that she would never have taken part in the expedition if she had not been convinced that the King intended to stay in France.

After a further two weeks, the dominant party in the Assembly, still hoping somehow to reconcile a traditional monarchy with reform, issued a statement on the matter of Varennes in which the guilt of the King was neatly fudged. Louis XVI and his family had in fact been 'abducted' by the Marquis de Bouillé and his son. Fersen, Goguelat, Choiseul and Damas were, among others, nominated as guilty. It was a fiction preserved by Bouillé in the proclamation which he now issued: that he had had no orders from the King. After a while the equerries were released and allowed to emigrate, the King and Dauphin bidding farewell to them with embraces. The Marquise de Tourzel, on the other hand, was allowed to resume her duties, having been saved from incarceration by the Queen's pleas about her ill health. As the new Constitution, so long discussed, neared completion, the King was still a necessary asset to the constitutionalist or Feuillant party;* his acceptance of the Constitution, leading perhaps to its acceptance by others abroad, was something to be negotiated. The 'Triumvir' of the Feuillants' leaders consisted of Alexandre de Lameth, the youngest of three brothers of noble birth but of democratic convictions; Adrien Duport, a proponent of judicial reform; and Antoine Barnave, who had recently spent two days in the Queen's company in the berlin.

It was La Fayette whose star was waning. Widely – if unfairly – blamed for the Varennes escape, he was defeated in October in the election for the Mayor of Paris by that very Pétion whose coarseness had caused so much disgust on the journey back. On the other hand the republicanism of the Feuillants' opponents naturally received a further impetus from the events of Varennes. These included Robespierre, the fastidious president of the Jacobins, with his daily dressed and powdered hair worthy of a courtier, and his 'catlike' appearance. This was the phrase of another Jacobin, Merlin de Thionville, the type of cat changing with time from domestic animal to wild cat and finally to 'the ferocious aspect of the tiger'. Why should a king alone be inviolable, he enquired pointedly: 'The people, aren't they inviolable too?' Then there was Georges Danton, with his contrastingly shaggy appearance – he described himself as having 'the rough features of liberty' – who had brought into being the extremist Cordeliers Club the previous year. Other opponents to the Feuillants were the journalists Camille Desmoulins and Jean Paul Marat, founder of the hostile newspaper *L'Ami du Peuple*, to whom 'Louis and Antoinette' were public enemies.[2] Lastly there was Jean Pierre Brissot, the son of a Chartres caterer. Much

---

* The name, like that of the Jacobins, derived from the former convent in which their meetings were held.

travelled in England and America, and founder of the newspaper *Le Patriote Français*, Brissot led the group that was later termed the Girondins, after the geographical area of France from which most of them came.

On 17 July, two days after the King's manufactured 'acquittal', a meeting was organized in the Champ de Mars at which republican petitions were presented at a kind of altar. Proceedings got off to a violent start when two men were discovered lurking beneath the altar. They had in fact no more political intent than to spy on the women's legs but they were executed as spies of a very different sort. The behaviour of the National Guards under La Fayette was far more lethal. Through some kind of fatal misapprehension, there was firing on the crowds and fifty people were killed. Although the extremist leaders were for the present obliged to lie low – Danton vanishing to England – a precedent had been set for the kind of interfactional warfare that would now rage in French politics. As for the 'tumult' in the capital city itself, that was well caught by an English visitor, Stephen Weston. Not only the French but every nation under the sun 'from Siam to California' was represented among the crowds thronging the streets, all wearing appropriate dress, including Cossacks, Jews, Americans – a 'Paul Jones' or a 'nephew of Benjamin Franklin' – as well as deserters from various military forces, whether that of the Marquis de Bouillé, the émigré Princes, or just the Turkish army.[3]

Although royalists – and optimists – hoped that the King might be the gainer in all this, the fact was that thanks to Varennes the reputation of Louis XVI had taken a severe knock. Marie Antoinette had, after all, no reputation left to lose; her unpopularity was now so great, reported the English ambassador, that if she had been released by the National Assembly, she would have been torn to pieces by the mob. There were renewed rumours that the Queen would be removed from her husband (and children) to be shut up in that convenient convent, after being tried for crimes against the nation. Maria Carolina in Naples, hearing of these ferocious prognostications, even thought that a convent might be the most secure refuge. 'I would give my life blood to save her,' wrote the Queen of

Naples to their mutual brother the Emperor Leopold, 'not to make her the Queen of France again, but that she may finish her sad days in a convent.' (The Archduchess Marie Christine, characteristically less compassionate, simply thought it might have been better for 'my poor sister' if she had never been married.) If these assaults on the Queen were nothing new, those on the King marked a distinct, and distinctly disagreeable, development in his relationship with those 'children', his subjects. Whatever the provocation, whatever the fudging, Louis XVI had tried to deceive the nation – and had been found out.[4]

'The King has reached the lowest stage of vileness,' wrote Manon Roland, the pretty, spirited and intelligent wife of a Girondin deputy, who had established a salon in Paris. 'He has been shown up nakedly by those around him; he inspires nothing but scorn ... People call him Louis the False or the fat pig. It is impossible to envisage a being so totally despised on the throne.' The picture given in *L'Ami du Peuple* was indeed of a 'Louis Capet' who was a hypocrite while being physically gross and 'consoling himself with the bottle'. To the Jacobin Club, he was 'perfectly contemptible'. It was a cunning intensification of the personal denigration of Louis XVI, as someone too base to occupy the dignified position he held at a time when that position itself was under attack. Meanwhile cartoonists abroad cheerfully made mock of the entire Varennes story, Gillray, for example, portraying the whole arrest as a slapstick comedy, while the King of England wondered when, if ever, the King of France would behave like a man. It was even believed – quite erroneously – that the greed of Marie Antoinette's 'beast of a husband' had been responsible for their capture because he would insist that they stop and eat at various places en route.'

It was hardly to be expected that the ordeal of Varennes would leave the Queen unaltered, mentally or physically. Her immediate emotions may be glimpsed in two letters written to Fersen at the end of June. The first is brief and begins baldly: 'Be reassured about us; we are alive.' The second is full of pauses like sighs: 'I exist ... How worried I have been about you,' and 'Don't write to me, that will expose us, and above all don't come here under any pretext ... We are in view of our guards day and night; I'm indifferent to it ... Be calm, nothing will happen to me ... Adieu ... I can't write any more to you ...' Using Count Esterhazy as an intermediary, the Queen sent Fersen two inexpensive rings with the fleur-de-lys on them, of the sort that were still generally on sale. One was inscribed: 'Coward who abandons them,' and the other: 'Many miles and many countries can never separate hearts.'[6]

The physical fullness of her childbearing years was rapidly disappearing; Léonard had mentioned her thin arms and sunken bust as early as 1789. In 1791 the Comte d'Hezecques called her outrightly thin, and a pastel portrait by Aleksander Kucharski that was begun this year for the Marquise de Tourzel shows a haggard middle-aged woman – one might almost say an old woman, although Marie Antoinette was not yet thirty-six.* Certainly the pastoral prettiness of Madame Vigée Le Brun's images has quite vanished; there is no rose here, no straw hat, no ribbons, only a Queen with a strong nose and chin, her single remaining good feature being her large, sad, wide-apart eyes.

When Marie Antoinette greeted Madame Campan on her return to the Tuileries for the first time after Varennes, she took off her cap to reveal hair that had gone quite white through her sufferings. The Queen had another ring sent to the Princesse de Lamballe containing a lock of the altered hair with an inscription making the point that the change was due to unhappiness: '*blanchis par malheur*'. The Princesse had fled in July, first to Brussels, then to Aix, finally to Spa where she resided as the Comtesse d'Amboisse. In fact Marie Antoinette's hair had probably been turning white or at least grey for some time, with traces noted by Count Esterhazy as early as 1786.† Later the Queen would ascribe white hairs at her temples to 'the trouble of 6 October', although her foster-brother Joseph Weber thought that the death of the first Dauphin had whitened it.[8] The colour,

* Since 1954 this portrait has been kept in the Queen's room at Versailles, having been preserved by Tourzel descendants.
† Although Queen Charlotte's hair did turn white overnight at the first madness of King George III when she was forty-four.[7]

of course, was not visible when her hair was being dressed or when she wore a simple cap; pomade, powder and no doubt dye covered up a great deal.

Nevertheless Marie Antoinette had not lost her ability to please, even to fascinate, when it was urgent for her to do so. At the end of the year Quentin Craufurd, the protector of Fersen's mistress and her supporter, paid the Queen a number of visits. He was impressed as so many others had been by her demeanour. 'All her movements were graceful,' he wrote. As for her appearance, 'The expression, so often used, "full of charms", is that which suited her in all its exactitude, and best described her whole person.'[9] It was a chivalrous reaction of the sort that Marie Antoinette was always able to evoke among those who had actually been in her presence. Among these was the Feuillant leader Antoine Barnave.

To reach Barnave, the Queen used an intermediary, the Chevalier François Regnier de Jarjayes, with whom she worked out a code of a fairly rudimentary nature. Bernardin de Saint-Pierre's great romantic novel *Paul et Virginie* was to be used as a code with Fersen,* with both parties careful to use the same edition; with Jarjayes, however, it was a question of the alphabet and numbers, Barnave being 2:1 for the first two letters of his name, and Jarjayes 10 for J. Jarjayes, a man in his mid-forties, had like Barnave been born in Grenoble. His wife was one of the Queen's waiting-women, an intimate who often slept in her room, and was – at least according to the Marquise de Tourzel who may have been jealous – preferred over Madame Campan. Jarjayes himself was a devoted servant of the royal cause and had already been employed on commissions to try to curb the ambitions of Artois when he was still in Turin.[10]

There had evidently been private conversations between the Queen and the handsome Barnave at the various stopping-places

---

* *Paul et Virginie*, first published in 1788 to universal admiration, concerned two young people brought up together in a state of innocence on an idyllic island (which was based on Mauritius). Rediscovering each other as adults in tragic circumstances, Paul and Virginie were finally united in 'the celestial paradise' after death, of which the earlier paradise of their youth had only been a prefiguration. It is easy to see how the plot might appeal to Marie Antoinette's sensibilities.

on the journey back from Varennes, in which Barnave, unlike Pétion, had shown 'respectful delicacy'. Barnave had expressed his growing conviction that the Revolution as such must be brought to an end in favour of liberal reforms and conciliation. In short, constitutionalists were not at all the same animals as the republicans. In a letter of early July, the Queen expressed herself as having been 'struck by his [Barnave's] personality' during the two days they spent together and later she also referred to his 'most animated and captivating eloquence' in a letter to her brother.[11]

Throughout the summer and autumn, the Queen was in constant communication with Barnave, although they did not in fact have any further private interviews until early October and then Alexandre de Lameth was present.* Naturally their association, once known, was given the usual lubricious spin. *Le Bordel Patriotique*, a pornographic play of 1791, had the Queen, Barnave, Bailly, La Fayette and the revolutionary known as *la belle Liègoise*, Théroigne de Méricourt, all involved in a chain of sexual acts. Count Fersen, more calmly, reported in his *Journal intime*: 'They say the Queen is sleeping with Barnave.'[13] The fact that these explicit charges were ludicrous did not mean that Barnave was not in some subtler way mesmerized by the Queen. And he saw himself as playing a crucial role, with her help, in persuading the King to accept the Constitution.

Barnave's most significant letter was written on 25 July. In this he outlined a new and happier future for Marie Antoinette, still Queen of France but a far more beloved Queen than in the past. He told her that she had misunderstood the nature of the Revolution so far, not realizing that it could actually be helpful to her position. It was true that the Queen had been the object of widespread resentment, but with her courage and character she could overcome this. The candour with which the Queen had always expressed her convictions – convictions hostile to recent political developments – would now work to her advan-

---

* This correspondence ended up in Sweden, the most probable explanation being that the Queen gave it to Fersen for safety.[12]

tage. If she openly supported the Constitution, she would be believed to be equally sincere.[14]

As August passed, Barnave, convinced that 'the monarchical principle is profoundly and solidly rooted', envisaged a new kind of constitutional court at the Tuileries. All evils would be at an end if the King and Queen managed to make themselves solidly loved – by implication leaving that tiresome incident of Varennes to be forgotten.

The King accepted the Constitution on 14 September. Publicly, he did so 'according to the wish of the great majority of the nation'. Privately, like the Queen, he thought that it would prove unworkable and that he would benefit from the subsequent upheaval. As 'King of the French' – with the Dauphin as the 'Prince Royal' – he allowed himself to be turned into a constitutional monarch of limited powers, but not actually bereft of them. The King could choose ministers and although he could not declare war, the new Legislative Assembly, which replaced the previous Constituent Assembly on 1 October, could only go to war if the King asked them to do so. The King was also considered to have immunity for actions he might take as monarch – something that incidentally did not apply to other members of his family. An English visitor in the Tuileries gardens would witness two soldiers keeping their hats on in the presence of the Queen while singing disgusting songs, on the grounds that there was no mention of *her* in the Constitution: 'She was owed no respect as the King's wife.'[15]

At the ceremony there was no throne and a simple chair painted with fleur-de-lys was provided for the King; the deputies also kept their hats on as he spoke. It was witnessed by Marie Antoinette from a private box. Afterwards the King flung himself down in an armchair and wept at the humiliation to which he had been subjected – and to which he had subjected his wife: 'Ah, Madame, why were you there? You have come into France to see —'. His words were interrupted by his sobs. The Queen put her arms round her husband as Madame Campan stood rooted to the spot. Finally the Queen ordered her: 'Oh, go, go.' The fact was that it was the uncomfortable power that he did retain – that of veto over new laws – that was likely to cause real trouble in the future. The veto was voted in by a majority of 300 out of 1000 deputies. In the new Assembly, any measure personally odious to the King had either to be accepted or vetoed. So the King would face a choice of being unhappy or unpopular.

The celebrations for the new Constitution included a ballet, *Psyche*, in which the Furies' torches lit up the theatre. Seeing the faces of the King and Queen in this glow of the underworld, Germaine de Staël, like the Duc de Choiseul at Varennes, was overwhelmed by presentiments of disaster. Yet the King and Queen graciously attended the fireworks in the Place Louis XV after the Constitution had been proclaimed at the Hôtel de Ville.* Virieu was much impressed by the 'fairyland' created by the lights and there were even a few cries of 'Long live the Queen'. The public reaction, however, was summed up by a slogan on a cobbler's wall which made support for the monarch conditional: 'Long live the King! If he is being honest.'[17]

In November, Barnave would praise the Queen for the 'courage and constancy' she had shown in helping the constitutional process. He was unaware that privately his heroine regarded the new Constitution as 'monstrous' and 'a tissue of absurdities', even if the King had no choice but to accept it. Since they had 'no force or means of their own', they could only temporize.[18] Like the King, the Queen believed that the Constitution had only to be put in place for it to be proved unworkable. Marie Antoinette's real desires for the future were focused in a very different direction.

It is clear from the Queen's correspondence with Mercy that following Varennes, she pinned her hopes on her brother, the Emperor Leopold. Although reproaches have been flung at Marie Antoinette for deceiving Barnave, this is to see politics from the point of view of the politician, not the Queen. The constitutionalist Barnave was using the Queen to manoeuvre his

---

* Two other visitors to the fireworks were Emma Hamilton and her husband Sir William, ambassador to the Neapolitan court; they were received by the Queen who took the opportunity to send a letter to Maria Carolina.[16]

own enemies. A captive, brought back to France like a trophy, Marie Antoinette was entitled to use any means at her disposal – and more than one – to try to secure her family's safety. The Queen did not as yet want an armed rescue. She agreed with Louis, as she told Fersen, that 'open force would bring incalculable danger for everybody, not only the King and his family but also all the French.'[9] Still less did she want, with her husband, to be 'in the tutelage of the King's brothers'.

Provence's successful escape introduced a fresh and extremely unwelcome complication into the situation since he was the next adult male in the line of succession. According to Mercy, Provence was already angling for the Regency when he passed through Brussels following his flight from Paris. There was a rumour that he had actually had himself declared Regent in August, on the grounds that the King was held under duress. This caused a frisson of horror at the Tuileries; even though the rumour was not actually true, it was a threat that would not go away. Marie Antoinette wrote explicitly of the harm it would cause. The Princes in the name of the Regent would give one set of orders and the Assembly another, so that the Princes would be seen to be in open opposition to the orders given in the name of the King. The Queen told the Russian Minister, Simolin, that the Princes would turn out to be far more demanding, far more counter-revolutionary than the King. In short, if the Princes were to be their liberators, 'they would soon act as masters'.[20]

Coblenz in the Electorate of Trier, south of Cologne, was where the belligerent royal Princes came finally to rest, joining the Princes of the Blood. Its ruler the Elector-Archbishop Clement, being a brother of the late Dauphine Maria Josepha, was thus uncle to Provence and Artois (and Louis XVI). Coblenz became a hotbed of royalist claims, some of them wild, all of them embarrassing to the real King of France who was languishing in the Tuileries. When Marie Antoinette's enemy Calonne arrived in Coblenz from his English exile, he too wanted the Regency claimed for Provence. In the meantime a mini-Versailles was created, with ostentatious deference to the Princes and even the royal bodyguards reinstated – this last to the intense anger of the King and Queen to whom these bodyguards, if they existed, rightfully belonged. The pleasure-loving aspect of the former court was resurrected too; there were gambling parties and dances until dawn, mainly centred around the Comte d'Artois, whom Fersen described as 'always talking, never listening, sure of everything, speaking only of force, not of negotiations'.[21]

Of course, if Provence succeeded in his self-promotion as Regent, there was still the question of whom he was to be Regent for – Louis XVI or his son. The idea of a Regency centring on the Dauphin was also floated in France by those who felt that Louis XVI was too inadequate or too compromised to perform the task, yet who did not wish to throw away the monarchical principle altogether. Cries of 'Long live our little King!' sometimes greeted Louis Charles as he took his exercise in the Tuileries gardens, an appealing figure, untainted by politics. What then of another possible candidate, the Duc d'Orléans, in the role of Regent? The flight of the Comte de Provence meant that Orléans was next in line of the adult males still inside France. But according to his son, Orléans had irrevocably decided to refuse the Regency; in any case his popularity had been much diminished by his lack of any positive action following the events of July 1789, and by 1791 it had waned still further.[22]

What Marie Antoinette had wanted in July was armed demonstrations of imperial power in their favour, which would, in effect, threaten the French and cause them to treat their monarch better, without incurring the hostility inevitably consequent upon an invasion. 'The foreign powers,' she wrote privately in mid-August, 'are the only ones that can save us.'[23] What she got at the end of the month was a declaration made at Pillnitz in Saxony.

The Emperor joined with the King of Prussia to declare the fate of the French monarchy as being 'of common interest' to the great powers, if their warnings about its ill treatment recently were not heeded. But for any concerted action to be taken, all the powers had to be in agreement. Although Artois, the Marquis de Bouillé and Calonne were present at Pillnitz, the declaration was in fact an extremely cautious document, intended to placate the Princes rather than spur them on further.

The Queen had a more positive scheme in mind. It was now, in her opinion, 'up to the emperor to put an end to the troubles of the French Revolution', since a French monarchy that was not under duress was needed in order to preserve the equilibrium in Europe. In order to achieve this, in an extremely long memorandum to Leopold, on 8 September, Marie Antoinette first mentioned the idea of an armed congress.[24] This was essentially seen by her as a means of *threatening* the French into better behaviour towards their King rather than using outright force. The powers, who would gather at Aix or Cologne as part of this armed congress, would thus declare France to be a monarchy, hereditary in the male line of the reigning branch, with no regency envisaged unless declared by the King himself. The latter would have free powers of communication and among other details the tricolour, that 'sign of troubles and seditions', would be abandoned as the flag of France.

Marie Antoinette devoted her energies to the subject of the armed congress in her private correspondence in the ensuing months. She wrote prodigious quantities of letters, often in code, sometimes using lemon juice as invisible ink and sometimes other means, which went wrong when water would not resurrect the letters. She despatched these missives by any safe courier she could find. Marie Antoinette lobbied the Bourbon King of Spain and the King of Sweden; later she also tackled Queen Maria Louisa of Spain, referring hopefully to 'the nobility of your character' as well as 'the double link of blood' that joined them.* With these and many other efforts, 'I hardly recognize myself,' she exclaimed at one point; was it really her speaking? To Fersen, Marie Antoinette confessed that she was 'exhausted by her writings'. She also touchingly admitted how afraid she was of forgetting something or 'saying something stupid'.[25]

---

* Not only were the Spanish Bourbons related to the French, but as the daughter of Madame Infante, Queen Maria Louisa was Louis XVI's first cousin; also the King of Spain's sister was married to the Emperor Leopold.

The light-hearted, unintellectual, pleasure-loving young woman of yesteryear at Versailles had developed into a formidably hard worker. Maybe it is true that as the Queen wrote at one point: 'It is in misfortune that you realize your true nature.' Or maybe it was 'the blood that runs in my veins' – the blood of Maria Teresa, to which she made increasing reference – that was responding to pressure. A year earlier she had wept with her ladies: 'How amazed my mother would be' if she could see her daughter in her present condition. Now she found inspiration in her memory. A third explanation is the most likely one: the Queen's growing determination, alluded to earlier, to preserve the heritage of her son, in whose veins Maria Teresa's blood also flowed: 'I hope that one day he will show himself a worthy grandson.'[26] Maternal ambition – or anguish – supplied the motive for the grinding work, to say nothing of the tricky diplomacy. 'The only hope that remains to me is that my son can at least be happy,' said Marie Antoinette; it was her reiterated theme.

The trouble with the idea of the armed congress was that it was a fantasy; furthermore, it was a fantasy of the Queen in which no one else shared. Where the Emperor Leopold was concerned, Marie Antoinette might perhaps have recalled her own wry words to Barnave in July. 'My influence over him is non-existent,' she wrote. 'He has regard for the family name and that is all.' Although the Queen was commenting at the time on her inability to secure Austrian acknowledgement of the Constitution, she was in fact all too prescient. It was *realpolitik* that would sway the Emperor Leopold. The Queen might see the French Revolution as 'an insurrection against all established governments', but the Emperor was far more likely to take up arms in the cause of a predatory Austria against a weakened France than in an ideological cause in favour of monarchy. The Emperor did indeed raise serious objections to the idea of the congress in November, questioning which authority in France he would deal with, while Prince Kaunitz thought the whole notion was a waste of time, not so much a fantasy as 'a chimera'. The Princes naturally detested a scheme that would have held them back. Even Louis XVI showed no enthusiasm for the armed congress. Marie Antoinette alone continued to term it 'the only useful and advantageous course'.[27]

Throughout the autumn, as Marie Antoinette pleaded secretly for an armed congress, Barnave took immense trouble over the details of her new role as Queen. He predicted the return of 'happy and serene' days for her if she took his advice. There was still to be panoply as befitted her royal position; for example, the Queen spent 1400 livres on a new court dress for the Feast of All Saints on the eve of her birthday, as she had always done. Louis XVI, said Barnave, was to wear the Cordon Rouge – the order of Saint-Louis – at the Assembly since it was a military order and soldiers would be pleased. One of Barnave's pre-occupations was the precise nature of the theatrical and operatic spectacles that the Queen attended. These were, after all, the traditional opportunities for public acclaim – and Barnave was enthusiastic for the Queen's attendance, so long as no unfortunate choices were made.[28]

Attendance at Grétry's *Richard I* in September, whose notorious song 'O Richard! O mon roi!' had sparked off the riots of 6 October, was considered by Barnave to be a mistake. The Queen should send for the Director and make sure that nothing so tactless took place in the future. Far better was her appearance, with her children, at the Théâtre de la Nation (formerly the Comédie Française) in late November to see *La Partie de Chasse de Henri IV*, an occasion that marked the return of the celebrated actor Préville to the stage. There were further royal appearances in December. On all these occasions the Queen was regally dressed, as she would have been under the former regime, and was happy to sit in the most prominent box. Only that closet counter-revolutionary Madame Elisabeth grumbled in her private letters at the necessity of showing herself on such occasions. 'My God! What fun!' she wrote sarcastically, although even the Princess had to admit, at some public applause the following year, that 'the French had some charming moments'.[29]

The projected return of Mercy was part of Barnave's intention that the Queen should actively encourage the émigrés to come back. Marie Antoinette, for her part, had never ceased to mourn his absence. Certainly Mercy in France would have acted as a more efficient liaison officer than the Queen's sporadic courtiers. In late December, the Comte de Narbonne, an illegitimate son of Louis XV who had become active in attempts at diplomacy between the royal family and the Emperor, added his pleas for Mercy to come back to France. To be fair to Mercy, his health at the time was wretched. But in his refusal, he managed as ever to stress his material concerns, worrying, for example, about his property at Valenciennes ('The municipality still hasn't sent me my four guns back'). If he did return, would his baggage be free of customs duties? That was essential. Mercy pointed out that he had just managed to extricate all his belongings from France, presumably with the exception of the guns, apart obviously from the house in Paris, which was still guarded by his Newfoundland dogs named Sultan, Castor, Castorine – and, presumably for his fierce temperament, Jacobin.*[30]

Barnave had more luck in convincing the Queen to recall the Princesse de Lamballe, still titular Superintendent of her Household, who had fled after Varennes. A good deal of persuasion was needed, because for a while the Queen was deeply opposed to the idea. In September, for example, she wrote to her former favourite, who was ill near Aix, bewailing 'the race of tigers' that had overwhelmed the kingdom and urging her to stay away from the country at all costs. Even though the acceptance of the Constitution, which had become necessary, would probably give some moments of relief from the tigers, the Queen still did not want the Princesse to fall into their cage: 'Ah, don't come my friend; come back as late as possible, your heart will be too disappointed, you will have too much to cry about with all our misfortunes, you who love me so tenderly.' Three days later she reiterated the prohibition: 'No, once again, don't come back, my dear heart; don't throw yourself in the mouth of the tiger; I've already got too many worries with my husband and my poor little children.' Her son, her *chou*

---

* Other people also gave a political twist to their dogs' names; the witty Prince de Ligne called two of his Turgot and Mirabeau because 'I always think of hunting dogs when I hear the names of "those Economists".'[31]

d'amour, was on her knees as she wrote and added his own signature: 'by the hand of the little Dauphin. Louis.'[32]

Nevertheless, on 29 September, the Queen engaged with Barnave that the Princesse de Lamballe would return, as 'a patriotic act and a pledge of her intentions'. A month later, in response to her mistress's messages, the faithful Princesse left Aix, and was back in Paris, via a visit to the Duc de Penthièvre, by mid-November. Prudently, she made her will in advance, making provision for charity – the Hôtel Dieu – and also the care of her little dogs. The Princesse was given an apartment close to the Queen's in the Tuileries. Although in certain quarters she was immediately accused of returning for 'lesbian practices', the Princesse de Lamballe actually resumed her ceremonial role at the Queen's side just as Barnave wished. On a more informal level, as one dog lover to another, the Princesse brought a little red-and-white spaniel for Marie Antoinette, to cheer the Tuileries; originally called Thisbée, its name was later transmuted into the cosier Mignon.[33]

Much later the Marquise de Tourzel would make out that the Queen, in requesting the Princesse de Lamballe's return, was doing her friend a favour; she enabled the Princesse to retain her position as Superintendent, which would otherwise have been terminated. It was true that the Queen dared not appoint a new household lest the old one be declared obsolete; as a result she suffered from lack of the ritual company of a court. With sublime ingratitude some of the grand ladies sulked at their perceived demotion under the new order, as, for example, the Duchesse de Duras who felt hardly used by the loss of her footstool. 'Nobody comes to my card parties,' exclaimed the Queen bitterly. 'The King goes solitarily to bed. No allowance is made for political necessity; we are punished for our misfortunes.'[34] Nevertheless the Marquise de Tourzel's interpretation cannot be reconciled with the total change in the Queen's attitude; in September she gave emotional warnings and in October a summons. For better or for worse it was Marie Antoinette, following the precepts of Barnave, who was responsible for the return of the Princesse de Lamballe to France.

The visible loyalty of the Princesse de Lamballe, in the public eye, contrasted with that of the émigré Princes. Since members of the former Constitutional Assembly were debarred from the new Legislative Assembly, the latter was inevitably more radical. On 31 October, influenced by Brissot and his Girondins, the Assembly proposed a decree by which those émigrés who did not immediately quit all armed camps abroad were guilty of conspiracy. For themselves, they were sentenced to death and confiscation of their property; but the properties of members of the same family who had not left France were also to be confiscated. On the advice of Barnave, the King exercised his veto on the measure. He also vetoed a measure that criminalized those French men and women who had stayed in France, but continued to attend non-juror Masses.

In other ways, however, the King still temporized. On 1 January 1792 Louis XVI received a New Year's deputation from the municipality of Paris; he did so with characteristic gaucheness, scarcely bothering to interrupt his game of billiards, and listening with apparent indifference to the various compliments bestowed. The Queen, on the other hand, having written her usual New Year's letter to Princesse Louise on 'the value of friends like you and yours' in misfortune, displayed herself in a new court dress of embroidered blue satin.[35] She did so with a panache that Barnave would have approved, had the Feuillant triumvir not begun to be disillusioned with the Queen's real intentions, just as the constitutionalist Feuillant party itself began to decline in power. Barnave retreated from Paris shortly after the New Year.

Nevertheless, on this day the King officially declared the émigré Princes to be traitors. And on 25 January a deputation from the Assembly brought a decree against the Emperor Leopold for Louis to sign. In another extremely long memorandum to her brother – 'long for me who is not used to it' – the Queen attempted to justify the fact that he did so. It was essential, she wrote, for the King to be seen to be faithful to the Constitution, and thus link himself to the 'national honour' that was being wounded by menaces and provocations from outside; only in this way could he rally the public confidence, which was gradually being stolen from him.[36]

Were there renewed plans for escape during this period? That would be a third strand to the Queen's policy, added to her private playing along with Barnave and her secret promotion of the armed congress. It would seem so. Rumours of a fresh escape there certainly were, stories that the King had got out disguised as a woman, and so forth. Naturally after Varennes the Tuileries was riddled with spies doubling as servants. One guard, hearing such a rumour, gave an order on his own initiative for the royal family to be locked up for an entire day. Fersen, having visited Turin and Vienna – where he had a sentimental reunion with the Duchesse de Polignac – was back in Brussels. On 19 October 1791 the Queen had told him, 'We have a project a little like that of June' for the middle of November and she promised to let him know more in about ten days' time. Nothing further was heard of this scheme.

It was left to King Gustav of Sweden, inspired not only by Fersen but by the monarchical solidarity that the Emperor seemed to lack, to seek fresh ways to rescue the royal family in the spring of 1792. King Gustav and Fersen parted company, however, on how the escape should be achieved. The Swedish King thought his fellow monarch should go alone but Fersen pointed to the danger of leaving the Queen and Dauphin behind in France as hostages. With his family in their power, it would be only too easy for the French to work on the 'feeble and irresolute' spirit of the King under such circumstances; alternatively they might well declare a Regency on behalf of the boy.[37]

For all the Queen's earlier prohibitions, Fersen arrived back in France in February, wearing disguise and travelling on a false passport (he had been named among the guilty 'abductors' of Varennes). The weather was so cold that Fersen could hear the wheels of the carriages crunching 'as they do in Sweden'. He lurked in the attic of Eléanore Sullivan's house, where he was discreetly passed food by his generous mistress, with Quentin Craufurd left in ignorance.[38]

Fersen returned to a France where 'a general cry of war was being heard', in the words of Marie Antoinette, and nobody had any doubts that war would soon take place. Brissot and the

Girondins were beginning to regard a struggle against the counter-revolutionary forces abroad as a cleansing process or 'a school of virtue'. It was Robespierre, the Jacobin, who made a far more cautious speech on the subject, pointing out how pleased the enemies of France would be if that country declared war, since it would provide them with a heaven-sent opportunity for their own aggression.[39] The alliance of Austria and Prussia on 7 February – those hereditary enemies now joined by a common cause of territorial aggrandizement – justified the observation.

Fersen managed to get into the Tuileries, using a side door. He saw the Queen on 13 February. They had not met since that farewell in the darkness at the Bondy *poste* over six months earlier. Fersen spent the night there, or, in a notorious phrase, which a subsequent editor of his *Journal intime* tried unsuccessfully to eliminate, '*Resté là*.'[40] Much has been made of this particular entry because the phrase was often used by Fersen to indicate spending the night with one of his numerous mistresses; this is the only occasion on which it has been found to apply to Marie Antoinette. It seems strange, however, to argue on the evidence of a solitary entry that this was the only time the Count and the Queen had sex. There may, after all, have been many other entries of '*Resté là*' that applied to 'Elle', as the Queen was known, which have not survived the late-nineteenth-century censor, Fersen's great-nephew Baron Klinckowström.

Fersen and Marie Antoinette had first met nearly twenty years ago and had been close for at least twelve of them; both were approaching middle age by the standards of the time; the Tuileries, with its National Guard whose presence Fersen noted with alarm, was not the free and easy Petit Trianon. If they had not made love before, they were unlikely to start now. It has been argued here that the Queen and Fersen did have an affair starting in 1783, petering out into a purely romantic relationship. Perhaps, then, there was a nostalgic fling at the Tuileries – one rather hopes so – or perhaps the phrase for once meant just what it said: 'Stayed there.'

Fersen needed primarily to see the King, which was a very different motive for his remaining within the Tuileries precincts overnight instead of risking another entry. On behalf of King Gustav he had to discuss the question of escape. But he got nowhere. It was not only the fact of continuing supervision but Louis XVI's own scruples that stood in the way; he had by now promised to remain in France on numerous occasions and the King, wrote Fersen, is 'an honourable man'. The most the King would do was agree to be guided through the forest by 'smugglers' to meet light troops in the event of an invasion. It was on this occasion that Louis made the melancholy confidence to Fersen quoted earlier on the subject of 14 July 1789. He should have gone to Metz then, he said; he had his opportunity and it had never come again. (Varennes was somehow obliterated from his memory.) Fersen lingered in Paris for a while, still concealed at the house of Eléanore Sullivan, although the Queen imagined that he had already left for Spain. He finally departed on 21 February, taking with him the dog Odin of whom a sibling had in happier days been presented to the Queen of France.

CHAPTER TWENTY-THREE

Violence and Rage

'It was a case of violence and rage on one side, feebleness and inertia on the other.'

Marie Antoinette to Count Mercy d'Argenteau
concerning 20 June 1792

On 20 April 1792, Louis XVI declared war upon what Marie Antoinette significantly described as 'the House of Austria'. The Marquise de Tourzel remembered how the King left the Tuileries for the Legislative Assembly with sadness painted on his face. Less compassionately, Madame de Staël described how Louis XVI looked left and right with the vacant curiosity of the short-sighted, and proposed war in the same flat voice as he would have proposed the least important measure in the world.[1] For the time being, Prussia was not mentioned although there were many denunciations of the Austro-Prussian defensive treaty of February. The Declaration of War followed an ultimatum of 5 April, calling for the removal of the émigré forces from their bases along the Rhine, which was ignored by Austria. The Feuillants, unwilling war-makers, gave way to a ministry of Girondins who had been pressing for a cleansing war since October.

Above all, Austria must avoid the appearance of meddling in the internal affairs of France, wrote Marie Antoinette to Mercy on 30 April. In another letter she emphasized the point again: 'The French will always repulse all political intervention by foreigners in their affairs.' In fact Marie Antoinette understood

Austria to be embarking on a mission to rescue the French royal family, not as a war of aggression to add territory to the Austrian Empire at France's expense. The latter project was unacceptable: she told the Dauphin's valet Huë firmly, for her 'the interests of France' came first – 'before everything'.[2]

Unfortunately there was a new Emperor in Austria. Leopold II died at the beginning of March, and was succeeded by his son, a man of a far more zealous and militaristic turn of mind. Francis II, Leopold's son, that boy whose birth had been greeted with such enthusiasm by Maria Teresa with her public announcement at the theatre, was now twenty-four. If his young wife, Maria Carolina's daughter, was said to resemble Marie Antoinette, more positive signs of family closeness hardly existed. Whatever the lack of an emotional bond between Marie Antoinette and Leopold, they had at least grown up in the same environment and shared the same august parentage. Francis II had never even met his aunt.

The Queen needed to bear in mind the trenchant warnings of Count Mercy. In February, Mercy had written in sharp terms to the French Queen about 'the lack of consideration by which in the Tuileries they allowed themselves to believe that all the conveniences of the Austrian monarchy should yield to those of France'. The previous summer there had even been a suggestion that the French King should be prepared to cede the border fortresses, such as Cambrai, Douai and Valenciennes, in exchange for imperial support as a kind of advance on expenses.[3]

If the Queen was hoping for rescue as a result of military action, the King's new Girondin ministry under General Dumouriez had a very different agenda. This was to be a national campaign in support of revolutionary ideals, or rather – a double negative – in opposition to counter-revolutionary ones. Hostility to 'the Austrian woman' was inevitably intensified by the war; she was now, in crude modern terms, an enemy alien. The Queen's anger at the idea of Austrian territorial claims on France would have been scarcely credible to those who demonized her. Instead, the Girondin orator Pierre Vergniaud pointed dramatically to the Tuileries itself: 'From here I can see the windows of a palace where counter-revolution is being plotted, where they are working out ways to plunge us once more into the horrors of slavery.' These were sentiments that found a more vulgar expression in the behaviour of the guards at the Tuileries, who, not content with insults, indulged with roars of laughter in a practice now called mooning.[4]

The beginning of a war that he had himself reluctantly declared provoked in Louis XVI one of those fits of silent gloom that were his customary reaction to an intolerable situation. Ten days in May passed without his speaking at all to his family, except for the terse words necessary to play backgammon with Madame Elisabeth. Marie Antoinette for her part saw it as her duty to provide Count Mercy and also Fersen, both in Brussels, with any details that she could glean about the conduct of the war. (However, the assassination of Gustav III and the coming to power of his brother as Regent, a man of very different political sympathies, meant that a Swedish rescue was no longer an option; as Fersen told the Queen, 'this loss is a cruel one'.)[5]

The Queen's new obsession was to avoid the dismemberment of France at the hands of Austria, particularly in the German-speaking east, that she imagined might take place if Austria lost Belgium in the west. This theme of distrust of Austria – the country that she nevertheless hoped would save them – was hammered home in her correspondence throughout the summer.

It is a nice point as to whether the Queen was a traitor for writing in her letters to Mercy such things as 'the plan is to attack by the Savoy and Liège' – even before the declaration of war. A coded letter of 5 June to Fersen reported that the army of General Luckner had been ordered by the Girondin ministry to attack without cease, although Luckner was against it and the troops were both ill supplied and disordered. Eighteen days later the Queen reported, also to Fersen, that Dumouriez was leaving for the army of Luckner the next day, with the intention of causing an insurrection in Brabant.[6] 'The Austrian woman' was, of course, ritually accused of treachery – by those who did not know of this correspondence – simply on the grounds of her birth. By her own lights, however, she was certainly not.

As she told Fersen on 23 June in an elliptical communication concerning the King: 'Your friend is in the greatest danger. His illness is making terrible progress ... Tell his relations about his unfortunate situation.'[7] Threatened, so she believed, with being 'put away' by the Jacobins, her son now seven years old being a target for schemes to take over his education, herself subject to daily menaces in the Tuileries, she still was convinced that she put 'the interests of France' first. In her view these interests were best served by the re-establishment of a proper unfettered monarchy. The present situation had, after all, been brought about by duress – to which in law no loyalty need be given. It was now clear to her that this re-establishment would not take place without some rescue at the hands of a foreign power and to this end she had no wish for the Girondins to win their war. But the army of her dreams was certainly not to be an army of occupation.

The ill-prepared French campaign against Austria in the Netherlands did not prosper. At the same time the Girondins continued to present Louis XVI with challenges that were predestined to provoke his veto. These included proposals for the deportation of non-juror priests and the establishment of a large body of provincial armed troops known as Confederates (*fédérés*) in a camp outside Paris. As the Girondin ministry foundered, slanderous rumours envenomed the King's new constitutional relationship with the country. The use of the King's veto became the subject of much popular indignation, Marie Antoinette receiving a new abusive nickname of 'Madame Veto'. The genesis of the next demonstration of people power, on 20 June, lay in the excited belief that the King intended to regain full power by force. The dismissal of the Girondins seemed positive proof of that, as Necker's dismissal had aroused rage three years earlier.

As 20 June was the anniversary of the flight to Varennes (to say nothing of the Tennis Court Oath in 1789), its approach was regarded with dread by the King, Queen and the much curtailed court. All felt unprotected. The King's new personal bodyguard under the Duc de Brissac, which had recently been granted him as part of the package of the Constitution, was removed again by the Girondins at the end of May. The National

Guards, so much less assured in their loyalties, returned. The Feast of Corpus Christi fell on 10 June this year; the gorgeous processions and radiant royal appearances were things of the past. The King made a brief showing alone in the chapel of the Tuileries. He was not in court dress. His air of stupor, the product of desperation, led to stories that he had been drunk.[8]

On 20 June itself, a mob of terrifying aspect was allowed into the Tuileries gardens by the National Guard. Sweating with the heat, they wore clothes so filthy that they could be smelt from the windows beneath which they demonstrated. These people carried pikes, hatchets and other sharp implements, which did not seem the less threatening because they were decorated with cheerful tricoloured ribbons. When they broke into the palace they were found to be also bearing some grisly symbols such as a gibbet from which a stained doll dangled, labelled 'Marie Antoinette à la lanterne'. (The traditional practical way in which Parisian crowds disposed of their enemies was to hang them from the nearest lamp-post.) A bullock's heart was labelled 'The heart of Louis XVI'; the horns of an ox bore an obscene reference to the King's cuckoldry.[9]

As members of the mob broke into the King's apartments, cries were heard of 'Where is he, the *bougre*?'[10] Then placards were thrust into Louis XVI's face with messages like 'Tremble, Tyrant!' When Sieur Joly, a dancer at the Opéra as well as a cannoneer in the National Guard, found the King, he saw the aged Duc de Mouchy, Marshal of France, sitting firmly in front of him, determined to protect his sovereign to the last with his own body.

Louis XVI behaved admirably. It was a situation where impassivity had its uses. He did not tremble. He adopted the small *bonnet rouge* proffered on the end of a butcher's pike with equanimity, being only surprised that such a low-class individual should address him simply as 'Monsieur' instead of 'Majesté'. The cap, despite the King's efforts to enlarge it, perched uneasily on his big head. But the King happily drank a toast to the health of the people. In a famous anecdote – probably true – he asked a grenadier to feel his heart and test whether it was beating any faster. It was not. Madame Elisabeth also behaved with great nobility. When she heard the death-threats to her sister-in-law, she tried to act as a decoy so that the hated Marie Antoinette could escape: 'Don't undeceive them, let them think that I am the Queen...'

Marie Antoinette, who must have expected a rerun of 6 October 1789, was helped to safety by her entourage. She had originally wished to take her place at the King's side, telling those who tried to stop her that they were trying to damage her reputation. However, the Queen was reminded by her servants that her presence might pose an additional danger to the King, who would certainly try to defend her if she was threatened and thus be killed himself. Furthermore the Queen must remember that she was 'also a mother' as well as a wife.[11]

Marie Antoinette took the point. Afterwards, having cowered with her children listening to the blows of hatchets on the panelling of the Dauphin's doors before getting away through a secret exit, the Queen was asked if she had been 'much afraid'. 'No,' she replied. 'But I suffered from being separated from Louis XVI at a moment when his life was in danger.' Instead, she had the consolation of staying with the children, which was also 'one of my duties'. When it was all over, the King sent for his family. There was a touching scene as Marie Antoinette rushed into his arms, the children fell at his knees and Madame Elisabeth, not to be left out, embraced her brother from behind.

The effects on the two children, whose world had once again been turned upside down, may be imagined. Afterwards one of the deputies of the Legislative Assembly, investigating how such an undisciplined attack could possibly have taken place, asked how old Madame Royale was – he called her 'Mademoiselle'. The answer was thirteen and a half but the Queen merely replied that her daughter was old enough to feel the horror of such scenes all too keenly. It was no wonder, as Pauline de Tourzel pointed out, that Marie Thérèse became increasingly serious and withdrawn, losing 'all the joy of childhood'. The Dauphin, who had been half extinguished by the vast *bonnet rouge* presented to him, could not speak at all. He simply hugged both his parents. The next morning, however, he came up with one of his poignant questions to the valet Huë, of the sort that were beginning to punctuate his family's ordeals. 'Is it still yesterday?' he asked, just as he had interrogated Huë about the turnaround at Varennes, and the Marquise de Tourzel on the morning after 6 October 1789.[12]

Despite the dozen deputies, including Pétion, who belatedly came from the Legislative Assembly to the King's assistance and the presence of the National Guards, proper order was not restored until the evening. By this time all the doors of the royal apartments were broken. As the Queen told Mercy afterwards, it was a case of 'violence and rage' on one side, 'feebleness and inertia' on the other – the side of the people who were supposed to protect them. All the same, she emphasized to Huë the need for discretion when he gave evidence at the ensuing investigation. 'No impression must be given,' she told him, 'that either the King or I retain the slightest resentment for what has happened.'[13]

Her real feelings, hardly surprisingly, were very different. Resentment was too mild a word for the panic she had experienced, for all the 'calm nobility' of her outward demeanour. This was particularly true of the danger to her children: 'Save my son,' the Queen had cried at one point. Madame Campan believed that it was as a result of the events of 20 June 1792 that Marie Antoinette turned to foreign aid as the only hope.[14] In fact, as we have seen, her decision predated the invasion of the Tuileries. The experience of this day amply confirmed – and indeed justified – what she felt already.

With the approach of 14 July, another potentially devastating anniversary, it was feared that worse was to come. Should the royal family attempt another precipitate flight as being the least bad option? Count Mercy, influenced by the attack of the mob on 20 June, thought it was. Schemes were discussed. One possibility was to head for Compiègne with La Fayette protecting them. Château Gallon, near Rouen in Normandy, was also mentioned, where the Duc de Liancourt – he who had broken the news of the 'revolution' to Louis XVI in 1789 – offered some loyal Norman troops. But from the coast of Normandy they might end by having to take ship to England. According

Silk cloth woven for Marie Antoinette for the summer furnishings of her own room at Versailles, 1785.

A group portrait by Mme Vigée Le Brun intended as a propaganda exercise to emphasise Marie Antoinette's role as royal mother; her second son, Louis Charles, is on her lap; unfortunately her fourth child, Madame Sophie, died as a baby and had to be painted out; the Dauphin, Louis Joseph, points to the empty cradle.

Marie Antoinette's second son, Louis Charles,
Duc de Normandie, born 27 March 1785, became Dauphin on
the death of his elder brother and was hailed by royalists
as King Louis XVII on the death of his father.

Louis XVI; despite his regal air here, contemporaries agreed that he could not in fact project majesty in real life.

Extract from Louis XVI's Journal concerning the flight to Varennes
on Monday 21 June: '*Départ à minuit de Paris, arrivé et arresté à
Varennes en Argonne à onze heures du soir.*'

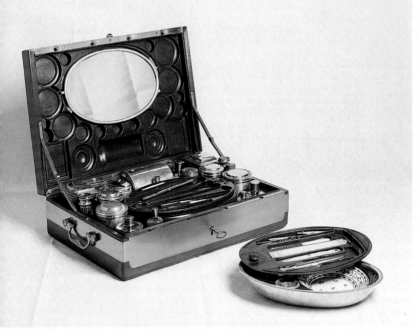

The *nécessaire* Marie Antoinette took with her to Varennes:
a combination of a dressing-case and a picnic basket.

Furniture made for Marie Antoinette by J-H Riesener: a mechanical table with the mechanism by Merklein and a secretaire.

Madame Campan (*née* Genet), the Queen's First Lady of the Bedchamber, who subsequently wrote her memoirs.

Porcelain coffee cup and saucer made to commemorate the birth of the first Dauphin, 1781.

Engraving of the march of the market-women on Versailles, 5 October 1789.

A cartoon of Marie Antoinette as a harpy tearing up *The Declaration of the Rights of Man* with her claws.

to Huë, the Queen shuddered away from the fate of the Stuart King James II; in 1689 he had fled in a fishing boat to France, never to regain his realm. Bertrand de Molleville offered another explanation: the Queen disliked Liancourt's previous democratic or constitutionalist views (just as she had never come to trust La Fayette).[15]

The real explanation for the Queen's reluctance to consider such schemes, leaving their plausibility aside, was different. For one thing, the capital might actually be safer than the French provinces, which were already the scene of revolutionary violence. Second and more importantly, Marie Antoinette believed that it was from Paris that the royal family would be rescued. Prussia entered the war in early July, and the joint Austro-Prussian army was now under the command of the Duke of Brunswick. She told Madame Campan that the Duke's plan, 'which he has communicated to us, is to come within these very walls to deliver us'.[16]

The commemoration of the fall of the Bastille, on 14 July, was attended by a host of Confederate troops, thronging into Paris from the provinces. The King attended on horseback. After his experience of 20 June, he consented to wear a thickly quilted under-waistcoat as a guard against possible assassination. The Queen, the children and Madame Elisabeth, with the Princesse de Lamballe and the Marquise de Tourzel in official attendance, went by carriage. The Marquise wept as she witnessed what she called 'the saddest ceremony': the King taking the oath to the patriotic 'Federation', while the Queen watched him through a spyglass. It was, however, the cries accompanying the ritual that were the most depressing element, rather than the oath itself. 'Down with the veto!' was frequently heard, along with acclamations for the Mayor: 'Long live Pétion, good old Pétion!' Most strident of all were the cries of 'Long live the *sans-culottes*!'* People waved branches, while banners with the

---

* This general term for a revolutionary activist – meaning literally without breeches – referred to the typical costume of baggy trousers, short jacket (*carmagnole*) and wooden sabots of the working class, whether small tradesman, labourer or vagrant.

same anti-monarchical messages bobbed up and down among the heads.[17]

In the following tense weeks, during the full heat of the Parisian summer, the quality of the royal family's life at the Tuileries deteriorated. All this year the King had been allowed a surprising freedom in riding to the environs of the city, including Saint Cloud and Meudon, as well as to the Bois de Boulogne, as his *Journal* bore witness. But in July there were no rides. On 20 July the sentence against that stormy petrel, Jeanne Comtesse de Lamotte Valois, was officially quashed by the Paris court as a deliberate affront to the monarchy, although the Comtesse herself was already dead in London, under circumstances which were, like the rest of her life, both scandalous and mysterious. This was a signal for further demonstrations of hostility, if any were needed. The next day the Queen reported to Fersen that the insults were now so terrible that none of them, not the King, the Queen nor Madame Elisabeth, dared walk in the gardens.[18]

It was a horrible, humid, brooding atmosphere as the nation – *la patrie* – was officially proclaimed in danger of invasion. Armed men paraded the streets singing the 'Ça Ira', that jaunty revolutionary song generally regarded as 'the signal of sedition', of which one key line ran: 'We shall hang all the aristocrats.' There were renewed distressing rumours that the Dauphin would be removed from his parents, with the possibility of a Regency in his name; the Girondins were said to actively favour this. One story suggested that the King had gone mad and was roaming crazily around the Tuileries – which of course made a Regency a necessity.[19] Marie Antoinette moved from her ground-floor apartment to one close to that of her husband and the Dauphin.

Into this world of suspicion and fear, the Brunswick Manifesto of 25 July came as a match to dry timber. The Duke of Brunswick himself was a veteran campaigner who had fought brilliantly for Prussia in the Seven Years' War and later for Prussia in the cause of the Stadtholder in Holland against the Patriots; he was an enlightened man who had been close to many of the *philosophes*. The manifesto was, however, fatally permeated with émigré sentiments. The French people were openly invited to rise up against 'the odious schemes of their oppressors' – that is to say, the existing government, for better or for worse. The Manifesto also threatened 'an exemplary and ever-memorable vengeance' and the 'total destruction' of Paris if the Tuileries was the subject of a further attack and if the King and royal family 'suffered even the slightest violence'. The campaign was intended 'to put an end to anarchy in the interior of France' as well as to deliver the royal family.[20]

Where now was Marie Antoinette's unreal dream of rescue by a force that would not interfere with the country's internal affairs? Nothing could have been more helpful to the republican sentiments in the opposition than this manifesto. They now had the excuse they needed to discuss openly the imperative to depose the King – and the means by which it should be done. On 31 July, one of the forty-eight administrative *sections* into which Paris was now divided, that of Mauconseil, publicly pronounced Louis XVI to be 'a despicable tyrant ... Let us strike this colossus of despotism.' In a grim way the Mauconseil resolution stood the Brunswick Manifesto on its head. Yes, the French people must indeed turn against the odious schemes of their oppressors – in order to declare with one accord: 'Louis XVI is no longer King of the French.'[21]

A few days earlier, a public dinner had been held in the ruins of the Bastille, at which calls were made for the fall of the monarchy, while petitions to that effect flooded into the Assembly. By 3 August, Pétion was able to ask for an end to monarchical government in the name of forty-six out of the forty-eight *sections*. The importation of further Confederate troops from the provinces, especially from Marseilles, described to Fersen by Marie Antoinette as 'the arrival of a great quantity of extremely suspicious strangers', signified the armed fist by which this message might shortly be struck home.[22]

The day of the Mauconseil *section* resolution, 31 July, was also the day of the King's last entry in his *Journal*; predictably it read 'Rien'. Louis XVI now took refuge in 'incessant' reading of the history of Charles I. He told his wife that everything that was happening in France was an exact imitation of what had happened during the English Revolution, and he hoped that his studies would enable him to do better than that monarch (from whom he was descended) in the coming crisis – for no one was in any doubt by now, whether revolutionary or monarchist, that the Tuileries was going to be attacked. On Sunday, 5 August, the King held his usual *lever* at the Tuileries. It was well attended by members of the current administration, which was rapidly losing its grip on power in the city. There was respect – of a sort – and Bertrand de Molleville even thought the occasion 'brilliant'. An English doctor, John Moore, recently arrived in Paris, reported a very different scene at the Palais-Royal. Adrenalin was flowing – republican adrenalin, any mention of the name of the King being generally received with hoots of derisive laughter.[23] Moore's experience was more prescient than that of Molleville.

The day of 9 August, hot as before, began with a delusive calm inside the Tuileries. The King, Queen, Madame Elisabeth and Marie Thérèse attended Mass as usual although one person present noted how the royal ladies never raised their eyes from their prayer books.* Outside, the news that the attack was planned for that night began to flow through the city. The young Comte de La Rochefoucauld, son of the Duc de Liancourt, was at a matinée at the Comédie Française when he heard the rumours that the crowds were beginning to assemble in the Faubourg Saint-Antoine. Immediately he returned to the Tuileries. The drums of the National Guard were sounded and a body of them arrived at the palace, saying they were 'voluntary soldiers in the service of the King'. Some members of the National Guard were, however, less reliable politically and there were already cries of 'No more King!' from among their number. There was another armed force of volunteer aristocrats, about 300 of them, some of whose weapons were rudimentary if heroic. The main defence of the King was expected to be provided by his ultra-loyal Swiss Guards.[24]

---

* This scene at Mass was subsequently the subject of a picture by the painter Marie Antoinette favoured, Hubert Robert.

The Cent-Suisses du Roi constituted an impressive body of crack troops. They led somewhat segregated lives in their barracks, preserving their own language and customs, although they had been in the service of the French King since the late fifteenth century and had a French colonel-in-chief, the Duc de Brissac. On ceremonial occasions, they still wore the ancient uniform of the liberators of Switzerland, but were otherwise dressed in blue uniforms braided in gold, with red breeches. When the Guards were drawn up in formation to the roll of their huge drums, wrote the Comte d'Hezecques, you would still think you saw 'the elite of a Swiss canton' marching against the oppressor.[25]

Tough and dedicated, the Swiss Guards were easily interpreted as symbols of the monarchy by its enemies. On 1 August one Swiss had written back to his homeland: 'The Confederates from Marseilles have announced that their objective is the disarmament of the Swiss Guards but we have all decided to surrender our arms only with our lives.' As the attack was expected, the Swiss Guards at the Tuileries were drawn up like 'real walls', their soldier-like silence in marked contrast to the perpetual din made by the much less professional National Guards.[26]

An extraordinary concession to the impending crisis was now made: the King's *coucher* was omitted. This ceremony had even taken place on the evening on 20 June, following the King's humiliation at the hands of the *sans-culottes*. Nothing could have made clearer the sense of a regime – a way of life – coming to an end. Instead, as the night wore on, the scene in the King's bedchamber was one of chaos, with people crowding in and sitting everywhere, on the ground, on chairs, on console tables. Even so, with an obstinate maintenance of standards, some minor members of the royal household tried to prevent anyone sitting down in the presence of the King. Louis XVI himself, having not undressed (or been undressed), was still wearing his purple coat and the wreckage of his formal powdered hairstyle. Camille Durand, of the National Guard volunteers, noticed how flushed the King was, his eyes extremely red.[27]

The Queen, Madame Elisabeth and their ladies did not

undress either; only the children went to sleep. At one o'clock Marie Antoinette and her sister-in-law lay down together on a sofa in one of the little rooms of the mezzanine floor. All of the adults were still awake when the raucous tocsins began sounding, summoning revolutionaries all over Paris to the long-anticipated assault. Durand in the Tuileries heard one tocsin at midnight, taking over as the clock's bell ceased to toll, as did John Moore. But the streets were still clear and Moore was not awakened again until two o'clock when his landlord informed him that the Tuileries was about to be attacked. La Rochefoucauld, sleeping at the Tuileries, was not awakened until 3 a.m. when he went down to the King. At four o'clock the Queen went to the King's bedchamber. When she came back, she informed Madame Elisabeth that the King refused to don his quilted waistcoat. He had done so on 20 June when he might have been the solitary target of an assassin. Now he was determined to share in the general fate on equal terms.[28]

But there was a more serious development. The Marquis de Mandat had been put in charge of the National Guard at the Assembly the day before with the instruction to 'repel force with force'. He was then called to the Hôtel de Ville by the new revolutionary Commune of Paris, which considered itself in charge of the National Guard. As Mandat left, he was struck down and killed by a bullet. The defence of the Tuileries was now in the hands of Pierre Louis Roederer, Procurator-General of the Paris Prefecture (*Département de la Seine*) and a deputy from Metz. The substitution was liable to cause additional dismay in such a critical situation since Roederer was inevitably regarded as the Assembly's man rather than the King's. Furthermore Roederer was timid and not absolutely sure of the limits of his authority.[29] At one point Madame Elisabeth tried to distract the Queen by drawing her attention to the red streaks beginning to appear in the sky: 'Sister, come and see the dawn rise.' Red sky in the morning – *rouge matin, chagrin* – is regarded as a bad omen in many countries; certainly the forewarning was justified on 10 August. By five o'clock one estimate had 10,000 men pressing towards the courtyards and gardens of the Tuileries.

The decision was now made that the King should inspect the

defences in order to improve morale. By this time 'pale as a corpse' but nevertheless composed, Louis XVI proceeded on his tour of the various posts about five o'clock; the Comte de La Rochefoucauld accompanied him. Marie Antoinette wished to go too with the children. Fifty years earlier the young Maria Teresa, under threat from Frederick II, had used the image of herself and the infant Joseph to arouse the chivalry of her subjects: 'What will become of this child?' Perhaps Marie Antoinette had in mind some similar appeal. The danger was, however, reckoned to be too great. As it was, the King's mission was an unfortunate failure. Not only did he fail to rise to such an occasion with the presence and oratory that it demanded, but he also exhibited himself to the scorn of the disaffected National Guards. And this proved to be contagious. To the horror of the royal party inside the Tuileries, the King was greeted with jeers. 'Good God! It is the King they are shouting at,' exclaimed Dubouchage, the Minister of the Navy.[30]

Afterwards Marie Antoinette confided to Madame Campan that it would have been better for the King to have remained inside rather than be subjected to such insults. Certainly, the idea that the National Guards could not be trusted contributed to the urgent debate now taking place between Roederer and the Queen as to whether or not the royal family should take refuge with the Assembly, situated on the far side of the Tuileries precinct. Roederer thought this course presented 'the least danger', whereas Dubouchage countered: 'You are proposing to hand over the King to his enemy!' Similarly disinclined to throw them all on the mercies of the Assembly, Marie Antoinette believed that it would be better to stay where they were. She pointed out to Roederer: 'Sir, there are some forces here.' The discussion was soon joined by the King, rather hot and breathless from his experiences but otherwise untroubled, even though one observer had compared him outside to an animal being furiously tormented by pursuing flies.[31]

The Queen was right about the forces. Estimates of numbers vary. However, with the Swiss Guards outside and those lining the Great Staircase, about 1000 in total, a force of the mounted gendarmerie of about the same size and the 300 or so aristocratic fighters determined to defend the King to the last, there were over 2000 armed men available, leaving aside those National Guards who would continue to protect their chief executive. Therefore it is possible at least that the Tuileries could have been held, with further consequences that can only be the subject of speculation.[32] In reality it was Roederer who won the argument by playing his ace: the Queen's natural concern for the safety of her family.

'Madame, do you really want to make yourself responsible for the massacre of the King, your children, yourself, to say nothing of the faithful servants that surround you?' he asked her. 'On the contrary, what would I not do to be the only victim?' she replied.[33] By this time there were growing noises outside, and the pounding on the main door had reached fever pitch.

Eventually, at eight o'clock, Marie Antoinette gave way. She agreed to take shelter with the Assembly. Her anguish was palpable but she contented herself with telling Roederer that she held him personally responsible for the safety of her husband and son. 'We can at least die with you,' replied Roederer. Although Marie Antoinette was the major advocate of remaining, she made 'no show of masculinity or heroics' in presenting her case, in the approving opinion of Roederer. As ever in a crisis, Marie Antoinette showed herself the forceful one who nonetheless could not bring herself finally to impose her will. The King could not make up his mind, but was inclined to favour staying put, since he had formed an incorrectly low estimate of the hostile numbers outside (due to his short-sightedness, perhaps). But the King went with the decision without fuss. He told the courtiers around him: 'I am going to the National Assembly.' Then he looked steadily at Roederer and glanced at the Queen. He raised his hand: 'Let's go [*Marchons*].'[34]

There were embraces and farewells – and brandy for the troops who would be left behind. Marie Antoinette made a gracious speech, in order to heal the jealousies between the National Guards and the aristocrats: 'Gentlemen, we all have the same interests ... These generous servitors will share your dangers, fight with you and for you to the last extremity.' Durand of the National Guard listened to a proclamation given in the Cour des Suisses: 'Citizen soldiers, soldier citizens, French and Swiss ... Our Chief of the Executive Power is menaced. In the name of the law it is forbidden to you to attack; but you are authorized to repel force with force.'

Most of the waiting-women were going to be left behind, the Queen with difficulty having secured Roederer's agreement to take the Princesse de Lamballe and the Marquise de Tourzel with them. The Princesse de Tarante who was staying offered to look after the latter's daughter Pauline. The women asked what they should do. 'We'll find you back here,' replied the Queen positively. 'If the King's downfall is decreed by the Assembly, he will accept it.' As a result, no one thought to provide the royal family with any personal belongings. The Queen's confidence in the outcome was paralleled by that of the King. He may have genuinely believed that his departure from the Tuileries would distract the mob and assuage its fury against the remaining inhabitants of the Tuileries. It was the Princesse de Lamballe who said grimly: 'We shall never come back.'[35]

The little procession that now filed its way through the western garden door, across a courtyard, to the site of the Assembly, consisted of six ministers as an additional escort as well as Swiss Guards and grenadiers from the National Guard. In spite of this, the crowd pressed round them. If the Princesse de Lamballe was fearful, Madame Elisabeth maintained the heroic religious composure of one about to be martyred; she even preached forgiveness to La Rochefoucauld, who could not help replying that he personally was only thinking of vengeance. Marie Antoinette attempted a semblance of cheerfulness but broke down every few minutes and had to wipe her eyes with her handkerchief. La Rochefoucauld, who gave her his arm, found that she was trembling uncontrollably.[36]

Only the Dauphin managed to maintain some kind of childish normality, kicking at the leaves. The King peered at the heaps gathered by the Tuileries gardeners and with a spark of animation at this interesting natural phenomenon observed: 'What a lot of leaves! They have fallen early this year.' Later the press was so great that the Dauphin had to be carried by a giant soldier above the heads of the crowd.

Deputies from the Assembly met them in the course of the journey and formally offered the King asylum. On arrival at the hall, however, the entire royal family with their attendants were penned into the reporters' box behind the chair of President Vergniaud. This was a recess about ten feet square, with a grating fully exposed to the sun. It was now ten o'clock. During the whole of a blazing hot day, they all remained there, apart from a rudimentary meal at about two o'clock served by one Dufour; he left an account of his adventure, including his successful search for the Queen's missing locket containing a miniature family portrait.*

So the future of the monarchy was debated between the extremist republican Jacobins and the more moderate Girondins. The King's words on arrival had been dignified: 'I have come here to avoid a great crime and I believe that I cannot be safer than in your midst.' Now he gazed at the Assembly through his lorgnettes without any visible emotion. The Queen was more agitated. By the evening the fichu of her dress was wet through with perspiration, while her handkerchief was soaked with mopping up her tears. She asked the Comte de La Roche-foucauld, who had managed to get into the box too, for his handkerchief. But the Comte did not dare to lend it to her; instead he went in search of another one.[37]

The reason for his refusal was that his handkerchief was saturated with blood. This came from staunching the wounds of the aged Vicomte de Maillé, one of the survivors of a frightful massacre, which began at the Tuileries about an hour and a half after the departure of the royal family. The responsibility for this orgy of killing would be long debated – and the details will always be subject to controversy. It seems probable that in the

* There were many accounts of this time by survivors; one person, however, who never mentioned her experiences during the next few days was Madame Royale, an unusual omission – her account of Varennes is very full – presumably indicating that it remained too painful to contemplate.

confusion, the King failed to give any order for a ceasefire when he left the palace. By the time the message was conveyed that the Swiss Guards should retreat and join him at the Assembly – a message that may not even have got through – the palace had been stormed and the fighting had begun. Possibly the first shot was fired by one of the Swiss. The republicans were in any case convinced that the Swiss had been ordered by the King to destroy them, and certainly the Swiss sold their lives dearly...[38]

And so began the killings, which left the Tuileries a shambles of blood, corpses, severed limbs, broken furniture and bottles. People were hurled out of windows, killed in cellars, stables and attics, and even in the chapel where some had sought sanctuary, pleading vainly that they had not fired their guns. Rioters broke open the King's wardrobe. Bloodstained hands were wiped on torn velvet mantles that once glittered with gold and the fleur-de-lys. The pike of an assailant, carried in triumph through the streets, was equally likely to be crowned with a fragment of Swiss uniform or a gobbet of human flesh. A young woman called Marie Grosholz, an apprentice sculptor in wax (who would be known to history as Madame Tussaud), never forgot the gravel stained with blood and littered with 'appalling objects' as the 'deep red sun' climbed up the sky. Many of those who tried to flee, whether Swiss or courtiers, were cut down by the mounted gendarmerie in the Place Louis XV. Paris became one huge abattoir, its gutters filled with the corpses of the Swiss, stripped naked and often mutilated. Traumatized wayfarers saw men kneeling in the streets and pleading for mercy before being beaten to death.[39]

Human decency did prevail in one instance. The terrified waiting-women, who had been left behind, cowered together in the Dauphin's apartments with the shutters drawn. At Pauline de Tourzel's suggestion, however, the rooms themselves were illuminated lest the women be mistaken for soldiers. When the *sans-culottes* burst in, they saw the candle-lit female reflections in the mirrors. With shouts of 'We don't kill women' and 'Get up, you trollop [*coquine*], the nation pardons you', the *sans-culottes* spared these victims at least.[40]

*

It was not until the evening that the royal family was released into the nearby accommodation that was to be theirs for the night. This was the sixteenth-century Convent of the Feuillants, which as their clubhouse had earlier given its name to the constitutionalists. The excuse given – that the Tuileries was uninhabitable – was true enough. Soon ordinary citizens would be queuing to goggle at the wreckage of the royal apartments where the Queen's wardrobe had also been pillaged and strewn around, with some people adorning themselves with fragments. Spectators included Thomas Paine, the staunch republican, who was mistaken for an English royalist; he was only saved by being taken equally incorrectly for an American. The progress of the King and Queen to and from the Assembly over the next few days was small in distance. Nevertheless there was plenty of opportunity for gross insult to the 'infamous Antoinette who wanted to bathe the Austrians in our blood' – insults delivered by hordes who were themselves heavily stained with the blood of Frenchmen. In the Place Vendôme they called for the head of the King and the entrails of the Queen.[41] The question remained as to whether the King was not now the Assembly's prisoner, his 'enemy's prisoner', as had been feared by Dubouchage.

The convent provided spartan accommodation only: four rooms with brick floors and whitewashed walls, except for the Queen's narrow cell, which had a green paper. The first need was for clothes; there was a desperate search for fresh linen. The Duchesse de Gramont provided some, while the Countess of Sutherland, the English ambassadress, who had a little boy the same age as Louis Charles, supplied clothes for him. The Princesse de Lamballe sent a note to the Princesse de Tarante asking for a chemise since she had not undressed for two days. About eleven o'clock at night they were visited by representatives of the Assembly to make sure they were still in their designated quarters. The Dauphin was crying. His mother explained that he was worried about the fate of his dear Pauline.[42]

All next day was spent listening to the debate, which would be summed up by the statement of the president, Vergniaud: 'The French people are invited to form a National Convention.

The Chief of the Executive Power [the King] is provisionally suspended from his functions.' In short, it was to be left to a National Convention, to be elected by the people, to decide the ultimate fate of the monarchy. The Queen had recovered her usual composure. That pleased no one, just as her misfortunes evoked no compassion. Doctor Moore attended the scene and remarked with surprise: 'Her beauty is gone!' A Frenchman nearby was convinced that her expression indicated 'rage and the most provoking arrogance'.[43]

At least the old regime struggled to recreate the conditions of the court in the unpromising surroundings of the convent. The King still managed to have his hair dressed. Dinner on 12 August – a day so hot that it became hazy – was a magnificent affair by most standards, if not those of Louis XVI. It included two soups, eight entrées, four roasts and eight desserts. An equally lavish supper followed. The Queen hardly touched her food. The King on the other hand ate heartily, 'as if he was in his own palace', which upset his wife. Further surviving servitors managed to get into the convent. These included Pauline, to the general joy. 'My dear Pauline, don't let us ever be separated again!' cried Marie Thérèse. Pauline also had escaped from the Tuileries with nothing but the clothes she had on; the royal ladies hastily began to adapt one of Madame Elisabeth's dresses for her.[44]

Then there was Madame Campan to whom Marie Antoinette showed a less optimistic face. Stretching out her arms to the First Lady of the Bedchamber, she said: 'It ends with us!' Madame Campan's sister, Madame Auguié, presented her mistress with twenty-five louis; lack of money, essential equipment for a prisoner dealing with jailers, was likely to prove as awkward in the future as lack of linen. In fact, other royal servants tried to present their master with funds before they were dismissed, until the King said that their own need was the greater.[45]

The whereabouts of an appropriate residence for the royal family was the new subject of debate in the Assembly. The original plan had been to use the Luxembourg Palace, former residence of the Comte de Provence. Then the revolutionary Paris Commune, which saw the guardianship of the royal family as its right – or perquisite – protested that the security there was not good enough; other places were dismissed on the same grounds. The Prince de Poix, who had accompanied the King on that progress to the Assembly, offered the family the Hôtel de Noailles. But the choice of the Commune was in fact the Temple, in the Marais district.[46] The Assembly, to whom the King had so happily entrusted himself and his family, where he expected to be 'never safer', now cheerfully abandoned their responsibility and allowed the Commune to have its way.

Painful negotiations followed as to how many attendants were to be allowed to the royal party. At one point Louis XVI, the suspended King, observed that his role model Charles I had at least been allowed to keep his friends with him until the day he mounted the scaffold. In the end the party that set out for the Temple at six o'clock on the evening of Monday, 13 August, consisted of the following: the five royals, the Princesse de Lamballe, the Tourzels, mother and daughter, Mesdames Thibault, Saint Brice and Navarre, the valets Chamilly and Huë.

Marat signed an article in *L'Ami du Peuple* in which he hailed 'The glorious day of the Tenth of August', which could be decisive for 'the triumph of liberty'. But he warned his readers not to give in to 'the voice of false pity'. There was not much danger of that as the thirteen-strong party set out in two heavy-laden carriages, drawn by only two horses apiece, which made progress intolerably slow. Altogether it took two and a half hours to reach the Temple. Along the way they saw the equestrian statue of Louis XIV, which had been toppled and smashed by the mob. One of the commissioners accompanying them, Pierre Manuel, Procurator-General of the Commune, remarked with satisfaction: 'That is how the people treat their kings.'

'It is pleasant that this rage is confined to inanimate objects,' commented the real-life King with a flash of acerbity.[47]

In the meantime a wag had affixed a placard to the Tuileries, 'House to Let', and miles away in the east the army of the Duke of Brunswick was on the march.

CHAPTER TWENTY-FOUR

The Tower

~

'You will see that they will put us into the Tower. They
will make that a real prison for us.'
Marie Antoinette to the Marquise de Tourzel,
13 August 1792

L anterns illuminated the walls of the Temple when the
royal party arrived, as though for a public festival, and a
great crowd of people chanted 'Long live the nation!'
That cry at least was a familiar one. More sinister was the gleeful
Marseillais chant of the guards:

Madame goes up into her Tower
When will she come down again?

It referred to the fact that the Temple was in fact two separate
structures. There was the gracious seventeenth-century palace
where the young Mozart had once played at the invitation of
the Prince de Conti, its governor; more recently it had belonged
to the Comte d'Artois. Then there was the Tower, sixty feet
high, a frowning mediaeval edifice that had once been part of
the old monastery of the Templar Order; this was divided into
a Great Tower and a Small Tower, with various turrets attached.
It lay in an ancient district not far from the Bastille and was not
much known to Parisians from other districts; some of those
who accompanied the royal family had never been there.

Marie Antoinette had always had a horror of the Tower.
Visiting her brother-in-law's palace, she had tried to persuade

him to have its grim adjunct knocked down.* One suspects that this was due more to dislike of a building so far from the pastoral spirit of the Petit Trianon than to some presentiment. Once at the Convent of the Feuillants, however, she had expressed genuine apprehension, exclaiming to the Marquise de Tourzel: 'You will see that they will put us into the Tower. They will make that a real prison for us.' Yet the public dinner served to the royal family on their arrival, together with the commissioners of the Commune who had accompanied them, did take place in the palace. They were all exhausted and Louis Charles fell asleep. There was a move to take the King alone to the Great Tower and leave the rest of them in the palace. In the end, however, orders came that the whole family was to be moved, for the time being, to the Small Tower while work was done to render the Great Tower both habitable and secure.¹

The Small Tower itself, that evening, could scarcely be described as comfortable for the royal party. The eyes of the two valets, Chamilly and Huë, met in silence over the uncurtained and verminous bedstead destined for Louis XVI.² (In spite of this, their master, characteristically, had a good night's sleep.) Indecent engravings in the room for Marie Thérèse were removed on her father's orders. Madame Elisabeth, Pauline de Tourzel and the waiting-woman Madame Navarre all had to sleep together in the kitchen. So they began the process of adaptation to their new home – or prison, the 'real prison' of Marie Antoinette's fears.

Security was, of course, immense. Four commissioners were in attendance at any one time, casting lots for the two who spent the night in the Tower. Twenty guards manned the gate. There were also elaborate precautions over the delivery of items such as books, linen and clothes. The lack of respect to the King – the suspended King – grieved Marie Thérèse. Instead of 'Sire' or 'Majesté', he was now 'Monsieur' or even 'Louis', this man whose own wife did not address him in public as

---

* Royalist pilgrims will not, however, find the Temple today; Napoleon did in 1808 what Marie Antoinette had wanted Artois to do: had it knocked down, specifically to avoid the creation of a hallowed site.

'Louis'. One particular jailer, Rocher, was found particularly detestable by the girl since he specialized in petty humiliations such as taking to his bed early, thus obliging the royal family to file past him. He loved the fact that the wicket gate was so low that the Queen herself had to bow her head before him to enter it, and then there was his deliberate manipulation of his pipe. Madame Elisabeth even asked one of the commissioners why Rocher smoked so persistently in their faces. 'No doubt because he likes it,' was the curt reply. Some of the commissioners also took pleasure in sitting down in the presence of the royal ladies and, as the weather grew colder, putting their feet on the firedogs to block the warmth.[3]

In spite of all this, the royal family was able to develop its own way of life, as prisoners do.[4] In luxury it was certainly a precipitate descent from the comparative ease of the Tuileries where they had spent the last two and three-quarter years. But as a regime it was not atrociously severe. The accommodation of the Small Tower was arranged to give the King a bedroom on the third floor and a little study in the turret. The Queen and others slept on the floor below him. On the first floor was an antechamber, a dining room and the unexpected asset of a book-lined turret. The King revelled in this library – 1500 books that had been the archive of the Knights of Malta. He read something like one book a day, frowning over Voltaire and Rousseau who, he said, had been 'the ruin of France'. The Queen had her beloved tapestry and at one point was able to send for her knitting needles from the Tuileries. The little dog Mignon was also brought in, since there were gardens for exercise.

Nobody had any kind of wardrobe – the Queen seems to have arrived with two dresses, one blue, one dark pink – but orders for lingerie were allowed to be given to the celebrated Madame Éloffe on arrival, and again on 15 and 18 August. In the next two months 25,000 livres would be spent on assorted items such as sheets, stockings, laundry and hats (black beaver tricornes for the Queen and Madame Elisabeth). Sailor suits were ordered for Louis Charles, and the King could still get his shoes from his usual cobbler, Giot, in the rue du Bac. Louis generally wore one of his two coats of plain chestnut brown, with metal filigree buttons, and a white piqué waistcoat. Marie Antoinette's outfits were similarly modest – loose pierrots of *toile de Jouy*, dresses of brown and white sprigged cotton and plain white dimity, worn with lace caps. She also practised the economy of making little changes to her costume with the aid of fichus and shawls. There was a payment of 600 livres to Rose Bertin for August and September; her business still flourished although the couturière herself had left the country in 1791. Much of this sum went on accessories and alterations.[5]

Food was still served liberally. The royal servants, knowing no other way of attending to their master, continued to produce the soups, entrées, roasts, fowls and desserts with which he was familiar. Louis XVI continued to drink – bordeaux, champagne and, what was considered abstemious, a single liqueur in the evening. In fact, the provision of food quickly assumed an additional importance because its acquisition necessitated trips into the outside world. There were three men in the kitchen, Turgy, Chrétien and Marchand, who had managed to infiltrate the Tower by pretending that they came on the orders of the Commune. The sympathetic Turgy used his thrice-weekly expeditions outside to acquire news and to pass on messages. There was certainly news to impart. The Prussian armies under the Duke of Brunswick crossed the French frontier on 19 August; Longwy fell four days later.

To Huë, Marie Antoinette emphasized as before that 'not one French fortress' must be given up to secure their liberty. If the royal family was freed, she said, they intended to go to Strasbourg in order to stop 'this important city', which 'must be preserved for France', becoming German once more. Huë was happily convinced that the daughter of Maria Teresa, the sister of Joseph II and Leopold II, the aunt of Francis II, had given way to 'the consort of the King of France and the mother of the heir to the throne'.[6] The fact was that for all her nationalistic words, the hopes of Marie Antoinette could hardly fail to rise as news of allied military successes percolated through to the prisoners.

On 19 August, however, the day that these armies crossed

the frontier, the little household in the Tower received a further devastating blow. The commissioners of the Commune announced that the surviving attendants, including the Princesse de Lamballe, the Marquise de Tourzel with Pauline, Chamilly, Huë and the waiting-women, were to be removed for interrogation. This was in keeping with a new order, prompted by the Commune, which set up a special tribunal to try royalists for crimes allegedly committed during the overthrow of the monarchy. Marie Antoinette made desperate pleas to keep the Princesse de Lamballe beside her, on the grounds that she was a royal relative. She wished to protect the vulnerable friend whom she had introduced into this perilous situation, judging the Tower to be safer than an ordinary prison. When the Princesse was removed with the others, the Queen urged the Marquise de Tourzel in a low voice to look after her, and try to answer for her where possible.[7] The Princesse and the Tourzels were now incarcerated in the La Force prison. Louis Charles, separated at last from his devoted Governess, shared the Queen's room. It was Huë who was, to the general pleasure and surprise, allowed to return after being interrogated about the flight to Varennes and (correctly) found to be innocent.

The three royal ladies were now without any female attendants. A couple called Tison with a daughter, another Pauline, were brought in to do the rough work of the establishment. No one liked the Tisons; the husband, in his late fifties, was gruff and unpleasant, the wife a hysteric more worried about her own comforts than those of the royal family she was supposed to serve. The next import permitted by the Commune was of a very different calibre. This was a valet named Hanet Cléry, who was intended to help Huë in his work, but when the latter was finally removed for good in early September, he became the effective manager of the tiny household. Cléry had been in Louis Charles's household since the boy's birth; he had escaped from the Tuileries on 10 August by jumping out of a window. (Seeing that Cléry wore a plain coat and carried no sword, a helpful Marseillais had offered him one of his own, in case Cléry wanted to participate in the killing.) Not only loyal and part of the inner network of royal servants, Cléry was also intelligent and resourceful. 'The faithful Cléry' would turn out to be an important witness to conditions in the Tower. Furthermore, additional joy, he had trained as a barber. Cléry could do the King's hair in the morning, and he could also move on to perform the same functions for the ladies whose hair had not been properly dressed for eight days. Hairdressing as ever being central to court life, even in this, the most modest of versions, Cléry used his sessions with the comb to pass on information discreetly.[8]

From time to time harsh sounds did penetrate the Temple. There was the monotonous daily chanting of that song 'Madame goes up into her Tower' by the guards. There were the insults shouted by the public – up to 400 of them – who had taken to behaving like tourists outside this new sight of Paris. 'We will strangle the little cubs and the fat pig' was one cry, 'Madame Veto shall dance from the lantern' another. On 25 August, the Feast of St Louis, which had been so splendidly celebrated with multiple illuminations in days gone by, Marie Thérèse heard the dreaded sound of the 'Ça Ira' at seven o'clock in the morning. Later the royal family learnt from the Procurator Manuel, one of the commissioners, that La Fayette had fled France. Manuel also handed over a letter from Mesdames Tantes, leading their pious lives in Rome. This was the last letter that the family received officially from outside, according to Marie Thérèse. The family was, however, unaware that in the evening Durosoy, the publisher of the royalist *Gazette de Paris*, was executed by a newfangled instrument called the guillotine.*[9]

From the point of view of the inhabitants of the Tower, therefore, the day of 2 September began like any other. The King was actually with Commissioner Daujon, watching a house being demolished outside the walls of the Tower in the interests of greater security, when the noise of cannon was heard. The King's great shout of laughter at the fall of a big stone was

---

* Its universal use had been decreed by the Assembly in March; not only was the guillotine considered a swift and thus humane instrument of justice, but it was also a symbol of the new equality – in this case equality in the face of death.[10]

interrupted. According to Daujon he turned pale, began to tremble, and in his cowardice 'forgot he was a man'. Marie Antoinette cried out: 'Save my husband!' This was echoed by Madame Elisabeth with: 'Have pity on my brother!'¹¹ Even if Daujon's charges were true, Louis XVI, who had been the subject of two apparently murderous assaults only recently, can hardly be blamed for his reaction. But indecisive and incapable of rising to an occasion as the King might be, he was not a coward as the events of 20 June had shown. It is far more likely that he feared for the safety of his family.

Marie Thérèse bore witness to their general bewilderment at this point: 'We didn't know what was happening.' Perhaps it was just as well. What was happening was a maniacal assault on the inhabitants of the Paris prisons, with some of the royal family's most beloved attendants still incarcerated in the La Force. These included the Marquise de Tourzel and Pauline – and that hate figure featured so often in obscene popular publications, the lesbian paramour of the 'Infamous Antoinette', the Princesse de Lamballe.

It will never be known for sure how many prisoners died, and there were similar massacres at Versailles and Rheims. Recent estimates make the Paris figure about 1300, the rates of killing varying from prison to prison. Were these assassins all foreigners to the city imported specially for the task? 'Greeks and Corsicans' with red caps and bare arms were mentioned, as well as southerners. Were they all drunk? Or was it, perhaps, the kind of wild blood-lust helped on by drink that can seize a whole mob, blotting out the sense of morality possessed by the individual? The ad hoc tribunals formed at the prisons certainly took pleasure in despatching most of those who were dragged before them to their deaths. The killings at the Bicêtre and the Salpêtrière prisons were especially frightful since these traditionally housed beggars and prostitutes, as well as boys and girls. Children as young as eight died, being found strangely hard to finish off: 'At that age it is hard to let go of life.' These totally apolitical figures fell victim to murderers, most of whom were in a kind of bloodthirsty delirium throughout the whole horrible proceedings. John Moore wrote in his diary: 'It is now past twelve at midnight and the bloody work goes on! Almighty God!"[12]

Yet the Paris theatres and restaurants did not close. A curious indifference to the whole matter gripped the city. A bourgeois family passing the prison of the Carmes, from which the most piteous cries were heard, was merely told by the father to quicken its steps. It was distressing, of course; nevertheless there were 'implacable enemies' of the nation who were being eliminated, in order that their own lives might be more secure.[13] This indifference found a parallel in the reaction of the political leaders. Robespierre took the convenient line that the will of the people was being expressed. Danton, if he did not inspire the killings, shrugged his shoulders and dismissed the fate of the prisoners with a coarse expletive. At the end of the day, the Girondins, who would have been in prison if Robespierre and Marat had had their way, were still safe, but the Jacobins were now in control.

At ten o'clock Commissioner Manuel told the royal family that the Princesse de Lamballe had survived. He was wrong. It was the Marquise de Tourzel who was miraculously acquitted in front of the tribunal of revolutionaries, while Pauline was spirited away to safety by a mysterious English Good Samaritan. A different destiny was reserved for the Princesse. Brought before the tribunal, she refused to denounce the King and Queen. The Princesse, who had once been too sensitive to bear the tribulations of ordinary life, found in herself the strength to answer with awesome composure: 'I have nothing to reply, dying a little earlier or a little later is a matter of indifference to me. I am prepared to make the sacrifice of my life.' So she was directed to the exit for the Abbaye prison – actually a code for execution. Once outside, in the courtyard of La Force, according to the testimony of a Madame Bault who worked there, 'several blows of a hammer on the head laid her low and then they fell on her.'[14]

Afterwards terrible stories were told of the fate of the Princesse de Lamballe; that she had been violated, alive or dead,* that her breasts and private parts had been hacked off

---

* This was certainly not impossible; many of the prostitutes were raped before

or, in another variant of savagery, her heart had been cooked and eaten. These stories were heard by many people in Paris at the time, the frequent use of the words 'fearful indignities … of a nature not to be related' and 'private infamies' as well as 'disembowelment' covering many possibilities.[15]

Unquestionably the Princesse's head was cut off and mounted on a pike. Her naked body was also ripped right open and her innards taken out, to be mounted on another pike. The corpse and the two grisly trophies were then paraded through Paris. The young Comte de Beaujolais, son of the Duc d'Orléans, who was doing his lessons at the Palais-Royal, was horrified to see the head of 'Tante' pass by, accompanied by her lacerated body. Along the way the head was thrust into the lap of the apprentice wax modeller Marie Grosholz. She was obliged to make a cast with 'the savage murderers' standing over her although, having been art teacher to Madame Elisabeth, Marie had known the Princesse and her hands trembled almost too much for her to work.[16]

It was now the firm intention of the crowd, fired up with wine and more wine, to take the head of the Princesse de Lamballe to the Temple so that the 'Infamous Antoinette' could bestow a last kiss on those sweet lips she had loved. This makes another story plausible: that a visit was paid to a barber along the way for the Princesse's hair to be dressed. For the Princesse's original coiffure could hardly have survived the assault of the hammers outside La Force, even if she had managed to preserve it during her fortnight inside. By the time the head on its pike appeared bobbing up and down outside the windows of the dining room of the Tower, the famous blonde curls were floating prettily as they had done in life, even if the face was waxen white. As a result the head was instantly recognizable.[17]

The King and Queen were upstairs, playing backgammon, when the head appeared outside the dining room, but Cléry saw it and so did Madame Tison who gave a loud cry; then they

being killed, as were even some of the very young girls, although Madame Bault's testimony makes it mercifully unlikely that the Princesse was still breathing at the time.

heard the frenzied laughter of 'those savages' outside. Upstairs the municipal officers had had the decency to close the shutters and the commissioners kept them away from the windows. But it was one of these officers who told the King, when he asked what all the commotion was about: 'If you must know, Monsieur, they are trying to show you the head of Madame de Lamballe.' Cléry too rushed in and confirmed what was happening.

Marie Antoinette, wrote her daughter, was 'frozen with horror'; it was the only time Marie Thérèse ever saw her mother's firmness abandon her.[18] Mercifully, the Queen then fainted away. But the crisis was not yet over. The 'savages', by climbing up some of the rubble of the destroyed houses, managed to get their pikes and their burdens higher up. They were still determined to secure the kiss of Marie Antoinette on the Lamballe's lips, or better still, her own head to join that of her favourite.

It was Commissioner Daujon who saved the day. His narrative confirms the fact that apart from the head, there was a huge blacksmith holding a pike with something – probably the heart – on it; another pike held a scrap of the dead woman's chemise, stained with mud and blood.[19] But Daujon would not permit the head to be brought inside. Instead the crowd was allowed to parade round the Tower with their pikes, and so the Queen never actually saw it, leaving the image, for better or for worse, to the eye of her appalled imagination. And Daujon prevented the entry into the Tower itself by the use of the tricolour ribbon on the door. 'The head of Antoinette does not belong to you,' he said with an authority that might have a sinister impact for the future. The rioting went on until about five o'clock. Later Marie Thérèse listened to the noise of her mother's weeping all through the night.

The head of the Princesse was subsequently rescued by a compassionate citizen, Jacques Pointel, who asked for it to be given burial in the cemetery for foundling children. But in the end the old Duc de Penthièvre managed to have body and head buried together in his family plot – where he expected to lie himself before long. It was Louis XVI who spoke the epitaph for the Princesse when he said that her conduct 'in the course of our misfortunes' – and he might have added, 'her own' –

amply justified the Queen's original choice of her as a friend.[20]

If the killings stopped, the chaos in Paris continued. During this period a band of enterprising professional robbers managed to lift a great many of the Crown Jewels from their storehouse, the Garde-Meuble in the Place Louis XV, because no one was guarding it. These jewels, said to be the finest royal collection in Europe, had been inventoried in June 1791 by the National Assembly at 23 million livres; the collection had been enhanced by the rich gifts of oriental sovereigns, especially Tippoo Sahib in the last years of the former regime. As Crown Jewels, they could not be disposed of by the King, unlike the gems conveyed abroad by Léonard on behalf of the Queen which, being 'mounted in Germany at a much earlier date', had been brought with her on her marriage and were thus her personal property. Over six nights, using a first-floor window, the thieves easily helped themselves to 7 million livres' worth, much of which was never seen again, including the fabulous pearls of Anne of Austria, which she had bequeathed to the Queens of France.*[21]

In the general disorder, everyone accused everyone else of the crime. The Girondins, for example, believed that Danton intended to use the proceeds to bribe the Duke of Brunswick to retreat. Of course Marie Antoinette was blamed. The execration in best-selling pamphlets and obscene engravings did not cease, many people expecting the Queen to take Jeanne de Lamotte Valois's former place in the Salpêtrière prison.[22] Any evil, including a daring jewel robbery brilliantly organized from a closed prison, could be attributed to her.

A new pamphlet, *Le Ménage royal en déroute*, whose subtitle was 'Open war between Louis XVI and his wife', had the drunken King beating up his wife, that 'sacrée' bitch. The truth of Temple life was very different. 'The way our family passed their days,' as Marie Thérèse put it, had an odd Rousseau-esque quality, if

---

* Others were tracked down and restored to France over the following two centuries; as late as 1976 the great Sancy diamond, which Marie Antoinette (and Maria Lesczinska) had worn in parures, was returned, thanks to an act of public-spirited generosity; with the Regent diamond, it is now in the Louvre.

one forgot the circumstances. It was Rousseau – once admired by the Queen, now blamed by the King for France's ills – who pronounced that 'the real nurse is the mother and the real teacher is the father.' These roles the royal couple now proceeded to fulfil in harmony. This was a very different kind of routine from that so cheerfully described by the young Dauphine Marie Antoinette in her letter home to her mother twenty-two years earlier: 'I put on my rouge and wash my hands in front of the whole world.' The Queen did not open her door until Cléry arrived. By this time the valet had already woken the King, dressed his hair and readied him to pray and read until breakfast – all with the door open so that the municipal officers could check him. Cléry then helped with the *toilette* of the women, doing their hair and teaching Marie Thérèse how to do her own on the Queen's instructions. A special sign was used when he had a bit of information to impart.[23]

Breakfast was at nine o'clock. After this, Cléry prepared the rooms, helped by Madame Tison, and the King gave Louis Charles his lessons. These included instruction in the works of Corneille and Racine, as well as writing; some of the seven-year-old Louis Charles's exercise books still survive.* The phrases he copied are poignant enough: 'Nationalement aimé', for example, emerging rather shakily first as 'Nrationnodement ainmé' and then as 'Nationnalement aiméen'. The signatures he practised had something of the former regime about them: 'Louis' and 'Louis Dauphin'. (Nevertheless, Cléry noted how tactful the boy was, never talking about the glories of Versailles and Saint Cloud or even life at the Tuileries.) Marie Antoinette taught her daughter, with Madame Elisabeth responsible for mathematics. It was then time for exercise in the garden, something that was obligatory whatever the weather, so that their rooms could be searched. However, Louis Charles enjoyed ball games with Cléry and noisy play, like hairdressing, also covered up incriminating conversation.

Dinner was at two o'clock, followed by a board or card game, which offered another good opportunity for private or coded

* Now in the Musée Carnavalet, Paris.

talk. After that Louis XVI, watched by the women, fell into a heavy sleep, lost to the world as he snored. Then there were more lessons and play for Louis Charles before bedtime and prayers, which were taken by his mother. The King might read aloud, generally from history books although that often proved a rather depressing experience. Madame Elisabeth concentrated on her prayer book, sometimes reciting the Mass of the day at the Queen's request. At supper the ladies took it in turn to sit by the Dauphin or to stay with the King. Bedtime was about eleven o'clock.

This account, however, omits one important feature of the royal day: the criers who appeared outside the Temple at seven o'clock in the evening. They were a principal source of news, since the gazettes were only provided when the war was going well for the French. It was from the criers, on 21 September, that they learnt that the French monarchy, having been suspended since mid-August, had officially come to an end. The National Convention, elected by manhood suffrage, now ruled France.

The next day the trumpets sounded. Soon there would be a revolution in the calendar as well as in the Constitution. In short, 22 September 1792 had been transformed into Day I of the month of Vendémiaire in Year I of the new era. Furthermore the last five days of September were designated '*les jours sansculotides*'. Names underwent their own revolution. Titles were already abolished and the Duc d'Orléans found himself offered a choice of two politically correct names; he chose Philippe Égalité over Publicola, the Roman consul who helped oust Tarquin Superbus. In the Temple, the new Elisabeth Capet unpicked the crowns from the linen of her brother, who was now Louis Capet (owing to the shortage of supplies, she had to wait until he was in bed). This was the surname of the dynasty that had ruled France until 1328; but Louis XVI, not only as a Bourbon but as a lover of history, disliked it; it was the name of his ancestors, not his own.[24]

The Prussian forces had captured Verdun on 3 September, news that was broken to the prisoners in the Tower by a woman in a house opposite who scrawled it on a big placard and held

it up to her window just long enough for them to read it. The
Duke of Brunswick predicted that he would be in Paris on 10
October. At rumours that the Prussians were about to invade
Paris, the jailer Rocher drew his sabre in the presence of the
King and vowed: 'If the Prussians come, I will personally kill
you.' Instead, an encounter at Valmy on 23 September was
inconclusive. Shortly afterwards Brunswick ordered a retreat on
that particular front. Louis kept his cool when presented with
the reverses of people who were presumed to be his allies and
came up with these emollient words: 'I have prayed for the
French to find that happiness which I have always wanted to
procure for them.'[25] Nevertheless, the inauguration of the Republic and the Valmy check marked the beginning of those increased
tribulations that many already believed must end with Louis
Capet's trial.

The King was separated from his family at the beginning of
October and taken alone to the Great Tower. This was a more
serious step than the removal of the Cordon Rouge from his
breast by Manuel, although that too was intended to signify
humiliation. The cries and protests of the Queen and the children
at the separation resulted in a dispensation that they were still
allowed to eat together, provided everyone spoke in 'loud and
clear French'. However, pen, ink, paper and pencils were
removed (although the royal ladies managed to conceal some);
potential hiding-places were found in hollowed-out peaches and
pockets cut in macaroons. The soap essence for shaving the
erstwhile King was suspected of being a poison. Scissors were
taken away. Louis watched Madame Elisabeth biting off a thread
as she embroidered and observed sadly: 'At your lovely house
at Montreuil, you had everything you needed. What a contrast!'
How could she have any regrets, replied Madame Elisabeth in
her ardent way, so long as she was sharing her brother's
misfortunes.[26]

Cléry and Turgy continued to be their mainstays, for although
Cléry was briefly taken away for interrogation he was allowed
to return. The news gathered on Turgy's shopping expeditions
would sometimes be passed on by him to Cléry by dint of the
men dressing each other's hair – yet another demonstration of

the uses of coiffure. As for Turgy, notes by Madame Elisabeth are still in existence with elaborate instructions for the signs that the serving-men should give: 'If the Austrians are successful on the Belgian frontier, place the second finger of the right hand on the right eye ... Be sure to keep the finger stationary for a longer or shorter time according to the importance of the battle.'[27]

At the end of October, Marie Antoinette, Madame Elisabeth and the children were moved into the new apartments in the Great Tower. Although the windows here were disagreeably barred, the accommodation itself had been freshly decorated and there were lavatories *à l'anglais*, which flushed with water. The room that Marie Antoinette shared with her daughter (Louis Charles was now to share his father's room) had a striped blue and green wallpaper; there was a green damask bed for Madame Elisabeth, white cotton curtains and valances, and a chest of drawers with a marble top.* There were some luxuries. One of the municipal officers, Goret, recalled being shown lockets of the blond hair of her children by Marie Antoinette, after which the erstwhile Queen rubbed her hands with one of the flower-essences she had always loved, passing them in front of Goret's face so he could share the sweet perfume.†[28] The food continued to be magnificent and to be served on silver; anything that was not eaten was distributed to the servants. There was always wine, which only the King drank.

When all the family in turn fell ill with colds and rheumatic fever, due to the fact that the Tower remained very damp, they were allowed after some argument to call the old royal doctor Le Mounier who was in his mid-seventies. Louis XVI was the sickest of them all, and there was, put crudely, an obvious

---

* This room has been recreated in a display at the Musée Carnavalet, Paris, which has some of the original artefacts including Madame Elisabeth's bed and dressing-table.

† There is also a story of Marie Antoinette seeking to console herself by sending for her erstwhile official draughtsman Redouté to paint the cactus known as the night-flowering cereus; if true, the cactus must have been acquired elsewhere than in her apartments; perhaps it was Redouté, able to maintain his position as an official draughtsman despite his royalist past, who brought or sent in the botanical drawing.[29]

danger of letting him die while in the custody of the Commune. Who would believe such a death was natural?

In the meantime the discussions over Louis Capet's trial raged in the Convention itself, while the French armies continued to be victorious. By the end of October, General de Custine had occupied the Rhineland, including Frankfurt and Mainz; in the south, Savoy and Nice had been captured. There was a further victory on 6 November at Jemappes, just west of Mons, for the troops under General Dumouriez, who had led the French at Valmy. Among those who now had to flee were the Archduchess Marie Christine, Count Mercy – and Fersen, who went to Düsseldorf. On 13 November the French pressed forward and entered Brussels. As a result, on 19 November the National Convention felt empowered to offer fraternal aid 'to any nation wishing to recover its liberty'. The ideological war was spreading, summed up by a decree of 15 December: 'War on the châteaux, peace for the cottages.'[30]

The favourable progress of the war from the French point of view was not the immediate catalyst of the former King's trial. This was provided by a coincidental and highly damaging discovery: the so-called iron chest (*armoire de fer*) in which Louis stored a number of his papers. It was the locksmith employed to install it, Gameau, who gave the game away. The revelations were actually more embarrassing than criminal. Here was the King's correspondence with Mirabeau, La Fayette and Dumouriez uncovered, rather than any proof of contacts with the Austrians. Barnave, however, was compromised and subsequently arrested. One draft in the King's handwriting reflected on the Varennes adventure, and insisted that his motives had been honourable: 'I had to escape any captivity.'[31] But a climate had been created in which the deceitful, manipulative Louis Capet could be portrayed as worthy of the nation's punishment.

This was a time when a translation of the trial of Charles I, in the English State Trials series, became a bestseller on the Paris bookstalls. One Frenchman told Doctor John Moore proudly that the behaviour of the English in the past – he cited the Wars of the Roses, the massacre of Glencoe and seventeenth-century Ireland – justified their own barbarities in the cause of freedom. At the theatre kings had to be tyrannical and rapacious if portrayed at all; the age of Grétry's noble Richard I had definitely passed.[32]

The sound of drums on 11 December announced the arrival of Pétion, accompanied by soldiers. The decree of the Convention was read to 'Louis Capet'; he was to be brought to its bar and interrogated. The former King merely commented that 'Capet' was inaccurate. At the Convention, he faced a massive denunciation for treason, ending with the events leading to Varennes: 'Louis left France as a fugitive in order to return as a conqueror.'

Before his father's departure, Louis Charles was taken away to join his mother. An act of gratuitous cruelty followed. It was decreed that Louis XVI could either continue to see his children, or agree to leave them with their mother during the coming proceedings against him; but Marie Thérèse and Louis Charles could not be in contact with both their parents. Nobly, Louis XVI decided to put his wife's passionate feelings for her children first. In this manner, Marie Antoinette, Madame Elisabeth and the children embarked on a yet sadder way of life. They were never allowed to visit 'Louis Capet' nor have any official communication with him whatsoever. This included 19 December, Marie Thérèse's fourteenth birthday, when Cléry brought her a little present from her father, an almanac for 1793 – but she was not permitted to see him.

It is true that the inventive Cléry started to conceal little crumpled notes in balls of string, once Louis was allowed paper to prepare his defence. The royal ladies responded by letting down their own missives on threads. But in principle, as Marie Thérèse wrote: 'He knew nothing of us, nor we of him but through the municipal officers.' The royal women became increasingly dependent either on the kindness of those officers who brought them newspapers (despite the frequently depressing contents) or on the criers outside. One loyal supporter, Dame Launoy, put a magic lantern in the third-floor window of a house near the Tower, and projected letters to give them news.

Commissioner Jacques Lepître who took up his position in mid-December was one of those kindly disposed. He realized that the harpsichord in the Tower was in too bad a state for Marie Antoinette to continue her daughter's lessons and agreed to replace it. Marie Antoinette gave him the name of the man she had generally used and a harpsichord, according to the accounts, duly arrived. A scrap of music was found there. It was Haydn's *La Reine de France*, one of his symphonies of the mid-1780s, which had been the Queen's favourite. 'How times have changed,' said Marie Antoinette. 'And we could not stop our tears,' wrote Lepître.[33]

Even with Cléry's scraps of paper, and the criers, a kind of unreality descended on the women. They were unaware of the long hours spent by the King with the gallant men who had agreed to act as his counsels. Chrétien de Malesherbes behaved with great style, addressing his master as 'Sire' and 'Majesté'. When asked at the Convention what made him so brave, he replied: 'Contempt for you and contempt for death.' Although Louis told Malesherbes that they should concern themselves with his trial 'as though I could win', two weeks after it started he spent Christmas Day preparing his last will and testament.[34] This was no time for 'Capets'; he wrote it as Louis XVI King of France and he gave the correct date in the Christian calendar, having no truck with 'Nivôse', as the month that began in late December would become. In every way it was the document of a committed son of the Catholic Church, and it also preached the Christian doctrine of forgiveness, especially to his son. If Louis Charles should be 'so unfortunate' as ever to become King, he should dedicate his whole life to his people's happiness; on no account was he to seek vengeance on his father's behalf. Louis remembered his other relations, including his brothers, his faithful servants such as Huë and Cléry, and he thanked his lawyers.

The King wrote with special loving kindness of his wife, commending his children to her: 'I have never doubted her maternal tenderness.' He also begged Marie Antoinette to forgive him 'all the ills she has suffered for my sake and for any grief that I may have caused her in the course of our marriage as she may be certain that I hold nothing against her.'*

The next day the trial began and the case was made for the defence. It was certainly not without merit in purely legal terms. Louis had been granted inviolability by the National Assembly; the veto had actually been awarded to him by the Constituent Assembly and was already in place at the Legislative Assembly before the bloodshed of 10 August began. As to the charges of treason, Gouverneur Morris commented drily to Thomas Jefferson on 21 December: 'To a person less intimately acquainted than you are with the History of human affairs, it would seem strange that the mildest monarch who ever filled the French throne … should be prosecuted as one of the most nefarious Tyrants that ever disgraced the Annals of human nature.'[35]

But of course none of this was relevant to that extremist party nicknamed 'the Mountain' after their high position on the seats of the Convention. Many of these argued that a trial in itself was totally unnecessary. Unlike the Girondins who saw the value of keeping the King alive as a hostage, Robespierre took the line that Louis Capet had already condemned himself to death by his actions.† The young revolutionary orator Saint-Just in his maiden speech thundered: 'Louis cannot be judged, he is already judged … He is condemned, or if he is not, the sovereignty of the Republic is not absolute.' He should be killed not for what he had done, but for what he was. This was, in fact, the best if the most ruthless answer to the fact that Louis Capet's trial flagrantly ignored the New Criminal Code of 1791; this decreed that an indictment by a special jury of accusation composed of several participants had to take place before there could be a trial.[37]

When voting began, the guilt of Louis was easily established. In total, 691 voted that he had conspired against the state, a few abstained but no one voted against. The question of the penalty that the former King should pay was far more

---

* These were surely traditional Christian sentiments, rather than Louis XVI forgiving Marie Antoinette at the last minute for her affair with Fersen.
† It was a point that Trotsky would later make against holding a trial of Tsar Nicholas II: putting the deposed monarch in the dock was to envisage the possibility at least of his innocence.[36]

complicated. There were arguments for confinement until the end of the war, followed by banishment. Thomas Paine, who had been elected to the Convention as a revolutionary hero, made a plea for Louis and his family to be sent to America at the end of the war. There, like the exiled Stuarts, they would sink into obscurity. Referring to the King's military support for independence, he besought the French not to let the tyrannical English have the satisfaction of seeing Louis die on the scaffold, 'the man who helped my much loved America to burst her fetters'.[38]

This was a move supported by Gouverneur Morris and the new ambassador to the United States, Edmund Genet, brother of Madame Campan.* At one point the Girondin leaders even thought that Genet would be the man 'to take Capet and his family with him' to the United States. The beguiling vision – of Louis happy as a country gentleman in Virginia, with Marie Antoinette in a gracious porticoed antebellum house recreating the life of the Petit Trianon, the children growing up as good American citizens – was not, however, destined to be fulfilled. Marat denounced Paine for his Quaker softness – the Quakers, among whom Paine had been brought up, being well-known opponents of capital punishment. Danton put it more pithily: revolutions could not be made with rosewater.[39]

In the end, after many voting complications, the death penalty was passed on 16 January 1793 by a narrow majority. The newly named Philippe Égalité, Louis' cousin and his closest adult male relative in France, was among those who voted for execution. In his own words Philippe Égalité was 'convinced that all who have attacked or will attack the sovereignty of the people deserve death'. When Louis was told of the verdict on the following day, it was the behaviour of his cousin that visibly pained him. His suffering was understandable. Even Orléans' own set was horrified by the vote, people weeping at his 'dishonour' and his own ADC throwing his uniform in the fire.[40]

There was still a question of a reprieve but that was rejected

---

* Hence the persistent tradition that country houses in the US, as for example in Maine, were prepared for the arrival of Marie Antoinette.

by a majority of seventy. It was not until 2 p.m. on Sunday, 20 January, that the former King was told that he was going to be put to death the following day, by the swift, humane guillotine. Louis asked for three days in which to prepare himself spiritually. This was denied him although a non-juror priest of Irish ancestry, the Abbé Edgeworth de Firmont, was admitted to the Tower. Otherwise Louis consoled himself with reading the account of the execution of Charles I. That evening it was the voices of the criers beneath the Tower that told the Queen and the rest of the royal family the fearful news. At this point the Convention relented. The family was allowed down to the King's apartments at seven o'clock.

It was a piteous scene. They had not seen Louis XVI for six weeks and Marie Thérèse found her father 'much changed'. But when Louis wept, it was not from fear, but for the sadness of parting from them and the tragedy of the situation into which he must perforce abandon them. Accepting his fate, Louis had asked the Convention to arrange for his family to be retired from the Tower 'to a place it thinks proper'. But who knew when that would be achieved and what that place might be? Nevertheless the King urged on his son the need to forgive the enemies who were about to cause his death, and he gave his children his final blessing.[41]

Marie Antoinette begged for them all to spend the night, this last night, together. Louis refused. He had much to do to prepare himself and needed peace. The scene as described by Cléry was heart-rending. The Queen huddled against the King, holding Louis Charles. The little boy clutched both his parents' hands tight, kissing them and crying. Elisabeth too clung to her brother. Marie Thérèse shrieked aloud.

In the end Louis only persuaded his family to leave by promising to see them again the next morning for a final farewell. 'I am not saying goodbye,' he said. 'Be sure that I shall see you again at eight o'clock tomorrow morning.'

'Why not seven o'clock?' pursued the Queen.

'Seven o'clock then.'

'Do you promise?' cried the Queen.

'I promise,' replied the King. He tore himself away and went into his bedroom. The sobs of the departing children reached Cléry through the walls.[42]

But Louis did not – could not – bring himself to keep his word. The three women lay sleepless upstairs, Marie Antoinette hardly having the strength to put her son to bed. But the man who came to see them at six o'clock the next morning wanted to fetch a prayer book, not conduct them to the King. There was an extraordinary silence over the city that morning, explained by the fact that the main gates had been locked and the usual bustle was therefore stilled. It was the sound of drumming shortly before half past ten, followed by loud 'shouts of joy' from the frantic spectators, that told the listeners in the Tower that the King was dead.[43]

Marie Antoinette could not speak. She was imprisoned in her own silent world of agony. But Elisabeth broke out, amid the piercing cries of the children: 'The monsters! They are satisfied now.'

PART SIX

Widow Capet

CHAPTER TWENTY-FIVE

Unfortunate Princess

~~~~~~~

'Unfortunate Princess! My marriage promised her a
throne; now, what prospect does it offer her?'
Louis XVI on the eve of his death, 1793

From the moment of the King's death onwards, Marie
Antoinette remained bowed down with a grief that went
too deep for words. It seems, according to the sympathetic
Commissioner Lepître, that she had still had some hope of a
reprieve for him; instead, they had 'let the best of Kings' perish.'
'The Widow Capet' was now her official designation, varied more
crudely with 'the woman Capet' and the frankly contemptuous
'Antoinette'; the traditional Habsburg prefix in honour of the
Virgin Mary was not for revolutionaries.

The widow's first wish was to see Cléry, who had attended
Louis XVI's last hours in the Temple and who might therefore
be expected to bear some message from him to the stricken
family. Madame Elisabeth and Marie Thérèse also privately
believed that the shock of the encounter might provoke 'a burst
of sorrow' that would relieve the Queen from her state of silent,
suppressed agony. In fact, Cléry had more than messages; he
also had the King's gold wedding ring, engraved *M.A.A.A. 19
Aprilis 1770* (for Marie Antoinette Archduchess of Austria, the
date being that of the proxy wedding in Vienna). Louis had told
Cléry to say that he only parted with it with his life. Then there
was a little parcel containing locks of his family's hair, 'so

precious to him' that the King had preserved them with great care in a silver seal that broke into three parts.[2]

Permission for the visit was, however, refused. After a few weeks the faithful servant was released from the Temple without either giving or receiving the consolation of a visit. He left the keepsakes behind him in the Tower, sealed up. Nevertheless they reached the royal family in the course of time by a circuitous route. One of those responsible for the prisoners, François Adrian Toulan, a Jacobin from Toulouse in his early thirties, had been won over to their cause by the spectacle of their plight; Marie Antoinette, with her love of nicknames, called him 'Fidèle'. It was Toulan who daringly broke open the seals and conveyed the keepsakes to their proper destination, leaving the municipal officers to think that a thief had been attracted to the royal arms on the silver.[3]

Marie Antoinette's other request met with more immediate success. She wanted suitable mourning clothes to which, as the widow of a King of France, she attached much symbolic importance; she could at least make this appropriate sign of respect for her late husband as she would have done during the previous regime. Marie Antoinette asked for a black taffeta cloak, fichu, skirt and gloves, all to be made up in 'the simplest possible way', as she told the municipal officer Goret; and she supplied the name and address of the right person. This was agreed although a request for black curtains and a black coverlet was refused. A dressmaker, Mademoiselle Pion, was allowed to come to the Temple and fit the mourning, also for the other ladies, over two days. A municipal officer had to be present at all times as she worked, but Louis Charles sprang about and with his childish play provided cover for some conversation.[4]

Otherwise the widow could not eat and would not even take the air because the route to the gardens meant passing the King's door. Seeing her pitiable state, her pallor and her emaciation, Goret remonstrated with Marie Antoinette in a kindly way on her duties to her children. He also arranged for seats in the circular gallery of the Tower so that Marie Antoinette could get some fresh air without making that traumatic journey. Nevertheless Marie Antoinette's condition was summed up by her daughter: 'She no longer had any hope left in her heart or distinguished between life and death; sometimes she looked at us with a kind of compassion which was quite frightening.' In the midst of her own suffering, Marie Thérèse was even relieved to have to report a cut foot on 25 January because it gave her mother the need to care for her.[5] Rejecting the prison doctor, Marie Antoinette managed to secure Brunier, the established doctor to the Children of France, along with the surgeon La Caze. After a month the girl was cured.

This explicit description of Marie Antoinette's original near-catatonic state by her daughter makes it unlikely that the Queen ceremonially hailed her son as King Louis XVII immediately on the morning of his father's death. Marie Thérèse, the prime witness, does not mention it.* Goret and Turgy, whose recollections were published after the Restoration in a newly joyful royalist atmosphere, referred more plausibly to Louis Charles being given in time 'the rank and the pre-eminence which the King had had' and his sitting on a special seat with a cushion and table – although that of course may have been due to his small size.[7] Open recognition of the boy as King would have been an astonishingly dangerous act on his behalf by Marie Antoinette on 21 January 1793 in a country where the monarchy had been abolished and his father had just been killed.

The title of Louis XVII, 'the little King', was of course accepted instantly abroad in royalist circles. At the same time the Comte de Provence seized the opportunity for which he had long been angling. This was the moment, as he saw it, to proclaim himself unilaterally as Regent of France for his seven-year-old nephew. He did so 'by right of birth' and according to the fundamental laws of the kingdom. Nevertheless the move aroused angry controversy. Some of the émigrés were shocked and the Austrians similarly frowned on it, believing that the claim neglected the superior one of Marie Antoinette, whatever her current situation. Other foreign powers followed Austria's

---

* Turgy implied that there was a salutation then and there, not in his *Recollections* of 1818, but in an interrogation of an impostor in 1817. But of course he could just as easily have tested an impostor with a false incident as with a true one.[6]

lead in refusing to recognize his new status. Count Mercy d'Argenteau was certainly quick to point out that the new Regent's rights were in fact much less well founded than those of Marie Antoinette.[8] It was, after all, only the Civil Constitution of 1791 (now suspended) that had divided the roles of Regent and Guardian; the ancient practice of France would have united them both in the person of the Queen Mother.

Ironically enough, existence in the Tower actually grew easier now that Louis was dead. 'The fury of the regicides was assuaged for the moment,' wrote Turgy. The municipal officers gave up their frequent visits, conversation among the Princesses was unsupervised, and they were able to give Turgy orders without indulging in subterfuge. Via Turgy, Huë managed once more to contact them. The truth was that the guards at least believed that their prisoners would soon be exchanged with Austria for prominent French captives and so were correspondingly gentle.[9]

Lepître gives an account of a musical evening on 7 February in which the 'young King' sang a lament on the death of his father, called 'La Piété Familiale', for which Lepître provided the simple words and Madame Cléry, an accomplished musician, composed the music. The municipal officers listened in silence, tears in their eyes, to the boy's voice accompanied by his sister on the harpsichord:

> *Tout est fini pour moi sur la terre*
> *Mais je suis auprès de ma mère.*
> (Everything is fled from me on earth
> But I am still at my mother's side.)

To his aunt Louis Charles also addressed a verse saluting her as his second mother.[10]

Such Temple servants as the Simons, husband and wife, were, at this juncture, no more than uncouth. Antoine Simon, a prominent member of the Commune, was despatched to be a general factotum at the Temple. A brusque uneducated cobbler whose business had failed, Simon was in his fifties, heavily built and already rather deaf. But the Municipal Goret bore witness that Simon took some trouble to fulfil the wants of the royal ladies, going from one to the other in his deliberate way: 'What is it that you need, Madame?' His wife Marie Jeanne, a cleaning woman, was no more cultivated, but she did have nursing skills, having gained prominence on 10 August by the 'rush of patriotism' with which she attended to the wounded.[11]

Goret overheard the Queen saying: 'We are very happy with our good Monsieur Simon who gets us whatever we ask for,' and this must have been at least partially true in early 1793. Marie Antoinette had, of course, a tradition of gracious behaviour towards her servants and the manners of the former regime did not die away so easily. In the high summer Madame Tison, always highly strung, would break down altogether, weeping and screaming and accusing herself of dreadful crimes towards the Queen and Madame Elisabeth. Needing eight men to hold her down, Madame Tison was carted off to the hospital, the Hôtel Dieu. Even then, at a time of great personal unhappiness, Marie Antoinette continued to send messages of enquiry about the welfare of 'poor Madame Tison'.

As to the Queen's future, an exchange of prisoners was a practice with a historical precedent. So was the reclamation of foreign princesses by their native country. In December, Count Mercy had recalled the case of the English Princess Caroline Matilda, divorced by the Danish King for adultery, who was reclaimed by her brother George III. For a short while Mercy played with the idea. Fearing for Marie Antoinette's assassination either in public or private, he believed that 'her august family' should apply to retrieve the former Archduchess of Austria from 'the vile brigands'. There was, after all, that marriage contract, which Mercy had investigated as long ago as October 1789, giving her the right to stay or go after her husband's death. But by 2 February 1793, Mercy had relapsed into the view that 'we should remain passive in this horrible crisis', for fear of making things worse, as he told the Comte de La Marck.[12]

Certainly there was no foregone conclusion about the fate of Marie Antoinette. There was no tradition of queen consorts, the weaker royal vessels, being tried and executed in history, whatever the tribulations of their male counterparts. (Mary Queen of Scots, executed in the late sixteenth century, was a queen in her own right.) The extremist Stanislas Fréron, a member of the 'Mountain' and editor of the outrageous *L'Orateur du Peuple*, had suggested before Louis' death that Antoinette should be dragged through the streets of Paris at the tail of a galloping horse, the fate of the seventh-century Brunnhilde at the orders of the Frankish King. Or perhaps she should be torn to pieces by dogs like Jezebel? Such suggestions belonged to the culture of demagogic violence rather than political statesmanship. At the end of January, Fersen, harrowed by reports of the Queen's 'much altered' physical state, held a conference with Quentin Craufurd, the Comte de La Marck and the veteran Russian Minister Jean Simolin, a keen admirer of the royal family. Should not the Emperor Francis II be persuaded to seek his aunt's release 'as a private individual'? In the end they held back for fear of provoking the Queen's trial. But by 9 February these apprehensions appeared to be groundless: 'I am beginning to hope a little,' Fersen wrote.[13]

So what did the 'villains' propose to do with their widowed captive? In one of his final conversations with his counsel Malesherbes, Louis XVI had pondered aloud on the same problem: 'Unfortunate Princess! My marriage promised her a throne; now, what prospect does it offer her?' There had been frequent rumours that Marie Antoinette would be put on trial ever since the return from Varennes; for example, the English royal family heard that 'the poor unhappy Queen' rather than Louis XVI was in danger of death from 'that tiger nation', and Earl Gower, the departing English ambassador, reported that the Queen would 'immediately be tried' after the attack on the prisons of 2 September.[14] But these gloomy predictions had not been carried out.

During the trial of Louis XVI, Robespierre had invoked Marie Antoinette's name only to make the point that she had no special status: 'As for his [Louis'] wife, you will send her before the courts, like all other persons charged with similar crimes.' Jean Baptiste Mailhe, a lawyer from Toulouse and part of the more moderate 'Plain' group in the Convention, as opposed to the radical 'Mountain', put across the same point: 'Of Antoinette we have said nothing.' The *ci-devant* (former)

Queen of France was no more sacred or inviolable than any other rebel or conspirator, and if there was a case to be made against her, it must be sent to an ordinary tribunal. Of this process, however, in the tense weeks following the King's execution, there was no sign. Meanwhile it was relevant that one of the options considered at length during Louis' trial had been banishment, including Paine's enterprising suggestion of exile to the United States. 'The banishment of all the Bourbons' was a revolutionary proposal, the reclamation of the former Archduchess a dynastic one, but they amounted to the same practical step: the departure of Marie Antoinette from France.[15]

In short, there seemed a real possibility that this humane procedure would take place. When Louis XVI, shortly before his death, had asked what would happen to those he left behind, he was told, reassuringly, that 'the nation, always great and always just' would concern itself with the future of his family. In the first week of February, Claude Antoine Moëlle, a member of the Paris Commune who was one of the Temple's commissioners, escorted Marie Antoinette up to her airing at the top of the Tower. She took the opportunity to ask him what the Convention intended to do with her. She would probably be reclaimed by the Emperor her nephew, replied Moëlle: 'any new excess' – he meant her death – would be 'a gratuitous horror' and contrary to policy.[16] The execution of the King had provided the Convention with closure in its need for purging bloodshed. This conversation, at which Marie Thérèse was also present, allowed for hopes to rise, not only that there would be no trial but that the Queen would be freed.

The poor health of the Queen gave an added impetus to the idea of mercy. This did not improve as the immediate shock of her husband's death wore off. Kucharski, who had been responsible for the portrait begun in 1791, now produced a yet more haggard image of the Queen in her widow's weeds; he may have made sketches in the Temple from life before reproducing the portrait in many versions. Tuberculosis was rife in her family; it had killed her eldest brother and her elder son, among other relations; she may have been in the early stages of it. But the Queen was also unquestionably suffering from haemorrhages, which had been part of the pattern of her troubled gynaecological history for many years and which now increased in frequency. There are various alternative explanations for this. She may have been experiencing the early onset of the menopause (Marie Antoinette was thirty-seven); she may have been suffering from fibroids; third, and most plausibly in view of her deteriorating physical condition, she may have been exhibiting the first signs of cancer of the womb. Marie Antoinette, whose health had for some years worried the ladies who were her intimates, was certainly by now an ill woman.[17]

In May, Doctor Brunier had to be called to Marie Thérèse who was 'at an age decisive for her sex'. (In her fifteenth year, Marie Thérèse was almost exactly the same age as Marie Antoinette had been when the latter reached puberty.) But the doctor also had to attend to the Queen, who was suffering from frequent 'convulsions' and fainting fits.[18] Whatever the cause, Marie Antoinette's was not by now what would be termed a good life, let alone a threatening one.

Unfortunately, there were several elements that militated against the merciful release of Marie Antoinette. First and foremost must be listed the indifference of the young Emperor. Even the Emperor Joseph II – who really loved his sister – had made it clear as long ago as August 1789 that it was in his own interest 'to be perfectly neutral in this business, no matter what may happen to the King and Queen'.[19] For his part, Francis II was simply not concerned over the fate of the unhappy aunt he had never met and who, as an agent of Habsburg dynastic politics, it had to be said, had not fulfilled her function. It did not help the Queen's cause, at home or abroad either, that the war now escalated. In the course of February crusading revolutionary France declared war on England, Spain and Holland. The tide, which had surged forward so strongly for the revolutionary armies under Dumouriez in the previous autumn, now turned in favour of the allies. The French had to evacuate Aix-la-Chapelle and abandon the siege of Maestricht, while the Austrians recovered Liège. It was inevitable that lethal political infighting in the Convention would, like the war itself, escalate.

In such struggles between the Jacobins and the Girondins, Marie Antoinette was once again a miserable pawn.

Private plans of escape, irrespective of the Emperor's intentions, were still afoot. One scheme involving the whole family was organized by 'Fidèle' Toulan and Lepître inside and the Chevalier de Jarjayes outside. Contact with Jarjayes had never been entirely broken; there were letters in which, for example, 'Roxane' stood for 'la Reine', 'Lucius' for Jarjayes, 'Fatime' probably for Madame Elisabeth and 'the old friend Mercinus' rather more obviously for Mercy himself. The scheme planned for early March involved the smuggling in of padded military overcoats to disguise the women's figures; wigs and battered and ragged trousers were intended for the children. The coasts of Normandy and England, once dismissed by the Queen, now promising salvation, were to be the target. The guardian Tisons, man and wife, were to be rendered insensible by narcotics mixed with their tobacco. Whether this latter-day 'Varennes-type' scheme had any feasibility at all was never tested; first Lepître lost his nerve and muddled the process of obtaining false passports. Then agitation due to the bad news of the war and food riots in Paris caused the city's barriers to be closed.[20]

The conspirators were left trying to persuade the Queen to escape alone, on the grounds that the rest of the family was not in danger. This Marie Antoinette resolutely refused to do, as she had always refused. 'We had a beautiful dream and that was all,' Marie Antoinette told Jarjayes. 'The interests of my son are the only guide I have, and whatever happiness I could achieve by being free of this place, I cannot consent to separate myself from him ... I could not have any pleasure in the world if I abandoned my children,' she wrote, adding, 'I do not even have any regrets.'[21]

Instead of attempting to flee herself, Marie Antoinette made a noble gesture of renunciation in favour of her two brothers-in-law. She despatched secretly via Jarjayes the silver seal with the lockets of hair to 'Monsieur, Comte de Provence' (no mention here of 'Regent') with a note signed M.A. This had a touching postscript from the two children 'M.T.' and 'Louis' (the simple name by which a monarch would sign himself). The girl wrote it 'on behalf of my brother and myself'. Both embraced their uncle 'with all their hearts', Madame Elisabeth adding her own initials at the end. Comte d'Artois got the engraved wedding ring; he was asked by Marie Antoinette to receive it as a symbol of their most tender friendship, Madame Elisabeth adding to her brother: 'How I have suffered for you.'[22]

Jarjayes had a second clandestine mission: to take an impression of the Queen's seal to 'the person you know came to see me last winter from Brussels' and to tell him at the same time that 'the device has never been more true'. This was Count Fersen who had spent that single night at the Tuileries in February 1792. The motto was '*Tutto a te mi guida*' – All things lead me towards you. The device was a pigeon in flight, which, Fersen noted in his *Journal intime*, was a mistake for his own arms which actually showed a flying fish. It took Jarjayes many months to get the impression to Fersen, and when he did receive it, it was, by coincidence, on the first anniversary of the execution of Louis XVI, a tragic memory that for Fersen would 'never be effaced'. However, the text of the message, surviving in two virtually identical versions – the Queen's letter to Jarjayes, and Fersen's notification of it in his *Journal intime* – make it clear that the bond between them, dependent and romantic on her side, romantic and chivalrous on his, had not been broken. This was the language of Julie to Saint-Preux in *La Nouvelle Héloïse*: 'Our souls touch at all points ... Fate may indeed separate us but not disunite us.'[23]

Lepître, Toulan and others were interrogated for overindulgence of the royal prisoners at the end of March on the word of the Tisons; Toulan was dismissed from the Tower. In other ways, the regime tightened. There were sudden night-time searches, intended to take the family by surprise but actually causing great fear and inconvenience. Not much was discovered beyond religious objects – pictures of the Sacred Heart of Jesus and a prayer for France. The man who led the searches was Jacques Hébert, founder of the newspaper *Le Père Duchesne*, which was the leading organ of the extremist Cordeliers. He, however, was a formidable adversary, and not someone to whom the Queen's plight or that of her children was likely to appeal.

On 18 March the Austrian army, under the Prince of Saxe-Coburg, inflicted a terrible defeat upon the French at Neerwinden, north-west of Liège. As a result the Austrians were able to retake Brussels and drive the French back out of the Austrian Netherlands. At the same time the Spanish crossed the French borders in the south. And in the Vendée the recent royalist rising was spreading rapidly. Nine days after Neerwinden, Robespierre in the Convention focused once more on Marie Antoinette's continued presence in the Temple – and the unresolved question of her punishment. It was manifestly intolerable that one 'no less guilty' than the late Louis Capet, 'no less accused by the Nation', should be left in peace to enjoy the fruit of her crimes out of some residue of superstitious respect for royalty.[24] Robespierre suggested to the Convention that the former Queen should be brought before the new Revolutionary Tribunal, which had been set up on 10 March, for her crimes against the State. Such notional crimes of 'the Austrian woman' were given further prominence when General Dumouriez, no longer the victorious revolutionary leader but the defeated general, absconded to the Austrians. Antoinette in the Tower was smeared by association.

On 6 April a new Committee of Public Safety was set up. Limited at first to nine members (including Danton) and meeting in secret, it would with time take over the conduct of the war. The next day Philippe Égalité and his third son, the *ci-devant* Comte de Beaujolais, were arrested. With other aristocrats, Orléans' sister – 'Citizeness Bourbon' – the Prince de Conti and Orléans' second son, Montpensier, they were sent to prison in Marseilles. It was as well for his own sake that Orléans' father-in-law, the Duc de Penthièvre, whose 'noble bearing' and 'loftiest virtues' had made him the last living link with 'the glory' that was his ancestors, did not live to see this day. This surviving grandson of Louis XIV had had his heart broken by the death of his beloved daughter-in-law the Princesse de Lamballe. It was a fate that he was said to have offered in vain a fortune to avert. But the shameful vote of his son-in-law for the death of the King was the ultimate blow and he never recovered, dying on 4 March.[25]

The events of the end of May, which led to the overthrow

of the Girondins as a party and the arrest of their leaders, had their impact on the Temple in the shape of yet greater security. Bars were put on the windows and shutters that were not always opened; the searches were increased. In spite of this, there was a pitiful if valiant attempt at rescue in June. It was instigated by the eccentric Baron de Batz, a man brave or foolhardy enough to try a last-minute rescue of the King on the scaffold, with the help of one of the police administrators of the prison, named Michonis. It failed when Simon was tipped off to the possibility of Michonis' treachery and paid an unscheduled late-night visit. Michonis talked his way out of trouble, suggesting that the whole incident had been a joke played on Simon.[26]

Attempts at exchanging Marie Antoinette for some of the French prisoners – four commissioners of the Convention – who had been brought over to Austria by Dumouriez when he fled to the allied side were no more successful. The imperial heart was not in it and by the beginning of August no progress had been made. Although the first-hand evidence vanished later for political reasons, it seems that Danton, a member of the Committee for Public Safety, also tried to negotiate some kind of deal with Francis II. But the latter was not prepared to make any concessions in return. In the meantime Marie Antoinette herself refused to consider a release that did not include her son. Maternal anxiety was interpreted by Danton as dynastic ambition and so that plan – insofar as it ever existed – collapsed.[27]

In mid-June the Pope announced the late King of France to be a royal martyr, killed purely for his religion: 'O triumphal day for Louis! ... We are sure that he has exchanged the fragile royal crown and the ephemeral lilies for an eternal crown decorated with the immortal lilies of the angels.' Two weeks later the real-life martyrdom of Marie Antoinette commenced. On the night of 3 July, commissioners arrived at the Tower and brusquely informed the Queen that her son was to be separated from her. They read the decree that the Convention had issued to this effect the day before, which had been spurred on by reports – without substance – that there was a plot to abduct the 'young King'. He was now to be removed to 'the most secure apartment of the Tower'.[28]

Louis Charles flung himself into his mother's arms, giving loud cries, and for her part Marie Antoinette behaved like a tigress whose cub was being taken away. For the next hour she absolutely refused to release her son. Threats to kill her left the Queen unmoved; only threats to kill Marie Thérèse produced some kind of reaction. In the end there was no way she could resist such an array of force any longer. Marie Antoinette no longer had the strength to dress her son – that was done by Marie Thérèse and her aunt – but had to be content with wiping his tears away.[29]

Louis Charles was aged eight years and three months; he had spent nearly half his life in captivity of one sort or another. He had become unnaturally circumspect and, above all, anxious to please. The rude 'peasant' health of which Marie Antoinette had once boasted to Princesse Louise was beginning to deteriorate in the confining conditions of the Tower. He had suffered from a fever in May and in June he was found to have a hernia in the groin. The celebrated truss-maker Hippoy Le Pipelet was allowed to bandage him. Pipelet noted that Louis Charles had also suffered an accident, which seemed insignificant at the time, if painful, but was to have grim consequences. He reported to the Temple authorities that Louis Charles, using a stick as a hobby-horse, had managed to bruise one of his testicles.[30]

That night and for many nights to come, the family left behind listened to the boy's sobbing, still audible from where he was kept. Marie Antoinette became obsessed with the prospect of having just one little glimpse of Louis Charles as he passed on his way to his exercise. There was one position in their apartments from where, by craning her neck, she could just see him as he passed. She spent whole days trying to do this. As Maria Carolina expressed it to her daughter, the wife of Francis II, just when 'time and resignation' seemed to have formed 'healing scars' following the King's death, Marie Antoinette's wounds had been 'torn open again'.[31]

Like all separations of children from parents in the name of ideology, this aim to retrain – or brainwash – the former

Dauphin was heart-rending for his family. The Commune's prosecutor, Chaumette, had declared the previous year: 'I wish to give him [Louis Charles] some education. I will take him from his family to make him lose the idea of his rank.'[32] The carrying out of this policy meant that Marie Antoinette's *chou d'amour*, petted, protected and loved in the way that few eighteenth-century children were, was given over to the altogether rougher care of the cobbler Simon. The new guardian was supposed to toughen up the little Capet and this he proceeded to do. The boy was beaten for crying so after a bit he ceased to cry. He was given wine, became tipsy and amused his jailers. He was taught their rough language, their obscenities, and, since it pleased them, took on such a way of talking as his own. This was simply the brutal way that the children of the people were tamed, and Louis Charles was thought to be a prime candidate for taming.

Marie Antoinette's own turn came a month later. It was once again the direction of the war that provoked a new official move against her. Many of the French soldiers were distracted in the west with the rebels of the Vendée. On 23 July the Austrian alliance recaptured Mainz. Then three days later they took Valenciennes, a victory that meant that Paris itself, too easily reached down the valley of the Oise, was in danger. On 1 August, Bertrand Barrère de Viruzac, president of the Convention and a member of the Committee of Public Safety, deliberately established the lethal connection. Was it 'our over-long for-getfulness of the Austrian woman's crimes ... our strange indifference towards the Capet family' that had given the nation's enemies a mistaken impression of its weakness?[33] If so, that could be remedied, and remedied immediately.

The security for the transfer of Marie Antoinette to the prison known as the Conciergerie was prodigious. All the doors of the Temple were checked during the day and the guards were told to regard themselves as being in a state of siege. At eight o'clock in the evening, the artillery in the courtyard was instructed to hold itself in readiness. It was a very hot, stuffy night, almost exactly a year since that hot night preceding a red dawn when the Tuileries had been stormed.

As a further precaution, they came for Marie Antoinette at

the dead hour when humanity's resistance is at its lowest, two o'clock in the morning. The Queen had undressed. As a foretaste of what was to come, she was not allowed the luxury of dressing in private; the municipals, headed by the once compliant Michonis, insisted on being in attendance, as though this frail, unarmed, middle-aged woman could somehow elude them. Marie Antoinette listened to the decree of the Convention against her without any visible emotion. She was then permitted to make up a little bundle of necessities, including a handkerchief and some smelling-salts. Marie Antoinette's last instruction to Marie Thérèse was to obey her aunt in all things and treat her as a second mother. On her passage downwards – Madame was finally coming down from her Tower – Marie Antoinette banged her head hard on the last and lowest beam. She was asked whether she was hurt. The former Queen replied blankly that she felt no pain at all.[34]

So the heavily armed party crossed the silent Temple gardens and went back into the palace itself, where that uncomfortable dinner had taken place on the first night of their imprisonment on 13 August 1792, a moment when Marie Antoinette still believed this princely residence was to be their prison. At the steps of the palace, there were two or three ordinary hackney carriages waiting and a body of soldiers. Marie Antoinette was conveyed as part of a strongly guarded cortège through the sleeping city, over the Pont Notre-Dame into the Conciergerie itself, beside the Palais de Justice. Her guards knocked loudly on the door with their bayonets.

It was the turnkey, Louis Larivière, who answered. He was extremely sleepy but even so he recognized the former Queen, all in black and dramatically pale, since as a boy he had once worked at Versailles as a pastry-cook. The jailer-registrar either did not or would not perform a similar feat of recognition. It was his duty to admit 'Prisoner no. 280', accused of having conspired against France. When he asked the new inmate for her name, she simply replied, 'Look at me.' One assumes that this answer sprang not so much from hauteur, as from the former Queen's inability to frame a suitable reply. Was she to be Marie Antoinette d'Autriche et Lorraine? *Ci-devant* Queen of

France? Or Antoinette Capet? The first two answers would have been unacceptable to her jailers, the last to herself. The heat was growing as the dawn began to break and Marie Antoinette had to wipe the sweat from her face with her handkerchief.[35]

Inside the prison her reception was more respectful. Madame Richard, the wife of the jailer, had been warned of her arrival during the previous day. After dinner she told her young maid Rosalie Lamorlière in a low voice: 'Tonight, Rosalie, we shan't go to bed. You will sleep on a chair. The Queen is going to be transferred from the Temple to this prison.' In order to prepare a suitable cell, General de Custine, who had commanded the French army in the Rhineland but was now accused of treachery, had to be turned out of the former Council Chamber. The two women did, however, manage to get hold of some good linen and a lace-edged pillow. With this they tried to soften the grim impression of the cell, brick-floored and quite damp, with its table and prison chairs; a warder had merely added from the prison store a canvas bed, two mattresses, a bolster, a light coverlet – and a bucket.[36]

Some time after three o'clock in the morning, Madame Richard hastily aroused Rosalie in her chair: 'Hurry, hurry, wake up, Rosalie,' she said, pulling at her arm. Trembling, the girl went down the long dark corridor and at the far end found the Queen already in Custine's cell. She was looking round at its spartan contents and then transferred her gaze in turn to Madame Richard and Rosalie. The latter had brought a stool from her own room. Marie Antoinette proceeded to climb on it and with the help of a convenient nail already in the wall, hung up her gold watch – a watch that Maria Teresa had given her.

The Queen then proceeded to undress. Rosalie offered to help. 'Thank you, my child,' replied Marie Antoinette. 'But since I no longer have anyone [of my household] with me, I will look after myself.' She spoke pleasantly and without any undue arrogance, according to Rosalie. Daylight grew stronger. The two women extinguished their torches and left. Marie Antoinette lay down alone on the bed, which the sympathetic Rosalie at least thought 'unworthy of her'.[37]

*

The Conciergerie was now the vast antechamber to the Revolutionary Tribunal, a warren full of people of all sorts who had incurred the suspicion of the state. On the Quai de l'Horloge of the Seine, it had once been a sumptuous royal palace hailed as more beautiful than any yet seen in France, taking its name from the concierge or keeper in charge of the King's residence. Since the late fourteenth century it had, however, been a much less comfortable prison. The Conciergerie's proximity to the river meant that most of its cells were damp, and given the age of the predominantly Gothic structure, most of them were also dark.

With the constant arrival and departure of prisoners, lawyers, hopeful or disappointed visitors, the general commotion of the Conciergerie was in complete contrast to the seclusion of the Temple with its tiny band of prized captives. In the case of Marie Antoinette, she was no longer a grand lady in Madame's Tower but an ordinary prisoner who would, like the rest of the occupants, soon be brought to judgement. But, of course, the widowed *ci-devant* Queen was also a figure of tragic celebrity – or notoriety, according to the point of view. With the connivance of good-natured jailers, intent on pleasing the public where possible (for money), Marie Antoinette now became one of the sights of the Conciergerie. Asked later whether she had recognized any particular individual, she was able to shrug and say with some plausibility: 'There were so many...'[38]

The Tower, before the King's death, had brought a kind of private family life of which most royal parents only dreamt; now the Conciergerie, in another reversal of expectations, removed all Marie Antoinette's privacy. The gendarmes were in the outer section of her cell day and night.* There was a half-curtain four

---

* There is a replica of a cell at the Conciergerie today. It shows the back of a black-clad figure, in a veil, reading a book, watched by a guard standing extremely close and peering over the screen. Tourists flock in and there is a susurration of the name in many languages and accents: 'Maree Antoinette ... Maria Antonietta ... Maria Antonia ... Marie.' Relics include a small beflowered water jug and a white linen napkin. The official notice, printed in French, English and German, refers to Marie Antoinette as 'a brilliant but carefree and extravagant personality', an image singularly at variance with the sight of the hunched widow.

feet high, which enabled her to wash, perform her natural functions and carry out her very limited *toilette*, for all of which the guards allowed her 'no liberty'.[39] But, of course, the public access, whether based on sympathy or ghoulish curiosity, together with the existence of fellow prisoners nearby, brought certain advantages undreamt of at the Temple.

It was relevant, for example, that there were many former nuns in the Conciergerie, imprisoned for their faith. Marie Antoinette saw one stretching up her hands, evidently in prayer on her behalf, out of the low barred window that looked on to the Women's Courtyard. Then there were non-juror priests inside the Conciergerie, and other clandestine priests who were still at liberty might be able to visit the former Queen in disguise. Saying the Mass required very little in the way of equipment; the forbidden pastors, as in all countries where a religion is proscribed, were becoming expert at organizing it. The presentation of an already consecrated Communion wafer was an even simpler matter. The eminent Abbé Emery was one of those known to have done this. The former Superior of the Seminary of Saint-Sulpice was imprisoned at the beginning of August, and, with the help of loyal clergy who brought him hosts wrapped in white handkerchiefs, continued his mission.[40]

In this context the story of a certain Mademoiselle Fouché – that she brought the non-juror Abbé Magnin into the prison to solace the Queen – is perfectly plausible. Mademoiselle Fouché was a young woman from a respectable family in Orléans; Magnin was the former Superior of the Little Seminary at Autun, now living in Paris disguised as a Fouché uncle under the name of 'Monsieur Charles'. Mademoiselle Fouché told of smuggling him in on several occasions; at one point Magnin spent an hour and a half with the Queen, courtesy of Richard and his 'good gendarmes' – plenty of time for confession and Communion.[41]

Marie Antoinette's religion had become increasingly important to her over the years as her ordeal intensified. The laughing girl, who had protested to the Abbé de Vermond that nothing would make of her a *dévote*, had developed into a woman who was markedly pious, much as her mother had been. At Easter 1792, still in the Tuileries, the Queen had got up at five o'clock in the morning to attend a secret Mass celebrated by a non-juror cousin of Madame Campan.[42] Her close relationship with her sister-in-law, ending in months of exclusive companionship, was also significant; political differences were forgotten, and at the Temple it had been back to the affectionate intimacy that the two had enjoyed when Marie Antoinette first arrived at Versailles, and Elisabeth became her little protégée – except that, where religion was concerned, Madame Elisabeth was now the leader.

The other possibility that this semi-public access presented was not so much spiritual nourishment as physical escape. It is difficult to estimate the seriousness of the various private attempts made to free the Queen while she was in the Conciergerie. However, unlike the 1791 flight, which might have been achieved but failed for extraneous reasons, one suspects that none of them had any real practical chance of success. In the case of the best-known attempt, the so-called Carnation Plot of late August and early September, the issue is clouded rather than clarified by the arrest of the conspirators and the subsequent testimonies, where all concerned tried to exonerate or protect themselves.

The plot took its name from the flower that a certain Alexandre de Rougeville dropped at the Queen's feet in her cell. Rougeville had formerly been part of the Comte de Provence's military establishment. He had plucked the carnation from the garden of his landlady Sophie Dutilleul. Rougeville had been introduced into the Conciergerie by the ever assiduous police administrator Michonis; the idea was for Marie Antoinette to be spirited away in a waiting carriage to the château of Madame de Jarjayes and so to Germany. Trembling, since she recognized a former Knight of the Order of Saint Louis, Marie Antoinette picked up the flower. Inside the petals was concealed a tiny note, which the Queen attempted to answer by pricking out a message with a pin. Huë heard that her response was 'negative'. But if she did indicate her readiness to escape, this plan foundered when Gilbert, one of the gendarmes who was in regular attendance in the Queen's cell, gave the game away.[43] Either he betrayed Marie Antoinette's confidence, envisaging danger to himself if she escaped, or he simply deduced what was going on from Rougeville's repeated visits and decided, for similarly self-preservative reasons, to have no part in it. Nevertheless one cannot help being sceptical as to how far the Queen really got on the path to freedom on this occasion.

The same sad scepticism must attend the Wigmakers' Conspiracy a few weeks later, in which a group of Parisian professionals whose work had depended on the lifestyle of the old regime, including pastry-cooks and lace-workers and lemonade-makers as well as the eponymous wigmakers, paid touching tribute to the Queen who had been their patroness and plotted to free her. The wigmakers and their colleagues were, however, betrayed. Another plot, in which the Baron de Batz was once more involved, was discovered thanks to an informer in the prison, Jean Baptiste Carteron.[44]

In later years, of course, it would be romantic to talk of trying and failing to free the tragic Queen of France. An example of this kind of enterprise (for which there is no independent corroboration) was provided by Charlotte Lady Atkyns, the pretty wife of an English baronet who had once been an actress at the Drury Lane Theatre. A friend of the Princesse de Tarante, she had formed a devotion to Marie Antoinette during her visits to France and conceived the idea of smuggling the Queen out of the Conciergerie. Putting both her thespian talents and her husband's money to good use, Charlotte Atkyns bribed a National Guard with 1000 louis to let her in, wearing his uniform. She then tried in vain to persuade the Queen to change clothes with her. Madame Guyot, head nurse at a hospice, had a similar plan – and a similar failure. She wanted to get the Queen transferred to her care, on the grounds of her health, whereupon she would be smuggled away to freedom, disguised as a young pregnant woman, Madame de Blamont.[45]

What is quite clear, however, is that these and other well-meaning private ventures were in marked contrast to the supine behaviour of Marie Antoinette's Austrian relations. The little people could get in, thanks to their obscurity, but practically speaking they could not get the Queen out. The great people with their armies and their treasuries had a much better chance of success – but showed no real signs of making the attempt.

Two of the Queen's supporters in Brussels, Count Fersen and the Comte de La Marck, were both driven frantic by the caution – or was it sheer indifference? – with which any idea of liberating the Emperor's aunt was greeted. Fersen, the man of action, suggested riding in from the Belgian frontier with a troop of gallant men and simply lifting the Queen from the Conciergerie. Mercy gave this idea a 'freezing' reception. Mercy's own notion, put to the allied commander, the Prince of Saxe-Coburg, was for some more measured military initiative. It was Coburg who poured cold water on this idea. The Queen might even be dead by now; besides, 'To menace savage men when you cannot do anything about it, is to make them yet more ferocious.' But perhaps the key sentence in Coburg's response was this: he had to think not only of the Queen, but of 'the real interests of the [Austrian] monarchy'.[46]

There was still the question of the four commissioners of the Convention brought over by Dumouriez. The Prince of Coburg did moot the possibility of an exchange with them in a postscript to a letter to Mercy in Brussels of 16 August. In his reply two days later, however, Mercy described such a plan as 'very delicate and not to be undertaken lightly'.[47] He proposed to reflect on it. And there the matter rested.

The Comte de La Marck supported what was, frankly, always the most promising approach. Marie Antoinette's freedom should literally be bought – and at a high price. The finances of the revolutionary government were in no better state than those of the former regime, thanks in both cases to the dangerous extravagance of financing foreign wars. By a law of 10 June, the contents of the royal palaces – 'the sumptuous furniture of the last tyrants of France' and 'the vast possessions which they reserved to their pleasure' – were now being sold off in aid of 'the defence of liberty'. This was often done at a loss: for example, a commode, two corner cupboards and a desk that had belonged to Louis XVI went for 5000 livres, whereas the desk alone had cost nearly 6000 in 1787. Urgency did not lead to good business practice. At the two-day August sale at the Petit Trianon of the former belongings of 'the woman Capet', including 'suites of furniture ... escritoires, consoles with marble tops, chairs with stools covered in damask and silk velvet ... glass and china for both pantry and parlour use', it was made clear that these objects could be transported to 'foreign parts' without any duty being paid. In a gesture that seemed to indicate that time now stood still at a deserted Versailles, all the Queen's clocks there were sold.*[48]

Like the precious objects with which she had once surrounded herself, 'the woman Capet' might have had considerable value to the Revolution as a hostage to be ransomed. La Marck reported to Mercy that a banker called Ribbes who had lent him 600,000 livres had contacts, including a brother, in Paris. He was prepared to go to the frontier and negotiate, possibly with Danton. For a moment, Mercy hesitated ... Then at the last moment he decided that the offer of money was unnecessary; it would be enough to offer a free pardon to the revolutionaries in the name of the Emperor once victory was achieved. In vain La Marck beseeched the diplomat 'not to wait for a response [from Austria] which may be too late', but to despatch another courier. His letter of 14 September was full of despair: 'They must understand in Vienna how painful, I might even say how amazing, it would be for the imperial government if history could say one day that forty leagues away from formidable and victorious Austrian armies, the august daughter of Maria Teresa has perished upon the scaffold without any attempt being made to save her.'[49] But nothing happened.

---

* The English royal family bought some of the belongings of the former King and Queen of France. As tends to happen when new regimes need money – Cromwell's Commonwealth and the Soviet Government come to mind – other more stable royal families benefited.

CHAPTER TWENTY-SIX

The Head of Antoinette

'I have promised the head of Antoinette. I will go and
cut it off myself if there is any delay in giving it to me.'
Hébert to the Committee of Public Safety,
2 September 1793

With touching faith in the family whose interests she
had tried for so long to serve, Marie Antoinette herself
continued to keep up the hope that her relations would
'reclaim' her. She told this to Rosalie Lamorlière, Madame
Richard's maid who had greeted her on arrival at the Conciergerie
and who now became the former Queen's devoted servant.
Rosalie's previous employer, a Madame Beaulieu, had been a
royalist and it was her son, an actor at the theatre close by the
Conciergerie, who had recommended the maid to the Richards.
Rosalie overcame her repugnance at working in a prison when
she found that the jailer and his wife did not try to check her
compassionate activities. Not only tender-hearted but naturally
quick, despite being virtually illiterate, Rosalie would in old age
dictate her memoirs of the Queen's prison-time, showing a
retentive memory for touching details. She described the Queen
in a reverie passing her two diamond rings endlessly from finger
to finger and back again, or looking up at the sound of a harp,
so poignantly reminiscent of her past life, and asking whether
some woman prisoner was playing (it was the daughter of one
of the glaziers currently working on her windows).[1]

Marie Antoinette's immediate need on arrival at the

Conciergerie in the early hours of the morning was clothing.
She had the black dress that she wore on her departure from
the Temple and acquired another white dress. Supplies of lingerie
were brought, handkerchiefs and black silk stockings. She had
fichus of crepe and muslin and a petticoat made of Indian
cotton. It was not much but it could be made sufficient with
the aid of Rosalie, a laundress and, for a while, old Madame
Larivière, mother of the turnkey, who had worked for the Duc
de Penthièvre for thirty years and therefore knew how things
should be done. It was Madame Larivière who skilfully patched
the black dress with muslin beneath the arms and at the hem
where it had become worn by the stones of the Temple, so that
her subsequent replacement by a Madame Harel was regretted.
At the Conciergerie the Queen's plum-coloured (*prunelle*) slippers
with their little heels *à la Saint Huberty* would become so coated
with rust that at one point a friendly guard scraped them down
with his sword.[2]

Another regret, felt keenly at the time according to Rosalie,
was the loss of the gold watch given to Marie Antoinette by her
mother, the good luck symbol that she had hung up herself so
carefully that first night. It was confiscated five days later. The
weather outside was boiling, the atmosphere in the Conciergerie
hot, humid and stinking; Marie Antoinette asked Rosalie to burn
juniper in her cell to cover up the smell of the primitive
sanitation. Yet in general the Queen showed that familiar spirit
of resignation towards her altered conditions that had marked
each step in the downward spiral of her fortunes. A white
ribbon was bought to dress her hair in the morning, an art at
which Rosalie became expert. It was Rosalie who brought in a
little cheap mirror with a red border and an oriental pattern on
its back. These few possessions came to be stored in a cardboard
box supplied by the maid, who was thanked by the Queen with
as much enthusiasm as if she had imported one of Riesener's
masterpieces.

Marie Antoinette was allowed Ville d'Avray mineral water,
from the Temple; the water from the Seine that was drunk by
the rest of the prisoners would no doubt have provided that
'natural death' that her desperate sister Maria Carolina was

beginning to think might be her happiest fate. She was given coffee for breakfast. The food – chicken, which she cut up extremely carefully and made last, and vegetables served on pewter – was the sort she liked; it was supplemented by the nourishing clear soup known as bouillon, on which Rosalie prided herself and which was the contemporary panacea for every nervous ill. The concierge and his wife, the Richards, were also well disposed towards their prisoner. Madame Richard had once sold haberdashery; she understood the need for comfort in small things. With her connivance (she was given the code name 'Sensible'), Huë himself got into the Conciergerie and managed to pass on news of the royal children to the Queen. A flush of emotion was produced in Marie Antoinette by the sight of the Richards' blond, blue-eyed child, Fanfan, introduced when she had been talking at length about her own missing family. She trembled, covered the boy with kisses and began to cry, so that Madame Richard judged it a mistake to introduce Fanfan again.[3]

It was Madame Richard who confided to Huë that her daily shopping was made easy by invoking the distinguished prisoner's name. When a fine melon was said to be destined for 'our unhappy Queen', the shopkeeper waived all charges. 'There are those among us who weep for her,' he told the concierge's wife. Rosalie had a similar experience buying peaches. The maid also put little bouquets on Marie Antoinette's small table from time to time, which led the Queen to confide in her sadly how she had had a 'real passion' for flowers in the past. This practice was later forbidden.

Marie Antoinette found solace from the aching boredom that is every prisoner's lot by watching the guards at their eternal card games. She had sent for her knitting-box from the Temple to continue making stockings for her son; the royal ladies, left behind, knowing 'how fond she was of this occupation', had hastily packed up all the silk and worsted they could find. But this was not permitted. Nor was she allowed needles for embroidery, so she began to pull out threads from the remains of the toile on the walls, and weave them into garters. And then there was reading. There is something touching about the fact that in confinement her taste turned to foreign adventures; *The Travels of Captain Cook*, lent to her by a subsequent jailer, became a favourite. *Un Voyage à Venise* amused Marie Antoinette because it contained references to people she had known in her youth.[4]

This form of existence, extremely confined but not completely intolerable, was brought to an end officially by the discovery of the Carnation Plot in early September. The indulgent Richards were taken away to be imprisoned themselves. They were replaced by the Baults, who were far more circumspect in their behaviour, given what had happened to their predecessors. Even if Bault was not a bad man at heart, according to Rosalie, Madame Bault did not have the elegant skills of Madame Richard, the former haberdasher. Marie Antoinette drew back from having her hair done by her when the concierge suggested it, declaring that henceforward she would dress it herself.*[5]

On 11 September the Queen was moved to another cell, the former pharmacy.† Although it too had a window on to the Women's Courtyard, this was to be semi-blocked. The inner and outer doors of the cell, which was divided between 'the widow Capet' and her gendarmes, were to be made much more secure.

Two long days of interrogation followed the Carnation Plot. The Queen met all the questioning not only with fortitude but also with a new kind of spirit, which one might also term bravado, if she had not been careful to couch her answers in suitably discreet terms.[8] There was no one to coach her, no tutor like Vermond, no parental-type ambassador like Mercy, yet Marie Antoinette showed both wit and cunning in her answers. That natural intelligence that the French had always doubted shone through, fortified by the resilience of character

---

* But Madame Bault, interviewed in old age by an early biographer of Marie Antoinette, Lafont d'Aussonne, struck him not only with her good memory but also with her grand manner: 'You would have thought you were dealing with a grand old countess, not a concierge's widow.'[6]

† This move has been doubted, but there are two good reasons to suppose it did take place; first, the records remain in the National Archives of the work that was done, together with the police order to do it. Second, Rosalie stated that the Queen remained only 'forty days' in the former Council Chamber, which fits this scenario.[7]

that she had had to develop – or go under. At her second interrogation, for example, she was cross-examined for nearly sixteen hours at a stretch – and yet at no point did she incriminate either herself or those who had (or had not) plotted to free her.

Marie Antoinette was particularly adroit at handling the delicate question of Louis Charles. When asked whether she had been interested in the military successes of France's enemies, she replied that she was interested in the success of the nation to which her son belonged. Which was that nation? 'Isn't he French?' answered Marie Antoinette. The question of Louis Charles's status came up and the privileges he might once have enjoyed that belonged to 'the empty title of king'. Marie Antoinette refused to be drawn on the subject, giving several versions of the same answer; she wanted France to be great and to be happy, nothing else mattered. Did she personally wish that there was still a king on the throne? Marie Antoinette replied that if France was content to have a king, she would like that king to be her son, but she was equally happy if France was content to be without a king. As to supporting the enemies of France: 'I regard as my enemies all those who would bring harm to my children.' She would not be more specific beyond repeating, 'Any kind of harm ... whatever might be harmful.'

All unknown to Marie Antoinette, the crucial meeting concerning her fate had taken place about the time of the alleged Carnation Plot and the decision had already taken place before its discovery. The subsequent revelation of the conspiracy was a coincidence – although it was a convenient one. This meeting of the Committee of Public Safety took place in secret and it lasted all night. By dawn the deaths of the Queen and the Girondins arrested at the end of May had been sealed.[9]

The leader in the call for the execution of 'the woman Capet' was Hébert. His reason, quite simply, was the need to bind the *sans-culottes* to them in an act of communal violence by shedding the blood of the *ci-devant* Queen. The death of Louis Capet had been specifically the work of the Convention, but that of

Antoinette should be the joint enterprise of the city of Paris, the Revolutionary Tribunal and the revolutionary army; the latter was in need of assurance since the French fleet at Toulon had gone over to the allies on 28 August. 'I have promised the head of Antoinette,' thundered Hébert. 'I will go and cut it off myself if there is any delay in giving it to me. I have promised it on your behalf to the *sans-culottes* who are asking for it, and without whom,' he emphasized, 'you will cease to be.'

In short, the best way to keep the people 'at white heat' was to grant them this sacrifice. 'This head' was to be for them; those of the Girondins arrested on 31 May were for the Committee. It was decided that both parties should be granted their desire. Suggestions that the former Queen might be kept as a hostage were swept away with the argument that Louis Charles Capet – 'Louis XVII' to the royalists – was hostage enough. The way was open for a Law of Suspects to be passed, in which all enemies of the people were to be tried immediately by a Revolutionary Tribunal.

Hébert's brutal exposition was in direct contrast to the sympathy that the former Queen's imagined condition in the Conciergerie was beginning to evoke in some generous hearts. In August, Germaine de Staël issued an impassioned plea, *Réflexions sur le Procès de la Reine*, whose author was simply described as 'Une Femme'. Necker's daughter, ten years younger than Marie Antoinette, was by now at Coppet in Switzerland, her father's home, having fled France after the September massacres. With two baby sons of her own, born in 1790 and 1792 respectively, Germaine sprang with zeal into a Rousseau-esque defence of Marie Antoinette as a 'tender mother'. The writer's ardour justified the Baronne d'Oberkirch's description of her: 'She is a flame.'[10]

A passionate introduction conjured 'you, women of all countries, all classes of society' to listen to her with the emotion that she herself felt. 'The destiny of Marie Antoinette contains everything that might touch your heart: if you are happy, she has had happiness; if you suffer, for one year and longer, all the pains of her life have torn her apart.' The conclusion was, from the point of view of the revolutionaries, even more lethal: a little boy on his knees – Louis Charles – was said to be demanding 'mercy for his mother'.[11]

This was the striking maternal image at one time put forward, with Marie Antoinette's connivance, by Madame Vigée Le Brun, which had once called for respect and now called for compassion. It was a far cry from that of the Infamous Antoinette, who was now held responsible by the pamphleteers for her 'savage spouse's' crimes as well as her own, thanks to her 'execrable counsels'. In contrast to the tender mother, how easy it was to suggest that this debauched creature should 'perish ignominiously on the scaffold' so that true revolutionaries could 'cement in blood' the liberty they had achieved. It might therefore become necessary to sully the maternal image and substitute for it something so vicious – even by the standards of the pamphlets so far – that there could be no question of letting such a monster live. In this connection a confidential piece of information supplied by the jailer Simon to Hébert at the end of September – that he had surprised young 'Charles Capet' masturbating – provided an exciting opportunity.[12]

The wretched boy was then induced to make a series of highly damaging allegations. Some of these were to do with a conspiracy to escape, supposedly organized by Commissioner Toulan. But it was the charge of sexual abuse on the part of his mother and aunt that was the nub of his story; how the two women together had taught him these 'very pernicious practices', making him lie in bed between them, and how the injury he had in his groin (a swollen testicle actually caused, as has been noted, by playing with a stick) was a result of this abuse. Such charges, apart from anything else involving the pious spinster Madame Elisabeth, would have been, in any other circumstances, ludicrous. But Louis Charles was an eight-year-old boy. He was now intent on pleasing the rough captors who had him helpless, plying him with drink when necessary, where once he had loved to please his mother and father. He therefore refused to retract his accusations even when confronted with his sister. Marie Thérèse was torn between shock and outrage. She did not absolutely understand what was being suggested, but knew enough to deny angrily that her brother had touched her 'where she should not be touched' in the course of their play. She signed her statement 'Thérèse Capet'.[13]

Stubbornly, Louis Charles persisted in his story even when his aunt was produced. Madame Elisabeth cried out in indignation that both his mother and herself had constantly tried to stop him in his habit, when the boy interrupted her, protesting that he had told the truth. But he became curiously vague about the details of the abuse beyond the fact that it had been done by 'the two of them together'. Had it happened by day or by night? At first he replied that he could not remember, then suggested that it had been in the morning. The consequence for Louis Charles was a breach with his sister, as well as his aunt, that would never be healed. It remained to be seen what the consequence would be for the mother he had been obliged to traduce.

Marie Antoinette underwent a secret preliminary interrogation on 12 October.[14] Two hours after she had gone to bed, on a night so cold that she had asked in vain for an extra blanket, she was roused. She was taken before the president of the Revolutionary Tribunal, Armand Martial Herman, a young ally of Robespierre, in the presence of Fouquier-Tinville, the public prosecutor. The idea was obviously to secure valuable material for the actual trial; in fact all the old canards were trotted out. She had given money to her brother the Emperor, taking part in nocturnal meetings with the Duchesse de Polignac in order to organize it. She had participated in that legendary orgy on 1 October 1789 at the royal bodyguards' dinner. Marie Antoinette denied all these charges, and when she was asked yet again whether she believed that monarchy was necessary to the happiness of France, she replied with circumspection that it was not up to an individual to decide about these things; she regretted nothing for her son so long as France prospered.

The most significant exchange – for the future – occurred when Marie Antoinette was accused of being the chief instigator of the 'treason of Louis XVI' in causing him to flee in 1791, as well as teaching him 'the arts of dissimulation'. Naturally she rebutted both charges. At the end of her interrogation Marie Antoinette was asked whether she wished to have counsel for the defence appointed. The answer was yes, she would like that. So she was taken back to her cell.*

Louis XVI had been allowed to work with his lawyers over a considerable period of time 'as though I could win'. No such privilege was accorded to Marie Antoinette. In fact the late appearance of her lawyers marked the first of many steps by which the female consort was treated a great deal more severely than the male sovereign. The distaste of the Revolution for the female sex in general – in ungrateful contrast to the role that women, intellectuals as well as market-women, had played in it earlier – did not bode well for the Widow Capet.

Women were at once inferior and dangerous, as witness the death of Marat at the hands of a young woman called Charlotte Corday in July. A supporter of the Girondins, Charlotte Corday had secured admittance to Marat's presence because her 'weaker' sex made it difficult to believe she constituted a threat; she had then proceeded to demonstrate her savagery by stabbing Marat in his bath, as Judith had executed Holofernes. She met the 'swift, humane' death of the guillotine four days later. Robespierre for one believed that the safest place for women was in the home, performing their traditional nurturing role. (In this he was in agreement with Rousseau, who thought that woman's 'glory' should reside 'in the esteem of her husband'.) Within a few weeks the various women's clubs that had urged on the Revolution would be officially suppressed. Since pre-revolutionary history was chequered with stories of cruel female rulers – to whom Marie Antoinette was regularly compared – it has been suggested that the misogyny of the Jacobin Revolution was inspired by the idea that powerful women belonged to the era of despotism. The domesticated apolitical Queen Charlotte of England was on a much more satisfactory course (from the

---

* It was believed by some after the Restoration that the Abbé Cholet gave the Queen a final Communion on the night of 12 October (the Abbé Magnin being ill) and that this was something permitted by Bault.[11] This seems a great deal more improbable than accounts of Masses and Communions under the Richards' regime, since security in the new cell was so much greater, with Marie Antoinette on the verge of trial. However, with this pious story, as with the romantic one of Fersen's last love-making in the Tuileries, one cannot help hoping that it was true.

male point of view) when she wrote that women could do much more good by staying out of public affairs and leading 'retired lives'.[16] This developing line of thought made the Widow Capet even more suspect.

The two lawyers permitted to Marie Antoinette were both at the Parisian bar: Chauveau-Lagarde (who had defended Charlotte Corday) and Tronson Doucoudray. Chauveau-Lagarde published an account of his experiences in 1816, describing how he had been in the country when he was summoned – he did not hesitate to accept – and therefore did not reach the Tuileries to inspect the mass of prosecution papers, to say nothing of the eight-page act of accusation itself, until the next day, 13 October. To visit their client, the counsels passed through the various wicket-gates of the Conciergerie to reach the divided cell with its iron-barred windows; on the left were the armed gendarmes, on the right Marie Antoinette in a plain white dress; the furniture consisted of a bed, a table and two chairs. Chauveau-Lagarde's knees trembled.[17]

Their first task was to persuade the Queen to write to the Revolutionary Tribunal and seek a delay so that the paperwork could be properly considered. She was extremely reluctant to do so, since it meant acknowledging the authority of the men who had killed Louis XVI, but in the end, with a sigh, the Queen picked up her pen. Addressing Herman as 'Citizen President', she asked for three days' respite: 'I owe it to my children to omit nothing that may be necessary to the justification of their mother.'[18]

The letter was not answered. The next day, Monday, 14 October, Marie Antoinette was collected shortly before eight o'clock in the morning and taken through the prison to the great chamber where Louis XVI had once held his *lits de justice* and which was now the seat of the Revolutionary Tribunal.

Marie Antoinette's appearance caused an immediate sensation in the crowded courtroom, thronged with cheerful spectators such as the inevitable market-women, as well as the necessary concomitants of justice, the president, Herman, the prosecutor, Fouquier-Tinville, and the jurors. The latter incidentally were not likely to give trouble to the Tribunal, just as the president would scarcely venture to cross the prosecutor. Some jurors were cronies of Robespierre, others came from humble professions, a cobbler, two carpenters and a hat-maker being among their number.

The *ci-devant* Queen looked ghastly. Here was a white-haired woman with sunken features whose extreme pallor was due as much to her persistent loss of blood as to her nine weeks' incarceration in the humid, airless Conciergerie. (Rosalie ascribed Marie Antoinette's condition to her lack of exercise, and tried to help her by cutting up her own chemises as cloths, but as has been discussed, it probably had a deeper cause.) Her haggard appearance contrasted bizarrely with the mental image that most of the spectators had of the accused. Marie Antoinette had, after all, been immured for over a year, and in the last months of her stay in the Tuileries had ventured out little in public for fear of hostility. If she was not the Austrian she-wolf, the ostrich with the harpy's face of the caricatures, then she was the glittering Queen with her diamonds and her nodding plumes, last seen properly in the glory days of the court at Versailles over four years before. As *Le Moniteur* admitted, Antoinette Capet was 'prodigiously changed'.[19]

She was nevertheless entirely composed as she stood in her widow's weeds, the worn black dress patched by Madame Larivière, and took the oath in the name of Marie Antoinette of Lorraine and Austria, widow of the King of France, born in Vienna. She described her age as being 'about thirty-eight' (the Queen was in fact two and a half weeks away from her birthday). She then looked about her at the courtroom, with what a hostile newspaper, *L'Anti-Fédéraliste*, called 'the serenity that habitual crime gives' but which was in fact the natural dignity in public inculcated since childhood. From time to time the Queen moved her fingers over the arm of her chair 'as though over the keyboard of her piano'; the diamond rings that she used to play with had been confiscated in the course of the searches following the Carnation Plot.[20]

The accused was allowed to sit down in an armchair on a little platform that put her on view, although the market-women, behind the balustrades, protested vociferously that the woman Capet ought to remain standing so that they could see her. The Tribunal's motive in granting this mercy was more prudent than kind; it would not have done for the prisoner to faint or collapse during the long hours of cross-examination that lay ahead, thus invoking unnecessary sympathy. Marie Antoinette merely murmured: 'Surely people will soon tire of hearing about my weaknesses.'

The first witness of the forty who would be called set the tone for much of what was to follow.[21] Laurent Lecointre was a former draper who had been second in command of the National Guard at Versailles during the events of October 1789. In his prolonged evidence Lecointre described feasts and orgies that had taken place at Versailles over a period of ten years, culminating in the notorious banquet of 1 October 1789 – at none of which, of course, he had been present. Cross-examined by Herman, Marie Antoinette gave a series of short, non-committal replies which equally set the tone for her responses: 'I do not believe so', 'I don't remember', 'I have nothing to say in reply.' With regard to those nocturnal meetings with 'the Polignac' at which the passing of money to the Emperor was planned: 'I have never been present at such meetings. The wealth amassed by the Polignacs was due to the paid positions they held at court.'

When Herman pressed her on the subject of Louis Capet's *séance* of 23 June 1789 and accused her of masterminding his speech, she was more explicit. It had become clear from her preliminary interrogation that the link between her evil counsels and the King's evil actions was one that the prosecution intended to demonstrate. 'My husband had great trust in me,' replied Marie Antoinette, 'so that he read me his speech but I did not allow myself to make any comment.' As to the idea of assassinating the majority of the people's representatives at this period with bayonets – a fantasy of the prosecution: 'I never heard talk of anything like that.'

Many of the witnesses who followed failed to rise above the level of scurrilous gossip or hearsay, when they were not purely inconsequential. The alleged discovery of wine bottles under the

Queen's bed after she left the Tuileries on 10 August 1792 was supposed to prove that she had deliberately made the Swiss Guards drunk in order to provoke a massacre of the French people. A maid called Reine Milliot reported a chat with the Comte (actually Duc) de Coigny in 1788 when he bemoaned the amount of gold that the Emperor was receiving because it would ruin France; she also testified that the Queen had planned to kill the Duc d'Orléans and had been reprimanded by the King. One Pierre Joseph Terrasson, employed at the Ministry of Justice, described how the Queen had cast 'the most vindictive look' upon the National Guards who escorted her back from Varennes, which proved to him that she was determined on vengeance.

The testimony of Hébert was more serious.[22] He, after all, had the evidence taken from 'young Capet' at his command. The products of his searches of the Temple were scarcely impressive – a picture of a pierced heart inscribed with the words *Jesus miserere nobis* or a hat in the room of Madame Elisabeth which had belonged to her dead brother. But the words of Louis Charles about La Fayette's involvement in Varennes (fabricated) and the gathering of outside intelligence while they were all in the Tower had more potential. Then he moved in for the kill. The physical condition of young Capet had noticeably deteriorated and Hébert was able to supply the reason: his mother and his aunt had taught him *pollutions indécentes*. Details followed, as a result of which there could be no doubt that there had been an incestuous relationship between mother and son.

After that Hébert stressed the deference with which young Capet had been treated after his father's death, when he was seated at the head of the table and served first. 'Did you witness it?' asked Marie Antoinette, making no comment on the shocking substance of Hébert's speech. Hébert agreed that he had not, but all the municipal officers certified that it had taken place. An examination concerning the Carnation Plot and Michonis's role in it all followed. It was in the course of this that one of the jurors intervened. 'Citizen President,' he said, 'I ask you to point out to the accused that she has not responded to the facts related by Citizen Hébert, regarding what took place between her and her son.' So Herman put the question.

It was a dramatic moment, as all contemporary accounts, however hostile, agreed. Marie Antoinette's marble composure deserted her. 'If I have not replied,' she said in a tone quite changed from the politely indifferent one she had been using, 'it is because Nature itself refuses to respond to such a charge laid against a mother.' The court record noted that here the accused appeared to be deeply moved. 'I appeal to all mothers who may be present,' she went on. A frisson went through the courtroom – a frisson of sympathy. As for the fickle market-women, some of them cried out in outrage that the proceedings ought to be stopped.

'Did I do well?' Marie Antoinette asked Chauveau-Lagarde in a low voice. He soothed her; she only had to be herself and she would always do well. But why the question? 'Because I heard one woman say to her neighbour: "See how arrogant she is."' The Queen's spirit in the face of such an intolerable slur was all too easily mistaken for disdain. And there was one juror, Doctor Souberbielle, who murmured scornfully: 'A mother like you…'[23]

The rest of the day and evening – the first two sessions lasted until 11 p.m. with a short break between them – produced less startling revelations. In fact very little in the way of tangible evidence was produced, with the Queen steadfastly refuting anything and everything that was put to her. Over Varennes, for example, she continued to deny the involvement of La Fayette, whose coincidental departure from the Tuileries after the King's *coucher* was thought to be highly suspicious. She answered all the other detailed questions laconically. For example, one query concerned the escape: 'How were you yourself dressed?' She replied: 'In the same dress I wore at my return.'

There was one intriguing moment when the name of the man who had purchased 'the famous carriage' was raised.

'It was a foreigner,' said Marie Antoinette.

'Of which nation?'

'Swedish.'

'Wasn't it Fersen who lived in Paris...?'

'Yes.'

Interestingly, no more was made of Fersen's involvement in the escape, suggesting that his relationship to the *ci-devant* Queen had not reached a wide audience.[24] The day ended with the examination of the two Richards and the gendarme Gilbert about the Carnation Plot, but once again no actual evidence was produced of Marie Antoinette's intent to escape and once again she admitted nothing.

The second session began at eight o'clock the following morning before Rosalie could bring the Queen her breakfast. It was 15 October, the Feast of St Teresa; a day of rejoicing in her childhood, it had been the name-day of her mother and in her adult life, that of her daughter. Now she was to spend her time in the courtroom, fasting until the late-afternoon break when Rosalie Lamorlière, aware that Marie Antoinette had had nothing to eat, brought in some of her special bouillon. Even then the maid's gesture was only partially successful. On a whim a girlfriend of one of the gendarmes, who wanted to boast of having met the former Queen, decided to serve her herself; in transporting the bouillon, she managed to spill half of it.[25]

The first witness was Charles Henri d'Estaing, once Governor of Touraine and a distinguished admiral who had spent much of his later life at Versailles.[26] He was pressed on the question of another putative royal flight – that of 5 October 1789, which had been stopped by the National Guard. Actually he bore witness that the Queen had refused to go, saying '*avec un grand caractère*' (determination) that if the Parisians came to assassinate her, she would die at the feet of the King. Marie Antoinette interrupted at this point. It was true. They had wanted the Queen to go, on the grounds that she was the only one in danger, but she had given the response quoted by d'Estaing.

Then Simon was called, to confirm revelations made by Louis Charles: how the Commissioner Dangé had taken him in his arms and in the presence of his mother declared: 'I wish you were King in place of your father.' Furthermore the boy had been treated as the King at table.

Finally, and more importantly, because for a moment it

seemed that some documentary proof was about to be offered, the Queen was questioned about 'the Polignac': had she corresponded with her since her detention? 'No.' Had she signed vouchers to enable her to draw on funds from the Civil List? 'No.' It was Fouquier-Tinville's turn to interrupt. Her denial was useless, for the vouchers signed by her would shortly be produced. Or rather, since they had been temporarily mislaid, evidence would shortly be heard from someone who had seen them.

This witness – François Tisset, who had gone through the Civil List papers after the sack of the Tuileries – deposed that he had seen the Queen's signature for sums of 80,000 livres, as well as other papers relating to large sums signed by the King, payments for Favras, Bouillé and others. Marie Antoinette pounced. What date was on the documents? One was 10 August 1792 and Tisset could not remember the other one. She could hardly have dated anything 10 August, replied the Queen scornfully, since, following the attack on the palace, she had been at the National Assembly since eight o'clock that morning.

Some of the evidence produced was more pathetic than treacherous. A little packet was shown to Marie Antoinette which she had brought from the Temple to the Conciergerie: 'Those are locks of hair of my children, the living and the dead, and of my husband.' A paper with figures written on it was to teach her son maths. Portraits were shown; one was of 'Madame de Lamballe', said Marie Antoinette. No one commented. Others proved to be of the Princesses (of Hesse) 'with whom I was brought up in Vienna'. Over the expenses of the Petit Trianon – which, incidentally, she was accused of building as well as decorating although it had been built in the previous reign – the former Queen did at last give a little ground. 'Perhaps more was spent than I would have wished.' Payments had mounted, little by little, and no one wished more than her to understand how it came about.

On one subject, however, Marie Antoinette was absolutely resolute. She had never met Jeanne Lamotte.

'You persist in denying that you knew her?'

'My intention is not to make a denial, but to tell the truth; that is what I persist in stating.'

When she sat for Kucharski's pastel portrait in the Temple, had she used the opportunity to receive news of what was going on in the Convention? 'No. He was simply a Polish painter who had lived in Paris for twenty years.' Other replies were equally staunch. As to Louis Capet's allegations that La Fayette (and Bailly) had been involved in Varennes: 'It is extremely easy to make a child of eight say anything you want,' replied Marie Antoinette significantly, no doubt having in mind the incestuous 'revelations' of the previous day.

Not all the witnesses exhibited the same spirit. While Doctor Brunier denied that he had exhibited all the 'servilities' of the *ancien régime* in treating the royal children,* Commissioner Dangé was more cautious. After he had denied making that fatal royalist whisper into the ear of Louis Charles, he was asked his opinion of the accused. If she was guilty, he replied, she must be judged. Was she a patriot? No. Did she want there to be a Republic? No.

The fortieth witness was followed by a final cross-examination of the prisoner. It was now getting on for midnight. Yet further charges of subverting the royal bodyguards and congratulating the Marquis de Bouillé on the 'massacre' at Nancy in 1790 were followed by a strange, almost nostalgic reference to her past. Since her marriage, had not Marie Antoinette conceived the project of reuniting (French) Lorraine and Austria? She had not.

'But you bear the name.'

'Because one has to bear the name of one's country,' replied Marie Antoinette.

Accused once again of teaching her son royalist precepts and putting him at the head of the table, to be served as King, she answered that he had been at the bottom of the table and she had served him herself.

At the very last, she was asked if she had anything further to say in her defence. 'Yesterday I did not know who the witnesses

---

* Meaning, literally, no more than the *former* regime, although the words *ancien régime* have come to have a weightier meaning.

were to be,' answered Marie Antoinette. 'I was ignorant of what they would say. Well, no one has articulated anything positive against me. I finish by observing that I was only the wife of Louis XVI and I had to conform to his wishes.' These were her last words to the court. Marie Antoinette, a woman in terrible health, had been in the courtroom something like sixteen hours, with only a few sips of bouillon to sustain her, having spent fifteen hours there the day before. Nevertheless these words focused on the real issue.

During the proceedings, it had been the constant harping on Marie Antoinette's 'evil ascendancy' over the 'feeble character' of Louis Capet that more than anything else revealed the insubstantiality of the judicial case against her. The traditional image of female weakness, a queen consort, devoid of responsibility and thus presumably of guilt for state actions, had to be replaced by that of a viciously powerful and dominating Messalina. Naturally the Queen herself denied Louis' feebleness: 'I never knew him to have such a character.' But the prosecution, by insisting to the contrary, could transfer the culpability of the former King entirely to the former Queen, and since the King's guilt had been proved in court, logically there was no need to prove that of the Queen further. The fact that nothing, as she herself said, had really been proved against her – there were charges of foreign correspondence and intrigues, but no evidence to support them – then became irrelevant.

Fouquier-Tinville now spoke at some length to a silent courtroom, followed by Chauveau-Lagarde. The prisoner was then taken out to an ante-room while the president of the Tribunal summed up for the jurors.[27] Marie Antoinette was therefore not in a position to listen to Herman's summation to the jurors. The key passage occurred halfway through. Her chief crimes were listed as follows: her secret agreements with foreign powers, including her brothers, émigré Princes and treacherous generals; her shipping of money abroad to help them; and lastly her conspiring with these powers against the security of the French State, both at home and abroad. 'If verbal proof was required,' declared Herman, 'then let the accused be paraded before the people of France; but if it was a question of material proof, that would be found among the papers seized from Louis Capet, listed already to the Convention.' These papers were, however, not produced.

Ignorant of what was being said, ignorant too of Hébert's secret command to the Convention – 'I must have the head of Antoinette' – the former Queen allowed herself to be buoyed up with the adrenalin that a bold performance, given against the odds, bestows. We have Chauveau-Lagarde's word for it that she was convinced she would be ransomed and sent abroad because nothing had been proved against her. There were others present of the same opinion; Madame Bault heard someone say: 'Marie Antoinette will get away with it; she answered like an angel. She will be deported.'[28] None of these people had experience of revolutionary justice or what was in effect a show trial, with the verdict predetermined. When she was brought back, she was handed the verdict of the jury, and told to read it. She was found guilty on all counts. Fouquier-Tinville then asked for, and was granted, the death penalty.

Asked if she had anything to say Marie Antoinette simply shook her head. It showed true courage, according to Chauveau-Lagarde, not to admit for a moment the shock she felt. Her head – the forfeit head of Antoinette – was held majestically high in a final display of dignity (or disdain) as she passed the barriers where the people were. To the sympathetic, the former Queen appeared to be in some kind of trance, so that she no longer saw or heard anything to do with her surroundings. She had to be prevented from slipping in the yard on the way back to her cell. It was past four o'clock in the morning and bitterly cold.

Marie Antoinette was now officially allowed writing materials. She used them to address a 'last letter' to Madame Elisabeth, heading it 'October 16. 4.30 in the morning'.

'I have just been condemned to death, not to a shameful death, that can only be for criminals, but in order to rejoin your brother. Innocent like him, I hope to demonstrate the same firmness as he did at the end. I am calm, as people are whose conscience is clear. My deepest regret is at having to abandon our poor children; you know that I only lived on for them and for you, my good and tender sister.'[29]

Believing (wrongly) that Marie Thérèse had been separated from her aunt, her mother dared do no more than send her blessing. There were instructions to both children to care for each other, and the elder in particular to look after the younger. As for Louis Charles: 'Let my son never forget his father's last words ... never try to avenge our deaths.' Marie Antoinette then raised the anguishing matter of the boy's allegations. 'I know how much pain this child must have given you. Forgive him, my dear sister; think of his age and how easy it is to make a child say what one wants, even things he doesn't understand.' It was the same point about Louis Charles's impressionable nature that she had made to the incoming Governess, the Marquise de Tourzel, and again at her trial.

As to religion, Marie Antoinette declared herself dying in the Catholic, Apostolic and Roman faith of her forefathers, in which she had been brought up, and which she had always professed. Here in prison she could expect no spiritual consolation; she did not even know whether there were any true – that is, non-juror – priests in the prison, but she would not in any case expose them to danger. (Although these words have been cited as proof that Marie Antoinette did not receive Communion while in the Conciergerie, she would hardly have given details of available non-jurors in a document that would undoubtedly be read by the authorities.)

'I ask God's pardon for all the sins that I have committed,' the Queen went on, and she asked pardon from all those she knew, but especially Madame Elisabeth, for any pain she might unwittingly have caused them – it was the same Christian formula that Louis XVI had used. 'I bid farewell to my aunts, and all my brothers and sisters. I had friends; the idea of being separated from them for ever, and their sufferings as a result, are one of the greatest regrets I take with me to my death; they should know that at the last moment I think of them.' Was it the Polignac? Was it Fersen? Both? Many others once part of her magic world? The Queen did not name them.

'Adieu my good and tender sister; may this letter reach you!

Think of me always; I embrace you with all my heart, as well as those poor beloved children. My God, it tears me to leave them for ever. Adieu, adieu, I now think only of my spiritual duties … They may bring me a [juror] priest here, but I solemnly declare here that I shall treat him as a total stranger.'* In due course the juror Abbé Girard was indeed imposed upon Marie Antoinette, being introduced into her cell, but she kept her word.

Yet the absence of a priest of her own kind emphasized the marked difference in the treatment of Marie Antoinette and Louis XVI at the last. Louis Capet had been allowed days to work with his lawyers for his defence, Marie Antoinette a few hours. The former King had his faithful valet and old friend Cléry with him up to the moment when he left the Temple. Almost too painful perhaps for Marie Antoinette to contemplate, she had been allowed to bring the children to him on the eve of execution for a final farewell. And he had been granted the services of the non-juror Abbé Edgeworth, not only the night before, but accompanying him right up to the scaffold. It was the Abbé Edgeworth, according to popular report, who told his royal master at the end: 'Son of Saint Louis, ascend to heaven.'[31] There were to be no such consoling words and no such company for Marie Antoinette.

There was only Rosalie Lamorlière, who came to her timidly at seven o'clock in the morning to see if she wanted any food. The maid had been woken to hear the verdict earlier, when she felt 'as if a sword had gone through her heart', and she spent the next few hours sobbing secretly in her room. Bault too was sad, Rosalie remembered afterwards, although being a jailer he was accustomed to such things. It was Rosalie therefore who was the witness to the Queen's despair. She found Marie Antoinette in her black dress lying on her bed, her head turned to the barred window, her hand against her cheek. Two lights

---

* But the 'last letter' never reached Madame Elisabeth. It was intercepted and given to Robespierre; it was unknown until 1816. It is now in the Archives Nationales showing the countersignature of Fouquier-Tinville, with three other signatures later. A note validates Marie Antoinette's handwriting ('*conforme à l'autographe*').[30]

were burning and the ever-present gendarmes were watching from the corner.[32]

The Queen wept as she refused to take any nourishment: 'My child, I need nothing. Everything is over for me.' Rosalie continued to offer the bouillon and some vermicelli that she had ready in her oven. Wearily the Queen agreed to the bouillon but took only a few mouthfuls before putting it aside. She had now eaten practically nothing for several days and was losing blood to an extent that Rosalie found frightening. At eight o'clock it was time to dress. Antoinette Capet was not allowed to wear her familiar black on the grounds that the crowd might insult the evil enchantress for daring to put on decent mourning. So she was left to wear her simple white dress of everyday; no one remembered that in the past white had been the mourning of the Queens of France.[33]

It was Rosalie too who was witness to the planned humiliation that was to be the lot of the woman Antoinette, where that of Louis Capet had been dignity even in death. First, she was obliged, for example, to get ready under the gendarmes' watchful eyes. When Marie Antoinette attempted to undress in a little niche between the wall and the bed, signing to Rosalie to shield her, one of the men came round and stood looking at her. Pulling her fichu round her shoulders, she pleaded with him: 'Monsieur, for decency's sake let me change my chemise in private.' The gendarme replied brusquely that his orders were to keep an eye on the prisoner at all times. The Queen sighed and changed as modestly as possible, stuffing the chemise, which was heavily bloodstained, into one of her loose sleeves, and hiding it in a crevice in the wall. To her white dress, she added a linen cap with pleated edges and two streamers that she took out of a box, which, with some black crepe, she made into an approximation of a widow's bonnet. For the rest of her costume she had to make do with what was there: the black silk stockings and plum-coloured shoes.

The humiliation continued when Charles Henri Sanson, fourth generation of his family to act as executioner, came to hack off her thin white hair with his enormous professional scissors. It got worse when they told the former Queen that her hands were to be bound. 'You did not bind the hands of Louis XVI,' Marie Antoinette protested at this point. But bound her hands were to be, and so tightly that her arms were dragged back behind her. The next humiliation occurred when the Queen was overcome with weakness. She asked to have her hands unbound in order to go and squat in the corner. That was grudgingly conceded. Having relieved herself, she meekly held out her hands to be bound again.[34]

The nature of death by 'Celestial Guillotine' or 'Sainte Guillotine, protectress of patriots' as contemporaries nicknamed it, was that it was essentially theatrical, a slow procession followed by a quick death.[35] In the case of Marie Antoinette, the procession that set off at eleven o'clock was also intended to be part of the ritual cruelty. She was installed in a cart rather than a carriage, drawn by the heavy horses known as *rosinantes*. When the former Queen instinctively went to sit in the back – her position in those magnificent carriages of Versailles – she was sharply corrected and told to sit with her back to the horses. A jolt of the cart nearly threw her down, and one of the gendarmes pointed out with satisfaction: 'There are none of your fine Trianon cushions here.'

The day was fine, slightly misty, and the deep cold of the night hours had gone. The huge crowds that lined the route to the guillotine at the Place de la Concorde listened to the cries of the escort: 'Make way for the Austrian woman!' and 'Long live the Republic!' The actor Grammont, ahead of the procession on horseback, stood up in his stirrups and waved his sword, shouting: 'Here she is, the infamous Antoinette, she is *foutue*, my friends!' Mainly the crowd heard these cries with satisfaction. The painter David, watching the Austrian woman from a window, drew her on her final journey in order to illustrate once and for all the contempt of the Habsburg Archduchess with her haughty indifferent expression and her pouting lip. A woman outside the Church of Saint-Roch spat at the cortège. Outside the Church of the Oratory one woman did hold up her laughing child, who was about the same age as Louis Charles, in a gesture of support, but on the whole the *ci-devant* aristocrats were discreet in their silent sympathy even if the police recognized them by their tight lips and sad expressions.[36]

Yet prolonged humiliation can in the end damage those who try to inflict it. Just as David's celebrated drawing done from the life as the prisoner passed can be interpreted as a final image of disdain – or unalterable calm dignity, depending on the point of view. Every account, every eyewitness, agreed on the unassailable composure with which Marie Antoinette went to her death. 'Audacious and insolent to the end,' wrote Hébert's *Le Père Duchesne* while *Le Moniteur* admitted more pedestrianly that she showed 'courage enough'. Virieu, the envoy of Parma, where her sister the Habsburg Amalia was the reigning Duchess, put it another way: Marie Antoinette never failed for a single instant either her great soul or the illustrious blood of the House of Austria. Only one moment did she falter and show some sudden emotion. This was at the sight of the Tuileries, bringing memories of the past and of her children. Her eyes momentarily filled with tears.[37]

By the time the cart reached the Place de la Concorde, she was sufficiently in command of herself to step easily down. Stepping lightly – 'with bravado' – she sprang up the steps of the scaffold despite her bound hands, pausing only to apologize to Sanson for stepping on his foot – 'I did not do it on purpose.' So she went willingly, even eagerly, to her death. And why should she not? Ten days earlier Maria Carolina had written of her sister: 'Everything that ends her torture is good.' Now that torture was about to end. 'This is the moment, Madame, to arm yourself with courage,' the juror Abbé Girard had said, still trying to press his spiritual services upon her in the face of her firm rejection. 'Courage!' exclaimed Marie Antoinette. 'The moment when my ills are going to end is not the moment when courage is going to fail me.'[38]

So the head of Antoinette, desired by Hébert, was cut off cleanly at twelve-fifteen on Wednesday, 16 October 1793, and exhibited to a joyous public. An unhinged man, who got under the scaffold and tried to bathe his handkerchief in the royal blood, was quickly taken away by the gendarmes.

CHAPTER TWENTY-SEVEN

Epilogue

'This prison can now serve as the laboratory of a new experience; to look without passion at the symbols of murders long past.'

Notice today in the Conciergerie

The journey – that journey which had begun in an imperial palace in Vienna and finished in a squalid cell in Paris – was completed. The body of Marie Antoinette with its severed head was taken unceremoniously to the graveyard off the rue d'Anjou, where Louis XVI had been interred nine and a half months previously. The people who had been crushed to death in the fireworks episode following the Dauphine's marriage had been buried there, as were, many years later, some of the Swiss Guards who died in the attack on the Tuileries. Now carts bearing fresh victims went to the rue d'Anjou every day.[1]

The gravediggers took time off to have their lunch, leaving the head and body on the grass unattended. This meant that the future Madame Tussaud was able to sculpt the Queen's lifeless face in wax; unlike her impression of the Princesse de Lamballe, however, this model was never exhibited. Two weeks later the bill for the interment came in: for the coffin six livres, for grave and gravediggers fifteen livres and thirty-five sous.[2]

Back at the Conciergerie, the effects of 'the Widow Capet' were listed. They were pitiful compared to the elaborate belongings that would be left by Philippe Égalité, *ci-devant* Duc d'Orléans, executed on 6 November. 'I vote for death,' shouted the derisive crowd as he passed, imitating the words with which he had condemned Louis XVI. Égalité died as he had lived, a rich man, going to the scaffold 'heavily powdered' and elegant, leaving behind waistcoats with silver buttons, breeches, cravats, dressing-gowns, sets of silver plate and a magnificent picnic basket. Everything that Marie Antoinette left was very plain: a few linen chemises and corsets in fine toile as well as some 'linge à blanchir', two pairs of black stockings, a lawn headdress, some black crepe, some batiste handkerchiefs, garters and two pairs of cotton 'pockets' which she used to carry her belongings inside her dress. She also left a box of powder, a 'big fine sponge' and a little box of pomade – the single last remnants of a *toilette* that in all its pomp had once preoccupied the whole of Versailles.[3]

These remains were distributed, according to custom, among the women prisoners of the Salpêtrière prison. Four years later those other objects that had been seized at the Temple and produced for trial were put up for auction. They included a small green morocco case for sewing things, and three little portraits in green shagreen cases. They raised a total of ten francs, fifteen centimes; everything else had been stolen.[4]

Public reaction in France to the death of the former Queen was ecstatic. Numerous congratulatory petitions were received by the Revolutionary Tribunal along these lines: 'It is fallen at last, the head of the haughty Austrian woman gorged with the blood of the people ...'; 'the execrable head of the Messalina Marie Antoinette ...'; 'Here is the second royal monster laid low ...'; 'The soil of France is purged of this pestilential couple.' A note of variety was struck by the District of Josselin, Department of Morbihan, which mentioned Marie Thérèse as being her mother's 'living portrait' and in character too; as for the boy, the teeth of the wolf-cub should be pulled out as soon as possible.

A Jacobin club in Angoulême made an outing to the foot of a so-called Tree of Liberty (these trees were popular symbols of the Revolution) 'to give thanks to the divinity that has rid us of this fury'. A choir then sang 'a sacred song'; it was the 'Marsellaise'. *Marie Antoinette au Diable* expressed the general theme of the pamphlets, whose voices were not stilled by her death. The former Queen had now claimed her place in hell, where she expected to find her mother and her two Emperor brothers, but 'as for my fat porpoise of a husband', that crass drunkard, 'I want to have nothing more to do with him.'

But as the news spread in the prisons of Marie Antoinette's 'greatness and courage' at the last, royalists there took comfort. Grace Elliott in Sainte Pélagie prison wrote of how they were all inspired by her example and hoped to follow it when the time came. Unfortunately the poor Comtesse Du Barry found herself unable to do so. The royal mistress, still beautiful at fifty, whiled her time away sitting on Grace Elliott's bed and telling her anecdotes of Louis XV and his court.[6] But when her time came to mount the scaffold, all composure deserted her. The Du Barry desperately but vainly tried to avoid her fate; she had, after all, been trained to give pleasure, not to die.

Outside, the royalist world tried to accommodate itself to the tragedy. The Duchesse de Polignac died shortly afterwards of what was generally believed to be a broken heart but was probably cancer accelerated by suffering. Her health had given way when the King was killed, her daughter had told Madame Vigée Le Brun, but at the news about the Queen, 'her charming face became quite altered and one could see death written there.' To Count Mercy d'Argenteau, however, in Brussels, the horrifying death was inevitably linked to the name of the Empress he had once served; his first reaction was nothing to do with Marie Antoinette but simple shock at seeing 'the blood of the great Maria Teresa shed upon the scaffold'.[7]

Fersen, also in Brussels, received the news on 20 October. For a while he felt quite numb, while Brussels society regarded him with silent and respectful pity. After that he kept 16 October – 'this atrocious day' – as a day of mourning for the rest of his life, for her who had been, as he told Lady Elizabeth Foster on 22 October, 'the model of queens and of women'. He was left with an ideal in his heart; memories of her sweetness, tenderness, goodness, her loving nature, her sensibility flooded over him in his correspondence with his sister. He told Sophie that Eléanore Sullivan could never replace Marie Antoinette – 'Elle' – in his heart.[8]

He did not know that his end, seventeen years after that of his heroine, was to be equally, if not more, violent than hers. The Count incurred the enmity of the Swedish crowd who were incited to believe that he had poisoned Christian, the Danish heir to the throne. At the funeral procession on 20 June 1810 – an ill-omened date – Fersen was set upon and torn to pieces, a fate that had been so often predicted for Marie Antoinette. He had never been repaid the prodigious sums that he had dispensed trying to save the King and Queen, his claim being shunted from royal to royal despite clear letters of proof.[9]

Maria Carolina, in Naples, was devastated in spite of her premonitions of disaster. Amélie, one of her string of daughters (like her mother, Maria Carolina had a vast family), always remembered being told of her aunt's death. The Queen took them all into the chapel to attend Mass and pray for Marie Antoinette. Amélie was then eleven and had already shed a few tears for the death of the first Dauphin whom she had fancied she might marry – they were of an age – and thus become Queen of France. Many years later, the unmarried Amélie fastened her affections on Louis Philippe, Duc d'Orléans since the death of Philippe Égalité. Maria Carolina had even tried to stop herself speaking French, so great was her horror of the people who had caused her sister's death, although in fact the habit turned out to be too strong.[10] Now she had to grit her teeth and accept that the twenty-eight-year-old Amélie would marry the son of the man who had voted for Louis XVI's death warrant – or no one.

In the end she accepted the suitor, by now stout and 'very Bourbon-looking', on condition that he spoke frankly to her about the past: 'I forgive you everything on condition that I know everything.' In this way Amélie became Queen of the French after 1830 when Louis Philippe displaced the Comte d'Artois, Louis XVI's last surviving brother, as monarch and took this title. As an old lady Queen Amélie would say that she believed it had always been her destiny to occupy the throne of France. Maria Carolina was left with the consolation that everyone recognized the deep affection that Marie Antoinette had borne her. 'My mother often spoke of you,' wrote Marie Thérèse. 'She loved you more than all her other sisters.'*[11]

There were many others for whom October would always be the month of 'sad memories', in the words of the Princesse de Tarante, and the 16th a day of solemn mourning 'when I cannot speak of anything but Her'.[12] Two people, however, who did not know of the Queen's death – they did not believe the criers outside the Temple – were her daughter Marie Thérèse and her sister-in-law Madame Elisabeth. The latter only discovered the truth shortly before her own execution in May 1794. Marie Thérèse, by now quite alone in the secluded prison, lived on in ignorance, a sad, abandoned and as it seemed, a forgotten figure.

She did not see her brother again before his death on 8 June 1795 at the age of ten. The cause was almost certainly the tuberculosis that had killed the first Dauphin, in this case exacerbated by conditions that were at best neglectful, at worst brutal. Since all the cosseting in the world and the fresh air of Meudon had not saved Louis Joseph from his pathetic fate, perhaps Louis Charles too was destined for an early death. Nevertheless what is known about his treatment indicated a level of callous indifference, the sins of the father (and the mother) being visited upon the child.

The announcement of the boy's death meant that the Comte de Provence in exile was at last free to claim the title of King of France. As Louis XVIII, he ascended a throne, he wrote, 'stained with the blood of my family'.[13] Since the new King was childless, the heir in the next generation was the twenty-year-old Duc d'Angoulême, son of the Comte d'Artois, the boy whose birth had caused Marie Antoinette such anguish in the days before her own marriage was consummated. Negotiations to free Marie Thérèse in exchange for revolutionary prisoners in Austria succeeded in December 1795 when she was just

---

* The French Bourbon pretenders to the throne today, headed by the Comte de Paris, are thus descended from Maria Carolina via Queen Amélie, not Marie Antoinette.

seventeen. There was then a brief squabble between Habsburgs and Bourbons over a suitable bridegroom among her first cousins for the 'orphan of the Temple', the sole surviving descendant of the martyred King. Louis XVIII won; the claims of the Duc d'Angoulême were preferred over those of the Archduke Charles, brother of the Emperor Francis II. Marie Thérèse became Duchesse d'Angoulême, but as a 'Child of France' – a King's daughter – her rank remained superior to that of her husband, a mere King's nephew.

Marie Thérèse enjoyed neither a happy marriage nor a happy life. The marriage was probably not consummated – in a strange echo of her mother's early years in France – and was certainly childless. There are thus no descendants of Marie Antoinette alive today. When she returned from exile at her uncle's side in 1814, the Duchesse d'Angoulême was received with sympathetic acclaim by the crowds, who had been brought up on the story of her sufferings. They saw an unappealing, red-faced woman with bad teeth, rather masculine-looking, who regarded them with ill-concealed loathing. She 'carried her head high like her mother' but lacked the softening grace; her voice was notably harsh.[14] The death of Louis XVIII in 1824 and the accession of Angoulême's father Artois as Charles X meant that for the six years of his reign Marie Thérèse enjoyed that title made famous by her mother, 'Madame la Dauphine'.

The abdication of Charles X in 1830 brought a further change of title for Marie Thérèse, at least in the opinion of devoted royalists. For just a few moments, the time it took his son to sign a second instrument of abdication, the former Duc d'Angoulême could be argued to have been King of France. In the years that followed, some well-wishers called Marie Thérèse 'Majesté' on the grounds that she was the last Queen of France (both the Comtesses de Provence and Artois had died – in 1810 and 1805 respectively). In principle, however, Marie Thérèse ended her life as her mother had begun hers, as 'Madame la Dauphine'.

It was not a happy life but in exile it was a long one. Marie Thérèse lived on until October 1851, when she was seventy-two, and died nearly sixty years after the execution of her mother. Her places of exile included Edinburgh and Prague, although she died at Frohsdorf near Vienna. In her own last testament she forgave 'with all my heart' those who had injured her, 'following the example' of both her parents. No doubt she did forgive her enemies. But it is to be doubted whether this sad, bitter, deeply conservative figure, obstinately old-fashioned – her dress was the despair of the Comtesse de Boigne – really had much forgiveness in her heart for what life had done to her.[15]

One of the problems that plagued Marie Thérèse and undoubtedly caused her much pain was the appearance of numbers of 'false Dauphins', at least forty of them, during the nineteenth century. It could not be easily accepted that Louis Charles had died in the Temple although recent DNA research has led to the conclusion that he did. This investigation was able to be made since one of the doctors who performed the autopsy on the boy's corpse took away his heart secretly; after a strange odyssey of thefts and recoveries, the heart came to rest in a crystal urn in Saint-Denis. Mitochondrial DNA testing, which concentrates on the scraps of genetic material found in the maternal line of descent, was done in two separate laboratories in Belgium and Germany; an announcement was made in April 2000 that the sequences were 'identical' with those of Marie Antoinette, two of her sisters and two living relatives on the maternal side.* 'Science has come to the rescue of history,' said a representative of the Spanish Bourbon royal line, the Duc d'Anjou, at the press conference.[16]

Some of the nineteenth-century stories of 'false Dauphins', who made their claims before science had performed its useful service to history, have a colourful flavour. There was, for example, the Frenchman Pierre Louis Poiret who ended up in the Seychelles archipelago; he had apparently been cared for by a cobbler called Poiret after being smuggled out of the Temple.

---

* DNA testing in 1993 had already showed that the most celebrated claimant, Karl Wilhelm Naundorf, who died in 1845, was extremely unlikely to be descended from Marie Antoinette.

His numerous descendants were given suitably Bourbon names including Louis Charles and Marie Antoinette. In the opposite hemisphere, a man known as 'Indian Williams' gave interviews in support of his claim. The son of Eunice Williams, kidnapped by a tribe of Native Americans, with a Native American father, 'Indian Williams' pointed to the fact that there was no record of his birth among the family records; he was, however, finally unmasked by Mark Twain among others.[17] But to Marie Thérèse, the romance of such implausible notions hardly appealed. Troubled as she might be by the claimants, for her, Louis Charles remained the brother who had so wickedly traduced their mother.

When Marie Thérèse first returned to France, she was escorted to the site of her parents' graves by Pauline de Tourzel, by now Comtesse de Béarn. It was seven o'clock in the morning and the Duchesse d'Angoulême wore an inconspicuous dress, with a veil over her hat. The ladies were conducted by Pierre Louis Desclozeaux, an old lawyer who lived at 48 rue d'Anjou with his son-in-law; he remembered the two interments and had subsequently tended the sites. When the cemetery was closed in 1794 – one of the last to be buried there was Jacques Hébert on 24 March – Desclozeaux made a garden out of the area, planting two weeping willows as a commemoration. Shown the place, Marie Thérèse trembled, fell on her knees and then prayed for the happiness of France – that prayer so frequently on both her parents' lips.[18]

The testimony of this good man – Desclozeaux's 'religious care' would be commemorated on his own tombstone – was important when the two royal bodies came to be exhumed, starting on 18 January 1815. The Queen's body was discovered first, deteriorated to a heap of bones, but with the head entire. According to Chateaubriand, who was a member of the party of inspection, it was recognizable by the special shape of the Queen's mouth, recalling that dazzling smile she had given him at Versailles nearly thirty years earlier. More prosaically, some of her hair and the two elastic garters that she wore to her execution were found, perfectly preserved. The Prince de Poix, in service right up to 10 August 1792, fell fainting backwards at the sight of these relics. The next morning the relics of Louis XVI were recovered.[19]

The remains of both King and Queen were held briefly at the house in the rue d'Anjou and prayers were said before they were sealed up in new coffins with appropriate inscriptions concerning the majesty and titles of the occupants. On 21 January 1815 there was a procession to the cathedral of Saint-Denis; it was the twenty-second anniversary of the execution of Louis XVI. This was the traditional resting-place of the Bourbon dynasty – where the Dauphin Louis Joseph had been interred, for example, in 1789 – but it had been horribly pillaged during the Revolution. The *caveau* (vault) of the Bourbons was now to be restored to due dignity.

In the main body of the cathedral today there is an idealized sculpture of the royal couple at prayer commissioned by the restored King. The crowned Louis XVI on his prie-dieu looks up to heaven, noble, even handsome, as though 'the son of St Louis' is indeed ready to ascend. Marie Antoinette, sculpted in décolleté and high-waisted gown of a later period, in necklace and earrings and wearing a long lace headdress, kneels submissively at his side with her eyes cast down. Below in the vault itself, the black marble tomb of Marie Antoinette, lying amid those of other Bourbons, enjoys a kind of last captivity behind bars ornamented with the fleurs-de-lys of France. In contrast to that of the Habsburg crypt in Vienna, the atmosphere of the *caveau* of the Bourbons is chilly and silent, and there are no flowers.

Two *chapelles expiatoires* were erected at the orders of Louis XVIII. One, designed as a classical mausoleum, marked the site where the royal remains were originally interred. It lies in the 'Square Louis XVI' as it is now termed, a pleasant green space off the Boulevard Haussmann. Inside are two marble groups, one depicting Louis XVI and the Abbé Edgeworth by Bosio, and one 'Marie Antoinette supported by Religion' by Courtot; the face of Religion has a strong resemblance to Madame Elisabeth. The second commemorative chapel, extensively restored in 1989, was erected at the Conciergerie, with altars and black velvet curtains heavily fringed in silver; the names of the three royal martyrs, Louis XVI and Madame Elisabeth as well as Marie Antoinette, are recorded, and there are paintings depicting such scenes as 'The Queen in the Conciergerie receiving the Succour of Religion', 'The Queen waiting to be conducted to the Conciergerie' and 'The Queen's Last Communion'.

'I will never be happy here. I can feel the Queen's ghost asking what I am doing in her bed.' Thus spoke Josephine, wife of the then First Consul Napoleon when he decided to move into the Tuileries in 1800. One can understand her dread; it was a palace still marked with the bloodstains from the Swiss Guards murdered there eight years previously. Did Napoleon placate the ghost of Marie Antoinette by studying and copying the marriage ceremonies of 1770 when he married another Archduchess of Austria in 1810? But the new Empress of France, Marie Louise, never felt completely at home in a country where the people had killed her great-aunt.[20]

Certainly the Queen's ghost has walked in the 200-odd years since her death – literally so, in the belief of some. The most celebrated and also the most controversial sighting is that by two English ladies, Charlotte Anne Moberly and Eleanor Jourdain, who were lost in the grounds of Versailles on 10 August 1901. Their account of seeing a beautiful fair-haired lady in an old-fashioned dress with some companions in the grounds of the palace was published ten years later under the title *An Adventure*. Given the fatal date of 10 August, the Misses Moberly and Jourdain came to the conclusion that they had somehow entered the reveries of the Queen while at the National Assembly on that date in 1792, looking back on her life at Versailles, coupled with the events of 5 October 1789 when she was brought news of the march of the market-women from Paris.

Various explanations have been put forward for this episode involving two eminently respectable 'donnish' women, in turn Principals of St Hugh's College, Oxford. Did the Misses Moberly and Jourdain see some real people – possibly actors – and trick them out with false memories? Perhaps they were influenced by the case of the medium Hélène Smith, which was discussed in a book published shortly before their own experience. Smith's spirit control was Cagliostro, who was allegedly madly in love with Marie Antoinette; as a result Smith was 'reincarnated' as the Queen in trances over several years. Recently, however, it has been suggested that there was some kind of emotional subtext to the women's adventure; since Moberly and Jourdain hardly knew each other in 1901, 'the vision of Marie Antoinette in some way ... made possible Moberly and Jourdain's lifelong homoerotic attachment'.*[21]

The idea of Marie Antoinette as a *tribade* – the eighteenth-century word for a female homosexual, based on the Greek word for friction – was sedulously preached at the time in lewd pamphlets as a means of abuse. But it has meant that her name, generally coupled with that of the Lamballe, has been entered more pleasantly in homosexual annals as worthy of honour. Marie Antoinette and the Lamballe rated a mention in Radclyffe Hall's novel of 1928, *The Well of Loneliness*, originally banned for its openly lesbian theme.[22] The poet of homosexuality, Jean Genet, was fascinated by the story of Marie Antoinette. She was one of the four women in history who interested him, as he once told a friend, the others being the Virgin Mary, Joan of Arc and Madame Curie. A foundling himself, he derived inspiration from the fact that Genet had been the maiden name of Marie Antoinette's favoured First Lady of the Bedchamber. It was indeed the story of Marie Antoinette's execution that was acted out by the eponymous characters in his 1947 play *The Maids* as part of their elaborate fantasies.

In modern terms, therefore, Marie Antoinette has become a gay icon. Whether or not the Queen was actually a *tribade* in the full sense of the word – it has been suggested here that her early feelings for the Lamballe and her intense attachment to the Polignac were more emotional than physical – this respect makes up for the coarse insults of her own time.

* In 1993 the title *The Ghosts of Versailles* was used as an opera composed by John Corigliano and with a libretto by William M. Hoffman, in which Marie Antoinette is the ghost and Beaumarchais falls in love with her, planning to revise history by rescuing her. This is not the only opera to touch on the life of the Queen, for *Marie Antoinette and Fersen*, composed by Daniel Börtz with a libretto by its director Claes Fellborn, was first performed in Stockholm by the Swedish Folk Opera in 1997. There have also been films and historical novels in abundance.

This is paralleled by the attachment that many romantically minded crowned heads have had to the memory of the unfortunate Queen. Ludwig of Bavaria made Linderhof, his favourite place, a replica of the Trianon. The Empress Eugénie, with no connection except that of rank, devoted herself to recovering some of Marie Antoinette's possessions for the Great Exhibition of 1867. From the point of view of hindsight, however, by far the most compelling attachment is that of Alexandra, the last Tsarina of Russia.* She had Marie Antoinette's picture on her desk in the Winter Palace. There was a Gobelin tapestry of the Queen and her children, after the family portrait by Madame Vigée Le Brun, presented by the President of France, in the Tsarina's corner drawing room at the Alexander Palace at Tsarskoe Seloe.[23]

Reopened as a museum in 1997, the Alexander Palace now has the tapestry restored to its former position. The official explanatory booklet states: 'This idyllic world was watched over by the sad and prophetic smile of Marie Antoinette of France ... Alexandra and the children may well have met Marie Antoinette's gaze as they left the palace for good at dawn on 1 August 1917.' The 'sad and prophetic' gaze of Marie Antoinette had already had an opportunity to look down on the Tsarina. In 1896, on a state visit to France, Alexandra was given Marie Antoinette's room in Versailles. She personally was delighted, but the arrangement was greeted with 'suppressed horror' by her entourage who found the association 'ominous'.[24]

A notice in the Conciergerie today adjures the visitor: 'This prison can now serve as the laboratory of a new experience; to look without passion at the symbols of murders long past.' Looking without passion is always a good plan where history is concerned. But is it really possible with regard to the career and character of Marie Antoinette? The two-hundredth anniversary of her birth in 1955 was marked by an eminent exhibition at

---

* Born a Princess of Hesse-Darmstadt and thus descended from Marie Antoinette's friend Princess Louise, Alexandra was a fourth cousin, four generations removed, of the French Queen; both traced descent back to the Landgrave of Hesse-Darmstadt, George II, whose granddaughter married the Emperor Leopold I.

Marie Antoinette was widely accused of lesbianism (as well as heterosexual promiscuity) in contemporary pornography; here the Queen and the Duchesse de Polignac embrace: 'I live only for you ... a kiss, my angel.'

Pastel of Marie Antoinette by
Alexandre Kucharski, c. 1792.

The head of the Princesse de Lamballe
paraded in front of the Temple.

The Tower attached to the palace
of the Temple where the royal family
was held from August 1792 onwards.

Marie Antoinette as a widow, 1793,
by Kucharski.

The Women's
Courtyard at
the Conciergeri
prison where
Marie Antoinet
was held from
August 1793 to
her death; her
barred windows
would have
looked out on i

Engraving of Marie Antoinette at her trial,
appealing to the mothers of France.

Drawing made from the life by Jacques Louis David of
Marie Antoinette with cropped hair and bound hands,
on her way to the guillotine.

Commemorative statues of Louis XVI and Marie Antoinette in the Cathedral of Saint-Denis, where their remains were reburied in the Bourbon vault in 1815, after the Restoration of the monarchy.

Versailles. Apart from pictures and sculpture, furniture and jewellery, its memorabilia included a corsage with the arms of the Dauphine embroidered on it, fragments of pink satin embroidered with jasmine, a white footbath garlanded with flowers and ornamented with illustrations of Aesop's fables, a pair of blue Chinese parrots once in her room at Versailles – and black silk stockings and garters such as she wore at her execution. Yet the British novelist and historian Nancy Mitford, herself the admiring author of a biography of the Pompadour, was moved to deliver a diatribe on the subject in the London *Times*. Marie Antoinette she considered 'frivolous without being funny' and a woman of 'monumental stupidity'.[25]

The year 1993, marking the two-hundredth anniversary of the Queen's death, found a gathering which included descendants of the faithful aristocrats at the site where she was guillotined, at the corner of the Place de la Concorde, opposite the entrance to the Tuileries. An actress from the Comédie Française read the Queen's last letter to Madame Elisabeth. But an interactive play put on around the anniversary, *Je m'appellais Marie Antoinette*, by André Castelot and Alain Decaux and produced by Robert Hossein, allowed the audience to vote on her fate, with the options of liberty, lifetime imprisonment – or execution. Although the majority voted, on the evidence given, for banishment, some still voted for execution. Marie Antoinette, who was recently estimated to be, with Napoleon, 'the most famous figure in the entire length and breadth of French history from Joan of Arc to Charles de Gaulle', continues to have her passionate admirers and her equally vehement detractors.[26]

Undoubtedly it is the death of Marie Antoinette that casts a glow of nobility over her life story. Some of her admirers understood this from the first, such as Horace Walpole who had once hailed her as Virgil's 'true goddess'. He reflected 'coolly' for three days before writing on the subject to his friend Mary Berry and then pronounced: 'Mine is not grief *now*. No, it is all admiration and enthusiasm!' The last days of 'that unparalleled Princess' with not one friend to comfort her were so superior to any death ever exhibited or recorded that he would not choose to revive her even if he could – unless of course she could be restored to a true happiness that would include her children. 'Let history or legend produce a similar model.'[27]

Certainly the 'greatness' at the end for which Marie Antoinette was much praised was true enough. 'Unhappy Queen! What courage and what firmness she has shown!' exclaimed Madame Adélaïde in September 1793 – the very aunt who had spoken so dismissively of *l'Autrichienne* twenty-three years earlier. 'How has she talked to all these villains! … *If only everything had depended on her!*'[28]

Let it be remembered, however, that this constancy was not a virtue that she exhibited on one solitary occasion in October 1793. On the contrary, Marie Antoinette faced a remarkable, even horrifying, tally of potentially violent assaults between 5 October 1789 and her death four years later. The howling invasion of Versailles, the events at the Tuileries of 20 June when she had to hide and the still more awful ones of 10 August, followed by the threats to her personally in the Tower during the September Massacres, as the crowd exhibiting the head of the Princesse de Lamballe wanted to acquire 'the head of Antoinette' as well; these were simply the most salient episodes. They leave out of the account other occurrences that were merely deeply unpleasant, such as the mobbing of the carriages intended for Saint Cloud and the slow torture of the return from Varennes, to say nothing of the gross, often maniacal threats to her person to which she had to listen almost daily – with the hope but not the absolute assurance that the words were empty.

On all these occasions Marie Antoinette experienced extreme fear, as we know from her private communications, quite apart from her dread on behalf of her children (and husband). Yet never at any time did she exhibit her distress publicly; her composure was so sublime as to be interpreted as contempt by her enemies until finally Hébert in *Le Père Duchesne* resorted to calling it the serenity of a habitual criminal. Courage like that did not come out of the blue. Nor could it be simply inherited, with due respect to those who casually attributed Marie Antoinette's bravery to the fact that she was the daughter of the great Maria Teresa. The Empress of Austria died in her bed at the age of sixty-three, surrounded by her family and servants, a very different, lonely fate being reserved for the Queen of France.

But a death, however noble, can never be the whole picture. The last weeks of Marie Antoinette's life also drew attention to the remarkable intelligence with which she faced her accusers. Her friend Georgiana Duchess of Devonshire, writing to her mother two weeks after the Queen's death, commented on this, how 'her answers, her cleverness, and greatness of mind' blazed forth in double splendour in view of her circumstances. The 'horror of making the child appear against her was what one should have hoped the mind of man incapable of,' added the Duchess. The Princesse de Tarante wondered that the Queen did not quote Julius Caesar's words, 'Et tu, Brute', regarding her son: 'Et toi aussi.'[29] Yet it was this dreadful accusation that gave the Queen her opportunity for a superb reply: 'Is there a mother amongst you ...' This instinctive intelligence, confounding those who routinely refer to her as 'vapid' and 'feather-brained', leads one to the crucial consideration where a biographical study is concerned. Given that her trial was a travesty, given that her treatment was inhuman, did Marie Antoinette nevertheless contribute to her own downfall?

In one important sense, Marie Antoinette was a victim from birth. That is to say, she was the victim of her mother's matrimonial alliances and the diplomatic ventures of the King of France. And princesses were of course 'born to obey', as Maria Teresa believed. Marie Antoinette was certainly not exceptional among the 'daughters of a great Prince' to be from birth 'the slave of other people's prejudices ... a sacrifice to the supposed public good' – Isabella of Parma's words. Hers was an uncommon story but it did not begin with an uncommon situation. Where she was exceptionally unlucky was to be shunted off to France in order to cement a Habsburg-Bourbon treaty, entered into after the Seven Years' War, which reversed traditional alliances. Yet this treaty was purely one of convenience for the great ones involved; it carried with it neither the hearts nor the minds of the French court. She was, after all, *l'Autrichienne* long before she appeared in France.

The political significance of her position was none of her making, any more than 'the little wife', as Maria Teresa called her, was herself responsible for the pitiful lack of preparedness with which she was despatched to France. Her education was woefully neglected until the death of one sister, and the moving up in the pecking order of another, meant that the last Archduchess was suddenly to be awarded the greatest position. Nevertheless the political implications of that position haunted Marie Antoinette from the first and followed her to the last.

As Dauphine and young Queen, this untrained girl was designated by her family to advance the interests of Austria in a role described by Joseph at one point as the 'finest and greatest ... that any woman ever played'.[30] There were many Austrian complaints over the years that she did not fulfil it. At the same time, Marie Antoinette was suspected by the French of exerting exactly the kind of petticoat influence that the Austrians criticized her for neglecting. There was scant sympathy in Austria for her position once she had lost her political value, more especially after the death of Joseph II, who for all his claims had at least loved her (one suspects that his affection was deeper than Maria Teresa's). The unalloyed Habsburg-Bourbon rivalry meant that France's internal troubles provided opportunities for predatory Austria.

The attitude of the Austrians towards Marie Antoinette in her last years was cold, where that of the French was brutal; both behaved according to the exigencies of their own situation, not hers. This extended right up to October 1793. Queens were not usually killed; imprisoned, yes; banished; but killed? Yet at the National Convention, Hébert called for the head of Antoinette to unite them all in blood. Like her marriage, Marie Antoinette's death was a political decision.

The final irony in all this was that Marie Antoinette was not by nature a political animal, a point on which Count Mercy frequently expatiated in despair. Left to herself, she would have carried out the role of queen consort in a graceful apolitical fashion, concentrating on the care of her children – she was indeed the 'tender mother' of Madame de Staël's plea – while adorning court functions. The effective collapse of Louis XVI in 1787, and periodically thereafter, meant that she really did have to assume control if they were not all to founder. But it is clear that she did so with much trepidation even if she surprised herself with her energy and her industry.

Curiously enough, Marie Antoinette's instinctive attitude to her role as Queen – as opposed to the political twist she attempted, in the main unsuccessfully, to give to it – pointed to the way that royal ladies would see their role in the future: leading those apolitical, 'retired' but charitable lives by which women could do the most good, in the words of Queen Charlotte. Individual acts of benevolence, private philanthropy, shedding an aura of kindness about her, above all *pleasing* – from childhood on, her love of pleasing people was one of her marked characteristics – all this was very much to Marie Antoinette's taste. As Besenval said, she was easily touched by the unfortunate.[31] Her famous care at the age of eighteen for the peasant injured in the royal stag-hunt, that much-disseminated image, was not an isolated incident but stood for a genuine, admirable compassion. The Marie Antoinette of the Tuileries in the spring of 1790, presiding over a charity committee, instructing her little boy on the need to care for unfortunate children, was a figure who would have fitted easily into the coming apolitical monarchies.

As for the simplicity she preferred, that, too, simply marked the transition from the grand baroque courts of the past to the more restrained versions of the nineteenth century with a strong domestic dimension. It was of course much criticized at the time – particularly by those left out or who suffered from the economies. Even Louis XVI felt that he had been at fault in approving such simple new ways just because they accorded so much with his own tastes. Nevertheless Mary Wollstonecraft, in *An Historical and Moral View of the Origin and Progress of the French Revolution* of 1794, surely carried such criticism rather far in blaming Marie Antoinette for throwing aside 'the cumbersome brocade of ceremony' that would have masked the French court's effeminate idle 'caprices' and general emptiness.[32] The truth was that the age of 'cumbersome brocade' was inevitably passing, as Marie Antoinette, like many people in touch with the *Zeitgeist*, knew by intuition, not by reason. Ironically enough, the Queen, so often seen as the epitome of the *ancien régime* in all its foolish, stilted splendour, actually disliked such ways. It was the life of Versailles that was going out of date, not that of the Petit Trianon.

This is not to say that Marie Antoinette – crushed as she might be between the nether and the upper millstone of Austria and France, and blamed for changes that were actually brought about by the passage of time – was without faults. She was unquestionably pleasure-loving. The loyal Goncourt brothers in their biography of 1858 exclaimed indignantly: 'In this century of women, nothing feminine is pardoned to the Queen.'[33] Certainly it was incumbent upon the First Lady of Versailles to lead in fashion or at any rate in feminine display.

In the pursuit of pleasure she was also extravagant. To point out that the French royal family as a whole, including Mesdames Tantes as well as the King's brothers and their wives, were prodigal in their spending is to explain the atmosphere in which she lived, but not to acquit her of the charge. Yet one might add to that defence not only the beauty that she created round about her but also a genuine appreciation of the arts, especially music in all its forms, which made her a generous patron. Finally, by what standards does one judge a royalty of great taste who spends too much money? (Charles I is the outstanding example.) Artistic or political? It is notoriously impossible to say.

One satiric pamphlet of 1792, *Les Adieux de la Reine à ses Mignons et Mignonnes*, was on stronger ground condemning the Trianon for its cost than when it listed the Queen's lovers of both sexes: Rohan, the 'vigorous Cardinal, Hercules of my burning and ferocious passion', and Jeanne Lamotte.[34] Such ostentatious spending was imprudent, and the acquisition of Saint Cloud for her own personal possession even more so. The atmosphere in which the details of the Diamond Necklace Affair would be believable – at least to her enemies – was created.

It is also true that Marie Antoinette as a young woman was

not particularly prudent, if not in fact as imprudent as these same enemies believed. 'My poor sister,' wrote Maria Carolina. 'Her only fault was that she loved entertainments and parties and this led to her misery.'[55] This was not the whole truth, although there was much truth in it. Many of her sins were venial, but nevertheless gave ammunition to those who had decided to criticize in the first place. If one takes, for example, the incident that led to the first personal attack, *Le Lever d'Aurore*, it was not a crime for a nineteen-year-old Queen, inspired by Rousseau-esque notions, to wish to see the dawn rising at Versailles. She was accompanied, after all, by Madame Étiquette herself, the Comtesse de Noailles, as well as by ladies and sisters-in-law. But there was a lightness of spirit there, that famous *légèreté* of which the French accused her and she accused the French. It vanished more or less with motherhood, certainly with the birth of her first son, Louis Joseph, by which she fulfilled at last 'the wishes of France'.

The question therefore arises as to how much this frivolity – which faded but left its impression behind – was the product of an extremely unhappy and, indeed, humiliating married situation for the first seven and a quarter years of her time in France. Once again politics played its part in this, since the suspicion inculcated in the Dauphin about his Austrian bride can hardly have helped the shy and uncouth young man to make love to her. Nevertheless this failure was of enormous importance to them both psychologically – whether it was due to Marie Antoinette's lack of adequate 'caresses', as Maria Teresa hinted, or to the Dauphin's physical disability or, more plausibly, to awkwardness on both their parts, as the Emperor Joseph believed. Marie Antoinette, whose self-esteem was hardly bolstered by her mother's incessant criticism, was branded a public failure. Louis XVI, a weak, indecisive but never malevolent character, also developed a sense of guilt towards his wife. He could never become the kind of strong dominant husband worthy of respect close to reverence, which Marie Antoinette had been taught in Vienna to expect. All he could do was dumbly resist her political influence with the aid of his ministers, as he did until 1787. When he was obliged to accept the

Constitution – i.e. in September 1791 – he expressed his sense of despair to her in tears: 'Madame, that you came from Austria for this!'

For Marie Antoinette arrived in France at the age of fourteen a highly dependent character, marked by a happy childhood association with her sister Maria Carolina. She looked round for repositories for her tender feelings, finding them first in the Princesse de Lamballe, more importantly in Yolande de Polignac and her family and circle. Although Marie Antoinette replied to the question of the Polignacs being 'gorged with gold' at her trial, by pointing out that they had become wealthy as a result of their *charges* or positions at court, that was to avoid the issue. It was she who had been instrumental in seeing that these *charges* and other emoluments were received. Whatever Yolande de Polignac's devotion, her appointment as Governess to the Children of France must be included among the Queen's mistakes. Pampered friends, whether King's mistresses or Queen's friends, never help the image of those who pamper them; Marie Antoinette, in the folly of her excessive patronage of the Polignacs, was no exception to this rule.

There was a further consequence to Louis XVI's publicly known impotence, about which satirists happily made up their crude rhymes. It provided ammunition against the Queen for allegations of lovers – if not her husband, then someone must be gratifying her – although the Queen was thought by those who knew her to have a fundamentally chaste nature. Her predisposition for chivalrous older men, or flirtatious foreigners, or some combination of the two, when she first arrived in France gave way to a romantic passion for Fersen, the man of action so unlike her husband. Otherwise there are no plausible linkings with the name of Marie Antoinette, who was in the meantime pilloried as the pattern of wicked, lubricious women in history. As Marie Antoinette wrote with truth to Yolande de Polignac, she did not fear poison: 'That does not belong to this century, it's calumny which they use, a much surer means of killing your unhappy friend.'[36] She was not the only one traduced in the eighteenth century, that age of *libellistes* and pornographic bestsellers; there were calumnies before and after her. But she was the one destroyed by the poison. A frequent charge made against 'Antoinette' was that she bathed in the blood of the French people; the truth of it was, of course, exactly the other way round.

Once the marriage of Louis XVI and Marie Antoinette was consummated, it can hardly be described as a bad marriage, as royal marriages go. Maria Teresa, for example, would have been happy to have had a husband who pointedly refused the mistresses that the court thoughtfully provided for him – although she might have missed the sexual performance of her own husband, the womanizing Francis Stephen. Yet there was an awkward side effect to this abstinence, so unfashionable in a monarch, which in the case of Louis XVI was a reproach to the morals of his grandfather: 'I do not wish to see the scenes of the previous reign renewed,' he once said.[37] It meant not only that the post of royal mistress was vacant, with many concomitant job opportunities thus missed, but also that the perceived political influence of the Queen was undiluted. For the King's distaste at the idea of a mistress, Marie Antoinette can hardly be blamed; yet somehow she was turned into the scapegoat of this upsetting of the natural order of things – as the French court saw it.

A scapegoat was in fact what Marie Antoinette became. Among other things, she would be blamed for the whole French Revolution, by those who optimistically looked to one 'guilty' individual as a way of explaining the complex horrors of the past. This view is epitomized by Thomas Jefferson, who wrote in his autobiography that if the Queen had been shut up in a convent, the whole Revolution would never have happened, an astonishingly draconian way of brushing aside the desperate need for reform in French society and government. The use of an animal or bird, who has the ills of the community heaped upon it before being driven out, has a long history in civilizations around the world. The name derived from the goat of the early Jews, described in Leviticus, presented alive before the Lord 'to make an atonement with Him' and then let go 'for a scapegoat into the wilderness'. But there were many similar procedures in other societies, some of them involving women or children, or disabled people, nearly all of them ending in some unpleasant ritual death for the 'scapegoats', who were stoned or hurled from a cliff, as a result of which the community was supposed to be purged of sins, or otherwise plague and pestilence.[38]

Marie Antoinette was not driven out into the wilderness, stoned or hurled from a cliff; yet in a subtler way she was treated as a scapegoat, while her eventual fate, if less barbaric, was not much less cruel. Given that it is evidently a deep primitive urge to blame one individual when things go wrong, what better scapegoat to discover in a monarchy in crisis than a foreign princess? There she is, a subversive alien, in the bed of the head of state, her blood corrupting the dynasty ... One only has to think of Henrietta Maria, French Catholic wife of Charles I in the years leading up to the English Civil War or, going forward to the nineteenth century, of the daughter of Queen Victoria, married to the Crown Prince of Germany, who was pilloried as 'the Englishwoman'. In France, hatred that focused on Marie Antoinette, the Austrian woman, left many of the population free to continue to reverence the King himself. Gouverneur Morris, a visitor from the republican United States, observed how many Parisians felt a kind of grief when the King was executed, 'such as for the untimely death of a beloved parent'.[39]

Compared to this lurid picture of an evil, manipulative, foreign wife, the real substance of Marie Antoinette became as a mere shadow. Having looked without passion at the extraordinary journey that was her life, one is drawn to the conclusion that her weaknesses, although manifest, were of trivial worth in the balance of her misfortune. Ill-luck dogged her from her first moment in France, the unwanted and inadequate ambassadress from a great power, the rejected girl-wife, until the end, when she was the scapegoat for the monarchy's failure. Let the Queen herself have the last word.[40] 'Oh my God,' she wrote in October 1790, 'if we have committed faults, we have certainly expiated them.'

Notes

〜

Full bibliographical details of the works cited in short form will be found in the list of Sources.

Abbreviations used

AN	Archives Nationales, Paris
BL	British Library MSS, London
Haus-Archiv	Haus-Archiv (Habsburg Archives), Hofburg, Vienna
PRO	Public Record Office, London
RA	Royal Archives, Windsor

Author's Note, pp. xv–xviii

1 Elon, p. 17.

Chapter 1: A Small Archduchess, pp. 3–15

1 Boutry, p. 19; Khevenhüller, III, p. 266. Marie Antoinette's natal horoscope shows at first sight a strong and helpful influence in Venus, the planet of love; she was born with Cancer rising, and the Sun in Scorpio; Venus was joined to the Sun and Mercury, and the Moon was in the Venusian house of Libra. However, the position of Mars, close to her Ascendant in Cancer, was extremely badly aspected by Saturn and squared by the Moon. Information supplied by Julia Parker.

2 Khevenhüller, III, p. 266.

3 Amiguet, pp. 157–8; Arneth & Geffroy, III, p. 270; Hamann, p. 52.

4 Weber, I, p. 2.

5 Campan, I, p. 32; Grimm, III, p. 46.

6 Khevenhüller, V, p. 108; IV, p. 49.

7 *Gluck*, p. 10.

8 Khevenhüller, III, p. 266.

9 Wheatcroft, p. 201.

10 Crankshaw, p. 16.

11 Beales, p. 23.

12 Moffat, p. 190.

13 Crankshaw, p. 10.

14 Wangermann, p. 283.

15 Khevenhüller, IV, p. 7.

16 MacDonogh, *Frederick*, p. 156.

17 Bernier, *Louis*, pp. x, 181 & note; Younghusband, p. 7.

18 Gooch, p. 165.

Chapter 2: Born to Obey, pp. 16–30

1 Vuaflart I, p. xviii.

2 Wormser, pp. 46, 52, 61, 154; Lever, *Marie-Antoinette*, p. 11.

3 Dutens, II, p. 214.

4 Klingensmith, p. 116; Armaille, p. 32.

5 Arneth & Geffroy, I, p. 356.

6 Beales, p. 34.

7 Wangermann, p. 302.

8 Beales, p. 34.

9 Ribeiro, *Dress*, p. 133.

10 Bruce, p. 455.

11 Wraxall, I, p. 317.

12 Crankshaw, p. 164.

13 Beales, *Mozart*, p. 4; Khevenhüller, V, p. 108.

14 Khevenhüller, V, p. 131.

15 Deutsch, p. 17.

16 Deutsch, p. 19; Solomon, p. 41.

17 Anderson, I, p. 198 note 1; Campan, I, p. 38; Arneth & Geffroy, I, p. 433.

18 Guest, p. 67.

19 Vocelka, p. 113; Crankshaw, p. 250.

20 Campan, I, pp. 32–3; Arneth & Geffroy, I, p. 404; Girard, p. 35.

21 Khevenhüller, VII, p. 113.
22 Wachter, pp. 75–6.
23 MacDonogh, *Frederick*, p. 273; Khevenhüller, V, p. 6.
24 Corti, p. 25; Vigée Le Brun, p. 115.
25 Beales, pp. 80, 84; Wraxall, II, p. 389.
26 Khevenhüller, *Theater*, pp. 223–4; Landon, I, p. 406.
27 *Tourzel*, p. 81; Hamann, p. 72.
28 Wraxall, II, p. 36; Ribeiro, *Dress*, p. 72.

Chapter 3: Greatness, pp. 31–47

1 Bearne, p. 43; *Lettres*, I, p. 27.
2 Dutens, I, p. 201.
3 Amiguet, pp. 90–2.
4 Deutsch, p. 457; Chalon, p. 24.
5 Khevenhüller, V, p. 6; Lamorlière, p. 243.
6 Moffat, p. 277.
7 Corti, p. 30.
8 Amiguet, pp. 90–1; Boutry, p. 12 note 5.
9 Boutry, p. 39; Roger King, *History of Dentistry*, Cambridge, UK, 1997, p. 12; Hamman, p. 25.
10 Oberkirch, p. 165.
11 Vuaflart I, p. 35; Lafont d'Aussonne, II, p. 164.
12 Younghusband, p. 198.
13 Campan, I, p. 79; Rand, 'Love, Domesticity', pp. 8–9; Younghusband, p. 129.
14 Campan, I, p. 79.
15 Acton, p. 128.
16 *Lettres*, I, p. 1.
17 Boutry, p. 21.
18 Younghusband, p. 131.
19 Arneth, *Marie Antoinette*, p. 13; Kenyon, p. 50; Stryiénski, p. 306.
20 Besenval, p. 461; Campan, I, p. 35 & note.
21 Weber, III, p. 247.
22 Stryiénski, p. 244; Girault de Coursac, pp. 45, 64; Nicolardot, p. 9.
23 Hezecques, p. 216; Girault de Coursac, pp. 105, 186; Nicolardot, pp. 15 *et seq*.
24 Girault de Coursac, p. 109.
25 Stryiénski, p. 364; Lever, *Louis XVI*, p. 52.
26 Nolhac, *Versailles*, p. 225; AN, K, 1015 no. 53ᵉ.

27 Boutry, p. 16.
28 Vuaflart I, pp. 18–19.
29 Boutry, p. 34.
30 Vuaflart I, p. 36.
31 Vuaflart I, pp. 35 *et seq.*
32 Boutry, p. 37; Campan, I, p. 36.
33 Armaille, pp. 50–1, 61; Arneth & Geffroy, I, p. 73; Oberkirch, p. 45.
34 Armaille, p. 59.
35 Haus-Archiv, Konv. 8.MA *Extraits de l'Histoire de France*, fols. 1–88, 1768.
36 Younghusband, p. 120; Boutry, p. 35.
37 Bernier, p. 35.

Chapter 4: Sending an Angel, pp. 48–64

1 Vuaflart I, p. 21.
2 Wachter, p. 13; Arneth & Geffroy, I, pp. lviii–lix.
3 Swinburne, I, p. 348; Campan, I, p. xiii.
4 Castelot, *Queen*, p. 15.
5 BL, Add. MSS 20, 707; Khevenhüller, VII, pp. 5, 8.
6 Vuaflart II, p. 7.
7 Boutry, p. 58; Amiguet, p. 120.
8 Boutry, pp. 58 *et seq.*
9 Corti, p. 44.
10 *Lettres*, I, p. lxix; *Landgrave Louise, passim.*
11 Arneth & Geffroy, I, p. 36; Younghusband, p. 272.
12 Boutry, p. 50.
13 Wheatcroft, pp. 226–7.
14 AN, K, 1015 no. 142; Saint-Priest, I, p. 117.
15 Boutry, p. 56.
16 Christoph, p. 311; Tillyard, p. 230.
17 Christoph, p. 23 & note 23, p. 226; Girard, p. 29 & note 1; Haus-Archiv, Familien-Akten Sammelbände (alt. 35) 55; Amiguet, p. 60.
18 Beales, p. 72; Bernard, p. 307.
19 Stryiénski, p. 247; *Diary of Dr Edward Lake*, ed. G. P. Elliott, 1847, I, p. 9.
20 Brooke, pp. 82–4; Lever, *Marie-Antoinette*, p. 27; Thomas, pp. 28–9.
21 Corti, pp. 32–4; Acton, p. 138.

22 Arneth & Geffroy, I, p. xx.

23 Acton, p. 132.

24 Arneth & Geffroy, I, pp. 1–6.

25 Arneth & Geffroy, I, p. 3.

26 Boutry, p. 58.

27 Boutry, p. 60; Castelot, *Queen*, p. 15.

28 Haus-Archiv, Familien-Akten 50, *Supplement to the Gazette de Vienne*, 18 April 1770.

29 Khevenhüller, VII, p. 6.

30 Khevenhüller, VII, p. 16.

31 Haus-Archiv, Familien-Akten 50, *Supplement to the Gazette de Vienne*, 18 April 1770; Khevenhüller, VII, p. 16.

32 Boutry, p. 62.

33 Nolhac, *Dauphine*, p. 46.

34 Nolhac, *Dauphine*, pp. 46–7.

35 Khevenhüller, VII, p. 18; Corti, p. 14; Ségur, p. 19; Weber, I, p. 5.

Chapter 5: France's Happiness, pp. 67–85

1 See Eiwes, *Brautfahrt der Marie Antoinette, passim*.

2 Amiguet, p. 11; Rocheterie, I, p. 14.

3 Klingensmith, p. 189; Haslip, p. 9; Bauchart, p. 243, no. 71.

4 Bombelles, I, p. 77.

5 Campan, I, p. 46.

6 Goncourt, p. 32.

7 Boutry, p. 77; Nolhac, *Dauphine*, p. 47.

8 Norton, p. 96.

9 Boutry, p. 72.

10 Arneth & Geffroy, I, p. 50.

11 Campan, I, p. 45; Rocheterie, I, p. 16.

12 BL, Add. MSS 20, 707; Campan (1988), p. 46 note 54; Nolhac, *Dauphine*, p. 47; Khevenhüller, VII, p. 21; Reiset, p. 38.

13 Reiset, p. 32.

14 Nolhac, *Dauphine*, p. 47; Campan, I, p. 45.

15 Oberkirch, pp. 42 *et seq*.

16 Boutry, p. 71.

17 Haynin, p. 65.

18 Besenval, p. 288; Saint-Simon, pp. 542–3.

19 Amiguet, p. 136.

20 Nolhac, *Dauphine*, p. 51.

21 Maxwell, p. 111; Croÿ, II, p. 373.

22 Cronin, p. 39; Campan, I, pp. 11–12.

23 *Northumberland*, p. 111; Nicolardot, p. 43.

24 Elliott, p. 27; Lever, *Philippe Égalité*, p. 31.

25 Bertin, p. 37; Sorel, pp. 10, 16.

26 Bernier, *Louis*, p. 226; *Northumberland*, p. 117; Choiseul, *Mémoires*, p. 198, p. 328 note 156.

27 Castelot, *Queen*, p. 29.

28 Dunlop, *Marie-Antoinette*, p. 71.

29 Ribeiro, *Fashion*, p. 26; Hezecques, p. 195; *Northumberland*, p. 111.

30 Nolhac, *Autour*, p. 158.

31 Campan, I, p. 59 & note; *Northumberland*, p. 112; Debriffe, p. 24.

32 Morel, p. 200; Campan, I, p. 52.

33 Bracelets now in the Victoria & Albert Museum; Sèvres at Waddesdon, Bucks.

34 *Northumberland*, p. 111; Nolhac, *Dauphine*, p. 53; Ségur, p. 22.

35 Nolhac, *Dauphine*, fac. p. 54.

36 Croÿ, II, pp. 393 *et seq.*

37 Amiguet, pp. 115, 140.

38 Christoph, p. 62.

39 MacDonogh, *Frederick*, p. 99.

40 Antonia Fraser, *King Charles II*, 1979, p. 349.

Chapter 6: In Front of the Whole World, pp. 86–107

1 Mansel, *Court*, p. 12.

2 Bluche, p. 87.

3 Chateaubriand, I, p. 203; Oberkirch, p. 338; Genlis, II, p. 198.

4 *La Tour du Pin*, pp. 55 *et seq.*

5 Blaikie, p. 197; Bombelles, I, p. 160; Young, p. 16.

6 Young, p. 84; Hezecques, p. 136.

7 Pimodan, p. 108 note 1; *Boigne*, I, p. 540; Genlis, I, p. 274.

8 Lever, *Louis XVI*, p. 33; Campan, I, p. 305.

9 Campan, I, p. 95.

10 Arneth & Geffroy, I, pp. 118–20.

11 *La Tour du Pin*, p. 44; Hezecques, p. 96.

12 Mansel, *Ligne*, p. 44; *Bachaumont*, I, p. 348.

13 Ligne, I, p. 199.

14 Corson, *Hair*, p. 275; Vigée Le Brun, p. 17; *Austen Papers*, p. 93.

15 Ribeiro, *Dress*, p. 109; Sagarin, pp. 39 *et seq.*; Ribeiro, *Fashion*, p. 144 note 25; Arneth & Geffroy, I, p. 19; Vigée Le Brun, p. 21.

16 Corson, *Make-up*, p. 218; Campan, I, p. 175.

17 Grimm, I, pp. 39–45.

18 Grimm, I, p. 46; BL Add. MSS 20, 707 fol. 171.

19 Croÿ, II, pp. 409, 426; *Tourzel*, p. 305.

20 Pimodan, pp. 40 *et seq.*

21 Arneth & Geffroy, I, p. 73.

22 Arneth & Geffroy, I, pp. vii, 69.

23 Haus-Archiv, Familien-Akten Sammelbände 12.

24 *Lettres*, I, pp. i *et seq.*, pp. xii, xviii.

25 *Bachaumont*, I, p. 491.

26 AN, K, 1015 nos. 147, 150, 167.

27 Arneth & Geffroy, I, p. 107; Vuaflart II, p. 89.

28 Kertanguy, p. 332.

29 Younghusband, p. 459.

30 Arneth & Geffroy, I, pp. 77–8.

31 Nolhac, *Versailles*, p. 280; Nolhac, *Autour*, pp. 160 *et seq.*

32 Arneth & Geffroy, I, p. 6.

33 Lever, *Louis XVI*, p. 70; *Northumberland*, p. 123; Amiguet, p. 161.

34 Arneth & Geffroy, I, pp. 21, 24.

35 Nicolardot, p. 25.

36 Arneth & Geffroy, I, pp. 93 *et seq.*

37 Vuaflart II, p. 67; Arneth & Geffroy, I, p. 196.

38 Arneth & Geffroy, I, p. 121.

39 *Lévis*, p. 84; Fleischmann, *Polignac*, p. 48.

40 *Bachaumont*, I, p. 373; Oberkirch, p. 182.

41 *Lettres*, I, p. 5.

42 Arneth & Geffroy, I, p. 88.

43 Vuaflart II, p. 53.

44 Nolhac, *Dauphine*, p. 82.

Chapter 7: Strange Behaviour, pp. 108–23

1 Bacourt, I, p. 31; Campan, I, p. 129, misdates the start of this relationship to winter 1775 since Mercy's evidence of 1771 is crucial; Arneth & Geffroy, I, p. 140.

2 Rousseau, *Nouvelle Héloïse*, p. 5.

3 Nicolardot, p. 68.

4 Arneth & Geffroy, I, pp. 149–51.

5 Hardman, p. 5; Arneth & Geffroy, I, p. 148.

6 Reiset, p. 62.

7 Arneth & Geffroy, I, pp. lviii–lix.

8 Arneth & Geffroy, I, p. 310 and *passim*.

9 Christoph, p. 23.

10 Arneth & Geffroy, I, pp. 6, 157–61.

11 Amiguet, p. 178; Reiset, p. 95.

12 Reiset, p. 50.

13 Reiset, p. 9.

14 Dormois, p. 106; Christoph, p. 52; Lever, *Louis XVIII*, pp. 21, 26, 49; *Véri*, I, p. 266; Reiset, p. 121.

15 Campan, I, p. 57; Pimodan, p. 110; Arneth & Geffroy, I, p. 222.

16 Arneth & Geffroy, I, p. 168.

17 Arneth & Geffroy, I, p. 218.

18 Arneth & Geffroy, I, pp. 234–6; Christoph, p. 62.

19 Arneth & Geffroy, I, pp. 260–1.

20 Arneth & Geffroy, I, p. 336.

21 Arneth & Geffroy, I, pp. 263–4.

22 Arneth & Geffroy, I, p. 321.

23 Bernier, *Louis*, p. 242.

24 Arneth & Geffroy, I, pp. 322–3, 329.

25 *Lettres*, I, pp. 32, 40.

26 *Thrale*, Appendix, p. 218; Arneth & Geffroy, I, p. 176.

27 *Lévis*, p. 107; Oberkirch, p. 160.

28 Hezecques, p. 40 & note.

29 Arneth & Geffroy, I, p. 328; Lever, *Louis XVI*, p. 72; Christoph, p. 172.

30 Christoph, p. 90.

31 Arneth & Geffroy, I, p. 435.

Chapter 8: Love of a People, pp. 124–39

1 Ségur, p. 50; Arneth & Geffroy, I, p. 316; for the Paris trip pp. 458–60.

2 Guest, p. 66.

3 Arneth & Geffroy, I, p. 460.

4 Christoph, p. 100.

5 Christoph, pp. 101, 105.

6 Flammermont, pp. 475–6 & note 1; Arneth & Geffroy, II, pp. 62, 88.

7 Arneth & Geffroy, II, p. 75.

8 Arneth & Geffroy, II, p. 79; Swinburne, II, p. 11; Amiguet, p. 213.

9 Amiguet, p. 216; Bluche, p. 30; Schama, p. 119; Campan, I, p. 124; Oberkirch, p. 208; Hezecques, p. 60.

10 Arneth & Geffroy, I, p. 59; *Lettres*, I, p. 55.

11 Arneth & Geffroy, I, pp. 355, 438, 444; II, p. 131; *Lettres*, I, p. 212.

12 Arneth & Geffroy, I, p. 11; II, pp. 191, 290.

13 Arneth & Geffroy, III, p. 28.

14 Lindqvist, p. 16; Aspinall, *George III*, p. 327; *Lévis*, p. 130; Bessborough, pp. 108–9.

15 Amiguet, p. 217; Söderhjelm, p. 34.

16 Söderhjelm, p. 37.

17 Pestelli, p. 78; Campan, I, p. 149; Howard, p. 112.

18 Howard, p. 107; Guest, pp. 67–8.

19 Howard, p. 109.

20 Demuth, pp. 231 *et seq.*; Eagles, p. 227; Howard, p. 244.

21 Demuth, p. 230; Johnson, p. 210.

22 Johnson, p. 211.

23 Besenval, p. 162; *Ségur Memoirs*, p. 8.

24 Besenval, pp. 164–6; Croÿ, III, pp. 82 *et seq.*

25 Campan, I, pp. 76 *et seq.*

26 Younghusband, pp. 563 *et seq.*; *Vergennes*, p. 6 & note 9.

27 Campan, I, p. 76.

Chapter 9: In Truth a Goddess, pp. 143–65

 1 Campan (1988), p. 69; *Lévis*, p. 69.

 2 Cottrell, p. 31; *Tilly*, p. 68.

 3 Ligne, I, p. 197; *Austen Papers*, p. 90.

 4 Platen, p. 94; *Thrale*, pp. 98, 125; Vigée Le Brun, p. 40.

 5 Besenval, pp. 180–1.

 6 Campan, I, p. 49; Grimm, I, p. 477; *Aeneid*, I, ll. 402–5; Nolhac, *Autour*, p. 19; Vigée Le Brun, p. 41.

 7 Bessborough, p. 30.

 8 *Thomas More Journal*, p. 458.

 9 *Lettres*, II, pp. 42–4.

10 *Lévis*, p. 65; *Ségur Memoirs*, p. 23.

11 Hardman, p. 88; Labourdette, p. 234.

12 *Vergennes*, pp. 170–1; Price, pp. 20–1; *Vergennes*, pp. 111–12.

13 Ligne, I, p. 131; Rogister, 'Maria Lesczinska'.

14 Pimodan, p. 145.

15 Arneth & Geffroy, I, p. liv; II, p. 165; Hardman, p. 95; Bacourt, I, p. 46; Choiseul, *Mémoires*, p. 300.

16 Sorel, p. 88; Campan, I, pp. 285, 299.

17 Maxwell, p. 123; Adams, p. 251.

18 Chalon, p. 10.

19 Kertanguy, pp. 61–2.

20 Campan, I, pp. 124, 129.

21 Sorel, pp. 89–92.

22 Polignac, p. 15; *Lévis*, p. 132; *Ségur Memoirs*, p. 113; Oberkirch, p. 210; Besenval, p. 192.

23 Arneth & Geffroy, II, p. 378; *Tilly*, p. 123.

24 *Lettres* , I, p. 81.

25 *Véri*, I, p. 231; Grimm, I, p. 345.

26 Pimodan, p. 148; *Véri*, I, p. 239.

27 Pimodan, p. 153.

28 Lever, *Louis XVI*, p. 186; Dunlop, *Marie-Antoinette*, p. 115; Morel, pp. 65, 203.

29 *Lettres*, I, pp. 90–1; Khevenhüller, VIII, p. 83; Schama, p. 51.

30 *Lettres*, I, p. 91; Arneth & Geffroy, I, p. 206.

31 *Boigne*, I, p. 55; Cronin, p. 13; Chalon, p. 17; Younghusband, pp. 21–2.

32 Rudé, *Crowd*, pp. 21–2; Cobb, *Police*, pp. xvii, 249, 263, 270.

33 Arneth & Geffroy, II, p. 360.

34 *Lévis*, pp. 176, 314, 409; Bombelles, I, p. 197; Price, p. 30.

35 *Vergennes*, pp. 218–19.

36 Campan, II, pp. 113–14; Arneth & Geffroy, II, p. 477.

37 Kertanguy, p. 111. Unfortunately, but perhaps predictably, little Jacques later turned into a violent revolutionary, eager to blot out his quasi-royal past.

38 Reiset, pp. 136 *et seq.*

39 *Lettres*, I, p. 109.

40 Almeras, pp. 215–19 & p. 215 note 1.

41 Arneth & Geffroy, II, p. 409.

Chapter 10: An Unhappy Woman? pp. 166–87

1 *Lettres*, I, p. 187; BL, MSS Zweig 171.

2 Flammermont, p. 99.

3 Arneth & Geffroy, II, p. 500.

4 Arneth & Geffroy, I, p. lxvi.

5 Ashton, p. 145; Saint-Priest, II, p. 99.

6 *Ségur Memoirs*, p. 29; Campan, I, 182.

7 Campan, I, p. 164; Besenval, p. 269.

8 *Lauzun*, p. 126.

9 *Boigne*, I, p. 139.

10 Arneth & Geffroy, I, p. lxix; Campan, I, p. 102.

11 Platen, p. 108; Eagles, *passim*; Arneth, *Marie-Antoinette*, p. 15.

12 Mansel, *Ligne*, p. 44; Vigée Le Brun, p. 51.

13 Bombelles, I, p. 108 & note 3, p. 311; *Esterhazy Mémoires*, pp. xix et seq.

14 Bernier, p. 217; Bombelles, I, p. 157; *Véri*, I, p. 400; Besenval, p. 270; *Ségur Memoirs*, p. 22.

15 Ligne, I, p. 199; Bacourt, I, p. 29; Laclos, p. 157.

16 Campan, I, p. 88.

17 Almeras, p. 201, p. 203 note 1.

18 Almeras, p. 206.

19 *Lettres*, I, p. 93; Almeras, p. 75 note 2.

20 Thomas, p. 43; *Lettres*, I, pp. 91, 109, 111.

21 Arneth & Geffroy, II, p. 306.

22 Langlade, p. 41; Ribeiro, *Art*, pp. 74–5; *Recollections of Léonard*, pp. 139, 152.

23 Higonnet, p. 297; Rice, p. 23; Oberkirch, p. 94.

24 Goodden, p. 70; Bernier, 'Eighteenth Century', p. 118.

25 Nouvion & Liez, pp. 1, 27; Oberkirch, pp. 145 *et seq.*; Garland, pp. 40–5; Bombelles, I, p. 302; *Lettres*, I, pp. 277 *et seq.*

26 Langlade, p. 41; *Léonard*, I, *passim*; *Léonard*, III, pp. 5 *et seq.*

27 Ségur, *Marie-Antoinette*, p. 92; Arneth & Geffroy, II, pp. 7–8.

28 Browning, *Despatches*, pp. 66–7; Kertanguy, p. 107; Labourdette, p. 165.

29 Younghusband, p. 330; Mansel, *Ligne*, p. 90.

30 *Bachaumont*, II, p. 40; Arneth & Geffroy, II, p. 162; Nolhac, *Trianon*, pp. 76 *et seq.*

31 Nolhac, *Trianon*, p. 103.

32 Campan, I, p. 108; II, p. 38; Bombelles, II, p. 105.

33 Price, pp. 48–9; Hardman, *Politics*, p. 50–1; Hardman, p. 47.

34 Haynin, pp. 92–4.

35 Arneth & Geffroy, III, pp. 22, 30; *Lettres*, I, pp. 139–40.

36 Arneth & Geffroy, III, p. 31.

37 Pimodan, p. 162.

38 Croÿ, IV, pp. 11–13.

39 Campan, I, p. 175.

40 Arneth, *Marie-Antoinette*, p. 43; Arneth & Geffroy, II, p. 443; Beales, p. 373; Arneth & Geffroy, III, p. 86.

41 Corti, p. 120.

42 Bernier, p. 217.

43 Arneth, *Marie-Antoinette*, pp. 4–18.

44 Beales, p. 374.

45 Nicolardot, p. 86.

46 Christoph, pp. 164, 172, 176, 178, 180; Flammermont, p. 329.

47 Flammermont, p. 103.

48 Beales, p. 374; Arneth & Geffroy, III, p. 80; Bernier, pp. 217–18.

49 Beales, p. 375 note 66.

50 Christoph, pp. 221, 234; Arneth & Geffroy, III, p. 113.

Chapter 11: You Shall Be Mine ... pp. 188–205

1 *Vergennes*, pp. 252–3; Labourdette, p. 104.

2 Christoph, p. 239.

3 Wraxall, I, p. 302; Beales, pp. 338 *et seq.*, pp. 386–8.

4 Price, p. 22.

5 Arneth & Geffroy, I, p. xxxvii; Wraxall, I, pp. 352–3; Beales, p. 425.

6 *Lettres*, p. 158 & note 1.

7 Arneth & Geffroy, I, p. xxxviii; Price, p. 22.

8 Arneth & Geffroy, III, pp. 168, 181; Flammermont, p. 359.

9 Haus-Archiv, Familien-Akten Sammelbände 55; Christoph, p. 246.

10 *Lettres*, I, p. 165; Christoph, p. 251.

11 Arneth & Geffroy, III, p. 211.

12 *Lettres*, I, p. 171.

13 *Lettres*, I, p. 173.

14 *Lettres*, I, p. 182; Campan, I, p. 188.

15 Bessborough, p. 31.

16 *Lettres*, I, p. 182.

17 The daughters of Joseph II, Leopold II, Amalia, Maria Carolina, Ferdinand and Marie Antoinette.

18 Anderson, I, p. 439; II, p. 541; Solomon, pp. 149–50; Beales, *Mozart*, p. 6, reports that Marie Antoinette 'seems to have done nothing for the Mozarts during their stay in Paris in 1778', without noting that it coincided with her first pregnancy.

19 Anderson, II, p. 564.

20 *Gluck*, pp. 134, 140, 161–3.

21 Söderhjelm, pp. 51, 57.

22 Söderhjelm, p. 58.

23 Lever, *Philippe Égalité*, pp. 162–172, 177.

24 Lever, *Philippe Égalité*, p. 181.

25 Campan, I, pp. 197 *et seq.*

26 Lever, *Louis XVI*, p. 336; Arneth & Geffroy, III, p. 278X.

27 *Tourzel*, p. 286; Nicolardot, p. 44.

28 Christoph, p. 341; Bombelles, I, p. 62; Arneth & Geffroy, III, p. 340.

29 Arneth & Geffroy, III, p. 277.

30 Croÿ, IV, p. 137; Campan, I, p. 201.

31 Arneth & Geffroy, III, p. 277.

32 *Fausselandry*, I, p. 157; Bluche, p. 20.

33 Rousseau, *Émile*, p. 5 note 1; *Lettres*, I, p. 189; Arneth & Geffroy, III, p. 270.

34 *Lettres*, I, p. 189; Nolhac, *Trianon*, p. 133.

35 Dutens Papers, no. 566, box 921.

36 Beales, p. 403.

37 Labourdette, p. 86; *Lettres*, I, p. 190.

38 Tussaud, p. 63; *Léonard*, I, p. 189; Guest, p. 143.

39 Labourdette, p. 107; *Lettres*, I, p. 198.

40 *Lettres*, I, pp. 195, 210.

41 Christoph, p. 293.

42 Christoph, p. 311.

43 PRO, SP 102/9 149, 152.

Chapter 12: Fulfilling Their Wishes, pp. 206–23

1 Solnon, p. 429; Arneth & Geffroy, II, p. 164.

2 *Fausselandry*, I, p. 80; Maza, ' "Bourgeois" ', p. 41; Huë, p. 466.

3 Ribeiro, *Dress*, p. 153; *Cradock*, p. 64.

4 AN, AE, I. 6 no. 2; Ribeiro, *Fashion*, p. 35.

5 Bessborough, p. 91.

6 Beales, pp. 172–3; Bombelles, I, p. 94.

7 Grimm, I, p. 203; Johnson, pp. 209 *et seq.*

8 *Landgrave Louise, passim.*

9 *Lettres*, I, pp. 208–10; Ribeiro, *Dress*, p. 153.

10 *Lettres*, I, p. 219.

11 Lamorlière, pp. 239–40; Lafont d'Aussonne, II, p. 61; Lucia Toñgiorgi Tomasi, *An Oak Spring Flora*, pp. 223–6, Upperville, Virginia, 1997; Mirault, p. 48; Nolhac, *Trianon*, p. 99; Nolhac, *Autour*, pp. 183–4; Corbin, p. 75.

12 Guest, p. 35.

13 Hemmings, pp. 226 *et seq.*; Nolhac, *Trianon*, p. 190.

14 Hemmings, p. 172.

15 Klinckowström, I, p. xxxiii; Söderhjelm, p. 69.

16 *Fausselandry*, I, p. 154; Devonshire MSS, 5th Duke, 265.

17 Klinckowström, I, p. xxxvi; Farr, *Fersen*, pp. 72–3.

18 Farr, *Fersen*, p. 73.

19 Söderhjelm, pp. 69, 73; Arneth & Geffroy, III, p. 417; Lindqvist, p. 62.

20 Girouard, p. 144; Bacourt, I, p. 36.

21 Fleischmann, *Polignac*, p. 32.

22 *Lettres*, I, p. 158; *Bachaumont*, II, p. 376; Swinburne, II, p. 12; Guest, p. 66.

23 Bombelles, I, p. 196.

24 Price, p. 61.

25 Hardman, pp. 63–4.

26 Arneth & Geffroy, III, p. 410.

27 Arneth & Geffroy, III, pp. 482, 492–6.

28 *Lettres*, I, p. 235.

29 *Vergennes*, p. 296.

30 Bombelles, I, p. 62; *Landgrave Louise*, pp. 20–1.

31 Arneth & Flammermont, I, p. 32.

32 Price, pp. 55–6.

33 Arneth & Flammermont, I, p. 54; Darnton, 'Lenoir', p. 545 & note 1; Nolhac, *Trianon*, p. 157.

34 Arneth & Flammermont, I, pp. 64, 66.

35 Castelot, *Queen*, pp. 174 *et seq.*

36 Lever, *Louis XVI*, p. 375.

37 *Bachaumont*, II, p. 271.

38 Platen, p. 111; Secher & Murat, pp. 18–19; Bombelles, I, p. 82.

Chapter 13: The Flowers of the Crown, pp. 227–51

1 *Lettres*, II, p. 9; Campan, I, p. 210.

2 Campan, I, p. 211.

3 Haynin, pp. 94–5, 127.

4 Morel, p. 230.

5 Arneth & Flammermont, I, pp. 68–9; Guest, p. 176; Bluche, p. 120; Oberkirch, p. 130; *Léonard*, I, p. 192.

6 *Gluck*, p. 192; Arneth & Flammermont, I, p. 71.

7 *La Tour du Pin*, p. 17; *Ségur Memoirs*, p. 184.

8 Fleischmann, *Polignac*, fac. p. 160; Flammermont, pp. 434–6; Gutwirth, p. 137.

9 Almeras, p. 322.

10 Bombelles, I, p. 85; Bluche, p. 17.

11 Nolhac, *Marie-Antoinette*, pp. 102 *et seq.*

12 Arneth & Flammermont, I, p. 77; Hardman, p. 69.

13 Price, p. 62; Arneth & Flammermont, I, p. 83.

14 Arneth & Flammermont, I, p. 290.

15 Blanning, *Joseph II*, p. 135; Arneth & Flammermont, I, p. 109; Langlade, p. 138; Haynin, p. 134; Campan, I, pp. 238–9.

16 Bombelles, I, p. 127; Reitlinger II, pp. 32, 41.

17 Grimm, I, pp. 361–74; Campan, I, p. 237.

18 Arneth & Flammermont, I, p. 187 & note 1, p. 300; Bacourt, I, p. 29.

19 Labourdette, p. 276.

20 *Lettres*, II, pp. 42–4 & note 1.

21 Bombelles, I, p. 157; *Lettres*, II, p. 23; Arneth & Flammermont, I, p. 151.

22 Haynin, pp. 136 *et seq.*, p. 139 note; Browne, pp. 28 *et seq.*

23 *Ségur Memoirs*, p. 116; *Boigne*, p. 52.

24 Browne, p. 27.

25 Arneth & Flammermont, I, p. 130.

26 Besenval, p. 545 note; Browne, p. 35.

27 Fleischmann, *Polignac*, p. 60; Bombelles, II, p. 77.

28 *Tilly*, p. 127.

29 *Esterhazy Mémoires*, p. 176.

30 Bombelles, I, pp. 252, 271.

31 Weber, I, pp. 71–2; Bombelles, I, p. 280; *Cradock*, p. 20; *Lettres*, II, p. 30.

32 Bluche, p. 188; *History Today*, April 1987, p. 3.

33 *Tilly*, p. 282; *Léonard*, I, p. 226.

34 *Boigne*, I, p. 42; Foster, 'Journal'.

35 Söderhjelm, p. 8; Farr, *Fersen*, pp. 101 *et seq.*; Webster, Appendix I, pp. 522–3; Castelot, *Queen*, pp. 179–80.

36 Söderhjelm, p. 386.

37 Söderhjelm, p. 80; Proschwitz, p. 119.

38 Söderhjelm, pp. 80–1.

39 Lindqvist, p. 67.

40 Söderhjelm, pp. 86–90.

41 Mansel, 'Militarisation'.

42 Nolhac, *Trianon*, pp. 200, 212; Gutwirth, p. 180, p. 404 & note 103.

43 Reiset, pp. 64–8, 70–1; Young, p. 70; Oberkirch, p. 196.

44 Nolhac, *Trianon, passim*; Oberkirch, p. 159; Nicolardot, p. 44.

45 Cronin, p. 129; Bombelles, I, p. 261.

46 Wilberforce, pp. 40–4; Ehrman, p. 111; Blaikie, p. 133.

47 Guest, p. 205; Haslip, p. 168.

48 *La Tour du Pin*, p. 57; Seward, p. 57.

49 Arneth-Geffroy, III, p. 114; Bauchart, pp. 227–32.

50 Bauchart, pp. 256–7.

51 Michon, pp. 245–59; Bauchart, p. 228.

52 *Lettres*, II, p. 33; BL, Add. MSS 33, 966; information of Mlle. Cécile Coutin, Association Marie-Antoinette; Landon, II, pp. 599, 608.

53 Bombelles, I, p. 327.

Chapter 14: Acquisitions, pp. 252–71

1 Bombelles, I, p. 327.

2 Campan, I, p. 246; Lever, *Philippe Égalité*, p. 274.

3 Hezecques, p. 26; *Boigne*, I, p. 53; Vigée Le Brun, p. 44.

4 Bombelles, I, pp. 208–9.

5 Oberkirch, p. 464.

6 *Thrale*, p. 206; Grimm, III, p. 167.

7 Oberkirch, p. 304; Campan, I, p. 271; Kertanguy, pp. 128–9.

8 Campan (1988), p. 179.

9 Söderhjelm, pp. 101–2; MacDonogh, *Reigning Cats*, p. 49; Adams, pp. 213–14; *Esterhazy Mémoires*, p. xxxv, note 1.

10 *Lettres*, II, pp. 39–41.

11 *Véri*, II, p. i.

12 Lindqvist, p. 248.

13 *Lettres*, II, pp. 49–50 & note 1; Arneth, *Marie-Antoinette*, p. 48.

14 Price, pp. 147–8; Augeard, p. 134; Blanning, *Joseph II*, p. 141–2.

15 Labourdette, p. 293; Price, p. 194; Arneth, *Marie-Antoinette*, p. 43.

16 Price, p. 32; Bombelles, I, p. 126; Bessborough, p. 108.

17 Hardman, p. 78.

18 Campan, II, p. 109; Hardman, p. 79.

19 Price, p. 147.

20 Verlet, p. 118; *Modes: Éloffe*, I, p. 2; Boyer, p. 39.

21 Verlet, p. 19; Reitlinger II, p. 42.

22 Verlet, pp. 39–40.

23 Verlet, p. 27; Boyer, pp. 30–1.

24 Reitlinger II, p. 41.

25 Boyer, pp. 78–80.

26 Campan, I, p. 152; *Bachaumont*, II, p. 147; Boyer, pp. 30, 83.

27 *Lettres*, I, p. 37 & note; Campan, I, p. 152.

28 Goodden, p. 38; Baillio, *Vigée Le Brun*, pp. 7–10; Vigée Le Brun, p. 37.

29 Vigée Le Brun, p. 43.

30 Malone, p. 13.

31 Bombelles, II, p. 401; Hedley, p. 73.

32 Haus-Archiv, Familien-Korrespondenz A55; *Lettres*, II, pp. 64, 66, 157; Stryiénski, p. 244.

33 Almeras, pp. 324–5.

34 Söderhjelm, p. 106.

35 Mossiker, pp. 200 *et seq.*; Campan, II, pp. 3 *et seq.*

36 Haynin, p. 196.

Chapter 15: Arrest the Cardinal! pp. 272–92

1 Haynin, pp. 167 *et seq.*

2 Campan, II, pp. 10 *et seq.*; Georgel, IV, pp. 2 *et seq.*

3 Pimodan, p. 226.

4 Mossiker, p. 273; Bombelles, II, p. 25; Mansel, *Ligne*, p. 25.

5 For example, to her cousin the Duchesse de Trémöille (1774), *Lettres*, I, p. 20; to Count Rosenberg (1775), BL, MSS Zweig 171; to the Comte d'Artois (1791), *Lettres*, II, p. 242.

6 AN, K, 162.

7 Oberkirch, pp. 116–17, 333, & note p. 528; Darnton, *Mesmerism*, p. 51.

8 *Vergennes*, p. 376.

9 Hardman, p. 82; Pimodan, p. 226.

10 Nolhac, *Trianon*, p. 216.

11 Maza, 'Diamond Necklace', p. 64, p. 85 note 7.

12 *Lettres*, II, pp. 75–6, 77–8.

13 Maza, *Private Lives*, p. 206 note 110; Maza, 'Diamond Necklace', p. 79.

14 Campan, II, p. 19.

15 AN, K, 162; Nolhac, *Marie Antoinette*, pp. 31–2.

16 Versailles 1955, no. 483; Morel, pp. 209–10; Mossiker, pp. 584–5, 611.

17 Delpierre, 'Bertin', p. 21; Langlade, p. 149; Bessborough, p. 106; Hezecques, p. 14.
18 *Lettres*, II, pp. 89, 106; Arneth & Flammermont, II, p. 3, 8, 12; Devonshire MSS, 5th Duke, 725.
19 Bombelles, II, p. 89; Söderhjelm, p. 107; Maza, 'Diamond Necklace', p. 74.
20 *Lettres*, II, p. 88.
21 Price, p. 176.
22 RA, Add. MSS Geo/9.17.
23 Mossiker, p. 461.
24 Campan (1988), p. 196.
25 Bessborough, pp. 108–9; Nicolardot, pp. 89 *et seq*.
26 Bombelles, II, p. 149.
27 Bombelles, II, p. 152.
28 Arneth & Flammermont, II, p. 38.
29 Arneth & Flammermont, II, p. 28.

Chapter 16: Madame Deficit, pp. 293–311

1 Arneth & Flammermont, II, p. 27; Arneth & Geffroy, III, pp. 340, 457; *Lettres*, II, pp. 85, 99.
2 Arneth & Flammermont, II, p. 38; Nolhac, *Trianon*, p. 220; Nolhac, *Marie-Antoinette*, p. 199; Arizzoli-Clémentel, pp. 16–18; Bombelles, II, p. 155.
3 Forrest, pp. 16 *et seq*.
4 Besenval, p. 426.
5 Ellis, p. 106; Hardman, pp. 87 *et seq*.
6 Arneth & Flammermont, II, pp. 66, 75–6.
7 Arneth & Flammermont, II, p. 80.
8 Arneth & Flammermont, II, p. 85.
9 Blanning, *Joseph II*, p. 137.
10 Pimodan, pp. 233–4.
11 Hardman, *Politics*, pp. 211 *et seq*.; Pimodan, pp. 231–2.
12 *Véri*, II, p. i; Ellis, p. 106; Hezecques, p. 8.
13 Flammermont, p. 120.
14 Foreman, p. 195.
15 Bacourt, I, p. 56; Devonshire MSS, 5th Duke, 822.
16 Hardman, p. 125.
17 Hardman, *Politics*, p. 91; Manceron, p. 311; Devonshire MSS, 5th Duke, 837.

18 Besenval, p. 422; Devonshire MSS, 5th Duke, 822; Mansel, *Court*, p. 9; Solnon, p. 518.

19 Ribeiro, *Art*, pp. 75–6; Baillio, 'Marie-Antoinette', *passim*; Goodden, p. 78.

20 *Modes: Éloffe*, I, p. 110; *Esterhazy Mémoires*, p. xxi.

21 'Modes et Révolutions', p. 14; Aspinall, *George III*, p. 331; Nolhac, *Marie-Antoinette*, p. 204.

22 Baillio, 'Marie-Antoinette', p. 52.

23 *Lettres*, II, p. 106; Secher & Murat, p. 146.

24 Campan, II, p. 42; Weber, II, p. 25.

25 Almeras, p. 398.

26 *Lettres*, II, pp. 108–9; Hardman, pp. 131–2.

27 Bessborough, p. 72; Young, p. 80.

28 *Lettres*, II, p. 115.

29 Haus-Archiv, Familien-Korrespondenz A66; *Lettres*, II, p. 112.

30 Dunlop, *Palaces*, pp. 163–73; Campan, II, pp. 163 *et seq.*

31 Devonshire MSS, 5th Duke, 872; *Lettres*, II p. 119.

32 Nicolardot, p. 74; Nolhac, *Trianon*, p. 221; Lever, *Philippe Égalité*, p. 274.

33 *Lettres*, II, p. 115.

Chapter 17: Close to Shipwreck, pp. 312–30

1 Manceron, p. 312.

2 *La Tour du Pin*, p. 90.

3 Bombelles, II, p. 217; Hezecques, p. 234.

4 Bombelles, II, p. 219.

5 *Lettres*, II, p. 121.

6 *Lettres*, II, p. 217; Staël, *Correspondance*, p. 250 note 2.

7 Hardman, p. 136; Staël, *Correspondance*, p. 255.

8 *Lettres*, II, p. 127.

9 *Léonard*, I, p. 257.

10 Söderhjelm, p. 121; Farr, *Fersen*, p. 126.

11 Higonnet, pp. 319–20.

12 Bacourt, I, p. 56.

13 Söderhjelm, p. 136.

14 Dard, pp. 19 *et seq.*; Lindqvist, p. 112.

15 Söderhjelm, p. 136.

16 Bombelles, II, pp. 240–1.

17 Saint-Priest, II, p. 80.

18 Klinckowström, I, pp. xliv–xlv; Adams, p. 233.

19 Bombelles, II, p. 269.

20 *Lettres*, II, pp. 129–30.

21 Browning, *Despatches*, II, pp. 138–40; Chinard, p. 53.

22 Darnton, *Best-Sellers*, p. 225; Bombelles, II, pp. 276–7.

23 Flammermont, p. 227.

24 Schama, p. 326.

25 *Léonard*, I, p. 260; Morris, I, p. 66.

26 Morris, I, p. 67.

27 Grouchy & Guillois, p. 88; Hezecques, p. 290.

28 *La Tour du Pin*, p. 84; Morel, p. 204.

29 Morel, p. 205.

30 Manceron, p. 463.

31 *La Tour du Pin*, p. 99.

32 Hezecques, p. 293; O'Brien, p. 59; Bombelles, II, p. 307; Hardman,
    p. 147; Manceron, p. 463.

33 Swinburne, II, p. 68; Nicolardot, pp. 41, 134.

34 Morris, I, p. 145.

35 Arneth, *Marie-Antoinette*, p. 239; Debriffe, p. 82.

36 Secher & Murat, pp. 188 *et seq.*; Bombelles, II, pp. 303 *et seq.*;
    Bertin, pp. 200–2; Vigée Le Brun, p. 99.

37 *Bertin*, p. 201.

38 Nicolardot, p. 135.

39 Secher & Murat, pp. 197–8.

40 Louis-Philippe, p. 30; Lever, *Philippe Égalité*, p. 313; Sorel, p. 175.

41 Goodden, p. 77; Bombelles, II, pp. 331 *et seq.*; Hardman, p. 149.

42 Young, p. 125; Dormois, p. 21.

Chapter 18: Hated, Humbled, Mortified, pp. 331–54

1 Young, p. 178; Almeras, p. 347; Fleischmann, pp. 134, 275–7;
   Cobb, *Police*, pp. 278 *et seq.*

2 Almeras, pp. 348–52, 404; Thomas, p. 175 *et seq.*

3 Almeras, pp. 343–5.

4 Morris, I, pp. 130–1; Rigby, pp. 41–2.

5 Hardman, p. 152; Grouchy & Guillois, p. 105.

6 Chateaubriand, I, p. 205.

7 Louis-Philippe, p. 30; Reiset, p. 165.

8 Pimodan, p. 241.

9 Hardman, p. 153.

10 Couty, p. 21; *Lettres*, II, p. 138.

11 Guest, p. 295.

12 Godechot, p. 325; Rudé, *Crowd*, p. 55 note 1.

13 Godechot, p. 24; Besenval, p. 28.

14 Nicolardot, p. 136.

15 Godechot, p. 325; Ribeiro, *Dress*, pp. 56–8.

16 Louis-Philippe, p. 43.

17 Hardman, p. 176.

18 *Lettres*, II, p. 131 & note 1.

19 Dormois, p. 83.

20 Swain, pp. 33–4.

21 RA, Add. MSS 15/8162; Jarrett, p. 165; Almeras, p. 281.

22 Browning, *Despatches*, p. 73.

23 Campan, II, pp. 50–1.

24 Klinckowström, II, p. 6.

25 Browning, *Despatches*, p. 246; Godechot, p. 260.

26 Feuillet de Conches, I, pp. 476–7; Pimodan, p. 245.

27 Forrest, p. 23.

28 *Lettres*, II, p. 137 note 1.

29 RA, Add. MSS 9/76.

30 Rudé, *Crowd*, p. 69.

31 *Tourzel*, pp. 11, 19.

32 *Lettres*, II, pp. 131–6; *Tourzel*, p. 20.

33 Campan, II, p. 70.

34 Webster, p. 66; Béarn, p. 35; Saint-Priest, II, pp. 6–7.

35 *L'Ami du Peuple*, 7 October 1789; Campan, II, p. 70.

36 Nicolardot, p. 138.

37 *Tourzel*, p. 22; Huë, pp. 7, 17; Saint-Priest, II, pp. 9–14.

38 *Marie Thérèse Journal*, p. 8; Huë, p. 7.

39 Klinckowström, I, p. li; Söderhjelm, pp. 135–6.

40 Lever, *Philippe Égalité*, p. 353; *Journal de Paris*, 7 October 1790.

41 *Tourzel*, pp. 22 *et seq.*; Campan, II, pp. 76 *et seq.*

42 Augeard, p. 196; *Marie Thérèse Journal*, p. 4; Elliott, p. 26.

43 *Tourzel*, p. 26; *La Rochejaquelein*, p. 10; but see Campan, II, p. 79.
    Campan, however, was not present at Versailles; Tourzel was.

44 Jarrett, p. 165.

45 Augeard, p. 196; *Marie Thérèse Journal*, p. 5.

46 Béarn, p. 36; Hardman, p. 172.

47 Klinckowström, I, p. li; Couty, p. 39; Louis-Philippe, p. 59.

48 Debriffe, p. 98.

49 *Léonard*, I, p. 291; Flammermont, p. 269.

Chapter 19: Her Majesty the Prisoner, pp. 357–76

1 *Lettres*, II, p. 144; Couty, p. 42.
2 Couty, p. 41.
3 Béarn, p. 42; Mansel, *Court*, p. 19.
4 Weber, II, p. 234.
5 Couty, p. 46.
6 Klinckowström, I, p. li; Sorel, pp. 180–1; Campan, II, pp. 83–5.
7 Campan (1988), p. 235; *Lettres*, II, pp. 147–9.
8 *Tourzel*, pp. 63–4; *Lettres*, II, p. 148.
9 Couty, p. 46; Reitlinger II, p. 50; Verlet, p. 135; Langlade, p. 204.
10 Mansel, *Court*, p. 21; Campan, II, pp. 90–6.
11 Béarn, p. 57; Debriffe, p. 99.
12 Mansel, *Court*, p. 19; RA, Add. MSS 43/2.
13 Béarn, p. 58.
14 Verlet, p. 184; Campan, II, p. 90; *Lettres*, II, pp. 173–4.
15 Campan, II, p. 87; Couty, pp. 62–4; Hezecques, p. 26; Thompson, p. 82; *Tourzel*, p. 37.
16 Campan, II, p. 213.
17 Elliott, p. 39; Yalom, p. 31; Huë, p. 143.
18 Bombelles, III, p. 83; Couty, p. 62.
19 *Journal de Paris*, 30 March 1790.
20 Béarn, pp. 48 *et seq.*; Huë, p. 165.
21 *Tourzel*, p. 79; *Journal de Paris*, 12 May 1790.
22 Campan, II, p. 107; Campan (1988), p. 247; Nicolardot, p. 138; *Tourzel*, p. 50; Hardman, p. 178.
23 *Lettres*, II, p. 137 note 1; Debriffe, pp. 105, 117.
24 *Tourzel*, p. 50.
25 Augeard, pp. 202 *et seq.*
26 Pimodan, pp. 248–9.
27 Augeard, p. 245; Saint-Priest, I, p. 49.
28 Mansel, *Louis XVIII*, p. 48; Campan, II, p. 103; *Véri*, I, p. 23.
29 Nicolardot, pp. 138–40; Campan, II, pp. 111–12.
30 *Lettres*, II, pp. 160, 197; Pimodan, p. 251; Haus-Archiv, Familien-Korrespondenz A, 26, 305.
31 *Lettres*, II, pp. 173–4.
32 *Lettres*, II, p. 166; Dormois, p. 42.
33 Söderhjelm, p. 145.
34 *Lettres*, II, p. 193.
35 *Lettres*, II, p. 191.
36 *Lettres*, II, p. 178; Louis-Philippe, p. 77; Cobban, p. 172.

37 Ribeiro, *Fashion*, p. 85; Schama, p. 511.

38 Huë, p. 172.

39 *Lettres*, II, pp. 188–9.

40 Hibbert, p. 309; Keane, p. 289; Pimodan, p. 303; Dutens, V, pp. 6–9; Feuillet de Conches, III, p. 364.

41 Burke, pp. 169–70.

Chapter 20: Great Hopes, pp. 377–95

 1 *Lettres*, II, pp. 202–3; Pimodan, p. 262.

 2 Campan, II, p. 134.

 3 Blanning, *Eighteenth Century*, p. 172; Hardman, p. 182; Campan, II, p. 125; *Tourzel*, p. 185.

 4 Keane, pp. 289 *et seq.*

 5 *Antonina*, II, p. 38; Fleischmann, *Pamphlets*, pp. 141, 147, 199.

 6 *Dictionnaire de Droit Canonique*, III, cols. 1153–9, 1942.

 7 Béarn, p. 54.

 8 Stryiénski, *Mesdames*, p. 264; *Journal de Paris*, 22 February 1791.

 9 Söderhjelm, *Barnave*, p. 259 note 1; *Lettres*, II, p. 224.

10 Hardman, p. 184; Couty, p. 88; Nicolardot, p. 141; Dormois, p. 96.

11 Dormois, pp. 43–5.

12 Haus-Archiv, Familien-Korrespondenz A26, 307.

13 Söderhjelm, *Barnave*, p. 263 note 1.

14 *Bouillé*, p. 39.

15 *L'Ami du Peuple*, 2 April 1791.

16 Crawford, pp. 437 *et seq.*

17 *Tourzel*, p. 194, p. 455, note; Versailles 1955, no. 645; Browning, *Varennes*, pp. 14–16, 52–76. Carlyle, in a colourful account – full, however, of inaccuracies – apostrophized it: 'Miserable new Berline! Why could not Royalty go in some old Berline similar to that of other men,' missing the point that the berlin was exactly that, rather than a recognizable royal vehicle: *French Revolution*, part II, p. 16; Dunlop, *Marie-Antoinette*, p. 295.

18 *Lettres*, II, p. 281 & note 3; Campan (1988), p. 443 note 167.

19 *Lettres*, II, pp. 230–1.

20 *Lettres*, p. 234.

21 Pimodan, p. 278.

22 Arneth, *Marie Antoinette*, p. 162.

23 *Lévis*, p. 211; *Lettres*, II, p. 231.

24 *Journal de Paris*, 20 April 1791; *Tourzel*, p. 172; Feuillet de Conches, II, p. 123.

25 Nouvion & Liez, p. 92; *Modes: Éloffe*, II, p. 120; Nicolardot, p. 142.

26 *Lettres*, II, p. 235.

27 Browning, *Varennes*, pp. 19 *et seq.*

28 *Bouillé*, pp. 46–8.

29 *Lettres*, II, p. 223.

30 *Bouillé*, p. 67; Browning, *Varennes*, p. 22 note 1.

31 *Tourzel*, p. 384.

32 *Lettres*, II, p. 312.

33 Damas, p. 219.

34 Söderhjelm, pp. 177–8; *Lévis*, p. 154.

35 *Lettres*, II, p. 251; Arneth, *Marie Antoinette*, p. 179; Feuillet de Conches, II, pp. 349–50.

36 *Tourzel*, p. 354; Morel, p. 213; Couty, p. 94.

37 Demuth, p. 247; Pimodan, p. 286.

38 Bombelles, III, p. 245; Weber, II, p. 324; Campan, II, p. 142.

39 Choiseul, *Relation*, pp. 39 *et seq.*; Feuillet de Conches, II, p. 95.

40 *Royal Memoirs*, I, pp. 15–16.

41 Reiset, pp. 190 *et seq.*; Mansel, *Louis XVIII*, p. 54.

Chapter 21: Departure at Midnight, pp. 396–415

1 Couty, pp. 94 *et seq.*

2 Keane, p. 313; Pimodan, p. 289.

3 Feuillet de Conches, II, pp. 101–25.

4 *Modes: Éloffe*, II, p. 234.

5 Valory, p. 273.

6 Valory, p. 281; *Tourzel*, pp. 190 *et seq.*

7 *Royal Memoirs*, I, pp. 20 *et seq.*

8 *Tourzel*, pp. 191–2.

9 Browning, *Varennes*, p. 12.

10 *Tourzel*, p. 195.

11 Choiseul, *Relation*, pp. 79 *et seq.*

12 Choiseul, *Relation*, p. 72.

13 *Tourzel*, p. 196.

14 Valory, p. 286; Marie Thérèse thought so, *Royal Memoirs*, I, pp. 30–1.

15 Damas, pp. 213 *et seq.*

16 Browning, *Varennes*, p. 30.

17 Raigecourt, pp. 199 *et seq.*

18 Deslon, p. 177.

19 Valory, pp. 295–304.

20 Browning, *Varennes*, p. 43; *Tourzel*, p. 202.

21 Valory, p. 304.

22 Deslon, p. 177; Damas, p. 250.

23 *Tourzel*, p. 231.

24 Debriffe, p. 137.

25 *Lévis*, pp. 218–20; Söderhjelm, *Barnave*, p. 35, note 3; *Tourzel*, pp. 207 *et seq.*; Amarzit, pp. 206 *et seq.*

26 *Tourzel*, p. 204; Dutens Papers, no. 938, box 923.

27 Elliott, p. 58; Browning, *Varennes*, p. 49; *Tourzel*, p. 205.

28 Grouchy & Guillois, pp. 277–8; Elliott, p. 63.

29 Nicolardot, p. 143; *Esterhazy Lettres* I, p. 237; Huë, p. 206 & note.

30 *Tourzel*, p. 207.

31 *Esterhazy Lettres* I, p. 238; Loomis, *Friendship*, p. 202.

32 See Choiseul, *Relation, passim; Bouillé*, p. 12 & *passim;* Damas; Valory; *Royal Memoirs*, I, *passim; Tourzel*, pp. 189, 453 & note.

33 Choiseul, *Relation*, pp. 111–16; *Bouillé*, p. 9.

34 Dormois, p. 193; *Bouillé*, p. 134.

35 Aspinall, *George III*, p. 547; Freeman, p. 70.

36 Lever, *Marie-Antoinette*, p. 559; Yalom, p. 150.

37 Nicolardot, pp. 128, 142.

Chapter 22: Up to the Emperor, pp. 416–35

1 Choiseul, *Relation*, p. 106.

2 Schama, p. 513; Rudé, *Robespierre*, p. 106; Amarzit, p. 216; Hampson, p. 53.

3 Weston, *Letters (1791)*, p. 92.

4 Devonshire MSS, 5th Duke, 1084, 1085; Corti, p. 18; Lever, *Louis XVIII*, p. 182.

5 Kelly, p. 31; Donald, p. 146; Browning, *Despatches*, p. 287; Devonshire MSS, 5th Duke, 1086.

6 *Lettres*, II, pp. 253, 254.

7 Hedley, p. 150.

8 Campan, II, p. 149; Sorel, p. 191; Lamorlière, p. 245; Weber, II, p. 23.

9 Söderhjelm, p. 250.

10 Söderhjelm, *Barnave*, pp. 18 *et seq.*; Campan, II, p. 178; *Lettres*, II, p. 392, note 3.

11 Söderhjelm, *Barnave*, pp. 39–40; Campan, II, pp. 150–1; Hardman, p. 200.

12 Söderhjelm, *Barnave*, pp. 14 *et seq.*

13 Thomas, p. 43; Söderhjelm, p. 229.

14 Söderhjelm, *Barnave*, pp. 54–61.

15 Feuillet de Conches, II, p. 427; Weston, *Letters (1792)*, p. 96.

16 Fraser, p. 170.

17 Yalom, p. 151; Weston, *Letters (1791)*, p. 282.

18 Söderhjelm, *Barnave*, p. 113; *Lettres*, II, pp. 268–9, 278.

19 *Lettres*, II, p. 255.

20 Pimodan, p. 296; *Lettres*, II, p. 286; Lever, *Louis XVIII*, pp. 162, 170; Louis-Philippe, p. 126.

21 Lever, *Louis XVIII*, p. 181; Mansel, *Louis XVIII*, p. 60; Daudet, p. 60.

22 Louis-Philippe, p. 92.

23 *Lettres*, II, p. 275.

24 *Lettres*, II, pp. 282–304.

25 *Lettres*, II, pp. 333, 360.

26 *Tourzel*, p. 80; *Lettres*, II, p. 275; Söderhjelm, p. 251.

27 Söderhjelm, *Barnave*, p. 47; *Lettres*, II, p. 292; Pimodan, p. 313.

28 Söderhjelm, *Barnave*, pp. 111 *et seq.*

29 Feuillet de Conches, II, p. 397.

30 Pimodan, pp. 319–20.

31 Mansel, *Ligne*, p. 85; Ligne, I, p. 286.

32 Feuillet de Conches, II, p. 284.

33 Söderhjelm, *Barnave*, p. 125 note 2, p. 143; Sorel, p. 199; Fleischmann, p. 246; MacDonogh, *Reigning Cats*, p. 49.

34 *Tourzel*, p. 303; Campan, II, p. 174.

35 Couty, p. 143; Nouvion & Liez, p. 94.

36 *Lettres*, II, pp. 364–78.

37 Browning, *Despatches*, pp. 150, 152; *Lettres*, II, p. 320; Klinckowström, I, p. lxvi; Söderhjelm, p. 236.

38 Castelot, *Queen*, p. 295.

39 Forrest, p. 113.

40 Stafsundarchive, AVF, *Dagböker*, V (1791–4); Söderhjelm, pp. 241–7.

Chapter 23: Violence and Rage, pp. 436–56

1 *Lettres*, II, p. 395 note 2; *Tourzel*, p. 296; Kelly, p. 45.

2 *Lettres*, II, pp. 396–7; Huë, p. 394.

3 Pimodan, pp. 296, 326.

4 Hampson, p. 111; Campan, II, p. 205.

5 Söderhjelm, p. 257.

6 *Lettres*, II, p. 398, 402.

7 *Lettres*, II, pp. 393, 399, 402.

8 *L'Ami du Peuple*, 11 June 1792.

9 Couty, pp. 166 *et seq.*; Campan, II, pp. 211 *et seq.*

10 Weston, *Letters (1792)*, p. 90.

11 Huë, pp. 263 *et seq.*

12 Béarn, p. 93; *Tourzel*, p. 294; Huë, p. 274.

13 *Lettres*, II, p. 406; Huë, p. 274.

14 Campan, II, p. 214.

15 Amarzit, p. 104; Couty, p. 190; Huë, p. 305; *Lettres*, II, p. 406 & note 2, p. 414; Molleville, II, pp. 174–5.

16 Campan, II, p. 239; Amarzit, p. 98.

17 *Tourzel*, p. 343.

18 Mossiker, p. 566; *Lettres*, II, p. 419.

19 Higonnet, p. 245.

20 *Lettres*, II, p. 420 note 1; Mayer, pp. 55–6; Arnaud-Bouteloup, pp. 363–6.

21 Schama, p. 612.

22 *Lettres*, II, p. 244.

23 Nicolardot, p. 148; Campan, II, p. 216; Couty, p. 194; Moore, I, p. 164.

24 Couty, pp. 197 *et seq.*; La Rochefoucauld, pp. 3 *et seq.*

25 Allen, pp. 14 *et seq.*; Hezecques, p. 135.

26 Campan, II, pp. 239 *et seq.*

27 La Rochefoucauld, p. 7; Couty, p. 215.

28 Moore, I, pp. 167 *et seq.*; La Rochefoucauld, pp. 13–14.

29 Jordan, p. 5.

30 Campan, II, p. 242; Crankshaw, p. 78; Couty, p. 220.

31 Huë, p. 332; Rocheterie, II, p. 272.

32 Allen, p. 80; Lever, *Marie-Antoinette*, p. 618; Hardman, pp. 220–1; Loomis, *Terror*, p. 194.

33 Huë, p. 333.

34 *Tourzel*, p. 364; Couty, p. 221; Allen, p. 91.

35 *Tarante*, p. 71; Allen, p. 92; La Rochefoucauld, pp. 22, 26.

36 La Rochefoucauld, p. 23.

37 *Journal de Paris*, 12 August 1792; Campan, II, p. 244; La Rochefoucauld, p. 40.

38 Allen, p. 101; Hardman, p. 221.

39 Weber, III, p. 109; Chapman, p. 571; *Tarante*, p. 77; Moore, I, p. 36; Maxwell, p. 186.

40 *Tarante*, p. 72; Béarn, p. 100.

41 Ribeiro, *Fashion*, p. 75 & note 31, p. 146; Keane, p. 318; Huë, p. 348.

42 *Tarante*, p. 97; *Tourzel*, p. 342.

43 Maxwell, p. 169.

44 *Journal de Paris*, 12 August 1792; Castelot, *Queen*, p. 315; Campan, II, p. 258; Béarn, p. 105; Lenotre, pp. 6–18.

45 Campan, II, p. 255.

46 Lenotre, pp. 31 *et seq.*

47 *L'Ami du Peuple*, 10 August 1792; *Tourzel*, p. 378; Lenotre, p. 32.

Chapter 24: The Tower, pp. 457–78

1 *Tourzel*, p. 374; *Royal Memoirs*, III, pp. 157–8.

2 Huë, pp. 355 *et seq.*

3 *Royal Memoirs*, III, p. 167; Lepître, p. 163.

4 *Royal Memoirs*, III, pp. 161 *et seq.*; Huë, pp. 355 *et seq.*

5 Nouvion & Liez, pp. 96–7 & note 2; Delpierre, pp. 27–32.

6 Huë, p. 394.

7 *Tourzel*, p. 382.

8 See *Cléry*, pp. 15, 26 & *passim*.

9 *Royal Memoirs*, III, p. 167; Couty, p. 270.

10 Arasse, p. 33.

11 Daujon, pp. 45 *et seq.*

12 Higonnet, p. 37; Cobb, *French*, p. 387 & note 4; Moore, I, p. 183; Loomis, *Terror*, p. 83.

13 Gueniffey, p. 237.

14 *Tourzel*, p. 389; *Bertin*, p. 306; Lafont d'Aussonne, I, pp. 52–3.

15 Morris, II, p. 540; Moore, p. 189.

16 Bertin, *Lamballe*, p. 326; Louis-Philippe, p. 261 & note; Chapman, p. 122; Tussaud, p. 272.

17 Bertin, *Lamballe*, p. 322; *Cléry*, pp. 31 *et seq.*

18 *Royal Memoirs*, III, pp. 174–5.

19 Daujon, pp. 59–61.

20 Fleischmann, *Terror*, p. 58; Lenotre, p. 79; Huë, p. 466.

21 Morel, pp. 213, 218–19, 234; 'Dix siècles de joaillerie', p. 40.

22 Moore, I, p. 271.

23 Fleischmann, p. 78; *Royal Memoirs*, III, pp. 183 *et seq.*; Rousseau, *Émile*, p. 15; *Cléry*, pp. 35 *et seq.*

24 Lever, *Philippe Égalité*, p. 447; *Cléry*, p. 45; Hardman, p. 226.

25 *Royal Memoirs*, III, p. 170.

26 Debriffe, p. 174.

27 Turgy, pp. 93–4; Loomis, *Terror*, p. 259.

28 *Cléry*, p. 210 & note 1 to p. 56; Goret, p. 127.

29 Mirault, p. 49; Wilfred Blunt and W. T. Stearn, *The Art of Botanical Illustration*, new revised edn, 1994, pp. 186–7 and note 5.

30 Blanning, *Revolution*, p. 65.

31 Couty, pp. 276–7; Freeman, pp. 1, 38, 50, 70.

32 Maxwell, pp. 179–80.

33 *Cléry*, p. 86; Lepître, p. 161 & note 1; Landon, II, pp. 594–5.

34 Dormois, pp. 201–4; Jordan, p. 127.

35 Morris, II, p. 591.

36 Walzer, p. 5; Figes, p. 639.

37 Jordan, pp. 58 *et seq.*, p. 102.

38 *Paine*, III, pp. 119–27.

39 *Paine*, IV, pp. x–xii; Jordan, pp. 196–7.

40 Jordan, p. 187; Elliott, p. 120.

41 *Royal Memoirs*, III, pp. 199–200, 203–4.

42 *Cléry*, pp. 104–5.

43 Turgy, p. 102.

Chapter 25: Unfortunate Princess, pp. 481–502

1 Lepître, p. 169.

2 *Royal Memoirs*, III, pp. 204–5; *Cléry*, p. 107; *Lettres*, II, p. 434.

3 *Lettres*, II, p. 438.

4 Lepître, p. 172 note 1; Goret, p. 144.

5 Goret, p. 144; *Royal Memoirs*, III, p. 206.

6 Furneaux, p. 119.

7 Goret, p. 149; 'Relation de Turgy', p. 112.

8 Lever, *Louis XVIII*, p. 200; Crawford, pp. 447 *et seq.*; Pimodan, p. 375.

9 Turgy, pp. 103 *et seq.*; Huë, p. 472.

10 Lepître, p. 159.

11 Lenotre, p. 150 & note 1.

12 Pimodan, pp. 372, 374; Bacourt, II, p. 368.

13 Higonnet, p. 138; Thomas, p. 68; Söderhjelm, p. 281.

14 Huë, p. 469; Aspinall, *Prince of Wales*, pp. 274, 276.

15 Rudé, *Robespierre*, p. 31; Walzer, p. 108; Jordan, p. 190.

16 Jordan, p. 210; Moelle, p. 211.

17 Salmon, p. 92; *Tarante*, p. 203; Saint-Priest, II, p. 98.

18 Pimodan, p. 377.

19 Blanning, *Joseph II*, p. 203.

20 *Lettres*, II, p. 426; Turgy, p. 104; Lepître, p. 178 note 1.

21 *Lettres*, II, p. 433.

22 *Lettres*, II, pp. 437–9.

23 Söderhjelm, p. 323; *Lettres*, II, p. 435; Rousseau, *Nouvelle Héloïse*, p. 47.

24 Lever, *Marie-Antoinette*, p. 640.

25 *Tourzel*, p. 385 & note p. 467.

26 Furneaux, p. 128.

27 Hampson, p. 120; Loomis, *Terror*, p. 257.

28 Jordan, p. 225; Arasse, pp. 70–1, p. 189 note 128; *Royal Memoirs*, III, pp. 222–3.

29 *Royal Memoirs*, III, pp. 223–4.

30 Furneaux, pp. 135–6.

31 Acton, p. 262.

32 Huë, p. 414.

33 Walter, *Procès*, p. 23.

34 *Royal Memoirs*, III, pp. 228–31; Lenotre, pp. 215–16.

35 Larivière, pp. 355–7; Saint-Priest, II, p. 97.

36 Lamorlière, pp. 228 *et seq.*

37 Lamorlière, pp. 230–1.

38 Walter, *Procès*, p. 27.

39 Lamorlière, p. 240.

40 Lenotre, pp. 295–7 & notes 1 & 2.

41 Fouché, pp. 308–19.

42 Campan, II, pp. 199–200.

43 Ségur, pp. 320 *et seq.*; Castelot, *Queen*, pp. 372 *et seq.*; Walter, *Procès*, p. 678; Huë, p. 151.

44 Cobb, *French*, pp. 48 *et seq.*

45 Barbey, p. 61; Lenotre, p. 292 note 1.

46 Klinckowström, II, pp. 82–3; Pimodan, pp. 388–91.

47 Pimodan, p. 396.

48 Verlet, p. 56; Reitlinger II, p. 130.

49 Bacourt, III, p. 418.

Chapter 26: The Head of Antoinette, pp. 503–26

1 Lamorlière, pp. 227 *et seq.*, p. 232 note 1, p. 246.

2 Lamorlière, p. 241.

3 Corti, p. 206; Huë, pp. 148–9; Lamorlière, p. 234.

4 *Royal Memoirs*, III, p. 233; Lamorlière, pp. 239–40; Lenotre, pp. 234–5 note 1.

5 Lamorlière, p. 236.

6 Lafont d'Aussonne, I, p. 52.

7 Campardon, pp. 55–7; AN, W296 & dossier F7.4392 cit. Castelot, p. 435.

8 Walter, *Procès*, pp. 26–36.

9 Fortescue, pp. 456–61.

10 Oberkirch, p. 191.

11 Staël, *Réflexions*, pp. v, xxx.

12 Walter, *Procès*, pp. 39 *et seq.*

13 Walter, *Procès*, p. 43.

14 Walter, *Procès*, pp. 45 *et seq.*

15 Lenotre, p. 301; Fouché, pp. 318–19; Castelot, pp. 418–20; but see Lafont d'Aussonne, I, p. 57.

16 Mills, p. 95; Forrest, p. 101; Maza, *Private*, p. 170; RA, Add. MSS GEO 21/91, 6 February 1787.

17 Chauveau-Lagarde, p. 3.

18 Chauveau-Lagarde, p. 5; *Lettres*, II, pp. 440–1.

19 Lamorlière, p. 249; Campardon, p. 229.

20 Walter, *Procès*, pp. 53, 98.

21 Walter, *Procès*, pp. 53 *et seq.*

22 Walter, *Procès*, pp. 59–61.

23 Walter, *Procès*, p. 61 & note 1; Chauveau-Lagarde, p. 23.

24 Walter, *Procès*, p. 63.

25 Lamorlière, p. 251.

26 Walter, *Procès*, pp. 68 *et seq.*

27 Walter, *Procès*, pp. 93 *et seq.*

28 Lenotre, p. 348; Castelot, *Queen*, p. 395.

29 Campardon, pp. 125–8 & note 1.

30 Lépinay & Charles, Annexes III, pp. 90 *et seq.*

31 In this form, probably invented by a journalist, although similar words seem to have been spoken; *Cléry*, p. 229 & note; Arasse, p. 90.

32 Lamorlière, pp. 252 *et seq.*

33 *Marie-Clothilde*, p. 152 note G: 'Des Deuils de cour et de famille'.

34 Lamorlière, pp. 252 *et seq.*

35 Arasse, p. 96.

36 Arasse, pp. 123 *et seq.*; *Le Moniteur*, 27 October 1793.

37 Campardon, p. 237; *Le Moniteur*, 27 October 1793; Grouchy & Guillois, p. 477; Walter, *Procès*, pp. 99–100.

38 Campardon, p. 232; Chalon, p. 469.

Chapter 27: Epilogue, pp. 527–48

1 Lenotre, p. 398.

2 Cottrell, p. 150; Lenotre, p. 394.

3 Fortescue MSS, p. 462; AN, W 15. 534/11.

4 Castelot, *Queen*, p. 439.

5 AN, C 279. C1. 730; Fleischmann, *Terror*, p. 324.

6 Elliott, p. 177.

7 Vigée Le Brun, pp. 2–3; Pimodan, p. 411.

8 Lindqvist, p. 204; Foster 'Journal', MSS; Söderhjelm, p. 315.

9 Pimodan, Appendix IV, pp. 438–43; Lindqvist, p. 215.

10 Bearne, pp. 114, 200; Corti, p. 207; Acton, p. 262.

11 Corti, p. 231.

12 Barbey, p. 243.

13 *Marie-Clothilde*, p. 224.

14 Yalom, p. 62.

15 Evans, p. 202; *Boigne*, I, p. 255.

16 Delorme, *Louis XVII, passim*, esp. pp. 93, 203–4.

17 A. W. T. Webb, *Story of the Seychelles*, 1964; John Demos, *The Unredeemed Captive: a family story from early America*, 1996, pp. 245 *et seq.*, p. 309 note 6.

18 Lenotre, pp. 398 *et seq.*; Béarn, pp. 223 *et seq.*

19 Chauteaubriand, III, p. 461; Lenotre, p. 410.

20 McLynn, p. 469; Bruce, pp. 302, 457.

21 C. A. Moberly & E. Jourdain, *An Adventure*, 2nd edn, 1913; Lucille Iremonger, *The Ghosts of Versailles: Miss Moberly and Miss Jourdain and their adventure*, 1957, p. 181; Castle, pp. 10, 112, 140.

22 Castle, pp. 143–4.

23 Figes, p. 277; Zeepvat, p. 4 *et seq.*

24 Baroness Sophie Buxhoeveden, *The Life and Tragedy of Alexandra Feodorovna*, 1928, pp. 100–10.

25 Versailles 1955; Mossiker, p. 582.

26 Information of Mlle Cécile Coutin, Association Marie-Antoinette; Higonnet, p. 295.

27 *Walpole*, pp. 264–5.

28 Sorel, p. 189.

29 Bessborough, p. 203; *Tarante*, p. 203.

30 Arneth & Flammermont, I, p. 290.

31 Prochaska, p. 17; Besenval, p. 181.

32 Huë, p. 466; Ribeiro, *Art*, p. 83.

33 Goncourt, p. 73.

34 Fleischmann, Appendix II, pp. 311–15.

35 Corti, p. 181.

36 Dormois, p. 98.

37 Bombelles, I, p. 196.

38 Ford, p. 140; Leviticus 16: 10; George Foot Moore, *Judaism in the First Centuries of the Christian Era*, New York, 1978, p. 55; James Frazer, *The Golden Bough: A Study in Magic and Religion*, abridged edn, 1922, pp. 540–2, 565, 568–9, 577–87.

39 Morris, II, p. 602.

40 Dormois, p. 43.

Sources

A full bibliography of the life and times of Marie Antoinette is impractical for reasons of space. This is a list of the principal sources consulted and also gives details of books cited in brief in the Notes. The place of publication is London (English) and Paris (French) unless otherwise stated.

Books

Acton, Harold, *The Bourbons of Naples (1734–1825)*, 1959

Adams, William Howard, *The Paris Years of Thomas Jefferson*, New Haven, US, 1997

Allen, Rodney, *Threshold of Terror: The Last Hours of the Monarchy in the French Revolution*, 1999

Almeras, Henri d', *Marie-Antoinette et les Pamphlets Royalistes et Révolutionnaires: avec une bibliographie...*, 1907

Amarzit, Pierre d', *Barnave: le conseiller Secret de Marie-Antoinette*, 2000

L'Ami du Peuple

Amiguet, Philippe, ed., *Lettres de Louis XV à son petit-fils l'Infant Ferdinand de Parme*, 1938

[AN] Archives Nationales, Paris

Anderson, Emily, ed., *The Letters of Mozart and his Family*, 2 vols., 2nd edn, New York, 1966

[*Antonina*] *Memoirs of Antonina, Queen of Abo, displaying her private intrigues ...*, trans. from the French, 2 vols., 1791

Arasse, Daniel, *La Guillotine et l'Imaginaire de la Terreur*, 1987

Arizzoli-Clémentel, Pierre, introd. & commentaries, *Views and Plans of the Petit Trianon at Versailles*, 1998

Armaille, Comtesse d', *Marie-Thérèse et Marie-Antoinette*, 3rd edn, 1893

Arnaud-Bouteloup, Jeanne, *La Rôle Politique de Marie-Antoinette*, 1924

[Arneth, *Marie Antoinette*] Arneth, Alfred von, *Marie Antoinette, Joseph II und Leopold II*, Leipzig, Paris & Vienna, 1866

[Arneth & Flammermont] d'Arneth, Alfred & Flammermont, Jules, *correspondance secrète du Comte de Mercy-Argenteau avec l'Empereur Joseph II et le Prince de Kaunitz*, 2 vols., 1889

[Arneth & Geffroy] d'Arneth, Alfred & Geffroy, M. A., *Marie-Antoinette: correspondance secrète entre Marie-Thérèse et le Comte de Mercy-Argenteau*, 3 vols., 1874

Ashton, Leigh, trans. & introd., *Letters and Memoirs of the Prince de Ligne*, 1927

Aspinall, A., ed., *The Correspondence of George, Prince of Wales, 1770–1812*, II, 1789–1794, 1964

Aspinall, A., ed., *The Later Correspondence of George III*, 2 vols., 1963–4.

Augeard, J. M., *Mémoires Secrètes...*, introd. M. Évariste Bavoux, 1866

Austen Papers, 1704–1856, ed. R. A. Austen-Leigh, 1942

[*Bachaumont*] *Mémoires Historiques, Littéraires, Politiques, Anecdotiques et Critiques de Bachaumont*, 2 vols., 2nd edn, 1809

Bacourt, M. Ad. de, ed., *Correspondance entre le Comte de Mirabeau et le Comte de La Marck pendant les années 1789, 1790 et 1791*, 3 vols., 1851

Baillio, Joseph, *Elisabeth Vigée Le Brun, 1755–1842*, Kimball Art Museum, Fort Worth, Texas, 1982

Baillio, Joseph, 'Marie-Antoinette et ses enfants par Mme Vigée Le Brun, pts I & II, *L'Oeil*, Lausanne, 1981

Barbey, Frédéric, *A Friend of Marie-Antoinette (Lady Atkyns)*, 1906

Bauchart, Quentin, *Les Femmes Bibliophiles*, 1826

[Bault] 'Relation de la femme Bault: veuve du concierge de la prison de la Conciergerie (11 September–16 October 1793): *see* Lenotre

[Beales] Beales, Derek, *Joseph II*; I, *In the Shadow of Maria Teresa*, Cambridge, 1987

Beales, Derek, *Mozart and the Habsburgs*, Stenton Lecture, University of Reading, Reading, 1993

Béarn, Pauline de, *Souvenirs de Quarante Ans 1789–1830*, nouvelle edn, 1868

Bearne, Mrs, *A Sister of Marie Antoinette: The Life-Story of Maria Carolina, Queen of Naples*, 1907

Bernard, J. F., *Talleyrand: A Biography*, 1973

Bernier, Olivier, *Louis the Beloved: The Life of Louis XV*, 1984

Bernier, Olivier, 'The Eighteenth Century Woman', Metropolitan Museum, New York, 1981

[Bernier] Bernier, Olivier, *Imperial Mother, Royal Daughter: the correspondence of Marie Antoinette and Maria Teresa*, 1969

Berry, Mary, *A Comparative View of the Social Life of England and France*, 1828

[Bertin] *Mémoires de Mademoiselle Bertin sur la Reine Marie-Antoinette*, 1824

[Bertin, *Lamballe*] Bertin, Georges, *Madame de Lamballe d'après des documents inédits*, 1888

Besenval, Baron de, *Mémoires sur la Cour de France*, introd. & notes Ghislain de Diesbach, 1987

Bessborough, Earl of, ed., *Georgiana: Extracts from the Correspondence of Georgiana, Duchess of Devonshire*, 1955

[BL] British Library MSS

Blaikie, Thomas, *Diary of a Scotch Gardener at the French Court at the End of the Eighteenth Century*, ed. & introd. Francis Birrell, 1931

Blanning, T. C. W., *The Eighteenth Century*, Oxford, 2000

Blanning, T. C. W., *Joseph II*, 1994

Blanning, T. C. W., *The French Revolution in Germany: Occupation and Resistance in the Rhineland 1792–1802*, Oxford, 1983

Bluche, François, *La Vie Quotidienne au Temps de Louis XVI*, 1988

[Boigne] *Mémoires de la Comtesse de Boigne née d'Osmond: du règne de Louis XVI à 1820*, ed. Jean-Claude Berchet, 2 vols., 1986

Bombelles, Marquis de, *Journal*, ed. Jean Grassion & Frans Durif, 3 vols., Geneva, 1977

[Bouillé] *Mémoire du Marquis de Bouillé (Cte Louis) sur le départ de Louis XVI au mois de juin, 1791 ...*, en réponse à la Relation de M. le Duc de Choiseul, 1823

Boutry, Maurice, *Le Mariage de Marie-Antoinette*, 1904

Boyer, Marie-France, *The Private Realm of Marie Antoinette*, trans. Jenifer Wakelyn, 1996

Brooke, John, *King George III*, foreword HRH the Prince of Wales, 1972

[Brosse, *Marie Thérèse*] Brosse, Jacques, ed., *Mémoire écrit par Marie-Thérèse-Charlotte de France sur la captivité des Princes et Princesses ses*

Parents, depuis le 10 août 1792 jusqu'à la mort de son frère: see Cléry

Browne, Rory, 'The Diamond Necklace Affair Revisited: the Rohan family and court politics', *Renaissance & Modern Studies*, XXXIII, Nottingham, 1989

Browning, Oscar, ed., *Despatches of Earl Gower... and the Diary of Viscount Palmerston*, Cambridge, UK, 1885

Browning, Oscar, *The Flight to Varennes and Other Historical Essays*, 1892

Bruce, Evangeline, *Napoleon and Josephine: An Improbable Marriage*, 1995

Burke, Edmund, *Reflections on the Revolution in France*, ed. Conor Cruise O'Brien, 1981

[Campan] Campan, Madame, *Memoirs of the Private Life of Marie Antoinette, Queen of France and Navarre*, 2 vols., 3rd edn, 1824

[Campan (1988)] *Mémoires de Madame Campan: première femme de chambre de Marie Antoinette*, ed. Jean Chalon, notes Carlos de Angulo, 1988

Campardon, M. Émile, *Marie-Antoinette a la Conciergerie (du 1er août au 16 octobre 1793)*, 2nd edn, 1864

Carlyle, Thomas, *The French Revolution: A History*, 2 pts., 1889

[Castelot] Castelot, André, *Marie Antoinette*, 1957

Castelot, André, *Le Procès de Marie Antoinette*, 1993

Castelot, André, *Queen of France: A Biography of Marie Antoinette*, New York, 1957

Castle, Terry, *The Apparitional Lesbian: Female Homosexuality and Modern Culture*, New York, 1993

Castries, Duc de, *Le Maréchal de Castries (1727–1800)*, 1979

Chalon, Jean, *Chère Marie-Antoinette*, 1988

Chapman, Pauline, *The French Revolution as Seen by Madame Tussaud Witness Extraordinary*, 1989

Chateaubriand, Vicomte de, *Mémoires d'Outre-Tombe*, ed. Edmond Biré, 6 vols., 1898–1900

Chauveau-Lagarde, avocat, leur défenseur, *Note historique sur le procès de Mme Elisabeth*, 1816

Chinard, Gilbert, *Trois Amitiés Françaises de Jefferson d'après sa Correspondance Inéditée avec Mme de Bréhau, Mme de Tessé et Mme de Corny*, 1927

Choiseul, Duc de, *Mémoires*, preface Jean-Pierre Guiccardi, notes Philippe Bonnet, 1987

Choiseul, M. le Duc de, *Relation du départ de Louis XVI*, 1822

Christoph, Paul, *Maria Theresia und Marie Antoinette: ihr geheimer briefwechsel*, Vienna, 1958

[*Cléry*] *Journal de ce qui s'est passé à la Tour du Temple pendant la captivité de Louis XVI par M. Cléry, valet du chambre du roi et autres mémoires sur le Temple*, ed. Jacques Brosse, 1987

Cobb, Richard, *The French and Their Revolution*, ed. David Gilmour, 1998

Cobb, Richard, *The Police and the People*, Oxford, 1970

Cobban, Alfred, *A History of Modern France*; I, *1715–1799*, pbk, 2nd edn, 1962

Corbin, Alain, *The Foul and the Fragrant: Odour and the Social Imagination*, pbk, 1996

Corson, Richard, *Fashions in Make-up: From Ancient to Modern Times*, 1972

Corson, Richard, *Fashions in Hair: The First Five Thousand Years*, 1965

Corti, Conte Egon Caesare, *Ich, ein Tochter Maria Theresias: ein Lebensbild der Königin Marie Karoline von Neapel*, Munich, 1950

Cottrell, Leonard, *Madame Tussaud*, 1951

Coutts & Co. MSS, London

Couty, Mathieu, *La Vie aux Tuileries pendant la Révolution, 1789–1799*, 1988

[*Cradock*] *Journal de Madame Cradock, Voyage en France (1783–1786)*, ed. Mme. O. Dolphin, 1896

Crankshaw, Edward, *Maria Theresa*, pbk, 1983

Crawford, Katherine B., 'Regency Government in early modern France: gender substitution and the construction of monarchical authority', D.Phil. dissertation, University of Chicago, 1997

Cronin, Vincent, *Louis and Antoinette*, 1974

Croÿ, Duc de, *Journal inédit 1718–1784*, ed. Vicomte de Grouchy & Paul Cottin, 4 vols., 1906

[Damas] 'Rapport de M. le Comte Charles de Damas': *see Bouillé*

Dard, Émile, *Un rival de Fersen: Quintin Craufurd*, 1947

Darnton, Robert, *The Forbidden Best-Sellers of Pre-Revolutionary France*, 1996

Darnton, Robert, 'The Memoirs of Lenoir, Lieutenant de Police of Paris, 1774–1785', notes & documents, EHR, LXXXV, 1970

Darnton, Robert, *Mesmerism and the End of the Enlightenment in France*, Cambridge, Mass., 1968

Daudet, Ernest, *Histoire de l'émigration: Coblentz 1789–1793*, 1890

[Daujon] 'Relation de Daujon, Commissionaire de la Commune (août 1792–Octobre 1793)' *see Lenotre*

Debriffe, Martial, *Madame Elisabeth: la princesse martyre*, 1997

Delorme, Philippe, *Louis XVII, La Verité: sa mort au Temple confirmée par la science*, 2000

Delorme, Philippe, *Histoire des Reines de France: Marie-Antoinette*, 1999

Delpierre, Madeleine, 'Rose Bertin, les marchandes de modes et la Révolution': *see* 'Modes et Révolutions'

Delpierre, Madeleine, 'La garde-robe de la famille royale au Temple': *see* 'Modes et Révolutions'

Demuth, Norman, *French Opera: Its Development in the Revolution*, Horsham, Sussex, 1963

[Deslon] 'Relation de M. Deslon': *see Bouillé*

Deutsch, O. E., *Mozart: A Documentary Biography*, 1965

Devonshire MSS: 5th Duke's Group, Devonshire Collections, Chatsworth

Dickens, A. G., ed., *The Courts of Europe: Politics, Patronage and Royalty 1400–1800*, 1977

'Dix siècles de joaillerie française', Musée du Louvre 13 mai–3 juin 1962, Ministère d'État Affaires Culturelles, 1962

Donald, Diana, *The Age of Caricature: Satirical Prints in the Reign of George III*, 1996

Dormois, Jean-Pierre, ed., *Lettres de Louis XVI et de Marie-Antoinette, 1789–1793*, 1988

Doyle, William, *Origins of the French Revolution*, 3rd edn, Oxford, 1999

[Dufour] 'Relation de Dufour (10–13 août 1792)': *see* Lenotre

Dunlop, Ian, *Marie-Antoinette: A Portrait*, 1993

Dunlop, Ian, *Royal Palaces of France*, 1985

Dunlop, Ian, *Versailles*, 1956

[Dutens] Dutens, Louis, *Memoirs of a Traveller Now in Retirement*, 5 vols., 1806

Dutens Papers, Coutts & Co. MSS

Eagles, Robin, 'Francophilia and Francophobia in English Society 1748–1783', D.Phil. thesis, Oxford, 1996

Ehrman, John, *The Younger Pitt: The Years of Acclaim*, pbk, revised edn, 1996

Eiwes, Carmen, *Die Brautfahrt der Marie Antoinette 1770: festlichen, zeremoniell und standische Rahmenbedungen...*, Hamburg, 1992

Elliott, Grace Dalrymple, *Journal of My Life During the French Revolution*, 1859

Ellis, Joseph P., *American Sphinx: The Character of Thomas Jefferson*, New York, 1998

Elon, Amos, *Founder: Meyer Amschel Rothschild and His Time*, 1996

[*Esterhazy Lettres I*] *Lettres du Cte Valentin Esterhazy à sa femme, 1784–1794*, introd. & notes Ernest Daudet, 1907

[*Esterhazy Lettres II*] *Nouvelles Lettres du Cte Valentin Esterhazy à sa femme, 1792–1795*, pub. Ernest Daudet, 1909

[*Esterhazy Mémoires*] *Mémoires du Cte Valentin Esterhazy*, introd. & notes Ernest Daudet, 1905

Evans, Joan, *Madame Royale*, 1959

Farr, Evelyn, *Marie-Antoinette and Count Axel Fersen: the untold love story*, 1995

Farr, Evelyn, *Before the Deluge: Parisian society in the reign of Louis XVI*, 1994

[*Fausselandry*] *Mémoires de Madame la Vicomtesse de Fars Fausselandry, ou Souvenirs d'une octogénaire*, 3 vols., 1830

Fersen, Axel von, *Dagböker: see* Stafsundarchive

Feuillet de Conches, F., *Louis XVI, Marie-Antoinette et Madame Elisabeth: lettres et documents inédits*, 6 vols, 1864

Figes, Orlando, *A People's Tragedy: The Russian Revolution 1891–1924*, pbk, 1997

Flammermont, Jules, *Les Correspondances des Agents Diplomatiques Étrangers en France avant la Révolution*, 1896

Fleischmann, Hector, *Behind the Scenes in the Terror*, 1914

Fleischmann, Hector, *Madame de Polignac et la Cour galante de Marie-Antoinette*, 1910

[Fleischmann] Fleischmann, Hector, *Les Pamphlets Libertins contre Marie-Antoinette d'après des Documents Nouveaux*, 1910

Ford, P. L., ed., *Autobiography of Thomas Jefferson*, 1914

Foreman, Amanda, *Georgiana: Duchess of Devonshire*, 1998

Forrest, Alan, *The French Revolution*, 1995

[Fortescue] H.M.C. 14th Report, App. Pt. V, (MSS of J. B. Fortescue, preserved at Dropmore, II) 1894

Foster, Lady Elizabeth, 'Journal', Dormer MSS

[Fouché] 'Souvenirs de Madame Fouché, redigés en 1824 par M. le Comte de Rosiano': *see* Lenotre

Fraser, Flora, *Beloved Emma: The life of Emma, Lady Hamilton*, 1986

Freeman, Andrew, *The Compromising of Louis XVI: the* armoire de fer *and the French Revolution*, Exeter, 1989

Furneaux, Rupert, *The Bourbon Tragedy*, 1968

Garland, Madge, 'Rose Bertin: Minister of Fashion', *Apollo Magazine*, January 1968

Genlis, Mme la Comtesse de, *Dictionnaire critique et raisonné des Étiquettes de la Cour*, 2 vols., 1818

Georgel, Abbé, *Mémoires pour servir à l'histoire des événements de la fin du dix-huitième siècle...*, 6 vols., 1817

Girard, Georges, ed., *Correspondance entre Marie-Thérèse et Marie-Antoinette*, 1933

Girault de Coursac, P., *L'Éducation d'un roi: Louis XVI*, 1972

Girouard, Mark, *Life in the French Country House*, 2000

[*Gluck*] *The Collected Correspondence of Christoph Willibald Gluck*, ed., Hedwig & E. H. Mueller von Asow, 1962

Godechot, Jacques, *The Taking of the Bastille July 14th, 1789*, 1970

Goncourt, Edmond & Jules de, *Histoire de Marie-Antoinette*, preface Robert Kopp, 1990

Gooch, G. P., *Louis XV: The Monarchy in Decline*, Westport, Conn., 1976

Goodden, Angelica, *The Sweetness of Life: A Biography of Elisabeth Louise Vigée Le Brun*, 1997

[Goret] 'Relation de Municipal Goret': *see* Lenotre

Grimm, Baron de, *Mémoires Historiques, Littéraires et Anecdotiques ...*, *depuis 1770 jusqu'en 1792*, 4 vols., 1813–14

Grouchy, Vicomte de & Guillois, Antoine, *La Révolution Française racontée par un diplomat étranger* [n.d.]

Gueniffey, Patrice, *La Politique de la Terreur: essai sur la violence révolutionnaire 1789–1794*, 2000

Guest, Ivor, *The Ballet of the Enlightenment: The Establishment of the Ballet d'Action in France, 1770–1793*, 1996

Gutwirth, Madelyn, *The Twilight of the Goddesses: Women and Representation in the French Revolutionary Era*, New Brunswick, 1992

Hamann, Brigitte, *Ein Herz und viele Kronen: das leben der Kaiserin Maria Theresia*, Vienna, 1998

Hampson, Norman, *Danton*, 1978

Hardman, John, *French Politics 1774–1789: From the Accession of Louis XVI to the Fall of the Bastille*, pbk, 1995

[Hardman] Hardman, John, *Louis XVI*, 1993

Haslip, Joan, *Marie Antoinette*, 1987

Haus-Archiv (Habsburg Archives), Hofburg, Vienna

Haynin, Éric de, *Louis de Rohan: le cardinal 'collier'*, 1997

Hazen, Charles Downer, *Contemporary American Opinion of the French Revolution*, Baltimore, 1897

Hedley, Olwen, *Queen Charlotte*, 1975

Heidenstam, O.-G. de, ed., *The Letters of Marie Antoinette, Fersen & Barnave*, trans. Winifred Stephens & Mrs Wilfred Jackson, 1926

Hemmings, F. W. J., *Theatre and State in France, 1760–1905*, Cambridge, 1994

Hezecques, Felix d', Comte de France, *Souvenirs d'un page de la cour de Louis XVI*, 1983

Hibbert, Christopher, *George III: A Personal History*, pbk, 1999

Higonnet, Patrice, *Goodness Beyond Virtue: Jacobins During the French Revolution*, Cambridge, Mass., 1998

Howard, Patricia, *Gluck: An Eighteenth-century Portrait in Letters and Documents*, Oxford, 1995

Huë, Francis, *The Last Years of the Reign and Life of Louis XVI*, trans. R. C. Dallas, 1806

Hunt, Lynn, 'The Many Bodies of Marie Antoinette: political pornography and the problem of the feminine in the French Revolution': *see* Hunt

[Hunt] Hunt, Lynn, ed., *Eroticism and the Body Politic*, Baltimore, 1991

Jarrett, Derek, *Three Faces of Revolution: Paris, London and New York in 1789*, 1989

Johnson, James H., 'Musical Experience and the Formation of a French Musical Public', *Journal of Modern History*, 64, 1992

Jordan, David P., *The King's Trial: The French Revolution vs Louis XVI*, Berkeley, Los Angeles, 1979

Journal de Paris

Kaplan, Laurence S., *Jefferson and France: An Essay on Politics and Political Ideas*, New Haven, US, 1967

Keane, John, *Tom Paine: A Political Life*, 1995

Kelly, Linda, *Women of the French Revolution*, 1987

Kenyon, John, *The History Men: The Historical Profession in England Since the Renaissance*, 1983

Kertanguy, Inès de, *Secrets de cour: Madame Campan au service de Marie-Antoinette et de Napoléon*, 1999

Khevenhüller-Metsch, Fürsten Johann Joseph, nach den Tagebucheintragungen des, *Theater, Feste und Feiern zur Zeit Maria Theresias 1742–1776*, Vienna, 1987

[Khevenhüller] Khevenhüller-Metsch, Rudolf & Schlitter, Hans, eds, *Aus der Zeit Maria Theresias: Tagebuch des Fürsten Johann Joseph Khevenhüller-Metsch*, 8 vols., Vienna & Leipzig, 1907–1925

Klinckowström, Baron R. M. de, *Le Comte de Fersen et La Cour de France: extraits des papiers…*, 2 vols., 1878

Klingensmith, S. J., *The Utility of Splendor, Ceremony, Social Life, and Architecture at the Court of Bavaria, 1600–1800*, Chicago, 1993

Labourdette, J. F., *Vergennes: ministre principal de Louis XVI*, 1990

Laclos, Pierre Ambroise Choderlos de, *Les Liaisons Dangereuses*, trans. Richard Aldington, pbk, 1987

Lafont d'Aussonne, M., *Mémoires secrets et universels des malheurs et de la mort de la Reine de France*, new edn, 2 vols., 1836

La Messaline Française ou les Nuits de la Duchesse de Polignac… par l'Abbé Compagnon de la Suite de la Duchess de Polignac, 1790

[Lamorlière] 'Relation de Rosalie Lamorlière, servante à la Conciergerie (août-octobre 1793): *see* Lenotre

[*Landgrave Louise*] *Lettres de la Reine Marie-Antoinette à la Landgrave Louise de Hesse-Darmstadt*, 1865

Landon, H. C. Robbins, *Haydn: Chronicle and Works*, I, *1732–1765*, 1980; II, *1766–1790*, 1978

Langlade, Émile, *Rose Bertin: Creator of Fashion at the Court of Marie-Antoinette*, 1913

[Larivière] 'Relation de Louis Larivière, Porte-Clef à la Conciergerie': *see* Lenotre

La Rochefoucauld, François de, *Souvenirs du 10 août 1792 et de l'Armée de Bourbon*, 1929

[*La Rochejaquelein*] *Memoirs of the Marchioness of La Rochejaquelein*, Edinburgh, 1816

[*La Tour du Pin*] *Escape from Terror: The Journal of Madame de La Tour du Pin*, ed. & trans. Felice Harcourt, 1979

[*Lauzun*] *Memoirs of the Duc de Lauzun*, trans. & with app. C. K. Scott Moncrieff, introd. Richard Aldington, 1928

Lenotre, G., *La Captivité et la Mort de Marie-Antoinette*, 1938

[*Léonard I*] *Recollections of Léonard, Hairdresser to Queen Marie Antoinette*, trans. E. Jules Meras, 1912

[*Léonard II*] *Souvenirs de Léonard, Coiffeur de La Reine Marie-Antoinette*, preface M. Jules Claretie, introd. & notes MM. Maurice Vitrac & Arnould Galopin [n.d.]

Lépinay, François Macé & Charles, Jacques, *Marie-Antoinette du Temple à la Conciergerie*, 1989

[Lepître] 'Relation de Jacques-François Lepître (decembre 1792–octobre 1793)': *see* Lenotre

[*Lettres*] *Lettres de Marie-Antoinette*, ed. Maxime de la Rocheterie & le Marquis de Beaucourt, 2 vols., 1895

Lever, Évelyne, *Philippe Égalité*, 1996

Lever, Évelyne, *Marie-Antoinette*, 1991

Lever, Évelyne, *Louis XVIII*, 1988

Lever, Évelyne, *Louis XVI*, 1985

[*Lévis*] *Souvenirs-Portraits de Gaston de Lévis (1764–1830) suivis de Lettres Intimes de Monsieur Comte de Provence*, introd. & notes Jacques Dupâquier, 1993

Ligne, Prince de, *Memoirs, Letters and Miscellaneous Papers*, introd. & preface C-A. Sainte-Beuve & Madame de Staël-Holstein, 2 vols., 1899

Lindqvist, Herman, *Axel von Fersen: séducteur et aristocrate*, trad. Claude Roussel, 1995

Loomis, Stanley, *The Fatal Friendship: Marie Antoinette, Count Fersen and the Flight to Varennes*, New York, 1972

Loomis, Stanley, *Paris in the Terror June 1793–July 1794*, 1965

Louis-Philippe, *Memoirs 1773–1793*, trans. & introd. John Hardman, foreword Henri Comte de Paris, New York, 1977

MacDonogh, Giles, *Frederick the Great*, 1999

MacDonogh, Katharine, *Reigning Cats and Dogs*, 1999

McLynn, Frank, *Napoleon: A Biography*, 1997

[*Magnin*] 'Déclaration de l'abbé Magnin (1825)': *see* Lenotre

Malone, Dumas, *Jefferson and his Time*, II, *1784–1792*, Boston, US, 1951

Manceron, Claude, *The French Revolution*, V, *Blood of the Bastille, 1787–1789*, New York, 1987

Mansel, Philip, *Le Charmeur de l'Europe: Charles-Joseph de Ligne (1735–1814)*, 1992

Mansel, Philip, *The Court of France 1789–1830*, pbk, 1991

Mansel, Philip, 'The Militarisation of European Monarchies 1688–1918', Anglo-American Conference of Historians, University of London, July 1988

Mansel, Philip, *Louis XVIII*, 1981

[*Marie-Clothilde*] *Lettres Inédites de Marie-Antoinette et de Marie-Clothilde de France...*, ed. Comte de Reisen, 2nd edn, 1877

[*Marie-Thérèse Journal*] *Journal de Marie-Thérèse de France, Duchesse d'Angoulême, 5 octobre 1789–2 septembre 1792*, corrigé et annoté par Louis XVIII ..., introd. Baron Imbert de Saint-Amand, 1894

[*Marie-Thérèse Mémoire*] *Mémoire écrit par Marie-Thérèse-Charlotte de France*

... *depuis le 10 août 1792 jusqu'à la mort de son frère arrivé le 9 juin 1795*, 1892

Maxwell, Constantia, *The English Traveller in France 1698–1815*, 1932

Mayer, Arno J., *The Furies: Violence and Terror in the French and Russian Revolutions*, Princeton, NJ, 2000

Maza, Sarah, 'The "Bourgeois" Family Revisited: Sentimentalism and Social Class in Prerevolutionary French Culture': *see* Rand

Maza, Sarah, 'The Diamond Necklace Affair Revisited (1785–1786): The Case of the Missing Queen': *see* Hunt

Maza, Sarah, *Private Lives and Public Affairs: The Causes Célèbres of Prerevolutionary France*, Berkeley, CA, pbk, 1993

La Messaline Française ou les Nuits de la Duchessee de Polignac... par l'Abbé Compagnon de la Suite de la Duchesse de Polignac, 1790

Michon, L.-M., 'Les Livres de Musique de Marie-Antoinette', *Bulletin du Bibliophile et du Bibliothecaire*, 6, 1954

Mills, Hazel, '"Recasting the Pantheon"? Women and the French Revolution', *Renaissance & Modern Studies*, XXXIII, Nottingham, 1989

Mirault, M., *Notice sur Joseph Redouté, membre de la Société, Annales de la Société Libre des Beaux-Arts, XIII*, 1843

[*Modes: Éloffe*] *Modes et Usages au temps de Marie-Antoinette, Livre-Journal de Madame Éloffe, Marchande de Modes, Couturière Lingère Ordinaire de la Reine*..., ed. Comte de Reisen, 2 vols., 1885

'Modes et Révolutions 1780–1804', 8 fevrier–7 mai 1989, Musée de la Mode et du Costume, Palais Galliéra, 1989

[Moelle] 'Relation de Moelle, Membre de la Commune': *see* Lenotre

Moffat, Mary Maxwell, *Maria Theresa*, 1911

Molleville, Bertrand de, *Private Memoirs*, 2 vols., Boston, US, 1909

Le Moniteur

Montjoye, M., *Histoire de Marie-Antoinette-Josephe-Jeanne de Lorraine, Archiduchesse d'Autriche*, nouvelle edn, 2 vols., 1814

Moore, John, M.D., *A Journal during a Residence in France, from the beginning of August, to the middle of December, 1792*..., 2 vols., Boston, 1794

Morel, Bernard, *The French Crown Jewels: The Objects of the Coronations of the Kings and Queens of France Followed by a History of the French Crown Jewels from François I up to the Present Time*, trans. Elsie Callander, Margaret Curran & Agnes Hall, preface Michel Bapst, heir to the jewellers of the crown of France, Liège, 1988

[Morris] Morris, Gouverneur, *A Diary of the French Revolution, 1789–93*, 2 vols., 1939

Morris, Marilyn, *The British Monarchy and the French Revolution*, 1998

Mossiker, Frances, *The Queen's Necklace*, 1961

Newton, William R., *L'Espace du roi: la cour de France au château de Versailles 1682–1789*, 2000

Nicolardot, Louis, ed., *Journal de Louis XVI*, 1873

Nolhac, Pierre de, *Autour de la Reine*, 1929

Nolhac, Pierre de, *La Dauphine Marie-Antoinette*, 1929

Nolhac, Pierre de, *Versailles au XVIII* Siècle*, 1926

Nolhac, Pierre de, *The Trianon of Marie-Antoinette*, 1925

Nolhac, Pierre de, *Marie-Antoinette*, 1905

[Northumberland] *The Diaries of a Duchess: Extracts from the Diaries of the First Duchess of Northumberland (1716–1776)*, ed. James Greig, foreword the Duke of Northumberland, 1926

Norton, Lucy, *First Lady of Versailles: Marie Adélaïde of Savoy, Dauphine of France*, 1978

Nouvion, Pierre de & Liez, Émile, *Mlle. Bertin, un ministre des modes sous Louis XVI*, 1911

Oberkirch, Baronne d', *Mémoires sur la cour de Louis XVI et la societé française avant 1789*, 1989

O'Brien, Conor Cruise, *The Long Affair: Thomas Jefferson and the French Revolution, 1785–1800*, 1996

[Paine] *The Writings of Thomas Paine*; III & IV, *1791–1804*, ed. Moncure D. Conway, New York, 1899

Pestelli, Giorgio, *The Age of Mozart and Beethoven*, Cambridge, UK, 1984

Phillipson, Nicholas, *Hume*, 1989

Pimodan, Comte de, *La Comte F.-C. de Mercy-Argenteau: ambassadeur imperial à Paris sous Louis XV et sous Louis XVI*, 1911

Platen, Carl Henrik von, *Stedingk*, Stockholm, 1995

Polignac, Comtesse D. de, *Mémoires de Madame la Duchesse de Polignac…*, 1796

Price, Munro, *Preserving the Monarchy: The Comte de Vergennes, 1774–1787*, Cambridge, UK, 1995

[PRO] Public Record Office

Prochaska, Frank, *Royal Bounty: The Making of a Welfare Monarchy*, 1995

Proschwitz, Gunnar von, ed., *Gustaf III: The Man Behind the Myth – A Self-Portrait in Letter Form*, Viken, Sweden, 1992

[RA] Royal Archives, Windsor Castle

Marie Antoinette

[Raigecourt] 'Relation de M. le Comte Charles de Raigecourt': *see Bouillé*

[Rand] Rand, Richard, ed., *Intimate Encounters: Love and Domesticity in Eighteenth-Century France*, Princeton, NJ, 1997

Rand, Richard, 'Love, Domesticity and the Evolution of Genre Painting in Eighteenth-Century France': *see* Rand

Reiset, Vicomte de, *Joséphine de Savoie, Comtesse de Provence 1753–1810*, d'après des documents inédits, 1913

[Reitlinger I] Reitlinger, Gerald, *The Economics of Taste*; I: *The Rise and Fall of Picture Prices*, 1961

[Reitlinger II] Reitlinger, Gerald, *The Economics of Taste*; II: *The Rise and Fall of Objets d'Art Prices Since 1750*, 1963

La Révolution Française, 1791

Ribeiro, Aileen, *The Art of Dress: Fashion in England and France 1750–1820*, 1995

Ribeiro, Aileen, *Dress in Eighteenth-Century Europe*, 1984

Ribeiro, Aileen, *Fashion in the French Revolution*, 1988

Rice, Howard C. Jr., *Thomas Jefferson's Paris*, Princeton, NJ, 1976

Rigby, Dr, *Letters from France etc. in 1789*, ed. Lady Eastlake, 1880

Rocheterie, Maxime de la, *The Life of Marie Antoinette*, trans. Cora Hamilton Bell, 2 vols., 1893

Rogister, John, 'Maria Lesczsinska', Society of Court Studies, conference, University of London, September 1999

[*Roland*] *Memoirs of Madame Roland*, ed. Paul de Roux, 1986

Rousseau, Jean-Jacques, *Émile*, trans. Barbara Foxley, 1921

Rousseau, Jean-Jacques, *La Nouvelle Héloïse: Letters of Two Lovers, Inhabitants of a Small Town at the Foot of the Alps*, trans. & abridged Judith H. McDowell, 1968

Royal Memoirs on the French Revolution..., by Madame Royale, Duchess of Angoulême and Monsieur, now Louis XVIII, in 3 vols., 1823

Rudé, George, ed., *Robespierre*, New Jersey, 1967

Rudé, George, *The Crowd in the French Revolution*, Oxford, 1959

Sagarin, Edward, ed., *Cosmetics, Science and Technology*, New York, 1957

Saint-Priest, Comte de, *Mémoires: Règnes de Louis XV et de Louis XVI*, 2 vols., 1929

Saint-Simon, Duc de, *Historical Memoirs*, ed. & trans. Lucy Norton, 1967

Salmon, Xavier, Conservateur au musée national des châteaux de Versailles et Trianon, *Les Pastels*, Musée National de Versailles

Schama, Simon, *Citizens: A Chronicle of the French Revolution*, 1989

596

Secher, Reginald & Murat, Yves, *Un prince méconnu: le Dauphin Louis-Joseph, fils aîné de Louis XVI*, 1998

Ségur, Marquis de, *Marie Antoinette*, 1927

[*Ségur Memoirs*] *Memoirs of Louis Philippe Comte de Ségur*, ed. & introd. Eveline Cruikshanks, 1960

Seward, Desmond, *Marie Antoinette*, 1981

[Söderhjelm] Söderhjelm, Alma, *Fersen et Marie-Antoinette*, 1930

Söderhjelm, Alma, ed., *Marie-Antoinette et Barnave: correspondance secrète (juillet 1791–janvier 1792)*, 1934

Solnon, Jean-François, *La Cour de France*, pbk, 1987

Solomon, Maynard, *Mozart: A Life*, pbk, 1996

Sorel, Albert-Émile, *La Princesse de Lamballe: une amie de la Reine Marie Antoinette*, 1933

Staël, Madame de, *Correspondance Générale*; I, *Lettres de Jeunesse*, ed. Béatrice W. Jasinski, 1962

Staël, Madame de, *Réflexions sur le Procès de la Reine, par Une Femme*, ed. Monique Cottret, Montpellier, 1994

Stafsundarchive, AVF (1755–1810), National Archive, Stockholm

[Stryiénski] Stryiénski, Casimir, *La Mère des Trois Derniers Bourbons: Marie-Josèphe de Saxe et la cour de Louis XV*, 1902

Stryiénski, Casimir, *Mesdames de France: filles de Louis XV*, documents inédits, 3rd edn, 1911

Swain, Virginia E., 'Hidden from View: French women authors and the language of rights, 1727–1792': *see* Rand

Swinburne, Henry, *The Courts of Europe at the Close of the Last Century*, 2 vols., 1895

[*Tarante*] *Souvenirs de la Princesse de Tarante, 1789–1792*, 1901

Thomas, Chantal, *La Reine scélérate: Marie-Antoinette dans les pamphlets*, 1989

Thomas More Journal, ed. Wilfred S. Dowden, Associated University Press, Texas, 6 vols., 1983–1991

Thompson, J. W., ed., *English Witnesses of the French Revolution*, Oxford, 1938

[*Thrale*] *The French Revolution of Mrs Thrale and Dr Johnson*, ed. Moses Tyson & Henry Guppy, Manchester, 1932

[*Tilly*] *Memoirs of the Comte Alexandre de Tilly*, introd. Havelock Ellis, 1933

Tillyard, Stella, *Aristocrats: Caroline, Emily, Louisa and Sarah Lennox 1740–1832*, pbk, 1995

[*Tourzel*] *Mémoires de Madame la Duchesse de Tourzel, Gouvernante des Enfants de France de 1789 à 1795*, 1986

[Turgy] 'Relation de Turgy: garçon servant au Temple (10 août 1792–13 octobre 1793)': *see* Lenotre

Tussaud, Madame, *Memoirs and Reminiscences of France*, ed. François Hervé, 1838

[Valory] 'Précis Historique par le Comte de Valory (François-Florent)': *see Bouillé*

[*Vergennes*] *Louis XVI and the Comte de Vergennes: correspondence 1774–1787*, ed. John Hardman and Munro Price, Voltaire Foundation, Oxford, 1998

[*Véri*] *Journal de l'Abbé Véri*, introd. & notes Baron Jehan de Witte, preface Pierre de Nolhac, 2 vols., 1928–30

Verlet, Pierre, *French Royal Furniture*, New York, 1963

[Versailles 1955] Château de Versailles: 'Marie-Antoinette, Archiduchesse, Dauphine et Reine: 16 mai–2 novembre, 1955', ed. Mlle. Marguerite Jallut, Conservateur au Musée de Versailles, Éditions des Musées Nationaux, 1955

Vigée Le Brun, Madame, *Souvenirs*, 3rd revised edn, New York, 1880

Vocelka, Karl, *Die Privat Weld des Habsburger: Leben und Alltag einer Familie*, Styria, 1998

[Vuaflart I] Vuaflart, Albert & Bourin, Henri, *Les Portraits de Marie-Antoinette*; I, *L'Archiduchesse*, 1909

[Vuaflart II] Vuaflart, Albert & Bourin, Henri, *Les Portraits de Marie-Antoinette*; II, *La Dauphine*, 1910

Wachter, Friederike, 'Die Erziehung der Kinder Maria Theresias', dissertation, Vienna, 1968

[*Walpole*] *Letters of Horace Walpole*, selected by W. S. Lewis, introd. R. W. Ketton-Cremer, 1951

Walter, Gérard, ed., *Le procès de Marie-Antoinette: 23–25 vendémiaire an II (14–16 octobre 1793)*, Actes de tribunal révolutionnaire, 1993

Walter, Gérard, *Le Comte de Provence*, 1950

Walter, Gérard, *Marat*, 1933

Walzer, Michael, ed., *Regicide and Revolution: Speeches at the Trial of Louis XVI*, Cambridge, UK, 1974

Wangermann, E., 'Maria Theresa: a reforming monarchy': *see* Dickens

Weber, Joseph, *Mémoires concernant Marie Antoinette Archiduchesse d'Autriche, Reine de France...*, 3 vols., 1804

Webster, Nesta H., *Louis XVI and Marie Antoinette: During the Revolution*, 1937

Weston, Stephen, *Letters from Paris During the Summer of 1791*, 1792

Weston, Stephen, *Letters from Paris During the Summer of 1792, with Reflections*, 1793

Wheatcroft, Andrew, *The Habsburgs*, 1995

Wilberforce, R. I. & S., *The Life of William Wilberforce*, I, 1838

Wormser, Olga, *Marie-Thérèse, Impératrice*, 1961

Wraxall, N. W., *Memoirs of the Courts of Berlin, Dresden, Warsaw and Vienna in the Years 1777, 1778 and 1779*, 2 vols., 1799

Yalom, Marilyn, *Blood Sisters: The French Revolution in Women's Memory*, New York, 1993

Young, Arthur, *Travels in France and Italy During the Years 1787, 1788 and 1789*, introd. Thomas Okey, New York [n.d.]

Younghusband, Lady, *Marie-Antoinette: Her Early Youth (1770–1774)*, 1912

Zeepvat, Charlotte, 'Phoenix on the Neva', *Royalty Digest*, August 1999

Zweig, Stefan, *Marie Antoinette: The Portrait of an Average Woman*, trans. Eden & Cedar Paul, New York, 1933

Zweig MSS, British Library

Index

Adélaïde, Madame (Louis XV's
daughter): names MA *l'Autrichienne*,
56; appearance, 76–7; formal address,
89; wishes to accompany MA to
Paris (1772), 124–5; leaves for Rome,
380; uncompromising attitude to
new ways, 380; on MA's death, 540

Adhémar, Comte d', 212, 217, 239, 260

*Adieux de la Reine à ses Mignons et
Mignonnes* (pamphlet), 544

Agoult, Vicomte d', 391, 394, 403

Aiguillon, Emmanuel Armand, Duc d',
116, 119, 137, 147, 152, 261

Aiguillon, Louise Félicité Duchesse d',
117

Aix-la-Chapelle, Peace of (1748), 11

Albert, Prince of Saxe-Teschen: marries
Marie Christine, 32; rivalry with
Durfort, 52; MA allowed to write to,
58; visits Versailles, 293; in Belgium,
298, 395; exiled, 370–1

Alexandra, Empress of Nicholas II of
Russia, 538

Alsace: risings (1789), 360

Amalia, Archduchess of Austria (MA's
sister): marriage prospects, 15, 32,
35; place in family, 25; character, 27,

Amalia, Archduchess of Austria – *contd*
57; at brother Joseph's wedding, 29;
mother's advice to on marriage, 57;
departure on marriage, 64; wedding,
83; breach with mother, 120; political
intrigues, 120

Amelia, Princess of Saxony, 42

Amélie, Queen of the French (Maria
Carolina's daughter), 530

American Revolution, 176, 180, 188,
203–4, 213, 220, 230 *see also* United
States of America

Ami du Peuple, L' (newspaper), 348, 417,
419

Ami du Roi, L' (newspaper), 383

Andouins, Captain d', 402

Angoulême, Duchesse d' *see* Marie
Thérèse Charlotte (MA's daughter)

Angoulême, Louis Antoine de
Bourbon, Duc d', 162, 185, 253, 311,
531

Anne of Austria, Regent of France, 82,
150, 414, 467

Anti-Fédéraliste, L' (newspaper), 513

Antwerp, 233, 259

Aquitaine, Duc d', 40

Aranda, Pedro Abarca y Bolea, Count
d', 127–8

available from
THE ORION PUBLISHING GROUP

All Orion/Phoenix titles are available at your local bookshop or from the following address:

Mail Order Department
Littlehampton Book Services
FREEPOST BR535
Worthing, West Sussex, BN13 3BR
telephone 01903 828503, *facsimile* 01903 828802
e-mail MailOrders@lbsltd.co.uk
(Please ensure that you include full postal address details)

Payment can be made either by credit/debit card (Visa, Mastercard, Access and Switch accepted) or by sending a £ Sterling cheque or postal order made payable to *Littlehampton Book Services*.
DO NOT SEND CASH OR CURRENCY.

Please add the following to cover postage and packing

UK and BFPO:
£1.50 for the first book, and 50p for each additional book to a maximum of £3.50

Overseas and Eire:
£2.50 for the first book plus £1.00 for the second book and 50p for each additional book ordered

---

BLOCK CAPITALS PLEASE

name of cardholder ....

delivery address
(if different from cardholder)

address of cardholder ....

postcode ....

postcode ....

☐ I enclose my remittance for £.................................

☐ please debit my Mastercard/Visa/Access/Switch (delete as appropriate)

card number

expiry date   Switch issue no.

signature ....

prices and availability are subject to change without notice